THE TRAVELING
SALESMAN PROBLEM

THE TRAVELING SALESMAN PROBLEM

A Guided Tour of Combinatorial Optimization

edited by

E. L. Lawler
University of California, Berkeley

J. K. Lenstra
Centre for Mathematics and Computer Science, Amsterdam

A. H. G. Rinnooy Kan
Erasmus University, Rotterdam

D. B. Shmoys
Harvard University, Cambridge, MA

A Wiley–Interscience Publication

JOHN WILEY & SONS
Chichester · New York · Brisbane · Toronto · Singapore

Library of Congress Cataloging in Publication Data:
Main entry under title:

The Traveling salesman problem.

   Includes index.
   1. Combinatorial optimization.   2. Traveling-salesman
problem. I. Lawler, Eugene L.
QA164.T73   1985   511'.6   85–3158
ISBN 0 471 90413 9

British Library Cataloguing in Publication Data:

The Traveling salesman problem.—(Wiley–Interscience
   series in discrete mathematics)
   1. Mathematical optimization   2. Combinations
I. Lawler, E.L.
   511'.6   QA402.5

ISBN 0 471 90413 9

Printed and bound in Great Britain

Preface

A weary salesman plodded down a dusty country road, his broken-down car far behind him. At last he came upon a farmhouse. 'I'd like to let you spend the night,' said the farmer, 'but there is a problem. My daughter is home from the university and all the beds are taken.'

Before explaining how this salesman's problem was resolved, let us give you, the reader, some background information about this book. Sometime in 1980 we conceived of the idea of a book only on the traveling salesman problem that could serve both as a text for advanced courses in combinatorial optimization and as a standard reference for workers in the area. Though we did not wish to write the book ourselves, we did want it to appear as if it had been written by no more than four persons. We drew up a list of the foremost authorities on the various facets of the traveling salesman problem and approached them with the idea. Their enthusiastic responses were heartening. Their subsequent cooperation and high level of professionalism in carrying out their writing assignments have made our editorial duties less arduous than they might otherwise have been.

As editors it has been our responsibility to establish certain policies and conventions for this book. One decision we made, with no hesitation, was to refer to the traveling 'salesman' rather than to the traveling 'salesperson.' We felt that the book would grow out of its size if we would include background material on graph theory, linear programming, and network flows; the reader is referred to standard works such as Wilson [1972], Bondy & Murty [1976], Lawler [1976], Papadimitriou & Steiglitz [1982], and Chvátal [1983]. We decided that there should be no subject index, because it is our presumption as editors that the book is organized so logically that no reader could have difficulty in locating a given topic. We also decided not to have an author index, since the bibliography indicates for each entry the sections in which it is cited.

The editors wish to thank the Royal Irish Academy in Dublin for their cooperation in permitting us to photograph Sir William Rowan Hamilton's Icosian game and to reprint it. The preparation of the book was materially aided by support from NSF Grant MCS-8311422, the Centre for Mathematics and Computer Science (CWI) in Amsterdam and the Erasmus University in Rotterdam. We also wish to thank James Cameron and Ian McIntosh of John Wiley & Sons for their helpfulness and encouragement.

And now, what happened to the salesman at the beginning of this preface? The daughter appeared. Pretty she was, and no fool. Sizing up the situation, she declared, 'You don't belong here. Not at all. This is a serious book of mathematics. As far as we are concerned, you don't exist!'

E. L. Lawler, Berkeley
J. K. Lenstra, Amsterdam
A. H. G. Rinnooy Kan, Cambridge, MA
D. B. Shmoys, Cambridge, MA

November 1984

Table of contents

Contributors

E. BALAS
Graduate School of Industrial
Administration
Carnegie-Mellon University
Pittsburgh, PA 15213, U.S.A.

N. CHRISTOFIDES
Department of Management Science
Imperial College of Science and
Technology
Exhibition Road
London SW7 2BX, U.K.

V. CHVÁTAL
School of Computer Science
Burnside Hall
McGill University
805 Sherbrooke Street West
Montreal, P.Q., Canada H3A 2K6

R. S. GARFINKEL
College of Business Administration
University of Tennessee
Knoxville, TN 37916, U.S.A.

P. C. GILMORE
Department of Computer Science
University of British Columbia
2075 Westbrook Mall
Vancouver, B.C., Canada V6T 1W5

B. L. GOLDEN
College of Business and Management
University of Maryland
College Park, MD 20742, U.S.A.

M. GRÖTSCHEL
Lehrstuhl für Angewandte
Mathematik II
Universität Augsburg
Memminger Strasse 6
8900 Augsburg, F.R.G.

A. J. HOFFMAN
IBM Thomas J. Watson Research
Center
P.O. Box 218
Yorktown Heights, NY 10598,
U.S.A.

D. S. JOHNSON
AT&T Bell Laboratories
600 Mountain Avenue
Murray Hill, NJ 07974, U.S.A.

R. M. KARP
Computer Science Division
Evans Hall
University of California
Berkeley, CA 94720, U.S.A.

E. L. LAWLER
Computer Science Division
Evans Hall
University of California
Berkeley, CA 94720, U.S.A.

J. K. LENSTRA
Centre for Mathematics and
Computer Science
P.O. Box 4079
1009 AB Amsterdam
The Netherlands

M. W. Padberg
*Graduate School of Business
Administration
New York University
100 Trinity Place
New York, NY 10006, U.S.A.*

C. H. Papadimitriou
*Computer Science Department
Stanford University
Stanford, CA 94305, U.S.A.*

C. H. Papadimitriou
*Department of Computer Science
National Technical University of
Athens
9 Heroon Polytechneiou Street
Zografou 624
Athens, Greece*

A. H. G. Rinnooy Kan
*Econometric Institute
Erasmus University
P.O. Box 1738
3000 DR Rotterdam,
The Netherlands*

D. B. Shmoys
*Aiken Computation Laboratory
Harvard University
Cambridge, MA 02138, U.S.A.*

J. M. Steele
*Department of Civil Engineering
Princeton University
Princeton, NJ 08540, U.S.A.*

W. R. Stewart
*School of Business
College of William and Mary
Williamsburg, VA 23185, U.S.A.*

P. Toth
*Istituto di Automatica
Università di Bologna
Viale Risorgimento 2
40136 Bologna, Italy*

P. Wolfe
*IBM Thomas J. Watson Research
Center
P.O. Box 218
Yorktown Heights, NY 10598,
U.S.A.*

The Traveling Salesman Problem
Edited by E. L. Lawler, J. K. Lenstra,
A. H. G. Rinnooy Kan, D. B. Shmoys
© 1985 John Wiley & Sons Ltd.

1

History

A. J. Hoffman, P. Wolfe

IBM Thomas J. Watson Research Center, Yorktown Heights

1 INTRODUCTION

If a salesman, starting from his home city, is to visit exactly once each city on a given list and then return home, it is plausible for him to select the order in which he visits the cities so that the total of the distances traveled in his tour is as small as possible. Let us assume he knows, for each pair of cities, the distance from one to the other. Then he has all the data necessary to find the minimum, but it is by no means obvious how to use these data in order to get the answer. This book is a survey of research on this problem. We call it the *traveling salesman problem* (TSP). This chapter gives some of the historical background of the TSP.

The importance of the TSP comes not from the wealth of applications (there are not many salesmen clamoring for an algorithm, and the number of other cases where the mathematical model of the TSP precisely fits an engineering or scientific situation have not to date been numerous), but from the fact that it is typical of other problems of its genre: *combinatorial optimization*. We are trying to minimize total distance, so the problem is one of optimization; but we cannot immediately employ the methods of differential calculus by setting derivatives to zero, because we are in a combinatorial situation: our choice is not over a continuum but over the set of all tours.

A different optimization method comes from linear programming. This branch of mathematics, whose continuous history began in the late 1940s with George Dantzig, treats the problem of finding the minimum of a linear function on a polyhedron described by a system of linear equations and

1

inequalities in nonnegative variables. Since the points at which the minimum is attained must include a vertex of the polyhedron, and the number of vertices is finite, linear programming can in principle be used as a tool of combinatorial optimization. Part of our story is about the effort to realize this principle in the case of the TSP. So both history and current developments witness interplay between the TSP and linear programming. Many of the prominent people in the early years of linear programming are in our story, and prominent people from earlier epochs of combinatorial mathematics contributed to precursors of the TSP.

There are three aspects of the history of any mathematical problem: how it arose, how research on it influenced other developments in mathematics, and how the problem was finally solved. If, as in the TSP, the problem is to develop an algorithm that satisfies formal or informal standards of efficiency, then the TSP has not yet been solved. In fact, the TSP is the most prominent of the unsolved combinatorial optimization problems, the first problem described in the book *Computers and Intractability* [Garey & Johnson, 1979], and the most common conversational comparator ('Why, it's as hard as the traveling salesman problem!'). And that is why it continues to influence the development of optimization concepts and algorithms; other chapters in this volume will attest to its present influence, and we will make remarks on the past.

2 CYCLES AND MESSENGERS

One of the earlier problems, still prominent in combinatorial mathematics, arises in the theory of graphs. By a *graph* we mean a finite set of vertices, some pairs of which are joined by edges. A *cycle* in a graph is a set of vertices of the graph which is such that it is possible to move from vertex to vertex, along edges of the graph, so that all vertices are encountered exactly once, and that we finish where we started. If a cycle contains *all* the vertices of the graph, it is called Hamiltonian (from the name of the 19th century Irish mathematician, Sir William Rowan Hamilton). The TSP for a graph with specified edge lengths is the problem of finding a Hamiltonian cycle of shortest length. Conversely, the problem of deciding whether a graph has a Hamiltonian cycle is a special case of the TSP: if we assign all the edges of the graph length 0, and for each missing edge we create an edge of length 1, we have a new graph that does have Hamiltonian cycles. Solving the TSP for it will yield a Hamiltonian cycle for the new graph which has either total length 0, and is thus a Hamiltonian cycle for the original graph, or has positive length, showing that there exists no such cycle.

In Chapter 2 of a marvelous book [Biggs, Lloyd & Wilson, 1976], the authors point out that even prior to Hamilton such questions had long been considered. For example, both Euler [1759] and Vandermonde [1771] discuss the problem of the *knight's tour*. A knight's tour is a Hamiltonian cycle for the graph whose vertices are the 64 squares of a chessboard, with two vertices adjacent if and only if a knight could move in one step from one square to the other.

The Reverend T. P. Kirkman may have been the first to consider Hamiltonian cycles in a general context [Kirkman, 1856]. He asserted a sufficient condition for a polyhedral graph to admit such a cycle, and also showed that a polyhedron on an odd number of vertices, in which each face has an even number of edges, cannot have such a cycle.

Incidentally, Kirkman's association with combinatorial mathematics goes far beyond the question of polyhedral cycles, with which his name is rarely associated, or the famous puzzle of the fifteen schoolgirls, with which it always is. In a fascinating sketch of his career [Biggs, 1981], it is pointed out that Kirkman, among other achievements, was an early creator of the theory of combinatorial designs and undertook massive investigations of the combinatorial classification of polyhedra.

Hamilton's entrance into the subject occurred at almost the same time. He invented a system of noncommutative algebra [Hamilton, 1856], for which the actions of the basis elements could be interpreted in terms of paths on the regular dodecahedron. Hamilton named this algebra the *Icosian Calculus* (adjacent vertices on the dodecahedron correspond to adjacent faces of the icosahedron) [Hamilton, 1858; Riversdale Colthurst, 1944], and used the graphical interpretation as the basis for a puzzle, marketed under the title 'The Icosian Game' (see Figure 1.1). The game consisted of various problems, such as finishing a cycle when the first five positions are given. The apparatus of the game was a circular wooden board on which the edges of the graph were grooved, with holes for the vertices, and twenty numbered pieces to put in the holes. Amazingly, the dealer who marketed the game also included excerpts from Hamilton's scholarly account of the Icosian calculus and its origin in systems of noncommutative roots of unity [Jaques, 1859].

Another version, in which the vertices of a solid dodecahedron represented important cities, was known as the 'Traveller's Dodecahedron'. A thread looped around pegs at the vertices to form a cycle was 'a voyage around the world'. From *traveller* to *traveling salesman* is not a big verbal or conceptual step, but we do not know if that step was ever consciously taken.

A more direct precursor of the TSP, in which the lengths of the edges play a prominent role, was given by Menger [1930]. It arose in connection with 'a new definition of curve length' that Menger proposed: that the length of a curve be defined as the least upper bound of the set of all numbers that could be obtained by taking each finite set of points of the curve and determining the length of the shortest polygonal graph joining all the points. 'We call this the *messenger problem* (because in practice the problem has to be solved by every postman, and also by many travelers): finding the shortest path joining all of a finite set of points, whose pairwise distances are known. Of course, this problem can always be solved by a finite number of

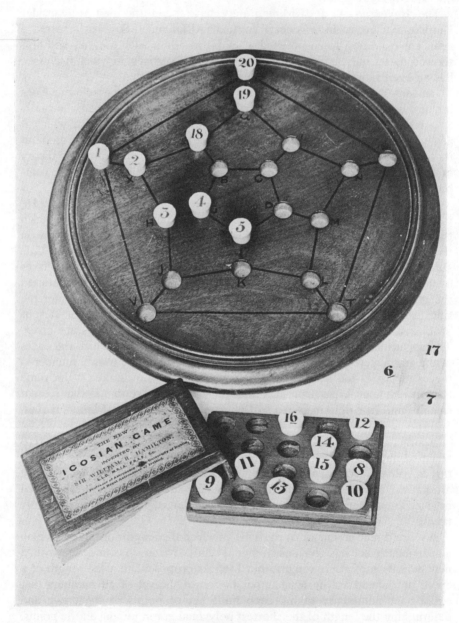

Figure 1.1   The Icosian Game (Photographed by Terri Russell. Copyright ©
1983 by the Royal Irish Academy. Reprinted with permission.)

trials. No rules are known that would reduce the number of trials to less than the number of permutations of the given points. The rule of proceeding from the origin to the nearest point, then to the nearest point to that, and so on, does not generally give the shortest path.'

Menger's statement of the problem does not require a cycle, just a path containing all vertices. But although that is only a small difference, it does not seem that the TSP descended directly from Menger's inquiry. For that matter, we do not know if Menger ever returned to his proposed definition of curve length.

3 THE BIRTH OF THE TRAVELING SALESMAN

The first use of the term 'traveling salesman problem' in mathematical circles may have been in 1931–32, as we shall explain below. But in 1832, a book was printed in Germany entitled *Der Handlungsreisende, wie er sein soll und was er zu thun hat, um Aufträge zu erhalten und eines glücklichen Erfolgs in seinen Geschäften gewiss zu sein. Von einem alten Commis-Voyageur* ('*The Traveling Salesman, how he should be and what he should do to get Commissions and to be Successful in his Business. By a veteran Traveling Salesman*'). Although devoted for the most part to other issues, the book reaches the essence of the TSP in its last chapter: 'By a proper choice and scheduling of the tour, one can often gain so much time that we have to make some suggestions. . . . The most important aspect is to cover as many locations as possible without visiting a location twice . . .' [Voigt, 1831; Müller–Merbach, 1983].

We do not know who brought the name TSP into mathematical circles, but there is no question that Merrill Flood is most responsible for publicizing it within that community and the operations research fraternity as well. He recalls being told about it by A. W. Tucker in 1937 'when I was struggling with the problem in connection with a school-bus routing study in New Jersey' [Flood, 1956]. Flood writes that Tucker remembered hearing of it from Hassler Whitney at Princeton University. Tucker has written to the editors of this volume: 'I cannot confirm or deny the story that I heard of the TSP from Hassler Whitney. If I did (as Flood says), it would have occurred in 1931–32, the first year of the old Fine Hall (now Jones Hall). That year Whitney was a postdoctoral fellow at Fine Hall working on Graph Theory, especially planarity and other offshoots of the 4-color problem. . . . I was finishing my thesis with Lefschetz on n-manifolds and Merrill Flood was a first year graduate student. The Fine Hall Common Room was a very lively place – 24 hours a day' [Tucker, 1983].

This would seem to make Whitney the entrepreneur of the TSP – possibly as a messenger from Menger – but Whitney remembers no connection whatever between himself and the TSP. Our inclination, nevertheless, is to rely on Flood's memory, even if Tucker and Whitney cannot confirm it.

The TSP now had a name and – starting at least as early as the late

1940s – a persistent and effective herald in Merrill Flood. John Williams urged Flood in 1948 to popularize the TSP at the RAND Corporation, at least partly motivated by the purpose of creating intellectual challenges for models outside the theory of games. In fact, a prize was offered for a significant theorem bearing on the TSP. There is no doubt that the reputation and authority of RAND, which quickly became the intellectual center of much of operations research theory, amplified Flood's advertizing.

Another reason for the popularity of the problem was its intimate connection with prominent topics in combinatorial problems arising in the then new subject of linear programming, namely the assignment problem and, more generally, the transportation problem, which we shall discuss briefly in the next section. The TSP was like those other problems, but apparently harder to solve, and the challenge became as intriguing for others as it was for Flood.

And, of course, the TSP became popular because it had a name that reminded people of other things. The traveling salesman was one of the classic personalities of American mythology, with a special chapter in the annals of ribald humor, and some of the disproportionate attention which the TSP has received in the world of combinatorial optimization must surely be credited to the resonances of its title.

4 THE SEMINAL PAPER

The appearance of 'Solution of a large-scale traveling-salesman problem' [Dantzig, Fulkerson & Johnson, 1954] in the *Journal of the Operations Research Society of America* was one of the principal events in the history of combinatorial optimization. It is important both for what it did and for the future developments it inspired. To understand its significance we need some background material: in linear programming, especially the assignment and transportation problems, and on the state of the art of combinatorial optimization at the time the paper appeared.

The assignment problem is to choose n elements – one from each row and column – of an $n \times n$ matrix $C = (c_{ij})$ so that the sum of the elements chosen is as small as possible. There are $n!$ possible ways of making this choice, so an effective algorithm must do something other than considering all choices. A linear programming approach is to consider the polyhedron P in n^2-space specified by all matrices $X = (x_{ij})$ satisfying the conditions

$$x_{ij} \geqslant 0, \qquad \sum_j x_{ij} = 1 \quad \text{(all } i\text{)}, \qquad \sum_i x_{ij} = 1 \quad \text{(all } j\text{)}$$

and to minimize $\sum_{i,j} c_{ij} x_{ij}$.

The reason is that, according to Birkhoff [1946], the vertices of P are precisely all matrices X in which every row and column contains exactly one 1 and has all other entries 0. Thus the $n!$ vertices of P correspond to the $n!$ choices, and $\sum c_{ij} x_{ij}$ calculates the score of each choice. Further, since the best score is reached at a vertex, linear programming algorithms can be used to solve the problem.

The transportation problem is more general than the assignment problem. Mathematically, it is the problem of choosing an $m \times n$ matrix $X = (x_{ij})$ such that

$$x_{ij} \geqslant 0, \qquad \sum_j x_{ij} = a_i \quad \text{(all } i\text{)}, \qquad \sum_i x_{ij} = b_j \quad \text{(all } j\text{)}$$

so that $\sum c_{ij} x_{ij}$ is minimum. Here a_i and b_j are given nonnegative integers with $\sum_i a_i = \sum_j b_j$. The transportation problem [Hitchcock, 1941] models this situation: at each of m sources i $(i = 1, \ldots, m)$ an amount a_i of a certain commodity is available, and at each of n destinations j $(j = 1, \ldots, n)$ the amount b_j of that commodity is required. It costs exactly c_{ij} to send one unit of the commodity from source i to destination j; how can we ship so as to satisfy all the requirements and minimize the total cost?

We have already noted in Section 1 Dantzig's development of linear programming as a class of mathematical models with widespread applications, together with a robust algorithm – the simplex method – for solving linear programming problems. By 1953, there existed effective codes implementing the simplex method in general and special adaptations for the significant special case of transportation and assignment problems. Linear programming was an important force in sponsoring the early UNIVAC computers, as well as the SEAC at the National Bureau of Standards, because of U.S. Air Force funding in support of computations required by it and other planning tools developed by Dantzig and his associates in the Office of the Air Controller. Most of the linear programming problems solved were transportation problems, which are problems in combinatorial optimization. In addition, purely mathematical developments were showing that theoretical as well as algorithmic topics in combinatorial mathematics could be usefully viewed in the context of linear programming.

It is also interesting to note some other work on combinatorial optimization by Dantzig, Fulkerson and Johnson appearing that remarkable year. They gave a method of solving a tanker scheduling problem [Dantzig & Fulkerson, 1954]. The solution arrived several years after the model became obsolete, but has survived nevertheless because the method can also be used to study basic questions of combinatorial theory. Ford and Fulkerson wrote their first report on flows in networks [Ford & Fulkerson, 1956], initiating a major topic, and Selmer Johnson [Johnson, 1954] derived a fascinating result on the scheduling of jobs through processors in a flow shop, the first significant combinatorial theorem in the subject of machine scheduling.

Veterans of that epoch recall its excitement and collective euphoria: they knew they were in on the ground floor of something, but it was not evident how large a structure would be erected above the foundation. The TSP, however, was not yielding to these developments, even though there was reason to hope it might. Let us return to the assignment problem described above.

If c_{ij} is the distance from city i to city j, then the TSP is very similar to the assignment problem. We would interpret $x_{ij} = 1$ to mean that the salesman on his tour moves from city i to city j. But a solution to the assignment problem might, under this interpretation, be a set of *subtours*. Taken altogether, each city is visited exactly once, but in a set of disconnected subtours; this would not solve the TSP. So we certainly have to impose the additional condition *no subtours*, which can be expressed mathematically by 2^{n-1} additional inequalities along with those given above. Unfortunately, the set of vertices of the new polyhedron Q, unlike the set of vertices of the old polyhedron P, may contain matrices with entries other than 0 to 1; so we must impose the additional condition that each entry in X must be 0 or 1. These moves have created two difficulties. The first is that we have, instead of $2n$ equations in nonnegative variables, an enormous number of extra inequalities to consider. A more serious difficulty is that the requirement that the variables be 0 or 1 is a requirement of integer linear programming, a subject which was only a dream in the early 1950s.

Now consider the set of all matrices X which satisfy the TSP requirements (i.e., they are matrices with entries only 0 or 1 describing full tours). Suppose one knew, in addition to the inequalities forbidding subtours, all other inequalities needed to create a new polyhedron R whose vertices were precisely the tours: then, in principle, linear programming could be applied. Mathematically, the specification of R can be described as finding the facets of the convex hull of the tours; but it had been shown that the description of facets was complicated [Heller, 1955; Kuhn, 1955a]. (These papers of Kuhn and Heller seem to be the earliest published attempts to find the facets of the convex hull of a set of vectors given by a combinatorial description, apart from Birkhoff's theorem quoted above, that the doubly stochastic matrices are the convex hull of the permutation matrices.) Nevertheless, after hearing one of Kuhn's lectures, Dantzig, Fulkerson and Johnson at RAND speculated that, starting from an optimal or nearly optimal tour, it might be possible to prove optimality by invoking only a few additional inequalities (called *cuts*). (Fulkerson had in earlier years been Flood's assistant at RAND, and had learned graph theory from writing up notes of lectures that Tucker had given on the subject at Flood's request.) The method seemed to work out on small problems, so they moved to a 49-city problem (Washington, D.C. and a large city in each of the then 48 states).

Starting from a solution worked out with strings on a model (which was in fact optimal), Dantzig, Fulkerson and Johnson had nevertheless to face the possibility that billions of cuts might be needed. An optimistic Dantzig wagered one dollar with a pessimistic Fulkerson: Dantzig contended that the number of cuts needed would be at most 25, Fulkerson that it would be at least 26. The result was very close: Dantzig remembers that it turned out to be 26, but the published paper says that only 25 were needed.

Commenting on the RAND work on the TSP over ten years later, Gomory wrote: 'I do not see why this particular approach stopped where it did. It should be possible to use the same approach today, but in an algorithmic manner' [Gomory, 1966]. In a discu: ion following the presentation of Gomory [1966], he added, 'Sometimes even the sheer number of faces is not a deterrent if we have some systematic way of getting at them. . . . And the trouble with the TSP is that we have not, up to now (I still think that it can be done), been able to produce enough of them easily enough . . . .' With hindsight, we see that he was completely correct. However, it took fifteen more years before the insights that were being developed could make full automation of large-scale TSP solution conceivable.

Thus Dantzig, Fulkerson and Johnson not only solved a sizable TSP, but showed that the concept of cutting planes was relevant to integer linear programs generally, since it applied to the TSP particularly, and that the complexity of the facet structure of a combinatorial optimization problem approached in the style of linear programming was not an insuperable obstacle to solving it. In addition they used, perhaps for the first time, the concept of branch and bound, about which there is more in Section 5 and much more in Chapter 10. All we shall say here is that the later development of this idea has been an indispensable ingredient in the solution of most of the practical combinatorial optimization problems arising in integer linear programming.

It was clear at the time of its publication that 'Solution of a large-scale traveling-salesman problem' was a very substantial achievement, even though the authors scrupulously and accurately refused to claim the development of a general algorithm. But it is remarkable, reading it retrospectively, how much of the scope and philosophy of later developments of combinatorial optimization are envisioned in this successful attack on one instance of the TSP.

5   INTEGER PROGRAMMING: CUTS AND FACETS, BRANCH AND BOUND

Assume that we have a polyhedron P, and we wish to minimize, among the integer points of P, a linear objective function. This is the general problem that integer (linear) programming addresses. Let us consider the convex hull Q of the integer points of P. If we knew in advance, or could generate systematically all the inequalities defining the facets of Q, then the simplex method applied to the facets of Q would solve the integer programming problem. Now for an arbitrary P, the facets of Q are not available. Nevertheless, building on the work of Heller and Kuhn mentioned in the preceding section, and the work of Gomory summarized in the next paragraph, facts about and techniques for discovering *some* facets of Q for *some* P have become useful in both practice and theory (see Section 8 below, Chapters 8 and 9, and papers by Edmonds [1965a] and Grötschel & Padberg [1979a, 1979b]).

Gomory invented several algorithms [Gomory, 1958, 1960, 1963] which, in principle, could find all facets of Q, but had as their aim merely finding an optimum for a given objective on Q. Each of the algorithms involved systematic generation of cutting planes which would excise part of P but leave Q intact. It is not difficult to find cutting planes with this property, but it was a major achievement to show how to develop these cuts so that, after a finite number of steps, the optimum vertex of the intersection of P with the half-spaces generated by the cuts would indeed be the optimum on Q.

Gomory's elegant algorithms have continued to affect the theory of integer programming, but they are not widely used in practice. The most popular computing method (especially when only some of the variables are required to be integral) is that of *branch and bound*. Its general approach is to take a variable x required to be an integer, but whose current value is not, by *branching* on nearby integer values or considering both the cases: x is at least the closest larger integer, or x is at most the closest smaller integer. This leads to the construction of a *search tree*, with nodes corresponding to linear programs with various restrictions, and which do not grow past nodes where some *bounds* on the value of the solution indicate that the tree need not be explored beyond such nodes. The concept seems to have appeared first in the celebrated paper [Dantzig, Fulkerson & Johnson, 1954] although the term *branch and bound* was first used – and in the context of the TSP – by Little, Murty, Sweeney & Karel [1963]. An exposition of concepts of branch and bound is given in Chapter 10, but it is worth noting here the contributions of Eastman, who developed the first branch and bound algorithm based on subtour elimination, and of Croes, whose proposal for a solution scheme also embodied a branch and bound philosophy [Eastman, 1958; Croes, 1958]. It seems to have been Land and Doig who first pointed out that this philosophy was relevant to general integer programming [Land & Doig, 1960].

An important way of finding bounds for branch and bound algorithms has become known as *Lagrangean relaxation*, which is described in Chapter 10. Held and Karp were the first to use a version of this general procedure [Held & Karp, 1970, 1971]. It was for the TSP, but, again, became a general tool for hard problems in combinatorial optimization.

6 EASY AND HARD PROBLEMS

By the end of the 1960s, it was well appreciated that there appears to be a significant difference between hard problems such as the TSP, for which the only available optimization algorithms are of an enumerative nature, and easy problems such as the assignment and transportation problems, for which *good* algorithms exist – a term coined by Edmonds [1965a] to describe solution methods whose running time increases at most polynomially with problem size. There was empirical evidence that all the enumerative methods developed for the TSP and other hard problems behaved much worse, and it seemed reasonable to conjecture that problems like the TSP were of such inherent complexity that the computational effort demanded by any method for their solution would grow superpolynomially with problem size.

That conjecture is still unverified, but developments in theoretical computer science around 1970 provide a much stronger foundation for its formulation as well as a much better understanding of the way in which the hard problems are related to each other.

From three fundamental papers [Cook, 1971; Karp, 1972; Levin, 1973], the insight emerged that many of the problems suspected to be inherently hard are all computationally equivalent, in the sense that a polynomial algorithm for one of them could be used to solve all others in polynomial time as well. Roughly speaking, the way to establish these results is first to show that these problems all allow (polynomially bounded) formulations as integer programming problems, and then to prove that integer programming in turn is a special case of certain individual hard problems (including the TSP). These latter problems are called $\mathcal{NP}$-hard. The concepts of *computational complexity theory* generated much research during the 1970s. An impressive survey is presented by Garey & Johnson [1979]; see also Chapter 3.

Although the $\mathcal{NP}$-hardness of the TSP does not imply that exponential worst-case running times for its solution are unavoidable, it does serve to reinforce one's belief that the existence of a polynomial algorithm for the TSP is extremely unlikely: the consequences of such an algorithm are dramatic beyond belief. A proof, however, has not been forthcoming so far, and as a result the conjecture is gaining in status and respectability every year.

Of course, the probable intractability of the general TSP does not exclude the possibility of polynomial solution procedures for special cases of the problem. In fact, one of the most surprising aspects of computational complexity theory is that a sharp borderline appears to exist that separates the easy problems from the hard ones. On one side of the border, one finds special cases of hard problems that can be proved to be $\mathcal{NP}$-hard in themselves, such as the Euclidean TSP, where the cities are given as points in the two-dimensional plane and their distances are computed according to the Euclidean metric. On the other side, one finds problems that look very similar to one of the hard problems but nevertheless turn out to be solvable in polynomial time, such as the TSP with an upper triangular distance matrix (i.e., $c_{ij} = 0$ if $i > j$). The first special TSP whose structure led to a polynomial algorithm was a job sequencing problem [Gilmore & Gomory, 1964]. In later years, it was notably the Soviet literature that concentrated on the identification of other easy TSPs. Chapter 4 gives the first comprehensive account of these *well-solvable* special cases of the TSP.

7 COPING WITH $\mathcal{NP}$-HARDNESS

Computational complexity theory confirmed earlier suspicions about the inherent complexity of the TSP, but of course the story does not end there.

Difficult problems still have to be solved, and one of the more practical consequences of the $\mathcal{NP}$-hardness of a problem is that it limits the choice to three solution strategies. To start with, we may not accept the apparent difficulty of the problem at hand and try to find some special structure that places it in a well-solved subclass. If that does not work out, there is no guarantee that an optimal solution can be found in a reasonable amount of time, and we can compromise on either of two dimensions: we insist on the optimality of the solution (and risk spending a lot of time), or we insist on a fast solution method (and accept the possibility of a suboptimal solution).

The first option is receiving a good deal of attention in other sections of this chapter. The history of using *cutting planes* and *branch and bound* has already been reviewed in Section 5, and their combination has impressive algorithmic consequences, as Section 8 will testify. Another enumerative optimization method, the recursive technique of *dynamic programming*, has also been applied to the TSP [Bellman, 1962; Held & Karp, 1962]. Due to its enormous storage requirements, dynamic programming can only solve relatively small problem instances. However, the method has useful theoretical running time characteristics (see Chapter 6) and is the basis for an effective bounding procedure in practical routing algorithms (see Chapter 12).

The second option, that of *approximation*, is undoubtedly the one most frequently chosen in practice. The TSP has again served as a playground in which many ideas for the approximate solution of combinatorial optimization problems were first developed and tested. Heuristic methods can be conveniently divided according to whether they *construct* a single feasible solution, or whether they systematically try to *improve* a given initial solution. In the former category, there are TSP heuristics such as the nearest neighbor rule, whose suboptimality was already noted by Menger [1930]. In the latter category, one finds the famous edge-exchange procedures from Lin [1965] and Lin & Kernighan [1973], that are foreshadowed by Flood [1956].

The *design* of approximation algorithms immediately leads to the *analysis* of their performance as a relevant research question. Given a heuristic, what can be said about the value it produces relative to the optimal one? There are three different ways in which one may try to answer this question.

There first way is strictly *empirical*. The heuristic is applied to a set of test problems and the solution values obtained are compared to the optimal solution values or, if the latter are not known, to lower bounds on those values or to the values produced by other heuristics (see Chapter 7). The difficulties with this approach are the generation of proper test problems that are in some sense representative and the proper statistical interpretation of the results. Nevertheless, for many years this was the only approach available. Experiments like these suggested, for example, that the Lin–Kernighan heuristic offered an attractive combination of high solution quality and low running time.

Towards the end of the 1960s, a second approach started to become popular; it was first proposed in the context of multiprocessor scheduling

[Graham, 1966, 1969]. The idea here is to derive bounds on the worst possible deviation from the optimum that the heuristic could produce and to devise bad problem instances for which the heuristic actually achieves this deviation (see Chapter 5). Such a *worst-case* analysis provides a *performance guarantee* that may be pessimistic but at least will never be violated. For the Euclidean TSP, the heuristic that amounts to doubling a minimum spanning tree and eliminating multiple visits to cities, was for a long time the best known method in a worst-case sense; its maximum error is 100%. In 1976, two important results were published. Christofides [1976] presented an elegant heuristic whose maximum error is 50% (and this is still the best worst-case result known today). And Sahni & Gonzalez [1976] showed for the general TSP that guaranteeing any fixed maximum error is just as hard as finding the optimum.

It should be mentioned at this point that, as early as 1955, a worst-case result of a quite different nature was obtained [Few, 1955]. For the Euclidean TSP in the unit square, Few gave an algorithm that constructs a tour of length at most $\sqrt{2n}+1.75$. No better result is known today.

The obvious difficulty with the worst-case approach is that our entire judgement of a heuristic could be based on its poor performance on some pathological problem instances. Empirical evidence, collected as under the first approach, may well suggest that such bad behavior is extremely rare. In such a situation, it would be attractive to conduct a rigorous analysis of the behavior of the heuristic in a probabilistic sense. Can anything be said, for example, about its expected error?

Again, the TSP led the way in opening up the whole area of research on the *probabilistic* analysis of combinatorial algorithms (see Chapter 6). In 1975, building on an old result from Beardwood, Halton & Hammersley [1959], Karp showed that a heuristic for the Euclidean TSP, which partitions the set of cities into subsets and concatenates the optimal tours through each of these, produces a worst-case error that, as a function of n, grows more slowly than the expected optimal solution value [Karp, 1977]. Thus, for sufficiently large n, the expected error becomes as small as desired.

The first difficulty with the probabilistic approach is that it presupposes the specification of a probability distribution over the set of all TSP instances (in the above case, the assumption is that the cities are uniformly distributed over a rectangle). The problem of deciding whether such a distribution is reasonable is comparable to the problem of finding a proper set of test problems.

The second difficulty is that almost all results of this nature tend to be asymptotic ones: they hold for 'sufficiently large' n. Not much is known about the convergence properties of asymptotically optimal heuristics, and their performance need not be competitive for realistic values of n. But then, probabilistic analyses should be seen more as an explanation for the observed behavior of some design principle than as a performance guarantee of some sort.

The three approaches discussed above have provided a wealth of approximation algorithms for the TSP. Surprisingly, the next development raises hopes that the optimal solution of large problem instances would be possible after all.

8 THE 318-CITY PROBLEM

A TSP of 318 cities is not the largest problem ever tackled; work has been reported on a problem having 6,406 cities [Kirkpatrick, 1984]. That problem may actually have been solved, but the 318-city problem is the largest problem *known* to have been solved [Crowder & Padberg, 1980]. It is the largest of the ten symmetric TSPs solved by Crowder and Padberg. For seven of these problems, the optimal solutions were established for the first time. Some of these had in fact been previously solved, but optimality had not been proved, so it was not known that they had been solved.

As Crowder and Padberg state, their distant point of departure was the RAND work of 1954; but their elaborate procedure, a sequel to one that had been already described [Padberg & Hong, 1980], used almost every device that has been mentioned so far.

It had three main phases. The first phase used the Lin–Kernighan heuristic to find a good starting tour [Lin & Kernighan, 1973], and then applied a simplex-based procedure to a linear programming problem composed initially of the degree-two constraints. During the course of this work suitable subtour elimination and, more generally, *comb* constraints [Chvátal, 1973a; Grötschel & Padberg, 1979a, 1979b] were derived and used to augment the current linear programming problem. These derived constraints had the property that they did not exclude feasible tours, but that the augmented problem was a tighter linear programming relaxation of the TSP. When the constraint generation procedure could no longer easily identify candidate constraints, the augmented linear programming problem was solved to optimality, yielding a true lower bound on the minimum tour length of the TSP.

The second phase involved fixing a subset of variables in the TSP to either 0 or 1. This procedure, first employed in this context in the RAND work, utilized the upper bound of the tour length from the Lin–Kernighan heuristic, and the solution value and reduced costs from the linear programming problem solved in phase one. For the 318-city problem this allowed more than 49,000 of the 50,403 variables to be fixed (most at 0, of course), thus reducing the number of variables in the problem to about three percent of its original number.

In the third phase, the reduced problem was treated as a 0–1 problem, utilizing MPSX-MIP/370 for its solution. The 0–1 solution to this problem was either an optimal solution to the reduced TSP – this solution, taken in conjunction with the variables fixed at 1 in phase two, yielded an optimal solution for the original TSP – or defined a collection of subtours for the reduced problem. In the latter case, appropriate constraints to exclude the current 0–1 solution were generated and adjoined to the problem, which was then resolved. For the 318-city problem, the 0–1 linear programming problem required two such augmentations before yielding the optimal tour. The total CPU time for the third phase on the IBM 370/168 was just under six minutes. (For a more detailed account of this work see Chapter 9.)

Crowder and Padberg conclude: 'We cannot report any failure of the proposed methodology. . . . In our view this fact points to the suitability of facet-defining cutting-planes for the purpose of proving optimality in hard and difficult combinatorial optimization problems. . . . We are confident that problems involving 1,000 cities and more are amenable to exact solution by today's technology.'

It is important to emphasize that their calculation did not employ the automatic generation of cutting planes, as envisaged by Gomory [1966], but the automatic derivation, where possible, of facets of the convex hull of tours. The problem of finding violated facets (of a certain type) is, in each combinatorial optimization problem approached by linear programming, a significant computational problem in its own right. Whether to settle for cutting plane formulas easy to calculate (as in Section 4), or to spend more time looking for facets – and when to switch to branch and bound – are significant strategic and tactical issues in combinatorial optimization. The TSP has been the central forum in which these issues have been raised and tested.

Exercises
1. Find the earliest references to the TSP in your national literature.
2. Try to discover any work following on Menger's definition of curve length, or his messenger problem (cf. [Verblunsky, 1951]).
3. Cutting planes, branch and bound, and Lagrangean relaxation are themes of combinatorial optimization for which the TSP was a principal stimulation. Can the same claim be made
(a) for the TSP's influence on $\mathcal{NP}$-completeness, or
(b) on the topic of describing facets of the convex hull of the incidence vectors of a combinatorially described set, or
(c) on the worst-case analysis of heuristic algorithms, or
(d) on the probabilistic analysis of heuristic algorithms?

The Traveling Salesman Problem
Edited by E. L. Lawler, J. K. Lenstra,
A. H. G. Rinnooy Kan, D. B. Shmoys
© 1985 John Wiley & Sons Ltd.

2

Motivation and modeling

R. S. Garfinkel
University of Tennessee, Knoxville

1 MOTIVATION

The TSP is seductively easy to state. It takes no mathematical background to understand the problem and no great talent to find good solutions to large problems. Thus it is fun to work on, continuously inviting recreational problem solvers.

On the other hand, the TSP has resisted all efforts to find a 'good' optimization algorithm (see Chapter 3) or even an approximation algorithm that is guaranteed to be effective (see Chapter 5). Thus the TSP contains both of the elements that have attracted mathematicians to particular problems for centuries: simplicity of statement and difficulty of solution. Furthermore, there is no reason to believe that this attraction will diminish in the years to come.

There are also practical reasons for the importance of the TSP. Many significant real-world problems can be formulated as instances of the TSP. In this chapter we try to indicate some of these applications of the TSP model. In doing so, we shall have reason to describe various problem transformations, related combinatorial problems, and generalizations of the basic TSP.

2 APPLICATIONS

Despite the fact that the traveling salesman model applies directly to a very useful-sounding situation, namely that of a salesman wishing to minimize his travel distance, most of the reported applications are quite different. That is, seemingly unrelated problems are solved by formulating them as instances of the TSP. The applications described below are intended to impress the reader with the versatility of the TSP model.

2.1 Vehicle routing

By vehicle routing we mean the problem of determining for a fleet of vehicles which customers should be served by which vehicles, and in what order each vehicle should visit its customers. Constraints generally include capacities of the vehicles as well as time windows for the customers. Some algorithms for this problem use the TSP model for the subproblem of ordering each vehicle's customers. In light of soaring fuel costs this is clearly a very timely problem. It will not be discussed further in this chapter, the reader being advised to refer to Chapter 12, which deals solely with this application.

2.2 Computer wiring

The following type of problem occurs repeatedly in the design of computers and other digital systems. A system consists of a number of modules and several pins are located on each module. The physical position of each module has been determined. A given subset of pins has to be interconnected by wires. In view of possible future changes or corrections and of the small size of a pin, at most two wires are to be attached to any pin. In order to avoid signal cross-talk and to improve ease and neatness of wiring, the total wire length should be minimized.

Let c_{ij} denote the actual distance between pin i and pin j. If any number of wires could be attached to a pin, then an optimal wiring would correspond to a minimum spanning tree which can be found efficiently by various algorithms. However, the degree requirement implies that we must find a minimum length Hamiltonian path. If we create a dummy pin 0, with $c_{0j} = c_{j0} = 0$, for all j, then the wiring problem becomes an $(n+1)$-city symmetric TSP [Lenstra & Rinnooy Kan, 1975].

Note that a more difficult problem results if the positions of the modules are not chosen in advance but are to be chosen so as to minimize the total wire length for all subsets of pins that have to be connected. This placement problem is often reformulated as a quadratic assignment problem, which we describe in Section 4.3.

2.3 Cutting wallpaper

Suppose we wish to cut n sheets of wallpaper from a single long roll of paper. Sheet i starts at position s_i and finishes at position f_i, with respect to a pattern that repeats at one unit intervals. (Thus, $f_i = s_i + l_i$ (mod 1) where the length of sheet i is l_i pattern units.) The amount of wallpaper that is wasted if sheet j is cut from the roll immediately after sheet i is then

$$c_{ij} = \begin{cases} s_j - f_i & \text{if } f_i \leq s_j, \\ 1 + s_j - f_i & \text{otherwise.} \end{cases}$$

Or equivalently,

$$c_{ij} = s_j - f_i \text{ (mod 1)}. \tag{1}$$

Now suppose that when we begin cutting, the end of the roll is at position f_0 and that after cutting the last sheet we must make one final cut to restore the roll to the same starting point $s_0 = f_0$. If we now create a dummy sheet 0, with starting and finishing points s_0, f_0, the problem of cutting the n sheets from the roll so as to minimize total wastage is an $(n+1)$-city TSP with distance matrix defined by (1) [Garfinkel, 1977]. In Chapter 4 we shall see that this special case of the TSP can be solved in a time of $O(n \log n)$.

2.4 Job sequencing

Consider the problem of sequencing n jobs on a single machine. The jobs can be done in any order and the objective is to complete all of them in the shortest possible time. Assume that the machine must be in a certain state S_j (e.g. rotation, temperature, pressure, cutting thickness, paint color, or whatever) in order to do job j and that the beginning and ending state for the machine is S_0.

Let the time required to complete job j directly after job i be

$$t_{ij} = c_{ij} + p_j,$$

where c_{ij} is the time required to transform the machine from S_i to S_j and p_j is the actual time to perform job j (with $p_0 = 0$). For a given cyclic permutation π of $\{0, \ldots, n\}$, the time required to complete all the jobs is

$$\sum_{i=0}^{n} (c_{i\pi(i)} + p_{\pi(i)}) = \sum_{i=0}^{n} c_{i\pi(i)} + \sum_{j=1}^{n} p_j.$$

Since the sum of all p_j's is a constant, it follows that the job sequencing problem is a TSP.

An interesting variation of this application given by Gilmore & Gomory [1964] is described in Chapter 4. In this application the state S_j is a numerical value (e.g. furnace temperature), and c_{ij} is the integral of a function whose limits are the ending state of job i and the beginning state of job j. (There are different functions to be integrated for increasing and for decreasing the state variable.) The problem is shown to have a special structure leading to a polynomial algorithm.

In this context it is also interesting to note that the flow shop sequencing problem with no wait in process can also be formulated as a TSP of this form. See Exercise 1 and Chapter 4, Exercise 29.

2.5 Clustering a data array

Suppose an $m \times n$ data array $A = (a_{ij})$ is given, where a_{ij} measures the strength of the relationship between row i and column j of the matrix. Examples of such arrays are given by McCormick, Schweitzer & White [1972] and Lenstra & Rinnooy Kan [1975]. If i and j are row and column indices then, for instance, row i could be a marketing technique and column j an application for which the technique has been successfully used.

The objective is to permute the rows and columns of A so that relationships between subsets of rows and columns become clear. For example the array of Figure 2.1(a) does not display any strong relationships, but in Figure 2.1(b) it is seen after suitable row and column permutations that rows 1, 3 and 5 are related to columns 1 and 3, and similarly rows 2 and 4 to columns 2 and 4.

$$
\begin{array}{c}
1 \\ 2 \\ 3 \\ 4 \\ 5
\end{array}
\begin{bmatrix}
1 & 0 & 1 & 0 \\
0 & 1 & 0 & 1 \\
1 & 0 & 1 & 0 \\
0 & 1 & 0 & 1 \\
1 & 0 & 1 & 0
\end{bmatrix}
\qquad
\begin{array}{c}
1 \\ 3 \\ 5 \\ 2 \\ 4
\end{array}
\begin{bmatrix}
1 & 1 & 0 & 0 \\
1 & 1 & 0 & 0 \\
1 & 1 & 0 & 0 \\
0 & 0 & 1 & 1 \\
0 & 0 & 1 & 1
\end{bmatrix}
$$
$$
\begin{array}{cccc} 1 & 2 & 3 & 4 \end{array} \qquad\qquad \begin{array}{cccc} 1 & 3 & 2 & 4 \end{array}
$$
$$
\text{(a)} \qquad\qquad\qquad \text{(b)}
$$

Figure 2.1

In order to make concrete the intuitive notion that Figure 2.1(b) represents a better clustering structure than Figure 2.1(a), a *measure of effectiveness* (*ME*) of a row and column permutation is introduced by McCormick, Schweitzer & White [1972]. Let ρ and σ be permutations of the row and column indices. In other words, if B is the matrix formed by the permutation, then b_{ij} corresponds to the original $a_{\rho(i)\sigma(j)}$. If we create a dummy row 0 and a dummy column 0 each composed of 0's, and respect the convention that $\rho(m+1) = \sigma(n+1) = \rho(0) = \sigma(0) = 0$, then

$$ME(\rho, \sigma) = \tfrac{1}{2} \sum_{i=1}^{m} \sum_{j=1}^{n} a_{\rho(i)\sigma(j)}(a_{\rho(i)\sigma(j-1)} + a_{\rho(i)\sigma(j+1)} + a_{\rho(i-1)\sigma(j)} + a_{\rho(i+1)\sigma(j)}).$$

$$(2)$$

In words, $ME(\rho, \sigma)$ is the sum of the products of adjacent elements in the permuted array. Thus, the ME of Figure 2.1(a) is 0, while that of Figure 2.1(b) is 11.

But equation (2) reduces to

$$\sum_{i=0}^{m} \sum_{j=1}^{n} a_{\rho(i)j} a_{\rho(i+1)j} + \sum_{j=0}^{n} \sum_{i=1}^{m} a_{i\sigma(j)} a_{i\sigma(j+1)},$$

so that $ME(\rho, \sigma)$ decomposes into two optimization problems with objectives $ME(\rho)$ and $ME(\sigma)$, each of which can be modeled as a TSP [Lenstra, 1974]. The key idea in doing this is to think of $\sigma(j)$ as the jth city visited. Then, the distance matrix for the row problem is

$$c_{ij} = -\sum_{k=1}^{n} a_{ik} a_{jk}$$

and for the column problem is

$$c'_{ij} = -\sum_{k=1}^{m} a_{ki} a_{kj}.$$

(The negative signs have been introduced to convert a maximization problem into a minimization problem.) For the example of Figure 2.1, the distance matrices are

$$C = \begin{array}{c} 0 \\ 1 \\ 2 \\ 3 \\ 4 \\ 5 \end{array} \begin{bmatrix} - & 0 & 0 & 0 & 0 & 0 \\ 0 & - & 0 & -2 & 0 & -2 \\ 0 & 0 & - & 0 & -2 & 0 \\ 0 & -2 & 0 & - & 0 & -2 \\ 0 & 0 & -2 & 0 & - & 0 \\ 0 & -2 & 0 & -2 & 0 & - \end{bmatrix} \qquad C' = \begin{array}{c} 0 \\ 1 \\ 2 \\ 3 \\ 4 \end{array} \begin{bmatrix} - & 0 & 0 & 0 & 0 \\ 0 & - & 0 & -2 & 0 \\ 0 & 0 & - & 0 & -2 \\ 0 & -2 & 0 & - & 0 \\ 0 & 0 & -2 & 0 & - \end{bmatrix}$$
$$\begin{array}{cccccc} 0 & 1 & 2 & 3 & 4 & 5 \end{array} \qquad\qquad \begin{array}{ccccc} 0 & 1 & 2 & 3 & 4 \end{array}$$

Results for some real applications are given by Lenstra & Rinnooy Kan [1975]. For a related problem the reader is referred to Hubert & Baker [1978].

Exercise

1. Suppose there are n jobs that require processing by m machines in the same order. That is, each job must be processed by machine 1, then by machine 2, ..., and finally by machine m. Each machine can work on at

most one job at a time and once it begins work on a job it must work on it to completion, without interruption. The amount of time machine h must process job i is denoted by p_{hi} ($h = 1, \ldots, m$, $i = 1, \ldots, n$). Further suppose that once the processing of a job is completed on machine h, its processing must begin immediately on machine $h + 1$ ($h = 1, \ldots, m - 1$). This means that we have a *flow shop* with *no wait in process*.

Show that the problem of sequencing the jobs so that the last job is completed as early as possible can be formulated as an $(n + 1)$-city TSP. (Create a dummy job requiring zero units of processing on each machine.) Specifically, show how the c_{ij} values for the TSP can be expressed in terms of the p_{hi} values. It is suggested that c_{ij} represent the amount of idle time required on machine 1 if job j immediately follows job i. *Note*: This problem can be solved efficiently for the special case of two machines by an algorithm of Gilmore & Gomory [1964]. See Chapter 4, Exercise 29.

3   SIMPLE TRANSFORMATIONS TO THE TSP

It surely did not escape the reader's attention that there was something a little contrived in our formulation of each of the problems in Sections 2.2 to 2.5. As soon as we appeared to have obtained a shortest Hamiltonian path problem, we made it into a standard TSP by introducing, respectively, a dummy pin, dummy sheet of wallpaper, dummy job, or dummy matrix row and column. This is just a simple example of a problem transformation that is useful in dealing with the TSP. Our purpose in this section is to review some other such transformations, as a prelude to a discussion of related combinatorial problems in the next section.

3.1   Shortest Hamiltonian paths

Let $C = (c_{ij})$ be an $n \times n$ matrix, where c_{ij} is the distance from vertex i to vertex j in an n-vertex directed network. Suppose our objective is to find a shortest Hamiltonian path in the network, without concern for the endpoints of the path. As we have indicated above, this problem is equivalent to an $(n + 1)$-city TSP whose distance matrix is obtained from C by appending an $(n + 1)$-st row and column of 0's. What if our objective is to find a shortest Hamiltonian path from a specified vertex s to another specified vertex t? Then this problem is equivalent to an $(n - 1)$-city TSP in which s and t are replaced by a single city, say u, and the distance matrix is C', where

$$c'_{ij} = \begin{cases} c_{sj} & \text{if } i = u, \\ c_{it} & \text{if } j = u, \\ c_{ij} & \text{otherwise.} \end{cases}$$

And what if the object is to find a shortest Hamiltonian path from vertex s to any other (unspecified) city? In this case the problem is equivalent to an n-city TSP with distance matrix obtained by setting all the entries in column

s of C to 0. (For any Hamiltonian path starting at s and ending at j, there is a Hamiltonian cycle of exactly the same length containing arc (j, s), and conversely.)

And what about transformations in the other direction? That is, suppose we have an n-city TSP specified by an $n \times n$ matrix C. How can we reformulate the problem as a shortest Hamiltonian path problem? If we are allowed to specify the endpoints of the path, we can create a second copy t of any given vertex s and let s and t be the endpoints. If we are not allowed to specify the endpoints of the path, we can nevertheless force s and t to be the endpoints of a shortest path, by setting c_{is} and c_{tj} to very large numbers.

3.2 Repetition of cities

Suppose that we have a problem that is like an ordinary TSP, except that we are to visit each city *at least once* instead of *exactly once*. How do we transform this problem to an ordinary TSP? Simply replace the given $n \times n$ distance matrix C by a new $n \times n$ distance matrix C', where

c'_{ij} = the length of a shortest path from i to j (in terms of the distances given by C).

(The matrix C' can be computed in time $O(n^3)$ by a variety of known methods, provided there are no directed cycles that are negative in length.) We leave it to the reader to justify this result.

And what about the converse transformation? That is, suppose somebody were to offer us a computational procedure for solving the 'at least once' problem. How could we use this procedure to solve a TSP instance specified by a given $n \times n$ matrix C? Note that if we add a constant M to each entry of C, we add exactly nM to the length of each Hamiltonian cycle, and a still larger value to any closed sequence of arcs that visits each city at least once and some city more than once. Accordingly, all we need do is make M very large and we shall accomplish our objective.

Note that if $c'_{ij} = c_{ij} + M$, where M is a sufficiently large number, then the matrix C' satisfies the triangle inequality of metrics:

$$c'_{ik} \leqslant c'_{ij} + c'_{jk}, \qquad \text{for all } i, j, k.$$

It follows that, with regard to *optimization*, there is no loss in generality in assuming that an instance of the TSP satisfies the triangle inequality. As we shall learn in Chapter 5, however, this assumption does make a considerable difference so far as *approximation* is concerned.

3.3 Multiple salesmen

The m-salesman problem is a simplified model of the vehicle routing problem dealt with in Chapter 12. Suppose each of n cities must be visited by one of m salesmen. Each salesman begins and ends his subtour at a predetermined home base. A fixed cost d_j is incurred if salesman j is employed. The objective is to minimize the sum of the fixed costs and the costs (lengths) of the tours. It will be shown that this *m-salesman problem* can be transformed into an ordinary TSP with the addition of $m-1$ additional vertices [Bellmore & Hong, 1974].

Let the m salesmen be indexed from 0 to $m-1$ such that

$$d_0 \le d_1 \le \ldots \le d_{m-1}.$$

Add $m-1$ additional vertices to the graph, denoted $-1, \ldots, -(m-1)$, and let the home base be vertex 0. Also, add the following sets of arcs to A, the

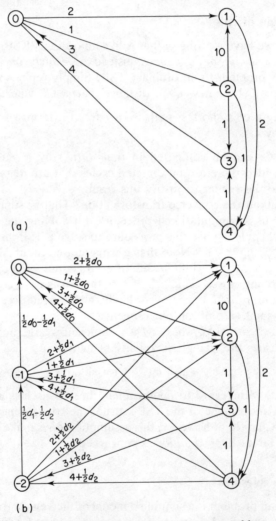

(a)

(b)

Figure 2.2   (a) Digraph for m-salesmen problem.
(b) Transformed digraph for TSP

original set of arcs: arc $(-i, j)$ for all i if $(0, j) \in A$; arc $(j, -i)$ for all i if $(j, 0) \in A$; arc $(-i, -(i-1))$ for $i = 1, \ldots, m-1$. The lengths c'_{ij} of the arcs in the transformed network are given by:

$$
\begin{aligned}
c'_{ij} &= c_{ij}, & i, j &= 1, \ldots, n, \\
c'_{-i,j} &= c_{0j} + \tfrac{1}{2} d_i, & i &= 0, \ldots, m-1, j = 1, \ldots, n, \\
c'_{j,-i} &= c_{j0} + \tfrac{1}{2} d_i, & i &= 0, \ldots, m-1, j = 1, \ldots, n, \\
c'_{-i,-(i-1)} &= \tfrac{1}{2} d_{i-1} - \tfrac{1}{2} d_i, & i &= 1, \ldots, m-1.
\end{aligned}
$$

Examples due to Bellmore & Hong [1974] of original and transformed networks are given in Figure 2.2. To interpret a tour in the transformed graph, consider for example $(0, 1, 4, -2, -1, 2, 3)$. This is interpreted as: salesman 0 visits cities 1 and 4; salesman 2 is not used; salesman 1 visits cities 2 and 3. The reader can verify that the cost of this tour consists of the original distances plus $d_0 + d_1$.

In some cases it may be desirable to solve a TSP with symmetric costs. It can be noted that the above transformation does not yield symmetric costs even if the original problem is symmetric. Hong & Padberg [1977] and Rao [1980] have shown that the transformation given above can be modified to yield a symmetric TSP. In particular, the Rao transformation is a direct extension of that of Bellmore & Hong.

Exercises
2. Justify the transformation from the *at least once* problem to the *exactly once* problem given in Section 3.2.
3. Verify the correctness of the Bellmore–Hong transformation given in Section 3.3.

4   GENERALIZATIONS OF THE TSP AND RELATED PROBLEMS
In this section we discuss the relationship of the TSP to several other more-or-less standard combinatorial optimization problems.

4.1   The assignment problem

Let x_{ij} be a 0–1 variable indicating whether or not the salesman goes directly from city i to city j, and c_{ij} be the corresponding distance. The length of his tour is then

$$
\sum_{i=1}^{n} \sum_{j=1}^{n} c_{ij} x_{ij} \tag{3}
$$

which is to be minimized. Clearly

$$
\sum_{j=1}^{n} x_{ij} = 1, \qquad i = 1, \ldots, n, \tag{4}
$$

Figure 2.3

since a unique city is visited directly after each city, and similarly

$$\sum_{i=1}^{n} x_{ij} = 1, \qquad j = 1, \ldots, n. \tag{5}$$

Now, (3), (4), (5) describe the well-solved *assignment problem*. It follows that the TSP must involve some additional complications, else there would be no need for this volume. In particular, the missing constraints in the above formulation involve *subtours*. For example, if $n = 4$ then $x_{12} = x_{21} = x_{34} = x_{43} = 1$ and $x_{ij} = 0$ otherwise satisfies (4), (5) but represents the two subtours $(1, 2)$, $(3, 4)$ of Figure 2.3 rather than a single tour. Thus, the assignment problem is a *relaxation* of the TSP or, equivalently, the TSP is the *restriction* of the assignment problem obtained by adding the constraint

'no subtours allowed'.   (6)

4.2 Integer linear programming

There are a number of ways to enforce (6) mathematically. For instance, (6) can be replaced with

$$\sum_{i \in S} \sum_{j \in S} x_{ij} \leqslant |S| - 1 \tag{6a}$$

or with

$$\sum_{i \in S} \sum_{j \in \bar{S}} x_{ij} \geqslant 1 \tag{6b}$$

for every proper, nonempty subset S of $N = \{1, \ldots, n\}$ where $|\cdot|$ denotes cardinality. Clearly any subtour violates (6a) and (6b) for some S. (In Figure 2.3, $S = \{1, 2\}$ or $\{3, 4\}$). Of course (6a) and (6b) represent a large number of constraints: $2^n - 2$ to be exact. However, these formulations, due to Dantzig, Fulkerson & Johnson [1954], do have at least one characteristic of good formulations, namely a well-solved relaxation.

A more compact variation of (6a) or (6b) is proposed by Miller, Tucker & Zemlin [1960]. Arbitrarily designate vertex 1 to be the home base. Then the constraints

$$u_i - u_j + n x_{ij} \leqslant n - 1, \qquad i, j = 2, \ldots, n, \tag{6c}$$

where u_i and u_j are arbitrary real numbers, block all tours not containing vertex 1. To see that (6c) in conjunction with (4), (5) blocks subtours, consider an arbitrary subtour $(i_1, \ldots, i_k)$ where $1 \notin \{i_1, \ldots, i_k\}$. If a set of x_{ij}

satisfying (4), (5) represents more than one subtour, then clearly it also represents at least one subtour not containing vertex 1. But addition of the constraints (6c) represented by this subtour yields $nk \le (n-1)k$ which is clearly false since $n, k \ge 2$. Furthermore, every TSP tour remains feasible with these additional constraints. Every tour can be assumed to start at city 1. If city i is visited jth after 1, let $u_i = j$. As an example, consider the tour $(1, 4, 3, 2)$. For this, set $u_1 = 0$, $u_4 = 1$, $u_3 = 2$, and $u_2 = 3$. It is straightforward to verify that this procedure works in general.

Note that the model (3), (4), (5), (6c) with x_{ij} binary is a mixed integer program since it has $n-1$ continuous variables, and that (6c) represents only $(n-1)^2$ constraints. It is also shown by Miller, Tucker & Zemlin [1960] that an extension of the TSP can be modeled in the same way. Suppose the salesman visits the cities in a number of subtours, each beginning and ending at city 1, and no subtour can contain more than p cities. Then (6c) can be replaced with

$$u_i - u_j + px_{ij} \le p - 1, \qquad i, j = 2, \ldots, n. \tag{6d}$$

Of course, since city 1 can be visited more than once, the conditions $\sum_{j=1}^{n} x_{1j} = 1$ and $\sum_{i=1}^{n} x_{i1} = 1$ should be eliminated.

Now that we have shown that the TSP can be modeled using $O(n^2)$ constraints, it is interesting to note that a further reduction to $O(n)$ constraints can be achieved while solving a considerable generalization of the TSP. This result is presented in Section 5.1.

4.3 The quadratic assignment problem

The quadratic assignment problem is to minimize

$$\sum_{i,j,p,q=1}^{n} d_{ijpq} x_{ip} x_{jq}$$

subject to

$$\left. \begin{array}{ll} \displaystyle\sum_{p=1}^{n} x_{ip} = 1, & i = 1, \ldots, n, \\[2ex] \displaystyle\sum_{i=1}^{n} x_{ip} = 1, & p = 1, \ldots, n, \\[2ex] x_{ip} \in \{0, 1\}, & i, p = 1, \ldots, n. \end{array} \right\} \tag{7}$$

The problem was originally stated in a slightly less general form by Koopmans & Beckmann [1957] as a model of a plant location problem. In this problem

$$d_{ijpq} = c_{ij} t_{pq},$$

where t_{pq} is the number of units of a commodity to be shipped from plant p to plant q, and c_{ij} is the unit shipping cost from location i to location j. The variable x_{ip} is an indicator of whether or not plant p is assigned to location i.

Before discussing the transformation by Lawler [1963] of the TSP to the quadratic assignment problem, it is important to note that a solution to the TSP can be thought of as a cyclic permutation of the integers $1, \ldots, n$. Then x_{ip} can be interpreted as an indicator of whether or not city i occupies the pth place in the permutation (i.e. is the pth city visited). For instance, if the proposed tour is $(3, 6, 4, 2, 1, 5)$ then $x_{31} = x_{62} = x_{43} = x_{24} = x_{15} = x_{56} = 1$ and $x_{ij} = 0$ otherwise.

It is easy to see that this definition of x also satisfies the constraints (7). This definition does not lend itself to a linear model, however, since there is no cost corresponding to x_{ip}. A quadratic objective can be used instead, since if $x_{ip} = 1$ and $x_{j,p+1} = 1$ then the cost incurred is c_{ij}. Thus the TSP can be written as a quadratic assignment problem in which $C = (c_{ij})$ is the original distance matrix and $T = (t_{pq})$ is a cyclic permutation matrix. That is, $t_{p,p+1} = 1$ for $p = 1, \ldots, n-1$, $t_{n1} = 1$ and $t_{pq} = 0$ otherwise.

4.4   The longest path problem

The problem of finding a longest path in a network between a specified pair of vertices does not seem to differ from the problem of finding a shortest path. This follows because maximization and minimization problems can be converted into one another by multiplying the objective (i.e. the arc lengths) by -1. It may, therefore, seem confusing that the shortest path problem is classified as easy while the longest path problem is hard. The reason for the difference is that the shortest (longest) path problem is only easy as long as there are no cycles of total negative (positive) length. Since arc lengths are generally positive, the distinction follows. The TSP, in turn, can be transformed into a longest path problem which generally contains cycles of positive length.

To transform the TSP to the longest path problem, first transform the given instance of the TSP, with arc lengths c_{ij}, to an instance of the Hamiltonian path problem, with arc lengths c'_{ij}, as indicated in Section 3.1. Then replace each arc length c'_{ij} by $c''_{ij} = M - c'_{ij}$, where M is suitably large, i.e. a number larger than the sum of the n largest c'_{ij} values. A longest path (with no repeated vertices) from s to t with respect to the arc lengths c''_{ij} is a shortest Hamiltonian path from s to t, and conversely [Hardgrave & Nemhauser, 1962].

The transformation from the longest path problem to the TSP is a bit more complicated. Suppose we wish to find a longest path from vertex 1 to vertex n in a digraph such as that in Figure 2.4(a). First multiply each arc length by -1, to convert the problem to a shortest path problem (with negative cycles). Then create $2(n-2)$ new vertices and $4n-7$ new arcs, with lengths $-M$ and $-\frac{1}{2}M$, where M is a very large number, as shown in Figure 2.4(b). We assert that a shortest Hamiltonian cycle in the new digraph has the property that the part of the cycle from vertex 1 to vertex n is a shortest path (and hence a longest path in the original digraph) and that the part of

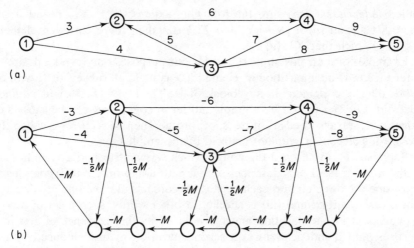

Figure 2.4   (a) Digraph for longest path problem. (b) Transformed digraph for TSP

the cycle from vertex n to vertex 1 has length exactly $-(2n-3)M$. We leave verification of this assertion to the reader as an exercise.

4.5   Minimum spanning trees

A *spanning tree* of a graph is a tree connecting all vertices. The solution to the problem of finding a spanning tree of minimum total length was one of the early successes of combinatorial optimization. The title of the pioneering paper [Kruskal, 1956] is certainly significant: 'On the shortest spanning subtree of a graph and the traveling salesman problem'. Every Hamiltonian path is a spanning tree, and a spanning tree is a Hamiltonian path provided it satisfies the additional constraint

'no vertex of the tree has degree greater than two'.   (9)

Thus, the minimum spanning tree problem is a relaxation of the TSP, and the TSP is a restriction of the minimum spanning tree problem.

In Chapter 10, it is described how Lagrangean multipliers can be used in an attempt to enforce the constraint (8). One approach is to employ so-called *subgradient optimization* so as to find (normalized) values of the Lagrangean multipliers for which the length of a minimum spanning tree is as large as possible. This results either in a shortest Hamiltonian path or in a good lower bound on its length.

4.6   Matroid intersection

Matroid theory provides still another perspective on the TSP. A *matroid* consists of a finite *ground set* E and a nonempty collection $\mathscr{I}$ of subsets of E, called *independent sets*, with the following axioms: (i) if $X \subseteq Y$ and $Y \in \mathscr{I}$ then $X \in \mathscr{I}$, and (ii) if $|X| < |Y|$ and $X, Y \in \mathscr{I}$ then there exists an element $e \in Y - X$ such that $X \cup \{e\} \in \mathscr{I}$.

Examples of matroids abound, but for our purposes only two kinds are of interest. Let Π be a partition of E and let $\mathscr{I}$ contain all subsets of E with no more than one element in any block of Π. Then $M = (E, \mathscr{I})$ is a *partition* matroid. Let $G = (V, E)$ be a graph and let $\mathscr{I}$ contain all acyclic subsets of edges, i.e., subsets of edges of trees, or forests. Then $M = (E, \mathscr{I})$ is called the *cycle* (or *polygon* or *graphic*) matroid of the graph G.

Suppose $G = (V, E)$ is a digraph in which we want to find a Hamiltonian path. A set of $n - 1$ arcs describes such a path if and only if it (i) contains at most one arc directed into each vertex, (ii) contains at most one arc directed out of each vertex, and (iii) is acyclic. In other words, such a set of arcs is independent in one partition matroid induced by the incidence of arcs into vertices, and is independent in a second partition matroid induced by the incidence of arcs out of vertices, and is also independent in the cycle matroid of the digraph (for which the directions of arcs are irrelevant).

Thus the Hamiltonian path problem reduces to the following: Given three matroids $M_i = (E, \mathscr{I}_i)$, $i = 1, 2, 3$ does there exist a set $X \subseteq E$, with $|X| = n - 1$, such that $X \in \mathscr{I}_1 \cap \mathscr{I}_2 \cap \mathscr{I}_3$. This formulation is tantalizing because there are good, polynomial-time algorithms for the *matroid intersection* problem [Lawler, 1976] in which there are only two matroids. However, there are no good algorithms known for intersecting three or more matroids.

In the case at hand, the intersection problem for the two partition matroids is simply a *bipartite matching* (or *assignment*) problem. The intersection problem for either one of the partition matroids and the cycle matroid is a *branching* (or *directed spanning tree*) problem, for which very efficient specialized algorithms are also known. But there are very few clues as to how to intersect all three matroids efficiently.

Exercises

4. Prove that the problem (3), (4), (5), (6d) represents the extension of the TSP described in Section 4.2.
5. Consider the following problem. There are two salesmen and $2n$ cities. During a period of n days, each salesman is to visit a different city each day. It does not make any difference which salesman visits which city. However, each evening the two salesmen are to confer by long-distance telephone. The cost of a call between cities i and j is, say, d_{ij}. It is desired to minimize the sum of the distances c_{ij} that the salesmen travel, plus the sum of the telephone charges d_{ij}. Formulate this as a quadratic assignment problem.
6. Verify the correctness of the transformation from the longest path problem to the TSP given in Section 4.4.
7. (a) Prove that the following *greedy algorithm* due to Kruskal [1956] solves the minimum spanning tree problem: Choose the edges, from smallest to largest, rejecting an edge for the spanning tree only if its introduction into

the solution would create a cycle with some of the edges already chosen. (Ties between edges can be broken arbitrarily.)

(b) Show that a minimum spanning tree satisfies the following very strong property. If T is a minimum spanning tree, then when T is compared with any other spanning tree T', the kth shortest edge of T is at least as short as the kth shortest edge of T', for $k = 1, 2, \ldots, n - 1$.

5 VARIANTS OF THE TSP

In this section we consider three variants of the TSP: the bottleneck TSP, the time-dependent TSP and the stochastic TSP.

5.1 The bottleneck TSP

In the *bottleneck* TSP the objective is to minimize the *longest* intercity distance that the salesman travels, instead of the *sum* of these distances. Otherwise the problem is the same as the ordinary TSP.

As an example of the bottleneck TSP, consider an assembly line with work stations arranged sequentially. There are n jobs to be performed on a product moving along the line and these jobs can be done in any order. The time required to do job j directly after job i is, as in the case of job sequencing in Section 2.4,

$$t_{ij} = c_{ij} + p_j,$$

where c_{ij} is the setup time and p_j is the actual time required to perform job j. If the objective is to sequence the jobs so as to minimize the cycle time of the assembly line, then the bottleneck criterion is appropriate.

Note that the optimality of a solution to the bottleneck TSP depends not on the magnitudes of the c_{ij} but only on their relative values. For example, the matrices

$$C_1 = \begin{bmatrix} 0 & 17 & 8 \\ 3 & 0 & 7 \\ 15 & 11 & 0 \end{bmatrix}, \qquad C_2 = \begin{bmatrix} 0 & 8 & 4 \\ 2 & 0 & 3 \\ 7 & 6 & 0 \end{bmatrix}$$

have identical solutions. In fact, it is easy to see that the order-preserving mapping

$$c'_{ij} = 2^{c_{ij}}$$

transforms an instance of the bottleneck TSP into an instance C' of the ordinary TSP (provided that all c_{ij} values are different). However, such a transformation is of largely theoretical interest, since the bottleneck problem is generally much easier to solve directly.

More useful is the fact that the bottleneck TSP reduces to the Hamiltonian cycle problem. To see this, note that one wants to find the smallest value t such that there exists a Hamiltonian cycle in the subgraph containing arcs (i, j) for which $c_{ij} \le t$. By applying binary search, an optimal solution to the bottleneck TSP can be found by solving $O(\log n)$ Hamiltonian cycle problems.

The analysis of random bottleneck TSPs is facilitated by the fact that any order-preserving transformation of the c_{ij} yields a bottleneck problem with the same ranking of solutions. Suppose the values c_{ij} are independent observations of a random variable with continuous distribution (or cumulative density) function F. In such a problem each c_{ij} can be replaced by $c'_{ij} = F(c_{ij})$. The c_{ij} are then independent observations of a random variable uniformly distributed on $[0, 1]$. This observation makes it possible to predict the value of an optimal solution to a large random bottleneck TSP with great confidence [Garfinkel & Gilbert, 1978].

5.2 The time-dependent TSP

Consider a variation of the TSP in which there are n time periods, indexed by t, and where c_{ijt} is the cost of going directly from city i to city j in period t. Variables x_{ijt} are correspondingly defined, so that the objective is to minimize

$$\sum_{i=1}^{n} \sum_{j=1}^{n} \sum_{t=1}^{n} c_{ijt} x_{ijt}. \tag{9}$$

It is easy to see that (9) should be minimized subject to:

$$\sum_{j=1}^{n} \sum_{t=1}^{n} x_{ijt} = 1, \qquad i = 1, \ldots, n, \tag{10a}$$

$$\sum_{i=1}^{n} \sum_{t=1}^{n} x_{ijt} = 1, \qquad j = 1, \ldots, n, \tag{10b}$$

$$\sum_{i=1}^{n} \sum_{j=1}^{n} x_{ijt} = 1, \qquad t = 1, \ldots, n, \tag{10c}$$

$$\sum_{j=1}^{n} \sum_{t=2}^{n} t x_{ijt} - \sum_{j=1}^{n} \sum_{t=1}^{n} t x_{jit} = 1, \qquad i = 2, \ldots, n, \tag{11}$$

where it is assumed for simplicity that the tour begins and ends in city 1. The constraints (11) insure that for all vertices i, $2 \le i \le n$, the time that i is entered is one less than the time that i is exited. This forces the tour to start at vertex 1; other than that, all other tours remain feasible. The constraints (11) serve to block all subtours not containing city 1, for if city $i^* \ne 1$ were in such a subtour and i^* were exited at p and entered at $p + \delta$, $\delta \ge 1$, then the left side of (11) for $i = i^*$ would be $-\delta$. Thus (11) permits only one tour.

The formulation (9), (10a,b,c), (11) contains n^3 variables and $4n - 1$ constraints, a very compact representation of this generalized TSP. Surprisingly, as shown by Fox, Gavish & Graves [1980], the number of constraints can be reduced to n by replacing (10a,b,c) with

$$\sum_{i=1}^{n} \sum_{j=1}^{n} \sum_{t=1}^{n} x_{ijt} = n. \tag{10d}$$

To show this, first note that the above argument did not use the constraints (10c), which are superfluous. Further, (11) implies

$$\sum_{j=1}^{n} \sum_{t=2}^{n} tx_{ijt} \geq 1, \qquad i = 2, \ldots, n. \tag{12}$$

In order for (12) to hold, it is necessary that

$$\sum_{j=1}^{n} \sum_{t=2}^{n} x_{ijt} \geq 1, \qquad i = 2, \ldots, n.$$

This, in turn, implies the stronger constraint that

$$\sum_{j=1}^{n} \sum_{t=2}^{n} tx_{ijt} \geq 2, \qquad i = 2, \ldots, n. \tag{13}$$

By similar reasoning, (11) and (13) imply that

$$\sum_{j=1}^{n} \sum_{t=1}^{n} x_{jit} \geq 1, \qquad i = 2, \ldots, n,$$

so that each vertex i, $2 \leq i \leq n$, has at least one arc entering it and at least one arc leaving it. Summation of the constraints (11) and simplifying gives

$$\sum_{i=2}^{n} \sum_{t=2}^{n} tx_{i1t} - \sum_{j=2}^{n} \sum_{t=1}^{n} tx_{1jt} - \sum_{i=2}^{n} \sum_{j=2}^{n} x_{ij1} = n - 1. \tag{14}$$

Recall that the purpose of (11) was, in part, to force the tour to begin and end at vertex 1. Therefore, we want $x_{i1t} = 0$, $t \neq n$; $x_{1jt} = 0$, $t \neq 1$; and $x_{ij1} = 0$, $i \neq 1$. We can impose these restrictions without introducing any additional constraints by either substituting these values into the existing constraints or setting the appropriate objective function coefficients to infinity. These restrictions simplify (14) to

$$\sum_{i=2}^{n} nx_{i1n} - \sum_{j=2}^{n} x_{1j1} = n - 1,$$

from which it follows that

$$\sum_{i=2}^{n} x_{i1n} \geq 1 \quad \text{and} \quad \sum_{j=2}^{n} x_{1j1} \geq 1.$$

Therefore, vertex 1 also has at least one arc entering and at least one arc leaving it. By (10d), every vertex must have exactly one arc both entering and leaving it. This is equivalent to (10a,b). The proof that no subtour exists which does not contain vertex 1 follows exactly as before.

The usefulness of this surprisingly compact formulation has yet to be shown, although it certainly warrants investigation. It is interesting to note, however, that the (non-time-dependent) TSP can be represented with only n constraints at the expense of increasing the number of variables from n^2 to n^3.

5.3   More on the time-dependent TSP

In this section, two other formulations of the time-dependent TSP by Picard & Queyranne [1978] are given. Since this work is derived from a one-machine scheduling problem, it is natural to assume that the machine has initial and final states denoted by 0 and $n+1$ respectively. Each state corresponds to a configuration that allows a particular job to be processed.

A model that is a direct extension of one given by Hadley [1964] for the TSP is as follows: Let x_{ijt} be an indicator variable for the transition from state i to state j at time t. Then the objective is to minimize

$$\sum_{j=1}^{n} c_{0j0}x_{0j0} + \sum_{t=1}^{n-1}\sum_{i=1}^{n}\sum_{j=1}^{n} c_{ijt}x_{ijt} + \sum_{j=1}^{n} c_{j,n+1,n}x_{j,n+1,n}$$

subject to

$$\sum_{j=1}^{n} x_{0j0} = 1,$$

$$x_{0j0} = \sum_{k=1}^{n} x_{jk1}, \qquad j = 1,\ldots,n,$$

$$\sum_{i=1}^{n} x_{ijt} = \sum_{k=1}^{n} x_{jk,t+1}, \qquad t = 1,\ldots,n-2, \qquad j = 1,\ldots,n,$$

$$\sum_{i=1}^{n} x_{ij,n-1} = x_{j,n+1,n}, \qquad j = 1,\ldots,n,$$

$$x_{0j0} + \sum_{i=1}^{n}\sum_{t=1}^{n} x_{ijt} = 1, \qquad j = 1,\ldots,n,$$

$$x_{ijt} \in \{0, 1\}, \qquad \text{all } i, j, t.$$

Note that this formulation is much less compact than that of Fox, Gavish & Graves [1980], yet it does have the desirable property that all of the constraint coefficients are in the set $\{-1, 0, 1\}$. Computational experience has indicated that it is a viable model.

Another interesting formulation of the same problem is also given by Picard and Queyranne. It is based on the graph of Figure 2.5 where $n = 4$ and vertex (i, t) means that job i is done in period t. A path from 0 to $n+1$ represents a feasible solution if every city is visited exactly once.

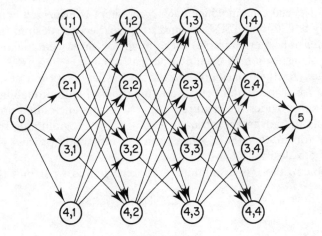

Figure 2.5

Then an appropriate formulation is to minimize

$$\sum_{p \in P} l(p)x_p$$

subject to

$$\sum_{p \in P} a_i^p x_p = 1, \qquad i = 1, \ldots, n,$$

$$x_p \in \{0, 1\}, \qquad \text{all } p \in P,$$

where P is the set of paths from 0 to $n + 1$, $l(p)$ is the length of a path $p \in P$ and a_i^p is the number of visits to state i in path p.

This type of formulation is different from those previously seen in this chapter since it uses an extremely large set P to index the variables. Clearly enumeration of P is out of the question for large problems, yet effective solution techniques can be based on a formulation such as this.

5.4 A stochastic TSP

It is possible to conceive of many realizations of stochastic traveling salesman models. One such model, along with various applications, is due to Derman & Klein [1966].

Consider a set of n components to be inspected over an infinite horizon. The cost of inspecting component j directly after component i is given by c_{ij}. Inspection times are constant and inspection frequencies over the infinite horizon are given. Inspection frequencies can be interpreted deterministically, in the sense that if the desired inspection frequency of component i is $\frac{1}{5}$ then component i will be inspected every five periods. This interpretation leads to two inherent difficulties.

First, the special case in which each component is inspected equally often is obviously a TSP, and TSPs are hard to solve. Second, desired frequencies may be infeasible. For example, there might be three components and the frequency of inspection of each component is $\frac{1}{2}$.

This leads to the consideration of stochastic decision rules. That is, component j is inspected directly after component i with probability p_{ij}. This interpretation provides the required inspection frequencies in a probabilistic sense. It has the advantage of leading to a linear programming solution. It also allows for an element of surprise in the inspection process which may very well be a desirable feature.

The problem, then, is to minimize the expected cost per unit time,

$$\sum_i \sum_j \pi_i p_{ij} c_{ij}$$

subject to

$$\sum_i \pi_i p_{ij} = \pi_j = b_j, \qquad j = 1, \ldots, n,$$

$$\sum_j \pi_j = 1,$$

$$\pi_j \geq 0,$$

where π_j is the steady-state probability of inspecting component j, and b_j is the corresponding required frequency of inspection. Derman and Klein point out that in order for the model to be valid, the underlying Markov chain must have exactly one ergodic class. Additional constraints are added in order to guarantee that condition and to permit the solution of the Markov decision model by linear programming.

Exercise

8. Show that the constraints (10c) are implied by (10a,b) and (11).

The Traveling Salesman Problem
Edited by E. L. Lawler, J. K. Lenstra,
A. H. G. Rinnooy Kan, D. B. Shmoys
© 1985 John Wiley & Sons Ltd.

3

Computational complexity

D. S. Johnson
AT&T Bell Laboratories, Murray Hill

C. H. Papadimitriou
Stanford University; National Technical University of Athens

1 INTRODUCTION

In the last decade or so a theory of *computational complexity* has developed, based on rigorous methods for evaluating algorithms and for classifying problems as 'hard' or 'easy'. This theory is deeply indebted to the field of combinatorial optimization, which has provided it with invaluable motivation, insight, and paradigms. The TSP is probably the most important among the latter. It has served as a testbed for almost every new algorithmic idea, and was one of the first optimization problems conjectured to be 'hard' in a specific technical sense [Edmonds, 1965a].

In this chapter we shall be studying the complexity of the TSP, while providing an introduction to the general area of computational complexity. Section 2 provides an introduction to the notion of an algorithm and to different measures of its 'complexity'. Section 3 shows how we can restrict our attention to *decision problems* (problems with a 'yes' or 'no' answer), and divide these into equivalence classes according to their difficulty. Section 4 then proves that even very restricted versions of the TSP are likely to be very hard (they are, in the technical jargon, $\mathcal{NP}$-complete). Section 5 concludes the chapter by examining the complexity of problems related to the TSP, as well as complexity aspects of various proposed *approaches* to the TSP.

2 ALGORITHMS AND COMPLEXITY

2.1 Algorithms

An *algorithm* is a step-by-step procedure for solving a problem. This concept can be formalized in a number of ways, for instance in terms of *Turing machines* or of *computer programs* in some programming language such as FORTRAN or ALGOL (assuming the semantics of the language have been precisely specified). However, the informal notion of 'algorithm' as a step-by-step procedure will suffice for most of our discussions, as will the following informal notion of 'problem' (the thing an algorithm 'solves').

A problem can be viewed as consisting of a *domain* containing the *instances* of the problem, together with a *question* that can be asked about any one of the instances. For example, an instance of the TSP is composed of a number n of cities and an $n \times n$ distance matrix C, and the question asked by the TSP is 'What is the shortest tour for the n cities?' Our standard format for describing problems will consist of a generic description of an instance in the problem's domain, followed by a statement of the problem's question, posed in terms of the generic instance. A description of the TSP in this format goes as follows:

TSP

INSTANCE: Integer $n \geqslant 3$ and $n \times n$ matrix $C = (c_{ij})$, where each c_{ij} is a nonnegative integer.

QUESTION: Which cyclic permutation π of the integers from 1 to n minimizes the sum $\sum_{i=1}^{n} c_{i\pi(i)}$?

Note that in this definition we restrict the intercity distances to be integers, a convention we shall follow throughout this chapter. In practice, one might expect intercity distances to occasionally have fractional parts, or even be irrational numbers. However, irrational numbers are approximated by rationals for computer representation, and one can always convert the rational distances to integral values simply by multiplying by an appropriate scale factor. We shall assume that all this has already been done.

An algorithm is said to *solve* a problem P if, given any instance *I* of *P* as input data, it will generate the answer of P's question for *I*. An algorithm for the TSP must thus, given any *n* and *C* as above, generate the corresponding minimum length tour (cyclic permutation).

One classical result in the theory of algorithms is that there are well-defined mathematical problems for which no algorithms can exist (for a discussion see Lewis & Papadimitriou [1981]). Although, given a particular instance, one may be able to come up with an answer for that instance, there is no general procedure that will apply to *all* instances. By comparison, the situation with the TSP is much better (at least in theory). There definitely is an algorithm for the TSP, namely, Algorithm A of Figure 3.1. It generates all tours, evaluates each, and picks the best. This algorithm embodies the widely used technique known to practitioners as 'brute force', and even though we shall postpone a detailed analysis of its efficiency, it should already be clear that efficiency is not its strong point.

ALGORITHM A

Input: An integer $n \geqslant 3$ and an $n \times n$ distance matrix C of nonnegative integers.

Output: The shortest tour of n cities.

begin

    $\text{min} := \infty$;

    for all cyclic permutations π of $\{1, 2, \ldots, n\}$ **do**

    begin

        $\text{cost} := \sum_{i=1}^{n} c_{i\pi(i)}$;

        if $\text{cost} < \text{min}$ **then**

        begin

            $\text{min} := \text{cost}$; $\text{besttour} := \pi$

        end

    end;

    output besttour

end

Figure 3.1

A better algorithm is Algorithm B in Figure 3.2. This algorithm finds, for each *i*, the shortest path from city 1 to city *i* that visits all the other nodes in $\{2, 3, \ldots, n\}$. Once these paths are found it is a simple matter to compute

ALGORITHM B

Input and **Output:** As in Algorithm A.

begin

    for $i = 2, 3, \ldots, n$ **do**

        begin

        $\text{cost}[\{i\}, i] := c_{1i}$; $\text{bestpath}[\{i\}, i] := (1, i)$

        end;

    for $j := 2, 3, \ldots, n-1$ **do**

        for each $S \subseteq \{2, 3, \ldots, n\}$ with $|S| = j$ **do**

            for each $i \in S$ **do**

            begin

            $\text{cost}[S, i] := \min_{k \in S - \{i\}} \{\text{cost}[S - \{i\}, k] + c_{ki}\}$;
            let k be the city that achieves this minimum;
            $\text{bestpath}[S, i] := \text{bestpath}[S - \{i\}, k]//(i)$

            end;

    $\text{mincost} := \min_{k \neq 1} \{\text{cost}[\{2, 3, \ldots, n\}, k] + c_{k1}\}$;
    let k be the city that achieves this minimum;
    $\text{besttour} := \text{bestpath}[\{2, 3, \ldots, n\}, k]$;
    output besttour

end

Note: $//$ stands for concatenation of sequences of cities. For example, $(1, 3)//(2, 5, 4) = (1, 3, 2, 5, 4)$.

Figure 3.2

the shortest tour (this is what the last two assignments of Algorithm B are doing). To find these paths, the algorithm solves a more general problem. For any $S \subseteq \{2, \ldots, n\}$ and $i \in S$, let an (S, i) path be a path which starts at city 1, visits each city in S exactly once, and no other city, and ends up in city i. Let $\text{cost}[S, i]$ stand for the length of the shortest (S, i) path. Then $\text{cost}[S, i]$ satisfies the following equation, where $|S| \geqslant 2$:

$$\text{cost}[S, i] = \min_{k \in S - \{i\}} \{\text{cost}[S - \{i\}, k] + c_{ki}\}.$$

What Algorithm B does should now be clear. It 'builds up' the values of $\text{cost}[S, i]$ for larger and larger sets S until $\text{cost}[\{2, 3, \ldots, n\}, i]$ is obtained for $i = 2, 3, \ldots, n$. The array *bestpath* is used to record for each S and i the path which achieves cost$[S, i]$.

Putting together the solutions of bigger and bigger subproblems to obtain an overall solution is an algorithmic technique of wide applicability, known as *dynamic programming* (see Bellman & Dreyfus [1962]). The particular algorithm is due to Held & Karp [1962].

For another example of the use of dynamic programming, let us consider the following problem that would seem to be closely related to the TSP.

SHORTEST PATH
INSTANCE: As in TSP.
QUESTION: What is the shortest path from city 1 to city n?

Note that, unlike the TSP, the shortest path problem makes no insistence that cities other than 1 and n be visited by the path. Here we define cost$[i, j]$, for each city $i \neq 1$ and integer $j \geq 1$, to be the length of the shortest path from 1 to i containing j or fewer edges. We have for $j > 1$,

$$\text{cost}[i, j] = \min\left\{\text{cost}[i, j-1], \min_{k \neq i, 1}\{\text{cost}[k, j-1] + c_{ki}\}\right\}.$$

ALGORITHM C

Input: As in Algorithm A.

Output: The shortest path from city 1 to city n.

begin

    for $i = 2, \ldots, n$ **do begin** cost$[i, 1] := c_{1i}$; bestpath$[i, 1] := (1, i)$ **end**;

    for $j = 2, 3, \ldots, n$ **do**

        for $i = 2, 3, \ldots, n$ **do**

        begin

        cost$[i, j] := \min_{k \neq 1, i}\{\text{cost}[k, j-1] + c_{ki}\}$;
        let k be the city that achieves this minimum;
        bestpath$[i, j] :=$ bestpath$[k, j-1]//(i)$;
        if cost$[i, j-1] <$ cost$[i, j]$ **then**

            begin
            cost$[i, j] :=$ cost$[i, j-1]$; bestpath$[i, j] :=$ bestpath$[i, j-1]$
            end

        end;

    output bestpath$[n, n-1]$

end

Figure 3.3

This equation is the key to the dynamic programming embodied in Algorithm C, shown in Figure 3.3.

Superficially, Algorithms B and C look very similar. As we shall see, from the standpoint of computational complexity they are worlds apart. Algorithm B, and in fact every known algorithm for the TSP, has much more in common with the brute force of Algorithm A than it does with the dynamic programming of Algorithm C.

2.2 Estimating running time

Let us estimate the running time of Algorithms A, B and C. In order that our analyses provide general information, we shall express running time as a function of the number n of cities, rather than just determine it for a particular instance. In order to make our analyses independent of the speed of the particular computer which might be used to execute the algorithm, we shall count 'steps' instead of machine cycles, and shall use O-notation ('big O' notation) to express the running time function. To say that an algorithm's running time is $O(f(n))$ means that there is some constant c such that the algorithm's running time on all inputs of size n is bounded by $cf(n)$. The precise value of c would depend on the computer used.

Algorithm A takes time $O(n!)$. The main loop is repeated $(n-1)!$ times, once for each cyclic permutation of $\{1, \ldots, n\}$. Each execution of the loop takes time $O(n)$ in generating the next tour, evaluating cost, and updating besttour (if necessary). Multiplying, we obtain the $O(n!)$ estimate.

Much of the effort of Algorithm B is concentrated in the triply nested loop. Let us assume that j is fixed. Then the innermost loop takes time at most cj for some $c>0$ (the minimization is over $j-1$ items, and the sequences bestpath are about j long). The loop is repeated for each subset of $\{2, 3, \ldots, n\}$ that contains j elements, and for each of the j elements in each subset. Summing over all j's we have

$$\sum_{j=2}^{n-1} \binom{n-1}{j} cj^2 \leqslant c[2^{n-1}(n-1)^2] = O(n^2 2^n).$$

The rest of Algorithm B (the initial loop and the computation of besttour) are of linear complexity, and their contribution is absorbed in the O-notation. Thus, Algorithm B takes time $O(n^2 2^n)$.

For Algorithm C, the body of the inner loop is executed $(n-1)^2$ times, and takes $O(n)$ times per execution. This yields an overall bound of $O(n^3)$.

2.3 Worst-case and average-case analysis

Algorithms A, B and C are all very well behaved, in the following sense: One can predict quite accurately the number of steps required for an instance, and the prediction does not vary from one instance to another with the same size n. On the other hand, there are many algorithms that can take a number of steps which varies wildly among instances of the same size (a famous example is the simplex algorithm for linear programming [Klee & Minty, 1972]). If we are to have a complexity function which takes on a single value for each size, there are essentially two approaches we can take. We can either count the *average* or the *maximum* number of steps, over all inputs of size n.

The second method of analysis, called *worst-case analysis*, has an obvious disadvantage: 'pathological' cases are allowed to determine the complexity, even though they may be exceedingly rare in practice. *Average-case analysis*, on the other hand, also has its drawbacks. We must choose a probability distribution for the instances, and finding a mathematically tractable one that also models the instances encountered in practice is not always easy (or even possible). Most clever algorithms introduce a great deal of *statistical dependence* among their individual stages, and average-case analysis becomes a very complicated task when independence cannot be assumed. Finally, whereas worst-case analysis at least provides a 'guarantee' to the user of an algorithm, average-case analysis often provides a prediction that one can have confidence in only if one has to solve a large number of instances. If you must solve a particular instance of a problem, and your algorithm performs abysmally on it, there is little consolation in knowing that you have just encountered a statistically insignificant exception.

Thus we shall take the worst-case approach in the rest of this chapter, a choice that rewards us with the elegant theory of $\mathcal{NP}$-completeness. The average-case approach will be pursued in Chapter 6.

2.4 Polynomial time

We have chosen a measure of the performance of an algorithm: the number of steps spent on an instance, maximized over all instances of size n, and expressed as a function of n (up to a constant multiple). What we have yet to do is specify a relationship between this measure and the question of whether the given algorithm is a 'good' one or not.

Ideally, we would like to call an algorithm 'good' when it is sufficiently efficient to be usable in practice, but this is a rather vague and slippery notion. An idea that has gained wide acceptance in recent years is to consider an algorithm 'good' if its worst-case complexity is bounded by a polynomial function of n. For example, Algorithm C is a 'polynomial-time algorithm' and hence 'good', but Algorithms A and B are not. They are both 'exponential' in the sense that their worst-case complexity grows at least as fast as c^n for some $c > 1$. (Although there are 'subexponential' functions such as $n^{\log n}$, which are neither polynomially bounded nor exponential, for simplicity in what follows we shall often use the term 'exponential' to refer to any algorithm whose worst-case complexity is not bounded by a polynomial.)

The difference between polynomials and exponentials becomes clear if

Table 3.1   A comparison of the growth of some polynomial
functions (above) to that of certain exponential functions
(below).

Function	Approximate values		
n	10	100	1,000
$n \log n$	33	664	9,966
n^3	1,000	1,000,000	10^9
$10^6 n^8$	10^{14}	10^{22}	10^{30}
2^n	1,024	1.27×10^{30}	1.05×10^{301}
$n^{\log n}$	2,099	1.93×10^{13}	7.89×10^{29}
$n!$	3,628,800	10^{158}	4×10^{2567}

one takes an 'asymptotic' point of view. Although a given exponential
function may initially yield smaller values than a given polynomial function,
there always is an N such that for all $n \geqslant N$, the polynomial is the winner.
See Table 3.1. Furthermore, polynomial-time algorithms are in a better
position to take advantage of technological improvements in the speed of
computers. Suppose that we have two algorithms, one running in time
$O(n^3)$, the other in time $O(2^n)$, both of which can solve a problem with
$n = 100$ in one hour. If we get a new computer which is twice as fast, the
polynomial-time algorithm can now in one hour solve instances with
$n = 126$, a *multiplicative* factor of 1.26, whereas our exponential algorithm
can only obtain an *additive* improvement, to $n = 101$.

There are also a number of mathematical niceties that reward us for
concentrating on the distinction between polynomial and exponential.
Polynomials have mathematical properties that make them appealing as the
basis for a theory. You can add two polynomials, multiply them, and
compose them, and the result will still be a polynomial. Polynomial time has
a long-standing place in the abstract theory of computation. There are a
wide variety of 'reasonable' theoretical models for computers, from Turing
machines to random access machines, with many varieties of each, but each
model can simulate any other one with only a *polynomial* loss in efficiency.
Thus a polynomial time algorithm for one model corresponds to a polynomial-time algorithm in each of the others. (For details, see Aho, Hopcroft &
Ullman [1974] or Hopcroft & Ullman [1979]). Furthermore, if one concen-
trates on polynomial time, one can ignore differences in the choice of input
size parameters, an issue that is worth further discussion.

Our definition of *input size* can have a significant effect on the function we
derive for the worst-case complexity of an algorithm. For instance, consider
an instance of the TSP with n cities. We have been using the number of
cities as the variable in our complexity measures. A reasonable alternative
would be the number $m = n^2$ of entries in the distance matrix. If we use *this*
as our measure of input size, Algorithm A suddenly 'speeds up' from $O(n!)$

to $O(\sqrt{m}!)$, and Algorithm C 'speeds up' from $O(n^3)$ to $O(m^{3/2})$. Notice, however, that Algorithm A remains exponential and Algorithm C remains polynomial. Thus, if we are only interested in the distinction between polynomial and exponential algorithms, we are given a wide latitude in our choice of input measures and hence can ignore fine details.

There is, however, one proviso: our measure of input size must reflect (to within a polynomial) the actual length of a concise encoding of the instance in question, as it would be input to a computer (i.e., as a sequence of symbols). Assuming that all the intercity distances are integers that fit into a single computer word, say of size 32, the number of cities is a measure of input size which meets this requirement, since the actual encoding length would be $32n^2$. If the intercity distances are allowed to be arbitrarily large integers, we would need to use a more sophisticated measure of input size, for example $m = n^2 \log_2(\max\{c_{ij}\})$, that would take into account the number of bits required to represent those distances (the requirement that we consider only concise encodings means that numbers must be represented in a positional notation such as binary, so that the size of a number is proportional to its logarithm, rather than its value). For a more detailed discussion of input size and encodings, see Garey & Johnson [1979].

Thus there are both practical and theoretical reasons for identifying the distinction between 'good' and 'bad' algorithms with the distinction between those algorithms that run in polynomial time and those that do not. Proposals to this effect were first made, in the mid-1960s, by Alan Cobham [Cobham, 1964] and Jack Edmonds [Edmonds, 1965a], and the significance of polynomial time was hinted at much earlier in Von Neumann [1953]. It was Edmonds who proposed the precise terminology 'good' for 'polynomial time'. Subsequent work and in particular the theory of $\mathcal{NP}$-completeness, which we shall be discussing shortly, have widened the acceptance of this equation as the best available way of tying the empirical notion of a 'practical algorithm' to a precisely formalized mathematical concept.

Of course, as with all mathematical modeling of real-world phenomena, there is room for 'experimental errors'. The simplex algorithm for linear programming, although it has exponential worst-case complexity [Klee & Minty, 1972], has been a constant success in practice. The recently discovered ellipsoid algorithm for linear programming [Khachian, 1979] on the other hand, is provably polynomial, but for now it seems to have been abandoned as a practical alternative, despite much initial enthusiasm.

There is also, of course, the possibility of such contrasts as an $O(1.001^n)$ exponential algorithm with a polynomial-time algorithm that runs in time proportional to n^{80} or $10^{100}n$. However, for the most part such contrasts are more potential than real. Algorithms with such running times do not appear that often in practice. Moreover, once a polynomial algorithm is discovered for a problem, it is often the case that a sequence of improvements produces a version that is also of practical use. The real breakthrough is in finding that *first* polynomial-time algorithm. In a sense, finding a better exponential time algorithm is just a matter of more cleverly organizing a brute force approach, whereas to make the jump to polynomial time requires a real insight into the nature of the problem at hand, *if* the jump can be made at all.

Exercises
1. How much *space* is required by Algorithm B? Describe a version of Algorithm B that requires only polynomial space.
2. Show that the space requirements of Algorithm C are $O(n2^n)$.
3. Give an $O(n^2)$ algorithm for SHORTEST PATH.

3 $\mathscr{P}$ AND $\mathscr{NP}$

3.1. Decision problems

Just as we can classify an algorithm as good or bad, depending on whether or not it has polynomial time complexity, we can classify a *problem* as 'hard' or 'easy' depending on whether or not it can be solved by an algorithm with polynomial time complexity. It is on the basis of this distinction that an elegant theory of the complexity of problems has been developed.

For uniformity, this theory formally restricts itself to *decision problems*, that is, problems whose question requires only a 'yes' or 'no' answer. (As we shall see, this does not restrict the applicability of the theory.) Many problems are naturally expressed as decision problems. An example, about which we will have much to say later, is the following well-known problem from graph theory.

HAMILTONIAN CYCLE
INSTANCE: A graph $G = (V, E)$.
QUESTION: Is there a cycle (closed sequence of edges) in G passing through each vertex in V exactly once?

The TSP is not a decision problem, as its question asks for the shortest tour, not a 'yes' or 'no' answer. However, the TSP (and *any* optimization problem) can be easily reformulated as a decision problem, by adding a *bound B* to the input data. For example, the decision version of the TSP would be as follows:

TSP DECISION
INSTANCE: Integer $n \geq 3$, an $n \times n$ matrix $C = (c_{ij})$, where each c_{ij} is a nonnegative integer, and an integer $B \geq 0$.
QUESTION: Is there a cyclic permutation π of the integers from 1 to n such that

$$\sum_{i=1}^{n} c_{i\pi(i)} \leq B?$$

It is clear that if there is a polynomial-time algorithm for the TSP, then there is a polynomial-time algorithm for its decision problem version. This is true for all optimization problems, as long as the cost of a given feasible solution can be computed in polynomial time (a quite reasonable assumption). What is more remarkable is that, for the TSP (and many other problems), the converse is also true.

Consider the algorithm TSPTOUR depicted in Figure 3.4. TSPTOUR generates an optimal tour for any TSP instance, so long as it is provided with a subroutine TSPDECISION that solves TSP DECISION.

ALGORITHM TSPTOUR

Input: An integer n, and an $n \times n$ distance matrix C with nonnegative integer entries.

Output: A revised matrix C in which all but n of the entries have been increased to $n \max_{i,j} \{c_{ij}\} + 1$. The n unchanged entries correspond to the edges used in an optimum tour.

begin

    comment The algorithm TSPTOUR calls as a subroutine an assumed algorithm TSPDECISION(n, C, B) which solves the decision problem version of the TSP;

    low := 0;

    high := $n \max_{i,j} \{c_{ij}\}$;

    while low $\neq$ high **do**

        if TSPDECISION $\left(n, C, \left\lfloor \dfrac{\text{low} + \text{high}}{2} \right\rfloor \right)$ = 'yes'

            then high := $\left\lfloor \dfrac{\text{low} + \text{high}}{2} \right\rfloor$

            else low := $\left\lfloor \dfrac{\text{low} + \text{high}}{2} \right\rfloor + 1$;

    comment At this point high = low and their joint value is the cost of the optimal tour;

    optimum := high;

    for $i = 1, 2, \ldots, n$ **do**

    for $j = 1, 2, \ldots, n$ **do**

        begin

        remember := c_{ij};

        c_{ij} := $n \max_{i,j} \{c_{ij}\} + 1$

        if TSPDECISION(n, C, optimum) = 'no'

            then c_{ij} := remember

        end

end

Figure 3.4

The first part of TSPTOUR computes the length of an optimal tour, using 'binary search'. We start out knowing that the optimal length lies between $low = 0$ and $high = nc_{max}$, where $c_{max} = max_{i,j}\{c_{ij}\}$. This is because a tour contains n links, none of which is longer than the maximum intercity distance. We use TSPDECISION to determine in which half of this range the optimum length actually resides, by applying it to the original instance with the bound $B = \left\lfloor \dfrac{low + high}{2} \right\rfloor$. If the answer is 'yes' we know that B is a new upper bound on the optimal length; otherwise $B + 1$ is a new lower bound. In either case, the size of the range has been halved. The process is repeated until the upper and lower bounds coincide, in which case they both equal the optimum length. The total number of iterations is no more than $\lceil \log_2(nc_{max}) \rceil$, since the size of the range is halved at each iteration.

At this point we know the optimal tour length but do not yet have an optimal tour. The second part of TSPTOUR constructs such a tour. It does this by going through the intercity links in order, and checking which links may be deleted, again using TSPDECISION. If a tour of the optimum length still exists when c_{ij} is increased to $nc_{max} + 1$, we know that there is an optimal tour not containing a link between cities i and j. Otherwise, an optimal tour that does not contain any of the earlier links with increased lengths *must* contain a link between i and j, so we return c_{ij} to its original value. After we have tested all the c_{ij}, the only ones that will retain their original values will be a set corresponding to the links on an optimal tour. (Since no optimal tour can contain one of the $(nc_{max} + 1)$-length links, there must be an optimal tour using only links which had their original length restored, and any unnecessary link would *not* have had its length restored.)

The running time of TSPTOUR depends on that of TSPDECISION. This subroutine is called $\lceil \log_2(nc_{max}) \rceil + n^2$ times, which is a polynomial function of $n \log_2(c_{max})$, the 'accurate' input size measure for the TSP described in the previous section. Thus if TSPDECISION runs in polynomial time, TSPTOUR will have a time complexity function which is the product of two polynomials and is hence polynomial itself. We thus have the following result.

Theorem 1 *There is a polynomial-time algorithm for the TSP if and only if there is a polynomial-time algorithm for* TSP DECISION.

Analogous results can be proved for most optimization problems. Thus, if we are only interested in the distinction between polynomial and non-polynomial, we lose little in the way of generality by restricting attention to decision problems.

3.2 Polynomial reductions

We now introduce a method for relating the complexities of different decision problems. It is every mathematician's dream to reduce the problem he is working on to a problem that has already been solved. In computational complexity there is an analogous notion: the *polynomial reduction*.

We say a problem A is *polynomial-time reducible* to a problem B if there is an algorithm for A which uses a subroutine for B, and the algorithm for A runs in polynomial time when the time for executing each call of the subroutine is counted as a single step (note that this implies that the subroutine can only be called a polynomially bounded number of times). For example, the algorithm TSPTOUR in Figure 3.4 is a polynomial reduction from the TSP to TSP DECISION.

The usefulness of this notion of reduction stems from the following lemma, which can be proved easily using the fact that the composition of two polynomials is a polynomial.

Lemma 1 *If there is a polynomial-time reduction from* A *to* B, *and there is a polynomial time algorithm for* B, *then there is a polynomial-time algorithm for* A.

There are basically three kinds of reductions:

(1) *Reductions that prove a problem is easy,* by reducing it to a problem already known to be solvable by a polynomial-time algorithm. This is the traditional use of reduction; for example, Ford & Fulkerson [1962] describe many such reductions.
(2) *Reductions that prove a problem is hard,* by showing that some known 'hard' problem reduces to it. Some early examples are in Dantzig, Blattner & Rao [1967]. Section 4 will contain a series of such reductions.
(3) *Reductions that prove nothing,* because they reduce problem A of unknown complexity to a problem B that is (or is suspected to be) hard.

A great many reductions of this third kind have appeared in the last three decades. A by now quite famous problem, for which all known algorithms have exponential time complexity (and work poorly in practice too), was most frequently the target in these reductions.

INTEGER PROGRAMMING
  INSTANCE: An $m \times n$ integer matrix $A = (a_{ij})$, an m-vector $b = (b_1, b_2, \ldots, b_m)$ of integers.
  QUESTION: Is there an n-vector x of nonnegative integers such that $Ax = b$, i.e. $\sum_{j=1}^{n} a_{ij}x_j = b_i, 1 \leq i \leq m$?

Versions of this problem with inequalities instead of equalities, or which ask for an x which minimizes a linear function $\sum_{j=1}^{n} c_j x_j$, can all be shown to be equivalent to this decision problem version [Papadimitriou & Steiglitz, 1982]. However, quite different-looking problems can also be reduced to it, and even though such reductions 'prove nothing', they can still provide a nice illustration of the concept of reducibility.

As an example, let us show how to reduce HAMILTONIAN CYCLE to INTEGER

PROGRAMMING. Given a graph $G = (V, E)$ where $V = \{1, 2, \ldots, N\}$, we can write an integer program $I(G)$ such that $I(G)$ has a solution if and only if G has a Hamiltonian cycle. $I(G)$ has N^2 variables x_{ik}, $i, k = 1, \ldots, N$. The intended meaning of x_{ik} is the following: $x_{ik} = 1$ if vertex t is the kth vertex of the Hamiltonian cycle, and $x_{ik} = 0$ otherwise. This can be expressed by the following equations and inequalities:

$$\sum_{k=1}^{N} x_{ik} = 1, \qquad i = 1, \ldots, N, \tag{1}$$

$$\sum_{i=1}^{N} x_{ik} = 1, \qquad k = 1, \ldots, N, \tag{2}$$

$$x_{ik} + x_{j,k+1} \leqslant 1 + e_{ij}, \qquad i, j, k = 1, \ldots, N, \tag{3}$$

where $e_{ij} = 1$ if $\{i, j\} \in E$ and $e_{ij} = 0$ otherwise; and $x_{i,N+1}$ stands for $x_{i,1}$, for all i. The inequalities of (3) can be turned into equalities by using *slack variables* $s_{ijk} \geqslant 0$ and replacing (3) by $x_{ik} + x_{j,k+1} + s_{ijk} = 1 + e_{ij}$, $i, j, k = 1, \ldots, N$. The requirement that the x_{ik} have only 0 or 1 as potential values is automatically ensured by equations (1) and (2). Writing all these equations in matrix form we get an instance $I(G)$ of INTEGER PROGRAMMING in which $m = N^3 + 2N$ and $n = N^3 + N^2$. It is easy to verify that the desired solution x exists for $I(G)$ if and only if G has a Hamiltonian cycle.

The polynomial reduction from HAMILTONIAN CYCLE to INTEGER PROGRAMMING is now straightforward. Given G we construct $I(G)$, which clearly can be done in polynomial time, and then call the hypothetical algorithm for INTEGER PROGRAMMING, using the 'yes' or 'no' outcome of that algorithm as our answer. There is a special name for polynomial reductions of this simple type, which are between decision problems and use the hypothetical sub-routine exactly once, returning its answer as their own. They are called *polynomial transformations*. We say that HAMILTONIAN CYCLE is *polynomial transformable* to INTEGER PROGRAMMING (notation: HAMILTONIAN CYCLE $\propto$ INTEGER PROGRAMMING).

The integer program $I(G)$, which was the result of the transformation above, belongs to the important class of *0–1 programs* that is, integer programs with the additional constraint $x_j \in \{0, 1\}$ for all variables x_j. 0–1 PROGRAMMING is a special case of INTEGER PROGRAMMING, since the constraint $x_j \in \{0, 1\}$ can be expressed by introducing a new variable x_j' and the equation $x_j + x_j' = 1$. Thus 0–1 PROGRAMMING can be no 'harder' than the general problem. We show below that it is no 'easier' either, by giving a polynomial transformation from INTEGER PROGRAMMING to it (this will be a reduction of type (2) above). The proof requires a relatively recent result, which we state without proof [Borosh & Treybig, 1976; Papadimitriou, 1981].

Lemma 2 *Suppose A and b make up an instance of* INTEGER PROGRAMMING, *and let s be the sum of the logarithms of the absolute values of the entries in*

A and b, plus m + n. Then the instance (A, b) has a solution if and only if it has a solution satisfying $x_j < 2^{p(s)}$, for all variables x_j, where p is a fixed polynomial independent of A and b.

Note that s, as defined in the lemma, constitutes a valid measure of input size as discussed in Subsection 2.4. Thus, the lemma in effect says that, if there is a solution, then there is one whose size is bounded by a polynomial in the instance size (each x_j requires only $O(p(s))$ symbols).

Theorem 2   INTEGER PROGRAMMING $\propto$ 0–1 PROGRAMMING.

Proof   Given an instance I of INTEGER PROGRAMMING, we transform I to an equivalent 0–1 program $Z(I)$ as follows: For each variable x of I we create $p(s)$ 0–1 variables $x_0, x_1, \ldots, x_{p(s)-1}$ for $Z(I)$, where s and p are as in Lemma 2, with the interpretation that $x = \sum_{j=0}^{p(s)-1} x_j 2^j$. We then rewrite the equations of I using this substitution, and obtain $Z(I)$. That $Z(I)$ is equivalent to I (i.e., has a solution if and only if I does) follows from Lemma 2 and the fact that a nonnegative integer less than $2^{p(s)}$ can be written (in a unique way) as the sum of powers of 2 from $2^0 = 1$ to $2^{p(s)-1}$. That this is a polynomial transformation follows from the fact that s, as defined in Lemma 2, is a valid measure of input size for INTEGER PROGRAMMING. $\square$

In Section 4 we shall show that INTEGER PROGRAMMING is polynomial-time transformable to even more restricted special cases of itself. In doing so we shall use the following particular desirable property of polynomial transformations, again proved using the fact that the composition of two polynomials is a polynomial.

Lemma 3   *If there are polynomial transformations T_1 from A to B and T_2 from B to C, then there is a polynomial transformation T_3 from A to C.*

In other words, polynomial transformability is transitive. (A similar result holds for polynomial reducibility.)

3.3   The classes $\mathcal{P}$ and $\mathcal{NP}$

We now define the first of two important classes of decision problems. The class $\mathcal{P}$ consists of all those decision problems for which a polynomial-time algorithm exists. In view of Theorem 1 and the discussion in Section 2.4, the crucial question involved in determining the complexity of the TSP can be formalized as follows: 'Is TSP DECISION in $\mathcal{P}$?'

In this chapter we present evidence that strongly suggests that the answer to this question is 'no', but we shall not be able to provide a rigorous proof. Proofs that problems are not in $\mathcal{P}$ do exist. If a problem is undecidable and hence not solvable by *any* algorithm, it is certainly not in $\mathcal{P}$. In addition, many decidable problems can be shown to require exponential time [Lewis & Papadimitriou, 1981]. Unfortunately, there is a sense in which TSP DECISION is qualitatively 'easier' than any of the problems so far shown to be outside of $\mathscr{P}$, and so new techniques would seem to be required if it is to be proved inherently exponential.

The characteristics of TSP DECISION which make it 'easier' than the provably hard problems, are shared with a wide variety of other natural combinatorial optimization problems. Over the past two decades three different but equivalent formulations have been proposed for these characteristics. Together they define a class of decision problems we call $\mathscr{NP}$.

The first definition involves the *succinct certificate property*. HAMILTONIAN CYCLE, 0–1 PROGRAMMING and TSP DECISION all have this property. Any 'yes' instance (i.e., a graph that has a Hamiltonian cycle; a system of linear equations that has a 0–1 solution; a distance matrix whose optimal tour length is less than a given bound B) has a succinct 'certificate': a mathematical object of small size that establishes beyond doubt that the instance indeed warrants a 'yes' answer. (For the above problems the certificates are: a Hamiltonian cycle; a 0–1 vector satisfying the equations; and a tour of length B or less, respectively). The certificate must be *succinct*, i.e., of size bounded by a polynomial in the instance size, and there must be a polynomial-time *certificate-checking algorithm* which, given an instance and a supposed certificate, determines whether the certificate is indeed valid. All 'yes' instances must possess at least one such certificate, and no 'no' instance can have any. It may be very difficult to discover a certificate for a 'yes' instance, but, once discovered, it can be exhibited and checked in an efficient manner.

This can be made a bit more formal as follows. A decision problem A has the succinct certificate property if and only if there is another decision problem $C \in \mathscr{P}$ (the certificate-checking problem for A) whose instances are of the form (I, S), where I is an instance of A and S is an object whose size is bounded by a polynomial in the size of I, and such that the following are equivalent:

(1) I is a 'yes' instance of A;
(2) There is an S such that (I, S) is a 'yes' instance of C.

There are clearly many interesting and important decision problems, in addition to the ones already mentioned, that have the succinct certificate property: By Lemma 2, INTEGER PROGRAMMING, though more general than 0–1 PROGRAMMING, has the succinct certificate property itself. Furthermore, it can be argued that the decision problem versions of all 'reasonable' combinatorial optimization problems have the property. Such problems ask about the existence of certain combinatorial objects (vectors, circuits, tours, etc.) whose costs, lengths, etc., obey a certain bound. Such objects are 'succinct' according to our definition, and their costs can be computed efficiently (if the cost function is 'reasonable'). Hence the objects themselves can play the role of the certificates for these problems. The class of problems that satisfy the succinct certificate property was introduced by Edmonds [1965b], who called them problems with *good characterizations*.

A second way of defining a broad class of decision problems including TSP DECISION involves the concept of a *nondeterministic algorithm,* an unrealistic but theoretically useful tool, with a long history in complexity theory. A nondeterministic algorithm is like an ordinary algorithm, except that it is equipped with one additional, extraordinarily powerful instruction:

go to both label 1, label 2.

Executing this instruction divides the computation into two parallel processes, one continuing from each of the two instructions indicated by *label 1* and *label 2.* By encountering more and more such instructions, the computation will branch like a tree into a number of parallel computations that potentially can grow as an exponential function of the time elapsed. (See Figure 3.5). If *any* of these branches reports 'yes' then we say that the overall nondeterministic algorithm has answered 'yes'. The answer is 'no' if none of the branches ever reports 'yes'. The asymmetry parallels that of the succinct certificate property: 'Yes' instances have a succinct proof of their 'yes-ness', but 'no' instances may not have a succinct proof of their 'no-ness' – how can one succinctly certify that a graph has *no* Hamiltonian cycle?

We say a nondeterministic algorithm solves a decision problem in polynomial time if (a) for each instance it gives the correct answer, as defined above, and (b) the number of steps used by the first of the branches to

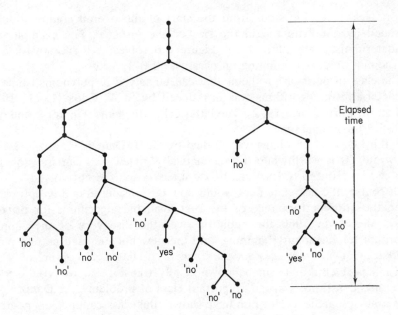

Figure 3.5 A possible execution history of a nondeterministic algorithm. Branching points are executions of **go to both** instructions. The answer of this computation is 'yes', because there is at least one leaf with answer 'yes'

ALGORITHM N

Input: An $m \times n$ integer matrix A, integer m-vector b.

Output: 'Yes' if there is an $x \in \{0, 1\}^n$ such that $Ax = b$, and 'no' otherwise.

begin

    for $j := 1, \ldots, n$ **do**

        begin
        go to both zero, one;
        zero: $x_j := 0$; **goto** again;
        one: $x_j := 1$;
        again: **continue**
        end;

    if $x = (x_1, \ldots, x_n)$ satisfies $Ax = b$
    then output 'yes'
    else output 'no'

end

Figure 3.6

report 'yes' (counting steps from the start of the overall computation) is bounded by a polynomial in the size of the instance. For example, the nondeterministic algorithm N of Figure 3.6 solves 0–1 PROGRAMMING in polynomial time by examining, in parallel, all 0–1 vectors.

The class of decision problems that can be solved in polynomial time by nondeterministic algorithms was introduced by S. A. Cook [Cook, 1971] and R. M. Karp [Karp, 1972]. The latter called the class $\mathcal{NP}$, for $\mathcal{N}$ondeterministic $\mathcal{P}$olynomial time.

A third class of problems was studied by G. B. Dantzig [Dantzig, 1960]. He wrote, 'It is worthwhile to systematically review and classify problems that can be reduced to [INTEGER PROGRAMMING] and thereby solved.'

Of course, the last statement would now be considered overly optimistic, given the poor performance of the best available algorithms for INTEGER PROGRAMMING. In 1960 the euphoria over the discovery of the simplex algorithm for linear programming, and the new but untested cutting plane approach for INTEGER PROGRAMMING, were fueling such optimism. Still, decision problems that can be polynomially transformed to INTEGER PROGRAMMING constitute a broad, important class of problems. As Dantzig and numerous researchers after him have shown, this class contains many graph problems, some nonlinear programming problems, and the decision problem versions of the TSP and a host of other combinatorial problems.

The following remarkable theorem, a paraphrase of results due to Cook, states that the three classes we have just defined are *one and the same class*.

Theorem 3 [Cook, 1971]   *Let* A *be a decision problem. Then the following are equivalent.*
(1) A *has the succinct certificate property.*
(2) A ∈ *NP*.
(3) A *is polynomial-time transformable to* INTEGER PROGRAMMING.

Sketch of proof.   We shall not give a complete proof of this theorem (for a rigorous proof, see Cook [1971] or Aho, Hopcroft & Ullman [1974], Garey & Johnson [1979], Lewis & Papadimitriou [1981] or Papadimitriou & Steiglitz [1982]). Two of the three implications are easy, however.

(1)⇒(2)   If A has the succinct certificate property, then a nondeterministic algorithm for A can be designed as follows. First, branch out the computation so that all potential certificates can be examined in parallel. Since the certificate is succinct, this can be accomplished while the computation tree still has only polynomial depth. Then, for each of the potential certificates (still in parallel), deterministically check its validity using the polynomial-time certificate-checking algorithm for the problem. If a succinct certificate exists, at least one of the branches of the computation will return a 'yes' answer in polynomial time. (This is exactly what the nondeterministic algorithm N of Figure 3.6 is doing).

(3)⇒(1)   If A is polynomially transformable to INTEGER PROGRAMMING, then every 'yes' instance of A has a succinct certificate: the solution, as specified in Lemma 2, to the integer program that is the result of the transformation. By Lemma 2 this solution will be succinct, and the certificate-checking algorithm merely needs to construct the integer program corresponding to the given instance of A (using the polynomial transformation) and then check to see whether the proposed certificate is indeed a solution.

(2)⇒(3)   This is the hard part. We need first to define more precisely our model of nondeterministic algorithms. This can be done in a number of ways, for instance, in terms of *nondeterministic Turing machines* [Aho, Hopcroft & Ullman, 1974; Garey & Johnson, 1979; Lewis & Papadimitriou, 1981]. Our model will essentially be a set of *rules* whereby we can move from one 'state' of the computation to the next (possibly in more than one way because of nondeterminism). What the proof would then show is that INTEGER PROGRAMMING is expressive enough to enable us to represent these rules by linear equations in appropriate 0–1 variables (not unlike the transformation from HAMILTONIAN CYCLE to INTEGER PROGRAMMING, although considerably more involved). The full details are omitted, but see Exercise 7.   □

The equivalences shown in Theorem 3 establish the class *NP* as an important, stable concept. A crucial question thus arises, concerning the relationship between *NP* and the previously introduced class *P* of problems solvable in polynomial time. Since ordinary 'deterministic' algorithms are a special case of nondeterministic algorithms (those nondeterministic algorithms which do not use the **go to both** instruction), it follows immediately that $\mathcal{P} \subseteq \mathcal{NP}$. Is $\mathcal{P} = \mathcal{NP}$? In other words, can we simulate deterministically any nondeterministic algorithm without sacrificing more than a polynomial amount of time? This seems extremely unlikely. Any direct way of performing such a simulation takes exponential time (due to the potential that a nondeterministic algorithm has for generating an exponential number of parallel computations after only a polynomial number of nondeterministic 'steps'). Furthermore, researchers have for years been attempting without success to find polynomial-time algorithms for certain problems in $\mathcal{NP}$, such as the TSP. If it were discovered that $\mathcal{P} = \mathcal{NP}$, and, as if by some master stroke, all those frustrating problems suddenly became polynomially solvable, these researchers (and many others) would be greatly surprised. Thus it is widely conjectured that $\mathcal{P} \neq \mathcal{NP}$. However, no proof of this conjecture has yet been found. This question is the central open problem in computer science today, and one of the most important open problems in mathematics.

Since $\mathcal{NP}$ contains TSP DECISION, we cannot hope to show that the TSP is intractable (not solvable in polynomial time), unless we first prove $\mathcal{P} \neq \mathcal{NP}$, an apparently awesome task. We can, however, do something almost as good. In the next section we show that the two conjectures, $\mathcal{P} \neq \mathcal{NP}$, and TSP DECISION $\notin \mathcal{P}$, are equivalent. The key concept is that of $\mathcal{NP}$-*completeness*.

Exercises

4. We are asked to determine an unknown number x between 0 and M by asking questions of the form 'is $x > a$?' for different a's of our choice. Show that this cannot be done with fewer than $\lceil \log_2(M+1) \rceil$ questions in the worst case. (Therefore the 'binary scarch' technique employed in the algorithm of Figure 3.4 is optimal.)

5. The WANDERING SALESMAN problem is the same as the TSP, except that the salesman can start his tour in any city, and does not have to return to the first city in the end.

(a) Give a polynomial-time transformation from TSP DECISION to WANDERING SALESMAN DECISION.

(b) As (a), but with the transformation the other way around.

6. Let x, y and z be integer valued variables. Using an additional 0–1 valued variable s, write a system of inequalities/equalities that can be satisfied if and only if $x = |y - z|$.

7. A *nondeterministic Turing machine* with *time bound n* can be viewed as a machine operating on a sequence $x_1, x_2, \ldots, x_n$ of *memory cells*, one of which is specified as *active* at any given time, and each of which can contain either a 0 or a 1. The computation proceeds in a stepwise fashion, through a sequence of n configurations. Let the variable $x_i[t]$ represent the contents of cell x_i in configuration $t, 1 \leq i \leq n, 1 \leq t \leq n$, and the variable $a[t]$ be the index of the active cell in that configuration.

(a) Write a set of linear equations and inequalities that enforce the fact that, for $1 \leqslant i \leqslant n$ and $1 \leqslant t < n$, if cell x_i is not active in configuration t, then it has the same contents in both configurations t and $t+1$. If necessary, you may use auxiliary variables, but their number should be bounded by a polynomial function of n.

(b) The *program* for a nondeterministic Turing machine can be viewed as consisting of a finite set $\{1, 2, \ldots, q\}$ of *states* and a finite set of *rules* of the form $\langle s, y, s', y', \Delta \rangle$, where s and s' are states, $y, y' \in \{0, 1\}$, and $\Delta \in \{-1, +1\}$. Such a rule is taken to mean that if, in configuration t, the state is s and the contents of the active cell x_i is y, then one option for configuration $t+1$ is that the state be s', the contents of x_i be y', and the new active cell be $x_{i+\Delta}$. There can be at most two rules with any given pair $\langle s, y \rangle$ as first components (in which case the two options correspond to the 'go to both' instruction of a nondeterministic algorithm). Let the variable $s[t]$ represent the state in configuration t. Write a set of linear equations and inequalities that enforce the fact that, for a given pair of rules $\langle s, y, s_i, y_i, \Delta_i \rangle$, $i \in \{1, 2\}$, one of the two options will always occur when the state is s, the contents of the active cell is y, and the configuration is t.

(c) A nondeterministic Turing machine program can be used to solve a decision problem as follows: First, give the nondeterministic Turing machine an 'adequate' time bound n, and initialize to 0 all n of its memory cells except for the first few, which are loaded with a binary representation of the instance I in question. Let the initial active cell be x_1 and the initial state be 1, and start applying rules to obtain a sequence of configurations. If there is a way of applying rules so that the state of configuration n is q, then the answer is 'yes,' otherwise 'no.' Write a system of equations and inequalities that force the initial configuration to have $s[1] = 1$ and $a[1] = 1$, the memory cells to be properly initialized for an instance represented by the string $u_1, u_2, \ldots, u_L$ of 0's and 1's, and the final configuration to have $s[n] = q$.

(d) You are now almost all the way to proving that if a decision problem A is in $\mathcal{NP}$, then it is polynomial-time transformable to INTEGER PROGRAMMING. The fact that $A \in \mathcal{NP}$ can be shown to mean that there is a polynomial p_A and a nondeterministic Turing machine program PROG_A that can solve A when given a time bound of $p_A(L)$, where L is the input size for I [Garey & Johnson, 1979; Lewis & Papadimitriou, 1981]. The desired polynomial-time transformation is based on this nondeterministic Turing machine program and its associated polynomial. Essentially all we need is parts (a), (b) and (c) of this exercise, modified so that $n = p_A(L)$ and the states and rules are those given by PROG_A. Fill in the details and show that the number of variables, equations, and inequalities are bounded by a polynomial in L, the exact polynomial depending on the PROG_A and p_A.

4 $\mathcal{NP}$-COMPLETENESS

4.1 Definition

We say that a decision problem A is $\mathcal{NP}$-complete if (a) $A \in \mathcal{NP}$ and (b) every problem in $\mathcal{NP}$ is polynomially transformable to A. The complexity of an $\mathcal{NP}$-complete problem is intimately related to our conjecture that $\mathcal{P} \neq \mathcal{NP}$. By (a), if $\mathcal{P} = \mathcal{NP}$ and A is $\mathcal{NP}$-complete, then $A \in \mathcal{P}$. On the other hand, by (b) and Lemma 1, if $A \in \mathcal{P}$ then $\mathcal{NP} = \mathcal{P}$. Thus if A is $\mathcal{NP}$-complete, it is solvable in polynomial time if and only if $\mathcal{P} = \mathcal{NP}$. If, as is widely believed, $\mathcal{P} \neq \mathcal{NP}$, then none of the $\mathcal{NP}$-complete problems can be in $\mathcal{P}$.

During the past decade, many problems have been proved to be $\mathcal{NP}$-complete. Garey & Johnson [1979] present a list of over 300 examples. We have already discovered one in this chapter: it follows directly from Theorem 3 that INTEGER PROGRAMMING is $\mathcal{NP}$-complete! In this section we shall show that TSP DECISION is also $\mathcal{NP}$-complete. This is our main negative result concerning the TSP; it is the strongest negative result one can hope to prove, short of establishing that $\mathcal{P} \neq \mathcal{NP}$.

One need not prove a new version of Theorem 3 every time one wants to show a new problem $A \in \mathcal{NP}$ to be $\mathcal{NP}$-complete. By the transitivity of polynomial transformability, all we need show is that some *already known* $\mathcal{NP}$-complete problem B transforms to A.

At this point we have only one 'known' $\mathcal{NP}$-complete problem: INTEGER PROGRAMMING. However, by Theorem 2 a second one can be quickly added to our list, since that theorem provides a polynomial transformation from INTEGER PROGRAMMING to 0–1 PROGRAMMING. From this start, a whole family tree of $\mathcal{NP}$-complete problems can be generated, although we will concentrate on that part of the tree that leads to the TSP. (Historically, the ancestral $\mathcal{NP}$-complete problem was not INTEGER PROGRAMMING, but a problem in mathematical logic called SATISFIABILITY – see Exercise 8, and Cook [1971], Aho, Hopcroft & Ullman [1974], Garey & Johnson [1979] and Papadimitriou & Steiglitz [1982]. However, any $\mathcal{NP}$-complete problem can serve as a root of the family tree, and INTEGER PROGRAMMING is a convenient choice for our purposes here.)

We note in passing that there are many problems which can be solved in polynomial time if and only if $\mathcal{P} = \mathcal{NP}$, but which do not make it into the family tree for technical reasons. For example, the TSP itself (optimization version) cannot be $\mathcal{NP}$-complete because it is not a decision problem, even though it is equivalent in complexity to TSP DECISION which *is* $\mathcal{NP}$-complete. A problem in $\mathcal{NP}$ to which an $\mathcal{NP}$-complete problem is polynomially *reducible* (but not known to be transformable) also may not be called $\mathcal{NP}$-complete, even though it has the same claim to intractability as any $\mathcal{NP}$-complete problem. Finally, there are decision problems which satisfy part (b) of the definition but not (a) (they are not known to be in $\mathcal{NP}$). For all these kinds of problems we have reserved the term $\mathcal{NP}$-*hard*. A problem (decision or otherwise) is $\mathcal{NP}$-hard if all problems in $\mathcal{NP}$ are polynomially reducible (not necessarily transformable) to it.

4.2 Special cases

We shall actually be proving complexity results for a number of different special cases of the TSP. We say problem A is a special case of problem B if both problems ask the same question and the domain of A (the set of possible instances) is a subset of the domain of B. A special case may be easier than the general problem (Chapter 4 presents polynomial-time algorithms for a number of special cases of the TSP), or it may be just as hard (*most* interesting special cases of TSP DECISION are just as $\mathcal{NP}$-complete as the general problem, as we shall see shortly). A special case cannot be harder (as long as there is an efficient way to tell instances that belong to the special case domain from those that don't).

Figure 3.7 depicts the position of the TSP within a hierarchy of special cases, with specialization increasing as we go down the figure. The general, asymmetric TSP is near the top. Above it we have *generalizations* of the TSP, some of which will be discussed in Chapter 5. A standard special case

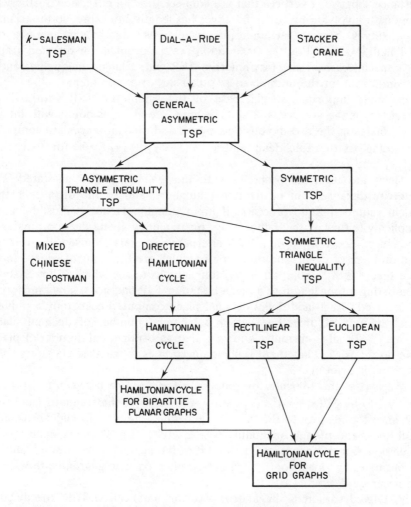

Figure 3.7   Special cases and generalizations of the TSP

is the symmetric TSP (restricted to only those instances where $c_{ij} = c_{ji}$ for all cities i and j) – this special case is often what people mean when they refer to the 'TSP'.

Another way to restrict the general TSP is to require that the distance matrix satisfy the *triangle inequality*: $c_{ij} + c_{jk} \geq c_{ik}$ for all i, j, k. Of course, we may ask that *both* conditions be satisfied, in which case we obtain an important special case, examined in Chapter 5. The (mixed) CHINESE POST-MAN problem (defined in Exercise 11 and discussed more fully in Chapter 5) can be considered as a (further) special case of the TSP with asymmetric distance matrices that obey the triangle inequality.

HAMILTONIAN CYCLE, a purely graph theoretic problem, can be viewed as a special case of the symmetric TSP with triangle inequality. Given a graph $G = (V, E)$, we can think of it as a $|V| \times |V|$ distance matrix with distance 1 between vertices that are connected by an edge, and 2 otherwise (any path involving two or more edges has length 2 or more, so the triangle inequality is obeyed). A Hamiltonian cycle exists if and only if there is a tour of length $|V|$. Similarly the HAMILTONIAN CYCLE problem for directed graphs is a special case of the (asymmetric) TSP with triangle inequality, and a generalization of the undirected HAMILTONIAN CYCLE problem.

Another important special case of the symmetric TSP with triangle inequality is the EUCLIDEAN TSP. The cities are given as points with integer coordinates in the two-dimensional plane, and their distances are computed according to the Euclidean metric: $\sqrt{(x_1 - x_2)^2 + (y_1 - y_2)^2}$ for two cities (x_1, y_1) and (x_2, y_2).

There are technical problems with the EUCLIDEAN TSP as stated. The intercity distances can be irrational numbers, and so the distance matrix might require infinite precision if input directly. Hence it must be given implicitly (either by the values of c_{ij}^2, or by merely giving the coordinates of the cities). Secondly, even if such alternative formats are used, there is still the problem of evaluating tour lengths which are the sums of square roots. See Figure 3.8. In comparing two tour lengths to see which is better (or in comparing a tour length to a given bound in TSP DECISION), how much work is involved? Each additional decimal place computed costs only a polynomial amount of time, but *will* a polynomial number of decimal places suffice? All that is currently known is that an exponential number of places will do the trick. Thus there is some question as to whether EUCLIDEAN TSP DECISION is even in $\mathcal{NP}$.

We bypass this difficulty by redefining the distance between (x_1, y_1) and (x_2, y_2) to be $\lceil \sqrt{(x_1 - x_2)^2 + (y_1 - y_2)^2} \rceil$, the value of the standard Euclidean distance rounded up to the next integer. This (discrete) Euclidean distance still obeys the triangle inequality (see Exercise 12). There is some loss of precision, but this can be moderated if in the beginning we multiply all city coordinates by an appropriately large number, so as to guarantee the degree of accuracy desired.

A related variant is the RECTILINEAR (or MANHATTAN) TSP: the distance

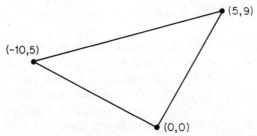

Figure 3.8 What is the length of the perimeter of this triangle? If calculated with the results truncated to the fifth significant digit, the answer is 36.999; to the eighth significant digit it is 37.000 145. There is no known method to predict the number of significant digits that are necessary in order to compare a sum of square roots to an integer

between (x_1, y_1) and (x_2, y_2) is $|x_1 - x_2| + |y_1 - y_2|$ (no problems of precision here).

At the bottom of our chart is a final special case. Suppose that in EUCLIDEAN TSP DECISION, the bound B equals the number n of cities. Since each city has integer coordinates, each pair of cities is at least distance 1 apart. Thus a tour of the desired length exists if and only if there is a Hamiltonian cycle in the graph G whose vertices are the cities, with edges only between those cities that are distance 1 apart in the plane. Such a graph is called a *grid graph* (because it is a vertex-induced subgraph of the infinite grid).

We shall show that HAMILTONIAN CYCLE FOR GRID GRAPHS, the ultimate special case of the TSP, is $\mathcal{NP}$-complete. Since complexity propagates upwards, this will imply that all the decision problems in the tower of Figure 3.7 are $\mathcal{NP}$-complete. (A separate proof is needed for the mixed CHINESE POSTMAN problem, which is also $\mathcal{NP}$-complete – see Papadimitriou [1976].) Our proof will follow from a series of transformations, starting with 0–1 PROGRAMMING and proceeding through two main intermediate problems: EXACT COVER and HAMILTONIAN CYCLE (the unrestricted version).

4.3 From 0–1 PROGRAMMING to EXACT COVER

Theorem 2 showed how to polynomially transform INTEGER PROGRAMMING to 0–1 PROGRAMMING. We now show how to transform the latter problem to a further special case: the one in which the matrix A is a 0–1 matrix and the vector b is all ones. This special case has a name: the EXACT COVER problem. It has the following interpretation. We are given a family $F = \{S_1, \ldots, S_n\}$ of subsets of a set $U = \{u_1, \ldots, u_m\}$. U corresponds to the set of rows A, and the columns of A are the characteristic vectors of the S_j. We are asked to find an *exact cover* of U, i.e., a subfamily $C \subseteq F$ such that each $u_i \in U$ is in *exactly one* of the subsets $S_j \in C$. C corresponds to a 0–1 solution x for $Ax = b$.

We shall show how to transform any 0–1 program $Ax = b$ to an equivalent one that conforms to the restriction of EXACT COVER. First, we must get rid of the negative entries in A. For each variable x we introduce a new variable x' and a new equation $x + x' = 1$. Then we replace x by $(1 - x')$ in each equation from A where x had a negative coefficient, yielding a new equation with x' instead of x and a positive coefficient instead of a negative one. The equations resulting after all such substitutions have been made may have new values for the constant on their right-hand side. If any right-hand side is negative, we know that the 0–1 program has no solution (all coefficients and variables must be nonnegative, so the result cannot be negative). We can then construct a trivial instance of EXACT COVER having no solution, such as $0x = 1$, and be guaranteed that the answer for the constructed instance is the same as that for $Ax = b$.

Assuming that all right-hand sides are nonnegative, let $A'x = b'$ be the new 0–1 program. This is not yet an instance of EXACT COVER, since A' could have fairly large integers as entries, as could b'. In order to replace these with 0–1 entries, we consider the binary representations of the coefficients in each equation, and write appropriate equations to capture binary additions.

We illustrate this by an example. Suppose we had the equation

$$6x_1 + 5x_2 + 7x_3 + 11x_4 = 12.$$

The binary expansions of 6, 5, 7, 11 and 12 are 0110, 0101, 0111, 1011 and 1100, respectively. We write the following four equations, one for each *bit* of the coefficients, the least significant first:

$$x_2 + x_3 + x_4 = 0 + 2z_1;$$
$$x_1 + x_3 + x_4 + z_1 = 0 + 2(z_2 + z_3);$$
$$x_1 + x_2 + x_3 + z_2 + z_3 = 1 + 2(z_4 + z_5);$$
$$x_4 + z_4 + z_5 = 1.$$

The z_i represent *carry bits*, and we may need up to n of these for each row. When we rewrite equations so that all variables are on the left-hand side, we once again get negative coefficients (-2) which we remove by replacing $-2z$ by $z' + z'' - 2$ in its equation and adding the new equations $z + z' = 1$ and $z + z'' = 1$. After having performed these substitutions we at last obtain a collection of equations, all of whose coefficients are 0 to 1. The right-hand sides, however, can be anywhere from 0 to $2n + 1$, and our definition of EXACT COVER requires that they all equal 1.

We get around this final obstacle as follows. If the right-hand side is 0, the equation can simply be dropped, and all its variables set to 0 in (and hence dropped from) the other equations. Suppose we have an equation whose right-hand side is equal to $k > 1$ and whose left-hand side has l nonzero coefficients. We replace the equation by $k + 2l$ new equations with right-hand side equal to 1. For example, the equation

$$x + y + z + w = 3$$

would be replaced by the following eleven equations:

$$x + x' = 1;$$
$$x_1 + x_2 + x_3 + x' = 1;$$
$$y + y' = 1;$$
$$y_1 + y_2 + y_3 + y' = 1;$$
$$z + z' = 1;$$
$$z_1 + z_2 + z_3 + z' = 1;$$
$$w + w' = 1;$$
$$w_1 + w_2 + w_3 + w' = 1;$$
$$x_1 + y_1 + z_1 + w_1 = 1;$$
$$x_2 + y_2 + z_2 + w_2 = 1;$$
$$x_3 + y_3 + z_3 + w_3 = 1.$$

Consider the first two equations. If $x = 0$ then all three of x_1, x_2 and x_3 must be 0. If $x = 1$ then exactly two of x_1, x_2 and x_3 must be 0 and the third must be 1. Analogous statements hold for the y_i, z_i and w_i, due to the next six equations. Thus the three final equations can be satisfied if and only if exactly three of x, y, z and w are equal to 1; precisely the requirement of our original equation.

To summarize our transformation: we first remove the negative coefficients from A, halting prematurely if this leaves a negative entry in b. We then reduce the coefficients of A to 0, 1 and -2 by replacing each equation by a set of equations that simulate it using bit-wise addition. Then the -2 coefficients are removed, leaving only certain entries in b as potential troublemakers. If any entry in b is 0 the corresponding equation is dropped, along with its variables. If any entry exceeds 1 the corresponding equation is again replaced by a set of equations that simulates it, and we at last have an instance in which all entries in A are 0 or 1 and all entries in b are 1, as required by EXACT COVER. Each step only adds a number of equations and/or variables that is bounded by a polynomial in m and n (the dimensions of A) and in the number of bits required to represent the largest entry in A or b. Thus the transformation is a polynomial transformation and we have proved the following result.

Theorem 4   0–1 PROGRAMMING $\propto$ EXACT COVER.

Since EXACT COVER is clearly in $\mathcal{NP}$, this means that EXACT COVER is

$\mathcal{NP}$-complete. Something even stronger can be said:

Corollary 1 EXACT COVER *is $\mathcal{NP}$-complete even when restricted to instances where each row of A contains exactly two or three entries equal to 1 (set terminology: each element is contained in either two or three sets).*

Proof   We show how to transform EXACT COVER to this restricted version of itself. Equations with no nonzero coefficients are either tautologically true ($0 = 0$), in which case they can be dropped, or tautologically false ($0 = 1$), in which case the instance has no solution and we transform it into a trivial one in the required format which has no solution (e.g., $x + y = 0$, $y + z = 0$, $x + y + z = 1$). Equations with one nonzero coefficient (e.g., $x = 1$) give the value of the corresponding variable, which then can be substituted in all other equations. The resulting A will still have all 0–1 entries, and all entries of b are 1 or less. If any such entry is negative, there is again no solution, and we proceed as above. If any entry is 0, then drop the equation, and also drop all variables that appear in this equation from all other equations.

Finally, consider an equation in which four or more variables have coefficient 1:

$$x_1 + x_2 + x_3 + \ldots + x_k = 1, \qquad k \geqslant 4.$$

We replace this equation by the following system of $2k - 5$ equations, having y_i's as new variables:

$$x_1 + x_2 + y_1 = 1;$$
$$y_1' + x_3 + y_2 = 1;$$
$$\vdots$$
$$y_{k-3}' + x_{k-1} + x_k = 1;$$
$$y_1 + y_1' = 1;$$
$$\vdots$$
$$y_{k-3} + y_{k-3}' = 1.$$

It is left as an exercise to verify that this system is equivalent to the above equation. $\square$

4.4   From EXACT COVER to HAMILTONIAN CYCLE

We shall present a transformation from the restricted form of EXACT COVER given in Corollary 1 to HAMILTONIAN CYCLE. Our construction employs several 'special-purpose subgraphs' (*gadgets* in the jargon of $\mathcal{NP}$-completeness). Take, for example, the graph H shown in Figure 3.9(a). It has a very useful property, described by the following lemma.

Lemma 4 *Suppose that a graph $G = (V, E)$ contains the graph $H = (W, F)$ of Figure 3.9(a) in such a way that no vertex in $V - W$ is adjacent to any of*

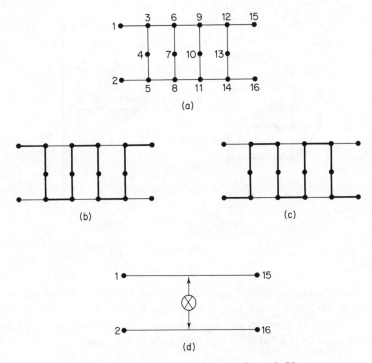

Figure 3.9   The exclusive-or subgraph H

the vertices 3 through 14. Then if C is a Hamiltonian cycle of G, C must traverse H in one of the two ways shown in Figure 3.9(b) and 3.9(c).

Proof Since C is a Hamiltonian cycle, it must traverse all four paths $(3, 4, 5)$, $(6, 7, 8)$, $(9, 10, 11)$ and $(12, 13, 14)$ (in one direction or the other) as this is the only way to pick up the vertices 4, 7, 10 and 13. Also, exactly one of the edges $\{6, 9\}$ and $\{8, 11\}$ must be traversed. If both are traversed, then the cycle $(6, 7, 8, 11, 10, 9, 6)$ is formed. If neither, then both $\{3, 6\}$ and $\{5, 8\}$ must be traversed, and the cycle $(3, 4, 5, 8, 7, 6, 3)$ is formed. If edge $\{6, 9\}$ is traversed, then the traversal shown in Figure 3.9(b) results, all choices being forced; if $\{8, 11\}$, it is then the one in 3.9(c). □

What Lemma 4 really says is that subgraph H behaves as a *pair of edges* $\{1, 15\}$, $\{2, 16\}$, with the additional constraint that a Hamiltonian cycle of G must traverse *exactly one* of these edges. For this reason we call H an *exclusive or* subgraph, using the symbolic representation of Figure 3.9(d).

For our construction we shall use two more special-purpose subgraphs, graphs J and K shown in Figures 3.10(a) and (b). Their 'crucial properties' are stated in Lemma 5.

Lemma 5 (a) *In graph J (Figure 3.10(a)), any Hamiltonian path from vertex 1 to vertex 2 traverses exactly two of the edges in $\{e_1, e_2, e_3\}$; further-*

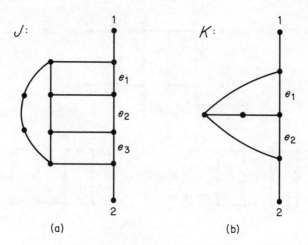

Figure 3.10　The graphs J and K

more, for any subset of two of these edges there is such a Hamiltonian path traversing them. (b) In graph K (Figure 3.10(b)), any Hamiltonian path from vertex 1 to vertex 2 traverses exactly one of the edges in $\{e_1, e_2\}$, and for each of these edges there is a Hamiltonian path from 1 to 2 traversing it.

The proof is straightforward exhaustion of all possibilities, similar to the proof of Lemma 4.

We can now describe our transformation from the restricted form of EXACT COVER to HAMILTONIAN CYCLE. Suppose we are given an instance $Ax = b$ of the restricted form of EXACT COVER, i.e., A is 0–1, b contains all 1's, and there are either two or three entries equal to 1 in each row of A (i.e., each equation involves two or three variables). We need to construct a graph $G = (V, E)$ such that G has a Hamiltonian cycle if and only if $Ax = b$ has a 0–1 solution.

Graph G contains, for each of the m equations in $Ax = b$, a copy of the graph J or the graph K, depending on whether the equation has three or two variables, respectively. These copies are linked together in series (see Figure 3.11). For each variable x, the graph contains a pair of parallel edges. These pairs are also linked in series, and two more edges are added to join the equation series and the variable series into a loop.

Note that, thus far, G certainly has a Hamiltonian cycle. It traverses the graphs J and K one after another (leaving out one e_i edge in each, according to Lemma 5), and then the pairs of parallel edges, one after the other, leaving out either the left or the right copy of each pair. As Figure 3.11 indicates, however, we are not yet finished with our construction of G. Using copies of the *exclusive or* subgraph of Figure 3.9(a), we are going to connect edges of G in such a way that G no longer automatically has a Hamiltonian cycle, but has one if and only if $Ax = b$ has the desired solution.

$x_1 + x_2 + x_3 = 1$

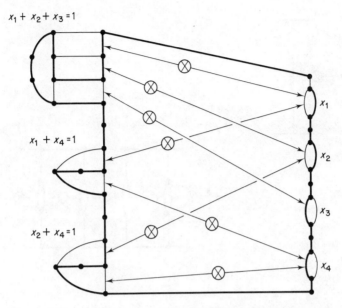

Figure 3.11   An example of the transformation from EXACT
COVER to HAMILTONIAN CYCLE

There are 2^n ways in which the Hamiltonian cycle can traverse the series of parallel edges on the right of Figure 3.11. Each of these will correspond to each of the 2^n possible solution vectors x. If the left edge from the pair corresponding to variable x_j is in the circuit, we take this to mean that $x_j = 1$ (as with x_3 and x_4 in this figure); if the right, then $x_j = 0$ (as with x_1 and x_2).

We use the *exclusive or*'s and the copies of J and K to assure that the resulting solution vector actually satisfies the equations: If the kth variable of an equation is x_j, we use an *exclusive or* to connect the e_k edge of the J or K graph corresponding to the equation to the left copy of the pair corresponding to x_j (see again Figure 3.11). A Hamiltonian cycle now will exist if and only if there is a way of traversing the pairs of parallel edges (i.e., a 0–1 n-vector x) such that in each copy of a J or a K on the left (i.e., in each equation) exactly one of the e_j's is not traversed (i.e., exactly one of the corresponding variables has value 1). Thus G has a Hamiltonian cycle if and only if $Ax = b$ has a 0–1 solution, and we have proved the following theorem.

Theorem 5   (*Restricted*) EXACT COVER $\propto$ HAMILTONIAN CYCLE.

Hence HAMILTONIAN CYCLE is $\mathcal{NP}$-complete. As with EXACT COVER, we can actually show that a restricted version of HAMILTONIAN CYCLE remains $\mathcal{NP}$-complete, using a slight modification of our proof. The graphs that we constructed are already quite constrained. All vertex degrees are either 2 or 3. Also the graph is 'almost planar': it can be arranged on the plane so that

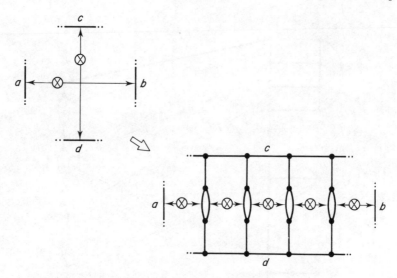

Figure 3.12   The 'crossover'

only exclusive-or subgraphs cross each other (there are four such crossings in Figure 3.11). Each crossing can be replaced by the 'crossover' configuration of Figure 3.12 (right), thus obtaining a planar graph with the same degree bounds. Finally, we can render our graph bipartite (a graph is bipartite if the vertices can be assigned colors black and white, in such a way that no edge joins two vertices with the same color). Each copy of *H*, *J* and *K* is already bipartite, as is the series of parallel edges. The only trouble spot could be the *exclusive or*'s of Figure 3.11. But these can be made bipartite by using the model of *exclusive or* shown in Figure 3.13 instead of that in Figure 3.9(a) (the crossovers of Figure 3.12 can be dealt with similarly). We thus have proved the following.

Corollary 2   HAMILTONIAN CYCLE *is* $\mathcal{NP}$-*complete even when restricted to planar, bipartite graphs with vertex degrees either 2 or 3.*

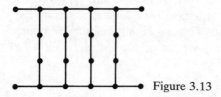

Figure 3.13

4.5   From HAMILTONIAN CYCLE to HAMILTONIAN CYCLE FOR GRID GRAPHS

Recall that a *grid graph* is a finite, vertex-induced subgraph of the *infinite grid,* i.e., the infinite graph with set of vertices $Z \times Z$ and set of edges

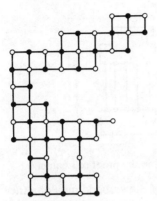

Figure 3.14   A grid graph

$\{\{(x, y), (x', y')\} : |x - x'| + |y - y'| = 1\}$ (see Figure 3.14). In this subsection we show that HAMILTONIAN CYCLE is $\mathcal{NP}$-complete even in the extremely special case of grid graphs. We have already argued that this problem is an extremely restricted special case of the TSP.

We first need a result concerning graph embeddings. An *embedding* of a planar graph G (with all degrees 2 or 3) into the grid is a function which maps the vertices of G to distinct vertices of the grid, and edges of G to vertex-disjoint paths (except for common endpoints) in the grid. Figure 3.15 shows an example. The *extent* of the embedding is the side of the smallest square that contains the images of all vertices and all edges of the graph – the extent of the embedding shown in Figure 3.15 is 4.

Lemma 6   *Any planar graph with n vertices and f faces (and all vertices of degree 2 or 3) has an embedding of extent $n + f$ or less.*

Proof   Recall that, if a graph is planar, then for each of its faces there is a planar representation in which that face is the *external* face (i.e., the one whose boundary is the boundary of the representation of G). We prove, by induction on the number of faces f, that, for any graph G as above, there is an embedding of extent $n + f$ or less, such that (a) a designated face is the external face of the embedding, and (b) each degree-2 vertex in the external

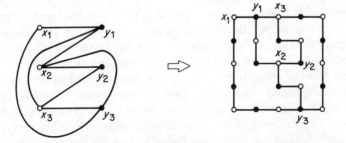

Figure 3.15   A color-preserving embedding of a planar bipartite graph

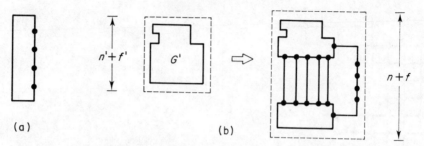

Figure 3.16   The basis (a) and the induction step (b) in the proof of Lemma 6

face is embedded so that it is the rightmost point of the embedding along the horizontal line drawn through it.

This is certainly true when $f = 2$ (i.e., G is a polygon as in Figure 3.16(a)). If $f > 2$, consider the graph G' obtained from G by choosing a face adjacent to the designated one, and deleting all edges and degree-2 vertices common to the two faces. G' has $n' \leqslant n$ vertices and $f' = f - 1$ faces. By induction, we can embed G' on an $(n'+f') \times (n'+f')$ square so that the combined face is external and (b) holds. We then add new vertices and edges to obtain an embedding of G, possibly replacing certain edges of G' by vertical paths, as shown in Figure 3.16(b). The addition increases the extent by at most 1 plus the number of new vertices. The lemma follows.   □

We shall show that HAMILTONIAN CYCLE for planar, bipartite graphs with degrees 2 or 3 is polynomially transformable to HAMILTONIAN CYCLE FOR GRID GRAPHS. Given a graph G in the former class, we shall construct in polynomial time a grid graph G' such that G' has a Hamiltonian cycle if and only if G has one.

We assume that G is given to us, along with a planar representation of itself (such a representation is available as a result of our construction in the proof of Theorem 5, and, if missing, can be generated in linear time from a standard description of the graph using the techniques of Hopcroft & Tarjan [1974]). Our first step is to embed G onto the grid as per Lemma 6 – it is easy to see that the construction in the proof of Lemma 6 can be implemented in polynomial time.

We wish to do this so that the embedding preserves the bipartiteness of G, in the following sense: Recall that in a bipartite graph the nodes can be divided into 'black' and 'white' classes, with the edges going from one class to the other. Assume that such a coloration has been assigned to G (this can be easily done in linear time). The grid is *itself* bipartite – we can color all vertices black whose coordinates have an even sum, and color all other vertices white. We wish our embedding to be 'color preserving', i.e., white vertices of G go to white vertices of the grid, and black to black. To do this, we first embed G as per Lemma 6, then multiply the scale by two so that all the vertices of G have black images, and then move all the images of white vertices one position to the right, as in Figure 3.17.

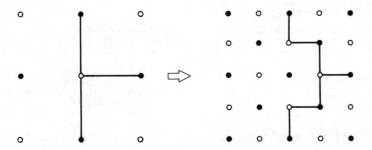

Figure 3.17   How to make an embedding color-preserving

This embedding will be our basic 'plan' for the construction of the grid graph G. For our final construction we shall expand the scale again (by a factor of 9), and replace the vertex and edge images by *boxes* and *tentacles*, respectively (defined below), which will simulate the vertices and edges of G.

A *box* is the 3×3 grid graph shown in Figure 3.18. As is easily checked, the box has the following agreeable property.

Lemma 7   *For all i, j, $1 \leq i < j \leq 4$, there is a Hamiltonian path from p_i to p_j (as identified in Figure 3.18) containing all four edges e_1, e_2, e_3 and e_4.*

Tentacles are built from *strips*. A strip is a grid graph like the one shown in Figure 3.19(a). Its *endpoints* are a, b, c and d. Two otherwise disjoint strips can be combined by identifying two adjacent endpoints of one with an endpoint and an adjacent vertex of the other, as in Figure 3.19(b). The endpoints of the combination are the two pairs of adjacent degree-2 vertices. We can continue adjoining new strips as long as we like, as in Figure 3.19(c). The result is called a *tentacle* if the only induced edges are those of the original strips. The grid graph in Figure 3.19(c) is a tentacle. A key property of tentacles is the following, proved by a parity argument.

Lemma 8   *In a tentacle there is a Hamiltonian path between two endpoints if and only if one is black and the other is white.*

A Hamiltonian path between two adjacent endpoints in a tentacle is called a *return path*; between two nonadjacent ones, a *cross path*.

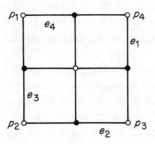

Figure 3.18   The box

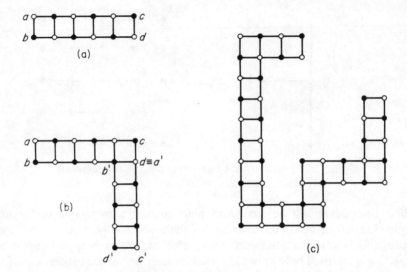

Figure 3.19   A strip (a), a combination of two strips (b), and a tentacle (c)

We are now ready to describe the grid graph G'. As mentioned above, we first multiply the scale of our previous embedding by 9, a factor big enough to open up space for the construction, and odd enough to preserve parity. We then expand each vertex which is the image of a node in G to a box, centered at that vertex (see Figure 3.20). Note that the corners of a box corresponding to a white vertex of G are all white, and analogously for the black vertices. The paths corresponding to edges of G are then expanded into tentacles. If the edge was $\{u, v\}$, where u is a white vertex of G and v is a black vertex, then the tentacle has two endpoints adjacent to vertices of the box corresponding to u, and only one endpoint adjacent to the vertex of the box corresponding to v. (For example, take $u = x_2$ and $v = y_2$ in Figure 3.20.) It is easy to see that this can always be done, because of the parity-preserving property of our embedding.

We now claim that G' has a Hamiltonian cycle if and only if G has one. First suppose that G has a Hamiltonian cycle C. The corresponding tour of G' follows the image of C in G'. A tentacle corresponding to an edge of C is traversed by a cross path, thus linking the two boxes corresponding to its endpoints. Boxes corresponding to black vertices of G are traversed by a Hamiltonian path from an endpoint of the tentacle corresponding to the 'incoming edge' of C, to an endpoint of the tentacle corresponding to the 'outgoing edge'.

A box corresponding to a white vertex is traversed analogously, except that a detour is made (around e_1, e_2, e_3 or e_4) to traverse by a return path any tentacle corresponding to an edge of G with the given white vertex as endpoint that is *not* in C (there can be at most one such detour per box since the maximum vertex degree in G is three). The existence of the

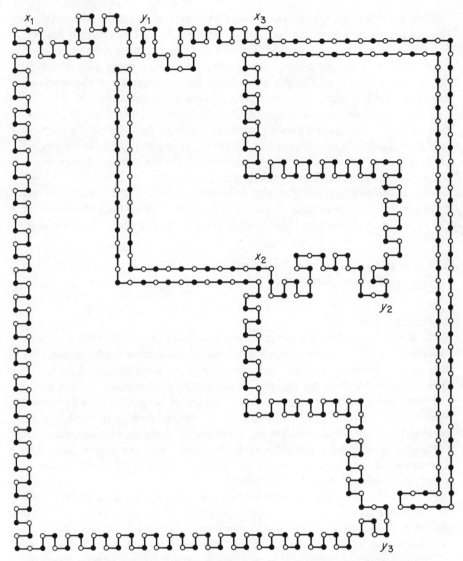

Figure 3.20   The grid graph G' corresponding to the embedding of Figure 3.15, and a
Hamiltonian cycle corresponding to $(x_1, y_1, x_3, y_2, x_2, y_3)$

required paths through boxes and tentacles is guaranteed by Lemmas 7 and
8. See Figure 3.20.

Conversely, suppose G' has a Hamiltonian cycle C'. Each black box of G'
has at most three edges to the outside world in G' (*external edges*). Hence
exactly two of these must be used in C', with the corresponding tentacles
traversed by cross paths. In the case where a black box has three external
edges in G', the tentacle corresponding to its untraversed external edge
must be picked up by a return path from its other endpoint.

Now consider the white boxes of G'. Each is adjacent to two or three tentacles, at least one of which must be traversed by a cross path if the box is to be connected to the outside world by C'. Since C' must contain an even number of the external edges for any box, and since a cross path uses only one of a pair of external edges, this means that exactly two of the tentacles associated with a white box must be traversed by cross paths.

Finally, consider the subgraph of C of G consisting of those edges of G that correspond to tentacles of G' traversed by cross paths of C'. All vertices in this subgraph have degree two. Moreover, the subgraph is connected since tentacles traversed by return paths in C' do not connect boxes in C'. Thus C is the desired Hamiltonian cycle for G.

This completes the proof of the following theorem, which has been our ultimate goal in this section (a goal that has taken us so long to reach that the reader may wish to go back to Sections 4.1 and 4.2 for a reminder of its significance).

Theorem 6 [Itai, Papadimitriou & Szwarcfiter, 1982]   HAMILTONIAN CYCLE *is $\mathcal{NP}$-complete even when restricted to grid graphs.*

Exercises
8. A *Boolean variable* is a variable assuming only the values **true** and **false**. Boolean variables can be combined by the operations **or**, **and** and **not** very much the same way that real variables can be combined by $+$, $\times$ and $\sqrt{\ }$. A *literal* is either a Boolean variable or the negation of one (an expression of the form **not** x, where x is a Boolean variable). A *clause* is the **or** of several literals. A *Boolean expression in conjunctive normal form* is the **and** of a set of clauses. Such an expression is *satisfiable* if there is an assignment of values to the Boolean variables in it that make the expression **true**. The SATISFIABILITY problem is the following: Given a Boolean expression in conjunctive normal form, is it satisfiable?
(a) Show that SATISFIABILITY can be considered a special case of 0–1 PRO-
    GRAMMING.
(b) Show that SATISFIABILITY is $\mathcal{NP}$-complete.
(c) Show that SATISFIABILITY remains $\mathcal{NP}$-complete even if there are three
    literals in each clause. (This problem is called 3-SATISFIABILITY.)
(d) Give a polynomial-time transformation from 3-SATISFIABILITY to the
    CLIQUE problem (given a graph G and an integer k, is there a completely
    connected set of k nodes in G?). (*Hint*: Construct a graph with seven
    vertices for each clause of the Boolean expression.)
9. (a) The DIAL-A-RIDE problem is the WANDERING SALESMAN problem of Exercise 5, only now the cities are divided into *origins* and the correspond-ing *destinations*, and the tour is required to visit each origin before the corresponding destination. Show that this problem is $\mathcal{NP}$-complete, and that the dynamic programming algorithm B can be modified to solve this problem. What is the time complexity of this algorithm?

(b) Repeat part (a) for the version of the TSP in which we are also given n integers $k_1, \ldots, k_n$, and we are asked for the shortest tour that visits city 1 k_1 times, city 2 k_2 times, and so on. (It may cost to go from a city to itself.)

10. There are four versions of the HAMILTONIAN CYCLE problem: HAMILTONIAN CYCLE, HAMILTONIAN PATH, DIRECTED HAMILTONIAN CYCLE, DIRECTED HAMILTONIAN PATH (the obvious definitions). Give polynomial-time transformations between all these problems.

11. The CHINESE POSTMAN problem is the following: Given a *mixed* graph (i.e., a graph with both directed and undirected edges), with a cost for each directed and undirected edge, find the shortest closed walk of the graph (path with possible repetitions of nodes and edges) that visits each directed and undirected edge at least once, always traversing the directed edges in the proper direction. Show that this problem is a special case of the asymmetric TSP with triangle inequality. (*Hint*: The cities are the midpoints of the edges.)

12. Show that the Euclidean distances among integer points on the plane, rounded up to the next integer, satisfy the triangle inequality.

13. (a) Show that the Euclidean WANDERING SALESMAN problem (Exercise 5) is $N P$-complete.

(b) Show that it is $N P$-complete to determine whether a set of points on the plane has a minimum spanning tree which is a path. (*Hint*: The construction in the proof of Theorem 6 is useful in both parts.)

14. Show that the HAMILTONIAN CYCLE problem remains $N P$-complete even when restricted to planar graphs with all vertices of degree *exactly* three.

15. The BOTTLENECK TSP is the version in which one tries to minimize the *maximum* among the distances traversed, not their sum. Show that the BOTTLENECK TSP is $N P$-complete even in the Euclidean case.

16. In the m-PROCESSOR NO WAIT FLOW SHOP scheduling problem, the goal is to schedule a collection of *jobs* $\{J_i : 1 \le i \le n\}$ so as to minimize the finishing time of the last job. Each job J_i consists of a sequence of m tasks. For each $k, 1 < k \le m$, the kth task has to be performed by the kth processor, requires time $J_i[k]$, and has to be started as soon as the $(k-1)$st task is completed by the $(k-1)$st processor (i.e., with 'no wait' between tasks). A schedule corresponds to an ordering of the jobs, with the first task of $J_{p(1)}$ starting on the first processor at time 0, and, for $1 < i \le n$, the first task of $J_{p(i)}$ starting as soon as possible subject to the constraint that, for $1 \le k \le m$, the kth processor cannot begin executing the kth task of $J_{p(i)}$ until it has finished the kth task of job $J_{p(i-1)}$.

(a) Show that this scheduling problem is a special case of the TSP.

(b) Show that the problem 'Given m, a set J of jobs, and a deadline D, can the jobs be scheduled so that the last task finishes by time D?' is $N P$-complete. (*Hint*: see Lenstra, Rinnooy Kan & Brucker [1977].) If this is an insufficient challenge, show that the problem is actually $N P$-complete even when m is fixed at 3 (without looking at Röck [1984]). (*Note*: the case that m is fixed at 2 is well solved; see Chapter 4, Section 13, Exercise 29(b).)

5 MORE BAD NEWS

In the previous section we saw that even very special cases of the TSP were
$\mathcal{NP}$-complete and hence likely to be intractable. In this section we examine
the complexity of a number of problems related to the TSP, and of some
approaches to solving the TSP. As we shall see, the outlook continues to be
bleak.

5.1 Suboptimality

In Chapter 5, we shall prove some negative results concerning the possibility
of even *approximating* the optimal solution of the general TSP. A similar
issue is that of *suboptimality*. As we have seen, finding an optimal tour is
likely to be a hopeless task. What about recognizing an optimal tour when
we see one? This can be formulated as the following decision problem.

TSP SUBOPTIMALITY
INSTANCE: An instance (n, C) of the TSP and a tour π of the n cities.
QUESTION: Is π suboptimal, i.e., is there a second tour π' of shorter
length?

TSP SUBOPTIMALITY is clearly in $\mathcal{NP}$; an optimal tour can, as in TSP
DECISION, serve as a certificate for any 'yes' instance. Unfortunately, this is
about the best we can say, as the problem is itself $\mathcal{NP}$-complete. This is a
consequence of the following result, derived by Papadimitriou & Steiglitz
[1977].

Theorem 7   *Given an undirected graph $G = (V, E)$ with a Hamiltonian cycle
C, it is $\mathcal{NP}$-complete to determine whether G has a second Hamiltonian cycle.*

Proof   We use a transformation from the HAMILTONIAN CYCLE problem.
Suppose $G = (V, E)$ is a graph. We show how to add an artificial Hamiltonian cycle to G, such that the edges of this cycle cannot 'mix' with other
edges of G to form a new Hamiltonian cycle. This is done by replacing each
vertex v of G by the subgraph S pictured in Figure 3.21(a), which uses the

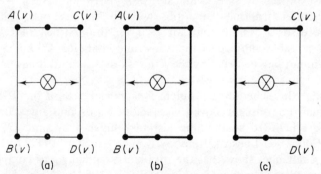

Figure 3.21   Vertex substitute for the proof of Theorem 7,
with the two possible ways it can be traversed

exclusive-or of the previous section. We then add edges $\{A(u), B(v)\}$ and $\{A(v), B(u)\}$ for each edge $\{u, v\}$ in the original graph. We obtain our artificial Hamiltonian cycle by ordering the vertices of G (arbitrarily) as $v_1, v_2, \ldots, v_n$ and adding the edges $\{C(v_i), D(v_{i+1})\}, 1 \le i < n$, and $\{C(v_n), D(v_1)\}$.

Subgraph S can be traversed by a Hamiltonian cycle in just two ways, shown in Figures 3.21(b) and 3.21(c). By our construction, all copies of S must be traversed in the same way. If they are traversed as in Figure 3.21(c), then we get our artificial cycle. If as in Figure 3.21(b), then we get a cycle if and only if G had one. □

Corollary 3 *TSP* SUBOPTIMALITY *is* $\mathcal{NP}$-*complete even in the case of symmetric distances matrices that obey the triangle inequality.*

Proof Let $G' = (V', E')$ be the graph produced by the above construction. The vertices in V' will be the cities, and the intercity distances $d(u, v)$ will be defined as follows:

$$d(u, v) = \begin{cases} 4, & \text{if } \{u, v\} \notin E'; \\ 3, & \text{if } \{u, v\} = \{C(v_n), D(v_1)\}; \\ 2, & \text{if } \{u, v\} \in E' - \{C(v_n), D(v_1)\}. \end{cases}$$

Note that the corresponding distance matrix will obey the triangle inequality.

The shortest possible tour length is $2|V'|$, and, furthermore, such a tour cannot use any nonedges of G' or any 'artificial' edges (if it used one artificial edge, it would have to use $\{C(v_n), D(v_1)\}$). Hence a tour of length $2|V'|$ exists (and our artificial tour, having length $2|V'| + 1$, is suboptimal) if and only if the original graph had a Hamiltonian cycle. □

The $\mathcal{NP}$-completeness of TSP SUBOPTIMALITY has some interesting consequences concerning the effectiveness of *local search heursitics* for the TSP. These issues will be examined in Chapter 5.

5.2 Restricted spanning tree problems

The TSP can be viewed as a special case of the following spanning tree optimization problem. Let us fix a family F of *prototype trees*, such as the family of paths (Figure 3.22(a)), that of stars (Figure 3.22(b)), or the remaining families shown in Figure 3.22. (The notion of a family of trees can be made formal [Papadimitriou & Yannakakis, 1982].) The *optimization problem for F* is defined as follows: Given a symmetric distance matrix C, find the shortest spanning tree which is isomorphic to a tree in the family F of prototypes.

If F is the family of paths, then we have the TSP (actually, the 'PATH TSP' or WANDERING SALESMAN problem, which is equivalent to the TSP, see Exercise 5). For the family of stars (Figure 3.22(b)) the problem is trivial –

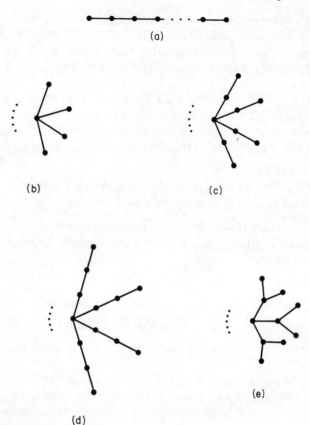

Figure 3.22   Families of trees

just try each possible center. For the family of Figure 3.22(c), the problem
turns out to be equivalent to the polynomial-time solvable WEIGHTED MATCH-
ING problem (see Exercise 24). On the other hand, the problem corresponding to the family of trees in Figure 3.22(d) is $\mathcal{NP}$-hard, as it is intimately
related to 3-DIMENSIONAL MATCHING [Garey & Johnson, 1979]. The question
that arises is, 'How can we tell the hard families of prototypes from the easy
ones?' In other words, what distinguishes the families of 3.22(a) and 3.22(d)
from those of 3.22(b) and 3.22(c)?

The answer involves what is called the *dissociation number* $d(T)$ of a tree
T. Given a tree T, $d(T)$ is the smallest number of vertices whose deletion
reduces the tree into a collection of isolated edges and vertices. For
example, a path with n vertices has dissociation number $\lceil n/3 \rceil$. The following theorem becomes a generalization of the result that the TSP is $\mathcal{NP}$-hard.

Theorem 8 [Papadimitriou & Yannakakis, 1982]   *If F is a family of trees
and there is an $\varepsilon > 0$ such that for each $T = (V, E)$ in F, $d(T) > |V|^{\varepsilon}$, then the
optimization problem for F is $\mathcal{NP}$-hard.*

The (unconstrained) MINIMUM SPANNING TREE problem can, of course, be solved in polynomial time (e.g., see Papadimitriou & Steiglitz [1982]). The discussion above reveals that this tractability is not particularly robust. Add a few side conditions on the desired trees and you may well find yourself facing the TSP. Another example of this nonrobustness comes from the following variants, one for each $k \geq 2$.

DEGREE-k MINIMUM SPANNING TREE
INSTANCE: Integer $n \geq 3$, $n \times n$ distance matrix C.
QUESTION: What is the shortest spanning tree for C in which no vertex has degree exceeding k?

DEGREE-2 MINIMUM SPANNING TREE is the TSP (again the WANDERING SALESMAN version) and hence it is $\mathcal{NP}$-hard. It is not difficult to show that DEGREE-k MINIMUM SPANNING TREE is $\mathcal{NP}$-hard for *any* $k \geq 2$ (Exercise 18(a)). An interesting question remains however: What is the complexity of the *Euclidean* special cases of these problems?

It can be shown (see Exercise 18(b)) that the minimum spanning tree of a set of integer coordinate points on the plane *never* contains a vertex of degree 6 or greater. Hence there is a polynomial-time algorithm for EUCLIDEAN DEGREE-k MINIMUM SPANNING TREE for all $k \geq 5$: namely, the algorithm which simply finds the shortest unconstrained minimum spanning tree. On the other hand, from Section 4 and Exercise 5 we have that EUCLIDEAN DEGREE-2 MINIMUM SPANNING TREE (the EUCLIDEAN TSP, that is) is $\mathcal{NP}$-hard. This leaves us with two cases: $k = 3$ and $k = 4$. Papadimitriou & Vazirani [1984] have shown that EUCLIDEAN DEGREE-3 MINIMUM SPANNING TREE is $\mathcal{NP}$-hard; EUCLIDEAN DEGREE-4 MINIMUM SPANNING TREE is still open.

5.3   More on complexity classes

In this section we discuss some distinctions that will be meaningless if it turns out that $\mathcal{P} = \mathcal{NP}$, but in the more likely event that $\mathcal{P} \neq \mathcal{NP}$ give us ways of showing that certain variants of the TSP are even 'harder' than the basic decision problem version. To do this we must first revisit the classes $\mathcal{P}$ and $\mathcal{NP}$ and their vicinity. The general hypothesis is that $\mathcal{P}$ and $\mathcal{NP}$ are related as in Figure 3.23, that is, $\mathcal{P} \neq \mathcal{NP}$ and all the $\mathcal{NP}$-complete problems belong to $\mathcal{NP} - \mathcal{P}$. There are other classes of interest. The class $co\mathcal{NP}$ contains the *complements* of all problems in $\mathcal{NP}$. For instance, the complement of TSP DECISION is given as follows:

TSP [COMPLEMENT]
INSTANCE: Integer $n \geq 3$, $n \times n$ distance matrix C, integer B.
QUESTION: Is it true that all tours have costs exceeding B?

This is the same as TSP DECISION except that the 'yes' and 'no' answers have been reversed. Similarly, HAMILTONIAN CYCLE [COMPLEMENT] asks

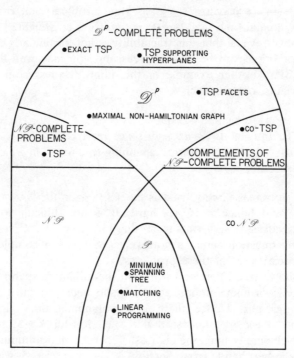

Figure 3.23   A conjectured topography of $\mathcal{P}$, $\mathcal{NP}$, and
their vicinity

whether a given graph has *no* Hamiltonian cycle, INTEGER PROGRAMMING
[COMPLEMENT] asks whether a given integer program has *no* solution, and so
on.

Due to the basic asymmetry in the definition of $\mathcal{NP}$, it seems quite likely
that $\mathcal{NP} \neq co\mathcal{NP}$. (What could be a succinct certificate of the fact that every
tour has cost *exceeding* B? A listing of all tours together with their lengths
would be a certificate, but it certainly would not be succinct.) However, no
proof that $\mathcal{NP} \neq co\mathcal{NP}$ is yet known, and for good reason: it would imply
$\mathcal{P} \neq \mathcal{NP}$ (Exercise 19(c)). What is certain, however, is that the complements
of the $\mathcal{NP}$-complete problems are the least likely members of $co\mathcal{NP}$ to be in
$\mathcal{NP}$, exactly as the $\mathcal{NP}$-complete problems are the least likely members of
$\mathcal{NP}$ to be in $\mathcal{P}$ (see Exercise 19(a)).

We can use $\mathcal{NP}$ and $co\mathcal{NP}$ to define a class that apparently includes even
harder problems, namely the class $\mathcal{D}^p$. This class contains just those problems which are the *intersection* of a problem in $\mathcal{NP}$ with one in $co\mathcal{NP}$. That
is, each problem X in $\mathcal{D}^p$ is defined by two problems X_1 and X_2 over the
same set of instances, with $X_1 \in \mathcal{NP}$ and $X_2 \in co\mathcal{NP}$, such that the answer for
X is 'yes' if and only if the answers for *both* X_1 and X_2 are 'yes'. Here are
two typical problems from this class.

EXACT TSP
INSTANCE: Integer $n \geq 3$, $n \times n$ distance matrix C, integer B.
QUESTION: Is the cost of an optimal tour *exactly* equal to B?

MAXIMUM NON-HAMILTONIAN GRAPH
INSTANCE: Graph $G = (V, E)$.
QUESTION: Is it true that (a) G has no Hamiltonian cycle, and (b) if we add *any* edge to E then a Hamiltonian cycle results?

EXACT TSP is the intersection of TSP DECISION, which is in $\mathcal{NP}$, with the variant of TSP [COMPLEMENT] which asks if all tours have length B or greater, and is in $co\mathcal{NP}$. MAXIMUM NON-HAMILTONIAN GRAPH is the intersection of the two problems suggested by the two parts (a) and (b) of its question. Problem (a) is in $co\mathcal{NP}$ and (b) is in $\mathcal{NP}$. Note that $\mathcal{NP}$ and $co\mathcal{NP}$ are both contained in $\mathcal{D}^p$, since any problem is equal to itself intersected with the trivial problem that always answers 'yes' and hence is in both $\mathcal{NP}$ and $co\mathcal{NP}$ (since it is in $\mathcal{P}$).

In analogy with $\mathcal{NP}$, a problem in $\mathcal{D}^p$ is said to be $\mathcal{D}^p$-complete if all problems in $\mathcal{D}^p$ are transformable to it. Since $\mathcal{D}^p$ contains all the problems in both $\mathcal{NP}$ and $co\mathcal{NP}$, $\mathcal{D}^p$-complete problems are potentially even worse than the $\mathcal{NP}$-complete ones. Papadimitriou & Yannakakis [1984] have shown the following.

Theorem 9   EXACT TSP *is $\mathcal{D}^p$-complete.*

We do not know whether MAXIMUM NON-HAMILTONIAN GRAPH is also $\mathcal{D}^p$-complete. However, it does have a property (shared by the $\mathcal{D}^p$-complete problems) that shows that it is even 'harder' than the $\mathcal{NP}$-complete problems.

Theorem 10   *If* MAXIMUM NON-HAMILTONIAN GRAPH *is in $\mathcal{NP}$, then $\mathcal{NP} = co\mathcal{NP}$.*

Proof   Suppose that it is in $\mathcal{NP}$. We show that this would imply HAMILTONIAN CYCLE [COMPLEMENT] is also in $\mathcal{NP}$, which, by Exercise 19(a), implies that $\mathcal{NP} = co\mathcal{NP}$. HAMILTONIAN CYCLE [COMPLEMENT] would be in $\mathcal{NP}$ because any graph with no Hamiltonian cycle would have the following succinct certificate: a set of additional edges that makes it *maximal* non-Hamiltonian, together with a succinct certificate that the augmented graph is indeed maximal non-Hamiltonian. The latter exists by our hypothesis.   □

It can be shown that the $\mathcal{D}^p$-complete problems have an even stronger property: if they are in either $\mathcal{NP}$ or $co\mathcal{NP}$, then $\mathcal{NP} = co\mathcal{NP}$ (see Exercise 19(b)). Thus the sense in which EXACT TSP and MAXIMAL NON-HAMILTONIAN GRAPH are 'harder' than TSP DECISION and the other $\mathcal{NP}$-complete problems is as follows: Assuming $\mathcal{NP} \neq co\mathcal{NP}$, these problems do not have the succinct certificate property (nor does the complement of EXACT TSP), whereas all the $\mathcal{NP}$-complete problems do. Note, however, that this is about the only sense in which these problems are 'harder'. All of the above problems (including the TSP) are polynomially *reducible* to each other (if not trans-formable) and hence they can all be solved within the same running time bounds (to within a polynomial). If $\mathcal{P} = \mathcal{NP}$ they will all be in $\mathcal{P}$.

Nevertheless, the distinctions made above are of importance from a theoretical point of view, and we shall make further use of them in the next subsection.

5.4 The complexity of the TSP polytope

The TSP is one of many combinatorial optimization problems, easy and hard, which can be reformulated as follows:

$$\text{minimize } c'x$$

$$\text{subject to } x \in V,$$

where c is a cost vector (in the case of the TSP, a representation of the distance matrix C in vector form), x is the vector to be optimized (an $\binom{n}{2}$-dimensional vector of unknowns for the n-city symmetric TSP), and V is a finite set of 'feasible' vectors (for the TSP, V consists of the characteristic vectors of all tours, considered as sets of edges).

The advantage of this formulation is that, because the objective function is linear, the optimization problem above is equivalent to the following problem:

$$\text{minimize } c'x$$

$$\text{subject to } x \in CH(V),$$

where $CH(V)$ is the *convex hull* of the set V, i.e., the smallest convex polytope that contains all the vectors in V (see Grünbaum [1967], and Chapters 8 and 9). Minimizing linear functionals over convex polytopes is supposed to be well understood – this is what linear programming and the simplex algorithm are all about [Dantzig, 1963], not to mention the ellipsoid algorithm [Khachian, 1979].

One catch is that it takes exponentially many inequalities to describe $CH(V)$ in the case of the TSP. The polyhedron $CH(V)$ has, literally, just too many faces. This does not immediately disqualify it, however. The *polyhedral* approach has worked before in the presence of this impediment, most notably in the case of the weighted matching problem [Edmonds, 1965c]. What seems more serious is that the convex polytope for the TSP is tarnished by a number of negative complexity results that strike at the very core of the known polyhedral techniques. These results suggest that, despite early promise, the polyhedral approach may prove to be no more of an 'answer' for the TSP than any of the other methods that have been tried so far (with so little success).

Let us first consider the complexity of *facets*. A facet of a d-dimensional polytope is a face of dimension $d - 1$. Alternatively, it is an inequality satisfied by all vertices of the polytope, and satisfied with equality by d *affinely independent* vertices (see Grünbaum [1967], and Chapter 8). If the TSP were to be solved, like weighted matching, by applying a variant of the simplex algorithm to the optimization problem over $CH(V)$, we would need at the very least a complete 'characterization' of all the facets of the TSP polytope. Such a characterization has been for a long time the 'Holy Grail' for researchers in the field. Increasingly more complex classes of facets have been discovered [Dantzig, Fulkerson & Johnson, 1954; Chvátal, 1973a; Maurras, 1975; Grötschel, 1980a; Grötschel & Padberg, 1979b], but no satisfactory conclusion of the search is in sight. Complexity theory yields an explanation for this failure. A satisfactory characterization of the facets of the TSP polytope would mean, at the very least, that the following problem is in $\mathcal{NP}$.

TSP FACETS
INSTANCE: an integer n, plus an inequality $\sum_{j=1} a_j x_j \leq b$ with b and the coefficients a_j all integers.

QUESTION: Is the given inequality a facet of the symmetric TSP polytope for n cities?

The following result was recently shown by Papadimitriou & Yannakakis [1984].

Theorem 11 MAXIMUM NON-HAMILTONIAN GRAPH $\propto$ TSP FACETS.

Thus, by Theorem 11, we have that TSP FACETS is 'harder' than the $\mathcal{NP}$-complete problems.

Corollary 4 *If* TSP FACETS $\in \mathcal{NP}$, *then* $\mathcal{NP} = co\mathcal{NP}$.

The same corollary can be proved using linear programming duality [Karp & Papadimitriou, 1982]. The proof of Theorem 11 has as a byproduct the construction of a new natural and 'dense' class of facets of the TSP polytope.

A variant of the TSP FACETS problem is TSP SUPPORTING HYPER-PLANES, the problem of recognizing valid inequalities for the TSP polytope that are 'tight' (i.e., satisfied with equality) for at least one vertex (not necessarily $d = \binom{n}{2}$ affinely independent ones). Facets are always supporting hyperplanes, but not vice versa. For this problem there is a stronger result, proved by a transformation from EXACT TSP.

Theorem 12 [Papadimitriou & Yannakakis, 1984] TSP SUPPORTING HYPERPLANES *is* $\mathcal{D}^p$-*complete*.

Let us now turn to the question of *adjacency* on the TSP polytope. An *edge* of a convex polytope is a one-dimensional face of the polytope. Two vertices are adjacent if they are the endpoints of an edge. Since the simplex algorithm moves toward optimality by walking along the edges of the polytope [Papadimitriou & Steiglitz, 1982, Section 2.9], an understanding of the edges of the TSP polytope should be a prerequisite for attacking the TSP polyhedrally. One way of formulating this problem is the following:

TSP NONADJACENCY

INSTANCE: An integer n, plus two tours π and π' of n cities.

QUESTION: Are π and π' non-adjacent vertices of the TSP polytope for n cities?

Unfortunately, the prospects are not good here either.

Theorem 13 [Papadimitriou, 1978]   TSP NONADJACENCY *is $\mathcal{NP}$-complete.*

A final problem is that of deciding whether a given rational point lies within the TSP polytope or not. Answering such a question would be essential if we wished to attack the TSP using the ellipsoid algorithm, as suggested by Browne [1979], for example. As might be expected, this problem too is $\mathcal{NP}$-complete [Papadimitriou & Yannakakis, 1982b].

For a different perspective on the polyhedral approach, see Chapters 8 and 9. We suspect readers have had their fill of bad news by now, and so we shall stop here. Subsequent chapters will show that, despite an overall bleak picture, there are many corners of the world where a traveling salesman can find an occasional ray of light.

Exercises

17. LINEAR PROGRAMMING is the same as INTEGER PROGRAMMING, except that *rational* solutions (not just integer ones) are allowed.

(a) Show that LINEAR PROGRAMMING $\in \mathcal{NP}$.

(b) Use the duality theory of linear programming (see Papadimitriou & Steiglitz [1982]) to show that LINEAR PROGRAMMING $\in co\mathcal{NP}$. (Note that both (a) and (b) follow trivially from the ellipsoid algorithm for linear programming [Khachian, 1979], so do not use that result.)

18. (a) Show that DEGREE-k MINIMUM SPANNING TREE problem is $\mathcal{NP}$-complete, for all $k > 1$.

(b) Show that EUCLIDEAN DEGREE-5 MINIMUM SPANNING TREE is polynomial. (*Hint*: Can the minimum spanning tree of a planar set of points with integer coordinates have a node of degree 6 or more?)

(c) Show that EUCLIDEAN DEGREE-3 MINIMUM SPANNING TREE problem is $\mathcal{NP}$-complete.

19. (a) Show that, if the complement of an $\mathcal{NP}$-complete problem is in $\mathcal{NP}$, then $\mathcal{NP} = co\mathcal{NP}$.

(b) Show that, if a $\mathcal{D}^p$-complete problem is in $\mathcal{NP}$ or in $co\mathcal{NP}$, then $\mathcal{NP} = co\mathcal{NP}$.

(c) Show that, if $\mathcal{P} = \mathcal{NP}$, then $\mathcal{NP} = co\mathcal{NP}$.

20. (a) Show that any problem in $\mathcal{NP}$ can be solved in time $O(2^{p(n)})$ for some polynomial p.

(b) Show that any problem in $\mathcal{NP}$ can be solved in polynomial *space*.

(c) Repeat (a) and (b) for the class $\mathcal{D}^p$.

21. (a) Show that $\mathcal{NP}, co\mathcal{NP} \subseteq \mathcal{D}^p$.

22. Show, by using the duality theory of linear programming that, if TSP FACETS $\in \mathcal{NP}$, then $\mathcal{NP} = co\mathcal{NP}$.

23. (a) Show that TSP FACETS $\in \mathcal{D}^p$.

(b) Show that the problem of telling whether a given rational point is an interior point of the TSP polytope is in $\mathcal{NP}$.

(c) Show that the problem of telling whether two given TSP tours on n cities are nonadjacent vertices of the TSP polytope is in $\mathcal{NP}$.

24. In the weighted matching problem [Edmonds, 1965c], one is given a graph with a weight assigned to each edge, and asks for the *matching* (i.e., set of edges, no two of which share an endpoint) which has maximum weight. Show that the problem of finding, given a matrix over an odd number of cities, the shortest spanning tree isomorphic to the 'double star' of Figure 3.22(c), can be reduced to the weighted matching problem. Note that you must turn a minimization problem into a maximization problem in order to do this.

25. Show that the problem UNIQUE TOUR, asking whether there is exactly one tour in a given instance of the TSP that has a specified length B, is in $\mathcal{D}^p$. Give evidence that the problem UNIQUE OPTIMAL TOUR (does the instance have a unique optimum tour?) is *not* in $\mathcal{D}^p$ (*Hint*: see Papadimitriou [1984].)

The Traveling Salesman Problem
Edited by E. L. Lawler, J. K. Lenstra,
A. H. G. Rinnooy Kan, D. B. Shmoys
© 1985 John Wiley & Sons Ltd.

4

Well-solved special cases

P. C. Gilmore
University of British Columbia, Vancouver

E. L. Lawler, D. B. Shmoys
University of California, Berkeley

1 INTRODUCTION

Despite the general pessimism contributed by both theory and practice, there is a bright side to the TSP. Many special cases can be easily and efficiently solved. We survey these special cases in this chapter, with the expectation that the reader will find them interesting, instructive and possibly even useful.

There are two broad categories of special cases of the TSP. In one category are problems that are special because of restrictions on the matrix C of arc lengths. For example, C may be upper triangular or a circulant matrix. In a second category are problems in which the TSP is to be solved over a network with a particular structure but with no restriction on the lengths of the arcs. For example, the network may have limited bandwidth.

The majority of the results presented here involve special cases of the first type, with the best known example being the single state-variable sequencing problem [Gilmore & Gomory, 1964]. The solution to this problem involves first solving an assignment problem for the distance matrix C and then patching together subtours so as to obtain an optimal solution to the TSP. Since several other special cases involve a similar approach, we have introduced a general theory of subtour patching in an effort to unify results.

Several of the results in this chapter are either new or are presented in an original manner. For example, we believe the formulation of the wallpapering problem presented here is original, and we have obtained more general results than were known previously. In addition, we believe the results on bandwidth-limited graphs and the generalizations of the Gilmore–Gomory model are original. Some of the results contained in this chapter were drawn from the Soviet literature, and were largely unknown in the West. Unpublished notes by E. Ya. Gabovich were extremely valuable in pointing out the most important (and the most obscure) Soviet results.

Throughout this chapter we will make extensive use of concepts related to the symmetric group of permutations on n elements. It is expected that the reader has some familiarity with the concepts, so we briefly note only some of the more important points. Consider an arbitrary permutation ϕ; $\phi(i) = j$ denotes that i is mapped to j by ϕ. Since the set of all permutations on n elements forms a group, for any two permutations τ and ϕ there exists a unique permutation ψ such that $\tau = \phi\psi$. As is customary, $\rho\phi(i)$ denotes $\rho(\phi(i))$ and also $\tau^{-1}(j) = i$ is equivalent to $\tau(i) = j$. It is well known that every permutation ϕ has a unique set of disjoint factors. We write permutations in their factored form, e.g. if $\tau(1) = 2$, $\tau(2) = 1$, $\tau(3) = 4$, and $\tau(4) = 3$ we write that $\tau = (1, 2)(3, 4)$.

There is a one-to-one correspondence between permutations and feasible solutions to the assignment problem; $\phi(i) = j$ has the interpretation that element c_{ij} is used in the assignment. Therefore, tours correspond to permutations where all of the elements (cities) are contained within one factor, that is, cyclic permutations or cycles. Also note that cycles on disjoint sets of elements commute, in contrast to the case of two arbitrary permutations. For an assignment that is not a tour, factors correspond to subtours. The cost of a permutation ϕ is

$$c(\phi) = \sum_{i=1}^{n} c_{i\phi(i)}.$$

Often we will modify one assignment ϕ by multiplying it by another permutation ψ; we will be interested in the additional cost of this permutation

$$c\phi(\psi) = c(\phi\psi) - c(\phi)$$

above the original cost of ϕ. When the bottleneck criterion is used we will denote the bottleneck cost

$$\bar{c}(\phi) = \max_i \{c_{i\phi(i)}\}$$

and, parallel to the case above, we let

$$\bar{c}\phi(\psi) = \bar{c}(\phi\psi) - \bar{c}(\phi).$$

We have indicated only the basic concepts about the symmetric group of permutations that will be used throughout the chapter; the interested reader is referred to Herstein [1975] for a more comprehensive treatment.

2 THE CONSTANT TSP

In this section we consider conditions on the distance matrix C under which all Hamiltonian cycles have the same length. For such a *constant* TSP, one simply needs to find *any* Hamiltonian cycle in the underlying network.

Let $\mathbf{C}$ be the collection of all $n \times n$ matrices C such that $c(\tau)$ is constant for all cyclic permutations τ of the n cities. $\mathbf{C}$ is evidently a linear subspace of the space of all $n \times n$ matrices. That is, if $C_1, C_2 \in \mathbf{C}$, with $c_1(\tau) = \alpha_1$, $c_2(\tau) = \alpha_2$, then $C' = \lambda_1 C_1 + \lambda_2 C_2 \in \mathbf{C}$, because $c'(\tau) = \lambda_1 \alpha_1 + \lambda_2 \alpha_2$ for all τ.

Lemma 1 *The dimension of $\mathbf{C}$ is $2n - 1$.*

Proof Let $T = \{\tau^{(1)}, \tau^{(2)}, \ldots, \tau^{(\omega)}\}$, where $\omega = (n-1)!$, denote the set of all cyclic permutations on n cities. Let

$$t_{ij}^{(k)} = \begin{cases} 1 & \text{if } \tau^{(k)}(i) = j, \\ 0 & \text{otherwise.} \end{cases}$$

It follows that

$$-1 = -\frac{1}{n} \sum_{\substack{i,j=1 \\ i \neq j}}^{n} t_{ij}^{(k)}, \qquad k = 1, 2, \ldots, \omega. \tag{1}$$

In order for a matrix C to belong to $\mathbf{C}$, there must exist a number α such that

$$\sum_{\substack{i,j=1 \\ i \neq j}}^{n} t_{ij}^{(k)} c_{ij} - \alpha = 0, \qquad k = 1, 2, \ldots, \omega. \tag{2}$$

Equations (2) give us a homogeneous system in $n(n-1)+1$ variables $(c_{12}, c_{13}, \ldots, c_{n,n-1}$, and $\alpha)$. The coefficient matrix for this system has ω rows and $n(n-1)+1$ columns. The column vectors will be denoted by $t_{ij} = (t_{ij}^{(1)}, \ldots, t_{ij}^{(\omega)})^T$ $(i, j = 1, 2, \ldots, n; i \neq j)$ and $t_\alpha = (-1, \ldots, -1)^T$. By (1), we see that t_α is a linear combination of the t_{ij}. Further,

$$t_{1h}^{(k)} = \frac{1}{n-2} \sum_{\substack{i,j=2 \\ i \neq j}}^{n} t_{ij}^{(k)} - \sum_{i=2}^{n} t_{ih}^{(k)}, \qquad k = 1, \ldots, \omega,$$

$$t_{h1}^{(k)} = \frac{1}{n-2} \sum_{\substack{i,j=2 \\ i \neq j}}^{n} t_{ij}^{(k)} - \sum_{j=2}^{n} t_{hj}^{(k)}, \qquad k = 1, \ldots, \omega,$$

so that t_{1h} and t_{h1}, $h = 2, \ldots, n$, are linear combinations of the t_{ij} with $i, j \neq 1$.

We claim the remaining $(n-1)(n-2)$ vectors t_{ij} $(i, j = 2, \ldots, n; i \neq j)$ are linearly independent. For suppose that

$$\sum_{\substack{i,j=2 \\ i \neq j}}^{n} \lambda_{ij} t_{ij}^{(k)} = 0, \qquad k = 1, \ldots, \omega.$$

Consider the cyclic permutation $\tau^{(k)} = (1, 2, \ldots, n)$ with $t_{23}^{(k)} = t_{34}^{(k)} = \ldots = t_{n-1,n}^{(k)} = 1$, $t_{ij}^{(k)} = 0$ otherwise, and also the permutations $(1, 3, 4, \ldots, n-1, n, 2)$, $(1, 4, 5, \ldots, n, 2, 3), \ldots, (1, n, 2, \ldots, n-3, n-2, n-1)$. (Note that we have eliminated t_{12}, t_{n1} from the problem.) From these permutations we obtain

$$\lambda_{23} + \lambda_{34} + \ldots + \lambda_{n-2,n-1} + \lambda_{n-1,n} = 0,$$

$$\lambda_{34} + \lambda_{45} + \ldots + \lambda_{n-1,n} + \lambda_{n,2} = 0,$$

$$\vdots$$

$$\lambda_{n,2} + \lambda_{23} + \ldots + \lambda_{n-3,n-2} + \lambda_{n-2,n-1} = 0.$$

Adding all of these equations yields

$$\lambda_{23} + \lambda_{34} + \ldots + \lambda_{n-1,n} + \lambda_{n,2} = 0.$$

Subtracting this equation from each of the former ones gives

$$\lambda_{23} = \lambda_{34} = \ldots = \lambda_{n-1,n} = \lambda_{n,2} = 0.$$

In this way we can prove that all $\lambda_{ij} = 0$.

Thus, the rank of the coefficient matrix is $(n-1)(n-2)$. It follows that the dimension of **C** is $n(n-1)+1-(n-1)(n-2) = 2n-1$. $\square$

Let R_i (C_j) be the $n \times n$ matrix whose ith row (jth column) contains ones and all other elements are zeros.

Lemma 2 *Any subset of $2n-1$ matrices from the set $\{R_1, \ldots, R_n, C_1, \ldots, C_n\}$ is a basis of **C**.*

Proof The $2n$ matrices $R_1, \ldots, R_n, C_1, \ldots, C_n$ all belong to **C**, but they are not linearly independent, since

$$\sum_{i=1}^{n} R_i = \sum_{j=1}^{n} C_j.$$

It is easily seen, however, that any $2n-1$ of them are linearly independent and thus, by Lemma 1, form a basis of **C**. $\square$

Theorem 1 *The only matrices C for which all cyclic permutations on the n cities have the same length are those of the form $c_{ij} = a_i + b_j$.*

Proof Follows immediately from Lemma 2. $\square$

Consider a transformation $C' = t(C)$ on distance matrices for which there exist constants α and β such that

$$c'(\tau) = \alpha + \beta c(\tau)$$

for all tours τ. Such a transformation is called a *linear admissible transformation*; depending upon the sign of β, it preserves or reverses the total ordering of tours according to length.

Theorem 2 *The only linear admissible transformations are those obtained by adding constants a_i to the ith row and b_j to the jth column of a scalar multiple of C.*

Proof Let $C' = t(C)$ be such that $c'(\tau) = \alpha + \beta c(\tau)$ for all tours τ. Defining $C'' = C' - \beta C$, we have $c''(\tau) = \alpha$ for all τ. By Lemma 2, C'' is a linear combination of $R_1, \ldots, R_n, C_1, \ldots, C_n$. Hence $C' = C'' + \beta C$ can be obtained in the way stated in the theorem. $\square$

Theorems 1 and 2 follow from results of Berenguer [1979] which were originally stated for the multisalesman problem (see also Gabovich [1976]). The proof of Lemma 1 is adapted from Lenstra & Rinnooy Kan [1979]. Note that Theorem 1 remains true if the adjective 'cyclic' is deleted. That is, matrices of the form $c_{ij} = a_i + b_j$ are also the only ones for which all permutations, i.e. assignments, have the same length.

Let $G = (V, A)$ be an arbitrary digraph and C be a distance matrix such that

$$c_{ij} = \begin{cases} a_i + b_j & \text{if } (i, j) \in A, \\ +\infty & \text{otherwise.} \end{cases}$$

Then the TSP is simply the problem of finding one of the Hamiltonian cycles, if any, in G. If G has some special structure, this may be easy. For example, if G is the line digraph of an Eulerian digraph then G is necessarily Hamiltonian and the problem is easily solved [Syslo, 1973]. Other cases in which it is easy to find a Hamiltonian cycle are discussed in Chapter 11.

It does not seem to be possible to obtain such simple conditions on the matrix C so that all Hamiltonian cycles to have the same bottleneck length. However, the reader should keep some simple facts in mind, as indicated by the following propositions.

Proposition 1 *Adding a constant to all elements of C adds the same constant to the bottleneck length of each tour.*

Proposition 2 *If C and C' are two matrices whose elements are similarly ordered, i.e.*

$$c_{ij} \leqslant c_{kl} \quad \text{if and only if} \quad c'_{ij} \leqslant c'_{kl},$$

then the ordering of tours according to bottleneck length is the same for both C and C'.

Proposition 3 *Let $k \leq \bar{c}(\tau^*)$, where τ^* is a bottleneck optimal tour. Then replacing C by C', where*

$$c'_{ij} = \max\{c_{ij}, k\}$$

leaves the bottleneck length of all tours unchanged.

Suppose ϕ is a bottleneck optimal assignment for C. Then by Propositions 1 and 3, the matrix C', where

$$c'_{ij} = \max\{c_{ij} - \bar{c}(\phi), 0\},$$

is nonnegative and preserves the order of tours with respect to the bottleneck criterion.

Exercise
1. Devise an algorithm to test whether or not a given matrix C is of the form $c_{ij} = a_i + b_j$.

3   THE SMALL TSP

In this section we examine the TSP for small matrices. The results presented are due to Gabovich [1970]. Let us call an $n \times n$ matrix C *small* if there exist n-dimensional vectors a and b such that $c_{ij} = \min\{a_i, b_j\}$. For simplicity of notation, assume that $a_1 \leq a_2 \leq \ldots \leq a_n$. A small matrix where all of the a_i and b_j are distinct is said to have *distinct values*. Let d_i be the ith smallest of the $2n$ distinct values a_i and b_j and then let $D = \{d_1, d_2, \ldots, d_n\}$. In addition, let $d = \sum_{i=1}^{n} d_i$. Consider solving the TSP for the distance matrix C. The length of an optimal tour can be found easily, and is limited to only a handful of different values.

Theorem 3 *Let C be a small matrix with distinct values. The length of an optimal tour for C is d if and only if one of the following three conditions holds:*
(S1)   *For some city i, both a_i and b_i are in D.*
(S2) $D = \{a_1, a_2, \ldots, a_n\}$.
(S3) $D = \{b_1, b_2, \ldots, b_n\}$.

Proof   Suppose that (S1) holds. The cities can be partitioned into four sets: those with neither a_i nor b_i in D; those with only a_i in D; those with only b_i in D; those with both a_i and b_i in D. Call these sets D_0, D_a, D_b and D_2, respectively. By a very simple counting argument, $|D_0| = |D_2|$. Construct a tour as follows. Start at a city in D_2. Then, in any order, visit the cities of D_a. Next, go to a city in D_0. This is followed by visiting the cities of D_b in any order. The tour is completed by visiting the remaining cities in D_2 and D_0 alternately; that is, one from D_2, then one from D_0, and so on. It is not hard to see that the cost of this tour is d. Since the values are distinct, each arc of a tour must have a different value, and thus the cost of any tour must be at least d. Next suppose that (S2) holds. This is a constant TSP and the cost of any tour is d. The same is true for (S3).

Finally, assume that (S1), (S2), and (S3) all do not hold. It follows that $D = \{a_1, \ldots, a_k, b_{k+1}, \ldots, b_n\}$ for some $1 \leq k \leq n-1$. Suppose that a tour of length d existed. The costs of the arcs in this tour must correspond precisely to those costs in D. Therefore, in this tour some arcs have costs that correspond to a values and some that correspond to b values. Therefore, at some point in the tour an arc with cost b_i must be followed by one with cost a_j. But for this to happen, i must equal j, which is impossible. $\square$

A set of costs $D = \{d_1, d_2, \ldots, d_n\}$ *dominates* another set of costs $D' = \{d_1', d_2', \ldots, d_n'\}$ if there exists a permutation σ such that $d_{\sigma(i)} \geq d_i'$ for $i = 1, \ldots, n$. Furthermore, a set of costs $D = \{d_1, d_2, \ldots, d_n\}$ is *feasible* if there exists a tour τ and a permutation σ such that $c_{i\tau(i)} = d_{\sigma(i)}$ for $i = 1, \ldots, n$. An almost identical proof will give a slightly stronger version of Theorem 3.

Theorem 3' *Let C be a small matrix with distinct values. Let $D' = \{d_1', d_2', \ldots, d_n'\}$ be a subset of $\{a_1, a_2, \ldots, a_n, b_1, b_2, \ldots, b_n\}$ such that any other subset that it dominates is infeasible. Then there exists a tour that uses precisely those costs if and only if one of the following three conditions holds:*
(S1') *For some city i, both of the values a_i and b_i are in D'.*
(S2') $D' = \{a_1, a_2, \ldots, a_n\}$.
(S3') $D' = \{b_1, b_2, \ldots, b_n\}$.

In Theorem 3, it was shown that d cannot be attained under certain conditions. In this case, what is the optimal value? This question is answered by the next result.

Theorem 4 *Let C be a small matrix with distinct values. The length of the shortest tour for the TSP given by C is either d, $d - d_n + d_{n+1}$, or $\min\{d - d_n + d_{n+2}, d - d_{n-1} + d_{n+1}\}$. Furthermore, suppose that the optimal cost is not d; then the optimal cost is greater than $d - d_n + d_{n+1}$ if and only if one of the following three conditions holds:*
(S4) $k = 1; d_n = b_2; d_{n+1} = a_2.$
(S5) $k = n-1; d_n = a_{n-1}; d_{n+1} = b_{n-1}.$
(S6) $2 \leq k \leq n-2$; *either* $(d_n = a_k \text{ and } d_{n+1} = b_k)$ *or* $(d_n = b_{k+1} \text{ and } d_{n+1} = a_{k+1})$.
Here k is the largest index i such that $a_i \in D$, the set of the n smallest values.

Proof Since the case of an optimal tour of length d was completely characterized by Theorem 3, assume that the optimal tour costs more than d. The next best possible value is $d' = d - d_n + d_{n-1}$, and to see if this can be attained, consider $D' = D \cup \{d_{n+1}\} - \{d_n\}$. By Theorem 3', d' is attainable if and only if D' satisfies (S1'), (S2') or (S3').

It is possible to list precisely those cases when all three of these conditions fail. As indicated in the proof of Theorem 3, if the optimal value is not d,

$D = \{a_1, \ldots, a_k, b_{k+1}, \ldots, b_n\}$. First, note that if $d_n = b_i$ and $d_{n+1} = b_j$, (S1')
will be satisfied. Therefore, for all three to fail, either $d_n = a_k$, or
$d_{n+1} = a_{k+1}$. Suppose that $d_n = a_k$; it is easy to see that condition (S1') will be
satisfied unless $d_{n+1} = b_k$. If d_{n+1} does equal b_k, then $D' =$
$\{a_1, \ldots, a_{k-1}, b_k, \ldots, b_n\}$. If $k = 1$, this implies that (S3') holds; otherwise
(S1'), (S2'), and (S3') all fail to hold. Finally, suppose that $d_{n+1} = a_{k+1}$.
Again, condition (S1') will hold unless $d_n = b_{k+1}$. In this case, $D' =$
$\{a_1, \ldots, a_{k+1}, b_{k+2}, \ldots, b_n\}$. If $k = n - 1$, it follows that (S2') is satisfied, but
otherwise all three conditions fail. These cases are precisely those stipulated
by (S4), (S5) and (S6).

To complete the proof of the theorem, suppose that d' is not attainable. It
is straightforward to show that the restrictions placed on d_n and d_{n+1} insure
that both $D - \{d_n\} \cup \{d_{n+2}\}$ and $D - \{d_{n-1}\} \cup \{d_{n+1}\}$ must satisfy one of (S1'),
(S2') and (S3'). Since both $d - d_n + d_{n+2}$ and $d - d_{n-1} + d_{n+1}$ are attainable,
the optimum is simply the minimum of the two values. $\square$

It is interesting to consider the case where the values a_i and b_i are not
necessarily distinct.

Theorem 5 *Consider an instance of the TSP given by a small distance
matrix. The length of an optimal tour is equal to d if and only if one of the
following four conditions holds:*
(S7) *(S1), (S2) or (S3) holds.*
(S8) $d_n = d_{n+1}$; *none of (S4), (S5) and (S6) holds.*
(S9) $d_n = d_{n+1} = d_{n+2}$.
(S10) $d_{n-1} = d_n = d_{n+1}$.

Proof Left as an exercise. $\square$

Exercises
2. Prove Theorem 5.
3. Formulate and prove the theorem corresponding to Theorem 4 when a_i
and b_i are not assumed to be distinct.
4. Construct an $O(n)$ time algorithm to find an optimal tour for small
matrices. (The input must be a and b.) *Hint:* It is possible to find the median
of n numbers in $O(n)$ time.
5. Prove that if C is a symmetric small matrix then the length of the optimal
tour is d.

4 CIRCULANT MATRICES

In this section we show how to find a shortest Hamiltonian path in the case
that C is a circulant matrix. Although we do not know of a polynomial
algorithm for the TSP for circulants, the Hamiltonian path result does
enable us to obtain an approximate solution that is quite close to the
optimum in many cases.

A *circulant* is an $n \times n$ matrix of the form

$$
\begin{bmatrix}
c_0 & c_1 & c_2 \ldots c_{n-2} & c_{n-1} \\
c_{n-1} & c_0 & c_1 \ldots c_{n-3} & c_{n-2} \\
c_{n-2} & c_{n-1} & c_0 \ldots c_{n-4} & c_{n-3} \\
\vdots & & & \vdots \\
c_1 & c_2 & c_3 \ldots c_{n-1} & c_0
\end{bmatrix}.
$$

The cells (i, j) such that $(j - i) = k \pmod{n}$ have the same value c_k; these cells comprise the kth *stripe* of C. Note that each stripe yields a feasible solution to the assignment problem defined by C.

Theorem 6 [Garfinkel, 1977] *The number of subtours in the assignment given by the kth stripe is* $\gcd(k, n)$.

Proof Cities i and j are in the same subtour if and only if there exist integers m_1, m_2 such that $j - i = m_1 k + m_2 n$. It follows from elementary number theory that i and j are in the same subtour if and only if $i = j \pmod{g}$, where $g = \gcd(k, n)$. Hence there are $\gcd(k, n)$ subtours, each of which contains $n/\gcd(k, n)$ cities. $\square$

Corollary 1 *If* $\gcd(k, n) = 1$, *then the kth stripe yields a Hamiltonian cycle.*

Corollary 2 *If n is prime then each stripe, other than the 0th, yields a Hamiltonian cycle.*

Let $c_{k(0)} \leq c_{k(1)} \leq c_{k(2)} \leq \ldots \leq c_{k(n-1)}$ and let

$$
g_0 = \gcd(k(0), n),
$$
$$
g_{i+1} = \gcd(k(i+1), g_i).
$$

Lemma 3 *A lower bound on the length of a shortest Hamiltonian path is given by*

$$
(n - g_0)c_{k(0)} + (g_0 - g_1)c_{k(1)} + \ldots + (g_{n-2} - g_{n-1})c_{k(n-1)}.
$$

Proof sketch Ignore directions of arcs and consider the undirected multi-graph that results. Edges from stripe $k(0)$, with cost $c_{k(0)}$, yield a subgraph with g_0 connected components. Edges from stripes $k(0)$ and $k(1)$ yield a subgraph with g_1 connected components, and so forth. It is now seen that a shortest spanning tree, such as one obtained by Kruskal's algorithm, has length equal to the asserted lower bound. Since every Hamiltonian path is a spanning tree, the length of a shortest spanning tree is a lower bound on the length of a shortest Hamiltonian path. $\square$

Theorem 7 [Bach, Luby & Goldwasser, 1982] *The nearest neighbor rule, starting from any city, yields a shortest Hamiltonian path.*

Proof sketch Show that the nearest neighbor rule yields a Hamiltonian path whose length is equal to the lower bound given in Lemma 3. $\square$

Corollary 3   *The nearest neighbor rule, starting from any city, yields a tour that differs in length from the optimum by no more than* $c_{k(n-1)} - c_{k(0)}$.

Proof   No tour can be shorter than the length of a shortest Hamiltonian path plus $c_{k(0)}$. The nearest neighbor rule chooses one arc in addition to a shortest Hamiltonian path and its length cannot exceed $c_{k(n-1)}$.   □

We comment that the Hamiltonian path produced by the nearest neighbor rule is optimal in a very strong sense – its kth shortest arc is as short as the kth shortest arc in any other Hamiltonian path. In particular, the path is bottleneck optimal.

Exercises
6. Let C be an $n \times n$ circulant, where

$$c_k = ak + b \pmod{n}$$

with $\gcd(a, n) = 1$. The elements of C are thus $0, 1, 2, \ldots, n-1$.
(*a*) Show that $g_1 = 1$ for C (where $c_{k(0)} = 0$, $c_{k(1)} = 1$). (*Hint*: It may be easiest to show $\gcd(k(1) - k(0), n) = 1$, which implies the desired result.)
(*b*) Show that the length of any Hamiltonian cycle is a multiple of n.
(*c*) Use the above results to show that the nearest neighbor rule yields an optimal Hamiltonian cycle.

7. (*Open question*) Is there a polynomial-time algorithm for solving the TSP for circulants, or is this problem $\mathcal{NP}$-hard?

5   UPPER TRIANGULAR MATRICES

We say that C is *upper triangular* if $i \geqslant j$ implies $c_{ij} = 0$. In this section we shall show that the TSP for upper triangular matrices is essentially as easy as the assignment problem [Lawler, 1971].

Lemma 4   *Let C be upper triangular and ϕ be an assignment that is optimal subject to the constraint that $\phi(n) = 1$. Then $c(\phi)$ is a lower bound on the length of an optimal tour.*

Proof   Call an arc (i, j) *backward* if $i \geqslant j$; for such an arc $c_{ij} = 0$. Let τ be an optimal tour. Remove each backward arc from the part of τ that extends from city n to city 1. The result is a set of paths, each extending from a city j to a city i, with $j \leqslant i$. Now turn each of these paths into a cycle by adding a backward arc from i to j. The result is an assignment ϕ with $\phi(n) = 1$ and $c(\phi) = c(\tau)$.   □

Theorem 8   *Let C be upper triangular and ϕ be an assignment that is optimal subject to the constraint that $\phi(n) = 1$. Then $c(\phi)$ is equal to the length of an optimal tour τ that can be easily constructed from ϕ.*

Proof   Let ϕ be an assignment that is optimal subject to the constraint that

$\phi(n) = 1$. If ϕ is not a tour then it consists of s subtours, where $s \geq 2$, each of which contains at least one backward arc (as defined in the proof of Lemma 4). Remove arc $(n, 1)$ from the subtour containing cities 1 and n and any one backward arc from each of the other subtours. The result is a set of paths, one extending from city 1 to city n, and the others from j_1 to i_1, j_2 to $i_2, \ldots, j_{s-1}$ to i_{s-1}, where $j_1 > j_2 > \ldots > j_{s-1}$ and $i_1 \geq j_1 > j_2$, $i_2 \geq j_2 > j_3$, $\ldots, i_{s-1} \geq j_{s-1} > 1$. Now add backward arcs (n, j_1), $(i_1, j_2), \ldots, (i_{s-2}, j_{s-1})$, $(i_{s-1}, 1)$ to obtain a tour τ with $c(\tau) = c(\phi)$. Since, by Lemma 4, $c(\phi)$ is a lower bound on the length of an optimal tour, τ is optimal. $\square$

Note that an assignment ϕ that is optimal subject to the constraint that $\phi(n) = 1$ is easily obtained by applying any algorithm for the assignment problem to the $(n-1) \times (n-1)$ matrix C' that results from the deletion of column 1 and row n from C. Standard assignment algorithms require no more than $O(n^3)$ time. The construction of an optimal tour, as indicated in the proof of Theorem 8, requires considerably less time. The reader may be interested in verifying that the construction requires no more than $O(n)$ time.

As a simple example, let

$$
C = \begin{bmatrix}
0 & -1 & 7 & -20 & 3 & -2 & 5 \\
0 & 0 & 12 & 8 & 16 & 9 & 8 \\
0 & 0 & 0 & 3 & 7 & 6 & 2 \\
0 & 0 & 0 & 0 & 4 & 4 & 9 \\
0 & 0 & 0 & 0 & 0 & -18 & -1 \\
0 & 0 & 0 & 0 & 0 & 0 & 3 \\
0 & 0 & 0 & 0 & 0 & 0 & 0
\end{bmatrix}.
$$

Then

$$
C' = \begin{bmatrix}
-1 & 7 & \mathbf{-20} & 3 & -2 & 5 \\
\mathbf{0} & 12 & 8 & 16 & 9 & 8 \\
0 & 0 & 3 & 7 & 6 & \mathbf{2} \\
0 & \mathbf{0} & 0 & 4 & 4 & 9 \\
0 & 0 & 0 & 0 & \mathbf{-18} & -1 \\
0 & 0 & 0 & \mathbf{0} & 0 & 3
\end{bmatrix}
$$

and an optimal solution to the assignment problem is indicated in bold face. This is converted to an optimal solution to the TSP as shown in Figure 4.1.

Exercises
8. Devise a procedure to determine whether or not a matrix C can be made upper triangular by adding constants to its rows and columns and by

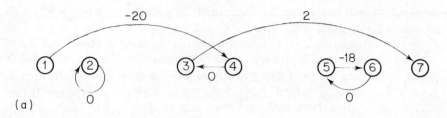

(a)

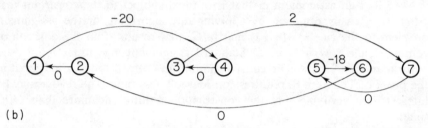

(b)

Figure 4.1   (a) Optimal solution to assignment problem. (b) Optimal solution to
TSP

renumbering the cities (effecting a symmetric permutation of rows and
columns). (*Hint*: Guess at the identity of the cities to be numbered 1 and n.
This determines the constants to be added to rows and columns, almost
uniquely. Then see if it is possible to renumber the remaining $n-2$ cities to
achieve upper triangularity. This question is essentially equivalent to determining whether or not a given matrix is the adjacency matrix of an acyclic
digraph.)

9. Suppose C is upper triangular and nonnegative. Show that the length of a
shortest path from city 1 to city n is equal to the length of an optimal tour.
(This means that an $O(n^2)$ shortest path computation suffices, instead of an
$O(n^3)$ assignment computation.)

10. What adaptations of the algorithm of this section are required to solve
the bottleneck TSP? (The bottleneck assignment problem can be solved in
$O(n^{2.5} \log n)$ time [Hopcroft & Karp, 1973].)

11. An author is writing a book with n sections. She would prefer that
certain sections precede others, because of the relationships in their contents. She is able to specify a partial order, $\leq$, describing the desired
precedence relations. How should she order the sections so as to minimize
the number of times that there is a section x in the book immediately
preceding y, with $x \not\leq y$? Formulate as a TSP with an upper triangular
distance matrix. (*Note*: A feasible solution to the TSP may not be consistent
with the partial order, in the sense that there may be a section x preceding a
section y, with $y \leq x$. If consistency with the partial order is demanded, the
resulting 'optimal linear extension' problem is known to be $\mathcal{NP}$-hard.)

6 GRADED MATRICES

We say that a matrix C is *graded across its rows* if $c_{ij} \le c_{i,j+1}$ for all i, j, and *graded up its columns* if $c_{ij} \ge c_{i+1,j}$ for all i, j. A matrix is *doubly graded* if it is graded both across its rows and up its columns.

The TSP is $\mathcal{NP}$-hard for graded (even doubly graded) matrices since any matrix can be made doubly graded by a linear admissible transformation, that is, by adding constants to its rows and columns. However, it is possible to obtain a useful approximation result for graded matrices, as we show below. In Section 10 we show that there is a polynomial algorithm for obtaining an optimal solution to the bottleneck TSP for graded matrices.

Theorem 9 *Let C be nonnegative and graded up its columns. Given an optimal assignment ϕ it is easy to construct a tour τ such that*

$$c(\tau) \le c(\phi) + \max_j \{c_{1j}\}.$$

Proof If ϕ is a tour, let $\tau = \phi$. Else choose one city from each of the $m \ge 2$ subtours of ϕ, and let these cities be $i_1, i_2, \dots, i_m$, with $i_1 < i_2 < \dots < i_m$. Remove arcs $(i_1, \phi(i_1)), \dots (i_m, \phi(i_m))$ from ϕ and substitute arcs $(i_2, \phi(i_1))$, $(i_3, \phi(i_2)), \dots, (i_{m-1}, \phi(i_{m-2})), (i_m, \phi(i_{m-1}))$ and $(i_1, \phi(i_m))$. From

$$c_{i_1\phi(i_1)} \ge c_{i_2\phi(i_1)},$$

$$c_{i_2\phi(i_2)} \ge c_{i_3\phi(i_2)},$$

$$\vdots$$

$$c_{i_{m-1}\phi(i_{m-1})} \ge c_{i_m\phi(i_{m-1})},$$

it follows that

$$c(\tau) \le c(\phi) + c_{i_1\phi(i_m)} - c_{i_m\phi(i_m)}$$

$$\le c(\phi) + \max_j \{c_{1j}\}. \quad \square$$

As a very simple example, let

$$C = \begin{bmatrix} 5 & 4 & 3 & 2 & 1 & \mathbf{0} \\ 4 & 3 & 2 & 1 & \mathbf{0} & 0 \\ 3 & 2 & 1 & \mathbf{0} & 0 & 0 \\ 2 & 1 & \mathbf{0} & 0 & 0 & 0 \\ 1 & \mathbf{0} & 0 & 0 & 0 & 0 \\ \mathbf{0} & 0 & 0 & 0 & 0 & 0 \end{bmatrix} \tag{3}$$

with an optimal assignment ϕ indicated by the bold entries. Note that ϕ has three subtours: $(1, 6)$, $(2, 5)$ and $(3, 4)$. Letting $i_1 = 1$, $i_2 = 2$, $i_3 = 3$, we convert ϕ to a tour τ as shown in Figure 4.2. This gives us $c(\tau) = c(\phi) + c_{31} - c_{61} = c(\phi) + 3$.

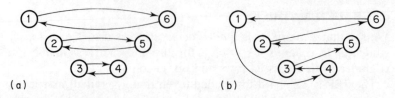

Figure 4.2   (a) Optimal assignment ϕ. (b) Tour τ obtained from ϕ

7 PYRAMIDAL TOURS

Let us say that a tour τ on cities $1, 2, \ldots, n$ is *pyramidal* if, for each city j, $1 < j < n$, either $\tau^{-1}(j) < j < \tau(j)$ or $\tau^{-1}(j) > j > \tau(j)$. In other words, τ is pyramidal if it is of the form $(1, i_1, \ldots, i_r, n, j_1, \ldots, j_{n-r-2})$, where $i_1 < i_2 < \ldots < i_r$ and $j_i > j_2 > \ldots > j_{n-r-2}$.

An equivalent characterization of pyramidal tours is as follows. Let Δ_n denote the set of all pyramidal tours on cities $1, 2, \ldots, n$. Then $\Delta_2 = \{(1, 2)\}$ and Δ_{n+1}, for $n \geqslant 2$, contains all permutations of the form $(n, n+1)\tau$ or $\tau(n, n+1)$, where $\tau \in \Delta_n$, and only such permutations.

For any distance matrix C it is possible to compute a shortest pyramidal tour by the following dynamic programming scheme. Let $C(i, j)$ denote the length of a shortest Hamiltonian path from i to j on cities $1, 2, \ldots, \max\{i, j\}$, subject to the condition that the path passes through cities in descending order of index from i to 1 and then through the complementary subset in ascending order of index from 1 to j. By the usual sort of argument involving the principle of optimality, we have

$$
C(i, j) = \begin{cases}
C(i, j-1) + c_{j-1,j} & \text{for } i < j - 1, \\
\min_{k < i} \{C(i, k) + c_{kj}\} & \text{for } i = j - 1, \\
C(i-1, j) + c_{i,i-1} & \text{for } i > j + 1, \\
\min_{k < j} \{C(k, j) + c_{ik}\} & \text{for } i = j + 1.
\end{cases} \tag{4}
$$

It is possible to compute $C(i, n)$ and $C(n, i)$ for all $i < n$ in $O(n^2)$ time, starting from the initial conditions $C(1, 2) = c_{12}$ and $C(2, 1) = c_{21}$. The length of a shortest pyramidal tour is then given by

$$\min\{C(n-1, n) + c_{n,n-1}, C(n, n-1) + c_{n-1,n}\}.$$

Let us now consider conditions under which we can be assured that there exists an optimal tour that is pyramidal. For a given matrix C, let

$$d_{ij} = c_{ij} + c_{i+1,j-1} - c_{i,j-1} - c_{i+1,j}, \tag{5}$$

where by definition $c_{ij} = 0$ if $i = n+1$ or $j = 0$. It is easy to establish that

$$c_{ij} = \sum_{k=i}^{n} \sum_{l=1}^{j} d_{kl}.$$

If the matrix $D = (d_{ij})$, as defined by (5), is nonnegative, we say that C is a (*cumulative*) *distribution* matrix generated by the *density* matrix D.

Lemma 5 *If C is a distribution matrix then*

$$c_{ij'} + c_{i'j} \geqslant c_{ij} + c_{i'j'},$$

for all $i < i'$, $j < j'$.

Proof Left as an exercise. $\square$

Corollary 4 *If C is a distribution matrix then the identity permutation $\iota(i) = i$ is an optimal assignment.*

Proof Let ϕ be an optimal assignment. If ϕ is not the identity permutation, then there are cities i, i' with $i < i'$ such that $\phi(i) > \phi(i')$. Apply Lemma 5, with $j' = \phi(i)$, $j = \phi(i')$, to obtain an assignment ϕ', where $\phi'(i) = j$, $\phi'(i') = j'$, $\phi'(k) = \phi(k)$ for $k \neq i$, i', and $c(\phi') \leqslant c(\phi)$. A finite sequence of such rearrangements yields the identity permutation, which must therefore be optimal. $\square$

Theorem 10 *If C is a distribution matrix then there exists an optimal tour that is pyramidal.*

Proof We prove the result by induction on the number of cities. The theorem is trivially true for two cities. So let us assume it is true for $n - 1$ cities and consider a problem with n cities. Let τ be an optimal tour. If τ is not pyramidal then there is a 'peak' $j \neq n$ such that $\tau^{-1}(j) < j > \tau(j)$. (The reader may care to show that the number of 'peaks' is equal to the number of 'valleys,' where a valley j is such that $\tau^{-1}(j) > j < \tau(j)$.) Let $i = j$, $i' = \tau^{-1}(j)$, $j' = \tau(j)$ and apply Lemma 5. The result is a permutation τ', with $\tau'(j) = j$, $\tau'(i') = j'$, $\tau'(k) = \tau(k)$ for $k \neq i'$, j and with $c(\tau') \leqslant c(\tau)$. The permutation τ' has two subtours, one containing j only and the other containing the other $n - 1$ cities. By inductive assumption, if the latter subtour is not pyramidal, it can be replaced by a pyramidal tour of no greater length. (A submatrix of a distribution matrix is a distribution matrix.) We now 'patch' j back into τ'. Let i be such that $i < j < \tau'(i)$. Now apply Lemma 5 with $i' = j$ and $j' = \tau(i)$. The result is a pyramidal tour τ'' on the n cities with $c(\tau'') \leqslant c(\tau') \leqslant c(\tau)$ and the theorem is proved. $\square$

As a simple application of Theorem 10, consider the distribution matrix C generated by the density matrix D, where

$$C = \begin{bmatrix} 4 & 16 & 20 & 23 & 40 \\ 3 & 12 & 15 & 17 & 33 \\ 3 & 10 & 13 & 15 & 31 \\ 1 & 4 & 5 & 6 & 18 \\ 0 & 3 & 3 & 4 & 14 \end{bmatrix}, \quad D = \begin{bmatrix} 1 & 3 & 1 & 1 & 1 \\ 0 & 2 & 0 & 0 & 0 \\ 2 & 4 & 2 & 1 & 4 \\ 1 & 0 & 1 & 0 & 2 \\ 0 & 3 & 0 & 1 & 10 \end{bmatrix}.$$

Solving for a shortest pyramidal tour by the recurrence relations (4), we obtain $\tau = (1, 4, 5, 3, 2)$ with $c(\tau) = 45$.

As we have seen, if the matrix C is a distribution matrix then the TSP can be solved in $O(n^2)$ time by applying the dynamic programming technique for finding a shortest pyramidal tour. As we show in the excercises below and in the next section, there are other conditions under which there exists an optimal tour that is pyramidal so that the same dynamic programming technique can be applied. In Section 13 we shall show that there are also special cases of distribution matrices for which it is possible to solve the TSP in less than $O(n^2)$ time.

Exercises
12. Prove that the two characterizations of pyramidal tours given at the beginning of this section are equivalent.
13. Prove that C is equivalent to a distribution matrix by a linear admissible transformation if and only if $d_{ij} \geq 0$ for $i = 1, 2, \ldots, n-1$, $j = 2, 3, \ldots, n$, where d_{ij} is as defined by (5).
14. Prove Lemma 5.
15. Suppose that

$$c_{ik} \geq \max\{c_{ij}, c_{jk}\},$$
$$c_{ki} \geq \max\{c_{ji}, c_{kj}\},$$

for all $i < j < k$. Prove that there exists a *bottleneck* optimal tour that is pyramidal.
16. Let $a_1 \geq a_2 \geq \ldots \geq a_n \geq 0$, $0 \leq b_1 \leq b_2 \leq \ldots \leq b_n$. Show that each of the following matrices is a distribution matrix:
(a) $c_{ij} = a_i + b_j$.
(b) $c_{ij} = a_i b_j$.
(c) $c_{ij} = |a_i - a_j|$.
(d) $c_{ij} = \min\{a_i, b_j\}$.
(e) $c_{ij} = \max\{a_{n-i+1}, b_j\}$.

8   THE DEMIDENKO CONDITIONS

In the previous section it was shown that for certain classes of matrices, there must be an optimal tour that is pyramidal. It was further shown that an optimal pyramidal tour can be found in $O(n^2)$ time. In this section, we show that a broad class of matrices has the property that there exists an optimal tour that is pyramidal. This result subsumes several results from the Soviet literature, which show that more restricted classes of matrices have optimal solutions that are pyramidal (for example, see Exercise 17).

The class of TSP instances C is defined by a set of conditions, each of which depends only on four cities. For any four cities, $(i, j, j+1, l)$ where

$i < j < j+1 < l$, the following conditions must hold: the path

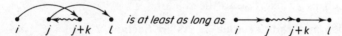

$$\tag{6}$$

and the symmetric condition that the path

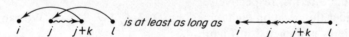

$$\tag{7}$$

the pair of arcs

$$\tag{8}$$

and its symmetric counterpart that the pair

$$\tag{9}$$

First, two preliminary lemmas are given.

Lemma 6 *Let $C \in \mathbf{C}$, and i, j, $j+1, \ldots, j+k$, $l \in \{1, \ldots, n\}$ where $i < j$, $j+k < l$, and $1 \leq k \leq n-j-1$. It follows that*

is at least as long as

and that, symmetrically,

is at least as long as

(Throughout this section, a 'wiggly' arc from i to j denotes the path i, $i+1, \ldots, j$. In addition, from here on, the obvious $\geq$ will be used to denote the words 'is at least as long as'.)

Proof By induction on k. For $k = 1$, these inequalities reduce to the conditions (6) and (7) which must hold (since $C \in \mathbf{C}$). Suppose that the lemma were true for $k-1$. Then,

$\geq$

by the inductive hypothesis. But, by (6),

$\geq$

Add the two inequalities to get

The arcs $(i, j+k-1)$ and $(j+k-1, l)$ on both sides cancel, giving the desired result. The symmetric case has an exactly parallel proof. □

Consider the conditions

$$\text{(10)}$$

and

$$\text{(11)}$$

for arbitrary (i, j, k, l) where $i < j < k < l$. Clearly these conditions imply (8) and (9); however, the converse is also true.

Lemma 7   *The conditions* (8) *and* (9) *hold for arbitrary* $(i, j, j+1, l)$, $i < j < j+1 < l$, *if and only if conditions* (10) *and* (11) *hold for arbitrary* (i, j, k, l) *where* $i < j < k < l$.

Proof   Left as an exercise to the reader. □

Consider an arbitrary tour τ. As in Section 7, call i a *peak* of τ if $\tau^{-1}(i) < i > \tau(i)$; call i a *valley* of τ if $\tau^{-1}(i) > i < \tau(i)$; otherwise i is called an *intermediate term*. $P(\tau)$, $V(\tau)$ and $I(\tau)$ denote the sets of peaks, valleys and intermediate terms, respectively.

Consider the cycle on eight cities, $\tau = (1, 3, 5, 4, 7, 8, 6, 2)$. We can 'graph' this cycle as is depicted in Figure 4.3.

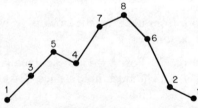

Figure 4.3

In Figure 4.3 it is easy to see that 5 and 8 are the only peaks, whereas 1 and 4 are the only valleys. For every peak $i \in P(\tau)$, define the set $S(\tau, i)$ to be the *slopes* of the peak; that is, include all points that form a decreasing sequence by repeatedly applying τ to i, or repeatedly applying τ^{-1} to i, up to, but *not* including the next valleys. Therefore, in the above example, $S(\tau, 5) = \{3, 5\}$ and $S(\tau, 8) = \{7, 8, 6, 2\}$. Furthermore, if τ is pyramidal there is exactly one peak, n, and $S(\tau, n) = \{2, 3, \ldots, n\}$.

The following lemma gives an equivalent characterization of pyramidal tours.

Lemma 8 *A tour τ is pyramidal if and only if it satisfies the following condition: for any peak $k \in P(\tau)$, $3 \leqslant k \leqslant n$, and any i, $0 \leqslant i \leqslant k-3$,*

$$\{k, \ldots, k-i\} \subset S(\tau, k) \Rightarrow (k-i-1 \in P(\tau) \text{ or } k-i-1 \in S(\tau, k)).$$

Proof Let k be a peak in $P(\tau)$. Suppose that the property above does not hold for some k and i within the specified range, but does hold for all j, $k > j > i$. In this case, k and i will be called a *bad* (k, i) pair. The claim is that τ is pyramidal if and only if there are no bad pairs. For a pyramidal tour τ, $S(\tau, n) = \{2, \ldots, n\}$, so by checking the boundary conditions, it follows that no bad pairs exist. To prove the other direction, assume that a tour has no bad pairs. Find the peak k of smallest size. Consider $S(\tau, k)$; for some i, $k - i \in S(\tau, k)$ and $k - i - 1 \notin S(\tau, k)$. But τ has no bad pairs, and by the choice of k, $k - i - 1$ is not a peak. Therefore, $k - i \leqslant 2$, and since the valleys on either side of k must be less than $k - i$, both of these valleys must be 1. But then k is the only peak, and hence τ is pyramidal. $\square$

Theorem 11 [Demidenko 1979] *Let $C \in \mathbf{C}$. For any tour τ there exists a pyramidal tour τ_0 of no greater cost.*

Proof We shall make critical use of Lemma 8. Suppose that τ is a nonpyramidal tour. We give a construction for finding a pyramidal tour of no greater cost by eliminating all of the bad pairs in τ. For any bad pair (k, i), the structure of the peak k and its relationship to $k - i - 1$ is limited to a small number of cases. For each of these cases we define an *elementary* transformation that removes the bad pair without increasing the length of the tour. These elementary transformations are used to construct a set of *composite* transformations. These composite transformations will have the following property: if (k, i) is the bad pair that a particular transformation is designed to remove, not only does it fix (k, i), but no new bad pair (k', i') with $k' - i' \geqslant k - i$ is created. Thus, by finding the bad (k, i) pair with the largest $k - i$ and fixing that pair, these composite transformations can be used to remove all bad (k, i) pairs where $k - i \geqslant 3$.

To complete the proof of the theorem, all that is left is to show is that these composite transformations can indeed be constructed. The proof given by Demidenko is very technical and only a sketch of it is given here.

Consider an arbitrary bad pair (k, i) for some permutation τ. There are two basic cases: either (I) $k - i - 1 \in V(\tau)$, or (II) $k - i - 1 \in S(\tau, l)$, $l > k$. (Since none of $k - 1, \ldots, k - i$ are peaks, note that $k - i - 1$ cannot be on a slope of a peak lower than k.) Within both of these cases there are several subcases. For case I, $k - i - 1$ can either be a valley of the peak k, or it can be a valley of another peak. From this breakdown we get the three cases that are depicted in Figure 4.4, and their mirror images. In case I(b), as well as in the cases that follow, the point $k - 1 + q$ denotes the smallest point on

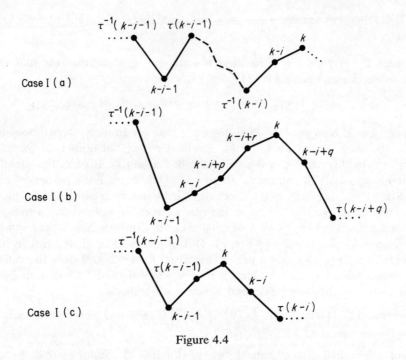

Figure 4.4

the right slope that is larger than $k-i$. The points $k-1+p$ and $k-i+r$ are, respectively, the consecutive points on the left slope that are just lower and just higher than $k-i+q$. (Note that r need not be $p+2$.)

Consider case I(a). The elementary transformation for this case alters the tour by visiting city $k-i-1$ in between cities $\tau^{-1}(k-i)$ and $k-i$. This is depicted in Figure 4.5. The dashed line superimposed on the original tour indicates the tour after the transformation has been made.

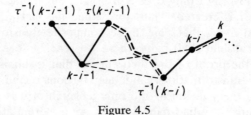

Figure 4.5

To prove that the new tour is no longer than τ, two cases must be considered. Suppose that $\tau^{-1}(k-i-1) > \tau(k-i-1)$. In this case, the relevant arcs of τ are as depicted in Figure 4.6. The dashed arc from $k-i$ to $k-i-1$ is a dummy arc that will cancel out at the end. This technique of adding dummy arcs is a very powerful tool, and it requires a bit of cleverness to determine which arcs are the correct ones to add. Condition (6) can be

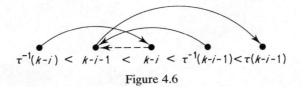

$$\tau^{-1}(k-i) \ < \ k-i-1 \ < \ k-i \ < \ \tau^{-1}(k-i-1) < \tau(k-i-1)$$

Figure 4.6

used to show that the collection of arcs in Figure 4.7 is no longer than the collection in Figure 4.6.

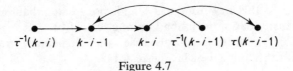

$$\tau^{-1}(k-i) \qquad k-i-1 \qquad k-i \quad \tau^{-1}(k-i-1) \quad \tau(k-i-1)$$

Figure 4.7

Applying condition (11) to the collection of arcs in Figure 4.7 we get the desired result; that is, the solid arcs in Figure 4.8 are precisely the arcs that replace the solid arcs in Figure 4.6 depicting τ.

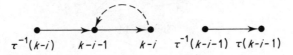

$$\tau^{-1}(k-i) \qquad k-i-1 \qquad k-i \quad \tau^{-1}(k-i-1) \quad \tau(k-i-1)$$

Figure 4.8

The case $\tau(k-i-1) < \tau^{-1}(k-i-1)$ is left as an exercise to the reader. It is important to note that this transformation already has the property that no new bad pairs (k', i') are created where $k'-i' \geqslant k-i$.

Next consider case I(b). In this case, the elementary transformation is more complicated; the resulting tour is depicted Figure 4.9.

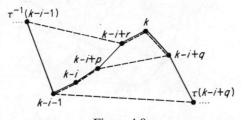

Figure 4.9

As above, it can be shown that the new tour is no longer than τ. However, it is not true that no new bad pairs (k', i') are created that have $k'-i' \geqslant k-i$. In fact, it is easy to see that $(k, i-r)$ has become a bad pair. However, as shown by the graph of the new tour, the essential structure of the tour is exactly as it was before that transformation, only the left slope is shorter. The result of repeated applications of similar transformations to τ is given in

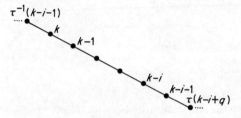

Figure 4.10

Figure 4.10, and this new tour has length no greater than τ. This is the composite transformation to fix bad pairs in case I(b).

Next consider case I(c). In this case, the elementary transformation changes τ into the tour given in Figure 4.11.

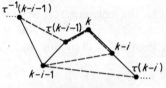

Figure 4.11

Again, we must form a composite transformation. This is done is a manner very similar to the case above.

Finally, considering case II, $k-i-1 \in S(\tau, l)$, $l>k$; $k-i-1$ can either be an intermediate term on a 'left slope' or a 'right slope'. The two cases and their elementary transformations are shown in Figure 4.12.

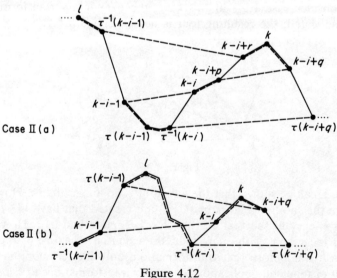

Figure 4.12

It is left as a somewhat tedious exercise to show that the necessary composite transformations can be formed, and that the resulting tours in these cases are indeed no longer than τ. $\square$

Exercises
17. [Klyaus, 1976] Suppose that

$$c_{ij} + c_{ji} \geq 0,$$
$$c_{ik} \geq c_{ij} + c_{jk},$$
$$c_{ki} \geq c_{ji} + c_{kj},$$

for all $i < j < k$.
(a) Prove that these conditions are a special case of the Demidenko conditions.
(b) Prove directly that there exists an optimal tour that is pyramidal. (*Hint:* Structure a proof similar to that of Theorem 10 of Section 7.)
18. Prove Lemma 7.
19. Complete the proof of Theorem 11. (This exercise should be attempted only by those who have a great deal of stamina. An interesting open problem is to find a more elegant proof for this result.)

9 THE THEORY OF SUBTOUR PATCHING

In this section we shall consider the following strategy for finding an optimal tour: First find an optimal assignment ϕ. If ϕ is a tour, it is clearly an optimal tour, and we are done. Otherwise, it consists of several cycles or subtours. Modify ϕ so as to patch these subtours together to yield a single tour τ that is optimal. Thus our strategy is: Given an *optimal* assignment ϕ, find a ψ such that $\phi\psi$ is an *optimal* tour.

Our first task is to investigate conditions on ψ under which $\phi\psi$ is a tour. We shall assume that the reader is familiar with the notion of a hypergraph. (A hypergraph is like an ordinary graph except that its 'hyperedges' may be incident to arbitrary subsets of vertices, and not only to subsets of size two.)

Let $P = \{\rho_1, \rho_2, \ldots, \rho_m\}$ be a set of (not necessarily disjoint) cycles on subsets of $V = \{1, 2, \ldots, n\}$. Let $H = (V, P)$ be a hypergraph with vertex set V and with hyperedges corresponding to cycles in P. The hyperedge for ρ_i is incident to exactly those elements of V on which ρ_i acts. For example, if we have $\rho_1 = (2, 3, 4)$, $\rho_2 = (1, 5)$, $\rho_3 = (1, 3, 2, 4)$, then $H = (V, P)$ is as shown in Figure 4.13. Note that $\tau = \rho_1\rho_2\rho_3 = (1, 2, 3, 4, 5)$ is a tour.

A hypergraph $H = (V, P)$ is *disconnected* if it is possible to partition its vertex set V into two nonempty parts S and T such that no hyperedge is incident to a vertex in S and also to a vertex in T. A hypergraph is *connected* if it is not disconnected.

Theorem 12 *If $\tau = \rho_1\rho_2 \ldots \rho_m$ is a tour, then $H = (V, P)$ is connected.*

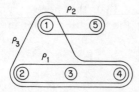

Figure 4.13   Hypergraph $H(V, P)$

Proof   Consider the contrapositive. Suppose $H = (V, P)$ is disconnected. Then there exist nonempty S and T such that $\rho_i(j) \in S$ if and only if $j \in S$, for all cycles ρ_i and cities j. Thus $\tau(j) \in S$ if and only if $j \in S$, where $\tau = \rho_1 \rho_2 \ldots, \rho_m$, and τ cannot be a tour. $\square$

Corollary 5   *Let ϕ, ψ have factors ϕ_i, $i = 1, 2, \ldots, r$, and ψ_j, $j = 1, 2, \ldots, s$, respectively. If $\phi\psi$ is a tour then $H = (V, \{\phi_i\} \cup \{\psi_j\})$ is connected.*

Corollary 5 gives a necessary condition on ψ for $\phi\psi$ to be a tour. We now seek a sufficient condition.

A hypergraph $H = (V, P)$ with n vertices and m edges $\rho_1, \ldots, \rho_m$ is a *tree* if it is connected and if

$$\sum_{i=1}^{m} (|\rho_i| - 1) = n - 1,$$

where $|\rho_i|$ is the number of vertices incident to ρ_i. Note that this definition generalizes the well-known condition for a graph G to be a tree, i.e. G is connected and $m = n - 1$. Also note that this definition allows a tree to have edges that are incident to a single vertex and that such edges (self loops) can be added to or deleted from the hypergraph without affecting its status as a tree. It is a straightforward exercise to show that if $H = (V, P)$ is connected, then

$$\sum_{i=1}^{m} (|\rho_i| - 1) \geq n - 1.$$

It follows that if $H = (V, P)$ is a tree, then the deletion of any edge ρ_i, with $|\rho_i| \geq 2$, disconnects H. Moreover, any edge ρ_i must be incident to exactly one vertex in each of the subtrees formed by its deletion. With these observations, it is not difficult to provide an inductive proof of the following.

Theorem 13   *If $H = (V, P)$ is a tree, then $\tau = \rho_1 \rho_2 \ldots \rho_m$ is a tour (where the order in which the cycles ρ_i are multiplied to obtain τ is immaterial).*

Corollary 6   *Let ϕ, ψ have factors ϕ_i, $i = 1, 2, \ldots, r$, and ψ_j, $j = 1, 2, \ldots, s$, respectively. If $H = (V, \{\phi_i\} \cup \{\psi_j\})$ is a tree then $\phi\psi$ is a tour.*

We can now reinterpret the procedure for upper triangular matrices presented in Section 5. The permutation ψ that is found is in the form of a single cycle acting on exactly one city in each subtour of ϕ. It follows that $H = (V, \{\phi_i\} \cup \{\psi_j\})$ is a tree and, by Corollary 6, $\phi\psi$ is a tour. The tour $\phi\psi$ is optimal because $c(\phi)$ is a lower bound on the length of a tour and

$c(\phi\psi) = c(\phi)$. (Recall that in this case ϕ is not necessarily an optimal assignment, but is only optimal subject to the condition that $\phi(n) = 1$; the fact that $c(\phi)$ is a lower bound is a nontrivial result.)

The case of upper triangular matrices suggests that we investigate conditions under which there exists a ψ such that $H = (V, \{\phi_i\} \cup \{\psi_j\})$ is a tree and $\phi\psi$ is an optimal tour either of the ordinary or the bottleneck variety. For simplicity, when considering the bottleneck TSP, we shall always assume that $\bar{c}(\phi) = 0$, in order to have $\bar{c}\phi(\psi) = \bar{c}(\phi\psi)$. (If this is not so, apply the transformation $c_{ij} := \max\{0, c_{ij} - k\}$, where k is the value of a bottleneck optimal assignment.)

Theorem 14 *Let ψ have factors ψ_j, $j = 1, 2, \ldots, s$. Then*

$$c\phi(\psi) = \sum_j c\phi(\psi_j),$$

$$\bar{c}\phi(\psi) = \max_j \{\bar{c}\phi(\psi_j)\}.$$

Proof Note that

$$c\phi(\psi_j) = c(\phi\psi_j) - c(\phi)$$

$$= \sum_i c_{i,\phi\psi_j(i)} - \sum_i c_{i,\phi(i)}$$

$$= \sum_{i\,:\,\psi_j(i)\neq i} c_{i,\phi\psi_j(i)} - \sum_{i\,:\,\psi_j(i)\neq i} c_{i,\phi(i)}.$$

It follows that

$$\sum_j c\phi(\psi_j) = \sum_{i\,:\,\psi(i)\neq i} c_{i,\phi\psi(i)} - \sum_{i\,:\,\psi(i)\neq i} c_{i,\phi(i)}$$

$$= \sum_i c_{i,\phi\psi(i)} - \sum_i c_{i,\phi(i)}$$

$$= c(\phi\psi) - c(\phi)$$

$$= c\phi(\psi).$$

The proof for $\bar{c}\phi(\psi)$ is similar. $\square$

Theorem 14 tells us that we can deal with the factors of ψ independently of each other. This fact is useful, but by itself does not help us much in finding a ψ such that $\phi\psi$ is an optimal tour. We shall adopt the approach of building up ψ as the product of transpositions (cycles of length two). Of necessity, these transpositions will generally not be factors of ψ (i.e. they will not be disjoint), so Theorem 14 will not apply.

As an example, suppose we have an eight-city problem, with $\phi = (1, 2, 3)$, $(4, 5)$, $(6, 7)$, (8). The hypergraph $H = (V, \{\phi_i\})$ is as shown in Figure 4.14(a). If we add edges for the transpositions $(2, 4)$, $(5, 7)$ and $(7, 8)$, we obtain the hypergraph tree shown in Figure 4.14(b). By Theorem 13, postmultiplication of ϕ by the transpositions $(2, 4)$, $(5, 7)$, $(7, 8)$, in any order, results in a

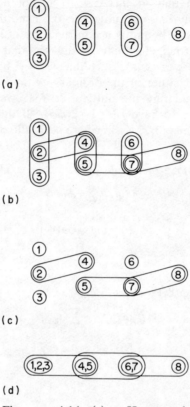

(a)

(b)

(c)

(d)

Figure 4.14 (a) Hypergraph $H(V, \{\phi_i\})$. (b) Tree obtained by adding transpositions. (c) Graph of transpositions. (d) Tree of transpositions after contraction of subtours ϕ_i

tour. The order in which the transpositions are multiplied determines ψ. For example, we can have either

$$\psi = (2, 4)(5, 7)(7, 8) = (2, 4)(5, 7, 8)$$

or

$$\psi = (2, 4)(7, 8)(5, 7) = (2, 4)(5, 8, 7).$$

But no matter in what order the transpositions are multiplied, the cyclic factors ψ correspond to the connected components of the graph of transpositions, as shown in Figure 4.14(c).

With respect to a given optimal assignment ϕ, let us assign a *length* to each transposition (i, j):

$$c\phi((i, j)) = c_{i\phi(j)} + c_{j\phi(i)} - c_{i\phi(i)} - c_{j\phi(j)},$$

or

$$\bar{c}\phi((i, j)) = \max \{c_{i\phi(j)}, c_{j\phi(i)}\}.$$

We can find a minimum length set of transpositions $\rho_1, \rho_2, \ldots, \rho_t$ such that the hypergraph $H = (V, \{\phi_i\} \cup \{\rho_j\})$ is a tree, by solving a minimum spanning tree problem for the (multi)graph that is obtained by contracting each of the hyperedges of $H = (V, \{\phi_i\})$. (Note that after contraction of the subtours $(1, 2, 3)$, $(4, 5)$, $(6, 7)$ the transpositions $(2, 4)$, $(5, 7)$, $(7, 8)$ form a tree as shown in Figure 4.14(d).) We shall say that a set of transpositions is a *minimum spanning tree* (with respect to ϕ) if it is an optimal solution to such a spanning tree problem.

What relationship is there between the length of a minimum spanning tree and the length of an optimal tour? In the following two theorems we state conditions under which a minimum spanning tree yields a lower bound or an upper bound on the length of an optimal tour.

Theorem 15 *Given an optimal assignment ϕ with respect to matrix C, suppose for any cyclic permutation ρ there exists a set T of transpositions connecting the same subtours in which there are cities on which ρ acts, such that $c\phi(T) \leq c\phi(\rho)$ (or $\bar{c}\phi(T) \leq \bar{c}\phi(\rho)$). Then if T is a minimum spanning tree, $c\phi(T) \leq c\phi(\tau)$ (or $\bar{c}\phi(T) \leq \bar{c}\phi(\tau)$), where τ is an optimal tour.*

Proof Let τ be an optimal tour and let $\psi = \phi^{-1}\tau$ have factors $\psi_1, \ldots, \psi_s$. Then $c\phi(\psi) = \sum c\phi(\psi_j)$, by Theorem 14. By hypothesis, there exists a connecting set of transpositions T_j for each ψ_j, with $c\phi(T_j) \leq c\phi(\psi_j)$. Moreover, there exists a tree $T \subseteq T_1 \cup T_2 \cup \ldots \cup T_s$ that spans all the subtours of ϕ with $c\phi(T) \leq c\phi(\psi)$. The proof of the bottleneck case is similar. $\square$

Theorem 16 *Given an optimal assignment ϕ with respect to matrix C, suppose for any set T of transpositions there exists a cyclic permutation ρ, acting on the same cities acted on by the transpositions in T such that $c\phi(\rho) \leq c\phi(T)$ (or $\bar{c}\phi(\rho) \leq \bar{c}\phi(T)$). Then if T is a minimum spanning tree, $c\phi(T) \geq c\phi(\tau)$ (or $\bar{c}\phi(T) \geq \bar{c}\phi(\tau)$), where τ is an optimal tour.*

Proof Let T be a minimum spanning tree. Consider the graph with vertex set V and edge set T (as in Figure 4.14(c)). Each connected component of this graph is a tree T_j and by hypothesis there exists a cyclic permutation ψ_j, acting on the same cities spanned by T_j, for which $c\phi(\psi_j) \leq c\phi(T_j)$. By Corollary 6, $\phi\psi$ is a tour, where the permutation ψ has the ψ_j as its factors. By Theorem 14, $c\phi(\psi) = \sum_j c\phi(\psi_j)$. Hence there exists a tour $\phi\psi$ whose length is bounded from above by $c\phi(T)$. The proof of the bottleneck case is similar. $\square$

In the sections that follow we shall consider some special classes of matrices for which the hypotheses of Theorems 15 or 16, or both, are satisfied.

Exercise

20. Show that if $H = (V, P)$ is connected then

$$\sum_{i=1}^{m} (|\rho_i| - 1) \geq n - 1.$$

10   THE BOTTLENECK TSP FOR GRADED MATRICES

We shall now apply the theory developed in the previous section to obtain an efficient algorithm for solving the bottleneck TSP for graded matrices. (Recall that in Section 6 we gave an algorithm for obtaining an approximate solution for the ordinary TSP for the same class of matrices.)

Let C be graded up its columns and let ϕ be a bottleneck optimal assignment. (Such an assignment can be found in $O(n^2)$ time; see Exercise 21.) Without loss of generality, assume

$$c_{ij} \geq \bar{c}(\phi), \qquad \text{for all } i, j. \tag{12}$$

If (12) does not hold, then apply the transformation

$$c_{ij} := \max\{0, c_{ij} - \bar{c}(\phi)\}$$

(this transformation preserves grading).

Suppose we now permute the columns of C into the order $\phi(1)$, $\phi(2), \dots, \phi(n)$. Assuming that (12) holds, we now have a *permuted* upper triangular matrix C^ϕ that is graded up its columns. (Note the c_{ij} still refers to the (i, j)th entry of the original matrix; $c_{i\phi(j)}$ designates the (i, j)th entry in the permuted matrix.) As an example, consider the permuted version of the matrix (3):

$$C^\phi = \begin{bmatrix} 0 & 1 & 2 & 3 & 4 & 5 \\ 0 & 0 & 1 & 2 & 3 & 4 \\ 0 & 0 & 0 & 1 & 2 & 3 \\ 0 & 0 & 0 & 0 & 1 & 2 \\ 0 & 0 & 0 & 0 & 0 & 1 \\ 0 & 0 & 0 & 0 & 0 & 0 \end{bmatrix}. \tag{13}$$

$$ \quad 6 \quad 5 \quad 4 \quad 3 \quad 2 \quad 1$$

Here, as suggested by the listing of indices at the bottom of the matrix, $\phi(1) = 6$, $\phi(2) = 5, \dots, \phi(6) = 1$.

We first want to show that the lower bound property of Theorem 15 holds. We must show that, for any cyclic permutation ρ, there exists a tree T of transpositions, spanning the same subtours of ϕ in which there are cities on which ρ acts, such that $\bar{c}\phi(T) \leq \bar{c}\phi(\rho)$. So let ρ be an arbitrary cycle. Because C^ϕ is a permuted upper triangular matrix,

$$\bar{c}\phi(\rho) = \max\{c_{i,\phi\rho(i)} \mid i < \rho(i)\}.$$

Because C is graded up its columns, we have for all $i \leq i' < \rho(i)$,

$$\bar{c}\phi((i', \rho(i))) = c_{i',\phi\rho(i)} \leq c_{i,\phi\rho(i)} = \bar{c}\phi((i, \rho(i))).$$

It follows that the set of transpositions

$$T = \{(i', \rho(i)) \mid i \leq i' < \rho(i)\} \tag{14}$$

connects the cities acted on by ρ, with $\bar{c}\phi(T) = \bar{c}\phi(\rho)$. If this set of transpositions is not a tree then transpositions can be removed from the set to obtain a tree T satisfying the hypotheses of the theorem.

In our example (13), ϕ has three subtours: $(1, 6)$, $(2, 5)$, $(3, 4)$. Let $\rho = (1, 6, 2, 4)$, with $\bar{c}\phi(\rho) = \bar{c}\phi((1, 6)) = c_{11} = 5$. The set defined by (14) is

$$T = \{(1, 6), (2, 6), (3, 6), (4, 6), (5, 6), (2, 4), (3, 4)\}.$$

From this set we can select, for example, $(4, 5)$ and $(5, 6)$ to obtain a tree. Note that $\bar{c}\phi((4, 5)) = c_{42} = 1$ and $\bar{c}\phi((5, 6)) = c_{51} = 1$, so the bottleneck length of this tree is unity.

Now let us show that the upper bound property of Theorem 16 holds. We must show that for any tree T of transpositions there exists a cyclic permutation ρ, acting on the same cities spanned by T, such that $\bar{c}\phi(\rho) \leq \bar{c}\phi(T)$. Let us define a partial order $\leq$ on transpositions: $(i, j) \leq (i', j')$ if $i' \leq i$ and $j \leq j'$, where $i < j$ and $i' < j'$. Now remove from T all transpositions that are not maximal with respect to the partial order. The remaining transpositions are of the form $(i_1, j_1), (i_2, j_2), \ldots, (i_r, j_r)$, where $i_1 < i_2 < \ldots < i_r$, and i_1, j_r are the cities of smallest and largest index spanned by T. Because the transpositions in T connect the cities on which they act, we must have $j_1 \geq i_2$, $j_2 \geq i_3, \ldots, j_{r-1} \geq i_r$. Let $k_1 > k_2 > \ldots > k_s$ be the cities different from $i_1, i_2, \ldots, i_r, j_1, j_2, \ldots, j_r$ that are acted on by transpositions in T.

For example, suppose $T = \{(1, 3), (2, 4), (3, 7), (4, 5), (5, 6)\}$. The transpositions in T that are maximal with respect to $\leq$ are $(i_1, j_1) = (1, 3)$, $(i_2, j_2) = (2, 4)$, $(i_3, j_3) = (3, 7)$, and $k_1 = 6$, $k_2 = 5$. Note that $j_1 = 3 > i_2 = 2$, $j_2 = 4 > i_3 = 3$.

We assert that if we take the sequence $(i_1, j_1, i_2, j_2, \ldots, i_r, j_r, k_1, \ldots, k_s)$, strike out the second occurrence of any index from within it, and treat the result as a cycle ρ, we have $\bar{c}\phi(\rho) \leq \bar{c}\phi(T)$, as required. (The reader is asked to verify this fact as an exercise.) In the case of our running example (13), suppose $T = \{(4, 5), (5, 6)\}$. Then we obtain $\rho = (4, 5, 6)$, with $\bar{c}\phi(\rho) = 1 \leq \bar{c}\phi(T) = 1$.

The algorithm for solving the bottleneck TSP for graded matrices is as follows:

(1) Find a bottleneck optimal assignment ϕ. This requires $O(n^2)$ time.
(2) Determine the subtours of ϕ. This can be done in $O(n)$ time.
(3) Find a minimum spanning tree T of transpositions spanning the subtours of ϕ. This can be done in essentially $O(n^2)$ time by the current champion algorithm [Gabow, Galil & Spencer 1984].

(4) For each connected component T_i of the graph $G(V, T)$, find a cyclic permutation ψ_i, with $\bar{c}\phi(\psi_i) \le \bar{c}\phi(T_i)$, as described above. This requires at most $O(n \log n)$ time.

(5) Multiply ϕ by ψ in $O(n)$ time.

It is seen that the overall running time is essentially $O(n^2)$, the time required for the minimum spanning tree computation. As we shall see, this time bound can be reduced for the more specialized case of permuted doubly graded matrices.

Recall that a matrix is *doubly graded* if it is both graded across its rows and up its columns, i.e. both $c_{ij} \le c_{i,j+1}$ and $c_{ij} \ge c_{i+1,j}$.

Theorem 17 *If C is doubly graded then a bottleneck optimal tour is given by the permutation* $(1, 2, \ldots, n-1, n)$.

Proof Suppose we apply the nearest neighbor rule, starting at city 1. We shall show by induction that the path $1, 2, \ldots, k$ contains no arc longer than the longest arc in a bottleneck optimal tour. Combining this result for $k = n$ with the fact that $(n, 1)$ must be as short as any arc from n, we get the desired result. The basis is easy, since $(1, 2)$ must be as short as any arc leaving 1. Suppose, by the inductive assumption, the path $1, 2, \ldots, j$ contains no arc longer than the longest arc in a bottleneck optimal tour. Since arc $(j, j+1)$ is as short as any arc from the subset of cities $\{1, 2, \ldots, j\}$ to the subset $\{j+1, \ldots, n\}$ the path may be extended to $j+1$. $\square$

A matrix C is *permuted doubly graded* if there exists a permutation ϕ such that both $c_{i\phi(j)} \le c_{i\phi(j+1)}$ and $c_{i\phi(j)} \ge c_{i+1,\phi(j)}$.

Theorem 18 *If C is permuted doubly graded with respect to ϕ, then ϕ is a bottleneck optimal assignment.*

Proof Left as an exercise. $\square$

The principal difference between the ordinary graded case, discussed above, and the permuted doubly graded case is that in the latter case there exists a minimum spanning tree composed of only transpositions of the form $(i, i+1)$. Since there are at most $n-1$ transpositions to consider the time bound for the spanning tree computation can be reduced to essentially $O(n)$.

In order to prove the assertion of the previous paragraph, it is sufficient to show that

$$\bar{c}\phi(i', i'+1) \le \bar{c}\phi(i, j),$$

for all $i \le i' < j$. We leave the details to the reader as an exercise.

Exercises

21. Show that it is possible to solve the bottleneck assignment problem for graded matrices in $O(n^2)$ time. (*Hint:* Assuming that C is graded up its columns, consider the following procedure. Find the smallest element in row

1. Suppose that this is in column k. Then cross out row 1 and column k and repeat.)

22. Justify the assertion that the sequence $(i_1, j_1, i_2, j_2, \ldots, i_r, j_r, k_1, \ldots, k_s)$, with the second occurrence of any index removed, yields a cycle ρ with $\bar{c}\phi(\rho) \leq \bar{c}\phi(T)$.

23. Note that the proof of Theorem 17 shows that the nearest neighbor rule constructs a bottleneck optimal tour if one starts from city 1. Show that the nearest neighbor rule does not necessarily yield a bottleneck optimal tour if one starts from any other city.

24. Let C be graded up its columns and 'contragraded' across its rows, i.e. both $c_{ij} \geq c_{i,j+1}$ and $c_{ij} \geq c_{i+1,j}$. Show that $(n, n-1, n-2, \ldots, 2, 1)$ is a bottleneck optimal tour.

25. Prove Theorem 18.

11   AN APPLICATION: CUTTING WALLPAPER

The problem dealt with in this section was formulated and solved in the context of reading records from a rotating storage device [Fuller, 1972]. A much more specialized version of this problem was dealt with by Garfinkel [1977].

Suppose we are to cut $n-1$ sheets of wallpaper from a very long roll of stock with a pattern that repeats at intervals of one unit. Sheet i, $i = 1, 2, \ldots, n-1$, starts at s_i (mod 1) and finishes at f_i (mod 1), with reference to the zero point of the pattern. If we cut sheet i from the roll immediately before sheet j, the intersheet waste is the distance from f_i to s_j, i.e.

$$c_{ij} = \begin{cases} s_j - f_i & \text{if } f_i \leq s_j, \\ 1 + s_j - f_i & \text{otherwise,} \end{cases} \tag{15}$$

$$= s_j - f_i \,(\text{mod } 1).$$

(Suppose the roll begins at the zero point on the pattern and after cutting our $n-1$ sheets from the roll we must make one more cut to restore the roll to the zero point. In other words, we must minimize the total intersheet waste, rounded up to the nearest pattern unit. To formulate this problem as a TSP, we introduce an nth dummy sheet with $s_n = f_n = 0$.

For example, suppose we wish to cut four sheets of wallpaper, with $s_1 = 0.1$, $s_2 = 0.8$, $s_3 = 0.6$, $s_4 = 0.4$ and $f_1 = 0.8$, $f_2 = 0.7$, $f_3 = 0.7$, $f_4 = 0.2$. After creating a dummy fifth sheet with $s_5 = f_5 = 0$, we obtain a five-city TSP with

$$C = \begin{bmatrix} 0.3 & 0.0 & 0.8 & 0.6 & 0.2 \\ 0.4 & 0.1 & 0.9 & 0.7 & 0.3 \\ 0.4 & 0.1 & 0.9 & 0.7 & 0.3 \\ 0.9 & 0.6 & 0.4 & 0.2 & 0.8 \\ 0.1 & 0.8 & 0.6 & 0.4 & 0.0 \end{bmatrix}.$$

Let us apply a linear admissible transformation to the matrix $C = (c_{ij})$ by adding f_i to row i and subtracting s_j from column j. The result is a $(0, 1)$ matrix C', where

$$c'_{ij} = \begin{cases} 0 & \text{if } f_i \leqslant s_j, \\ 1 & \text{otherwise.} \end{cases} \tag{16}$$

If the sheets are indexed so that $f_1 \geqslant f_2 \geqslant \ldots \geqslant f_n$, the matrix C' is graded up its columns. In the case of our example, we now have

$$C' = \begin{bmatrix} 1 & 0 & 1 & 1 & 1 \\ 1 & 0 & 1 & 1 & 1 \\ 1 & 0 & 1 & 1 & 1 \\ 1 & 0 & 0 & 0 & 1 \\ 0 & 0 & 0 & 0 & 0 \end{bmatrix}.$$

For any tour τ, $c(\tau) = c(\tau') + \sum s_j - \sum f_i$. In other words, the cost of an optimal tour for the TSP for C' differs from the cost of an optimal tour for the TSP for C by a constant, $\sum s_j - \sum f_i$.

Since the matrix C' is graded up its columns, we can apply Theorem 9 and solve an assignment problem over C' to obtain an approximate solution to the TSP whose length differs from that of an optimal tour by no more than the value of the largest element in C', namely one unit. However, we can do better than this. In the following we shall show how to obtain a strictly optimal solution and, moreover, to obtain it in $O(n \log n)$ time.

There is a trick that simplifies matters and this involves changing the zero point of the pattern. Suppose we add a constant δ to each of the f_i and s_j values and redefine the problem in terms of f'_i and s'_j values, where

$$f'_i = f_i + \delta \quad (\text{mod } 1),$$
$$s'_j = s_j + \delta \quad (\text{mod } 1).$$

Such a translation does not affect the matrix C, as defined by (15), since

$$s'_j - f'_i = s_j - f_i \quad (\text{mod } 1).$$

However, this translation does change the matrix C' as defined in (16).

In the case of our example, if we take $\delta = 0.3$, we obtain $s'_1 = 0.4$, $s'_2 = 0.1$, $s'_3 = 0.9$, $s'_4 = 0.7$, $s'_5 = 0.3$, and $f'_1 = 0.1$, $f'_2 = 0$, $f'_3 = 0$, $f'_4 = 0.5$, $f'_5 = 0.3$. The matrix C' then becomes

$$C' = \begin{bmatrix} 0 & 0 & 0 & 0 & 0 \\ 0 & 0 & 0 & 0 & 0 \\ 0 & 0 & 0 & 0 & 0 \\ 1 & 1 & 0 & 0 & 1 \\ 0 & 1 & 0 & 0 & 0 \end{bmatrix}.$$

Suppose it is possible to find a δ such that C' can be made upper triangular and doubly graded after (independent) permutations of rows and columns. If such permutations exist, they can be effected by renumbering so that $f'_1 \geqslant f'_2 \geqslant \ldots \geqslant f'_n$ and then applying a permutation of ϕ to the columns so that $s'_{\phi(1)} \geqslant s'_{\phi(2)} \geqslant \ldots \geqslant s'_{\phi(n)}$. Since the permuted matrix is upper triangular, we have $c'(\phi) = 0$. Since C' is a $(0, 1)$-matrix, it follows from Theorem 9 that an optimal tour τ is such that either $c'(\tau) = 0$ or $c'(\tau) = 1$. But the case $c'(\tau) = 0$ holds if and only if there is a tour with bottleneck length zero. And we know how to find a bottleneck optimal tour, in essentially $O(n)$ time, by the methods of the previous section.

Now all that remains is to show that it is always possible to find a δ such that the matrix C' becomes upper triangular and doubly graded after permutations of its rows and columns. This will be achieved if we can find a δ such that the largest s'_i is no smaller than any of the n f'_i values, the second largest s'_i is no smaller than $n-1$ of the f'_i values, and so forth.

To see that there is such a δ, we adapt a problem and its solution of Lovász [1979, Problem 21, p. 27]. Suppose we are to walk around a circle on which there are n points f_i at which we are paid one dollar and n points s_i at which we must pay one dollar. Is there any point on the circle at which we can start with an empty wallet and never be financially embarrassed? And if so, how can we find this point?

The solution: Take a wallet full of money and start walking around the circle, starting at any point. Since we take in \$$n$ and give out \$$n$, we have the same amount of money in our wallet when we return to the starting point. Now remember where on the circle we had the least money. This was surely in an interval between an s_i and an f_i. Make that f_i our new starting point, i.e. set $\delta = -f_i$, and we shall have accomplished our objective.

To summarize the procedure for the wallpapering problem:

(1) Sort the f_i and s_i values, in $O(n \log n)$ time.
(2) Find the value δ and an optimal assignment ϕ in $O(n)$ time.
(3) Apply the algorithm for solving the bottleneck TSP for permuted doubly graded matrices. This requires essentially $O(n)$ time.
(4) If the bottleneck optimal tour found in (3) has zero length, it is an optimal solution to the problem. Else apply the approximation method of Theorem 9, to obtain an optimal tour. In this case, since an optimal assignment ϕ is already known, only $O(n)$ additional time is required.

The running time for solving the problem is dominated by the $O(n \log n)$ time required to sort the f_i and s_i values.

In the case of our example, an optimal solution is given by the tour $(1, 4, 3, 2, 5)$, with a length of 1.5.

Exercise

26. We have formulated the wallpaper cutting problem with the objective of minimizing total waste, rounded up to the nearest pattern unit. To do this,

we introduced a dummy sheet n, with $s_n = f_n = 0$. Now suppose we wish to minimize the absolute amount of waste. That is, the roll begins at the zero point of the pattern and we are charged for the total amount of paper used, regardless of where we make our final cut with reference to the zero point. To do this, let us replace the dummy job with a 'pseudo-job' n with $f_n = 0$ and s_n being equal to the f_i of whatever job precedes it. Then

$$c_{in} = s_n - f_i$$
$$= f_i - f_i$$
$$= 0,$$
$$c_{nj} = s_j - f_n$$
$$= s_j.$$

Investigate what happens to coefficients c'_{in}, c'_{nj} for the pseudo-job when the pattern origin is translated. In particular, show that it is unnecessary to consider the pseudo-job in finding a new origin.

12 PERMUTED DISTRIBUTION MATRICES

We say that C is a *permuted* distribution matrix if there exists a permutation ϕ such that $C^\phi = (c_{i\phi(j)})$ is a distribution matrix. Recall that in Section 7 it was shown that the identity permutation is an optimal assignment for a distribution matrix; that is, the main diagonal of the matrix constitutes an optimal assignment. Therefore, if C is a permuted distribution matrix where C^ϕ is a distribution matrix, then ϕ is an optimal assignment for C. Throughout this section ϕ will be used to denote the optimal assignment for which C^ϕ is a distribution matrix.

In this section we show that permuted distribution matrices always have optimal tours that are of a specific form. In the following two sections we use this result to compute optimal tours for special cases of permuted distribution matrices.

Consider a permutation $\tau = \phi\psi$ where ϕ is an optimal assignment. The assignment τ is said to be *basic* relative to ϕ if $H = (V, \{\phi_i\} \cup \{\psi_i\})$ is a tree. Furthermore, τ is *pyramidal* with respect to ϕ if each of the factors of ψ is a pyramidal cycle. Finally, τ is *dense* with respect to ϕ if each of the subtours of ψ acts on a set of cities of the form $\{i, i+1, \ldots, i+k\}$.

The following theorem is the main result of this section.

Theorem 19 *Let C be a permuted distribution matrix. Then C has an optimal tour $\tau = \phi\psi$ where τ is basic, pyramidal, and dense with respect to ϕ.*

This theorem will follow from a number of intermediate results about the structure of assignments and tours for permuted distribution matrices.

Lemma 9 *Let C be a permuted distribution matrix. If $\tau = \phi\psi$ is a permutation such that $H = (V, \{\phi_i\} \cup \{\psi_i\})$ is connected, then there exists a permutation*

$\sigma = \phi\rho$ where $H = (V, \{\phi_i\} \cup \{\rho_i\})$ is connected, σ is pyramidal with respect to ϕ, and $c(\sigma) \leqslant c(\tau)$.

Proof This result follows from Theorem 10, which states that any distribution matrix has a pyramidal optimal tour. Consider the distribution matrix C^ϕ; any submatrix of C^ϕ is also a distribution matrix. Furthermore, the cost $c\phi(\psi_i)$ is the cost of the subtour ψ_i with respect to the matrix C^ϕ. This factor ψ_i is a tour for some submatrix of C^ϕ. Thus, by Theorem 10, there is some pyramidal tour ρ_i for this submatrix of C^ϕ with no greater cost. Therefore, $c\phi(\rho_i) \leqslant c\phi(\psi_i)$.

By repeating this procedure for each factor ψ_i we obtain a permutation $\rho = \prod_i \rho_i$ such that $\sigma = \phi\rho$ is pyramidal with respect to ϕ, and $c\phi(\rho) \leqslant c\phi(\tau)$. Furthermore, since ρ_i and ψ_i act on an identical set of cities, $(V, \{\phi_i\} \cup \{\rho_i\}) = (V, \{\phi_i\} \cup \{\psi_i\})$ which is connected. $\square$

Throughout this section we will refer to the following example.

$$C = \begin{bmatrix} 8 & 24 & 16 & 32 & 40 & 56 & 48 & 64 \\ 7 & 21 & 14 & 28 & 35 & 49 & 42 & 56 \\ 6 & 18 & 12 & 24 & 30 & 42 & 36 & 48 \\ 5 & 15 & 10 & 20 & 25 & 35 & 30 & 40 \\ 4 & 12 & 8 & 16 & 20 & 28 & 24 & 32 \\ 3 & 9 & 6 & 12 & 15 & 21 & 18 & 24 \\ 2 & 6 & 4 & 8 & 10 & 14 & 12 & 16 \\ 1 & 3 & 2 & 4 & 5 & 7 & 6 & 8 \end{bmatrix}.$$

This has an optimal assignment $\phi = (2, 3)\,(6, 7)$ and is generated by a density matrix $D = (d_{ij})$ where $d_{ij} = 1$ for all i, j. Consider the tour $\tau = \phi\psi = (2, 3)\,(6, 7)\,(1, 4, 2, 5)\,(3, 7, 8) = (1, 4, 3, 6, 7, 8, 2, 5)$; $c(\tau) = 160$. The factor $(1, 4, 2, 5)$ is not pyramidal. It does correspond to a tour in the submatrix of C^ϕ,

$$\begin{bmatrix} 8 & 16^* & \mathbf{32} & 40 \\ 7 & 14 & 28 & \mathbf{35^*} \\ 5^* & \mathbf{10} & 20 & 25 \\ \mathbf{4} & 8 & 16^* & 20 \end{bmatrix}$$

where the bold-face entries indicate the costs used. Using the techniques described in Section 7, we find an optimal pyramidal tour for this matrix. This optimal tour, indicated by the starred entries, corresponds to the factor $(1, 2, 5, 4)$. Thus the transformation indicated in Lemma 9 yields the permutation $\tau_2 = (2, 3)\,(6, 7)\,(1, 2, 5, 4)\,(3, 7, 8) = (1, 3, 6, 7, 8, 2, 5, 4)$; $c(\tau_2) = 151$.

By the definition of a permuted distribution matrix, if C is a permuted distribution matrix, then for all $i < l$ and $j < m$,

$$c_{i\phi(m)} + c_{l\phi(j)} \geqslant c_{i\phi(j)} + c_{l\phi(m)}. \tag{17}$$

Lemma 10   *Let C be a permuted distribution matrix. If $\tau = \phi\psi$ is a permutation that is pyramidal with respect to ϕ such that $H = (V, \{\phi_i\} \cup \{\psi_i\})$ is connected, then there exists a permutation $\sigma = \phi\rho$ that satisfies the following conditions:*

(a) *$H = (V, \{\phi_i\} \cup \{\rho_i\})$ is connected;*
(b) *σ is pyramidal and dense with respect to ϕ; and*
(c) *$c(\sigma) \leq c(\tau)$.*

Proof   Assume that $\tau = \phi\psi$ is not dense with respect to ϕ. We first check whether there exist two factors of ψ, ψ_p and ψ_q, where the peaks of ψ_p and ψ_q are j_p and j_q, respectively, and the valleys of ψ_p and ψ_q are i_p and i_q, where $i_p < i_q < j_p < j_q$.

If there are two such overlapping factors, we shall show how to construct a permutation $\sigma = \phi\rho$ where the factors of ρ are identical to ψ, with the exception of ψ_p and ψ_q; these factors have been combined into one new factor ψ_{pq} that acts on the set of cities that is precisely the union of the sets of cities acted on by ψ_p and ψ_q. Furthermore, $c\phi(\psi_p\psi_q) \geq c\phi(\psi_{pq})$.

First consider the simplest such case, where j_p is the only city on which ψ_p acts that is greater than i_q, and i_q is the only city on which ψ_q acts that is smaller than j_p. Let $l = \psi_p^{-1}(j_p)$ and $m = \psi_q^{-1}(i_q)$; by our assumptions about ψ_p and ψ_q we know that $l < i_q < j_p < m$. Form $\psi_{pq} = \psi_p\psi_q(l, m)$; this patches the two pyramidal factors into one pyramidal factor. It is not hard to see that the cost of this patching operation, $c\phi(\psi_{pq}) - c\phi(\psi_p\psi_q)$, is $c_{m\phi(j_p)} + c_{l\phi(i_q)} - c_{l\phi(j_p)} - c_{m\phi(i_q)}$, which is nonpositive, since C satisfies (17). Therefore, $\rho = (\prod_{i \neq p,q} \psi_i)\psi_{pq}$ satisfies the properties specified in the previous paragraph.

Next consider the case where ψ_p acts on some other city k where $j_p > k > i_q$. In this case we shall transform ψ_p and ψ_q into two new pyramidal factors ψ_p' and ψ_q' where j_p has been inserted into ψ_q (and has been deleted from ψ_p); furthermore, $c\phi(\psi_p\psi_q) \geq c\phi(\psi_p'\psi_q')$. By repeated use of this transformation, and the analogous one that inserts the valley of ψ_q into ψ_p, we eventually reach the easy situation dealt with above. At this stage, the two factors can be patched into one pyramidal factor that acts on all of the cities acted on by ψ_p and ψ_q.

Therefore, suppose that ψ_p acts on k, $j_p > k > i_q$. Let $j_1 = \psi_p(j_p)$, $j_2 = \psi_p^{-1}(j_p)$, and $\psi_p' = \psi_p(j_p, j_2)$; this deletes j_p from the factor ψ_p. Find the city of ψ_q, say l, such that $l > j_p$ but $m = \psi_q(l) < j_p$. (Since $i_q < j_p$ and $j_q > j_p$ there must be some such l.) Let $\psi_q' = \psi_q(j_p, l)$; this inserts j_p into ψ_q between l and m. The difference of the costs is

$$c\phi(\psi_p\psi_q) - c\phi(\psi_p'\psi_q') = c_{j_2\phi(j_p)} + c_{j_p\phi(j_1)} - c_{j_2\phi(j_1)} + c_{l\phi(m)} - c_{l\phi(j_p)} - c_{j_p\phi(m)}$$

$$= (c_{j_2\phi(j_p)} + c_{j_p\phi(j_1)} - c_{j_2\phi(j_1)} - c_{j_p\phi(j_p)})$$
$$+ (c_{j_p\phi(j_p)} + c_{l\phi(m)} - c_{l\phi(j_p)} - c_{j_p\phi(m)}).$$

Since C satisfies (17), both parenthesized quantities on the right-hand side of this last equation are nonnegative. Notice that these transformations can be used to obtain a permutation $\sigma = \phi\rho$ where no two factors of ρ overlap in this interlaced manner, where σ is pyramidal with respect to ϕ and $H = (V, \{\phi_i\} \cup \{\rho_i\})$ is connected.

Next consider two pyramidal factors ψ_p and ψ_q where the peaks of ψ_p and ψ_q are j_p and j_q, respectively, the valleys of ψ_p and ψ_q are i_p and i_q, respectively, and $i_p < i_q < j_q < j_p$. Two such nested factors can be transformed in much the same way as was done above, to form a new factor ψ_{pq} that acts on all of the cities contained in ψ_p and ψ_q, and $c\phi(\psi_{pq}) \leqslant c\phi(\psi_p\psi_q)$. The essential idea is that the valley of ψ_q, i_q, can be deleted from that factor and inserted in the appropriate place into ψ_p while maintaining pyramidality, without increasing the cost. The details are exactly the same as the case above, and are left to the reader. By repeating this procedure, the two factors will be merged into one factor ψ_{pq}. As in the case above, it is easy to see that the required connectivity property is maintained as well.

As a result of the transformation mentioned above, we may assume without loss of generality that the factors ψ_r can be ordered so that the peak of ψ_r is less than the valley of ψ_{r+1}. If $\tau = \phi\psi$ is not dense with respect to ϕ, then one factor ψ_r must act on cities i and j, but not on k, $i < k < j$. There must exist some city l acted on by ψ_r such that $l < k$ but $m = \psi_r(l) > k$. Let $\psi_r' = \psi_r(l, k)$; this inserts k in between l and k in ψ_i. The change in the costs,

$$c\phi(\psi_r) - c\phi(\psi_r') = c(\phi\psi_r) - c(\phi\psi_r')$$

$$= c_{k\phi(k)} + c_{l\phi(m)} - c_{k\phi(m)} - c_{l\phi(k)},$$

is nonnegative, since C satisfies (17). This transformation does not affect the desired connectivity and pyramidality properties. As a result, we can transform $\tau = \phi\psi$ into a permutation $\sigma = \phi\rho$ where σ satisfies properties (a) through (c). □

Let us return to our example. The factors $(1, 2, 5, 4)$ and $(3, 7, 8)$ overlap; in fact, both 4 and 5 are greater than 3, the valley of $(3, 7, 8)$. As a result we first use the transformation that deletes 5 from $(1, 2, 5, 4)$ and inserts it into $(3, 7, 8)$. This yields $\tau_3 = (2, 3)(6, 7)(1, 2, 4)(3, 7, 8, 5) = (1, 3, 6, 7, 8, 5, 2, 4)$; $c(\tau_3) = 142$. Next we merge $(1, 2, 4)$ and $(3, 7, 8, 5)$ into $(1, 2, 4)(3, 7, 8, 5)$ $(2, 5) = (1, 2, 3, 7, 8, 5, 4)$.   Therefore $\tau_4 = (2, 3)(6, 7)(1, 2, 3, 7, 8, 5, 4) = (1, 3, 6, 7, 8, 5, 4)$ which is not a tour; $c(\tau_4) = 139$. Note that although τ_2 and τ_3 are tours, Lemmas 9 and 10 do not insure that the resulting permutations will be tours. Finally, τ_4 is still not dense with respect to ϕ; the factor $(1, 2, 3, 7, 8, 5, 4)$ omits 6. This is rectified by the last transformation $(1, 2, 3, 7, 8, 5, 4)(3, 6) = (1, 2, 3, 6, 7, 8, 5, 4)$. So $\tau_5 = (2, 3)(6, 7)(1, 2, 3, 6, 7, 8, 5, 4) = (1, 3, 7, 8, 5, 4)$; $c(\tau_5) = 136$.

A *(hyper)cycle* in a hypergraph $H = (V, \{\rho_i\})$ is an alternating sequence of hyperedges and vertices, $(\rho_0, i_1, \rho_1, i_2, \ldots, i_m, \rho_m)$ where $\rho_0 = \rho_m$, but $\rho_j \neq \rho_k$ and $i_j \neq i_k$ for all $\{j, k\} \subset \{1, \ldots, m\}$ and $i_j \in \rho_{j-1} \cap \rho_j$ for all $j = 1, \ldots, m$, $m > 1$. Note that this is just an extension of the usual definition for a cycle in a graph.

Lemma 11   *If a hypergraph is connected and is not a tree, then it contains a cycle.*

Proof   Left as an exercise to the reader.   □

Corollary 7   *Let $\tau = \phi\psi$ be a permutation that is dense and pyramidal with respect to ϕ and $H = (V, \{\phi_i\} \cup \{\psi_i\})$ is connected. Then there exists a permutation $\sigma = \phi\rho$ that is dense, pyramidal, and basic with respect to ϕ where $c(\sigma) \le c(\tau)$.*

Proof   Assume that τ is not basic with respect to ϕ. Since $H = (V, \{\phi_i\} \cup \{\psi_i\})$ is not a tree, and it is connected, there must exist some cycle in $H = (V, \{\phi_i\} \cup \{\psi_i\})$. Some hyperedge of this cycle must be a factor of ψ, say ψ_k; suppose that i and j are the cities (vertices) that link the hyperedge ψ_k in the cycle, where $i < j$. It is clear that either $\psi_k(i) > i$ or $\psi_k^{-1}(i) > i$; without loss of generality suppose that the former is true. Let $p = \psi_k(i)$ and let l be the city such that $l > i$ but $\psi_k(l) = m \le i$. (Note that either p or l is $i + 1$.) Then form $\psi_k' = \psi_k(i, l)$; ψ_k' has two pyramidal, dense factors ψ_{k1} and ψ_{k2} that together act on the same set of cities as the one factor ψ_k. Furthermore, the change in the costs,

$$c\phi(\psi_k) - c\phi(\psi_{k1}\psi_{k2}) = c_{l\phi(m)} + c_{i\phi(p)} - c_{l\phi(p)} - c_{i\phi(m)},$$

is nonnegative, since C satisfies (17). Most importantly, since ψ_k was part of a cycle, the transformation does not destroy the required connectivity constraint. In addition, the quantity $\sum (|\psi_i| - 1)$ must decrease by 1 as result of this transformation. Therefore, after a sufficient number of such splitting operations, the resulting permutation ρ is such that $\sigma = \phi\rho$ is basic with respect to ϕ.   □

Let us return one last time to our example. The hypergraph $H = (V, \{\{2, 3\}, \{6, 7\}, \{1, 2, 3, 6, 7, 8, 5, 4\}\})$ contains the cycle $(\{2, 3\}, 3, \{1, 2, 3, 6, 7, 8, 5, 4\}, 2, \{2, 3\})$. We perform the splitting operation $(1, 2, 3, 6, 7, 8, 5, 4)(2, 4) = (1, 2)(3, 6, 7, 8, 5, 4)$. So $\tau_6 = (2, 3)(6, 7)(1, 2)(3, 6, 7, 8, 5, 4) = (1, 3, 7, 8, 5, 4, 2)$ and $c(\tau_6) = 132$. The hypergraph $H = (V, \{\{2, 3\}, \{6, 7\}, \{1, 2\}, \{3, 6, 7, 8, 5, 4\}\})$ contains the cycle $(\{6, 7\}, 6, \{3, 6, 7, 8, 5, 4\}, 7, \{6, 7\})$. The factor $(3, 6, 7, 8, 5, 4)$ is split into $(3, 6, 5, 4)$ and $(7, 8)$ to give the tour $\tau_7 = (2, 3)(6, 7)(1, 2)(3, 6, 5, 4)(7, 8) = (1, 3, 7, 8, 6, 5, 4, 2)$ which is basic, pyramidal and dense with respect to $(2, 3)(6, 7)$. Furthermore, $c(\tau_7) = 128$.

By combining Lemma 9, Lemma 10 and Corollary 7 we get the desired result that every permuted distribution matrix has an optimal tour that is basic, dense, and pyramidal with respect to ϕ. This completes the proof of Theorem 19.

Exercises

27. Prove Lemma 11.
28. Construct a polynomial-time algorithm to determine if C is a permuted

distribution matrix; if C is a permuted distribution matrix the algorithm should output the corresponding density matrix and permutation ϕ.

13   AN APPLICATION: SEQUENCING A SINGLE STATE-VARIABLE MACHINE

A certain factory manufactures specialty refractory products. There are $n - 1$ different jobs that are ready for burning in the kiln. Job i requires a starting temperature s_i and after some prescribed variations in temperature (over which we have no control) the job is finished at temperature f_i. If job j immediately follows job i in the kiln, the temperature must be changed from f_i to s_j. The cost of changing the kiln temperature between jobs i and j is

$$c_{ij} = \begin{cases} \displaystyle\int_{f_i}^{s_j} f(x)\,dx & \text{if } f_i \leqslant s_j, \\[2mm] \displaystyle\int_{s_j}^{f_i} g(x)\,dx & \text{if } s_j \leqslant f_i, \end{cases} \tag{18}$$

where f and g are cost density functions. It is natural that f and g should be different functions, since the cost density for raising the temperature of the kiln is probably quite different from that for lowering it. Neither f nor g need be strictly nonnegative, but it conforms to reality to require that

$$f(x) + g(x) \geqslant 0$$

for all x. (Else one could cycle the temperature of the kiln up and down and make money without manufacturing anything.)

Our objective, of course, is to prescribe a sequence for the jobs that minimizes the total cost of changing the temperature of the kiln between jobs. In order to set this problem properly, we must specify an initial temperature f_n at which we find the kiln and a final temperature s_n at which we must leave it. We let s_n and f_n prescribe an nth dummy job and we have a proper TSP.

Let us index the jobs (which we hereafter call cities) so that $f_1 \leqslant f_2 \leqslant \ldots \leqslant f_n$. Let ϕ be a permutation such that $s_{\phi(1)} \leqslant s_{\phi(2)} \leqslant \ldots \leqslant s_{\phi(n)}$. We assert that when the columns of C have been permuted in this way, C^ϕ is equivalent by a linear admissible transformation to a distribution matrix. That is, for $1 \leqslant i \leqslant n-1$ and $2 \leqslant j \leqslant n$,

$$d_{ij}^\phi = d_{i\phi(j)} = c_{i\phi(j)} + c_{i+1,\phi(j-1)} - c_{i\phi(j-1)} - c_{i+1,\phi(j)} \geqslant 0.$$

(Recall Exercise 13, Section 7.) Specifically, for C defined by (18) we have

$$d_{i\phi(j)} = \int_a^b (f(x) + g(x))\,dx \geqslant 0,$$

where $a = \max\{f_i, s_{\phi(j-1)}\}$, $b = \min\{f_{i+1}, s_{\phi(j)}\}$ and $d_{i,\phi(j)} = 0$ if $a > b$.

Because C^ϕ is a distribution matrix, it follows from the results of the previous section that there exists an optimal tour $\phi\psi$, where ψ is minimal, dense, and pyramidal. Moreover, the lower bound property is satisfied and there exists a minimal spanning tree composed of transpositions of the form $(i, i+1)$. In order to obtain an efficient algorithm, we must now establish the upper bound property for such minimal spanning trees.

Our task quite simply is the following. Show that for all i, j, $i < j$, there exists a pyramidal cyclic permutation ψ acting on cities $i, i+1, \ldots, j$ such that

$$c\phi(\psi) = \sum_{h=i}^{j-1} c\phi((h, h+1)) = \sum_{h=i}^{j-1} d_{h\phi(h+1)}. \tag{19}$$

Our proof is by induction on the value of $j - i$. For $j - i = 1$, we have $c\phi((i, i+1)) = d_{i\phi(i+1)}$, so $\psi = (i, i+1)$. So assume there exists a pyramidal cycle ψ acting on $i, i+1, \ldots, j$ that satisfies (19). We shall show that this implies the existence of such a ψ' on $i, i+1, \ldots, j+1$.

Suppose we let $\psi' = (j, j+1)\psi$. Then city $j+1$ is inserted between j and its immediate predecessor $\psi^{-1}(j)$ in ψ. Let $\psi^{-1}(j) = k$ and we have

$$c\phi((j, j+1)\psi) = c\phi(\psi) + c_{k\phi(j+1)} + c_{j+1,\phi(j)} - c_{k\phi(j)} - c_{j+1,\phi(j+1)}$$

$$= c\phi(\psi) + d_{j\phi(j+1)} + \sum_{h=k}^{j-1} d_{h\phi(j+1)}.$$

On the other hand, if we let $\psi = \phi(j, j+1)$, then city $j+1$ is inserted between j and its immediate successor $\psi(j)$ in ψ. Let $\psi(j) = k$ and we have

$$c\phi(\psi(j, j+1)) = c\phi(\psi) + c_{j\phi(j+1)} + c_{j+1,\phi(k)} - c_{j\phi(k)} - c_{j+1,\phi(j+1)}$$

$$= c\phi(\psi) + d_{j\phi(j+1)} + \sum_{h=k+1}^{j} d_{j\phi(h)}.$$

But for $1 \leqslant h \leqslant j-1$ we have

$$d_{h\phi(j+1)} = \int_a^b (f(x) + g(x))\,dx,$$

where $a = \max\{f_h, s_{\phi(j)}\}$, $b = \min\{f_{h+1}, s_{\phi(j+1)}\}$. And for $2 \leqslant h \leqslant j$ we have

$$d_{j\phi(h)} = \int_{a'}^{b'} (f(x) + g(x))\,dx,$$

where $a' = \max\{f_j, s_{\phi(h-1)}\}$, $b' = \min\{f_{j+1}, s_{\phi(h)}\}$.

There are two possibilities:

(1) $f_j \leqslant s_{\phi(j)}$, in which case $f_{h+1} \leqslant s_{\phi(j)}$, $a \geqslant b$, and

$$d_{h\phi(j+1)} = 0, \qquad \text{for } 1 \leqslant h \leqslant j-1;$$

(2) $f_j > s_{\phi(j)}$, in which case $f_j > s_{\phi(h)}$, $a' \geqslant b'$, and

$$d_{j\phi(h)} = 0, \qquad \text{for } 2 \leqslant h \leqslant j.$$

Thus if $f_j \leqslant s_{\phi(j)}$, the desired permutation is $\psi' = (j, j+1)\psi$, whereas if $f_j > s_{\phi(j)}$ we want $\psi' = \psi(j, j+1)$. We have thus proved the following.

Theorem 20 *Let C^{ϕ} be a distribution matrix defined by (18). For any $i, j, i < j$, let $i \leqslant i(1) < i(2) < \ldots < i(r) \leqslant j-1$ be such that $f_{i(h)} \leqslant s_{\phi(i(h))}$, $1 \leqslant h \leqslant r$, and let $i \leqslant j(1) < j(2) < \ldots < j(s) \leqslant j-1$ be such that $f_{j(h)} > s_{\phi(j(h))}$, $1 \leqslant h \leqslant s$. Then*

$$\psi = (i(r), i(r)+1)(i(r-1), i(r-1)+1) \ldots (i(1), i(1)+1)$$

$$(j(1), j(1)+1) \ldots (j(s-1), j(s-1)+1)(j(s), j(s)+1)$$

is a pyramidal cyclic permutation acting on $i, i+1, \ldots, j$, with

$$c\phi(\psi) = \sum_{k=i}^{j-1} d_{k\phi(k+1)}.$$

We are now prepared to state the algorithm for solving the single state-variable machine sequencing problem [Gilmore & Gomory, 1964]:

(1) Sort the s_i, f_i values so that $f_1 \leqslant f_2 \leqslant \ldots \leqslant f_n$, $s_{\phi(1)} \leqslant s_{\phi(2)} \leqslant \ldots \leqslant s_{\phi(n)}$. This can be done in $O(n \log n)$ time.
(2) Find the subtours of the optimal assignment ϕ. This requires only $O(n)$ time.
(3) Find a minimum length tree T of $(i, i+1)$ transpositions spanning the subtours of ϕ. This requires computation of the values $d_{i\phi(i+1)}$, which we assume can be done in $O(n)$ time. A minimum spanning tree can be found in essentially $O(n)$ time.
(4) For each connected component T_j of the graph $G(V, T)$, find a pyramidal cyclic permutation as indicated by Theorem 20, and thereby find ψ. This requires only $O(n)$ time.
(5) Multiply ϕ by ψ to obtain an optimal tour. This requires $O(n)$ time.

Exercises
29. (a) You are given $n-1$ trapezoids, where each trapezoid j is specified by two parameters, a_j and b_j, $j = 1, 2, \ldots, n-1$, as shown in Figure 4.15(a). The object is to arrange these trapezoids in a line, no two of them overlapping (a typical feasible arrangement is shown in Figure 4.15(b)), so that the total length of the arrangement is as short as possible. Show that this problem can be formulated and solved as an n-city TSP of the Gilmore–Gomory type, with a distance matrix of the form (18). (b) Consider the following scheduling problem. There are $n-1$ jobs to be worked on by each of two machines. Job j requires a_j units of processing on the first machine and b_j units on the second. As soon as the processing of job j is completed on the first machine, its processing must begin on the second machine. (There is no buffering of jobs possible between the two machines.) The object is to find a sequence for the jobs such that all the jobs will be completed as early as possible. Verify that the trapezoid problem of part (a)

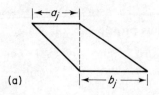

(a)

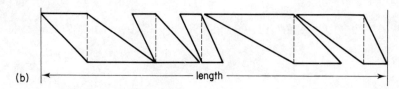

(b)

Figure 4.15   (a) Typical trapezoid. (b) Feasible schedule

is an appropriate model for this problem. (*Note*: The three-machine generalization of this problem is $\mathcal{NP}$-hard; see Röck [1984] and Chapter 3, Section 4, Exercise 16(b).)

30. [Gilmore & Gomory, 1964]. Let τ be an optimal tour for a problem instance with density functions f and g. Prove that τ is also an optimal tour for any problem instance with functions f' and g' where $f(x) + g(x) = f'(x) + g'(x)$. (The parameters f_i, s_i remain unchanged.)

31. [Gilmore & Gomory, 1964]. Suppose that $n-1$ jobs are to be sequenced on a machine with costs related to a single state-variable x. Assume that $g(x) = 0$. Prove the following:

(a) If the initial value of the state-variable must be f_n but its final value is unrestricted, then the sequencing problem is equivalent to a TSP with an additional job n with starting value s_n, where $s_n \leq \min_{1 \leq i \leq n} \{f_i\}$ and final value f_n.

(b) If any value of the state-variable is available at the beginning, but the final value must be s_n, then the sequencing problem is equivalent to a TSP with an additional job n with starting value s_n and final value f_n where $f_n \geq \max_{1 \leq i \leq n} \{s_i\}$.

(c) If any value of the state-variable is available at the beginning and its final value is unrestricted, the sequencing problem is equivalent to a TSP with an additional job n with

$$s_n \leq \min_{1 \leq i \leq n} \{f_i\},$$

$$f_n \geq \max_{1 \leq i \leq n} \{s_i\}.$$

32. Modify the algorithm to solve the bottleneck version of the Gilmore–Gomory TSP, subject to the assumption that $f(x) \geq 0$ and $g(x) = 0$.

33. Construct an example to show that a bottleneck optimal tour is not necessarily a shortest tour, for the Gilmore-Gomory TSP. Show that in the case $f_i \geq s_{\phi(i)}$ for all i, there is a tour that is optimal with respect to both criteria. (Assume $f(x) \geq 0$, $g(x) = 0$.)

14   THE TSP FOR PRODUCT MATRICES

An $n \times n$ matrix $C = (c_{ij})$ is called a *product* matrix if there exists two n-dimensional vectors a and b such that $c_{ij} = a_i b_j$ for all i, j. Recall that an $n \times n$ matrix C is called a *permuted distribution* matrix if there exist a nonnegative matrix D, and a permutation ϕ, such that $c_{i\phi(j)} = \sum_{k=i}^{n} \sum_{l=1}^{j} d_{kl}$. It is a straightforward exercise to show that all product matrices can be transformed into a permuted distribution matrix by a linear admissible transformation. In this section, we present negative and positive results for product matrices. We show that, in general, computing an optimal tour is $\mathcal{NP}$-hard, but for many special cases, including symmetric product matrices, there exists a polynomial-time algorithm.

Theorem 21 [Sarvanov, 1980]   *The TSP restricted to product matrices is $\mathcal{NP}$-hard.*

To prove this result, an intermediate problem is introduced. Before this can be done, some additional terminology must be defined. Let $\Pi = \{N_1, \ldots, N_m\}$ be a partition of $N = \{1, \ldots, n\}$. For any partition Π, let the *spine graph* of the partition be $G(\Pi) = (N, E)$ where $E = \{\{i, i+1\} \mid i \in N_k, i+1 \in N_l, k \neq l\}$. Let $G' = (N, E')$ be a subgraph of G. The vertex set of G' is the entire vertex set of G. Define the *partition graph* of G' to be $P(G') = (\Pi, E_P)$ where $E_P = \{\{N_k, N_l\} \mid$ there exists an i such that $i \in N_k$, $i+1 \in N_l$, $\{i, i+1\} \in E'\}$. All of these graphs are undirected. As an example, consider $\Pi = \{\{1, 4\}, \{2, 3\}, \{5\}\}$. The corresponding spine graph $G(\Pi)$ is given in Figure 4.16(a). For the subgraph G' shown in Figure 4.16(b), the corresponding partition graph $P(G')$ is given in Figure 4.16(c). In addition, call G' a *matching* if the degree of every vertex is 0 or 1.

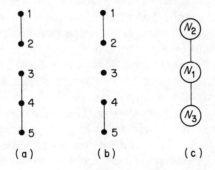

Figure 4.16   (a) $G(\Pi)$. (b) G'. (c) $P(G')$

Consider the following decision problem.

PARTITION GRAPH SPANNING TREE
INSTANCE: $N = \{1, \ldots, n\}$ and $\Pi = \{N_1, \ldots, N_m\}$, a partition of N.
QUESTION: If $G(\Pi) = (N, E)$ is the spine graph of Π, does there exist a
subgraph $G' = (N, E')$ of $G(\Pi)$ that is a matching, such that the partition
graph $P(G') = (\Pi, E_P)$ is a spanning tree of the vertex set Π?

A matching is said to be *good* if its partition graph is a spanning tree.

Notice that there is a connection between the tools that we have defined
for this problem and those that were defined for the theory of subtour
patching. The fact that a given set of $\{i, i+1\}$ edges form a spanning tree of
$P(G')$ implies that those edges, together with the hyperedges induced by the
partition (which correspond to a permutation ϕ) form a spanning (hypergraph) tree. Furthermore, the fact that the $\{i, i+1\}$ edges form a matching in
the spine graph implies that they could be factors of ψ and therefore their
costs are independent of each other.

Lemma 12 PARTITION GRAPH SPANNING TREE *is $\mathcal{NP}$-complete.*

Proof It is easy to verify that PARTITION GRAPH SPANNING TREE is in $\mathcal{NP}$. To
show that it is $\mathcal{NP}$-hard, we reduce from the Hamiltonian path problem for
cubic graphs (see Chapter 3). Recall that a cubic graph is a graph where the
degree of every vertex is three. Given a cubic graph $G = (V, E)$ we will
construct an instance of PARTITION GRAPH SPANNING TREE. Note that $|V| = n$
must be even and that $|E| = 3n/2$. The set N constructed is $\{1, 2, \ldots, 9n\}$
and there will be $3n$ parts in the partition; n each of types 1, 2 and 3 as we
shall define below. For each part N_{ij}, $i = 1, 2, 3$, $j = 1, \ldots, n$, the second
index may be thought of as corresponding to a vertex in V. From G,
construct   a   multigraph $G^+ = (V, E^+)$ where $E^+ = E \cup \{\{1, 2\},
\{3, 4\}, \ldots, \{n-1, n\}\}$. The $n/2$ new edges will remain distinguished through-
out this construction. Since the degree of every vertex of G^+ is 4, it is
Eulerian, so an Eulerian tour $T = \{e_1, e_2, \ldots, e_{2n}\}$ can be constructed in
polynomial time. The edges e_i are now oriented in the direction of the tour.
The partition $\Pi = \{N_{ij} \mid i = 1, 2, 3, j = 1, \ldots, n\}$ is constructed by 'following'
the Eulerian tour. It is easiest to understand the construction in terms of the
corresponding spine graph. To differentiate between vertices of G and
vertices of the spine graph, those of the spine graph will be called *elements*.
Suppose $e_1 = (v, w)$ and is not a distinguished edge; in this case the initial
portion of the resulting spine graph is shown in Figure 4.17(a). If (v, w) is
distinguished, then the alternate construction is shown in Figure 4.17(b).

In general, for any edge e_i, the next six elements will be used if it is
distinguished, and the next four otherwise. Furthermore, the same construction as above will be used. Suppose that $j-1$ elements have been used
before reaching $e_i = (v, w)$. Then add the construction shown in either Figure
4.18(a) or 4.18(b) depending on whether e_i is undistinguished or distinguished, respectively. Every N_{1v} and N_{2v} contains four elements, whereas

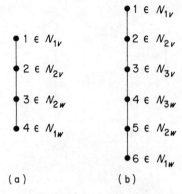

Figure 4.17

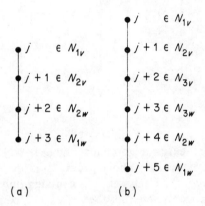

Figure 4.18

N_{3v} contains only one. Since the tail vertex of e_i is equal to the head vertex of e_{i-1}, the spine has $2n$ components, each of which corresponds to an edge of the tour. Now we must show that a suitable matching can be found if and only if G has a Hamiltonian path.

Suppose that $\{v_1, v_2, \ldots, v_n\}$ is a Hamiltonian path of G. For every distinguished edge, include in the matching the marked edges shown in Figure 4.19(a). For every edge in the Hamiltonian path, choose the edges as shown in Figure 4.19(b). There are $n/2 + 1$ components of the spine that have not yet been marked. By a simple counting argument, these components contain elements that belong to every N_{1v} and N_{2v}. All but one of the components will be marked as shown in Figure 4.20(a), and the last will be marked as depicted in either Figure 4.20(b) or 4.20(c). It is easy to see that the corresponding partition graph is the spanning tree given in Figure 4.21.

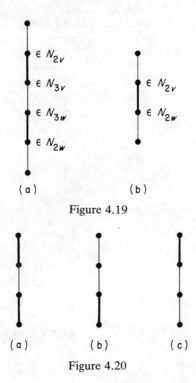

$$(a)\qquad\qquad (b)$$

Figure 4.19

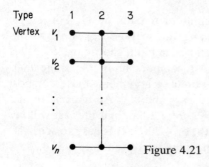

$$(a)\qquad\qquad (b)\qquad\qquad (c)$$

Figure 4.20

Suppose that there exists a good matching. It will be shown that the spanning tree must be of the above form. Consider the vertices of the partition graph of type 3. Each set N_{3v} contains only one element; thus there are only two possible sets that the vertex N_{3v} could be adjacent to in the spanning tree. Consider the component of the spine in which this element appears (see Figure 4.22). If the edge between the N_{3v} and N_{3w} elements were in the matching, the corresponding edge in the partition graph must be a separate component, and therefore could not be in the spanning tree. Thus, for every distinguished component of the spine $\{v, w\}$, the matching must contain the edges between the N_{2v}, N_{3v} and N_{2w}, N_{3w}

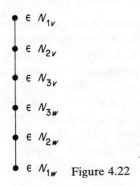

Figure 4.22

elements, as shown in Figure 4.19(a). Similarly, by examining the structure of the spine, it is easy to see that any N_{1v} must be adjacent only to the corresponding N_{2v} vertex in the spanning tree. Thus, the structure of the spanning tree is forced to be as depicted in Figure 4.23, and the tree is connected by forming a spanning tree on the vertices of type 2.

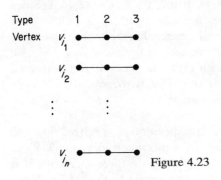

Figure 4.23

But what form can the tree take? In creating the edges shown, a maximal set of edges from the distinguished components of the spine has been forced to be in the matching. Thus all the $\{N_{1v}, N_{2v}\}$ edges have been taken from undistinguished components. Since the undistinguished components correspond to edges of G, each N_{2v} contains exactly three elements from these components. To form the $\{N_{1v}, N_{2v}\}$ edges, one of these has been used. Thus, for each v there are at most two available elements in the spine that are contained in N_{2v}. Therefore, in the spanning tree on vertices of type 2 in the partition graph, these vertices must all have degree at most 2. But the only spanning tree with each degree 1 or 2 is a Hamiltonian path. Thus the graph induced by the vertices of degree 2 is a Hamiltonian path. For each edge $\{N_{2v}, N_{2w}\}$ in the Hamiltonian path, there exists an edge $\{v, w\}$ in the original graph G. Therefore, G has a Hamiltonian path. $\square$

Lemma 13 PARTITION GRAPH SPANNING TREE $\propto$ TSP *for product matrices.*

Proof Given an instance of PARTITION GRAPH SPANNING TREE, we must construct a corresponding instance of the TSP for product matrices; that is, we must construct a product matrix C and a bound K such that C has a tour of length at most K if and only if the instance of PARTITION GRAPH SPANNING TREE admits a good matching.

Let $\Pi = \{N_1, \ldots, N_m\}$ be the partition of an instance of PARTITION GRAPH SPANNING TREE. Let ϕ be any permutation with the same cycle structure as Π. For example, if $\Pi = \{\{1, 4\}, \{2, 3\}, \{5\}\}$, then $\phi = (1, 4)(2, 3)(5)$. In general there may be many such permutations. The matrix C is given by a and b, where $c_{ij} = a_i b_j$ and $a_i = n - i + 1$ and $b_{\phi(j)} = j$. The bound for this instance of the TSP is $K = \sum_{i=1}^{n} i(n - i + 1) + m - 1$.

Since C is a permuted distribution matrix, an optimal assignment can be specified as the assignment that permutes the columns to yield a distribution matrix. It is not hard to see that ϕ is this permutation for C. This assignment has the cycle structure of Π and these cycles must be patched together to form an optimal TSP tour. The cost of the optimal assignment will always be $\sum_{i=1}^{n} i(n - i + 1)$.

Suppose that there exists a good matching, $E = \{e_1, \ldots, e_{m-1}\}$. If $e_i = \{j, j+1\}$, let ψ_i be the interchange $(j, j+1)$. It follows that $c\phi(\psi_i) = 1$. Since the partition graph generated by E is a spanning tree, it follows that $\tau = \phi\psi = \phi\psi_1\psi_2 \ldots \psi_{m-1}$ is a Hamiltonian cycle. Furthermore, since the interchanges ψ_i are disjoint, the cost of this tour is precisely K.

Now suppose that there is a tour τ with $c(\tau) \leq K$. Since C is a permuted distribution matrix, there must exist a tour τ' that is pyramidal and dense relative to ϕ with $c(\tau') \leq K$. Therefore, assume that $\tau = \phi\psi = \phi\psi_1\psi_2 \ldots \psi_p$ where the ψ_i are dense and pyramidal.

We will show that if ρ is not an $(i, i+1)$ transposition then $c\phi(\rho) \geq |\rho|$. The proof is by induction on $|\rho|$. For the basis of the proof consider $|\rho| = 3$. Since there are only two different dense pyramidal tours on three elements, it is simple to verify this case, and we leave it as an exercise to the reader. Next, we complete the induction by showing that if there exists a dense pyramidal permutation with $c\phi(\rho) < |\rho| = k + 1$, then there exists a dense pyramidal permutation ρ' with $c\phi(\rho') < |\rho'| = k$. Suppose that ρ is a dense pyramidal permutation on the cities $\{i, i+1, \ldots, i+k\}$ such that $c\phi(\rho) < k + 1$. Suppose that $\rho(i+k) = i+j$ and that $\rho^{-1}(i+k) = i+l$. Let $\rho' = \rho(i+l, i+k)$; ρ' is simply the cycle formed by deleting $i + k$. A straightforward computation gives that $c\phi(\rho) - c\phi(\rho') = (k-j)(k-l) \geq 1$ (actually it is at least 2) which shows that $c\phi(\rho') < |\rho'| = k$. This completes the proof that $c\phi(\rho) \geq |\rho|$ for $|\rho| \geq 3$. For transpositions ρ not of the form $(i, i+1)$ it is easy to see that $c\phi(\rho) \geq 2$. Thus we have proved the claim that for all factors ρ that are not $(i, i+1)$ transpositions, $c\phi(\rho) \geq |\rho|$.

Furthermore, since τ is a tour it follows from the fact that $H = (N, \{\phi_i\} \cup \{\psi_i\})$ must be connected, that $\sum_{i=1}^{p} |\psi_i| \geq m - 1 + p$. However, since the cost of the tour is at most K, $c\phi(\psi) \leq m - 1$. Suppose that q of the ψ_i are

$(j, j+1)$ transpositions. Then we find that

$$m-1 \geqslant c\varphi(\psi) = \sum_{i=1}^{p} c\phi(\psi_i) \geqslant \sum_{i=1}^{p} |\psi_i| - q \geqslant m-1+p-q.$$

Therefore, $p = q$ and all of the factors of ψ are $(i, i+1)$ transpositions. These transpositions must correspond to a matching that generates a spanning tree of the partition graph. □

This completes the proof of Theorem 21.

In the remainder of this section we turn to some more positive results for special classes of product matrices. The result presented here shows that there is a broad class of product matrices for which there is a polynomial-time algorithm.

Let ϕ be an arbitrary permutation and let Π be the corresponding partition of $\{1, \dots, n\}$. For simplicity of notation, let G_ϕ denote $P(G(\Pi))$, the partition graph of the spine graph of Π.

Theorem 22 *Let C be a permuted distribution matrix, and let ϕ be the optimal assignment where C^ϕ is a distribution matrix. If G_ϕ is a tree, then there is a polynomial-time algorithm to find an optimal tour for C.*

Proof Left to the reader as an exercise. □

Corollary 8 [Gaikov, 1980] *Let C be a product matrix such that $c_{ij} = a_i b_j$ and $a_1 \leqslant a_2 \leqslant \dots \leqslant a_n$. Let ϕ be the optimal assignment. If G_ϕ is a tree, then there is a polynomial-time algorithm to find an optimal tour for C.*

The Soviet literature contains a great number of papers with results that were superseded by Corollary 8. An easy corollary to this result is the case of the symmetric product matrices; that is $c_{ij} = a_i b_j$ and $c_{ij} = c_{ji}$.

Corollary 9 *For a symmetric product matrix C where $c_{ij} = a_i b_j$ and $a_1 \leqslant a_2 \leqslant \dots \leqslant a_n$, there exists a polynomial-time algorithm to find an optimal tour.*

Proof As noted above, an optimal assignment ϕ is given by the permutation that sorts the b's; that is $b_{\phi(1)} \geqslant b_{\phi(2)} \geqslant \dots \geqslant b_{\phi(n)}$. Since C is symmetric, $a_i b_j = b_i a_j$ for all i, j. Equivalently,

$$\frac{a_i}{b_i} = \frac{a_j}{b_j} = \lambda.$$

Thus, $a_i = \lambda b_i$. Therefore, ϕ is $(1)(2) \dots (n)$ or $(1, n)(2, n-1) \dots (\lfloor n/2 \rfloor, \lceil n/2 \rceil)$ depending on whether λ is negative or positive, respectively. In either case, G_ϕ is a path. □

Note that this shows that there are cases where the symmetric case of the TSP is provably easier than the asymmetric case, of course under the assumption that $\mathcal{P} \neq \mathcal{NP}$.

Exercises

34. Construct a polynomial-time algorithm that either constructs a and b, or shows that C is not a product matrix.

35. Prove Theorem 22. (*Hint:* The following observations may be useful in constructing a polynomial-time algorithm based on dynamic programming.

(a) There exists an optimal tour $\tau = \phi\psi$ that is basic, pyramidal and dense with respect to ϕ (see Section 12).

(b) Given the set of cities on which a factor of ψ acts, it is possible to compute the factor in polynomial time (see Section 7).

(c) Since more than one $(i, i+1)$ transposition may support the existence of a particular edge in the tree G_ϕ, it may be convenient to view G_ϕ as a 'multitree'. Note, however, that exactly one factor of ψ will contain both endpoints of a set of multiedges of the tree.

(d) Every factor of ψ corresponds to a path in G_ϕ. Determining the factors of ψ amounts to covering the edges of G_ϕ with paths. (Note that the paths will be edge-disjoint, but not vertex-disjoint.)

(e) Since the costs $c\phi(\psi_i)$ and $c\phi(\psi_j)$ are independent for disjoint factors, subproblems for edge-disjoint trees can be solved independently.

(f) Root G_ϕ at an arbitrary node. For each node v of G_ϕ, at most one edge to a child of v is contained on the path that includes v and the parent of v. Suppose that the edge to the child u is used on that path. Then the path covering problem for the subtree rooted at v with the subtree rooted at u deleted can be solved as an independent subproblem.

(g) Suppose that v is the endpoint of the path that includes its parent. (This is, in effect, the case of the root of G_ϕ as well.) The edge to each child of v must be covered by some path, and some (possibly more than one) of these paths pass through v. Thus, there is a matching problem among the children of v to determine which children (if any) get paired on a path through v.)

15 BANDWIDTH-LIMITED NETWORKS

Let A be the adjacency matrix of a digraph G. That is,

$$a_{ij} = \begin{cases} 1 & \text{if } (i, j) \text{ is an arc,} \\ 0 & \text{otherwise.} \end{cases}$$

It is customary to say that A and G have *bandwidth* k if $|i-j| > k$ implies $a_{ij} = 0$. The principal result of this section is to show that for any fixed k, there exists an algorithm with $O(n)$ running time that will solve the TSP for networks with bandwidth k. (The distance matrices for such a class of problem instances have the property that $c_{ij} = +\infty$ if $|i-j| > k$.)

Let H be a Hamiltonian cycle in an undirected graph of bandwidth k. Consider the subgraph H_j that H induces on vertices $1, 2, \ldots, j$ where $1 \le j \le n-1$. Each of the vertices $1, 2, \ldots, j-k-1$ has degree 2, because of the bandwidth of G. Moreover, H_j contains no cycles (else H is not a

Hamiltonian cycle), hence each connected component of H_j is a directed path. The endpoints of these paths are in the set $\{j-k, j-k+1, \ldots, j\}$.

Let us define an equivalence relation on the subgraphs induced by Hamiltonian cycles. For given j, subgraphs H_j and H_j' are *equivalent* if

(1) the degrees of vertices $j-k, j-k+1, \ldots, j$ are the same, and
(2) for each path (connected component) in H_j there is a path in H_j' with the same endpoints, and conversely.

The significance of the subgraphs H_j and the equivalence relation we have defined on them is suggested by the following observation. Let H be an optimal Hamiltonian cycle and let H induce H_j on vertices $1, 2, \ldots, j$. Then for each H_j' in the same equivalence class as H_j, it must be the case that $c(H_j') \geqslant c(H_j)$. Else a shorter tour H' could be obtained by removing the edges of H_j from H and substituting those of H_j'. It follows that we can state a necessary condition for the optimality of tours in terms of the lengths of shortest equivalent subgraphs.

It turns out that knowledge of shortest equivalent subgraphs is also sufficient to enable us to find an optimal tour. Our strategy is as follows. Having found a shortest subgraph in each equivalence class for vertices $1, 2, \ldots, j$, we then use this information to find a shortest subgraph in each equivalence class for $1, 2, \ldots, j+1$. Finally, having found a shortest subgraph in each equivalence class for $1, 2, \ldots, n$, we find an optimal tour.

Let S denote an equivalence class of subgraphs on $1, 2, \ldots, j+1$. Each subgraph H_{j+1} in S induces a unique subgraph H_j on vertices $1, 2, \ldots, j$. The equivalence class to which H_j belongs depends upon the set Δ of zero, one or two edges incident to $j+1$ in H_{j+1}. Conversely, for each equivalence class S' of subgraphs on $1, 2, \ldots, j$, there are various subsets Δ of edges incident to $j+1$ that yield legitimate subgraphs on vertices $1, 2, \ldots, j+1$, and each Δ yields a subgraph in a different equivalence class. Thus we can define a mapping τ where $\tau(S', \Delta)$ denotes the equivalence class of a subgraph in S', when the subgraph is augmented by the edges in Δ. ($\tau(S', \Delta)$ is undefined if the augmented subgraph is not legitimate.)

Let $C(S, j+1)$ denote the length of a shortest subgraph in the equivalence class S on $1, 2, \ldots, j+1$, and let $c_{j+1}(\Delta)$ denote the length of the subset Δ of edges incident to $j+1$. Then, by the usual sort of dynamic programming argumentation we have

$$C(S, j+1) = \min_{\Delta} \{C(S', j) + c_{j+1}(\Delta) \mid S = \tau(S', \Delta)\}. \tag{20}$$

Now notice that every Hamiltonian cycle H contains exactly two edges incident to vertex n, say $\{a, n\}$ and $\{b, n\}$. These edges determine the equivalence class $S_{a,b}$ to which H_{n-1} belongs. There are only a finite number of choices of a and b. Minimizing over them, we find that the length of a shortest tour is

$$\min_{a,b} \{C(S_{a,b}, n-1) + c_{an} + c_{bn}\}. \tag{21}$$

With appropriate initial conditions, equations (20) and (21) provide the basis for a dynamic programming solution to the TSP. We note that, for any fixed bandwidth k, the number of equivalence classes S, the number of sets Δ, and the number of choices of vertices a, b, is each fixed. It follows that the equations (20) and (21) can be solved in $O(n)$ time.

Of course, we should like to have an estimate of how rapidly the computational effort grows with k. The most difficult part of making such an estimate is to determine the number $N(k)$ of equivalence classes S for a given bandwidth k. We make a counting argument as follows. Let us partition the equivalence classes of subgraphs on $1, 2, \ldots, j$ into three groups, determined by the degree of vertex $j - k$:

(0) Vertex $j - k$ cannot have degree 0 unless $k \leqslant j \leqslant n - 1$, so we ignore this possibility.
(1) In the case vertex $j - k$ has degree 1, it is the endpoint of a path and the other endpoint is l, where $j - k + 1 \leqslant l \leqslant j$. For each of the $k - 1$ possibilities for l, there are $N(k - 2)$ equivalence classes, determined by the other $k - 2$ vertices between $j - k + 1$ and j.
(2) In the case vertex $j - k$ has degree 2, there are $N(k - 1)$ equivalence classes, determined by vertices $j - k + 1, \ldots, j$.

Thus we have

$$N(k) = N(k - 1) + (k - 1)N(k - 2), \tag{22}$$

with the initial conditions $N(1) = 0$, $N(2) = 1$. A tabulation of values as determined by (22) is as follows:

k	1	2	3	4	5	6	7	8	9	10	11	12	13
$N(k)$	0	1	1	7	11	46	112	434	1,130	5,236	18,536	76,132	298,564

Although $N(k)$ grows quite slowly at first, its growth rate soon becomes quite explosive. Noting that $N(k)$ is $O((k - 1)!)$ and that the number of Δ's is $O(k^2)$, we can easily verify that the running time of the dynamic programming computation, expressed in terms of both k and n, is $O((k + 1)! \, n)$.

The dynamic programming computation described here was suggested by ideas of Monien & Sudborough [1981] and Ratliff & Rosenthal [1983]. We leave certain extensions and generalizations as exercises.

Exercises

36. Extend the dynamic programming computation to the asymmetric bandwidth-limited TSP. Compute $N(k)$ for this case.
37. Consider the *stripe-width*-limited problem: $(j - i) > k \pmod{n}$ implies $c_{ij} = +\infty$. Show that the difficulty of solving the TSP for stripe-width k is about the same as for bandwidth $2k$.

16 REDUCIBLE NETWORKS

Some instances of the TSP can be easily solved, or at least significantly simplified, because the underlying network is wholly or partially *reducible*, as we shall describe.

Let $G = (V, A)$ be a directed graph. A *directed cut* of G is a bipartition of its vertex set V into nonempty subsets S, T such that no arc extends from a vertex in T to a vertex in S. (That is, all arcs extending across the cut are directed from S to T.) Let us say that a bipartition (S, T) defines an *almost directed cut* if there is exactly one arc (u, v) such that $u \in T$, $v \in S$.

If an instance of the TSP is defined over a network that contains a directed cut (S, T), then it clearly has no feasible solution, since there is no way to reach a city in S from a city in T. Suppose we have a network that contains an almost directed cut (S, T). Then we know that (u, v), the only arc from T to S, must be contained in any feasible tour and hence in an optimal tour, if one exists. It follows that we can delete from the network all arcs (u, y), where $y \neq v$, and (x, v), where $x \neq u$, because such arcs cannot be contained in a feasible tour. The elimination of such arcs may create additional almost directed cuts, where such cuts did not exist before.

Let us call a directed network *reducible* if it can be transformed to a tour by the deletion of arcs through the repeated discovery of almost directed cuts. (This notion of reducibility is, effectively, a generalization of the notion of reducibility for so-called flow graphs. See, for example, Hecht & Ullman [1972].) As a very simple example, the directed graph shown in Figure 4.24 is reducible and contains exactly one tour, namely $(1, 2, 3, 4)$. Even if a network is not reducible, the deletion of arcs through the discovery of almost directed cuts may yield a significant simplification.

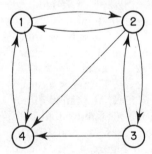

Figure 4.24   A reducible digraph

17 HALIN GRAPHS AND 3-EDGE CUTSETS

A *Halin graph* is constructed as follows: Start with a tree T in which each nonleaf vertex has a degree of at least three. Embed the graph in the plane and then add new edges to form a cycle C containing all the leaves of T in such a way that the resulting graph $H = T \cup C$ remains planar (see Figure 4.25.) These graphs were introduced by R. Halin as an example of a class of

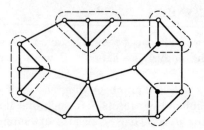

Figure 4.25   A Halin graph

edge-minimal planar 3-connected graphs. Halin graphs are Hamiltonian and
remain so if any single vertex is deleted. Also, every edge belongs to a
Hamiltonian cycle and the number of such cycles can grow exponentially
with the size of the graph.

Cornuéjols, Naddef & Pulleyblank [1985] have shown how to solve the
TSP when the underlying network is a Halin graph, or more generally, when
it can be decomposed by the discovery of 3-*edge cutsets*; we shall follow
their exposition closely. First some definitions.

An *edge cutset* of a connected (undirected) graph G is a minimal set of
edges whose deletion leaves a disconnected graph. If it contains exactly k
edges, then it is a k-*edge cutset*. The following is apparent: *Every Hamiltonian cycle contains exactly two edges of every 3-edge cutset.*

Let $H = T \cup C$ be a Halin graph. If T is a star, i.e. a single vertex v joined
to $n - 1$ other vertices, then H is a *wheel* and is the simplest type of Halin
graph. Suppose H is not a wheel, and let w be a nonleaf that is adjacent to
exactly one other nonleaf of T. (At least two such nonleafs must exist.) The
set of leaves of T adjacent to w, which we denote by $C(w)$, comprises a
consecutive subsequence of the cycle C. We call the subgraph of H induced
by $\{w\} \cup C(w)$ a *fan* and call w the *center* of the fan. In Figure 4.25 the
black nodes are the centers of the fans indicated by dashed lines. Now notice
that there are exactly three edges extending between a fan and the remainder of the Halin graph. These edges constitute a 3-edge cutset.

Let u and v be the endpoints of the portion of the cycle C that is induced
by $C(w)$. We know that any tour of H must enter and leave the fan at either
(a) u and w, (b) v and w, or (c) u and v, and describe a Hamiltonian path
within the fan between those pairs of vertices. For cases (a) and (b) the
Hamiltonian path is uniquely prescribed, as shown in Figure 4.26. And in
case (c) there are only a limited number of possibilities for the Hamiltonian
path as shown in the figure. It follows that we can easily compute the length
of a shortest Hamiltonian path for each of these three cases.

Now what we propose to do is this: We shall condense all the vertices of a
fan $\{w\} \cup C(w)$ into a single vertex x, thereby obtaining a smaller Halin
graph H'. The edges of the 3-edge cutset associated with the fan will have
their lengths modified in H' so that an optimal tour in H' is identified with
an optimal tour in H. We shall continue condensing fans in this way until

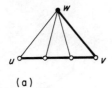

(a)

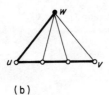

(b)

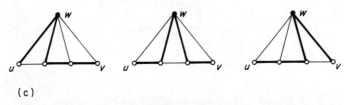

(c)

Figure 4.26 (a) Unique Hamiltonian path between u and w. (b) Unique Hamiltonian path between v and w. (c) All Hamiltonian paths between u and v

finally we obtain a Halin graph that is a wheel. (Wheels are easy to solve.) We shall then backtrace our steps, constructing an optimal tour in the original Halin graph.

In order to modify the lengths of the edges in the 3-edge custset, we need only solve a system of three linear equations in three unknowns. Let (w, w'), (u, u'), (v, v') be the edges of the 3-edge cutset, with lengths $c_{ww'}$, $c_{uu'}$, $c_{vv'}$, respectively. These edges become (x, w'), (x, u'), (x, v') in the condensed graph H', with lengths $c_{xw'}$, $c_{xu'}$, $c_{xv'}$. Let $C^*(u, w)$, $C^*(v, w)$, $C^*(u, v)$ denote the lengths of shortest Hamiltonian paths in $C(w)$ between u, w, between v, w and between u, v. Then we have the system

$$c_{xw'} + c_{xu'} = c_{ww'} + c_{uu'} + C^*(u, w),$$

$$c_{xw'} + c_{xv'} = c_{ww'} + c_{vv'} + C^*(v, w),$$

$$c_{xu'} + c_{xv'} = c_{uu'} + c_{vv'} + C^*(u, v).$$

We now illustrate with a small example. Consider the Halin graph in Figure 4.27(a). In order to condense the fan whose center is w_1 into a single

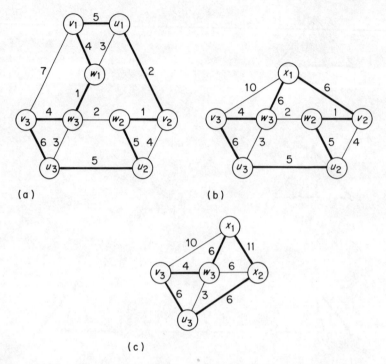

Figure 4.27   Solution of TSP for Halin graph

node x_1, we must solve the equations:

$$c_{x_1 w_3} + c_{x_1 v_2} = c_{w_1 w_3} + c_{u_1 v_2} + C^*(u_1, w_1)$$
$$= 1 + 2 + 9$$
$$= 12,$$

$$c_{x_1 w_3} + c_{x_1 v_3} = c_{w_1 w_3} + c_{v_1 v_3} + C^*(v_1, w_1)$$
$$= 1 + 7 + 8$$
$$= 16,$$

$$c_{x_1 v_2} + c_{x_1 v_3} = c_{u_1 v_2} + c_{v_1 v_3} + C^*(u_1, v_1)$$
$$= 2 + 7 + 7$$
$$= 16.$$

This yields the solution

$$c_{x_1 w_3} = 6,$$
$$c_{x_1 v_2} = 6,$$
$$c_{x_1 v_3} = 10,$$

and the network shown in Figure 4.27(b). Carrying the process one step further, we obtain the wheel shown in Figure 4.27(c) which has a shortest tour as shown by **wiggly** lines. This implies that the tour shown in Figure 4.27(b) is optimal and that in turn implies that the tour shown in Figure 4.27(a) is optimal.

Cornuéjols, Naddef & Pulleyblank [1985] have also given an explicit description of the traveling salesman polytope for a Halin graph.

Exercise
38. Consider the generalization of Halin graphs in which nonleaf nodes may have degree 2. Show how the TSP for such graphs can be solved by the approach described here.

18   CONCLUSION

In this chapter we have shown that a number of special cases of the TSP can indeed be easily solved. Among these cases are the constant TSP, the upper triangular TSP, the small TSP, the Demidenko TSP, the bottleneck TSP for graded matrices, the Gilmore–Gomory TSP, the bandwidth-limited TSP, and the TSP for reducible networks and Halin graphs. Many of our results were obtained through subtour patching and we have indicated some basic theory of this technique.

We have noted some interesting demarcations between easy problems and hard problems. The ordinary TSP is $\mathcal{NP}$-hard for graded matrices, whereas the bottleneck TSP is easy. The TSP is $\mathcal{NP}$-hard for asymmetric product matrices but easy for symmetric ones. It is easy to find a shortest Hamiltonian path for circulants, but there is not much we can say about the TSP for these matrices.

We hope that at least a few of the special cases dealt with in this chapter may have direct practical application. We believe, however, that in the long run the greatest importance of these special cases will be for approximation algorithms. Much remains to be done in this area.

The Traveling Salesman Problem
Edited by E. L. Lawler, J. K. Lenstra,
A. H. G. Rinnooy Kan, D. B. Shmoys
© 1985 John Wiley & Sons Ltd.

5

Performance guarantees for heuristics

D. S. Johnson
AT&T Bell Laboratories, Murray Hill

C. H. Papadimitriou
Stanford University; National Technical University of Athens

1 INTRODUCTION

The $\mathcal{NP}$-hardness of the traveling salesman problem, as discussed in Chapter 3, makes it unlikely that any efficient algorithm can be guaranteed to find optimal tours when the number of cities is large. There is thus a trade-off: we can have an algorithm that runs quickly, or one that finds optimal tours, but not one that does both simultaneously. Given this choice, practitioners usually opt for the former. They design efficient 'heuristic' algorithms that, while not guaranteed to find optimal tours, do find what one hopes are 'near-optimal' tours.

In this chapter we shall examine some of these heuristics, and discuss one approach toward making our 'hopes' for near-optimality more concrete. This approach involves proving 'performance guarantees': bounds on how far from optimal the constructed tour can be in the worst case. The following two chapters will consider two other approaches to the analysis of heuristics: probabilistic analysis and empirical testing. All three approaches are attempts to provide the prospective user of a heuristic algorithm with information that will help in answering the question 'How well will the algorithm perform (how near to optimal will be the tours it constructs) on the problem instances to which I intend to apply it?'

Each approach has its advantages and its drawbacks. Empirical analysis can be the most appropriate if the test problems on which it is based include or mirror instances currently under consideration. It can be quite misleading if care is not taken in the choice of test problems, or if the test problems chosen have very different characteristics from those at hand. Probabilistic (or average-case) analysis can tell us a lot, especially when we will be applying the algorithm to many instances having similar characteristics. However, by its nature, this type of analysis must make assumptions about the probability distribution on the class of instances, and if these assumptions are not appropriate, then the results of the analysis may not be germane to the instances at hand. Furthermore, probabilistic analysis cannot say anything definite about the performance of an algorithm on a *particular* instance, since any particular instance may be quite atypical.

Worst-case analysis, on the other hand, can provide guarantees that do hold for individual instances, and does not involve the assumption, implicit or explicit, of any probability distribution. The drawback here is of course that, since the guarantee must hold for all instances, even ones that may be quite atypical and pathological, there may be a considerable discrepancy between the behavior of an algorithm 'in practice' and the best performance guarantee that we can prove for it. As we shall see, one way to limit this drawback is to perform our worst-case analysis over classes of instances which, although they include the instances at hand, are restricted in such a way as to eliminate some of the worst pathologies.

A final problem with both probabilistic and worst-case analysis of heuristics comes from the rigorous nature of both approaches. Analyzing a heuristic in either way can be a very challenging mathematical task. Heuristics that yield nice probabilistic bounds may be inappropriate for worst-case analysis, and heuristics that behave well in the worst case are often exceedingly difficult to analyze probabilistically. In addition, many heuristics (including quite successful ones, such as that of Lin & Kernighan [1973]) do not seem to be susceptible to *either* type of analysis.

Nevertheless, a significant group of heuristics *have* proved analyzable, and in this chapter we shall survey the results that have been derived using the worst-case approach. These results for the most part concern the *symmetric* TSP, and so in what follows we shall assume a restriction to instances with symmetric distance matrices unless the asymmetric case is mentioned explicitly. In Section 2 we discuss the possibility of polynomial-time heuristics that provide good guarantees for *all* (symmetric) TSP instances, and show that this can only happen in the unlikely event that $\mathcal{P} = \mathcal{NP}$. In Section 3 we show that the situation is much better in the case where distances obey the triangle inequality. We examine a number of algorithms which find tours whose lengths are guaranteed to be at most twice optimal under this restriction, and one algorithm with an even better guarantee. Even here, however, there are still limits on our ability to find good approximations, and we discuss these in Section 4. Section 5 concludes our discussion of the symmetric TSP by mentioning an interesting result for the case when the distance function is Euclidean and all the cities lie in a unit square. In Section 6 we turn to a survey of performance guarantees for problems related to the TSP, such as the *k-traveling salesman problem*, the *stacker crane problem* and the *Chinese postman problem*. We conclude in Section 7 with a brief guide to the literature on the performance guarantee approach and the other kinds of combinatorial optimization problems to which it applies.

2 THE COMPLEXITY OF FINDING NEAR-OPTIMAL TOURS

2.1 General results

The first results we shall present concern the (symmetric) TSP when *no* restrictions are imposed. If A is a heuristic algorithm for the TSP and I is an instance of that problem, let A(I) be the length of the tour produced by A when it is applied to I, and let OPT(I) be the length of an optimum tour.

Theorem 1 [Sahni & Gonzalez, 1976] *Suppose there is a polynomial-time heuristic A for the TSP and a constant r, $1 \leq r < \infty$, such that for all instances I,*

$$A(I) \leq r \, \text{OPT}(I).$$

Then $\mathcal{P} = \mathcal{NP}$.

Proof We show that if such a heuristic existed, it could be used to solve the $\mathcal{NP}$-complete HAMILTONIAN CYCLE problem in polynomial time, thus implying that $\mathcal{P} = \mathcal{NP}$ by the arguments in Chapter 3. So suppose we are given a graph $G = (V, E)$ and we wish to know whether it has a Hamiltonian cycle. We will answer this question by constructing a corresponding instance I of the TSP and applying algorithm A to it.

Let the vertices of V be $1, 2, \ldots, n$, where $n \geq 2$. Our instance will have the vertices as cities, with a distance matrix defined as follows:

$$c_{ij} = \begin{cases} 1, & \text{if } \{v_i, v_j\} \in E, \\ rn, & \text{otherwise.} \end{cases}$$

Observe that if G has a Hamiltonian cycle C, then I has a tour of length n: merely traverse the cities in the order that the corresponding vertices of G are traversed in C. The edges of the tour all correspond to edges of G and hence each has length 1, for a total of n. Thus if A is applied to I in this case, it must yield a tour of length rn or less.

On the other hand, suppose G has *no* Hamiltonian cycle. Then any tour for I must contain at least one edge that does not correspond to an edge of G, and hence must have total length at least $rn + n - 1$. Thus if A is applied to I in this case, it must yield a tour of at least length $rn + 1$ (since $n \geqslant 2$).

This gives us our method for testing if G has a Hamiltonian cycle: Construct I and apply A to it. If $A(I) \leqslant rn$, then G has a Hamiltonian cycle. Otherwise, it does not.

Since I can be constructed in polynomial time if we are given G, and A is assumed to be a polynomial-time algorithm, the above testing procedure itself runs in polynomial time, as claimed, and the theorem is proved. □

In the light of Theorem 1, we see that no polynomial-time heuristic can hope to provide meaningful guarantees that apply to *all* instances of the TSP, except in the unlikely event that $\mathscr{P} = \mathscr{NP}$. (Moreover, if $\mathscr{P} = \mathscr{NP}$ then, as shown in Chapter 3, *optimal* traveling salesman tours could be found in polynomial time, and we probably would not be studying heuristics.)

2.2 Complexity of local search algorithms

There is a sense in which the situation with respect to the general TSP is actually a bit *worse* than is indicated by Theorem 1. Let us consider a widely used type of heuristic algorithm: *local search*. Algorithms of this type are discussed extensively by Papadimitriou & Steiglitz [1982]; we shall settle for a quick summary here. A local search algorithm is built around a 'neighborhood search procedure,' which, given a tour, examines all tours which are closely related to it and finds a shorter such 'neighboring' tour, if one exists. The definition of 'closely related' varies with the details of the particular local search heuristic. The particularly successful heuristic described by Lin & Kernighan [1973] defines the 'neighbors' of a tour to be those tours which can be obtained from it by doing a limited number of interchanges of tour edges with non-tour edges, as in Figure 5.1.

The overall process goes as follows. We start with some initial tour, chosen arbitrarily or generated by some other heuristic. If there is no neighboring tour which is shorter than our original tour, we halt with a tour which is at least a 'local' optimum. Otherwise, we use a shorter neighbor of our original tour as a new starting point, and repeat the procedure, looking for a better neighbor of this new tour. This process must eventually halt as there is only a finite number of possible tours.

The running time of a local search heuristic depends both on the amount of time needed for an application of the neighborhood search procedure and on the number of iterations that may be required (the number of times a tour can be improved before a local optimum is reached). By Theorem 1 we know that if a local search algorithm is to provide reasonable guarantees,

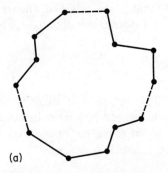
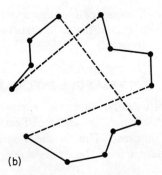

(a)   (b)

Figure 5.1 Example of the type of interchange that is used in the Lin–
Kernighan algorithm to construct 'neighboring' tours. A 'k-interchange'
involves the deletion and replacement of k edges. The Lin–Kernighan
algorithm uses a sophisticated method for choosing the value of k to be used
at any given time in the search. (a) Initial tour. (b) Tour that could be
obtained by a 3-interchange

one of these two factors must be exponential (assuming $\mathscr{P} \neq \mathscr{NP}$). However,
the following stronger statement can be made.

Theorem 2 [Papadimitriou & Steiglitz, 1977] *If* A *is a local search algorithm whose neighborhood search time is bounded by a polynomial, then,
assuming* $\mathscr{P} \neq \mathscr{NP}$, A *cannot be guaranteed to find a tour whose length is
bounded by a constant multiple of the optimal tour length, even if an
exponential number of iterations is allowed.*

Proof See Exercise 1. □

Even if neighborhoods requiring exponential search time are allowed,
local search algorithms based on interchange techniques can still get into
trouble. Papadimitriou & Steiglitz [1978] have constructed instances
where the second-best tour length is an arbitrary multiple of the optimal
length, and yet no second-best tour can be improved without interchanging
at least $3n/8$ edges (given a tour, there are an exponential number of
potential interchanges of this sort). Furthermore, there are an exponential
number of these 'second-best' tours, whereas there is only one optimal tour.
Thus, not only is it *possible* for a local search heuristic to get trapped far
from the optimal solution, it is almost unavoidable.

Exercise
1 [Proof of Theorem 2]. Suppose that A is an algorithm for the general TSP
that uses a polynomial-time heuristic to generate an initial tour, and then
attempts to improve the tour by local search using a polynomial-time
neighborhood search procedure. Show that there cannot be any constant
$r < \infty$ such that

$$A(I) \leqslant r \, OPT(I)$$

for all instances I, unless $\mathcal{P} = \mathcal{NP}$. (*Hint*: Note that in the proof of Theorem 1, the TSP instance constructed has at most $n + 1$ distinct possible values for tour lengths.)

3   THE TRIANGLE INEQUALITY

Fortunately, there is a restriction on the TSP which will exclude the pathological instances of Section 2, while leaving untouched most instances of interest. This is the restriction on the distance matrix introduced in Chapter 2 as the *triangle inequality*: For all i, j, $k \in \{1, 2, \ldots, n\}$,

$$c_{ik} \le c_{ij} + c_{jk}.$$

In other words, the shortest distance between two points (cities) is a straight line (direct route).

The triangle inequality is obeyed in geometric versions of the TSP (where cities correspond to points in a metric space and distances are computed according to the space's metric, be it Euclidean, rectilinear, or whatever). It also will hold in any version of the problem where distances correspond to the lengths of shortest paths in some graph. Indeed, it is safe to say that a substantial majority of the versions of the TSP encountered in practice obey this restriction for one reason or another.

Nevertheless, the triangle inequality provides a substantial restriction on the types of instances that must be dealt with by our worst-case analysis. For instance, it is easy to see that the instance constructed in the proof of Theorem 1 will fail to obey it in most cases. However, even with this restriction we must still take care in designing our heuristics.

3.1   Nearest neighbor algorithm

Consider the following simpleminded and appealing method for constructing a tour:

1. Start with a partial tour consisting of a single, arbitrarily chosen city a_1.
2. If the current partial tour is $a_1, \ldots, a_k$, $k < n$, let a_{k+1} be the city, not currently on the tour, which is closest to a_k, and add a_{k+1} to the end of the tour.
3. Halt when the current tour contains all the cities.

One obvious drawback of this algorithm is the fact that, although all earlier edges are in a sense 'minimal,' the final edge $\{a_n, a_1\}$ may be quite long. However, as a consequence of the triangle inequality, it can be no more than the total length of the rest of the tour, and hence one might still hope for some meaningful bound on the length of the overall tour. Unfortunately, by being 'greedy' at every step along the way, the nearest neighbor algorithm can get into trouble well before its last edge, with unpleasantly cumulative consequences. Let $\text{NN}(I)$ stand for the length of the tour constructed. Then we have the following result [Rosenkrantz, Stearns & Lewis, 1977].

Theorem 3 *For every $r > 1$ there exist n-city instances of the TSP, for arbitrarily large n, obeying the triangle inequality and such that*

$$NN(I) \geq r\,OPT(I).$$

Proof We use a modification of a construction presented by Rosenkrantz, Stearns & Lewis [1977]. For each $i > 0$ we construct an instance F_i for which the nearest neighbor algorithm performs poorly, finding a tour whose length is at least $(i+2)/6$ times the optimum length. Note that this ratio becomes arbitrarily large as i approaches ∞. The instances F_i are constructed recursively. F_1 is shown in Figure 5.2(a). As with all the subsequent F_i's, F_1 has three distinguished vertices (in the case of F_1, that's all it has): a left endpoint A, a midpoint B, and a right endpoint C. F_2 and F_3 are shown in Figure 5.2(b). The instance F_i, $i > 1$, is constructed from two copies of F_{i-1}, together with three additional cities, as shown in Figure 5.2(c). City E is the midpoint of F_i, and cities A and C' are the left and right endpoints, respectively. Note that only certain of the distances c_{ij} are specified in the figure. If c_{ij} is not specified in the figure, then it is taken to be the length of the shortest path between cities i and j along edges whose lengths *are* specified. This choice of lengths will guarantee that the triangle inequality is

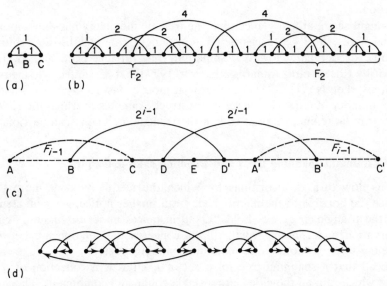

Figure 5.2 Examples used in Theorem 3 to prove lower bounds on the worst case behavior of the nearest neighbor algorithm. (a) F_1. (b) F_3: number of cities $= 21$. (c) Recursive construction of F_i, $i > 1$. F_i contains $3(2^i - 1)$ cities. (d) Tour found by nearest neighbor algorithm when applied to F_3. Length $= (i+2)2^i - 3 = 37$

satisfied (so long as the lengths of edges $\{B, D'\}$ and $\{B', D\}$ satisfy it, which is an exercise left to the reader (Exercise 3)).

It is an easy induction to show the number of cities in F_i is $3(2^i - 1)$. One possible tour would be to traverse the cities in order, from left to right, and then return directly to the starting point, and so we have $\mathrm{OPT}(I) \leqslant 6(2^i) - 8$. On the other hand, the nearest neighbor algorithm might, given a particularly inauspicious sequence of choices when confronted with 'ties' between potential nearest neighbors, find a tour of length $(i+2)2^i - 3$, as illustrated in Figure 5.2(d) for F_3. This tour consists of a Hamiltonian path of length $(i+1)2^i - 2$ from the left endpoint of F_i to its midpoint, plus a final edge back to the left endpoint, of length $2^i - 1$. The Hamiltonian path is constructed recursively, by first taking the path for the left copy of F_{i-1}, then jumping from the midpoint of that F_{i-1} to city D' of F_i, proceeding to the left endpoint of the right copy of F_{i-1}, following *its* bad Hamiltonian path to its midpoint, then jumping to D and taking a final edge to get to the midpoint E of F_i. We leave it to the reader to verify that this tour *could*, in fact, be generated by the nearest neighbor algorithm. $\square$

Note that, although for simplicity we have presented a collection of examples in which ties must be broken in unfortunate ways in order for the nearest neighbor algorithm to construct a bad tour, examples *can* be constructed (by appropriate minor modifications of the edge lengths) in which the bad tour is generated without ever encountering a tie-breaking situation.

It might seem, at first glance, that the triangle inequality has done nothing for us here, since the constructed tour length can still be an arbitrary multiple of optimal. However, something has, in fact been gained. It is shown by Rosenkrantz, Stearns & Lewis [1977] that, if the triangle inequality holds, then $\mathrm{NN}(I)/\mathrm{OPT}(I)$ can grow at most as fast as $O(\log n)$, where n is the number of cities. It is easy to construct examples in which the ratio is arbitrarily large, independent of n, if the triangle inequality can be violated.

3.2   Minimum spanning trees and traveling salesman tours

Let us now turn to algorithms for which the inequality does more than reduce the horrible to the merely bad. Until further notice, we shall assume that the triangle inequality holds for all instances under discussion. A key observation underpinning what follows concerns the relationship between traveling salesman tours and minimum spanning trees.

Recall that a spanning tree for a set of n cities is a collection of $n-1$ edges which join all the cities into a single connected component. There are a variety of low-order polynomial-time algorithms for constructing a spanning tree of minimum possible length, (e.g., see Aho, Hopcroft & Ullman [1974]). When the input is given in the form of the distance matrix C, the minimum spanning tree can be found in time $O(n^2)$, which is about the best one could hope for, since C is of size proportional to n^2 itself. Thus the minimum spanning tree problem, unlike the TSP, can be solved quite efficiently.

Moreover, this solution provides an immediate lower bound on the optimal tour length: Observe that deleting any edge from a tour yields a spanning tree consisting of a single path through all the cities. Thus the optimal traveling salesman tour must be strictly longer than the minimum spanning tree. We shall now see how the triangle inequality allows us to use the minimum spanning tree to obtain an *upper* bound on the optimal tour length as well.

Suppose we wished to visit all the cities, but were only allowed to use edges of the minimum spanning tree. See Figures 5.3(a) and 5.3(b). One approach we could use would be to start at a 'leaf' of the tree (vertex of degree 1), and apply the following strategy: If there is any untraversed edge leaving the current vertex, follow that edge to a new vertex. If all the edges from the current vertex have been traversed, go back along the edge by which the current vertex was first reached to the vertex from which it was visited. Halt when we eventually return to our starting vertex.

Those who are familiar with graph algorithms will recognize the above procedure as the well-known *depth first* traversal of the minimum spanning tree. It is not difficult to verify that it will indeed visit all the vertices (cities), and moreover that it will traverse no edge of the minimum spanning tree more than twice. It thus provides a route for visiting all the cities that has length no more than twice that of the minimum spanning tree, and hence, by

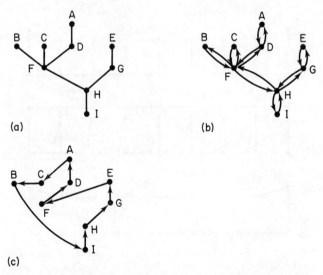

Figure 5.3   Using a minimum spanning tree to generate a tour. (a) A minimum spanning tree T. (b) Depth first transversal of T: IHGEGHFDADFCFBFHI. (c) Depth first traversal of T with 'shortcuts': IHGEFDACBI

the above remarks about lower bounds, at most twice the length of the optimum traveling salesman tour.

The only thing that prevents this traversal from being a traveling salesman tour is the fact that it may visit some cities more than once. Here is where the triangle inequality helps us. We can avoid repeated cities by introducing 'shortcuts' that do not increase the total length of the traversal.

Start, as before, at a leaf of the minimum spanning tree. However, whenever the depth first traversal would take us back to an already-visited city, skip ahead in the traversal and go directly to the next as-yet-unvisited city. (The direct route can be no longer than the previous indirect one.) If all cities have been visited, go back to the starting point. See Figure 5.3(c). We have now constructed an actual tour (it visits no city except the starting point more than once), and because its length is no more than that of the original depth first traversal, this tour has length at most twice that of the optimal tour.

We thus have a polynomial-time algorithm which obeys a quite reasonable performance guarantee (at least in comparison to the results we have seen so far in this chapter). The algorithm, which we shall call the *minimum*

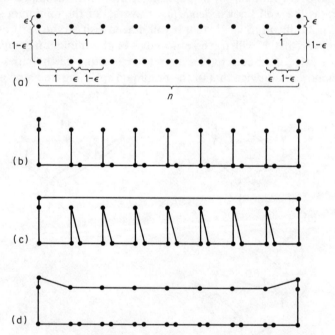

Figure 5.4 Examples of instances I of the Euclidean TSP where $\text{MST}(I)/\text{OPT}(I)$ approaches 2 (for ε small and n large). (a) Instance of Euclidean TSP. (b) Minimum spanning tree. Length $= n + (n+1)(1-\varepsilon) + 2\varepsilon$. (c) Doubled spanning tree tour, with shortcuts. Length $\sim 2n + 2n(1-\varepsilon)$. (d) Optimal tour. Length $\sim 2n + 2$

spanning tree algorithm, runs in overall time $O(n^2)$, as can be seen from the following summary:

1. Find a minimum spanning tree T for the given set of cities – $O(n^2)$.
2. Construct a depth first traversal of T – $O(n)$.
3. Introduce shortcuts into the depth first traversal to obtain a tour – $O(n)$.

Our above arguments yield the following often-rediscovered theorem,

Theorem 4 [Folklore]   *For all TSP instances I that obey the triangle inequality, if MST(I) is the length of the tour constructed by the minimum spanning tree algorithm applied to I, then*

$$\text{MST}(I) \leqslant 2 \, \text{OPT}(I).$$

That this is in fact the best such guarantee possible follows from the examples shown in Figure 5.4. Here we have instances for which $\text{MST}(I) = 2n - 1$ even though $\text{OPT}(I) = n$. Note that not only do the distances obey the triangle inequality, they are actually the Euclidean distances between points in the plane.

3.3   Variants on the minimum spanning tree algorithm

In this section we shall briefly describe four algorithms that have the same worst-case behavior as the minimum spanning tree algorithm. Although, at first glance, the algorithms look quite different (in fact more like the abysmal nearest neighbor algorithm of Section 2.1 than like the minimum spanning tree algorithm), the proofs of their performance guarantees hinge on basically the same arguments as were presented in the previous section. In essence, each of these algorithms corresponds to a method for generating a minimum spanning tree. For each edge added by the spanning tree algorithm to its partial spanning tree, the corresponding TSP algorithm adds a pair of edges to its partial tour(s) whose total length is at most twice that of the spanning tree edge. We shall leave the details of the proofs for Exercises 4 and 5, and concentrate on describing and comparing the algorithms themselves.

First, let us introduce some basic terminology, borrowed from Rosenkrantz, Stearns & Lewis [1977], who first presented these results. Suppose T is a partial tour (viewed as a set of edges) and k is a city not on T. Let $\text{TOUR}(T, k)$ be the partial tour obtained by *inserting* k into T as follows:

1. If T passes through a single city i, then $\text{TOUR}(T, k)$ is the two-city tour consisting of the edges $\{i, k\}$ and $\{k, i\}$.
2. If T passes through more than one city, let $\{i, j\}$ be the edge of T which minimizes $c_{ik} + c_{kj} - c_{ij}$, and construct $\text{TOUR}(T, k)$ by deleting edge $\{i, j\}$ and adding edges $\{i, k\}$ and $\{k, j\}$.

Define $\text{COST}(T, k)$ to be the length of $\text{TOUR}(T, k)$ minus the length of T.

The first of the algorithms is called the *nearest merger algorithm*. It starts with n partial tours, each consisting of a single city, and successively merges the tours until a single tour containing all the cities is obtained. If the current number of tours exceeds one, the tours T, T' that should next be merged are chosen so that $\min\{c_{ij} : i \in T$ and $j \in T'\}$ is as small as possible. The merging procedure goes as follows.

If T consists of a single city k, the merged tour is TOUR(T', k). If T' consists of a single city k', the merged tour is TOUR(T, k'). If both T and T' contain at least two cities, let i, j, k and l be cities such that $\{i, j\}$ is an edge of T and $\{k, l\}$ is an edge of T', and

$$c_{ik} + c_{jl} - c_{ij} - c_{kl}$$

is minimized. The merged tour is then obtained by deleting $\{i, j\}$ and $\{k, l\}$, and replacing them with $\{i, k\}$ and $\{j, l\}$. See Figure 5.5 for an illustration of the nearest merger algorithm in action.

The nearest merger algorithm corresponds to the well-known algorithm for generating minimum spanning trees due to Kruskal [1956]. The remaining three algorithms correspond to a minimum spanning tree algorithm presented by Prim [1957]. These three algorithms are superficially similar to the nearest neighbor algorithm of Section 3.1, although they are 'greedy' in a much more sophisticated manner. We will present them in order of increasing greed (where 'greed' indicates the extent to which the length of the new partial subtour is minimized at each step).

The least greedy of these algorithms, illustrated in Figure 5.6, is the

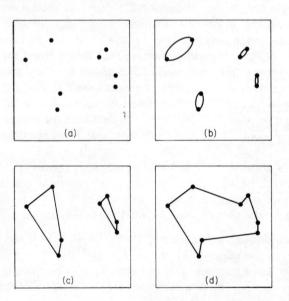

Figure 5.5 Snapshots of the nearest merger
algorithm in action

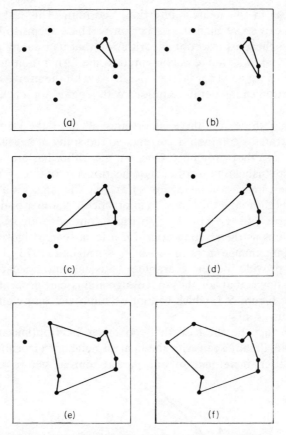

Figure 5.6   Snapshots of the nearest addition
algorithm in action

nearest addition algorithm:

Step 1.   Start with a partial tour consisting of a single, arbitrarily chosen city
i.

Step 2.   If the current partial tour T does not include all the cities, find those
cities k and j, j on the tour and k not, for which c_{kj} is minimized.

Step 3.   Let $\{i, j\}$ be either one of the two edges involving j in T, and replace
it by $\{i, k\}$ and $\{k, j\}$ to obtain a new tour including k.

The *nearest insertion algorithm* 'improves' on this slightly. It chooses k as
in Step 2 above, but instead of just putting k next to j, it finds the *best* place
to insert it. This is accomplished by letting the new partial tour be
TOUR(T, k).

Finally, the *cheapest insertion algorithm* makes the further (local) optimization of choosing k in Step 2 to be the city not on T which minimizes
COST(T, k) over all such cities, and then letting the new partial tour be

TOUR(T, k) as in the nearest insertion algorithm. This last optimization may be more expensive than the earlier ones. There seems to be no way to implement the cheapest insertion algorithm so that its running time is better than proportional to $n^2 \log n$, as compared to the $O(n^2)$ running times of the other algorithms we have considered so far. As with the previous algorithms, cheapest insertion can generate solutions with lengths approaching twice the optimal length.

The fact that these last three algorithms all have the same worst-case behavior illustrates a common occurrence in the study of heuristics, both for the TSP and for other problems. Once an algorithm has attained a certain threshold of sophistication, further modifications to 'optimize' it, even quite expensive ones, may not have any effect on the algorithm's worst-case behavior (helpful though they may be in practice). Another optimization one might be tempted to try would be to use a tour generated by one of the above algorithms as the starting point for a local search algorithm, perhaps by using the interchange method of Lin & Kernighan [1973]. However, this too fails to provide better guarantees. Rosenkrantz, Stearns & Lewis [1977] have shown that all the above algorithms can generate the length $2n - 1$ tour in Figure 5.7, which cannot be improved on by any number of interchanges up to $n/4$.

It might, in fact, be the case that too much local optimization is a bad thing. We have already seen with the nearest neighbor algorithm that trying to minimize each increment to our partial tour as we go along can be

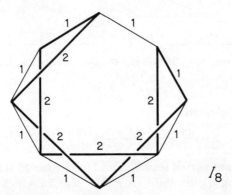

Figure 5.7 Example of an instance I_n, n even, such that I_n obeys the triangle inequality (when distances correspond to shortest paths along the edges shown in the figure), $\text{OPT}(I) = n$, and each of the four algorithms (nearest merger, nearest addition, nearest insertion, cheapest insertion) can, given appropriately bad choices when breaking ties, generate a tour of length $2n - 1$ (here shown by darker lines). This tour cannot be improved by any k-interchange, $k \leq n/4$

counterproductive. The above 'insertion' algorithms seem to avoid this difficulty, by using a different type of increment. However, consider the variant on our insertion algorithms that, instead of choosing the best city to insert next, chooses a city which is in a sense the *worst* candidate. The *farthest insertion algorithm* differs from nearest insertion in that the city chosen in Step 2 is the one which is *farthest* from the current partial tour T, i.e., that city k, not on T, which *maximizes* $\min\{c_{jk} : j \text{ is on } T\}$. Once we have chosen k we resume being greedy, and add it to the current tour in the best place it will fit, i.e., as in nearest insertion the next tour becomes $\text{TOUR}(T, k)$.

Although farthest insertion chooses the locally worst city to insert, rather than the best, there are reasons for thinking that this might not be a bad idea. The farthest cities must eventually be linked into the tour anyway; by putting them in first we establish an outline for the overall shape of the tour, which is then refined by adding in the cities which are close enough so that their addition does not have so major an effect on the overall tour length. As evidence, we observe that farthest insertion will actually construct optimal tours for the examples in Figures 5.4 and 5.7 which gave the other algorithms so much trouble. It was also the champion in limited empirical tests reported by Rosenkrantz, Stearns & Lewis [1977], who generated instances by randomly choosing points in the unit square and using Euclidean distance. (This is an interesting type of instance, about which we will have more to say in Section 5).

However, farthest insertion seems to be more difficult to analyze than the other insertion algorithms. It can be shown to generate tours which approach 3/2 times the optimal tour length, but new techniques will be required for determining what the actual upper bound is, since farthest insertion does not correspond in any direct way to an algorithm for generating minimum spanning trees.

In the next section we shall present an algorithm that can be *proved* to guarantee a tour length no more than 3/2 times the optimal length.

3.4 Christofides' algorithm

The algorithms presented in the last two sections (farthest insertion excepted) did not involve any substantial insights beyond the fact that a traveling salesman tour can be obtained by doubling a minimum spanning tree, in one way or another. Thus it is perhaps not surprising that they all had the same worst-case behaviors. If we are to improve on the 'factor of two' guarantee, we will need a new way of looking at things. This is provided by the concept of an *Eulerian graph*.

An Eulerian graph is a connected graph in which every vertex has even degree. It is not a difficult exercise to show that Eulerian graphs are precisely those graphs that contain an *Eulerian tour*, i.e., a cycle that passes through every edge exactly once. Moreover, given an Eulerian graph, such a tour can be found in $O(n)$ time using techniques from Aho, Hopcroft & Ullman [1974, Chapter 5]. Suppose we had an Eulerian graph with the cities of a TSP instance as its vertices. Then we could use the Eulerian tour for this graph to obtain a traveling salesman tour, merely by using the 'shortcut' technique of Section 3.3. In fact, the minimum spanning tree algorithm can be reinterpreted in precisely these terms.

We start with a minimum spanning tree, double its edges in order to obtain an Eulerian graph, find an Eulerian tour for this graph, and then convert it to a traveling salesman tour by using shortcuts. By the triangle inequality the traveling salesman tour can be no longer than the Eulerian tour and hence at most twice the length of a minimum spanning tree.

This suggests that if we want to find better traveling salesman tours, all we need is a better way of generating an Eulerian graph connecting the cities. (We cannot hope to find the *best* Eulerian graph. By the triangle inequality, a minimum length Eulerian graph that connects all the cities must have the same length as the minimum traveling salesman tour, and so its determination must be just as hard as the TSP itself.) The currently best method for generating such an Eulerian graph is due to Christofides [1976] and involves the concept of a *minimum weight matching*.

Given a set containing an even number of cities, a *matching* is a collection of edges M such that each city is the endpoint of exactly one edge in M. A *minimum weight* matching is one for which the total length of the edges is minimum. Such matchings can be found in time $O(n^3)$ (e.g., see Lawler [1976] or Papadimitriou & Steiglitz [1982]).

How do matchings come into the picture? Let us look once again at a minimum spanning tree T for a TSP instance. Certain of the vertices in T already have even degree and hence do not have to receive more edges if we wish to turn the tree into an Eulerian graph. The only vertices we need worry about are the ones with odd degree. Note further that there must be an even number of these odd-degree vertices, since the sum of all vertex degrees must be even (it counts each edge exactly twice). Thus one way to construct an Eulerian graph which includes T would be simply to add a matching for the odd-degree vertices (cities). See Figure 5.8. This would increase the degree of each odd-degree vertex by one, while leaving the even-degree vertices alone. It is not difficult to show that, if we add to T a *minimum weight* matching for its odd-degree vertices, we will obtain an Eulerian graph that has minimum length among those that contain T.

How long is this Eulerian graph? Consider Figure 5.9. This shows a traveling salesman tour, with the cities that correspond to odd-degree vertices in T emphasized. The tour determines two matchings M and M', indicated respectively by the bold and wavy lines in the figure. Let I denote the given TSP instance, and let LENGTH(T), LENGTH(M) and LENGTH(M') denote the sums of the edge lengths for T, M and M', respectively. By the triangle inequality, we must have

$$\text{LENGTH}(M) + \text{LENGTH}(M') \leq \text{OPT}(I),$$

so one of M and M' must have length less than or equal to OPT(I)/2. Thus

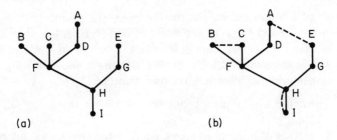

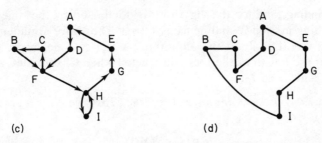

Figure 5.8   Snapshots of Christofides' algorithm in action.
(a) Minimum spanning tree *T*. (b) *T* plus a minimum cost
matching of its odd-degree vertices. (c) Euler tour of (b):
IHGEADFCBFHI. (d) Tour constructed by Christofides'
algorithm, using shortcuts: IHGEADFCBI

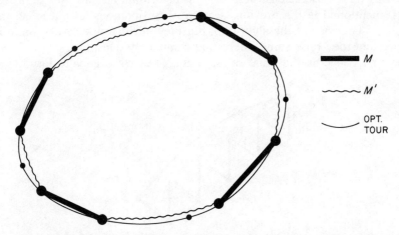

Figure 5.9   The two matchings induced by an optimal tour. The vertices
in the matchings are the odd-degree vertices in a minimum spanning
tree. By the triangle inequality, each matching edge is no longer than the
corresponding segment of the optimal tour, and so LENGTH(M)+
LENGTH(M') ⩽ OPT(I)

the length of a minimum weight matching for the odd-degree vertices of T must also be at most OPT(I)/2. Since LENGTH(T) is less than OPT(I), as argued in Section 3.3, we conclude that the length of the Eulerian graph constructed is at most (3/2)OPT(I). We thus have the following algorithm, named *Christofides' algorithm* after its inventor:

Step 1. Construct a minimum spanning tree T on the set of all cities in I $- O(n^2)$.

Step 2. Construct a minimum matching M^* for the set of all odd-degree vertices in $T - O(n^3)$.

Step 3. Find an Eulerian tour for the Eulerian graph that is the union of T and M^*, and convert it to a tour using shortcuts $- O(n)$.

The running time for the algorithm is dominated by the time for finding the matching in Step 2, and hence is $O(n^3)$. The above arguments yield the following theorem about the algorithm's worst-case behavior, where $C(I)$ stands for the length of the tour constructed when Christofides' algorithm is applied to instance I.

Theorem 5 *For any instance I of the TSP which obeys the triangle inequality,*

$$C(I) < \tfrac{3}{2}\text{OPT}(I).$$

This is the best possible guarantee provable for Christofides' algorithm, even in the Euclidean case, as follows from examples due to Cornuéjols & Nemhauser [1978] and illustrated in Figure 5.10.

We conclude this section with a brief discussion of some methods for improving on the tours constructed by this algorithm. As with the 'improvements' mentioned in the previous section, these methods do not affect the worst-case behavior of the algorithm, but they might well be worthwhile in practice and they raise some interesting complexity questions.

The first concerns the issue of 'shortcuts'. As we originally introduced

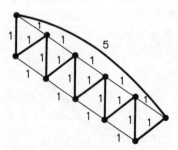

Figure 5.10 Example of an instance I of the Euclidean TSP for which $C(I) = \tfrac{3}{2}[\text{OPT}(I) - 1]$. In this case, OPT($I$) = 11 and $C(I) = 15$

them, the shortcuts taken in converting an Eulerian tour into a traveling salesman tour depended only on the city at which we chose to start. We only took shortcuts to bypass cities we had already encountered on our tour. However, a more general approach to shortcuts is possible. There is no reason why we must visit a city the first time it appears in the Eulerian tour and then bypass it each later time it appears. We only need insure that we visit it once. Thus we might, in order to obtain a shorter tour, bypass it the first two times it was encountered and then visit it on its third appearance. The question thus arises: How can we find the *best* way of making shortcuts to convert the Eulerian graph of the Christofides' algorithm into a traveling salesman tour? This turns out to be a question that was better left unasked: Papadimitriou & Vazirani [1984] have shown that the problem of finding the best set of shortcuts is $\mathcal{NP}$-hard.

The second issue concerns the question of *edge crossings*. This mainly arises in the two-dimensional Euclidean case (the idea of edges crossing is basically a planar notion), but since that is a quite common setting for the TSP, it is worth considering. It is possible for our algorithms to construct tours in which edges cross each other. It is easy to see that this can be suboptimal. See Figure 5.11. Edges {A, B} and {B, D} cross. If we were to delete them, then the tour could be reconnected by adding the pair of edges {A, B} and {C, D}. By the triangle inequality, this pair has total length no more than that of the original pair (with equality only if all four points are colinear). Thus we can remove the edge crossing without increasing the overall length of the tour.

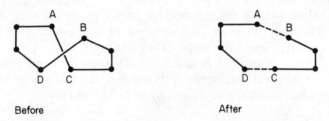

Before   After

Figure 5.11   An edge crossing in a tour and its removal

Unfortunately, in removing one edge crossing we might introduce a new one. One could envision an exponential sequence of minute improvements to our tour, each removing some crossings at the cost of creating new ones. The question thus arises: Is there a way to remove all the edge crossings in a tour in a reasonable amount of time, or is this also $\mathcal{NP}$-hard? In this case we are more fortunate. It can be shown by a clever argument presented by Van Leeuwen & Schoone [1985] that in fact the straightforward procedure of removing crossings, as above, must terminate in at most n^3 steps (for a hint, see Exercise 9). There are examples for which about n^2 steps are required.

Exercises

2. Let P be a path between cities i and j, involving one or more intermediate cities. Show that the triangle inequality implies that the length of P
is at least c_{ij}.

3. (a) Show that the instances F_i constructed in the proof of Theorem 3
obey the triangle inequality and have the claimed number of cities. (b) Show
that the nearest neighbor algorithm can produce the claimed tour, and that
this tour has the claimed length. (c) Show that the intercity distances in the
F_i can be modified by insignificant amounts so that the same tour is found
without any application of tie breaking rules (and the triangle inequality
continues to hold).

4. Prove that Theorem 4 holds when the minimum spanning tree algorithm
is replaced by the nearest merger algorithm. (*Hint*: Use the fact that
Kruskal's algorithm constructs a minimum spanning tree [Kruskal, 1956;
Aho, Hopcroft & Ullman, 1974, p. 174].)

5. Prove that Theorem 4 holds when the minimum spanning tree algorithm
is replaced by either the nearest addition, nearest insertion, or cheapest
insertion algorithm. (*Hint*: Use the fact that Prim's algorithm constructs a
minimum spanning tree [Prim, 1957].)

6. (a) Show that the farthest insertion algorithm can construct tours whose
lengths approach 3/2 times the optimal tour lengths. (b) Determine the
worst-case behavior of the farthest insertion algorithm. (*Hint*: Attempt part
(b) of this problem at your own risk, as it is currently still an open problem.)

7. Show that if an undirected graph has an Eulerian tour, it can be found in
polynomial time. Can you find the Eulerian tours in linear time?

8. Prove that finding the best set of shortcuts for Christofides' algorithm is
$\mathcal{NP}$-hard. (*Hint*: Modify the construction of Section 4.5 of Chapter 3.)

9. Prove that all crossings can be removed in n^3 steps from a traveling
salesman tour for cities in the plane. (*Hint*: For each edge, viewed as a line
segment, count the number of (infinite) lines that can be drawn through two
cities so as to intersect that segment. Show that the removal of a crossing
reduces the total count, for all edges, by at least one.)

4   APPROXIMATION SCHEMES

Christofides' algorithm provides the best guarantee (a ratio of 3/2) known
for any polynomial-time TSP heuristic when the only restriction on instances
is that they obey the triangle inequality. Even for instances where cities
correspond to points in the plane and the distance metric is Euclidean, the
Christofides' 3/2 guarantee is the best known. However, there may well exist
better, as yet undiscovered, algorithms for these types of instances. There
might even exist what is known as an *approximation scheme*.

An approximation scheme A for a problem is an algorithm which takes
two inputs: an instance I of the problem and an error bound $\varepsilon > 0$. It returns

a solution to the problem with value $A(I, \varepsilon)$ such that

$$\frac{|A(I, \varepsilon) - \text{OPT}(I)|}{\text{OPT}(I)} \leq \varepsilon. \tag{1}$$

Approximation scheme A will be especially appealing if it is what we call a *fully polynomial time approximation scheme*. Such a scheme is one whose running time is bounded by a function that is polynomial in both the instance size and $1/\varepsilon$. An example of a problem which has a fully polynomial time approximation scheme is the *knapsack problem*: Given a *knapsack capacity* C and a set $A = \{a_1, \ldots, a_n\}$ of items, each item a having an integer *size* $s(a)$ and value $v(a)$, find a subset $A' \subseteq A$ such that

$$\sum_{a \in A'} s(a) \leq C \quad \text{and} \quad \sum_{a \in A'} v(a) \text{ is maximized.}$$

This problem can be solved to within an error ratio of ε in time $O(n \log(1/\varepsilon) + (1/\varepsilon)^4)$ [Lawler, 1979]. (See also Ibarra & Kim [1976] and Garey & Johnson [1979].)

It would certainly be pleasant if such a fully polynomial time approximation existed for the TSP. We would then have a nice trade-off between the nearness to optimality we wished to guarantee, and the amount of time we were willing to spend in order to guarantee it. Unfortunately, the following theorem holds.

Theorem 6 *If $\mathcal{P} \neq \mathcal{NP}$ then there can be no fully polynomial time approximation scheme for the TSP, even if instances are restricted to points in the plane under the Euclidean metric.*

Proof Suppose A were such a scheme, and recall from Chapter 3 that the Euclidean TSP is $\mathcal{NP}$-complete even if all cities have integer coordinates, and we are asking if there is a tour of length n, where n is the number of cities. We shall show how A could be used to solve this Euclidean TSP problem in polynomial time.

Let I be an n-city instance. Note that if I does not have a tour of length n, it must have a tour of length at least $n - 1 + \sqrt{2}$, since the next shortest possible edge, after those of unit length, is $\sqrt{2}$. Since A is a fully polynomial time approximation scheme, its running time is bounded by $p(n, 1/\varepsilon)$ for some two-variable polynomial p. Suppose we were to set $\varepsilon = 1/(3n)$. Then the running time of A would be $p(n, 3n)$ and hence polynomial in n. Moreover, by the definition of approximation scheme, the solution returned by A must have a value $A(I)$ satisfying

$$\frac{A(I) - \text{OPT}(I)}{\text{OPT}(I)} \leq \frac{1}{3n}.$$

If a tour length n exists, this means that $A(I) \leq n + 1/3$. Otherwise, we must have $A(I) \geq \text{OPT}(I) \geq n - 1 + \sqrt{2} > n + 1/3$.

Thus, by one application of A with ε set to the value $1/(3n)$, we could tell in polynomial time whether or not I has a tour of length n. Since this would enable us to solve an $\mathcal{NP}$-complete problem in polynomial time, our claimed approximation scheme A cannot exist under the assumption that $\mathcal{P} \neq \mathcal{NP}$. $\square$

Although the possibility of a fully polynomial time approximation scheme is ruled out, there is still room (should we ever succeed in beating Christofides' algorithm) for an approximation scheme that, although it is not polynomial in $1/\varepsilon$, does have a running time which is polynomial in n for every *fixed* value of ε. Karp [1977] gives an example of what might be called a 'probabilistic' approximation scheme, for the case of the Euclidean TSP when all the points lie inside a unit square. This *adaptive dissection method* (cf. Chapter 6, Section 1) runs in time linear in n (though exponential in $1/\varepsilon$) and will guarantee that inequality (1) holds 'almost always'. This result can be recast into worst-case terms, but one comes up with a different form of 'guarantee' from the ratio-to-optimal guarantees we have discussed so far. We consider this different form of guarantee in the next section.

Exercise
10. (a) Show how to use 'dynamic programming' (as described in Chapter 3, Section 2.1), to solve the knapsack problem in time $O(nC)$, where n is the number of items and C is the knapsack capacity. (b) Design a fully polynomial time approximation scheme for the knapsack problem, based on your dynamic programming algorithm. (*Hint*: Note that if C is small, the above optimization algorithm is quite fast. The key idea is to replace instances with large values of C by instances with small values that 'approximate' them.)

5 THE TSP IN THE UNIT SQUARE

In this section we shall restrict attention to TSP instances in which all the cities lie within a square of unit width, and distances are measured using the Euclidean metric. See Figure 5.12. If we use $K(I, \varepsilon)$ to denote the length of

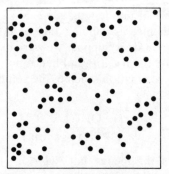

Figure 5.12 A unit square
containing n points

the tour found by the algorithm of Karp [1977] when the error bound is ε and the instance is I, we have the following result (see Chapter 6): For all instances I consisting of n cities and all $\varepsilon > 0$,

$$K(I, \varepsilon) \leq \mathrm{OPT}(I) + \varepsilon \sqrt{n}. \tag{2}$$

This is a *difference* rather than a ratio result. The bound has significance in the average case because, assuming the cities are uniformly distributed, the expected value of $\mathrm{OPT}(I)$ is proportional to $\sqrt{n}$. However, for some instances, e.g., those with $\mathrm{OPT}(I) = O(n^{1/4})$, the bound might not be very impressive at all. Nevertheless, there is a way of interpreting the above result that *does* provide a meaningful worst-case guarantee, if we are willing to consider what might be called *asymptotic* worst-case behavior.

For any $n > 0$, define

$$R_{\mathrm{OPT}}^n = \max\left\{\frac{\mathrm{OPT}(I)}{\sqrt{n}} : I \text{ has } n \text{ cities}\right\} \tag{3}$$

and

$$R_{\mathrm{OPT}}^\infty = \limsup_{n \to \infty} R_{\mathrm{OPT}}^n. \tag{4}$$

It can be shown that R_{OPT}^∞ exists and lies somewhere in the range from 1.07 to $\sqrt{2} = 1.414\ldots$ [Supowit, 1981]. Informally, these definitions imply that, as n grows very large, the worst that an optimal traveling salesman tour can be for n points in a unit square approaches $R_{\mathrm{OPT}}^\infty \sqrt{n}$.

Now, if we define $R_{K(\varepsilon)}^\infty$ analogously, by replacing $\mathrm{OPT}(I)$ by $K(I, \varepsilon)$ in (3), we can now reinterpret the guarantee of (2) as

$$R_{K(\varepsilon)}^\infty \leq (1 + \varepsilon) R_{\mathrm{OPT}}^\infty. \tag{5}$$

In other words, for n large there exist tours approximately as long as $R_{\mathrm{OPT}}^\infty \sqrt{n}$, and algorithm $K(\varepsilon)$ guarantees a tour which is no more than approximately $(1 + \varepsilon)$ times this. Such a guarantee doesn't say anything about nearness to optimality, but it does provide a bound on the tour length that is easily computable as a function of n. Such a bound can be quite useful for planning purposes.

If one is interested in a guarantee of this sort (rather than the average-case result for which algorithm K was designed), the best one could hope for would be an algorithm A satisfying

$$R_A^\infty = R_{\mathrm{OPT}}^\infty. \tag{6}$$

Surprisingly enough, such an algorithm has been found, even though the precise value of R_{OPT}^∞ has yet to be determined. The algorithm is described by Supowit, Reingold & Plaisted [1983], and is based on much the same ideas as algorithm K, although the dependence on ε is removed. Algorithm K works using a subroutine which finds optimal tours for sets of t cities, where t depends on ε, using (for instance) the dynamic programming algorithm described in Chapter 3. The modified algorithm finds optimal tours for sets of about $\log(\log n)$ cities, with the sets chosen by a slightly different partitioning algorithm, and the subtours combined into an overall tour according to a more complicated heuristic. The running time of the algorithm is $O(n \log n)$.

Exercises

11. Show that there exist sets of n points in the unit square for which the minimum traveling salesman tour must be at least $\sqrt{n}$ in length. (*Hint*: Place n points in the unit square so that no pair is closer than $1/\sqrt{n}$ apart.) Can you find a worse example?

12. The algorithm of Supowit, Reingold & Plaisted [1983] for the TSP in the unit square is based on a partitioning plan which divides the problem into subproblems each involving $\log(\log n)$ cities. Show that these subproblems can be solved in time $O(n \log n)$ overall, using the dynamic programming algorithm for the TSP presented in Chapter 3.

6 PERFORMANCE GUARANTEES FOR RELATED PROBLEMS

So far in this chapter we have been concerned only with the problem of finding traveling salesman *tours*. However, the techniques and results described so far readily extend to the case where we are looking for a *path* which visits all the cities (whether a starting point is specified of not – see Exercise 13).

We have also restricted our attention so far to the symmetric TSP, where $c_{ij} = c_{ji}$ for all cities i and j. When we turn to the asymmetric case (c_{ij} not necessarily equal to c_{ji}), the situation is quite different. Even if we restrict ourselves to instances which satisfy the triangle inequality, there are no known polynomial-time heuristics that can guarantee a solution within a constant ratio of the optimal solution. Many of the algorithms introduced in Section 3 can be generalized to apply to the asymmetric case, but their good guarantees do not carry over.

For instance, Frieze, Galbiati & Maffioli [1982] have shown that, although cheapest insertion guarantees a ratio of 2 in the symmetric case, it can be arbitrarily bad in the asymmetric case. In particular, there are instances that cause it to construct tours whose lengths are proportional to n times the optimal length, where n is the number of cities. Similar results hold for the nearest neighbor algorithm and various 'greedy' and 'interchange' heuristics. The brightest news currently available corresponds to the worst news we encountered in the symmetric case: There is a polynomial-time heuristic which, while still capable of generating tours whose length is an arbitrary multiple of optimal, never creates one of length exceeding $\log n \, \mathrm{OPT}(I)$. On the other hand, no complexity results have yet been proved that would imply that good heuristics for the asymmetric triangle-inequality TSP cannot exist (assuming $\mathcal{P} \neq \mathcal{NP}$). The asymmetric TSP thus remains a quite significant open area for further research.

In the following subsections we shall consider a number of variants on the basic TSP, and the approximation results that can be proven for them. Throughout we shall assume that the triangle inequality holds.

6.1 Many traveling salesmen

Let us now turn to a generalization of the symmetric TSP in which more than one salesman is allowed. In the k-traveling salesman problem (the k-TSP), an instance is a set of cities with a distance matrix C, as before, plus a specified *start city*, say city 1. We are looking for a collection of k subtours, each containing city 1, such that each city is in at least one subtour. This problem models the situation where k salesmen work for a company with a home office in city 1, and between them they wish to visit each city at least once. Thus each salesman must follow a route that takes him from the home office through some subset of the cities and then back to the home office, and every city must be on some salesman's route. See Figure 5.13. As a measure of the quality of a given collection of k routes, we take the length of the maximum length subtour in the collection. The goal is to minimize this maximum length.

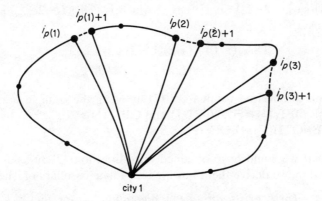

Figure 5.13 A traveling salesman tour split into subtours – one approach to the solution of the k-TSP

This problem was studied by Frederickson, Hecht & Kim [1978]. It of course reduces to the standard TSP when $k = 1$, but even when k is large, near-optimal solutions can still be found (though not quite as near to optimal as in the case of the 1-TSP). The best algorithm known starts with a standard traveling salesman tour T (generated by your favorite TSP heuristic), and proceeds to partition the given tour into k pieces. More precisely, suppose that $(1 = i_1, i_2, \ldots, i_n)$ is the order of the cities in T. Let L be the length of T, and let $c_{\max}$ be the maximum distance between any city and city 1.

k-Tour-splitting algorithm

Step 1. For each j, $1 \leq j < k$, define $p(j)$ to be the largest integer such that the length of the path in T from 1 to $i_{p(j)}$ does not exceed $(j/k)(L - 2c_{max}) + c_{max}$.

Step 2. Let the k subtours be $T_1 = (1, i_2, \ldots, i_{p(1)})$, $T_2 = (1, i_{p(1)+1}, \ldots, i_{p(2)})$, $\ldots$, $T_k = (1, i_{p(k-1)+1}, \ldots, i_n)$. See Figure 5.13.

Theorem 7 *Suppose T is a tour for an instance I of the TSP and satisfies $\mathrm{LENGTH}(T) \leq r\,\mathrm{OPT}(I)$. Let $\mathrm{TSA}_k(I, T)$ be the length of the longest of the k subtours generated by the k-tour-splitting algorithm when it is applied to T, and let $\mathrm{OPT}_k(I)$ be the length of the longest subtour in an optimal solution of the k-TSP for I. Then*

$$\mathrm{TSA}_k(I, T) \leq (r + 1 - 1/k)\mathrm{OPT}_k(I).$$

Proof The length of $T_1 \cap T$ is at most $(1/k)(L - 2c_{max}) + c_{max}$. Thus $\mathrm{LENGTH}(T_1) \leq (1/k)(L - 2c_{max}) + 2c_{max}$. For each j, $2 \leq j \leq k - 1$, $T_j \cap T$ has length at most $(1/k)(L - 2c_{max})$, since the path in T from city 1 to city $i_{p(j)}$ is at most $(j/k)(L - 2c_{max}) + c_{max}$ and the path from city 1 to city $i_{p(j-1)+1}$ is at least $((j-1)/k)(L - 2c_{max}) + c_{max}$. Thus $\mathrm{LENGTH}(T_j) \leq (1/k)(L - 2c_{max}) + 2c_{max}$. Finally, consider T_k. The length of T_k is at most $L - [((k-1)/k)(L - 2c_{max}) + c_{max}] + c_{max}$, which is $(1/k)(L - 2c_{max}) + 2c_{max}$, as before. Thus

$$\begin{aligned} \mathrm{TSA}_k(I, T) &\leq (1/k)(L - 2c_{max}) + 2c_{max} \\ &= (L/k) + 2(1 - 1/k)c_{max}. \end{aligned} \tag{7}$$

We obtain the desired result from (7) by using the triangle inequality to observe that $\mathrm{OPT}_k(I) \geq (1/k)\mathrm{OPT}(I)$ and $\mathrm{OPT}_k(I) \geq 2c_{max}$, and by recalling that $L = \mathrm{LENGTH}(T) \leq r\,\mathrm{OPT}(I)$. $\square$

Noting that we could have obtained our initial tour T by using Christofides' algorithm, we derive the following immediate corollary of Theorem 7.

Corollary 1 *There exists an $O(n^3)$ algorithm C_k for the k-TSP which guarantees*

$$C_k(I) \leq \left(\frac{5}{2} - \frac{1}{k}\right)\mathrm{OPT}_k(I).$$

The tour-splitting approach we have described is not the only method available. One might propose more direct methods for constructing the subtours, for instance using a greedy incremental approach that grew all k tours in parallel using nearest insertion techniques. However, Frederickson, Hecht & Kim [1978] have shown that this latter approach can, in the worst case, yield solutions which are $2k$ times optimal. This guarantee is considerably worse than the 5/2 bound (independent of k) for algorithm C_k, which remains the current champion for the k-TSP.

6.2 The stacker crane problem

The stacker crane problem is a generalization of the TSP in which the desired tour must contain certain edges, and must traverse them in specified directions. An instance is a set of cities (and corresponding distance matrix C) together with a set A of *arcs*, where each arc is an ordered pair of cities, and every city occurs in exactly one arc. The goal is to find a minimum length tour $(i_1, i_2, \ldots, i_m)$, possibly containing repeated cities, such that for each arc $(i, j) \in A$, there is some k such that $i_k = i$ and $i_{k+1} = j$.

The motivation for this problem is best expressed by ignoring stacker cranes entirely and considering delivery trucks. Suppose a truck must perform a collection of pickups and deliveries, subject to the constraint that each load that is picked up completely fills the truck and goes to a single destination, and hence no pickups or deliveries can be combined. If $(i, j) \in A$, this means that a load must be picked up at city i and delivered to city j. The goal is to save fuel by minimizing the total length of the route used to make all the pickups and deliveries. Note that if each pickup location is arbitrarily near to its corresponding destination, we get the TSP in the limit. It is in this sense that the stacker crane problem is a generalization of the TSP.

We shall discuss two heuristics for this problem, first presented by Frederickson, Hecht & Kim [1978], which have an interesting property. Both provide reasonable worst-case guarantees by themselves. However, if one applies each heuristic independently to a given instance I and then chooses the better of the two solutions generated, one obtains a solution for which a guarantee holds that is *stronger* than either of the individual guarantees.

The first of the two algorithms is best adapted to the case when the total length of the required arcs turns out to be large with respect to the optimal route length. It is based on the fact that a strongly connected directed graph in which every vertex has equal out- and indegrees has a *directed Eulerian tour*, i.e., there is a directed cycle in the graph which passes through each arc exactly once. As with Eulerian tours in undirected graphs, a directed Eulerian tour can be found in linear time if it exists.

Large arcs algorithm

Step 1. Construct a bipartite graph G_A with two vertices for each arc in A, one corresponding to the city at its head and one corresponding to the city at its tail. All edges connect head vertices to tail vertices. There is an edge between a head vertex a and a tail vertex b if and only if a and b are *not* head and tail of the same arc. The cost of an edge $\{a, b\}$ equals the distance between the cities corresponding to a and b. See Figure 5.14(b).

Step 2. Find a minimum cost bipartite matching M for G_A. Construct a directed graph G_B with a vertex for each city and an arc set A'

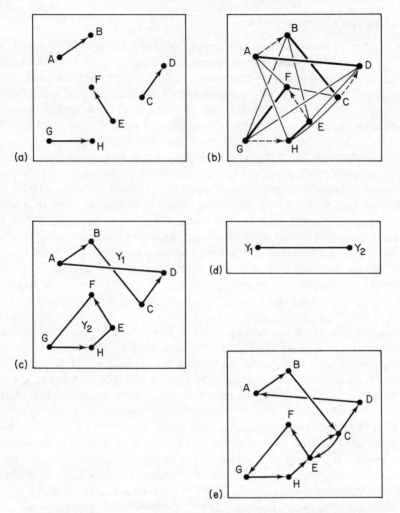

Figure 5.14   Snapshots of the large arcs algorithm for the stacker crane problem in action. (a) Stacker crane instance $A = \{(A, B), (C, D), (E, F), (G, H)\}$. (b) Graph G_A. Bold lines indicate minimum cost matching M. (c) Graph G_B: the set A of arcs plus matching M. (d) Graph G_C and a minimum spanning tree T for it. (e) Graph G_D obtained from G_B by adding two arcs for each edge in T

consisting of A together with an arc for each edge in M, directed from the city corresponding to its head endpoint to the city corresponding to its tail endpoint. This results in a graph consisting of $k \geqslant 1$ disjoint cycles, each made up of alternating arcs from A and M. See Figure 5.14(c).

Step 3. Construct a graph G_C, with a vertex for each of the k cycles of Step 2 and an edge between each pair of vertices, the length of $\{v, w\}$

being

$$\min\{c_{ij} : i \in R(v) \quad \text{and} \quad j \in R(w)\}$$

where, for each vertex u, $R(u)$ is the set of cities in the cycle corresponding to u. Find a minimum length spanning tree T of G_C. See Figure 5.14(d).

Step 4. Construct a new directed graph G_D from G_B by adding two arcs for each edge in T. The two arcs corresponding to an edge $\{v, w\}$ join the two cities $i \in R(V)$ and $j \in R(w)$ whose distance c_{ij} equals LENGTH($\{v, w\}$), and go in opposite directions. Note that graph G_D is strongly connected, it contains all the required arcs of set A, and each of its vertices has its indegree equal to its outdegree. Thus G_D has a directed Eulerian tour, and this is the stacker crane route which we output. See Figure 5.14(e).

Theorem 8 *The large arcs algorithm runs in time $O(|A|^3)$ and, for all instances I obeying the triangle inequality, finds a route whose length LA(I) satisfies*

$$\text{LA}(I) \leqslant 3\text{OPT}(I) - 2\text{LENGTH}(A)$$

where LENGTH(A) is the sum of the lengths of the arcs in A.

Proof The running time of the algorithm is dominated by the time for finding the minimum cost bipartite matching for graph G_A in Step 1. This matching problem can be solved in time $O(n^3)$, where n is the number of vertices (see Lawler [1976]). Since G_A has $|A|$ vertices, the claimed overall bound follows.

For the guarantee, we first note that any route R must contain all the arcs of A. Moreover, the order in which the arcs are encountered in R induces a matching (between the head of one arc and the tail of the next) of the form required by Step 1. By the triangle inequality, the length of this matching is bounded by the lengths of the edges in $R - A$. Thus the total cost of arcs in G_B is bounded by OPT(I).

The edges of $R - A$ must also induce a spanning tree for G_C, since R connects together all arcs of A. Thus the total length of the spanning tree created in Step 3 is bounded by OPT(I) $-$ LENGTH(A). Twice this amount gets added in when we create G_D from G_B, and so we conclude that the sum of the edge lengths in G_D, and hence in the large arcs route, is bounded by $3\text{OPT}(I) - 2\text{LENGTH}(A)$, as claimed. $\square$

Note as a corollary that we obtain LA(I) $\leqslant$ 3OPT(I) for all instances I, although the situation is actually better than this when LENGTH(A) is large relative to OPT(I). Our second algorithm is tailored to the case where LENGTH(A) is small relative to OPT(I). It uses a simple fact concerning Eulerian tours in *mixed graphs*. A mixed graph is one with both directed and undirected edges. An Eulerian tour of a mixed graph must go through each edge (directed or not) exactly once, respecting the directions of the directed edges. It is easy to see, by analogy with the directed and undirected cases, that if a mixed graph is strongly connected and each node is incident with an even number of edges and has equal in- and outdegrees, then the graph has an Eulerian tour. Unfortunately, this criterion is not a necessary condition, and precise necessary and sufficient conditions are considerably more complex to state (see Exercise 18). Fortunately, the above criterion *is* sufficient, and, in fact, when it holds the Eulerian tour can be found in linear time. This is all we need for our algorithm below (Step 6).

Small arcs algorithm

Step 1. Construct a graph G_A with a vertex for each arc in A, and an edge between each pair of vertices. The length of the edge between vertices corresponding to (i, j) and (k, l) is the minimum of c_{ik}, c_{il}, c_{jk}, and c_{jl}. See Figure 5.15(b).

Step 2. Compute the lengths of all shortest paths between vertices in G_A, and construct a new graph $G_{A'}$ with the same vertices and edges, but with edge lengths corresponding to the shortest paths in G_A (see

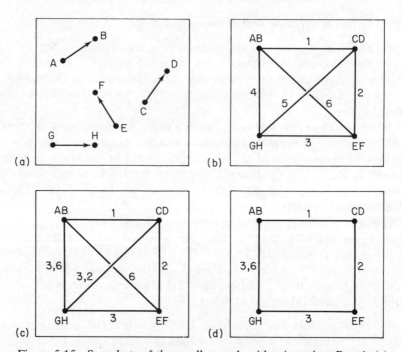

Figure 5.15 Snapshots of the small arcs algorithm in action, Part 1. (a) Stacker crane instance, as in Figure 5.14(a). (b) Graph G_A (the numbers on the edges are *not* lengths, but labels, for use in (c) below). (c) Graph $G_{A'}$ with distances corresponding to shortest paths in G_A (edge labels give the corresponding shortest path). (d) Tour T found for $G_{A'}$ by Christofides' algorithm

Figure 5.15(c); note that, whereas the edge lengths in G_A need not have obeyed the triangle inequality, those in $G_{A'}$ do). Apply Christofides' algorithm to find a traveling salesman tour T for $G_{A'}$. See Figure 5.15(d).

Step 3. Let E be the multiset of edges of G_A obtained by replacing each edge of T by the corresponding shortest path in G_A (recall that in a multiset, certain elements may occur more than once). Note that, by the action of Christofides' algorithm, each vertex of G_A is an endpoint for an even number of edges in E. See Figure 5.16(a).

Step 4. Construct a multigraph G_B (in a multigraph, multiple copies of edges are allowed), whose vertices are the cities, and whose edges correspond to the edges in E in the following fashion: If an edge $e \in E$ linked the vertices corresponding to (i, j) and (k, l) in G_A, it is represented in G_B by an edge joining that pair of cities, one from (i, j) and one from (k, l), which are the closest together, and hence whose distance equals LENGTH(e). See Figure 5.16(b).

Step 5. Construct a mixed graph G_C from G_B as follows. For each arc (i, j) in A, consider the vertices i and j in G_B. Cities i and j correspond to

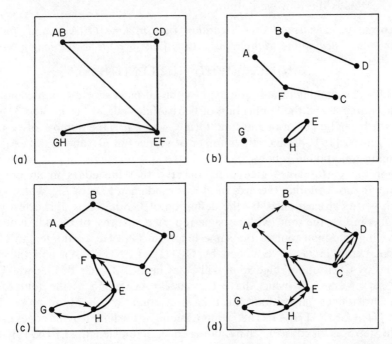

Figure 5.16 Snapshots of the small arcs algorithm in action, Part 2. (a) Set E of edges in G_A corresponding to tour T. (b) Multigraph G_B with edges corresponding to edges in E. (c) Graph G_C constructed by adding directed and undirected representatives of arcs in A to G_B. (d) Final directed multigraph, obtained by adding directed arc pairs to a mixed Euler tour of G_C

the same vertex in G_A. Since each vertex in G_A is the endpoint of an even number of edges in E, either i and j both have even degree in G_B or they both have odd degree. If both have even degree, add two directed edges, one in each direction. If both have odd degree, add an (undirected) edge between the two. Call this latter type of edge an *odd* edge, and let A_o be the set of arcs in A corresponding to odd edges. See Figure 5.16(c).

Step 6. Find a mixed Eulerian tour for G_C. If the length of the odd arcs which are traversed in a direction opposite to that of the corresponding arc in A_o exceeds $(1/2)\text{LENGTH}(A_o)$, reverse the direction of the tour.

Step 7. Turn G_C into a directed multigraph by associating with each undirected edge the direction in which it was traversed by the tour constructed in the previous step. For each incorrectly traversed odd arc, add two new arcs with the same endpoints, one arc going in each direction. See Figure 5.16(d). This new graph is a directed graph in which all vertices have indegree equal to their outdegree, and in which all arcs of A are present. It has an Eulerian tour and this is the tour we output.

Theorem 9 *The small arcs algorithm runs in time $O(|A|^3)$ and, for all instances I obeying the triangle inequality, finds a route whose length $\text{SA}(I)$ satisfies*

$$\text{SA}(I) \leq (3/2)\text{OPT}(I) + (1/2)\text{LENGTH}(A).$$

Proof The running time is bounded by the all-pairs shortest path computation in Step 1 and the application of Christofides' algorithm in Step 3, both of which can be performed in time $O(n^3)$, where n is the number of vertices (see Lawler [1976]). Since the number of vertices in G_A and $G_{A'}$ is $|A|$, the running time bound follows.

For the performance guarantee, observe that the edges in an optimal route R (not counting the arcs of A) will induce a tour of G_A which visits each vertex at least once. By the definition of $G_{A'}$ in terms of shortest path lengths in G_A, the tour (with possible repeated vertices) of G_A will induce a traveling salesman tour of the same length in $G_{A'}$. Hence the length of an optimal tour in $G_{A'}$ is bounded by $\text{OPT}(I) - \text{LENGTH}(A)$, and the tour found by Christofides' algorithm will be at most $3/2$ times this length. Thus the set of edges E, which have the same total length as the tour found by Christofides' algorithm, must have a total length of at most $(3/2)$ $[\text{OPT}(I) - \text{LENGTH}(A)]$. This is thus a bound on the length of the edges in G_B.

In Step 5, G_C is constructed by adding edges of total length $2\text{LENGTH}(A) - \text{LENGTH}(A_o)$ to G_B. In Step 7, we obtain our final graph by adding edges of total length at most $2[(1/2)\text{LENGTH}(A_o)] = \text{LENGTH}(A_o)$. Thus the total length of the route found is at most $(3/2)\text{OPT}(I) + (1/2)\text{LENGTH}(A)$, as claimed. $\square$

As a corollary we have that $\text{SA}(I) \leq 2\text{OPT}(I)$, since $\text{OPT}(I) \geq \text{LENGTH}(A)$, by definition. However, an even more significant result can be obtained by combining Theorems 8 and 9. Let *large or small arcs* be the compound algorithm that works by applying both the large arcs and the small arcs algorithms to an instance, and then outputting the better of the two routes that are found.

Theorem 10 *The large or small arcs algorithm runs in time $O(|A|^3)$ and, for all instances I obeying the triangle inequality, finds a route whose length $\text{LSA}(I)$ satisfies*

$$\text{LSA}(I) \leqslant \tfrac{9}{5}\text{OPT}(I).$$

Proof The running time bound follows since both the large arcs and small arcs algorithms obey the same bound. For the performance guarantee, we note that the small arcs algorithm provides the better guarantee whenever $\text{LENGTH}(A) \leqslant (3/5)\text{OPT}(I)$; otherwise large arcs is better. Thus we divide into cases depending on the value of $\text{LENGTH}(A)$. Suppose $\text{LENGTH}(A) \geqslant (3/5)\text{OPT}(I)$. Then, by Theorem 8, $\text{LA}(I) \leqslant 3\text{OPT}(I) - 2(3/5)\text{OPT}(I) = (9/5)\text{OPT}(I)$. On the other hand, suppose $\text{LENGTH}(A) \leqslant (3/5)\text{OPT}(I)$. Then, by Theorem 9, $\text{SA}(I) \leqslant (3/2)\text{OPT}(I) + (1/2)(3/5)\text{OPT}(I) = (9/5)\text{OPT}(I)$. Thus the desired bound is obeyed in both cases by $\min\{\text{LA}(I), \text{SA}(I)\}$. $\square$

The large or small arcs algorithm currently provides the best performance guarantee known for a polynomial-time heuristic for the stacker crane problem. It can be generalized to provide the same guarantee even in the absence of the triangle inequality, and even when arcs are allowed to share endpoints and there can be required cities which are not part of any arc [Frederickson, Hecht & Kim, 1978]. The technique of combining algorithms to obtain better guarantees than either algorithm provides separately can also be applied to other problems, as we shall see in the next section.

6.3 Problems of the postal service

The stacker crane problem is related to a number of other problems which are concerned more with traversing arcs (or edges) than with visiting vertices. The undirected analogue of the stacker crane problem is called the *rural postman problem* [Orloff, 1974]. Here we are given a set of required *edges* (rather than arcs) and ask for a route of minimum length which will traverse each edge at least once (the direction of traversal does not matter). This models the problem a mail-carrier might face in designing an optimum route, with each edge corresponding to a street along which the mail must be delivered. It is not difficult to see that a Christofides-like algorithm can guarantee a ratio of 3/2 for this problem [Frederickson, 1979]. We leave the details for Exercise 17.

The mail-carrier's problem becomes a bit more exciting when one-way streets must be contended with (unless the carrier is the old-fashioned type who still walks his route). In the *Chinese postman problem* an instance is a mixed graph $G = (V, E, A)$, where the edges and arcs represent the streets

(bidirectional and one-way) of a city, and the vertices correspond to intersections. The goal is to find a tour of this graph which visits every street at
least once (in the proper direction, if one-way), and has minimum possible
length. Note that this problem differs from the stacker crane and rural
postman problems in that the route is restricted to lie in the graph itself: the
only edges that may be traversed are those that are required (although each
may be traversed many times, if necessary). In the other two problems we
were assuming an underlying complete graph, along which the tours could
be routed.

The Chinese postman problem is $\mathcal{NP}$-hard [Papadimitriou, 1976]; however, this only holds true when the fully generality of mixed graphs is
allowed. For the case where all edges are directed or all are undirected,
optimal postman's routes can be found in polynomial time [Edmonds,
1965d; Edmonds & Johnson, 1973]. Thus it is only for the general case that
we need to resort to heuristics.

It is here that the compound algorithm approach yields another success.
Two heuristics, one due to Edmonds & Johnson [1973] and the other due to
Frederickson [1979], both generate routes that are no longer than twice
optimal in the worst case (and *can* generate solutions that are that bad).
However, as was the case with our stacker crane algorithms, each algorithm
performs well on the instances that confound the other. Thus the combined
algorithm, which takes the better of the two routes generated by the
algorithms, provides a guarantee that is better than that for either algorithm
individually. It outputs a route that is guaranteed to be no longer than 5/3
optimal [Frederickson, 1979].

Exercises

13. (a) Show that a traveling salesman *path* (a path that visits each city
exactly once) whose length is at most (3/2) times the optimal path length can
be found using a Christofides-like algorithm. (*Hint*: It may be necessary to
add new points to the instance so as to insure that the desired matching
exists.) (b) Show that the same bound can be obtained for the problem when
one of the endpoints of the path is specified in advance. (c) What if *both*
endpoints are fixed in advance?!

14. Show that, in the case of the aymmetric TSP, the cheapest insertion
algorithm can produce tours which are an arbitrary multiple of the optimal
tour length, even when the triangle inequality holds.

15. Show that if a directed graph G is strongly connected (i.e., for every
pair of vertices u, v there is a directed path from u to v) and is *Eulerian*
(every vertex v has indegree(v) = outdegree(v)), then G has a directed
Eulerian tour, and such a tour can be found in linear time.

16. Design an algorithm for the asymmetric TSP that, assuming the triangle
inequality holds, constructs a tour whose length is at most $(\log n)$OPT(I)
when I is an n-city instance. (*Hint*: There is a polynomial-time algorithm A

that, with the aid of graph matching techniques, finds a minimum length subset of intercity arcs so that every city has indegree = outdegree = 1 [Lawler, 1976; Papadimitriou & Steiglitz, 1982]. Such a subset has length at most OPT(I), although it may not be connected and so need not comprise a tour by itself, since it can yield as many as $n/2$ disjoint cycles. Use A as a subroutine to construct a strongly connected Eulerian graph with the cities as vertices. By an appropriate choice of the subsets of cities to which it is applied, this can be done in just log n iterations.)

17. Show that a (3/2) guarantee can be provided for the rural postman problem.

18. Let $G = (V, E, A)$ be a mixed graph that is strongly connected (for mixed graphs this means that there is a path from any vertex to any other vertex using undirected and directed edges, the latter in their proper direction). For each $v \in V$ let degree(v) be the number of edges $\{u, v\} \in E$, indegree(v) be the number of directed edges $(u, v) \in A$, and outdegree(v) be the number of directed edges $(v, u) \in A$. (a) Suppose that, for all vertices v, indegree(v) = outdegree(v) and degree(v) is even. Show that G has an Eulerian tour, which can be found in polynomial time (actually $O(|E| + |A|)$). (b) Show that G can contain an Eulerian tour even if the above condition does not hold. (c) Find necessary and sufficient conditions for G to have an Eulerian tour. (*Hint*: Think of conditions that must hold for every *set* of vertices.)

19. Show that the directed Chinese postman problem can be solved in polynomial time. (*Hint*: See Edmonds [1965d] and Edmonds & Johnson [1973] for the undirected and directed cases, respectively.)

20. (a) Show that the techniques used to solve the k-TSP, given a heuristic for the TSP, can be extended to the stacker crane problem, thus guaranteeing a $(14/5)-(1/k)$ ratio in the k-stacker cranes problem. (b) Apply the same techniques to the k-Chinese postmen problem. What type of bounds are obtained in the directed, undirected and mixed cases?

7 CONCLUSION

In this chapter we have surveyed work on performance guarantees for heuristic 'approximation' algorithms for the TSP and related problems. As we have seen, there is still much more room for improvement in the guarantees, but new algorithmic techniques may well be needed if such improvements are to be realized. (The successful algorithms to date have all relied on just a few basic ideas and constructs, such as minimum spanning trees, Eulerian tours and minimum cost matchings.)

For the reader interested in this approach to combinatorial optimization problems, there exists an extensive literature concerned with the application of the performance guarantee approach to other problems. We have already mentioned work on the knapsack problem [Ibarra & Kim 1976; Lawler 1979]. Another well-studied area is the bin packing problem and its variants. The survey by Coffman, Garey & Johnson [1984] provides a complete bibliography of work in this area as of 1983, where significant contributions were made by Johnson, Demers, Ullman, Garey & Graham [1974], Garey, Graham, Johnson & Yao [1976] and Baker, Coffman & Rivest [1980]. A related, and also extensively studied field is that of multiprocessor scheduling, where the performance guarantee approach was first applied successfully, in the work of R. L. Graham [Graham, 1966, 1969]. The above-mentioned survey by Coffman, Garey & Johnson [1984] also provides pointers to the literature in this area, as do Graham, Lawler, Lenstra & Rinnooy Kan [1979].

Concerning more purely combinatorial problems, Johnson [1974a, 1974b] examines algorithms for graph coloring and finds them wanting, while Johnson [1974a], Chvátal [1979] and Hochbaum [1982] consider various set covering heuristics. For an introduction to performance guarantees in general, see Garey & Johnson [1979] and Papadimitriou & Steiglitz [1982].

The Traveling Salesman Problem
Edited by E. L. Lawler, J. K. Lenstra,
A. H. G. Rinnooy Kan, D. B. Shmoys
© 1985 John Wiley & Sons Ltd.

6

Probabilistic analysis of heuristics

R. M. Karp
University of California, Berkeley

J. M. Steele
Princeton University

1 INTRODUCTION

One of the mysteries surrounding the TSP is the remarkably effective performance of simple heuristic solution methods. The properties of such heuristic methods are usually established empirically, simply by trying the methods and observing the quality of the results. The present chapter explores a complementary theoretical approach, in which it is assumed that problem instances are drawn from certain simple probability distributions, and it is then proven mathematically that particular solution methods are highly likely to yield near-optimal solutions when the number of cities is large. This analysis also reveals that the cost of an optimal solution to a random TSP is sharply predictable from the parameters of the underlying probabilistic model.

Two principal probabilistic models are discussed: a *Euclidean model*, in which the cities are points in *d*-dimensional Euclidean space and their

181

locations are drawn independently from the uniform distribution over the d-dimensional unit cube, and an *asymmetric model*, in which the elements of the distance matrix (c_{ij}) are drawn independently from the uniform distribution over $[0, 1]$ and neither symmetry nor the triangle inequality is assumed. Section 2, which treats the Euclidean model, and Section 3, which treats the asymmetric model, can be read independently. The reader should also refer to Chapter 11, where a *random graph model* is considered, in which the input is a random graph and the object is to determine whether a Hamiltonian cycle exists.

Within each of our two models certain predictions will hold true with very high probability when the number of cities is very large. In the d-dimensional Euclidean case it is predictable that the cost of an optimal solution will be close to a certain constant times $n^{(d-1)/d}$, where n is the number of cities, and that simple, efficient algorithms based on a 'divide-and-conquer' principle will yield near-optimal solutions. In the asymmetric case it is predictable that a near-optimal solution to the TSP can be obtained by patching together the cycles of an optimal solution to the assignment problem.

The study of random Euclidean TSPs was initiated in the pioneering paper by Beardwood, Halton & Hammersley [1959], where the following is proved:

Let $\{X_i\}$, $1 \le i < \infty$, be independent random variables uniformly distributed over the d-dimensional unit cube, and let L_n denote the Euclidean length of a shortest closed path which connects all the elements of $\{X_1, X_2, \ldots, X_n\}$. Then there is a constant c_d such that, with probability 1, $\lim_{n \to \infty} L_n n^{-(d-1)/d} = c_d$. We will give a new and brief proof of this classic result in Section 2.

The study of cellular dissection algorithms for the approximate solution of random TSPs in the plane was initiated by Karp [1976, 1977]. The locations of the n cities are assumed to be drawn independently from the uniform distribution over the unit square. The algorithms dissect the unit square into rectangular cells, each containing a small number of cities, construct an optimal tour through the set of cities in each cell, and then patch these subtours together into a tour through all the cities. Karp proposed a *fixed dissection method* in which all the cells are congruent squares, and an *adaptive dissection method* in which the locations of the cities determine the dissection. Refinements of the analysis of the fixed dissection method are due to Weide [1978] and Steele [1981]. The method is extended to higher dimensions by Halton & Terada [1982].

Section 2 presents the principal dissection methods, discusses their execution times and derives theoretical bounds on the quality of the solutions they produce. In each of the methods there occurs a parameter $s(n)$ giving the number of cells into which the unit d-dimensional cube is dissected. A typical, but simple, consequence of the results proved there is the following:

Assume that $s(n) = o(n)$, so that the average number of cities per cell grows without bound as $n \to \infty$. Let $L_n^F(X_1, X_2, \ldots, X_n)$ be the length of the tour produced by the fixed dissection method; then, with probability 1, $\lim_{n \to \infty} L_n^F n^{-(d-1)/d} = c_d$, where c_d is the same constant that appears in the statement of the Beardwood–Halton–Hammersley theorem. Thus we see that the length of the tour produced by the fixed dissection method has the same asymptotic behavior as the length of the optimal tour.

Section 3 is concerned with probabilistic properties of the asymmetric TSP. It is assumed that the distances c_{ij} are drawn independently from the uniform distribution over [0, 1]. Then the minimum cost of a tour is given by $\min_\pi \{\sum_i c_{i\pi(i)}\}$, where π ranges over the cyclic permutations of $\{1, 2, \ldots, n\}$. A closely related problem which can be solved in time $O(n^3)$ is the assignment problem: $\min_\sigma \{\sum_i c_{i\sigma(i)}\}$, where σ ranges over the permutations of $\{1, 2, \ldots, n\}$. An approximation algorithm for the TSP is presented which first solves the assignment problem to obtain a permutation σ, and then constructs a tour by patching together the cycles of σ. Let T^* be the cost of an optimal tour, and let T be the cost of the tour produced by the approximation algorithm. It is proven that $E[(T - T^*)/T^*] = O(n^{-1/2})$. Thus the approximation algorithm tends to give a near-optimal tour when n is very large.

2   PROBABILISTIC ANALYSIS OF THE EUCLIDEAN TSP

The Euclidean TSP is the problem of finding a closed path (tour) of minimum length through a given set of points in d-dimensional Euclidean space. We conduct a probabilistic analysis of this problem on the assumption that the points are drawn independently from the uniform distribution over the d-dimensional unit cube. The probabilistic analysis will be concerned both with the length of the optimal tour and with the lengths of the tours produced by certain *dissection algorithms*. Each of these algorithms dissects the unit cube into regions, constructs an optimal tour through the points in each region, and then patches these tours together to obtain a single tour through all the given points.

2.1   Some elementary facts about the TSP

It is clear that the shortest closed path through n given points is always a simple polygon (unless all the points are collinear) but it will be convenient in describing certain approximation algorithms to allow closed paths which make repeated visits to some of the given points. Such a closed path can easily be converted to a simple polygon of smaller length.

The following lemma, illustrated in Figure 6.1, will often be useful.

Lemma 1   *Let V be a set of points and E a multiset (i.e., a set which may contain repeated elements) of line segments joining pairs of points in V. Suppose that any two points in V can be joined by a path consisting of line*

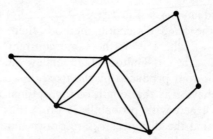

Figure 6.1   A multiset of line segments which determines a closed walk

segments from E. Then the following are equivalent:
 (i) *Every point in V is the endpoint of an even number of line segments in E.*
 (ii) *E can be decomposed into a union of edge-disjoint cycles.*
 (iii) *The line segments in E determine a closed walk through all the points in
      V.*

The following bound will be used repeatedly.

Lemma 2   *Let I_n be a set of n points in the d-dimensional unit cube, $d \geqslant 2$.
Then there is a closed walk through I_n of length $\leqslant dn^{(d-1)/d} + \delta_d n^{(d-2)/(d-1)}$,
where δ_d depends only on d.*

Proof   The proof is by induction on d, with $d = 2$ as the basis.

 Basis. Let $\Delta = 1/\lceil n^{1/2} \rceil$. Let the unit square be dissected into horizontal
strips $S_1, S_2, \ldots, S_{\lceil n^{1/2} \rceil}$ of width Δ. Adjoin to I_n new points at the right-
hand ends of the boundaries between S_1 and S_2, S_3 and S_4, $\ldots$, and at the
left-hand ends of the boundaries between S_2 and S_3, S_4 and S_5, $\ldots$, and call
the resulting set of points I'_n. Construct a closed walk which visits the points
in $S_1 \cap I'_n$ in left-to-right order, then visits the points in $S_2 \cap I'_n$ in right-to-
left order, etc., finally returning to the initial point from the last point of the
final strip. The length of this tour is

$$\leqslant \lceil n^{1/2} \rceil + \Delta(n + \lceil n^{1/2} \rceil) + \sqrt{2}$$
$$\leqslant 2\sqrt{n} + 2 + \sqrt{2}.$$

 Induction step. Assuming the result for d, we prove it for $d + 1$. Let
$\Delta = 1/\lceil n^{1/(d+1)} \rceil$. Let the unit cube in $\mathbb{R}^{d+1}$ be dissected into parallelopipeds
$S_1, S_2, \ldots, S_{\lceil n^{1/(d+1)} \rceil}$ by hyperplanes parallel to one of the coordinate axes
and a distance Δ apart. Adjoin to I_n an arbitrary new point on each of these
hyperplanes, and call the resulting set of points I'_n. Let $n_i = |S_i \cap I'_n|$. For
each i, construct a closed walk through the points in $S_i \cap I'_n$ as follows:

 (i) Project each of the points in $S_i \cap I'_n$ onto the hyperplane which forms
     the base of S_i.
 (ii) Find a closed walk of length $\leqslant dn_i^{(d-1)/d} + \delta_d n_i^{(d-2)/(d-1)}$ through the set of

projected points (this entails iterative use of the construction being described here).

(iii) Visit the points of $S_i \cap I'_n$ in the same order as the corresponding projected points are visited.

By Lemma 1, the union of the set of closed walks constructed in this way determines a closed walk through all the points in I'_n, and hence through all the points in the subset I_n.

The length of this walk is

$$\leq \sum_{i=1}^{\lceil n^{1/(d+1)} \rceil} (dn_i^{(d-1)/d} + \delta_d n_i^{(d-2)/(d-1)}) + (n + \lceil n^{1/(d+1)} \rceil)\, \Delta.$$

A concavity argument shows that this bound is maximized subject to $\sum n_i \leq n + 1/\Delta$ when each n_i is equal to $n\Delta + 1$, in which case the bound becomes

$$\frac{1}{\Delta} (d(n\,\Delta + 1)^{(d-1)/d} + \delta_d (n\,\Delta + 1)^{(d-2)/(d-1)}) + (n + \lceil n^{1/(d+1)} \rceil)\, \Delta$$

$$= (d+1)n^{d/(d+1)} + O(n^{(d-1)/d}).$$

This completes the induction step. $\square$

Lemma 2 is sufficient for our purposes, but stronger results are possible. Few [1955] has shown that there is a closed walk of length $\leq 2^{1/2} n^{1/2} + 1.75$ through any set of n points in the unit square. For higher dimensions, tight upper bounds on the length of the shortest closed walk through n points in the unit hypercube are given by Moran [1982].

2.2   The fixed dissection algorithm

Any method for the exact solution of the TSP can be used in conjunction with various divide-and-conquer strategies to produce interesting approximation algorithms for the Euclidean TSP. An example is the following *fixed dissection algorithm* [Karp, 1977; Halton & Terada, 1982]. Let the dimension d be fixed. Let $m(n)$ be an integer-valued nondecreasing function such that $m(n)^d$ is $o(n)$. Let $s(n)$ denote $m(n)^d$.

Fixed dissection algorithm

Input: A set I_n consisting of n points in the unit d-dimensional cube Q. Partition Q into $s(n)$ congruent subcubes Q_i. Construct an optimal tour through each nonempty set $I_n \cap Q_i$. Select an arbitrary element X_i from each nonempty set $I_n \cap Q_i$, and obtain a tour through $\{X_i\}$ using the construction in the proof of Lemma 2.

The tours within the subcubes, together with the tour through $\{X_i\}$, determine a closed walk through I_n.

2.3 Two asymptotic probabilistic results

The Euclidean TSP will be analyzed on the assumption that the cities are drawn independently from the uniform distribution over the d-dimensional unit cube. Let X_i, $1 \leq i < \infty$, be independent identically distributed (i.i.d.) random variables with the uniform distribution on $[0, 1]^d$. Let $I_n = \{X_1, X_2, \ldots, X_n\}$. For any finite set $S \subseteq [0, 1]^d$, let $L(S)$ denote the length of an optimal tour through S, and let $L^F(S)$ denote the length of the tour produced by the fixed dissection algorithm.

Theorem 1 [Beardwood, Halton & Hammersley, 1959] *With probability* 1,

$$\lim_{n \to \infty} L(I_n) n^{-(d-1)/d} = c_d.$$

(*Here, c_d is a constant depending on the dimension d.*)

Theorem 1 will be referred to as the BHH theorem.

Theorem 2 *With probability* 1,

$$\lim_{n \to \infty} L^F(I_n) n^{-(d-1)/d} = c_d.$$

Roughly stated, these theorems assert that the length of an optimal tour through n random points is sharply predictable when n is large, and that the fixed dissection method tends to give near-optimal solutions when n is large.

2.4 Probabilistic background

In this subsection we collect the principal definitions and tools from probability theory that will be used in our analysis of the Euclidean TSP. We do expect that the reader be familiar with some basic facts from elementary probability theory, such as $E[\sum X_i] = \sum E[X_i]$ and $\text{var}[cX] = c^2 \text{var}[X]$. A detailed introduction to probability theory is given by Feller [1968].

Markov's inequality

Let X be a nonnegative random variable with mean μ. Then, for $a \geq 1$, $\Pr[X > a\mu] < 1/a$.

Chebyshev's inequality

Let X be a random variable with mean μ and variance σ^2. Then $\Pr[|X - \mu| \geq a\sigma] \leq 1/a^2$.

Efron–Stein inequality [Efron & Stein, 1981]

Let $X_1, X_2, \ldots, X_n$ be i.i.d. random variables. Let $S = S(y_1, y_2, \ldots, y_{n-1})$ be any symmetric function of $n - 1$ random variables. Let $S_i =$

$S(X_1, X_2, \ldots, X_{i-1}, X_{i+1}, \ldots, X_n)$, and let Y be any random variable. Then

$$\text{var}[S(X_1, X_2, \ldots, X_{n-1})] \leq E\left[\sum_{i=1}^{n} (S_i - Y)^2\right].$$

McDiarmid's inequality

Let $X_1, X_2, \ldots, X_s$ be nonnegative integer random variables which sum to n and have the multinomial joint distribution; i.e.,

$$\Pr[X_1 = n_1, X_2 = n_2, \ldots, X_s = n_s] = \frac{n! \, s^{-n}}{\Pi n_i!}.$$

Let $f_1, \ldots, f_s$ be nonnegative nondecreasing functions. Then $\text{var}[\sum_{i=1}^{s} f_i(X_i)] \leq \sum_{i=1}^{s} \text{var}[f_i(X_i)]$.

Poisson process

The Poisson process on $\mathbb{R}^d$ with unit intensity formalizes the idea of scattering points at random in $\mathbb{R}^d$ so that the average number of points per unit volume is 1. The process is defined as a random function Π which associates with every measurable set $A \subset \mathbb{R}^d$ a random set of points in A such that:

(i) $A \subseteq B \Rightarrow \Pi(A) \subseteq \Pi(B)$;
(ii) the integer $|\Pi(A)|$ is a Poisson random variable with parameter $\lambda = \mu(A)$, where μ is Lebesgue measure;
(iii) $\Pi(A)$ and $\Pi(B)$ are independent if $\mu(A \cap B) = 0$;
(iv) conditioned on the event $|\Pi(A)| = k$, the k elements of $\Pi(A)$ are independently and uniformly distributed in A.

A Tauberian theorem [Schmidt, 1925; Bingham, 1981].

If $f(k)$ is monotone increasing, and if, as $\lambda \to \infty$, $\sum_{k=0}^{\infty} f(k) e^{-\lambda} \lambda^k / k! \sim c \lambda^\alpha$, $\alpha > 0$, then as $n \to \infty$, $f(n) \sim c n^\alpha$.

Stochastic convergence

Let $\{Y_n\}$, $1 \leq n < \infty$, be a sequence of random variables and let Y be a random variable. We say $Y_n \to Y$ in probability if, for every $\varepsilon > 0$, we have

$$\lim_{n \to \infty} \Pr[|Y_n - Y| > \varepsilon] = 0.$$

A stronger notion than convergence in probability is that of almost sure convergence (also called convergence with probability 1). We say $Y_n \to Y$ almost surely (a.s.) provided

$$\Pr\left[\limsup_{n \to \infty} Y_n = Y = \liminf_{n \to \infty} Y_n\right] = 1.$$

To reinforce understanding of the notion of almost sure convergence, the reader might focus on the fact that $\limsup_{n\to\infty} Y_n$, $\liminf_{n\to\infty} Y_n$ and Y are all random variables. To say $Y_n \to Y$ almost surely just means that with probability 1, all three of these random variables are equal.

The difference between convergence in probability and convergence almost surely is an important one both in theory and in practice. Particularly in the area of probabilistic analysis of algorithms it is valuable to preserve the distinction. An exercise is given later to show that convergence a.s. implies convergence in probability, but not the converse.

A key tool in the proof of almost sure convergence is the following.

Borel–Cantelli lemma

If, for every $\varepsilon > 0$, $\sum_{n=1}^{\infty} \Pr[|Y_n - Y| > \varepsilon] < \infty$, then $Y_n \to Y$ almost surely.

Complete convergence

The Borel–Cantelli lemma gives a sufficient condition for the almost sure convergence of Y_n to Y, but the condition is *not* necessary. When the condition

$$\sum_{n=1}^{\infty} \Pr[|Y_n - Y| > \varepsilon] < \infty, \forall \varepsilon > 0,$$

holds we say Y_n *converges completely* to Y.

In the section which follows we give a simple proof of the BHH theorem which rests on a subadditivity argument and the Efron–Stein inequality. These same tools were pushed a bit harder by Steele [1981] to prove complete convergence in place of almost sure convergence.

2.5   A simple proof of the BHH theorem

The notions of the preceding section will now be applied to give a simple proof of the BHH theorem.

Theorem 3   *Suppose X_i, $1 \leqslant i < \infty$, are i.i.d. with the uniform distribution on $[0,1]^d$. Let $I_n = \{X_1, X_2, \ldots, X_n\}$. Then $L(I_n)/n^{(d-1)/d} \to c_d$ almost surely, where c_d is a constant depending on the dimension d.*

Proof   To prove this theorem we first get the asymptotics of the expected values, i.e., we show $E[L(I_n)] \sim c_d n^{(d-1)/d}$ as $n \to \infty$. For this purpose it is handy to first consider a related situation in which the points are distributed according to a Poisson process.

Let Π denote the Poisson process on $\mathbb{R}^d$ with unit intensity; in particular, $\Pi([0,t]^d)$ denotes the set of points that fall in the cube $[0,t]^d$. Let $F(t) = E[L(\Pi([0,t]^d))]$. Then

$$F(t) = \sum_{n=0}^{\infty} \Pr[|\Pi([0,t]^d)| = n] E[L(\Pi([0,t]^d)) \mid |\Pi([0,t]^d)| = n].$$

Recalling that $|\Pi([0, t]^d)|$ has a Poisson distribution with parameter t^d, and noting that, by an obvious scaling argument, an optimal tour through n points drawn independently from the uniform distribution over $[0, t]^d$ has expected length $tE[L(I_n)]$, we obtain

$$F(t) = \sum_{n=0}^{\infty} e^{-t^d} \frac{t^{dn}}{n!} tE[L(I_n)], \tag{1}$$

so information about $F(t)$ should give us information about $E[L(I_n)]$.

By decomposing $[0, t]^d$ into congruent subcubes Q_i of side t/m and applying the fixed dissection algorithm, we obtain

$$L(\Pi([0, t]^d)) \le \sum_{i=1}^{m^d} L(\Pi(Q_i)) + t(dm^{d-1} + \delta_d m^{d(d-2)/(d-1)}).$$

The first terms come from the optimal tours within the subcubes. The second term is from the bound of Lemma 2 applied to a set of arbitrarily chosen points, one from each Q_i with $\Pi(Q_i) \ne \varnothing$. Taking expectations,

$$F(t) \le m^d F\left(\frac{t}{m}\right) + t(dm^{d-1} + \delta_d m^{d(d-2)/(d-1)}).$$

Setting $t = ms$, we obtain

$$\frac{F(ms)}{(ms)^d} \le \frac{F(s)}{s^d} + \frac{d}{s^{d-1}} + \delta_d \frac{m^{-1/(d-1)}}{s^{d-1}}, \qquad m = 1, 2, \ldots.$$

This inequality, together with the fact that $F(t)$ is monotone and $F(t)/t^d$ is bounded, implies that $F(t)/t^d$ approaches a limit c_d as $t \to \infty$.

Returning to (1) and letting $u = t^d$, we see

$$\sum_{n=0}^{\infty} E[L(I_n)] e^{-u} \frac{u^n}{n!} \sim c_d u^{(d-1)/d}.$$

Since $E[L(I_n)]$ is monotone, the Tauberian theorem of Section 2.4 tells us at once that

$$E[L(I_n)] \sim c_d n^{(d-1)/d}.$$

To bound the variances of the variables $L(I_n)$ we apply the Efron–Stein inequality with $S(X_1, X_2, \ldots, X_{n-1}) = L(I_{n-1})$ and $Y = L(I_n)$. This gives

$$\text{var}[L(I_{n-1})] \le E\left[\sum_{i=1}^{n} (L(\{X_1, X_2, \ldots, X_{i-1}, X_{i+1}, \ldots, X_n\}) - L(I_n))^2 \right]$$

$$= nE[L(I_{n-1}) - L(I_n)]^2.$$

Since $|L(I_{n-1}) - L(I_n)| \le 2 \min_{1 \le i < n}\{|X_i - X_n|\}$, an easy calculation shows $E[L(I_{n-1}) - L(I_n)]^2 = O(n^{-2/d})$, and hence

$$\text{var}[L(I_n)] = O(n^{(d-2)/d}).$$

This implies $\text{var}[L(I_n)n^{-(d-1)/d}] = O(n^{-1})$, and taking $n_k = k^2$ we get

$$\sum_{k=1}^{\infty} \text{var}\left[\frac{L(I_{n_k})}{n_k^{(d-1)/d}}\right] < \infty.$$

By Chebyshev's inequality, we have for any $\varepsilon > 0$

$$\Pr[|L(I_n) - E[L(I_n)]| \geqslant \varepsilon n^{(d-1)/d}] \leqslant \varepsilon^{-2} \text{var}\left[\frac{L(I_n)}{n^{(d-1)/d}}\right],$$

so, by the asymptotics of $E[L(I_n)]$, we have

$$\sum_{k=1}^{\infty} \Pr[|L(I_{n_k}) - cn_k^{(d-1)/d}| \geqslant \varepsilon n_k^{(d-1)/d}] = \sum_{k=1}^{\infty} \Pr[|L(I_n)/(n_k^{(d-1)/d}) - c| \geqslant \varepsilon] < \infty.$$

The Borel–Cantelli lemma then says,

$$L(I_{n_k}) \sim cn_k^{(d-1)/d} \text{ with probability 1 as } k \to \infty. \tag{2}$$

Since $n_{k+1}/n_k \to 1$ and $L(I_{n_k}) \leqslant L(I_n) \leqslant L(I_{n_{k+1}})$ for $n_k \leqslant n < n_{k+1}$, (2) implies the desired result that $L(I_n) \sim cn^{(d-1)/d}$ with probability 1 as $n \to \infty$. $\square$

2.6 Analysis of the fixed dissection algorithm

First we will recall our model and the procedure we have called the *fixed dissection* algorithm. By X_i, $1 \leqslant i < N$, we denote independent random variables with the uniform distribution on the unit cube Q in $\mathbb{R}^d$, and $L_n = L_n(X_1, X_2, \ldots, X_n)$ is just the length of the minimal tour through $\{X_1, X_2, \ldots, X_n\}$.

The fixed dissection algorithm consists of dividing the cube Q into s congruent subcubes Q_i, solving the TSP within each subcube for the data $Q_i \cap \{X_1, X_2, \ldots, X_n\} = D_i$, crudely touring a set R consisting of representatives of all of the non-empty D_i, and crudely deleting excess edges to convert the resulting closed walk to a simple polygon.

The main objective of this section is to prove two results which respectively assert the effectiveness and the efficiency of the fixed dissection algorithm. First we consider the effectiveness and give an elementary proof (not using BHH) that the ratio L_n^F/L_n converges completely to 1. Specifically, we prove the following.

Theorem 4   *If σ is an unbounded increasing function of n and $s = n/\sigma$, then*

$$\sum_{n=1}^{\infty} \Pr\left[\frac{L_n^F}{L_n} \geqslant 1 + \varepsilon\right] < \infty, \forall \varepsilon > 0.$$

The proof will be obtained by two reasonably easy lemmas, the first of which asserts that L_n is unlikely to be small compared to $n^{(d-1)/d}$. The proof of the first lemma is one of our listed exercises.

Lemma 3   *There exist constants $A > 0$ and $0 < \rho < 1$ such that for all $n \geqslant 1$,*

$$\Pr[L_n < An^{(d-1)/d}] \leqslant \rho^n.$$

The second lemma shows that L_n^F is bounded above by L_n plus a quantity which is *deterministically* small compared to $n^{(d-1)/d}$.

Lemma 4 *There is a remainder r_n such that*

$$L_n \leqslant L_n^F \leqslant L_n + r_n$$

and $r_n = O(n^{(d-1)/d} \sigma^{-1/(d(d-1))})$, where the O depends only on d (not on n or σ).

Proof Let T denote the optimal tour through $\{X_1, X_2, \ldots, X_n\}$. For each face F_{ij}, $1 \leqslant j \leqslant 2d$, of Q_i we consider the set of 'marks' where an edge of T which connects a point of $Q_i \cap \{X_1, X_2, \ldots, X_n\}$ to a point of $Q_k \cap \{X_1, X_2, \ldots, X_n\}$, $k \neq i$, intersects F_{ij}. We let M_{ij}, $1 \leqslant i \leqslant s$, $1 \leqslant j \leqslant 2d$, denote the sets of marks in F_{ij}. Trivially, the cardinality of M_{ij} (denoted by $|M_{ij}|$) is even and is bounded by $2n_i = 2 |Q_i \cap \{X_1, X_2, \ldots, X_n\}|$, the total number of points in Q_i.

We will now get an upper bound on L_n^F. Recalling the definition of L_n^F and the bound of Lemma 2, we get

$$L_n^F \leqslant \sum_{i=1}^{s} L_n(Q_i) + \{ds^{(d-1)/d} + o(s^{(d-1)/d})\}.$$

Our main task is to bound the sum above using parts of the optimal path and extra lengths of lower order. Let $Q_i \cap T$ denote the segments of T contained in Q_i. From each nonempty M_{ij}, $1 \leqslant j \leqslant 2d$, choose an arbitrary element as its representative. To obtain a tour through $Q_i \cap \{X_1, X_2, \ldots, X_n\}$, add segments to $Q_i \cap T$ as follows: for each nonempty M_{ij}, a tour through M_{ij}; a tour through the representatives of the nonempty sets M_{ij}; for each nonempty M_{ij} of even cardinality, a perfect matching of the elements of M_{ij}; for each M_{ij} of odd cardinality, a perfect matching of the elements of M_{ij} other than the representative; a perfect matching of the representatives of the M_{ij} of odd cardinality (there will be an even number of such representatives). Note that a perfect matching can be constructed by taking alternate edges of a tour through an even number of points. This procedure yields a walk through $Q_i \cap \{X_1, X_2, \ldots, X_n\}$ and the cost of this walk is bounded by

$$\text{length}(T \cap Q_i) + \sum_{j=1}^{2d} ((d-1) |M_{ij}|^{(d-2)/(d-1)} + \delta_{d-1} |M_{ij}|^{(d-3)/(d-2)}) s^{-1/d}$$

$$+ \{d(2d)^{(d-1)/d} + o((2d)^{(d-1)/d})\} s^{-1/d}$$

$$+ \sum_{j=1}^{2d} ((d-1) |M_{ij}|^{(d-2)/(d-1)} + \delta_{d-1} |M_{ij}|^{(d-3)/(d-2)}) s^{-1/d}$$

$$+ \{d(2d)^{(d-1)/d} + o((2d)^{(d-1)/d})\} s^{-1/d}.$$

Summing over all the cells of the dissection,

$$\sum L_n(Q_i) \leq L_n + 2\left(\sum_{i=1}^{s} \sum_{j=1}^{d} (d-1)|M_{ij}|^{(d-2)/(d-1)} + \delta_{d-1}|M_{ij}|^{(d-3)/(d-2)}\right)s^{-1/d}$$
$$+ 2\{d(2d)^{(d-1)/d} + o((2d)^{(d-1)/d})\}s^{(d-1)/d}.$$

Since $\sum_{i=1}^{s}\sum_{j=1}^{d}|M_{ij}| \leq 2n$ and the functions $x^{(d-2)/(d-1)}$ and $x^{(d-3)/(d-2)}$ are concave, the above expression is bounded above by the value it assumes when each M_{ij} is $2n/(sd)$. This gives

$$\sum L_n(Q_i) \leq L_n + O(n^{(d-2)/(d-1)}s^{1/(d(d-1))}) + O(s^{(d-1)/d}).$$

The substitution $n/\sigma = s$ completes the proof of the lemma. $\square$

Proof of Theorem 4   This is now easily given:

$$\Pr\left[\frac{L_n^F}{L_n} \geq 1 + \varepsilon\right] \leq \Pr[L_n < An^{(d-1)/d}] + \Pr[|L_n - L_n^F| \geq \varepsilon An^{(d-1)/d}].$$

The first summand is summable since it is dominated by a term going to 0 geometrically, and the second term is summable since it is 0 for all sufficiently large n. $\square$

The execution time of the fixed dissection method clearly has the same order as the time to solve all of the TSPs within the subcubes. We assume that dynamic programming [Bellman, 1962; Held & Karp, 1962] is used to solve the TSPs within the subcubes. Since dynamic programming solves an x-city TSP in time bounded by $f(x) = Ax^2 2^x$, the order of the execution time of the fixed dissection procedure is bounded by order of

$$T_n = \sum_{i=1}^{s} f(n_i)$$

where n_i denotes the number of elements of the set $Q_i \cap \{X_1, X_2, \ldots, X_n\}$. We shall derive upper bounds on the mean and variance of T_n. As a first step we bound the mean and variance of $f(n_i)$ for a fixed i. The random variable n_i has a binomial distribution:

$$\Pr[n_i = k] = \binom{n}{k}\left(\frac{1}{s}\right)^k \left(1 - \frac{1}{s}\right)^{n-k}.$$

Hence

$$E[f(n_i)] = \sum_{k=0}^{n} Ak^2 2^k \binom{n}{k}\left(\frac{1}{s}\right)^k \left(1 - \frac{1}{s}\right)^{n-k}$$

and

$$E[f(n_i)^2] = \sum_{k=0}^{n} A^2 k^4 4^k \binom{n}{k}\left(\frac{1}{s}\right)^k \left(1 - \frac{1}{s}\right)^{n-k}.$$

Using the identity

$$\sum_{k=0}^{n} k(k-1)\ldots(k-i+1)\binom{n}{k}x^k = n(n-1)\ldots(n-i+1)x^i(1+x)^{n-i}$$

one obtains, after some algebraic manipulation, that, as $n \to \infty$ and $s \to \infty$ in such a way that $\sigma = n/s \to \infty$, $E[f(n_i)] \sim 4A\sigma^2 e^\sigma$ and $\mathrm{var}[f(n_i)] \sim 256A^2\sigma^4 e^{3\sigma}$. Since expectations add, $E[T_n] \sim 4An\sigma e^\sigma$ and, by McDiarmid's inequality, $\mathrm{var}[T_n] \sim 256A^2 n\sigma^3 e^{3\sigma}$. Thus, for the specific choice $\sigma = [\log n]$, the expected execution time of the fixed dissection method is $O(n^2 \log n)$ and the variance is $O(n^4(\log n)^3)$.

2.7 The Euclidean directed TSP

Karp [1977] posed the problem of formulating a probabilistic model of the directed TSP for which one can find an algorithm that runs in polynomial time with high probability. One such formulation was given by Steele [1985]; although, as we will see, the available results are far less complete than for the undirected case.

To specify the model let X_i, $1 \leq i < \infty$, be independent random variables with the uniform distribution on $[0, 1]^2$. As the vertex set of a random graph G_n we take $V_n = \{X_1, X_2, \ldots, X_n\}$. To define a set of directed arcs for G_n we first suppose that for $1 \leq i < j \leq n$ there are independent Bernoulli random variables Y_{ij} which are also independent of V_n and for which $\Pr[Y_{ij} = 1] = \Pr[Y_{ij} = 0] = 1/2$. Now the directed arc set A_n for $G_n = (V_n, A_n)$ is defined by taking $(i, j) \in A_n$ if $Y_{ij} = 1$ and taking $(j, i) \in A_n$ if $Y_{ij} = 0$. This procedure yields a complete digraph G_n.

It is not necessarily apparent that there always exists a directed path through G_n; but, in fact, it is a classic result due to Rédei [1934] that any complete digraph has a path through all its vertices.

By a solution to the directed Euclidean TSP we mean here a *path* through V_n which has minimum Euclidean length. We denote this length by D_n.

The results established by Steele [1985] are the following.

Theorem 5   *There is a constant $0 < \beta < \infty$ such that as $n \to \infty$,*

$$E[D_n] \sim \beta\sqrt{n}.$$

Theorem 6   *There is a polynomial algorithm which provides a directed path through V_n which has length D_n^* satisfying*

$$E[D_n^*] \leq (1 + \varepsilon)E[D_n]$$

for all $\varepsilon > 0$ and $n \geq N(\varepsilon)$.

These results easily generalize to $[0, 1]^d$, but the extension to almost sure (or complete) convergence results seems to be considerably more difficult than in the undirected case. These extensions remain as open problems.

Exercises

1. Prove that the shortest closed walk through a set of n points in $\mathbb{R}^d$, not all of which are collinear, is a simple polygon.
2. Prove Lemma 3.

3. Give your own proof, independent of Lemma 2, of the following fact: Let S be a set of n points in the unit d-dimensional cube. Then $L(S) \leq a_d n^{(d-1)/d}$, where a_d depends only on the dimension d.

4. Prove that for each dimension d there exist constants $A_d > 0$ and $B_d < 1$ such that $\Pr[L(I_n) < A_d n^{-(d-1)/d}] < (B_d)^n$.

5. Derive the best lower and upper bounds you can on the constant c_d occurring in the statement of the BHH theorem.

6. The *strips method* for constructing a tour through n random points in the unit square dissects the square into $1/\Delta$ horizontal strips of width Δ, and then follows a zig-zag path, visiting the points in the first strip in left-to-right order, then the points in the second strip in right-to-left order, etc., finally returning to the initial point from the final point of the last strip. Prove that, when Δ is suitably chosen, the expected length of the tour produced by the strips method is $\leq 0{\cdot}93\sqrt{n} = O(\sqrt{n})$.

7. Let S be a set of points in the unit square Q, and let Q be dissected into rectangles Q_i. Prove: $\sum_i L(S \cap Q_i) \leq L(S) + \frac{3}{2} \sum per(Q_i)$, where $per(Q_i)$ is the perimeter of Q_i.

8. Generalize the preceding result to d dimensions.

9. Prove the following scaling principle: Let S be a set of n points drawn independently from the uniform distribution over $[0, t]^d$. Then $E[L(S)] = tE[L(I_n)]$.

10. Complete the proof that $F(t)/t^d$ approaches a limit.

11. Prove: $L(I_n) - L(I_{n-1}) \leq 2 \min_{i=1,2,\ldots,n-1} \{|X_n - X_i|\}$. Here $|X_n - X_i|$ denotes the Euclidean length of the vector $X_n - X_i$.

3 PROBABILISTIC ANALYSIS OF THE ASYMMETRIC TSP

In this section we consider a very general form of the TSP, in which the distances between cities are given by an arbitrary nonnegative $n \times n$ matrix (c_{ij}). Neither symmetry ($c_{ij} = c_{ji}$) nor the triangle inequality ($c_{ij} + c_{jk} \geq c_{ik}$) is required. The cost of an optimal tour is $\min_\pi \{\sum_i c_{i\pi(i)}\}$, where π ranges over the cyclic permutations of $\{1, 2, \ldots, n\}$.

The asymmetric TSP appears to be a tough nut to crack, since it is $\mathcal{NP}$-hard to construct a tour whose cost is within a constant factor of the cost of an optimal tour. Despite this evidence that the problem is difficult, there is a simple heuristic algorithm which, in most instances, will produce a near-optimal tour. This heuristic is based on solving a related problem called the *assignment problem*, and then using certain *patching operations* to convert the solution of the assignment problem into a tour. The assignment problem can be stated as follows:

$$\text{minimize} \sum_i c_{i\sigma(i)},$$

where σ ranges over the permutations (not just the cyclic permutations) of $\{1, 2, \ldots, n\}$. The assignment problem can be solved in $O(n^3)$ steps.

In order to validate this *patching algorithm* we conduct a probabilistic analysis on the assumption that the distances c_{ij} are drawn independently from the uniform distribution over $[0, 1]$. Let A^* be the cost of an optimal assignment for the $n \times n$ matrix (c_{ij}), let T^* be the cost of an optimal tour, and let T be the cost of the tour produced by the patching algorithm. Then $A^* \le T^* \le T$. The inequality $A^* \le T^*$ follows because the assignment problem is a relaxation of the TSP. The inequality $T^* \le T$ follows because T^* is the cost of an optimal solution of the TSP, and T is the cost of a feasible solution.

When the c_{ij} are drawn independently from the uniform distribution over $[0, 1]$, A^*, T^* and T become random variables. It is a surprising fact, first proved by Walkup [1970], that $E[A^*]$, the expected value of A^*, remains bounded as $n \to \infty$. Karp [1984] has proved that $E[A^*] < 2$ for all n. Lazarus [1979] has proved that $E[A^*] \ge 1 + 1/e + O(1/n)$. Computational experiments indicate that $E[A^*]$ is close to 1.6 when n is greater than 100.

Our main results here are that

$$E[T - A^*] < 2.33 n^{-1/2} \quad \text{and} \quad E\left[\frac{T - T^*}{T^*}\right] = O(n^{-1/2}).$$

Thus the expected cost of an optimal tour remains bounded as $n \to \infty$ and tends to be close to the cost of an optimal assignment. Moreover, the percentage difference between the cost of an optimal tour and the cost of the tour produced by the patching algorithm tends to be very small when n is large.

3.1 The assignment problem and the patching operation

Recall that the assignment problem asks for a permutation σ that minimizes $\sum_i c_{i\sigma(i)}$, while the TSP asks for a *cyclic* permutation π that minimizes $\sum_i c_{i\pi(i)}$. Thus the assignment problem is a relaxation of the TSP, and A^*, the cost of an optimal assignment, is a lower bound on T^*, the cost of an optimal tour. Computational experience indicates that this lower bound is often very tight. In Chapter 10, Balas and Toth report the following experiment.

> 'We generated 400 problems with $50 \le n \le 250$, with the costs independently drawn from a uniform distribution of the integers over the intervals $[1, 100]$ and $[1, 1000]$, and solved both the AP and the TSP. We found that on the average $v(\text{AP})[= A^*]$ was 99.2% of $v(\text{TSP})[= T^*]$. Furthermore, we found the bound to improve with problem size, in that for the problems with $50 \le n \le 150$ and $150 \le n \le 250$ the outcomes were 98.8% and 99.6%, respectively.'

Since an optimal assignment can be computed in $O(n^3)$ steps, and since A^* tends to be a tight lower bound on T^*, it is natural to solve the assignment problem as a first step towards the exact or approximate solution of the TSP. Balas and Toth survey several rather successful branch and bound algorithms for the directed TSP based on the use of A^* as a lower bound on T^*. In the present chapter we explore a patching algorithm which uses an optimal assignment as the starting point for the construction of a near-optimal tour. A similar algorithm was presented by Karp [1979], but the analysis presented here is simpler and the results are stronger.

The patching algorithm is based on a patching operation. To explain this operation it is necessary to discuss the cycle structure of a permutation. With any permutation τ we may associate a directed graph with vertex set $\{1, 2, \ldots, n\}$ and arc set $\{(i, \tau(i)) \mid i = 1, 2, \ldots, n\}$. Each connected component of this graph is a directed cycle. These components are called the cycles of τ and, of course, a cyclic permutation is a permutation that has only one cycle.

In general σ, the permutation which is the optimal solution of the assignment problem, will have many cycles. The patching algorithm converts σ to a cyclic permutation by a sequence of patching operations, each of which joins two cycles together. Let τ be a permutation, and let i and j be elements that occur in two distinct cycles C and D. Then the (i, j)-patching operation, depicted in Figure 6.2, joins C and D into a new cycle by

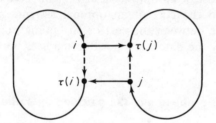

Figure 6.2   The (i, j)-patching operation

inserting the arcs $(i, \tau(j))$ and $(j, \tau(i))$ and deleting the arcs $(i, \tau(i))$ and $(j, \tau(j))$. This operation increases the cost of the permutation by

$$\Delta(\tau, i, j) = c_{i\tau(j)} + c_{j\tau(i)} - c_{i\tau(i)} - c_{j\tau(j)}.$$

The following is a statement of the patching algorithm.

Patching algorithm

begin
$\tau \leftarrow \sigma$;
{σ is the optimal assignment and τ is the permutation currently being processed}
while τ is not a cyclic permutation **do**
  begin
  let D_1 and D_2 be the two longest cycles in τ;

{the length of a cycle is the number of elements it contains, and ties are broken arbitrarily}
choose $i \in D_1$ and $j \in D_2$ to minimize the patching cost $\Delta(\tau, i, j)$;
perform the (i, j)-patching operation and call the new cycle τ
end;
$\pi \leftarrow \tau$
end.

3.2 A probabilistic bound on the largest cost in an optimal assignment

In preparation for the analysis of the patching algorithm, we show that, with high probability, $c_{i\sigma(i)}$ is very small for every pair $(i, \sigma(i))$ occurring in the optimal assignment. Let 'log' denote $\log_e$ and let 'lg' denote $\log_2$. Let

$$\alpha(n) = \frac{20 \log n (\lceil \lg(n+3) \rceil - 2)}{n}.$$

Lemma 5 *Let the elements of the $n \times n$ matrix (c_{ij}) be drawn independently from the uniform distribution over $[0, 1]$, and let σ be the optimal assignment. Then, with probability $1 - O(n^{-2})$, $c_{i\sigma(i)} \leq \alpha(n)$ for all i.*

The proof of Lemma 5 requires the concepts of an expanding matrix and an expanding digraph. Let A be an $n \times n$ matrix of 0's and 1's. For each set $S \subseteq \{1, 2, \ldots, n\}$, let $\Gamma(S) = \{j \mid \text{for some } i \in S, a_{ij} = 1\}$ and let $\Gamma^{-1}(S) = \{j \mid \text{for some } i \in S, a_{ji} = 1\}$. Then A is an *expanding matrix* if, for every $S \subseteq \{1, 2, \ldots, n\}$,

$$|\Gamma(S)| \geq \min\left\{2 |S| + 1, \frac{n+1}{2}\right\} \quad \text{and} \quad |\Gamma^{-1}(S)| \geq \min\left\{2 |S| + 1, \frac{n+1}{2}\right\}.$$

Thus an expanding matrix is one in which each small set of rows S 'hits' at least $2 |S| + 1$ columns, and each small set of columns hits at least $2 |S| + 1$ rows.

A digraph G with vertex set $\{1, 2, \ldots, n\}$ is called an *expanding digraph* if $A(G)$, the adjacency matrix of G, is an expanding matrix; here the $i - j$ element of $A(G)$ is equal to 1 if and only if (i, j) is an arc of G.

Lemma 6 *In an n-vertex expanding digraph, every vertex lies in a cycle of length $\leq 2 \lceil \lg(n+3) \rceil - 4$.*

Proof Let $d_G(i, j)$ denote the minimum number of arcs in a path of G from vertex i to vertex j. By inductive application of the fact that G is expanding, we obtain the following inequalities for all l:

$$|\{k \mid d_G(i, k) \leq l\}| \geq \min\left\{2^{l+1} - 1, \frac{n+1}{2}\right\}$$

and

$$|\{k \mid d_G(k, i) \leq l\}| \geq \min\left\{2^{l+1} - 1, \frac{n+1}{2}\right\}.$$

Setting $l^* = \lceil \lg(n+3)-2 \rceil$, we have $|\{k \mid d_G(i, k) \le l^*\}| \ge (n+1)/2$ and $|\{k \mid d_G(k, i) \le l^*\}| \ge (n+1)/2$. Note that if i is contained in either of the sets $\{k \mid d_G(i, k) \le l^*\}$ and $\{k \mid d_G(k, i) \le l^*\}$ then the lemma has been proved, and so we assume that this is not the case. Hence there exists a $k \ne i$ such that $d_G(i, k) \le l^*$ and $d_G(k, i) \le l^*$, and it follows that i lies in a cycle of length $\le 2l^* = 2\lceil \lg(n+3) \rceil - 4$. $\square$

Lemma 7 *Let $A = (a_{ij})$ be an $n \times n$ matrix of 0's and 1's whose elements are independent random variables such that, for each i, j, $\Pr[a_{ij} = 1] = 10 \log n/n$. Then $\Pr[A$ is not an expanding matrix$] = O(n^{-2})$.*

Proof Call a set $S \subseteq \{1, 2, \ldots, n\}$ row-faulty if $|S| \le n/4$ and $|\Gamma(S)| \le 2|S|$, and column-faulty if $|S| \le n/4$ and $|\Gamma^{-1}(S)| \le 2|S|$. Then A fails to be an expanding matrix if and only if there is a row-faulty or column-faulty set. The expected number of row-faulty sets is bounded above by

$$\sum_{k=1}^{\lfloor n/4 \rfloor} \binom{n}{k}\binom{n}{2k}(1-p)^{k(n-2k)}$$

where $p = 10 \log n/n$. Since

$$\binom{n}{k} \le \left(\frac{ne}{k}\right)^k, \quad \binom{n}{2k} \le \left(\frac{ne}{2k}\right)^{2k} \quad \text{and} \quad 1-p < e^{-p} = n^{-10/n},$$

the above summation is bounded above by

$$\sum_{k=1}^{\lfloor n/4 \rfloor} \left(\frac{ne}{k}\frac{n^2e^2}{k^2}n^{-10}n^{20k/n}\right)^k.$$

Since $k \ge 1$ and $n^{20k/n} \le n^5$ when $k \le n/4$, this summation is $\le \sum_{k=0}^{\lfloor n/4 \rfloor} (n^{-2}e^3)^k = O(n^{-2})$. Thus the expected number of faulty rows is $O(n^{-2})$. Similarly, the expected number of faulty columns is $O(n^{-2})$, and thus the probability that A fails to be an expanding matrix is $O(n^{-2})$. $\square$

Given the cost matrix (c_{ij}), define the 0–1 matrix $A(C) = (a_{ij})$ by

$$a_{ij} = \begin{cases} 1 & \text{if } c_{ij} < \dfrac{10 \log n}{n}, \\ 0 & \text{otherwise.} \end{cases}$$

By Lemma 7, $\Pr[A(C)$ is an expanding matrix$] = 1 - O(n^{-2})$.

Let G^σ be the digraph with vertex set $\{1, 2, \ldots, n\}$ and arc set $\{(i, j) \mid c_{i\sigma(j)} < 10 \log n/n\}$. Then G^σ is an expanding digraph if and only if $A(C)$ is an expanding matrix. Thus, $\Pr[G^\sigma$ is an expanding digraph$] = 1 - O(n^{-2})$. To complete the proof of Lemma 5, we need only prove the following lemma.

Lemma 8 *Let σ denote the optimal assignment for C. If G^σ is an expanding digraph then, for all i, $c_{i\sigma(i)} \le \alpha(n)$.*

Proof The proof is by *reductio ad absurdum*. Suppose G^σ is an expanding digraph and $c_{i\sigma(i)} > \alpha(n)$. By Lemma 6, G^σ contains a cycle of length $t \leq 2\lceil \lg(n+3) \rceil - 4$ from i to i. Let the successive vertices along this cycle be $i_1, i_2, \ldots, i_t$ where $i = i_1$. Consider the permutation ϑ given by:

$$\vartheta(i_1) = \sigma(i_2), \; \vartheta(i_2) = \sigma(i_3), \ldots, \vartheta(i_t) = \sigma(i_1)$$

and

$$\vartheta(j) = \sigma(j) \qquad \text{for} \qquad j \notin \{i_1, i_2, \ldots, i_t\}.$$

Then

$$\sum_{i=1}^{n} c_{i\vartheta(i)} - \sum_{i=1}^{n} c_{i\sigma(i)} = (c_{i_1\sigma(i_2)} + \ldots + c_{i_{t-1}\sigma(i_t)} + c_{i_t\sigma(i_1)})$$
$$- (c_{i_1\sigma(i_1)} + \ldots + c_{i_t\sigma(i_t)}).$$

But, by the way G^σ was constructed, each term in the first summation on the right-hand side is $\leq 10 \log n/n$. Also each term in the second summation is ≥ 0, and $c_{i_1\sigma(i_1)} > \alpha(n)$. It follows that

$$\sum_{i=1}^{n} c_{i\vartheta(i)} - \sum_{i=1}^{n} c_{i\sigma(i)} < \frac{10t \log n}{n} - \alpha(n) \leq 0,$$

contradicting the optimality of σ. $\square$

3.3 Analysis of the patching algorithm

Our main goal in this section is to derive an upper bound on the expected cost of converting the optimal assignment to a tour, using the patching algorithm.

Call the $n \times n$ matrix (c_{ij}) *exceptional* if its optimal assignment includes an arc of $\cos t > \alpha(n)$. By Lemma 5 the probability that a matrix is exceptional is $O(n^{-2})$, and thus the patching costs associated with exceptional matrices cannot contribute more than $O(n^{-1})$ to the overall expected patching cost. Call a cost c_{ij} *small* if $c_{ij} \leq \alpha(n)$, and *large* otherwise. Associate with (c_{ij}) a matrix $(\bar{c}_{ij})$ defined as follows:

$$\bar{c}_{ij} = \begin{cases} c_{ij} & \text{if } c_{ij} \text{ is small,} \\ \infty & \text{if } c_{ij} \text{ is large.} \end{cases}$$

If (c_{ij}) is not exceptional then (c_{ij}) and $(\bar{c}_{ij})$ have the same optimal assignment. Thus, for purposes of bounding the overall expected patching cost, we may assume that the optimal assignment is always computed using $(\bar{c}_{ij})$ instead of (c_{ij}). This means that, once a cost is determined to be large, it is never involved in the computation of the optimal assignment σ, and thus is not conditioned in any way by that computation. Thus, at the beginning of the patching process, the large costs may be treated as independent random variables, each of which is drawn from the uniform distribution over $(a(n), 1]$.

Now consider the patching step when cycle C, of length r, is patched into cycle D, of length m. Every arc occurring in C or D is of nonnegative cost. The cost of each arc (i, j) between C and D is either small ($\leq \alpha(n)$) or large ($> \alpha(n)$).

The costs c_{ij} of the large arcs between cycles C and D are independent random variables with the uniform distribution over $(\alpha(n), 1]$. This holds true at the beginning of the patching process, and none of the computations performed in previous patching steps involve these values, so it remains true at the present step. Thus, the cost of patching C into D is stochastically smaller than it would be if the costs of all arcs within C or D were 0 and the costs of all arcs between C and D were uniform over $(\alpha(n), 1]$. We analyze the patching algorithm under this pessimistic assumption.

Certain properties of the optimal assignment σ will be important for our analysis. First note that, since the c_{ij} are drawn independently from a continuous distribution, it will be true with probability 1 that no two permutations have the same cost and, as a consequence, that the optimal assignment is unique. Also, the optimal assignment is equally likely to be any one of the $n!$ permutations of $\{1, 2, \ldots, n\}$. To see this, define two $n \times n$ cost matrices to be equivalent if one of them can be obtained by permuting the columns of the other. Each matrix lies in exactly one equivalence class. Excluding events of probability 0 such as the occurrence of two equal columns, an equivalence class consists of $n!$ equally likely matrices, and each of the $n!$ permutations is the optimal assignment for exactly one of these matrices.

The fact that the optimal assignment is a random permutation is essential for our analysis. To give the reader a feeling for the cycle structure of a random permutation, we list the cycle structures of ten randomly generated permutations of 1000 elements. The cycle structure is given as $\langle a_1, a_2, \ldots, a_t \rangle$, meaning that the permutation has t cycles, and their respective lengths are $a_1, a_2, \ldots, a_t$ where $a_1 \leq a_2 \leq \cdots \leq a_t$.

$$\langle 2, 2, 3, 25, 49, 919 \rangle$$
$$\langle 1, 8, 9, 20, 24, 147, 781 \rangle$$
$$\langle 3, 6, 6, 10, 17, 42, 107, 156, 653 \rangle$$
$$\langle 1, 1, 6, 16, 58, 70, 75, 298, 475 \rangle$$
$$\langle 1, 9, 13, 16, 17, 35, 40, 41, 828 \rangle$$
$$\langle 1, 2, 3, 3, 21, 94, 139, 338, 399 \rangle$$
$$\langle 2, 3, 5, 28, 117, 332, 513 \rangle$$
$$\langle 1, 1, 10, 16, 95, 155, 722 \rangle$$
$$\langle 1, 2, 997 \rangle$$
$$\langle 45, 246, 709 \rangle$$

In these examples the number of cycles is small and very few elements lie in short cycles. The following facts about random permutations indicate that this tends to be true in general. In the following three facts let σ denote a random permutation of n elements.

Fact 1. The probability that element 1 lies in a cycle of length x is $1/n$, for $x = 1, 2, \ldots, n$.

Fact 2. The expected number of cycles in σ is

$$1 + \frac{1}{2} + \frac{1}{3} + \ldots + \frac{1}{n} \sim \log n.$$

Fact 3. The probability that exactly t elements lie in cycles of σ of length less than or equal to r is $\leq 1/\lfloor t/r \rfloor!$.

Lemma 9 *The conditional expectation of the total patching cost, given that the optimal assignment has cycle structure $\langle a_1, a_2, \ldots, a_t \rangle$, is*

$$\leq 2(t-1)\alpha(n) + \tfrac{1}{2}\sqrt{\pi} \sum_{k=1}^{t-1} \frac{1}{\sqrt{a_k(a_{k+1} + a_{k+2} + \ldots + a_t)}}.$$

Proof The algorithm performs $t-1$ patching operations. For $k = 1, 2, \ldots, t-1$, a step occurs in which a cycle D_1 of length a_k gets patched into the longest cycle D_2, which is of length $a_{k+1} + a_{k+2} + \ldots + a_t$. As discussed above, we may assume pessimistically that the arcs within D_1 and D_2 are of cost 0, and the arcs between D_1 and D_2 are independent random variables, each of which is the sum of two independent random variables drawn from the uniform distribution over $(\alpha(n), 1]$. A standard calculation shows that the expected value of the patching cost is

$$\leq 2\alpha(n) + \tfrac{1}{2}\sqrt{\pi} \frac{1}{\sqrt{a_k(a_{k+1} + a_{k+2} + \ldots + a_t)}}$$

and, summing over all the patching steps, the total patching cost is

$$\leq 2(t-1)\alpha(n) + \tfrac{1}{2}\sqrt{\pi} \sum_{k=1}^{t-1} \frac{1}{\sqrt{a_k(a_{k+1} + a_{k+2} + \ldots + a_t)}}. \qquad \square$$

Theorem 7 $E[T - A^*] \leq 2.33 n^{-1/2} + o(n^{-1/2})$.

Proof By Lemma 9,

$$E[T - A^*] \leq E\left[2(t-1)\alpha(n) + \tfrac{1}{2}\sqrt{\pi} \sum_{k=1}^{t-1} \frac{1}{\sqrt{a_k(a_{k+1} + \ldots + a_t)}} \right],$$

where $\langle a_1, a_2, \ldots, a_t \rangle$ is the cycle length distribution of a random permutation of $\{1, 2, \ldots, n\}$. By Fact 2, $E[t] \sim \log n$ so $E[2(t-1)\alpha(n)] = O((\log n)^3/n)$. If σ is a permutation with cycle structure $\langle a_1, a_2, \ldots, a_t \rangle$ then

$$\sum_{k=1}^{t-1} \frac{1}{\sqrt{a_k(a_{k+1} + \ldots + a_t)}} \leq \sum_{\{C | r(C) \leq n/2\}} \frac{1}{\sqrt{r(C)\max\{r(C), m(C)\}}},$$

where C ranges over the cycles of σ, $r(C)$ is the number of elements in cycle C, and $m(C)$ is the number of elements in cycles of length greater than $r(C)$.

Conditioning on the event that σ contains a given cycle C, we compute

$$E\left[\frac{1}{\sqrt{\max\{r(C), m(C)\}}}\right].$$

Let $r = r(C)$.

Case 1. $r < n^{0.6}$. The cycles of σ different from C form a random permutation σ' of $n - r$ elements. Hence $m(C)$ is distributed as $n - r - M(n - r, r)$, where the random variable $M(n - r, r)$ denotes the number of elements in cycles of length $\leq r$ in a random permutation of $n - r$ elements. Let $x = M(n - r, r)/(n - r)$. Then

$$\frac{1}{\sqrt{m(C)}} = \frac{1}{\sqrt{n-r}}\frac{1}{\sqrt{1-x}}.$$

Noting that

$$\frac{1}{\sqrt{1-x}} \leq 1 + 2x \qquad \text{for} \qquad 0 \leq x \leq 0.85,$$

we obtain

$$E\left[\frac{1}{\sqrt{\max\{r(C), m(C)\}}}\right] \leq \Pr[x \leq 0.85]\frac{1}{\sqrt{n-r}}E[1+2x \mid x \leq 0.85]$$

$$+ \frac{1}{\sqrt{r(C)}}\Pr[x > 0.85]$$

$$\leq E[1+2x]\frac{1}{\sqrt{n-r}} + \frac{1}{\sqrt{r(C)}}\Pr[x > 0.85].$$

Recalling the definition of x and using Fact 3:

$$\Pr[x > 0.85] = \Pr[M(n-r, r) > 0.85(n-r)] \leq \sum_{t=\lceil 0.85(n-r)\rceil}^{n-r} \frac{1}{\lfloor t/(n-r)\rfloor!}.$$

When $r < n^{0.6}$,

$$\sum_{t=\lceil 0.85(n-r)\rceil}^{n-r} \frac{1}{\lfloor t/(n-r)\rfloor!}$$

goes to 0 faster than D^{-n} for any positive constant D. Also, by Fact 1, $E[x] = r/(n-r)$. Hence

$$E\left[\frac{1}{\max\{r(C), m(C)\}}\right] \leq \frac{1}{\sqrt{n-r}}\left(1 + \frac{2r}{n-r} + o(D^{-n})\right),$$

where D is an arbitrarily large constant.

Case 2. $r \geq n^{0.6}$. In this case we use $1/\sqrt{\max\{r(C), m(C)\}} \leq 1/\sqrt{r}$.

Combining the bounds obtained in Cases 1 and 2 with the fact that the expected number of cycles of length r is $1/r$, we obtain

$$E\left[\sum_{k=1}^{t-1}\frac{1}{\sqrt{a_k(a_{k+1}+\ldots+a_t)}}\right]$$

$$\leq\sum_{r=1}^{\lfloor n^{0.6}\rfloor}r^{-3/2}\frac{1}{\sqrt{n-r}}\left(1+\frac{2r}{n-r}+o(D^{-n})\right)+\sum_{r=\lceil n^{0.6}\rceil}^{\lfloor n/2\rfloor}r^{-2}$$

$$\leq\left(\sum_{r=1}^{\infty}r^{-3/2}\right)\frac{1}{\sqrt{n}}+o(n^{-1/2})<2.65n^{-1/2}+o(n^{-1/2}).$$

Finally, applying Lemma 9, we have $E[T-A^*]\leq 2.33n^{-1/2}+o(n^{-1/2})$. $\quad\square$

We close by noting the following corollary, which establishes that the percentage difference between T, the cost of the tour produced by the patching algorithm, and T^*, the cost of the optimal tour, tends to be very small when n is large.

Corollary 1 $E\left[\dfrac{T-T^*}{T^*}\right]=O(n^{-1/2}).$

Proof Since $T^*\geq A^*$ it suffices to prove that $E\left[\dfrac{T^*-A^*}{A^*}\right]=O(n^{-1/2})$. This follows from three observations:

(i) $E[T-A^*]=O(n^{-1/2})$ (Theorem 7).
(ii) On all instances, $T-A^*\leq 2n$.
(iii) For every $\varepsilon>0$, $\Pr[A^*<1-\varepsilon]$ goes exponentially to 0 as $n\to\infty$. This is most easily seen by noting that $A^*\geq\sum_i\min_j\{c_{ij}\}$. $\quad\square$

3.4 Open questions

We mention two variants of the random directed TSP for which it should be possible to conduct a probabilistic analysis of approximation algorithms based on patching. The first of these is the random undirected TSP, in which the matrix (c_{ij}) is symmetric, and the elements on or above the main diagonal are drawn independently from the uniform distribution over $[0, 1]$. The second variant is the random directed TSP with repeated visits to cities permitted, so that, instead of tours, we deal with directed spanning walks.

It would also be of great interest to make a probabilistic analysis of branch and bound methods for the optimal solution of the directed TSP. One common branch and bound method makes use of the fact that the optimal solution of the assignment problem provides a lower bound on the cost of an optimal tour. The method develops a tree of problem instances, each of which is obtained from the original instance by setting certain costs c_{ij} to ∞, thus excluding tours which use the arc (i, j). Given such a derived instance I, let $\sigma(I)$ be the optimal solution of the assignment problem. If $\sigma(I)$ happens to be a cyclic permutation then it solves instances I of the

TSP, and there is no need to create descendants of I in the tree of problem instances. If the permutation $\sigma(I)$ is not cyclic then its shortest cycle determines its descendants. Suppose the shortest cycle of $\sigma(I)$ is $(i_0, i_1, \ldots, i_{k-1})$. Then $\sigma(I)$ maps i_0 to i_1, i_1 to i_2, ..., i_{k-1} to i_0. Every cyclic permutation must omit at leat one of these arcs. Accordingly, instance I has as its children instances $I_0, I_1, \ldots, I_{k-1}$ where I_j is obtained by setting $c_{i_j, i_{j+1 (\mathrm{mod}\, k)}}$ to ∞.

The general step of the branch and bound method is as follows. In the current tree of problem instances, let instance I be the leaf for which the cost of the optimal solution to the assignment problem is least. If $\sigma(I)$ is a cyclic permutation then it is the optimal tour for the original instance of the TSP. If $\sigma(I)$ is not cyclic then its shortest cycle determines k children which become leaves of the tree of instances. The process continues until a cyclic permutation is found.

Since the optimal assignment is equally likely to be any one of the $n!$ permutations of $\{1, 2, \ldots, n\}$, and exactly $(n-1)!$ of these permutations are cyclic, there is a $1/n$ chance that the solution of the original assignment problem will be an optimal tour (this chance can be increased to approximately e/n by setting the diagonal elements c_{ii} to ∞, and thus eliminating permutations with fixed points). If the problem instances occurring in the branch and bound tree were independent random instances then, independently at each step, there would be a $1/n$ chance of finding a cyclic permutation and terminating the branch and bound computation. Two papers have been published which make such an erroneous independence assumption and conclude thereby that the optimal tour can be found by branch and bound in polynomial expected time. Lenstra & Rinnooy Kan [1978] point out the error in one of these erroneous papers. A correct analysis of the branch and bound method remains to be made.

Exercises

12. Prove: For every matrix (c_{ij}), $T^* \geq A^*$.

13. Prove: In a random permutation of $\{1, 2, \ldots, n\}$, Pr[element 1 lies in a cycle of length r] $= 1/n$, for $r = 1, 2, \ldots, n$.

14. Prove: The expected number of cycles in a random permutation of $\{1, 2, \ldots, n\}$ is $1 + \frac{1}{2} + \frac{1}{3} + \ldots + 1/n$.

15. Prove: For every positive integer a, Pr[$\mu(n) \leq n/a$] $\leq 1/a!$. Here the random variable $\mu(n)$ denotes the length of a longest cycle in a random permutation of $\{1, 2, \ldots, n\}$.

16. Let (c_{ij}) be an $n \times n$ matrix in which every diagonal element c_{ii} is equal to ∞, and the off-diagonal elements are drawn independently from the uniform distribution over $[0, 1]$. Prove:

$$\text{Pr[the optimal assignment for } (c_{ij}) \text{ is a cyclic permutation]} \sim e/n.$$

17. Let $X(N)$ be the minimum of N independent random variables, each of which is the minimum of two independent samples from the uniform

distribution over $[0, 1]$. Prove:

$$E[X(N)] < \frac{1}{2} \sqrt{\frac{\pi}{N}}.$$

18. Prove or disprove: There exists a constant β such that, for every $\varepsilon > 0$,

$$\Pr[|A^* - \beta| > \varepsilon] \to 0 \qquad \text{as} \qquad n \to \infty.$$

Here A^* is the cost of the optimal assignment for a matrix (c_{ij}) whose elements are drawn independently from the uniform distribution over $[0, 1]$.

19. What happens to the distribution of $(T - T^*)/T^*$ when the elements of (c_{ij}) are drawn independently from the uniform distribution over $[a, 1]$, $a > 0$?

The Traveling Salesman Problem
Edited by E. L. Lawler, J. K. Lenstra,
A. H. G. Rinnooy Kan, D. B. Shmoys
© 1985 John Wiley & Sons Ltd.

7

Empirical analysis of heuristics

B. L. Golden
University of Maryland, College Park

W. R. Stewart
College of William and Mary, Williamsburg

1 INTRODUCTION

In previous chapters, worst-case analysis and probabilistic analysis of TSP heuristics are discussed. In this chapter, we focus on the *empirical analysis* of TSP heuristics. We interpret empirical analysis to mean *analysis originating in or based on computational experience*. The number of articles that are devoted, at least partially, to this topic is enormous. As the bibliography of this book bears witness, hundreds of procedures have been suggested for solving the TSP. With this fact in mind we make no attempt at being encyclopedic. We do, however, seek to accomplish in a coherent fashion the following:

(1) discuss some guidelines for the empirical analysis and comparison of TSP heuristics;
(2) discuss statistical methods for comparing TSP heuristics;

(3) summarize and update recent computational studies [Golden, Bodin, Doyle & Stewart, 1980; Adrabiński & Syslo, 1983];
(4) present the results of a new computational comparison of certain Euclidean TSP heuristics [Stewart, 1981];
(5) describe algorithms specifically designed for the asymmetric TSP;
(6) study statistical inference techniques for assessing deviations from optimality.

Whereas worst-case analysis and probabilistic analysis of heuristics are performed in a scientific manner, empirical analysis is often performed in a haphazard and subjective way. Our hope is that this chapter will help correct this situation.

While we devote most of the ensuing chapter to a discussion of ways in which to obtain high-quality solutions, heuristics possess attributes in addition to quality of solution that we feel should be kept in mind. These attributes are well recognized as valid criteria for the comparison of heuristic algorithms [Ball & Magazine, 1981] and include:

(a) running time;
(b) ease of implementation;
(c) flexibility;
(d) simplicity.

The running time required by a heuristic to solve a given problem is often a crucial consideration in choosing between competing approaches. Ease of implementation is also an important consideration. Difficult-to-code algorithms that require substantial amounts of computer time may not be worth the effort if they only marginally outperform an easy-to-code algorithm that is extremely efficient. Flexibility refers to the ability of an algorithm to handle problem variations. A TSP heuristic that can solve only undirected TSPs is, clearly, not as flexible as one that can solve both directed and undirected TSPs. With regard to simplicity, simply stated algorithms are more appealing to the user than cumbersome algorithms and they more readily lend themselves to various kinds of analysis.

The emphasis in this chapter will be on the development of more formal methods for comparing and analyzing heuristic algorithms and heuristic solutions for the TSP. In Section 2, statistical methods for comparing heuristics are introduced and illustrated. An expected utility approach is also tested. Section 3 provides a synopsis of computational experience gathered in previous studies of TSP heuristics. In Section 4, a new heuristic for the Euclidean TSP is presented, and extensive computational results and statistical tests are analyzed. Section 5 deals with the asymmetric TSP. In Section 6, the central issue is the development of point and interval estimates for the optimal solution.

2   STATISTICAL METHODS TO COMPARE HEURISTICS

Suppose that three heuristics (HEURISTIC X, HEURISTIC Y, and HEURISTIC Z) are applied to fifteen TSPs for which reasonable lower bounds on the

Table 7.1   Comparison of solutions for fifteen test problems (ratio = length/lower
bound)

Test problem number	Lower bound	HEURISTIC X		HEURISTIC Y		HEURISTIC Z	
		Length	Ratio	Length	Ratio	Length	Ratio
1	310	316	1.02	326	1.05	331	1.07
2	339	367	1.08	367	1.08	418	1.23
3	275	289	1.05	291	1.06	313	1.14
4	274	320	1.17	290	1.06	350	1.28
5	370	417	1.13	383	1.04	475	1.28
6	295	316	1.07	324	1.10	356	1.21
7	312	357	1.14	325	1.04	355	1.14
8	144	171	1.19	164	1.14	186	1.29
9	150	172	1.15	162	1.08	194	1.29
10	258	416	1.61	356	1.40	407	1.58
11	253	355	1.40	339	1.34	364	1.44
12	275	302	1.10	302	1.10	364	1.32
13	395	424	1.07	430	1.09	501	1.27
14	424	560	1.32	564	1.33	655	1.54
15	544	592	1.09	560	1.03	560	1.03

optimal solution value are known. The hypothetical results are displayed in
Table 7.1. They will be used to illustrate statistical techniques that may be
helpful in choosing among alternative heuristic algorithms. These techniques
presuppose that the test problems form a representative sample from the
problem class that the heuristics have been designed for. Although impossible to validate, this assumption does underline the importance of a proper
set of test problems to start from. Fortunately, in the case of the TSP, there
appears to be a fair consensus that certain benchmark test problems are the
ones to work with.

Which of the three heuristics from Table 7.1 is most accurate? In order to
answer this question, researchers tend to compile statistics and then identify
the heuristic that dominates the others or the one that comes closest to
dominating the others. Some measures of accuracy are provided in Table
7.2.

HEURISTIC Y dominates the other two heuristics with respect to the four
measures shown in Table 7.2 and HEURISTIC X outperforms HEURISTIC Z. Can
we say more about the apparent superiority of HEURISTIC Y? Is it statistically
significant, or could the results in Table 7.2 have occurred by chance? Is
there a more systematic procedure that we might follow in order to reach
the same conclusion? The answer is yes – we can apply the Wilcoxon signed
rank test, a well-known nonparametric statistical test [Pfaffenberger &
Patterson, 1981; Mosteller & Rourke, 1973], to compare any two of the
three heuristics.

Table 7.2   Comparison of performance of heuristics

	HEURISTIC X	HEURISTIC Y	HEURISTIC Z
Number of times heuristic is best or tied for best	7	10	1
Average percentage above lower bound	17.29	12.74	27.41
Average rank among three heuristics	1.80	1.43	2.77
Worst ratio of solution to lower bound	1.61	1.40	1.58

The Wilcoxon signed rank test assumes the following:

(1) the data consist of n matched pairs (x_i, y_i) with differences $d_i = x_i - y_i$;
(2) each d_i must be a continuous random variable;
(3) the distribution of each d_i must be symmetric;
(4) the pairs (x_i, y_i), $i = 1, 2, \ldots, n$, represent a random sample from a bivariate distribution.

The null hypothesis is that $E[x] = E[y]$ and the alternate hypothesis is either $E[x] \neq E[y]$, $E[x] > E[y]$, or $E[x] < E[y]$. The Wilcoxon test uses signed ranks of differences in order to assess the difference in *location* of two populations. In the context of comparing heuristics, the Wilcoxon test may be used to compare two heuristics at a time based on a set of n problems of varying size and structure. Below, x_i and y_i will correspond to percentages above the lower bound generated by the two heuristics for problem i. The Wilcoxon statistic W is computed in the following way. First, rank the absolute differences of the original measurements, $|d_i|$. If any $d_i = 0$, drop it from consideration and decrease n by one. If ties in absolute differences occur, average the ranks of the items involved in the tie and use the average as the rank of each tied item. Second, to the rank of the ith absolute difference attach the sign of $x_i - y_i$, and denote this signed rank by R_i. Finally, obtain the sum W of the signed ranks:

$$W = R_1 + R_2 + \ldots + R_n.$$

The null hypothesis should be rejected at the α significance level if

$$W > W_{1-\alpha/2} \quad \text{or} \quad W < W_{\alpha/2},$$
$$W > W_{1-\alpha}, \quad \text{or}$$
$$W < W_{\alpha},$$

depending upon whether the alternate hypothesis is $E[x] \neq E[y]$, $E[x] > E[y]$, or $E[x] < E[y]$. Critical values of the Wilcoxon signed rank test statistic are tabulated in many textbooks on nonparametric statistics. Furth-

Table 7.3   HEURISTIC X vs. HEURISTIC Y

x_i	y_i	$x_i - y_i$	Rank of $|x_i - y_i|$	Signed ranks R_i
1.94	5.16	-3.22	5	-5
8.26	8.26	0.00		
5.09	5.82	-0.73	1	-1
16.79	5.84	10.95	12	12
12.70	3.51	9.19	10	10
7.12	9.83	-2.71	4	-4
14.42	4.17	10.25	11	11
18.75	13.89	4.86	6	6
14.67	8.00	6.67	9	9
61.24	37.98	23.26	13	13
40.32	33.99	6.33	8	8
9.82	9.82	0.00		
7.34	8.86	-1.52	3	-3
32.08	33.02	-0.94	2	-2
8.82	2.94	5.88	7	7
				$W = 61$

ermore, for $n \geqslant 10$, the critical value W_α can be approximated by

$$W_\alpha = Z(\alpha)\sqrt{n(n+1)(2n+1)/6},$$

where $Z(\alpha)$ is the standard normal fractile such that a proportion α of the area is to the left of $Z(\alpha)$.

Let us now use the Wilcoxon signed rank test to compare HEURISTICS X and Y. The data of interest from Table 7.1 lead to the computations summarized in Table 7.3. Given the results displayed in Table 7.2, a one-sided test seems appropriate with the alternate hypothesis being $E[x] > E[y]$. If we set $\alpha = 0.05$, we obtain

$$\begin{aligned} W_{1-\alpha} &= Z(1-\alpha)\sqrt{n(n+1)(2n+1)/6} \\ &= (1.645)(28.62) \\ &= 47.08. \end{aligned}$$

This tells us that if the null hypothesis is true (and assumptions (1)–(4) are valid), then in only one out of twenty trials would W exceed 47.08. Since $W = 61$, we reject the null hypothesis and infer that HEURISTIC Y outperforms HEURISTIC X. In fact, there is less than an $\alpha = 0.02$ ($Z(1-\alpha) = 2.05$) chance of obtaining a W value as large as 61.

Next, we could compare HEURISTICS Y and Z. It is clear, however, from Table 7.1, that HEURISTIC Y outperforms HEURISTIC Z by a wide margin and that HEURISTIC Y is the most accurate of the three heuristics. We leave verification as an exercise for the reader.

Actually, one must be careful in applying the Wilcoxon signed rank test in the case where there are several heuristics in contention for the title 'most accurate'. This is due to the fact that if Y outperforms X at the α significance level and Y outperforms Z at the α significance level, this does not imply that Y is the most effective heuristic at the α significance level. In general, if HEURISTIC Y outperforms m heuristics at individual significance levels α_i, then HEURISTIC Y outperforms all m heuristics at a significance level of $1 - (1 - \alpha_1)(1 - \alpha_2) \ldots (1 - \alpha_m)$.

Several additional points regarding the Wilcoxon test should be made. First of all, we remark that there is a variation of this test known as the *sign test*. To illustrate, let us compare HEURISTICS X and Z. We seek to test the hypothesis that both procedures are equally accurate. If we subtract the solution values resulting from HEURISTIC X from those values resulting from HEURISTIC Z and record the sign of the difference, we obtain twelve pluses and three minuses. If we assume that $\Pr[z_i - x_i > 0] = 0.5$, then the probability that twelve or more positive differences are found is given by $\sum_{k=12}^{15} \binom{15}{k}(0.5)^k(0.5)^{15-k} = 0.018$. The inference would be that HEURISTIC X is superior to HEURISTIC Z. The Wilcoxon test is more powerful than the sign test. On the other hand, it requires stronger assumptions.

In dealing with three or more different heuristics, we should apply the Friedman test rather than apply the Wilcoxon test repeatedly. This test, which is an extension of the Wilcoxon matched pairs procedure, is the non-parametric analogue to the classical ANOVA test of homogeneity which, typically, is used to test the null hypothesis

$$H_0 : E[x_1] = E[x_2] = \ldots = E[x_k]$$

under the assumption of normal distributions with a common variance.

We illustrate the Friedman test on the data in Table 7.1 ($n = 15$ and $k = 3$). Let R_{ij} be the rank (from 1 to k) assigned to HEURISTIC j ($j = $ X, Y, Z) on problem i (lowest value gets rank of 1). In the case of ties, average ranks are used. Next, we calculate $R_j = \sum_{i=1}^{n} R_{ij}$ for $j = 1, \ldots, k$. The test statistic is given by

$$T_F = \frac{(n-1)\{B_F - nk(k+1)^2/4\}}{A_F - B_F},$$

where $A_F = \sum_{i=1}^{n} \sum_{j=1}^{k} (R_{ij})^2$ and $B_F = (1/n) \sum_{j=1}^{k} R_j^2$. The null hypothesis is rejected at level α if the test statistic exceeds the $1 - \alpha$ quantile of the F-distribution with $k - 1$ and $(n-1)(k-1)$ degrees of freedom. For more information on the Friedman test, see Conover [1980]. Using Table 7.4, we have that $A_F = 208.5$, $B_F = 194.23$, and $T_F = 14\{194.23 - (15)(3)(16)/4\}/14.27 = 13.96$. Since $T_F = 13.96 > F_{0.05,2,28} = 3.34$, we reject the null hypothesis that all three heuristics are equally accurate at $\alpha = 0.05$. We now have reason to perform further analysis to identify the 'best' of the three heuristics.

Table 7.4 Summary of calculations required by the Friedman test

Problem	HEURISTIC X	Rank HEURISTIC Y	HEURISTIC Z
1	1	2	3
2	1.5	1.5	3
3	1	2	3
4	2	1	3
5	2	1	3
6	1	2	3
7	3	1	2
8	2	1	3
9	2	1	3
10	3	1	2
11	2	1	3
12	1.5	1.5	3
13	1	2	3
14	1	2	3
15	3	1.5	1.5
R_j	27	21.5	41.5
$\sum_i R_{ij}^2$	56.5	33.75	118.25

The sign test, the Wilcoxon test and the Friedman test represent reasonable procedures for comparing heuristics. However, as these procedures are tests of location (specifically, mean or median) and not of distribution shape or dispersion, the results can be less than totally satisfying. With this in mind, we finally propose an *expected utility approach* for comparing two or more heuristics, which is both simple and useful although it rests on somewhat arbitrary assumptions.

The procedure is based on the notion that we seek a heuristic that performs well on the average and that very rarely performs poorly. In other words, we are concerned with *downside risk* as well as expected accuracy. The proposed expected utility approach incorporates our attitude towards risk in a *risk-averse* utility function. The procedure is outlined below:

Step 1. Fit a gamma distribution to the histogram of frequency vs. percentage deviation from lower bound.

Step 2. Select a risk-averse decreasing utility function of the form $u(x) = \alpha - \beta e^{tx}$, where α, β, $t > 0$.

Step 3. Calculate the expected utility for each heuristic and select the one that yields the largest value.

In Step 1, we use a gamma distribution for reasons of computational convenience. First, it has a simple density function with 0 as a minimum value. In particular,

$$f(x) = (x/b)^{c-1} e^{(-x/b)}/(b\Gamma(c)), \qquad \text{where} \qquad \Gamma(c) = \int_0^\infty e^{-u} u^{c-1}\, du.$$

Second, estimating parameters via the method of moments is trivial; we obtain

$$\hat{b} = s^2/\bar{x},$$
$$\hat{c} = (\bar{x}/s)^2,$$

where $\bar{x}$ and s^2 are the sample mean and sample variance (unadjusted). That is, $\bar{x} = (1/n) \sum_i x_i$ and $s^2 = (1/n) \sum_i (x_i - \bar{x})^2$. Third, the moment generating function is of the simple form

$$E[e^{tx}] = (1 - bt)^{-c}.$$

For Step 2, we propose a utility function that is constantly risk averse and that equals $\alpha - \beta e^{tx}$ when the percentage deviation from the lower bound is x. (See Keeney & Raiffa [1976] for more information regarding unidimensional utility theory.)

The expected utility is then easy to compute in Step 3, since

$$\int_0^\infty u(x)f(x)\, dx = \int_0^\infty \{\alpha - \beta e^{tx}\} f(x)\, dx$$
$$= \alpha - \beta E[e^{tx}]$$
$$= \alpha - \beta(1 - bt)^{-c}.$$

We illustrate this procedure by comparing the three heuristics from Table 7.1. We select a utility function where $\alpha = 600$, $\beta = 100$ and $t = 0.05$. The first two parameters can be chosen arbitrarily; the third parameter, t, gives a measure of risk aversion for the utility function. It should be pointed out that t must be less than $1/\hat{b}$ for each heuristic and that sensitivity analysis on t is trivial to perform; the former is due to the gamma moment generating function. From Table 7.5, we learn that HEURISTIC Y appears to be the most accurate of the three heuristics and that the rankings coincide with those determined previously.

Table 7.5   Comparing the accuracy of three heuristics using expected utility

	HEURISTIC X	HEURISTIC Y	HEURISTIC Z
$\bar{x}$	17.29	12.74	27.41
s	15.31	11.50	15.09
$\hat{b}$	13.56	10.38	8.31
$\hat{c}$	1.28	1.23	3.30
$\alpha - \beta(1 - \hat{b}t)^{-\hat{c}}$	173.5	354.0	11.7

Exercises

1. With respect to Table 7.1, with what level of significance could one conclude that HEURISTIC Y outperforms both HEURISTIC X and HEURISTIC Z, using only the sign test?

2. Repeat Exercise 1, but now use the Wilcoxon test in place of the sign test.

3 HEURISTICS FOR THE TSP

In this section, we review two earlier computational studies on TSP heuristics. Most of the test problems discussed in this section are Euclidean, although some non-Euclidean problems studied by Adrabiński and Syslo will also be discussed. A TSP is called *Euclidean* in this chapter when the locations to be visited all lie in the same plane and the cost of traveling between any pair of locations is given by the Euclidean distance between them.

The algorithms discussed in this section are either tour construction procedures, tour improvement procedures or composite procedures. *Tour construction procedures* build an approximately optimal tour starting from the original distance matrix. *Tour improvement procedures* start with a feasible tour and seek to improve the tour via a sequence of interchanges. *Composite procedures* apply tour construction procedures to begin with and tour improvement procedures next.

3.1 Tour construction procedures

In studying tour construction procedures, the following three components serve as key ingredients:

(1) the choice of an *initial subtour* (or starting point);
(2) the *selection* criterion;
(3) the *insertion* criterion.

In many tour construction procedures, the *initial subtour* is simply a randomly chosen city or self-loop. There are alternate ways of choosing a starting subtour. In fact, in dealing with Euclidean TSPs, several authors [Wiorkowski & McElvain, 1975; Or, 1976; Stewart, 1977; Norback & Love, 1977, 1979] have found that the convex hull provides an excellent initial subtour for insertion procedures. Recall that the convex hull of a set V of vertices is the smallest convex set that includes V. Since it has been shown by Flood [1956] that every Euclidean TSP has an optimal solution that visits the cities on the boundary of the convex hull in the same order as if the boundary of the convex hull itself were traced, this strategy is quite reasonable. In discussions that follow, *convex hull* will refer to the vertices on the boundary of the convex hull and the boundary itself which forms an initial subtour.

In addition to initial subtour construction, a distinction is made between deciding which city is *selected* to be inserted into the current subtour and where the city is to be *inserted*. While such decisions may be made at the same time (e.g., for the cheapest insertion procedure), several of the algorithms compared in this section employ different criteria for deciding *which* versus *where*. The choice of selection and insertion criteria can be critical to the success of a heuristic procedure. Figure 7.1 demonstrates how different insertion criteria might lead to different solutions. It is easy to see in Figure 7.1(a) that city k may be inserted in four ways. The greatest angle criterion would insert city k between cities l and m as in Figure 7.1(b) while the cheapest insertion criterion would insert it between cities i and j. The cheapest insertion route shown in Figure 7.1(c) is the shortest overall route in this case.

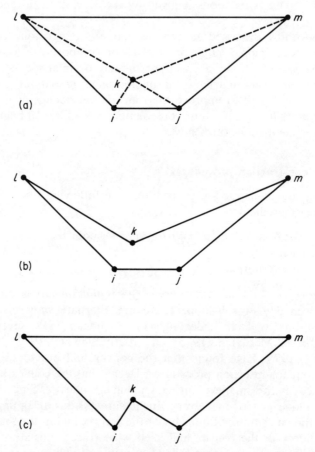

Figure 7.1   Comparison of insertion criteria. (a) Initial subtour with potential insertions. (b) Greatest angle insertion. (c) Cheapest insertion

The nearest addition, nearest insertion, cheapest insertion and farthest insertion heuristics were described in the previous chapter. In the next few pages, we outline some additional variants of the tour construction idea that have been proposed for the TSP in the literature. Some of these heuristics require an underlying Euclidean structure and then exploit this geometric structure, while others make no such restriction on the form of the TSP. In particular, any heuristic that uses the convex hull or the angle formed by three vertices assumes the vertices lie in Euclidean space.

Arbitrary insertion procedure [Rosenkrantz, Stearns & Lewis, 1977]

Step 1. Start with a subgraph consisting of city i only.
Step 2. Find city k such that c_{ik} is minimal and form the subtour (i, k).
Step 3. (*Selection*) Given a subtour, arbitrarily select city k not in the subtour to enter the subtour.
Step 4. (*Insertion*) Find the edge $\{i, j\}$ in the subtour which minimizes $c_{ik} + c_{kj} - c_{ij}$. Insert k between i and j.
Step 5. Go to Step 3 unless we have a Hamiltonian cycle.

Convex hull insertion procedure [Stewart, 1977]

Step 1. Form the convex hull of the set of cities. The hull gives an initial subtour.
Step 2. (*Insertion*) For each city k not yet contained in the subtour, decide between which two cities i and j on the subtour to insert city k. That is, for each such k, find $\{i, j\}$ such that $c_{ik} + c_{kj} - c_{ij}$ is minimal.
Step 3. (*Selection*) From all (i, k, j) found in Step 2, determine the (i^*, k^*, j^*) such that $(c_{i^*k^*} + c_{k^*j^*})/c_{i^*j^*}$ is minimal.
Step 4. Insert city k^* in subtour between cities i^* and j^*.
Step 5. Repeat Steps 2 through 4 until a Hamiltonian cycle is obtained.

Greatest angle insertion procedure [Norback & Love, 1977, 1979]

Step 1. Form the convex hull of the set of cities. The hull gives an initial subtour.
Step 2. (*Selection and insertion*) Choose the city k^* not in the subtour and the edge $\{i^*, j^*\}$ in the subtour such that the angle formed by the two edges $\{i^*, k^*\}$ and $\{k^*, j^*\}$ is maximum.
Step 3. Insert city k^* in subtour between cities i^* and j^*.
Step 4. Repeat Steps 2 and 3 until a Hamiltonian cycle is obtained.

Ratio times difference insertion procedure [Or, 1976]

Same as for greatest angle insertion except that Step 2 is replaced by the following step.

Step 2'. (*Selection and insertion*) Choose the city k^* not in the subtour and the edge $\{i^*, j^*\}$ in the subtour such that the product

$$\{c_{i^*k^*}+c_{k^*j^*}-c_{i^*j^*}\}\times\{(c_{i^*k^*}+c_{k^*j^*})/c_{i^*j^*}\}$$

is minimum.

3.2   Tour improvement procedures

The second stage in a composite algorithm is a tour improvement procedure. The best-known procedures of this type are the edge exchange procedures [Croes, 1958; Lin, 1965; Lin & Kernighan, 1973].

In the general case, r edges in a feasible tour are exchanged for r edges not in that solution as long as the result remains a tour and the length of that tour is less than the length of the previous tour. Exchange procedures are referred to as *r-opt* procedures where r is the number of edges exchanged at each iteration. Figure 7.2 illustrates the exchange procedure for $r = 3$. In this example, the three edges $\{i, j\}$, $\{l, k\}$ and $\{m, n\}$ are removed and replaced by $\{i, k\}$, $\{j, m\}$ and $\{l, n\}$.

In an *r*-opt algorithm, all exchanges of r edges are tested until there is no feasible exchange that improves the current solution. This solution is then said to be *r-optimal* [Lin, 1965]. In general, the larger the value of r, the more likely it is that the final solution is optimal. Unfortunately, the number of operations necessary to test all r exchanges increases rapidly as the

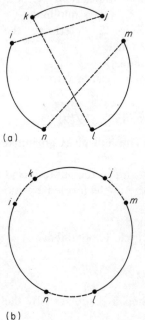

(a)

(b)

Figure 7.2   3-opt example. (a) Current tour. (b) Tour after exchange number of cities increases. As a result, values of $r = 2$ and $r = 3$ are the ones most commonly used.

Lin and Kernighan's more powerful (*variable r-opt*) algorithm, which decides at each iteration how many edges to exchange, is also used with regularity, especially when tight upper bounds are required as input to an optimal TSP procedure. Lin and Kernighan's algorithm requires considerably more effort to code than either the 2-opt or 3-opt approach. However, it produces solutions that are usually near-optimal.

Lin and Kernighan's algorithm decides dynamically at each iteration what the value of r (the number of edges to exchange) should be. Given that it has been decided to exchange s edges, a series of tests are performed to determine whether $s + 1$ edge exchanges should be considered. This continues until stopping conditions are satisfied. Potential exchanges are chosen to ensure that a new feasible tour can be formed at any stage in the process.

Referring to Figure 7.2, we now illustrate how the algorithm works. Let G_p^* be the improvement or savings that can be realized if the p edges currently under consideration are exchanged in order to generate a new tour. Roughly speaking, the procedure works as follows.

Step 1. Choose an initial tour.

Step 2. Set $G_0^* = 0$. Select any city as a starting city (e.g., city l) and consider one of the edges in the current tour adjacent to this city (e.g., $\{l, k\}$) for removal. Set $p = 1$.

Step 3. From the other end of this edge (city k) choose an edge that is not in the current tour (e.g., $\{k, i\}$) such that $g_1 = c_{lk} - c_{ki} > 0$. The edge is chosen so that g_1 is maximized.

Step 4. Having chosen $\{l, k\}$ to leave and $\{k, i\}$ to enter the solution in the previous iteration, the edge to leave in the pth iteration is uniquely determined. It must be the one of the two edges currently adjacent to city i such that upon removal the set of cities remains connected. In this case, $\{i, j\}$ must leave the solution. Note that adding an edge $\{j, l\}$ reconstructs a tour. Now $G_1^* = g_1 + c_{ij} - c_{jl}$. Let us suppose that $g_1 > G_1^* > 0$. Increment p by 1.

Step 5. Edge $\{j, l\}$ is not necessarily the edge chosen to enter the solution at this iteration. That is, we seek to find city q that maximizes $g_p = c_{ij} - c_{jq}$. Suppose $q = m$ and thus the edge chosen to enter is $\{j, m\}$. Calculate $G_p = \sum_{s=1}^p g_s$ and then $G_p^* = G_p + c_{mn} - c_{nl}$. Let $G^* = \max\{G_0^*, G_1^*, \ldots, G_p^*\}$.

We increment p and repeat Step 5 unless

(a) no further feasible swaps exist,

(b) the current configuration is already a tour,

(c) $G_p \leq 0$, or

(d) $G_p \leq G^*$.

If one of the above conditions holds, we construct the tour associated with the best of $\{G_1^*, G_2^*, \ldots, G_p^*\}$.

The entire process is repeated until every city has been used as a starting city and no further improvement has been found.

Recently, a modified 3-opt procedure has been proposed [Or, 1976] which considers only a small percentage of the exchanges that would be considered by a regular 3-opt, and which seems to work extremely well. This procedure, which we refer to as *Or-opt*, considers only those exchanges that would result in a string of one, two or three currently adjacent cities being inserted between two other cities. By thus limiting the number of exchanges that need to be considered, Or-opt requires significantly fewer calculations than 3-opt.

To understand how the Or-opt procedure works, we refer to Figure 7.3. For each connected string of s cities in the current tour (s equals 3 first, then 2, then 1), we test to see if the string can be relocated between two other cities at a reduced cost. If it can, we make the appropriate changes. For $s = 3$ in Figure 7.3(a), each string of three adjacent cities m, n, p in the current tour is considered for insertion between all pairs of connected cities i and j outside of the string. The insertion is performed if the total cost of the edges to be erased, $\{a, m\}$, $\{p, b\}$ and $\{i, j\}$, exceeds the cost of the new edges to be added, $\{i, m\}$, $\{p, j\}$ and $\{a, b\}$. After considering all strings of three cities, all strings of two cities and then all strings of one city are considered. When no further exchanges improve the solution, the algorithm terminates.

Even more recently, in a totally different approach to tour improvement, it has been argued [Kirkpatrick, Gelatt & Vecchi, 1982, 1983] that there is an analogy between combinatorial optimization problems such as the TSP and large physical systems of the kind studied in statistical mechanics. Some

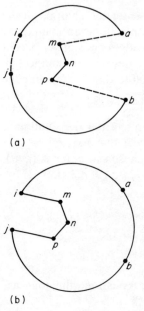

(a)

(b)

Figure 7.3 Or-opt example for string of $s = 3$ cities.
(a)   Current   tour.
(b) Improved tour

initial computational tests based on this model were performed on large TSPs and the results were somewhat encouraging. A brief description follows.

Statistical mechanics concerns itself with analyzing aggregate properties of large numbers of atoms in liquids or solids. The behavior is characterized by random fluctuations about a *most probable behavior*, namely the average behavior of the system at that temperature. An important question is: What happens to the system at extremely low temperatures? The low-temperature state may be referred to as the ground state or the lowest energy state of the system. Since low-temperature states are very rare, experiments that reveal the low-temperature state of a material are performed by a process referred to as *annealing*. The material under study is first melted and then the temperature is slowly lowered, with a long time spent at temperatures near freezing point. The period of time at each temperature must be sufficiently long to allow a thermal equilibrium to be achieved. Otherwise, certain random fluctuations will be frozen into the material and the true low-energy state will not be reached. The process can be likened to growing a crystal from a melt. If the temperature is lowered too quickly, the result may be glass or a crystal with many defects.

The annealing process is usually simulated using the following procedure: Given a configuration of the elements of the system, randomly displace the elements, one at a time, by a small amount and calculate the resulting change in the energy, ΔE. If $\Delta E < 0$ then accept the displacement and use the resulting configuration as the starting point for the next iteration. If $\Delta E \geq 0$ then the displacement is accepted with probability $\Pr[\Delta E] = \exp(-\Delta E/(k_b T))$ where T is the temperature and k_b is Boltzmann's constant.

The probabilistic aspect is implemented by comparing $\Pr[\Delta E]$ with a random variable drawn from a uniform distribution on the interval $(0, 1)$. Repetition of this step continues until equilibrium is achieved. At that point, the temperature is lowered and the procedure repeated.

The analogy we are seeking now presents itself. If we view each feasible solution to the TSP as a configuration of atoms and the objective value associated with each feasible solution as the energy of that system, then the optimal solution to the TSP is like the lowest energy state of the physical system.

Simulated annealing gives us a mechanism for accepting increases in objective value in a controlled fashion. At each temperature setting, we can accept an increase in the tour length with a certain probability. It is possible that accepting an increase will reveal a new configuration that will avoid a local minimum or at least a bad local minimum. Note that we always accept a decrease in the tour length. The effect of the method, however, is that one descends slowly. By controlling these probabilities, through the temperatures, we are in essence simulating many random starting solutions in a controlled, simultaneous fashion. An analogy similar to this is well known in statistical mechanics.

The attractiveness of using the simulated annealing approach for combinatorial optimization problems is that transitions away from a local
optimum are always possible when the temperature is nonzero. As pointed
out by Kirkpatrick *et al.*, the temperature is merely a control parameter; this
parameter controls the probability of accepting a tour length increase. As
such, it is expressed in the same units as the objective function. In implementing the approach, any improvement procedure could be used.

In order for the method to function well, a proper annealing schedule
must be developed. An *annealing schedule* is defined to be the sequence of
temperatures and the amount of time at each to reach equilibrium for that
temperature. Given this schedule of temperatures, $S = \{t_1, t_2, \ldots, t_n\}$, with
the sequence obeying $t_1 > t_2 > \ldots > t_{n-1} > t_n$, one can formally outline the
simulated annealing algorithm. Computational results to date have been
mixed; see Kirkpatrick, Gelatt & Vecchi [1982, 1983], Golden & Skiscim
[1983] and Johnson [1983] for details. Further experiments are in progress.

3.3 Computational studies

Two recent and comprehensive studies [Golden, Bodin, Doyle & Stewart,
1980; Adrabiński & Syslo, 1983] test the performance of a number of
heuristic algorithms that fit into the above categories. The main results of
the Golden *et al.* study are summarized in Table 7.6. In this table, the first,
second and third group of rows correspond to tour construction, tour
improvement and composite procedures, respectively. As a result, it is easier
to compare performance within each category. Table 7.6 is taken largely
from the original paper, although it has been updated by the inclusion of
data for an additional heuristic (the most eccentric ellipse method [Norback
& Love, 1977]). Also, the second column is slightly revised to include the
optimal solution rather than the previously best-known solution.

The test problems reported in Table 7.6 are the five 100-city Euclidean
TSPs presented first by Krolak, Felts & Marble [1971] and solved to
optimality by Crowder & Padberg [1980].

A unique feature of the Golden *et al.* computational comparison is their
study of the degeneration of algorithmic performance under conditions of
sparsity. In particular, they start with a completely filled-in distance matrix,
apply a number of heuristics, remove edges from the problem, reapply the
heuristics, and so on. The motivation behind such an experiment is to
determine how well certain heuristics solve sparse TSPs and to see if edges
can be ignored for larger problems (in order to conserve storage) without
having much of an adverse impact. Table 7.7 is given by Golden, Bodin,
Doyle & Stewart [1980] and displays some typical results. The density level l
is varied from 100% to 20% in Table 7.7 and is defined by

$$\bar{c} = \min\{c_{ij}\} + l[\max\{c_{ij}\} - \min\{c_{ij}\}];$$

all edges with lengths greater than $\bar{c}$ are erased.

Table 7.6   Computational results – percentage above the optimal solution

Heuristic	Problem no./Number of cities				
	24/100	25/100	26/100	27/100	28/100
Optimal solution	21,282	22,141	20,749	21,294	22,068
Nearest neighbor (all cities)	16.67	16.88	13.35	16.51	13.27
Nearest insertion (all cities)	18.69	17.81	22.96	14.44	20.33
Farthest insertion (all cities)	5.14	6.97	3.17	1.99	7.42
Arbitrary insertion (all cities)	4.46	3.50	3.28	2.90	5.03
Cheapest insertion (all cities)	12.07	11.67	20.83	12.97	12.16
Clarke and Wright (all cities)	1.62	3.77	6.37	3.41	2.85
Christofides' heuristic	7.53	3.93	5.36	14.44	8.51
Convex hull	3.64	2.52	2.54	2.35	3.45
Most eccentric ellipse method	2.90	8.33	19.70	7.10	12.70
Stinson's heuristic	36.45	18.94	25.00	18.06	21.16
2-opt (best of 25 runs)	1.11	3.05	0.51	3.27	3.24
3-opt (once)	7.82	2.87	3.30	1.15	1.40
Nearest neighbor (all cities), 2-opt, 3-opt	0.14*	1.46	1.06	0.73	2.46
Convex hull, 2-opt	0.94	1.94	1.60	2.04	3.22
Convex hull, 3-opt	0.37	1.46	1.06	0.35	2.46
2-opt (best of 50), 3-opt	0.81	1.44	0.53	1.74	0.18*
Christofides, 2-opt, 3-opt	2.51	1.40	1.53	0.17*	3.03
Arbitrary insertion from 10 cities, 3-opt from best tour	1.42	1.51	2.57	1.13	1.59
Arbitrary insertion from 10 cities, 3-opt from each tour	0.56	1.33*	1.20	0.66	1.06
Farthest insertion from 10 cities, 3-opt from best tour	1.17	3.09	0.58	2.34	2.60
Farthest insertion from 10 cities, 3-opt from each tour	0.46	1.57	0.49*	0.45	0.98

* An asterisk indicates best solution found for each problem.

Golden *et al.* reach the following conclusions.

1. Many of the tour construction procedures will find a traveling salesman tour to within 5% to 7% of optimality. However, these procedures outside of the convex hull approach are hard-pressed to do much better. Fortunately, most of these procedures are computationally efficient relative to other procedures proposed. As such, these procedures should be utilized when a reasonably effective solution is desired.
2. The tour improvement procedures, in particular the 2-opt (best of 25 runs) and 3-opt (once) with random starting solutions, operate with

Table 7.7 Computational results on problem 24 under conditions of sparsity –
          percentage above optimality

Heuristic	Density level (%)						
	100	80	60	50	40	30	20
Nearest neighbor (all cities)	16.1	16.1	16.1	16.1	∞	∞	∞
Nearest neighbor (all cities), 2-opt	2.5	2.5	2.5	2.5	∞	∞	∞
Nearest neighbor (all cities), 2-opt, 3-opt	0.3	0.3	0.3	0.3	8.3	∞	∞
2-opt (best of 25 runs)	1.1	1.2	1.7	1.9	1.2	2.4	∞
2-opt (best of 25 runs), 3-opt	0.6	0.2	1.2	0.9	0.2	0.9	∞
Arbitrary insertion from 10 cities	6.0	6.2	6.4	5.6	11.2	∞	∞
Arbitrary insertion from 10 cities, 2-opt from each tour	3.8	3.8	3.8	2.7	3.7	1.2	∞
Arbitrary insertion from 10 cities, 2-opt, 3-opt from each tour	1.4	1.4	1.4	0.2	1.8	0.4	∞
Farthest insertion from 10 cities	7.1	6.7	4.9	10.1	15.1	∞	∞
Farthest insertion from 10 cities, 2-opt from each tour	2.8	2.5	0.3	3.6	1.1	∞	∞
Farthest insertion from 10 cities, 2-opt, 3-opt from each tour	0.0*	2.1	0.0*	3.5	0.7	∞	∞

* An asterisk indicates best solution.

   approximately the same effectiveness and efficiency as the best of the
   tour construction procedures.
3. The three-step composite procedure will find a traveling salesman tour
   within 2% to 3% of optimality with high regularity. However, this
   approach is somewhat slower computationally than the tour construction
   or tour improvement procedures by themselves.
4. To reliably find a traveling salesman tour within 1% to 2% of optimality
   requires repeated application of the three-step composite procedure.
5. Under conditions of sparsity, where $100\% \geqslant l \geqslant 60\%$, the deterioration
   of algorithmic performance seems to be negligible.

   We now briefly summarize the second computational study Adrabiński &
Syslo, 1983]. Adrabiński and Syslo test a number of heuristics including the
nearest neighbor, nearest insertion, farthest insertion and nearest addition
procedures on twelve non-Euclidean problems. Only two of the problems
($n = 10$ and $n = 25$) satisfy the triangle inequality. We present some of their
findings in Table 7.8. The authors conclude that the farthest insertion
method is superior to the three other fast approximation algorithms tested.

Table 7.8 Computational results – percentage above the optimal solution

Heuristic	Problem no./n											
	1/10	2/10	3/10	4/20	5/25	6/27	7/27	8/33	9/42	10/48	11/57	12/120
Optimal solution	212	292	378	246	1711	3719	3336	10861	699	11461	12955	6942
Nearest neighbor (all cities)	0*	2.40	0.79	14.23*	3.52	9.55	4.05	7.83	23.60	5.90	11.24	18.77
Nearest insertion (all cities)	1.89	0*	0*	38.21	12.04	3.01	6.89	14.93	10.87	9.51	9.25	17.27
Farthest insertion (all cities)	0*	0*	0*	28.45	0*	0*	0.35*	0.62*	1.43*	0.11*	1.28*	3.06*
Nearest addition (all cities)	1.89	11.64	2.91	86.58	14.70	19.66	13.88	20.21	11.02	15.87	14.76	21.78

* An asterisk indicates best solution found for each problem.

In addition, they point out that the farthest insertion solutions are better to use as initial solutions in the r-opt algorithm [Lin & Kernighan, 1973] than solutions from the other three tour construction heuristics.

When the farthest insertion solution is used as a starting tour in the Lin–Kernighan procedure, the optimal solution is found for eight of the twelve problems; the largest deviation from optimality on the remaining four problems is only 1.2%.

Exercises

3. The nearest neighbor, nearest insertion, farthest insertion, arbitrary insertion and cheapest insertion algorthms are tour construction procedures that require about the same amount of effort to perform. Can one conclude statistically that the farthest and arbitrary insertion procedures are more accurate than the other three algorithms, based on Table 7.6?

4. Can one verify statistically that the farthest insertion procedure is indeed more accurate than its competitors, based on Table 7.8?

5. Prove that in a Euclidean TSP the optimal tour does not intersect itself.

6. Prove the convex hull result due to Flood mentioned in Section 3.1 as a direct consequence of Exercise 5.

7. Consider the following two versions of the farthest insertion procedure:

Farthest insertion procedure, version 1

Step 1. Start with a subgraph consisting of city i only.

Step 2. Find city k such that c_{ik} is maximal and form the subtour (i, k).

Step 3. (*Selection*) Given a subtour, find city k not in the subtour and city l in the current subtour such that $c_{lk} = \max_j\{\min_i\{c_{ij}\}\}$, where j denotes a city *not in* the current subtour and i denotes a city *in* the current subtour.

Step 4. (*Insertion*) Find the edge $\{i, j\}$ in the subtour which minimizes $c_{ik} + c_{kj} - c_{ij}$. Insert k between i and j.

Step 5. Go to Step 3 unless we have a Hamiltonian cycle.

Farthest insertion procedure, version 2

Same as for version 1, except that we replace Step 3 by Step 3′:

Step 3′. (*Selection*) Given a subtour, find city k not in the subtour farthest from any city in the subtour.

Write computer programs for both versions of the farthest insertion procedure and generate a set of 25 TSP instances. Compare the effectiveness of the two procedures using the Wilcoxon test.

8. How many of the $\binom{n}{3}$ 3-opt exchanges might the Or-opt procedure consider at each step?

4   TESTING A NEW HEURISTIC FOR THE EUCLIDEAN TSP

To demonstrate how carefully designed computational experiments can assist in assessing the merits of a heuristic solution method, we shall present such a computational analysis of a new composite heuristic for the Euclidean TSP.

4.1   The new heuristic

The new heuristic combines the insertion concept and the edge-exchange concept in a composite algorithm that exploits the special geometry inherent in Euclidean TSPs. It uses a convex hull as an initial subtour. It selects the city k to be inserted at each iteration on the basis of how large an angle is formed by the two edges that would touch k and the corresponding insertion cost. Finally, an Or-opt postprocessor is applied to improve the tour constructed in the first stage. The new algorithm will be referred to as CCAO (for Convex hull, Cheapest insertion, Angle selection and Or-opt). The steps are outlined in detail below.

CCAO procedure

Step 1. Form the convex hull of the set of cities. This gives the initial subtour.
Step 2. (*Insertion*) For each city k not yet contained in the subtour, identify the two adjacent cities i_k and j_k on the subtour such that $c_{i_k k} + c_{k j_k} - c_{i_k j_k}$ is minimized.
Step 3. (*Selection*) Select the city k^* that maximizes the angle between edges $\{i_k, k\}$ and $\{k, j_k\}$ in the subtour and insert it between i_{k^*} and j_{k^*}.
Step 4. Repeat Steps 2 and 3 until a Hamiltonian cycle is obtained.
Step 5. Apply the Or-opt procedure to the tour generated in Steps 1–4. When no further improvements are available, stop.

The example in Figure 7.4 illustrates how the CCAO algorithm works. First the convex hull is generated yielding a starting subtour consisting of cities 1, 7, 8, 9 and 10. In Step 2, each of the internal cities (2, 3, 4, 5, 6) is associated with a pair of connected cities from the initial subtour (the dashed lines in Figure 7.4(a)). In Step 3, the dashed lines that form the greatest angle identify the city to be inserted (city 6 in this case). Figure 7.4(b) shows the intermediate solution after the first two insertions (cities 6 and 4 in that order). Notice that cities 2, 3 and 5 are all associated with new city pairs. Figure 7.4(c) displays the final tour for stage one (Steps 1–4) after insertion of cities 2, 5 and 3, in that order. This tour is now tested by an Or-opt postprocessor. In this case, the tour from stage one is optimal and the Or-opt procedure will find no improvements.

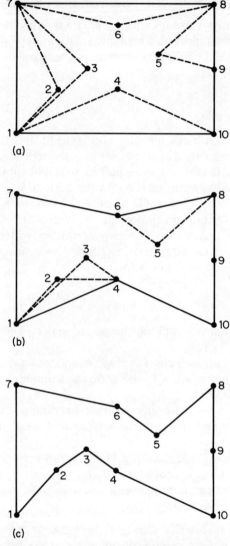

Figure 7.4 CCAO example. (a) Initial
subtour and insertions. (b) Intermediate
subtour and insertions. (c) Final tour

4.2 Computational results: the convex hull

The initial subtour for the CCAO procedure is given by the convex hull. We
start our computational analysis with an experimental justification of this
choice. Table 7.9 compares two of the insertion algorithms from Table 7.6
with and without the convex hull as a starting solution. The test problems
are the same five 100-city problems studied in Table 7.6.

Table 7.9   The value of the convex hull as an initial subtour – percentage above
optimal solution

Problem no.	Optimal solution	Cheapest insertion (%)	Convex hull cheapest insertion (%)	Farthest insertion (%)	Convex hull farthest insertion (%)
24	21,282	12.1	8.3	5.1	4.5
25	22,141	11.7	5.0	7.0	5.9
26	20,749	20.8	4.3	3.2	7.1
27	21,294	13.0	2.0	2.0	4.3
28	22,068	12.2	3.6	7.4	8.6

The cheapest insertion algorithm is substantially improved on all five problems by use of the convex hull. Although the farthest insertion algorithm is not comparably improved, the solutions for this algorithm with and without the convex hull are approximately the same. Since the cheapest insertion and farthest insertion solutions in columns 3 and 5 represent the best from 100 repetitions (see Table 7.6), the convex hull solutions are extremely attractive. For the five test problems, they require only about 1% of the computer execution time required by the non-hull procedures. The convex hull can be generated very quickly in practice (see Eddy [1977] for a FORTRAN implementation).

One additional observation can be made from Table 7.9 concerning the use of the convex hull. While the farthest insertion procedure outperforms the cheapest insertion procedure without benefit of the convex hull, when the convex hull is employed as the initial subtour, there is no such dominance in the end results. In fact, a reason for the farthest insertion procedure performing so well in the first place is that the farthest insertion procedure tends to generate a subtour closely resembling the convex hull on the early insertions.

4.3   Computational results: the CCAO procedure

This subsection presents three sets of computational results. The first set compares the performance of the CCAO procedure to published results for similar heuristic algorithms. These comparisons are performed on several standard test problems and are based on quality of solution.

The second set of computational results contrasts the performance of the convex hull cheapest angle insertion criteria for different selections of postprocessor (2-opt, 3-opt, Or-opt). The aim of this comparison is to reach some general conclusions about how much computation time must be spent in order to achieve a certain amount of improvement. More specifically, how much is the solution from the first stage improved by moving to each of the

Table 7.10 CCAO solutions versus published results (percentage over best known solution)

Problem no.	n	Best known solution	Best of first 11 & 14th algorithms from Table 7.6[a] (%)	Best of other 9 algorithms from Table 7.6[b] (%)	Greatest angle insertion, 2-opt (%)	Most eccentric ellipse method, 2-opt (%)	Convex hull, 2-opt (%)	CCAO (%)
24	100	21,282[c]	0.94	0.14	0.58	1.29	0.94	0.00
25	100	22,141[c]	1.94	1.30	4.86	3.35	1.93	0.97
26	100	20,749[c]	0.51	0.49	2.42	4.48	1.60	0.50
27	100	21,294[c]	1.99	0.17	1.74	2.62	2.04	0.97
28	100	22,068[c]	2.85	0.18	—	—	3.22	2.54
30	150	26,736	—	—	2.99	3.43	—	0.79
32	200	29,563	—	—	4.94	5.03	—	1.39
LK	318	43,865	—	—	0.69	1.34	—	0.06

[a] These algorithms are either stand-alone or employ a 2-opt procedure.
[b] These algorithms employ at least one 3-opt procedure.
[c] Optimal solution.

edge exchange procedures, and is the additional computational effort justified by the expected improvement?

The third set of computational tests takes the CCAO procedure and
versions of its more successful competitors, and compares solutions and
solution times on an extensive set of benchmark problems. Since the Or-opt
outperforms the 2-opt, the superiority exhibited by CCAO in the first set of
comparisons may simply be the result of a superior postprocessor and may
be unrelated to the tour construction procedure.

In Table 7.10, the results of CCAO on eight test problems are compared to published results for a number of other heuristic algorithms. The
first seven test problems are due to Krolak, Felts & Marble [1971]. The
optimal solutions for the five 100-city problems are from Crowder &
Padberg [1980]. The best solution for the 200-city problem was generated
by a man–machine interactive heuristic [Krolak, Felts & Marble, 1971]. The
best known solution for the 150-city problem was generated by a 3-opt
algorithm [Stewart, 1981]. The 318-city problem [Lin & Kernighan, 1973] is
solved here as a TSP for comparison with the other results. Lin and
Kernighan originally solved a shortest Hamiltonian path problem over 318
cities.

In Table 7.6, 21 different algorithms are compared. These results are
summarized in columns 4 and 5 of Table 7.10. Column 4 contains for each
problem the best result from the first eleven and the fourteenth of the 21
algorithms. These twelve algorithms have the common characteristic that
none of them makes use of an edge exchange procedure more powerful than
2-opt. The remaining nine algorithms summarized in column 5 all include a
3-opt postprocessor. Some of the algorithms even make use of multiple
3-opts from different starting solutions.

The CCAO algorithm appears to outperform the algorithms summarized
in column 4 of Table 7.10. Using a sign test, we see that there is only one
chance in 32 of observing such total dominance when columns 4 and 9 of
solutions are generated by equivalent algorithms. Thus, we conclude that the
CCAO algorithm is superior at the $\alpha = 0.03125$ level of significance. The
comparison of CCAO to column 5 is not quite so clear. Since it tests a larger
number of the possible exchanges of three edges, a 3-opt algorithm is
expected to consistently outscore the Or-opt procedure. And yet, there is no
evidence of dominance in Table 7.10; the results reported in column 5 are
only marginally better than those for the CCAO procedure.

Closer inspection of the nine algorithms with 3-opt (see Table 7.6) reveals
that the CCAO procedure outperforms one of the nine on all five 100-city
problems, four of the nine on four out of five problems, and three of the nine
on three out of five problems. Only one of the nine algorithms (farthest
insertion from 10 cities, 3-opt from each tour) gets better solutions than the
CCAO procedure on three of the five problems. The repeated application of
a 3-opt procedure makes this algorithm relatively expensive in terms of
computer time. And still, it is not clear that this last algorithm outperforms

the CCAO procedure. While it does not require Euclidean distances, it does require considerably more computer time than the CCAO algorithm.

Columns 6, 7 and 8 of Table 7.10 represent results for composite algorithms that are similar in nature to the CCAO procedure. The *greatest angle insertion* algorithm has already been described. The *most eccentric ellipse* method uses the convex hull as an initial subtour. Then, at each step, for every two adjacent cities i and j in the current subtour, the ellipse with i and j as foci and k on the ellipse itself is obtained. The city k (not yet in the subtour) that created the most eccentric (flattest) ellipse is placed between the two focal points of that ellipse and thus joins the subtour. The procedure continues until all cities have been added. The *convex hull* algorithm is very similar to the CCAO procedure and has already been discussed.

All three of these algorithms followed by a 2-opt produce effective solutions to the TSP. Each, however, is dominated by the CCAO procedure on the set of problems in Table 7.10. Testing the null hypothesis that there is no difference between the CCAO algorithm and each of its competitors in columns 6, 7 and 8 against the alternate hypothesis that the CCAO algorithm produces better solutions (using the sign test), results in acceptance of the alternate hypothesis in each case, at levels of significance of 0.0078, 0.0078 and 0.03125, respectively. In a test of the CCAO algorithm versus its three competitors, the conclusion is that the CCAO algorithm is superior to all three at a level of significance of 0.046. Although this domination is complete, it may be somewhat illusory since the CCAO procedure has the advantage of an Or-opt postprocessor, whereas the other three algorithms each use a 2-opt postprocessor. It is therefore conceivable that the dominance of the CCAO procedure is entirely attributable to choice of postprocessor. We address this point in Tables 7.11, 7.12 and 7.13.

In the second set of results referred to at the beginning of Section 4.3, we examine both the accuracy and efficiency of the three competing postprocessors. We discuss efficiency here since, in comparing heuristics for the TSP, computation time as well as quality of solution ought to be considered.

Some running time comparisons are easy to make. For example, all of the first-stage insertion algorithms should require approximately the same amount of time due to their structural similarity. On the other hand, postprocessors can require vastly different amounts of computer time due to obvious differences in their complexity. A 3-opt, for instance, should require substantially more computer time than a 2-opt if the two procedures are coded with equal care.

In developing the CCAO algorithm, three postprocessors were considered – a 2-opt, an Or-opt and a 3-opt. The choice of Or-opt over the other two was based on both the quality of the solutions produced and the corresponding execution times. In general, the Or-opt procedure yields solutions that are comparable to the 3-opt in terms of quality of solution in an amount of time closer to that of the 2-opt procedure.

Table 7.11 displays the results of the convex hull, cheapest insertion,

Table 7.11   Comparison of postprocessors (percentage over best known and incremental CPU times)

Problem no.	n	Best known solution value	CCA (%)	(sec)[a]	CCA2 (%)	(sec)[a]	CCAO (%)	(sec)[a]	CCA3 (%)	(sec)[a]
8	50	430	5.16	1.52	3.72	0.07	1.38	0.53	2.22	9.14
9	75	553	3.88	3.06	3.43	0.16	1.68	1.05	0.99	29.93
24	100	21,282[b]	1.84	4.92	0.94	0.62	0.00	3.42	0.00	68.34
25	100	22,141[b]	1.35	5.50	1.03	0.30	0.97	1.92	0.97	68.87
26	100	20,749[b]	2.29	5.20	1.12	0.84	0.50	2.68	0.58	72.55
27	100	21,294[b]	3.03	5.56	2.72	0.90	0.97	2.30	1.35	72.49
28	100	22,068[b]	4.54	4.61	3.55	0.49	2.54	2.05	2.03	72.99
30	150	26,736	3.34	11.12	0.81	3.95	0.79	5.59	0.12	237.54

[a] Seconds of CPU time on an IBM 370/158.
[b] Optimal solution value.

angle selection algorithm (CCA) as a stand-alone procedure and with each of the three postprocessors. The algorithms are designated CCA, CCA2, CCAO and CCA3 for the stand-alone, with 2-opt, with Or-opt and with 3-opt versions respectively. The test problems include problems 8 and 9 [Christofides & Eilon, 1972] and problems 24–28 and 30 [Krolak, Felts & Marble, 1971].

The CPU times under each postprocessor algorithm represent the amount of time the postprocessor adds to the CCA computation time. In other words, the CCA algorithm requires 4.92 CPU seconds for problem 24, but when a 2-opt is used as a postprocessor, the CCA2 algorithm requires 5.54 CPU seconds in all.

Two conclusions are clear from Table 7.11. First, the 3-opt postprocessor requires substantially more time than either the 2-opt or the Or-opt procedure. Second, the 2-opt postprocessor is dominated by the Or-opt and the 3-opt in terms of quality of solution (the probability of one of two equally effective algorithms producing superior solutions on eight out of eight problems is 0.004).

The Or-opt procedure should require about three times as much computer effort as the 2-opt procedure. The Or-opt procedure reported in Table 7.11 requires between 50% and 750% more time than the 2-opt procedure. These results are consistent with the factor of 3.

On the other hand, there is statistically no difference in quality of solution between the Or-opt and 3-opt solutions. For the eight problems reported on in Table 7.11, Or-opt produces better solutions than 3-opt on three of the eight, worse solutions on three of the eight, and the same solutions on the remaining two. The two algorithms have essentially the same performance.

The results from Tables 7.10 and 7.11 mesh together nicely. In Table 7.10, we see that the CCAO solutions are generally slightly better than each of the nine algorithms with 3-opt. From Table 7.11, we learn that the Or-opt and 3-opt postprocessors produce comparable solutions but that the former is much less time-consuming to perform. The experimental conclusion is that the overall performance of the CCAO procedure is excellent.

In the first two sets of computational experiments, we have focused on how well the CCAO procedure measures up against well-known algorithms studied in the literature. The third set of computational tests addresses the following question: Does the CCAO procedure outperform other relatively recent insertion algorithms because it uses the Or-opt procedure, as opposed to the more commonly used 2-opt procedure? The results, depicted in Tables 7.12 and 7.13, indicate that the CCAO algorithm is superior to each of these new insertion procedures even when they are followed by an Or-opt postprocessor.

The insertion algorithms tested in the third set of experiments have been discussed previously and are denoted as follows:

CC – convex hull cheapest insertion procedure;
RXD – ratio times difference insertion procedure;
GA – greatest angle insertion procedure;
CI – convex hull insertion procedure;
CCA – convex hull, cheapest insertion, angle selection procedure.

When an Or-opt postprocessor is attached to each of these algorithms, an O is appended to the corresponding abbreviation (e.g., CCA becomes CCAO).

The test problems come from several different sources. The first three problems are from Eilon, Watson-Gandy & Christofides [1971]. The nine problems 24–33 are from Krolak, Felts & Marble [1971]. The 318-city TSP is from Lin & Kernighan [1973]. The 105-city problem is extracted from the 318-city problem, and the 249-city problem is due to Gillett & Johnson [1976]. Only the problems due to Krolak, Felts & Marble have received extensive treatment in the literature, and only the solutions to problems 24–28 in Table 7.12 are known to be optimal [Crowder & Padberg, 1980]. The best solutions for the remaining problems are either from the literature or are generated by the algorithms described here.

The results from the five new insertion algorithms are reported in Table 7.12. Table 7.13 presents results when each of the algorithms is followed by an Or-opt postprocessor. The first column under each algorithm shows how close the solutions come to the best known solutions. In the second column under each algorithm, computer times are displayed. In Table 7.12 the time represents the execution time of the insertion algorithm on each problem, whereas in Table 7.13 it represents the amount of time used by the Or-opt postprocessor.

The CCA and CCAO algorithms outperform their competitors and offer good evidence of their superiority as seen in Tables 7.12 and 7.13 respectively. Several measures of performance are used in arriving at this conclu-

Table 7.12 Comparison of five new insertion algorithms without postprocessor

Problem no.	n	Best known solution	CC		RXD		GA		CI		CCA	
			Per-cent over (%)	CPU (sec)[a]	Per-cent over (%)	CPU (sec)[a]	Per-cent over (%)	CPU (sec)[a]	Per-cent over (%)	CPU (sec)[a]	Per-cent over (%)	CPU (sec)[a]
8	50	429.7	5.80	0.87	8.09	1.06	6.39	2.52	2.67[b]	1.01	5.16	1.52
9	75	552.9	5.96	1.82	7.09	2.15	9.40	6.60	4.29	1.93	3.88[b]	3.06
10	100	640.9	5.90	2.55	5.48	3.33	7.91	10.38	3.23[b]	3.09	4.90	5.34
24	100	21,282.0[c]	8.29	2.77	3.75	3.08	5.81	10.17	3.62	2.76	1.84[b]	4.92
25	100	22,141.0[c]	5.00	2.74	1.57	3.57	9.30	9.31	2.52	2.91	1.35[b]	5.50
26	100	20,749.0[c]	4.26	2.57	2.90	3.40	9.08	11.46	2.54	2.91	2.29[b]	5.20
27	100	21,294.0[c]	1.96	2.59	1.78[b]	3.25	11.00	10.46	2.35	3.07	3.03	5.56
28	100	22,068.0[c]	3.63	2.52	4.64	3.31	6.59	9.41	3.45[b]	2.79	4.54	4.61
105	105	14,383.0	3.68	2.83	4.42	3.74	6.29	10.52	5.73	4.10	2.37[b]	8.56
30	150	26,735.6	7.78	5.34	6.68	7.11	7.86	24.71	6.84	5.94	3.34[b]	11.12
31	150	26,216.4	4.80	5.53	5.67	7.21	16.74	26.19	3.49[b]	6.06	3.78	11.79
32	200	29,563.1	7.54	9.67	8.77	12.96	12.50	47.76	4.67	10.99	3.43[b]	22.21
33	200	29,678.2	8.24	9.90	7.79	11.69	8.13	41.40	6.09	11.17	4.27[b]	22.77
249	249	2,363.6	10.36	13.74	8.04	24.64	9.15	88.00	6.39	18.13	4.63[b]	37.21
318	318	43,864.7	6.93	22.71	6.89	34.44	7.50	158.20	6.51	31.75	4.03[b]	52.57

[a] IBM 370/158 at the College of William and Mary.
[b] Marks the best solution in each row.
[c] Optimal solution value.

Table 7.13   Comparison of five new insertion algorithms with Or-opt postprocessor

Problem no.	n	Best known solution	CCO		RXDO		GAO		CIO		CCAO	
			Per-cent over (%)	CPU (sec)[a]	Per-cent over (%)	CPU (sec)[a]	Per-cent over (%)	CPU (sec)[a]	Per-cent over (%)	CPU (sec)[a]	Per-cent over (%)	CPU (sec)[a]
8	50	429.7	2.79	0.56	2.31	0.47	1.74	0.87	2.29	0.43	1.38[b]	0.53
9	75	552.9	0.94[b]	2.06	4.09	2.04	1.85	2.51	1.74	0.96	1.68	1.05
10	100	640.9	3.09	3.55	1.33[b]	3.91	2.64	4.25	1.57	2.75	1.42	3.97
24	100	21,282.0[c]	0.00[b]	4.79	0.06	3.10	0.85	4.88	0.43	4.00	0.00[b]	3.42
25	100	22,141.0[c]	2.60	3.14	0.41[b]	2.56	1.45	4.47	0.97	2.01	0.97	2.42
26	100	20,749.0[c]	0.50	2.64	0.00[b]	2.15	1.39	4.07	0.50	2.30	0.50	2.68
27	100	21,294.0[c]	0.97[b]	2.02	0.97[b]	1.90	2.26	7.18	1.66	1.99	0.97[b]	2.30
28	100	22,068.0[c]	2.08	2.15	2.98	2.30	2.03[b]	3.06	2.58	1.76	2.54	2.05
105	105	14,383.0	0.08	3.38	0.78	5.01	0.62	5.44	1.40	4.65	0.00[b]	3.51
30	150	26,735.6	0.75	11.24	3.05	9.33	0.57[b]	13.82	1.60	8.98	0.79	5.59
31	150	26,216.4	0.81	9.62	0.00[b]	15.95	3.21	22.39	0.79	10.86	1.13	11.07
32	200	29,563.1	0.83[b]	28.90	3.76	25.09	4.49	45.93	2.27	24.06	1.39	15.13
33	200	29,678.2	2.26	37.52	1.99	35.62	0.13[b]	32.24	0.69	21.78	0.13[b]	25.65
249	249	2,363.6	3.75	65.53	4.00	55.98	1.83	77.71	1.74	57.98	0.00[b]	60.86
318	318	43,864.7	0.92	188.97	0.69	140.15	0.00[b]	173.20	2.01	83.36	0.06	98.66

[a] IBM 370/158 at the College of William and Mary.
[b] Marks best solution in row.
[c] Optimal solution value.

sion. We discuss these below.

1. The CCA and CCAO procedures are consistently closer to the best known solution than the other algorithms to which they are being compared. The CCA procedure generates solutions within about 5% of the best known solution on all fifteen problems. The CCAO procedure yields solutions that are within 2% of the best known solution on fourteen of the fifteen problems. The next best performance is turned in by the RXDO algorithm, with eleven solutions that are within 2%.
2. The CCA and CCAO procedures produce a larger number of best (with respect to the solutions generated by the five algorithms) solutions than the other algorithms. In Table 7.12, it is easy to see that the CCA algorithm finds the best solution to ten of the fifteen problems. The CI procedure obtains four best solutions. In Table 7.13, the CCAO procedure yields the best solution from among all the algorithms six times, while RXDO is next with the best solution on five occasions.
3. Other measures of evaluation are obtained by calculating the mean percentage ($\bar{x}$) and the standard deviation of percentage (s) above the best known solution for each algorithm in Tables 7.12 and 7.13. These statistics are provided in Table 7.14. The CCA procedure dominates each of the other stand-alone insertion algorithms on the basis of average performance (lowest $\bar{x}$) and consistency of performance (lowest s). The CCAO procedure has the best average performance among the five algorithms with postprocessors. Although the CIO algorithm has the lowest standard deviation, the standard deviation for the CCAO procedure is very close. Without specific distributional assumptions, no further statistical inference can be drawn.
4. In Table 7.15, we present average rankings for each of the heuristics studied in Table 7.12. The CCA procedure has the lowest average ranking among the stand-alone insertion algorithms.
5. The Friedman test is performed in Table 7.16. It indicates that there are significant differences in performance with respect to the five heuristics

Table 7.14   Mean and standard deviation of performance (%)

Insertion Algorithm	Stand alone		With Or-opt	
	$\bar{x}$ (%)	s (%)	$\bar{x}$ (%)	s (%)
CC	6.01	2.21	1.49	1.16
RXD	5.57	2.33	1.76	1.51
GA	8.91	2.83	1.67	1.19
CI	4.29	1.62	1.48	0.68
CCA	3.52	1.15	0.86	0.76

Table 7.15   Average rank for algorithms

	CC	RXD	GA	CI	CCA
Average rank for each column in Table 7.12	3.53	3.13	4.73	2.06	1.53

from Table 7.12 (note that $T_F > F_{0.05,4,56}$). While there is little doubt that such differences exist, there may be some question as to whether they are caused by the CCA procedure outperforming the other four heuristics, or one or more of the other heuristics simply performing very poorly. This question can be addressed by individual pairwise tests (such as the sign test or the Wilcoxon test) of the CCA heuristic versus each of the competing heuristics. We leave this as an exercise for the interested reader.

To summarize, the CCA and CCAO procedures have been shown to

Table 7.16   Friedman test applied to insertion heuristics

	Rank				
Problem no.	CC	RXD	GA	CI	CCA
8	3	5	4	1	2
9	3	4	5	2	1
10	4	3	5	1	2
24	5	3	4	2	1
25	4	2	5	3	1
26	4	3	5	2	1
27	2	1	5	3	4
28	2	4	5	3	3
105	2	3	5	4	1
30	4	2	5	3	1
31	3	4	5	1	2
32	3	4	5	2	1
33	5	3	4	2	1
249	5	3	4	2	1
318	4	3	5	2	1
R_j	53	47	71	31	23

$B_F = 769.9$
$A_F = 825$
$T_F = 23.98$
$F_{0.05,4,56} \approx 5.70$

outperform the other algorithms on the basis of a number of different criteria (see Exercises 9, 10 and 11). Another conclusion that is partially supported by the third set of computational results is that the quality of the final solution produced by an Or-opt postprocessor is directly related to the quality of the solution it receives as input. *Best-in, best-out* appears to be the general rule for edge exchange postprocessors, at least for Euclidean TSPs.

Exercises
9. From Table 7.11 it seems that the CCAO solutions dominate the CCA2 solutions. In all eight problems, the Or-opt procedure produces better solutions than the 2-opt procedure. Only in problems 24 and 30 are the solutions even close. With what level of significance can we conclude that the CCAO algorithm outperforms the CCA2 algorithm?
10. Apply the Friedman test to the heuristics in Table 7.13.
11. Compare the heuristics in Table 7.12 and the heuristics in Table 7.13 using the expected utility approach.

5 HEURISTICS FOR THE ASYMMETRIC TSP

As we have seen, much research attention has been focused on the design of heuristics for the symmetric TSP. The design of heuristics for the asymmetric TSP (where it is not necessarily the case that $c_{ij} = c_{ji}$) has been comparatively neglected. Furthermore, the heuristics developed for the asymmetric TSP, at least until recently, have not been as effective as their symmetric counterparts [Akl, 1980; Van Der Cruyssen & Rijckaert, 1978]. In this section, we focus on several heuristics for the asymmetric TSP that have been proposed in the last few years and that seem to be quite promising.

5.1 The minimum spanning digraph approach

We define a *minimum spanning digraph* as a subgraph of a complete digraph that spans all vertices and has minimum total length. It forms a spanning tree when directions are ignored. Equivalently, when directions are ignored, the graph is a minimum spanning tree with edge lengths $l_{ij} = \min\{c_{ij}, c_{ji}\}$.

We refer to the algorithm stated below as the minimum spanning digraph approach [Akl, 1980]. We present the steps briefly and then comment on them in more detail later on.

Step 1. Find a minimum spanning digraph of G.
Step 2. Add a set of arcs to the minimum spanning digraph after solving an appropriate transportation problem in order to make the digraph thus obtained Eulerian.

Step 3. Find an Eulerian tour in this digraph.
Step 4. Transform the Eulerian tour into a Hamiltonian cycle.

In Step 1, we apply a minimum spanning tree algorithm to an undirected
network with edge lengths l_{ij} as defined previously. If edge k in the
minimum spanning tree has length c_{ij}, it is directed from i to j; if the length
is c_{ji}, it is directed from j to i. By directing all the edges of the minimum
spanning tree, we obtain a minimum spanning digraph. In Step 2, we
identify vertices with excess indegree as supply points and vertices with
excess outdegree as demand points and solve an associated transportation
problem in order to balance the graph. Step 3 is straightforward [Nijenhuis
& Wilf, 1975]. Step 4 is also easy: Assume the Eulerian is $(v_1, v_2, \ldots, v_l)$,
where the v_i are not necessarily distinct vertices. A Hamiltonian cycle can
be formed by starting at v_1, moving to the right and introducing a vertex
into the Hamiltonian cycle only if it appears for the first time.

5.2 The savings method

The savings method was developed in the context of the vehicle routing
problem (see Chapter 12), but has also been studied in the context of the
TSP [Golden, 1977a; Frieze, Galbiati & Maffioli, 1982; Golden, Bodin,
Doyle & Stewart, 1980]. The motivation behind the procedure lies in the
fact that connections are made at each step so as to maximize the distance
saved over a previous configuration. The algorithm is as follows.

Step 1. Select any city as an origin and denote this as city 1.
Step 2. Compute savings

$$s_{ij} = c_{i1} + c_{1j} - c_{ij} \qquad \text{for} \qquad i, j = 2, 3, \ldots, n$$

(see Figure 7.5).
Step 3. Order the savings from largest to smallest.
Step 4. Starting at the top of the savings list and moving downwards, form
larger subtours by linking appropriate cities i and j. Repeat until a
tour is formed.

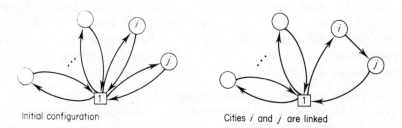

Initial configuration   Cities i and j are linked

Figure 7.5   A step in the savings method

The procedure can be repeated n times to allow each city a chance to serve as origin. The best solution obtained would then be listed as the answer.

5.3   The loss method

Loss methods have been proposed for symmetric [Webb, 1971] as well as asymmetric TSPs [Van Der Cruyssen & Rijckaert, 1978]. The procedure that we outline here for asymmetric TSPs fixes one arc in the tour at each step.

At an intermediate stage in the procedure, each city j falls into one of four categories as shown in Table 7.17.

Table 7.17

Case	A	B	C	D
Indegree	1	1	0	0
Outdegree	1	0	1	0

In the loss method, we compute a loss or opportunity cost for each city j other than those that belong to case A. Cities that satisfy the requirements of case A are no longer interesting in the sense that arcs in and out have already been determined and these decisions are never changed.

On the other hand, suppose city j belongs to category B. In Figure 7.6, we see that (j, k) and (j, k') are the cheapest and next cheapest arcs emanating

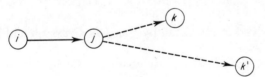

Figure 7.6   Loss method: Case B

from j such that no subtour is formed. The opportunity cost of not linking city j to its nearest neighbor is thus given by

$$\text{LOSS}(j) = c_{j,k'} - c_{j,k}.$$

That is, if arc (j, k) is not used, a loss of at least this much is incurred.

Similarly, suppose city j falls into category C. In Figure 7.7, we observe

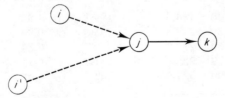

Figure 7.7   Loss method: Case C

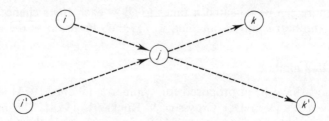

Figure 7.8   Loss method: Case D

that (i, j) and (i', j) are the cheapest and next cheapest arcs into city j such that no subtour is formed. The opportunity cost of not linking a nearest neighbor to city j is thus given by

$$LOSS(j) = c_{i',j} - c_{i,j}.$$

Figure 7.8 depicts the case D situation. Here (i, j) and (i', j) are the cheapest and next cheapest arcs into city j such that no subtour is formed and (j, k) and (j, k') are the cheapest and next cheapest arcs emanating from j such that no subtour is formed. Case D is the only one that is complicated. The difficulty arises in that $i = k$, $i' = k'$, $i = k'$ and $k = i'$ are all possible. Under the simplest scenario where i, i', k and k' are distinct cities, we find that

$$LOSS(j) = \max\{c_{i',j} - c_{i,j}, c_{j,k'} - c_{j,k}\}.$$

Case D is described in full detail by Van Der Cruyssen and Rijckaert via a flowchart.

At each step in the procedure, we compute $LOSS(j)$ for all cities j that fall

Table 7.18   Comparison for the asymmetric
TSP

n	Minina–Perekrest solution	Loss method solution	Ratio
20	184.9	189.1	1.02
30	217.8	205.6	0.94
50	239.9	200.7	0.84
70	255.4	181.7	0.71
100	321.6	208.4	0.65

in category B, C or D. Then we connect the city having the greatest loss with its most favorable neighbor.

Computational experiments comparing the loss method with a variant of the nearest neighbor algorithm of Minina & Perekrest [1975] have been performed [Van Der Cruyssen & Rijckaert, 1978]. The results, displayed in Table 7.18, indicate that the superiority of the loss method becomes more noticeable as n increases.

5.4 Further remarks

Many other heuristics have been proposed for the asymmetric TSP. A number of these are straightforward modifications of heuristics for the symmetric TSP [Frieze, Galbiati & Maffioli, 1982]. Others, such as the heuristic of Kanellakis & Papadimitriou [1980], require major revisions to symmetric TSP procedures, such as the one of Lin & Kernighan [1973].

The variable-depth edge exchange procedure of Lin and Kernighan, described in Section 3, is one of the few heuristics that *consistently* obtains near-optimal solutions to the symmetric TSP. The Kanellakis–Papadimitriou heuristic may be as successful with the asymmetric TSP; however, further experiments are necessary in order to confirm such a statement. Some extremely encouraging preliminary computational results with the Kanellakis–Papadimitriou heuristic are summarized in Table 7.19 (this table is borrowed from Kanellakis & Papadimitriou [1980]). In addition to the variable-depth arc exchange procedure for the asymmetric TSP, Kanellakis and Papadimitriou explain how to transform an asymmetric TSP on n cities into a symmetric TSP on $3n$ cities and discuss the implications from a practical point of view and in terms of computational complexity.

Table 7.19   Kanellakis–Papadimitriou heuristic

n	30	40	50	60	70	80	90
Number of trials	10	10	10	10	10	10	10
Number of distinct local optima found	2	4	2	4	4	5	5
Number of times optimum was found	8	5	6	2	2	2	2

A *patching algorithm* of Karp [1979] exploits the fact that the assignment problem is a relaxation of the TSP. This procedure and a probabilistic analysis of it are described in Chapter 6 of this book.

Exercises

12. Apply the minimum spanning digraph approach to the small example shown below. Verify that the length of the resulting tour is 94 units. What is the optimal solution?

$$
C = \begin{bmatrix}
\infty & 7 & 65 & 68 & 34 & 81 \\
19 & \infty & 22 & 27 & 59 & 29 \\
14 & 43 & \infty & 62 & 77 & 65 \\
76 & 53 & 64 & \infty & 6 & 51 \\
39 & 58 & 38 & 27 & \infty & 13 \\
46 & 67 & 27 & 11 & 38 & \infty
\end{bmatrix}
$$

13. Apply the savings heuristic to the example in Exercise 12. Does the solution improve if the modified savings function

$$
s_{ij}^{(\lambda)} = c_{i1} + c_{1j} - \lambda c_{ij}
$$

(with $\lambda = 0, 0.5, 1, 1.5, 2$) is applied?

14. Write computer programs for the minimum spanning digraph, savings, loss, and patching procedures and generate a set of twenty-five asymmetric TSP instances. Compare the effectiveness of the four procedures using some of the statistical techniques already discussed in this chapter.

6 STATISTICAL ESTIMATION OF THE OPTIMAL TOUR LENGTH

In this section, we approach the problem of analyzing heuristic solutions from a different perspective. Given a systematic procedure for generating independent heuristic solutions, we seek to obtain point and interval estimates for the optimal solution value using statistical inference [Klein, 1975; Golden, 1977b; Dannenbring, 1977; Golden, 1978; Golden & Alt, 1979; Ariyawansa, 1980; Los & Lardinois, 1982; Derigs, 1983].

Suppose we take S independent samples, each of size m, from a parent population which is continuous and bounded from below by a. If x_i is the smallest value in sample i, then let

$$
v = \min\{x_i \mid 1 \leq i \leq S\}.
$$

As m gets large, the distribution of x_i approaches a Weibull distribution with a as the location parameter [Fisher & Tippett, 1928]. The cumulative

Weibull distribution is given by

$$F_x(x_0) = \Pr[x \leqslant x_0] = 1 - \exp\left\{-\left(\frac{x_0 - a}{b}\right)^c\right\}$$

$$\text{for} \qquad x_0 \geqslant a \geqslant 0, b > 0, c \geqslant 0,$$

where a is the location parameter, b is the scale parameter and c is the shape parameter.

Researchers have been able to appeal to this fundamental result in statistical extreme-value distribution theory in order to derive accurate point estimates for the optimum [McRoberts, 1971; Golden, 1977b, 1978]. Specifically, the parent population consists of $(n-1)!/2$ tours with total costs bounded from below by a, the length of the optimal tour. The distribution is discrete but unless the problem is especially perverse (see Papadimitriou & Steiglitz [1978]) we can argue that its histogram can be approximated by a continuous distribution since the number of tours is so large. Each heuristic solution x_i ($i = 1, 2, \ldots, S$) is a local minimum relative to the 'swapping' operation from a large number of m possible tours. Furthermore, these heuristic solutions are independent to the extent that the initial tours are randomly chosen. (The above argument does not at all constitute a proof. There are, however, a number of related results [Patel & Smith, 1983; Boender, Rinnooy Kan, Stougie & Timmer, 1982; De Haan, 1981] in which the Weibull distribution or a variant arises when the feasible region is a convex or bounded set.)

Good estimates for the three parameters can be determined from a least squares/goodness-of-fit analysis [Golden, 1978]. One can also solve the maximum likelihood equations [Golden & Alt, 1979], using one of several methods [Zanakis, 1977].

In order to verify the argument that the heuristic solution values are Weibull distributed, we computed Kolmogorov–Smirnov statistics (assuming independence) in our point estimation experiments [Golden, 1978]. In all cases these statistics fall far below the critical value at the 0.05 level of significance, indicating that there is no reason to reject the Weibull hypothesis. In addition, it should be observed that the point estimate was always within 2.8% of the true optimal solution.

After point estimation, the next step is to develop a procedure for determining a confidence interval for a, the optimal TSP solution value. If we could say, for example, that the optimal solution is contained in the interval [975, 1000] with a certain confidence level for a particular problem, then we would have a useful tool for evaluating heuristic solutions and measuring deviations from optimality.

An interval estimation procedure which seems to perform quite satisfactorily is now presented [Golden & Alt, 1979]. From the cumulative Weibull distribution function we see that

$$F_{x_i}(a+b) = 1 - e^{-1} \approx 0.63,$$

which enables us to write

$$\Pr[v \leq a+b] = 1 - \Pr[v > a+b]$$
$$= 1 - \{1 - F_{x_1}(a+b)\}\{1 - F_{x_2}(a+b)\}\ldots\{1 - F_{x_S}(a+b)\}$$
$$= 1 - e^{-S},$$

or

$$\Pr[v - b \leq a \leq v] = 1 - e^{-S}.$$

This calculation should be interpreted to imply that, if the Weibull assumption is correct, then a will lie in the indicated interval in a fraction $1 - e^{-S}$ of our experiments. Since b is seldom known, a procedure for constructing an approximate confidence interval for the location parameter a is outlined below.

Step 0. Compute $x_1, x_2, \ldots, x_S$.
Step 1. Rearrange the observations from smallest to largest to obtain

$$v = x_{(1)}, x_{(2)}, \ldots, x_{(S)}.$$

Step 2. Determine good initial parameter estimates for a, b and c.
Step 3. Solve the maximum likelihood equations to obtain improved parameter estimates $\tilde{a}$, $\tilde{b}$, $\tilde{c}$.
Step 4. An approximate confidence interval is given by $[v - \tilde{b}, v]$.

Table 7.20, given by Golden & Alt [1979], displays the results of some preliminary computational experiments. Notice that the width of the confidence interval ($\tilde{b}$) is never more than about 6.5% of the optimal solution, and that the optimal solution is contained in the interval in every case. We expect this to be true almost always since $1 - e^{-S}$ approaches 1 very quickly as S increases. In these experiments, random starting tours were generated by the procedure RANPER [Nijenhuis & Wilf, 1975]; the tour improvement heuristic was the 2-opt procedure.

Since there are so few TSPs of over 100 cities where the optimal solution is known, we shall now take advantage of an asymptotic expected length formula for an optimal tour when the cities are distributed uniformly over a rectangular area of R units [Beardwood, Halton & Hammersley, 1959]. The expected length of the optimal tour is given by

$$L(n, R) = K\sqrt{nR}.$$

In the extensive computational experiments, the following empirical bounds on the constant K have been obtained [Stein, 1977]:

$$0.765 \leq K \leq 0.765 + \frac{4}{n}.$$

The expression $L(n, R)$ is discussed in more detail in Chapter 6.

In Table 7.21, also given by Golden & Alt [1979], networks of from 70 to 130 vertices were generated uniformly in a square of area 10,000,

Table 7.20 Computational results: $100(1 - e^{-S})$% confidence intervals[†]

Problem no.	v	$\bar{a}$	$\bar{b}$	$\bar{c}$	$[v - \bar{b}, v]$	Optimal solution value	Does interval include optimum?
24	21,518.99	21,454.77	926.36	1.76	[20592.63, 21518.99]	21,282	Yes
25	22,816.55	22,754.95	856.92	1.92	[21959.63, 22816.55]	22,141	Yes
26	20,971.54	20,763.87	1,260.75	2.31	[19710.79, 20971.54]	20,749	Yes
27	21,807.23	21,779.19	837.82	1.51	[20969.41, 21807.23]	21,294	Yes
28	22,382.39	22,190.20	1,415.64	2.62	[20966.75, 22383.39]	22,068	Yes
318-city short-est Hamiltonian path problem	41,415.00	41,365.38	609.58	1.96	[40805.42, 41415.00]	41,345	Yes

[†] For the above problems, $S = 50$ and $e^{-S} = 1.92874 \times 10^{-22}$. This implies that $1 - e^{-S}$ is practically 1.

Table 7.21   Computational results: $100(1 - e^{-S})\%$ confidence intervals[†]

n	v	$[v - \tilde{b}, v]$	Estimated optimal solution value $76.5\sqrt{n}$
70	659.39	$[621.61, 659.39]$	640.04
80	700.46	$[662.69, 700.46]$	684.24
90	747.24	$[711.50, 747.24]$	725.74
100	785.73	$[668.31, 785.73]$	765.00
110	832.44	$[720.79, 832.44]$	802.34
120	915.36	$[833.06, 915.36]$	838.02
130	917.56	$[825.84, 917.56]$	872.23

[†] For the first four problems, $S = 25$ and $e^{-S} = 1.38879 \times 10^{-11}$. For the last three problems, $S = 30$ and $e^{-S} = 9.35762 \times 10^{-14}$. Again, $1 - e^{-S}$ is practically 1.

heuristic solutions to the TSP were calculated, and Weibull interval estimates were computed where $0.765\sqrt{nR}$ was taken as the presumed optimal solution value.

For what it may be worth, the interval included the estimated optimum in all cases. Also, the intervals were fairly tight but not as tight as the intervals in Table 7.20. This is partially due to the fact that the sample size in Table 7.21 is smaller than in Table 7.20 (see Golden [1977b] for details).

The results displayed in Tables 7.20 and 7.21 are encouraging but a more extensive experiment is needed in order to further test the effectiveness of the confidence interval procedure. With this in mind, we generate 250 2-opt solutions to each of the problems 24–28. This yields ten sets of 25 solutions for each of the five 100-city TSPs for a total of fifty samples. For each sample, we compute approximate $100(1 - e^{-25})\%$ confidence intervals (note that $100(1 - e^{-25})$ is practically 100). In *all* fifty cases, the interval contains the optimal solution value. These results are summarized in Table 7.22.

A rather massive set of numerical experiments involving both the TSP and the quadratic assignment problem are described by Derigs [1983]. This work provides support for the confidence interval procedure.

In addition to analyzing a heuristic solution v to a particular combinatorial problem, Tables 7.20 and 7.21 provide a basis for comparing the accuracy of various heuristic procedures as well. For example, the heuristic solutions x_i to the 318-city problem were obtained by the Lin–Kernighan algorithm which is a substantial improvement on the 2-opt heuristic. From Table 7.20, we can see that the performance measure $\tilde{b}/v$ (a measure of relative interval width) is generally smaller when the more powerful heuristic is used. The heuristic solutions x_i studied in Table 7.21 were obtained by

Table 7.22   Width of confidence interval as percentage of
optimal tour length

| | Problem no. | | | | |
Sample	24	25	26	27	28
1	7.33	3.90	9.83	4.54	4.74
2	4.09	8.06	7.39	4.81	9.70
3	5.02	9.17	10.75	8.86	5.26
4	5.31	4.21	9.19	8.03	5.75
5	8.91	8.29	9.24	3.39	10.72
6	10.71	7.75	6.79	7.50	5.13
7	10.31	7.61	5.59	8.64	8.72
8	4.91	3.47	9.85	8.31	9.77
9	3.71	10.34	6.67	5.29	7.72
10	8.39	4.31	5.42	5.98	10.99

the Clarke–Wright savings algorithm which is not as powerful as the 2-opt procedure. Again the performance measure $\tilde{b}/v$ reflects this fact. That is, in a relative sense the intervals are tighter when using the 2-opt procedure. Thus, the more powerful the heuristic, the tighter are the confidence intervals that can be expected.

Exercise
15. The confidence interval for a discussed and tested in this section has been extended [Los & Lardinois, 1982] so that a $100(1-\alpha)\%$ interval $[v-b/T, v]$ may be obtained. Derive this result by letting

$$T = \left(\frac{-S}{\ln \alpha}\right)^{1/c}.$$

The Traveling Salesman Problem
Edited by E. L. Lawler, J. K. Lenstra,
A. H. G. Rinnooy Kan, D. B. Shmoys
© 1985 John Wiley & Sons Ltd.

8

Polyhedral theory

M. Grötschel
Universität Augsburg

M. W. Padberg
New York University

1 INTRODUCTION TO POLYHEDRAL THEORY

This chapter focuses on polyhedral aspects of the TSP from a theoretical point of view. It lays the foundation for Chapter 9, where algorithmic implications of the polyhedral results are discussed. In particular, it turns out that large classes of facet-defining inequalities can be efficiently identified and can be used as the backbone of computationally successful linear programming based algorithms for TSPs.

All algorithmic problems arising in connection with cutting plane genera-

The second author's work was partially supported by the College Interuniversitaire d'Etudes Doctorales dans les Sciences du Management, Belgium.

tion or facet identification are postponed to Chapter 9. We will deal in this chapter solely with *descriptive* results concerning the facial structure of traveling salesman polytopes.

A detailed treatment of the theory of polyhedra is presented in Bachem & Grötschel [1982], Grünbaum [1967], Rockafellar [1970] and Stoer & Witzgall [1970], as well as in some books on linear programming. For completeness, however, we shall summarize here those concepts and results from linear algebra and polyhedral theory which are necessary for our exposition.

If $x_1, \ldots, x_k \in \mathbb{R}^n$ and $\lambda_1, \ldots, \lambda_k \in \mathbb{R}$, then the vector $x \in \mathbb{R}^n$ with $x = \lambda_1 x_1 + \ldots + \lambda_k x_k$ is called a *linear combination* of the vectors $x_1, \ldots, x_k$. If the λ_i in addition satisfy $\lambda_1 + \ldots + \lambda_k = 1$, then x is called an *affine combination* of the vectors $x_1, \ldots, x_k$. If $x = \lambda_1 x_1 + \ldots + \lambda_k x_k$ is an affine combination such that $\lambda_i \geq 0$ for $i = 1, \ldots, k$, then x is called a *convex combination* of the vectors $x_1, \ldots, x_k$.

If $\varnothing \neq S \subseteq \mathbb{R}^n$, then the set of all linear (affine, convex) combinations of finitely many vectors in S is called the *linear (affine, convex) hull* of S and is denoted by $\text{lin}(S)$ $(\text{aff}(S), \text{conv}(S))$; by convention $\text{lin}(\varnothing) = \{0\}$, $\text{aff}(\varnothing) = \text{conv}(\varnothing) = \varnothing$. A set $S \subseteq \mathbb{R}^n$ with $S = \text{lin}(S)$ $(S = \text{aff}(S), S = \text{conv}(S))$ is called a *linear subspace (affine subspace, convex set)*.

One can show that a set $L \subseteq \mathbb{R}^n$ is a linear (affine) subspace if and only if there is an (m, n)-matrix A (an (m, n)-matrix A and a vector $b \in \mathbb{R}^m$) such that $L = \{x \in \mathbb{R}^n \mid Ax = 0\}$ $(L = \{x \mid Ax = b\})$. Affine subspaces of particular interest are *hyperplanes*, i.e. sets of the form $\{x \in \mathbb{R}^n \mid a^T x = a_0\}$ where $a \in \mathbb{R}^n - \{0\}$ and $a_0 \in \mathbb{R}$. Clearly, every affine subspace different from $\mathbb{R}^n$ is the intersection of hyperplanes.

A nonempty set $S \subseteq \mathbb{R}^n$ is called *linearly (affinely) independent*, if for every finite set $\{x_1, x_2, \ldots, x_k\} \subseteq S$, the equations $\lambda_1 x_1 + \ldots + \lambda_k x_k = 0$ $(\lambda_1 x_1 + \ldots + \lambda_k x_k = 0$ and $\lambda_1 + \ldots + \lambda_k = 0)$ imply $\lambda_i = 0$, $i = 1, \ldots, k$; otherwise S is called *linearly (affinely) dependent*. Every linearly (affinely) independent set in $\mathbb{R}^n$ contains at most $n(n+1)$ elements. Moreover, for sets S with at least two elements, linear (affine) independence means that no $x \in S$ can be represented as a linear (affine) combination of the vectors in $S - \{x\}$. All sets $\{x\}, x \neq 0$, are affinely and linearly independent, $\{0\}$ is linearly dependent but affinely independent. By convention, the empty set is linearly and affinely independent.

The *rank (affine rank)* of a set $S \subseteq \mathbb{R}^n$ is the cardinality of the largest linearly (affinely) independent subset of S, and the *dimension* of S, denoted by $\dim(S)$, is the affine rank of S minus one. A set $S \subseteq \mathbb{R}^n$ is called *full-dimensional* if $\dim(S) = n$; this is equivalent to saying that there is no hyperplane containing S.

It is clear from the definition that the affine rank of a set is equal to the affine rank of its affine hull. Moreover, if $0 \notin \text{aff}(S)$, i.e. if S is contained in a hyperplane $\{x \mid a^T x = a_0\}$ with $a_0 \neq 0$, then $\dim(S)$ is the maximum cardinality of a linearly independent set in S minus one.

The *rank of a matrix* is the rank of the set of its column vectors (which is the same as the rank of the set of the row vectors of the matrix). An (m, n)-matrix is said to have *full rank* if its rank equals $\min\{m, n\}$.

If S is a subset of $\mathbb{R}^n$, then $Ax = b$ is called a *minimal equation system* for S if $\text{aff}(S) = \{x \in \mathbb{R}^n \mid Ax = b\}$ and A has full rank.

A set $H \subseteq \mathbb{R}^n$ is called a *halfspace* if there is a vector $a \in \mathbb{R}^n$ and a scalar $a_0 \in \mathbb{R}$ such that $H = \{x \in \mathbb{R}^n \mid a^T x \leq a_0\}$. We say that H is the halfspace defined by the inequality $a^T x \leq a_0$, and we shall also say that (if $a \neq 0$) the hyperplane $\{x \mid a^T x = a_0\}$ is the hyperplane defined by $a^T x \leq a_0$.

An inequality $a^T x \leq b$ is called *valid* with respect to $S \subseteq \mathbb{R}^n$ if $S \subseteq \{x \in \mathbb{R}^n \mid a^T x \leq b\}$, i.e. if S is contained in the halfspace defined by $a^T x \leq b$. A valid inequality $a^T x \leq b$ for S is called *supporting* if $S \cap \{x \in \mathbb{R}^n \mid a^T x = b\} \neq \varnothing$. An inequality $a^T x \leq b$ valid with respect to S is called a *proper valid* inequality if S is not contained in the hyperplane $\{x \in \mathbb{R}^n \mid a^T x = b\}$. A valid inequality for S which is not proper is sometimes called an *implicit equation* for S.

A *polyhedron* is the intersection of finitely many halfspaces, i.e. every polyhedron P can be represented in the form $P = \{x \in \mathbb{R}^n \mid Ax \leq b\}$. Since an equation system $Dx = c$ can be written as $Dx \leq c$, $-Dx \leq -c$, every set of the form $\{x \in \mathbb{R}^n \mid Ax \leq b, Dx = c\}$ is a polyhedron. A bounded polyhedron (i.e. a polyhedron P with $P \subseteq \{x \in \mathbb{R}^n \mid \|x\| \leq B\}$ for some $B > 0$ where $\|x\|$ is, for example, the Euclidean norm of x) is called a *polytope*. Polytopes are precisely those sets in $\mathbb{R}^n$ which are the convex hulls of finitely many points, i.e. every polytope P can be written as $P = \{x \in \mathbb{R}^n \mid Ax \leq b\}$ (A an (m, n)-matrix, $b \in \mathbb{R}^m$), and as $P = \text{conv}(V)$ ($V \subseteq \mathbb{R}^n$, $|V|$ finite).

A subset F of a polyhedron P is called a *face* of P if there exists an inequality $a^T x \leq a_0$ valid with respect to P such that $F = \{x \in P \mid a^T x = a_0\}$. We say that the inequality $a^T x \leq a_0$ defines F. A face F is called *proper* if $F \neq P$. In fact, if $P = \{x \in \mathbb{R}^n \mid a_i^T x \leq b_i, i = 1, \ldots, k\}$ is a polyhedron and F is a face of P, then one can show that there exists an index set $I \subseteq \{1, \ldots, k\}$ such that $F = \{x \in P \mid a_i^T x = b_i, i \in I\}$. Similarly, if $P = \text{conv}(V)$ for a finite set $V \subseteq \mathbb{R}^n$ and if F is a face of the polytope P, then there exists a set $W \subseteq V$ with $F = \text{conv}(W)$.

If $a^T x \leq a_0$ and $b^T x \leq b_0$ are two valid inequalities for a polyhedron P and if $\{x \in P \mid a^T x = a_0\} = \{x \in P \mid b^T x = b_0\}$ (i.e. both inequalities 'define' or 'induce' the same face), we say that $a^T x \leq a_0$ and $b^T x \leq b_0$ are *equivalent* with respect to P.

A face which contains one element only is called a *vertex*. If $\{x\}$ is a vertex of P we shall simply say that x is a vertex of P. (The word 'vertex' is standard in polyhedral theory as well as in graph theory, so we will use it in two meanings. We made sure that there will be no confusion.) A *facet* F of a polyhedron P is a proper, nonempty face (i.e. a face satisfying $\varnothing \neq F \neq P$) which is maximal with respect to set inclusion.

Clearly, the set of feasible solutions of a linear programming problem $\max\{c^T x \mid Ax \leq b\}$ forms a polyhedron P. If c_0 is the optimum value of

$\max\{c^T x \mid x \in P\}$, then $c^T x \leqslant c_0$ is a supporting valid inequality for P, i.e. the set $F = \{x \in P \mid c^T x = c_0\}$ of optimum solutions is a face of P. If P contains a vertex, then every face contains a vertex. This implies in particular that every linear program over a polytope has at least one optimum vertex solution.

In order to apply linear programming techniques (the simplex method, the ellipsoid method, Karmarkar's method [1985], relaxation methods, etc.) polyhedra have to be given in the form $\{x \in \mathbb{R}^n \mid Ax \leqslant b\}$. In combinatorial optimization, however, polyhedra are usually given as the convex hulls of finite sets of points; thus a major problem is to find an inequality system defining such a polyhedron. Moreover, one wants to find inequality systems with as few inequalities as possible. For these purposes facets, i.e. facet-defining inequalities, are of particular importance.

Theorem 1 *Let $P \subseteq \mathbb{R}^n$ be a polyhedron and assume that A is an (m, n)-matrix, $b \in \mathbb{R}^m$ such that $\mathrm{aff}(P) = \{x \in \mathbb{R}^n \mid Ax = b\}$. Let F be a nonempty face of P, then the following statements are equivalent:*
(a) *F is a facet of P.*
(b) *F is a maximal proper face of P.*
(c) *$\dim(F) = \dim(P) - 1$.*
(d) *There exists an inequality $c^T x \leqslant c_0$ valid with respect to P with the following three properties:*
 (d$_1$) *$F \subseteq \{x \in P \mid c^T x = c_0\}$.*
 (d$_2$) *There exists $\bar{x} \in P$ with $c^T \bar{x} < c_0$, i.e. the inequality is proper.*
 (d$_3$) *If any other inequality $d^T x \leqslant d_0$ valid with respect to P satisfies $F \subseteq \{x \in P \mid d^T x = d_0\}$, then there exists a scalar $\alpha \geqslant 0$ and a vector $\lambda \in \mathbb{R}^m$ such that*

$$d^T = \alpha c^T + \lambda^T A,$$
$$d_0 = \alpha c_0 + \lambda^T b.$$

Conditions (c) and (d) provide the two basic methods to prove that a given inequality $c^T x \leqslant c_0$ defines a facet of a polyhedron P. In both cases, of course, one first has to check that $c^T x \leqslant c_0$ is valid and that P is not contained in $\{x \in \mathbb{R}^n \mid c^T x = c_0\}$. This is usually trivial.

The first method consists of exhibiting a set of $k = \dim(P)$ vectors (usually vertices of P) $x_1, x_2, \ldots, x_k \in P$ satisfying $c^T x_i = c_0$, $i = 1, \ldots, k$, and showing that these vectors are affinely independent. (If $c_0 \neq 0$, this is equivalent to showing that these k vectors are linearly independent.) Let us call this method the *direct method*. We shall encounter some cases where the direct method is easy to apply since the linear (or affine) independence of 'simply structured' vectors like unit vectors and simple modifications of these is easy to check.

In most (nontrivial) cases the second *indirect method*, based on condition (d) of Theorem 1, is more suitable, and it is as follows. One assumes the existence of a valid inequality $d^T x \leqslant d_0$ with $\{x \in P \mid c^T x = c_0\} \subseteq \{x \in P \mid d^T x = d_0\}$. Using the known equation system $Ax = b$ for P, one can determine a $\lambda \in \mathbb{R}^m$ such that $\bar{d} := d + A^T\lambda$ has certain useful properties, i.e. some of the coefficients of $\bar{d}$ are equal to the corresponding coefficients of the given c or the like. Then utilizing known properties of the points x in P satisfying $c^Tx = c_0$, one determines the still unknown coefficients of $\bar{d}$ iteratively. If it turns out that $\bar{d} = \alpha c + A^T\mu$ for some $\alpha \geq 0$ and $\mu \in \mathbb{R}^m$, then condition (d) of Theorem 1 implies that $c^Tx \leq c_0$ defines a facet of P.

Facets are of importance since they have to be known in order to obtain a minimal inequality representation of a polyhedron. Let $P \neq \mathbb{R}^n$ be a polyhedron; then a system of equations and inequalities $Dx = c, Ax \leq b$ is said to be *complete* with respect to P if $P = \{x \in \mathbb{R}^n \mid Dx = c, Ax \leq b\}$. (The equation system may be vacuous.) Let us call such a system *nonredundant* if $Ax \leq b$ contains no implicit equations and if the deletion of any equation or inequality of the system results in a polyhedron different from P. Any equation or inequality which can be deleted without changing the polyhedron is called *redundant*.

Theorem 2 *Let $P \subseteq \mathbb{R}^n$ be a polyhedron and $Ax \leq b, Dx = c$ be a complete and nonredundant system for P, where D is an (m, n)-matrix and A is a (k, n)-matrix. Then the following hold:*

(a) *$\operatorname{aff}(P) = \{x \in \mathbb{R}^n \mid Dx = c\}$ and $m = \operatorname{rank}(D)$.*

(b) *$\operatorname{aff}(P)$ and P have dimension $n - m$.*

(c) *Every inequality $a_i^T \leq b_i$ of the system $Ax \leq b$ defines a facet F_i of P, where $F_i = \{x \in P \mid a_i^Tx = b_i\}, i = 1, \ldots, k$.*

(d) *If $\bar{a}_i^Tx \leq \bar{b}_i, i = 1, \ldots, \bar{k}$,*
   $\bar{d}_i^Tx = \bar{c}_i, i = 1, \ldots, \bar{m}$,
   is any other complete and nonredundant system for P, then
   (d$_1$) *$k = \bar{k}, m = \bar{m}$,*
   (d$_2$) *$\bar{d}_i^T = (\lambda^i)^T D$ for some $\lambda^i \in \mathbb{R}^m - \{0\}$ $(i = 1, \ldots, m)$,*
   (d$_3$) *$\bar{a}_i^T = \alpha_i a_j^T + (\lambda^i)^T D$ for some $\alpha_i > 0, \lambda^i \in \mathbb{R}^m$, and $j \in \{1, \ldots, k\}$ $(i = 1, \ldots, \bar{k})$.*

Theorem 2(d) in particular implies that for a full-dimensional polyhedron P there is a complete and nonredundant inequality system $a_i^Tx \leq b_i, i = 1, \ldots, k$, such that every complete and nonredundant inequality system $\bar{a}_i^Tx \leq \bar{b}_i, i = 1, \ldots, \bar{k}$, satisfies $k = \bar{k}$ and $\bar{a}_i = \alpha_i a_i$ for some $\alpha_i > 0$ (after suitable indexing) and $i = 1, \ldots, k$. This justifies the statement that a full-dimensional polyhedron is defined by a *unique* (up to multiplication by positive scalars) nonredundant and complete inequality system. Moreover, for every facet F of P there is a unique (up to multiplication by a positive scalar) inequality defining F.

Suppose a polytope P is given as the convex hull of finitely many points (we will encounter such polytopes in the following), then Theorem 2(c) implies that in order to get a complete inequality description of P, for every facet of P one has to know (at least) one inequality defining it. Moreover, if we want to find a complete and nonredundant system $Ax \leq b, Dx = c$ for P, we have to prove that $Dx = c$ is a minimal equation system for P, that

$Ax \le b$ contains no implicit equations, that every inequality of $Ax \le b$ defines a facet of P and that $Ax \le b$ contains no equivalent inequalities, i.e. different inequalities defining the same facet of P.

The main purpose of this chapter is to introduce several large classes of inequalities which are valid for the polytope(s) associated with the TSP and to prove that these inequalities define nonequivalent facets of the polytopes. This will show that incredibly large numbers of inequalities are necessary to give a complete (and nonredundant) description of the traveling salesman polytopes.

2 POLYTOPES ASSOCIATED WITH THE SYMMETRIC AND ASYMMETRIC TSP

2.1 The general approach

The approach that we are going to describe here consists of associating polytopes with the TSP and other closely related problems. This approach is applicable to almost all other combinatorial optimization problems as well; see e.g. Padberg [1979] for a related survey concerning the facial structure of polyhedra related to covering, packing and knapsack problems. The area of research in which polyhedra related to combinatorial optimization problems are investigated is often referred to as 'polyhedral combinatorics' and its principal ideas are discussed next. (For general surveys of this subject see, e.g., Grötschel [1984], Pulleyblank [1983] and Schrijver [1983].)

Let E be a finite ground set and $\mathcal{I}$ be a set of subsets of E. With every element $e \in E$ we associate a variable x_e, i.e. a component of a vector $x \in \mathbb{R}^E$ indexed by e. (Rather than writing $\mathbb{R}^{|E|}$ we simply write $\mathbb{R}^E$.) With every subset $F \subseteq E$ we associate a vector $x^F \in \mathbb{R}^E$, called the *incidence* or *characteristic vector* of F, defined as follows:

$$x_e^F = \begin{cases} 1 & \text{if } e \in F, \\ 0 & \text{if } e \notin F. \end{cases}$$

Thus, every subset $F \subseteq E$ corresponds to a unique 0–1 vector in $\mathbb{R}^E$ and vice versa. Now we associate with $\mathcal{I} \subseteq 2^E$ the polytope $P_{\mathcal{I}}$ which is the convex hull of all incidence vectors of elements of $\mathcal{I}$, i.e.

$$P_{\mathcal{I}} := \text{conv}\{x^F \in \mathbb{R}^E \mid F \in \mathcal{I}\}. \tag{1}$$

It is easy to see that every vertex of $P_{\mathcal{I}}$ corresponds to a set in $\mathcal{I}$ and vice versa.

Now suppose 'weights' or 'distances' $c_e \in \mathbb{R}$ for all $e \in E$ are given and we want to find $F^* \in \mathcal{I}$ such that $c(F^*) := \sum_{e \in F^*} c_e$ is as small (or as large) as possible. Then we can solve this combinatorial optimization problem via the linear programming problem

$$\min\{c^T x \mid x \in P_{\mathcal{I}}\}, \tag{2}$$

since every optimum solution of the combinatorial optimization problem corresponds to an optimum vertex solution of (2) and vice versa. In order to apply linear programming techniques we need a complete (and, preferably, nonredundant) description of the polytope $P_{\mathcal{J}}$ by way of linear equations and inequalities. As we shall indicate later, such a *completeness* result will probably prove to be elusive for all $\mathcal{NP}$-complete problems, i.e. there is little hope that complete and nonredundant systems of linear equations and inequalities describing $P_{\mathcal{J}}$ will ever be found explicitly for 'hard' combinatorial optimization problems. But we shall also see that *partial* results can be of great computational help for the numerical solution of hard problems when used in conjunction with linear programming and branch and bound methods.

2.2 The TSP case

With respect to the symmetric TSP, the 'natural' polytopes to work with are the following. Let $K_n = (V, E)$ denote the complete graph on n vertices, i.e. for every two different vertices i and j there is exactly one edge $\{i, j\}$ linking i and j. Denote by $\mathcal{S}_n$ the set of all *tours* (*Hamiltonian cycles*) in K_n (note that we view cycles as sets of edges) and let $\tilde{\mathcal{S}}_n$ be the set of all subsets of tours, i.e. $\tilde{\mathcal{S}}_n = \{S \subseteq E \mid \text{there exists a tour } T \subseteq E \text{ with } S \subseteq T\}$. Then the polytope

$$Q_T^n := \text{conv}\{x^T \in \mathbb{R}^E \mid T \in \mathcal{S}_n\}$$

is called the (n-city) *symmetric traveling salesman polytope* and the polytope

$$\tilde{Q}_T^n := \text{conv}\{x^S \in \mathbb{R}^E \mid S \in \tilde{\mathcal{S}}_n\}$$

is called the (n-city) *monotone symmetric traveling salesman polytope*.

In the asymmetric case, we get two such canonical polytopes in the following way. Let $D_n = (V, A)$ be the complete digraph on n vertices, i.e. every two different vertices i and j are linked by two antiparallel arcs (i, j) and (j, i), let $\mathcal{T}_n$ denote the set of all (directed) *tours* (directed Hamiltonian cycles) in D_n, and let $\tilde{\mathcal{T}}_n$ denote the set of all subsets of tours in $\mathcal{T}_n$. Then

$$P_T^n := \text{conv}\{x^T \in \mathbb{R}^A \mid T \in \mathcal{T}_n\}$$

is called the (n-city) *asymmetric traveling salesman polytope* and

$$\tilde{P}_T^n := \text{conv}\{x^S \in \mathbb{R}^A \mid S \in \tilde{\mathcal{T}}_n\}$$

is called the (n-city) *monotone asymmetric traveling salesman polytope*.

Every symmetric TSP can be solved – in principle – via the linear programming problem

$$\min\{c^T x \mid x \in Q_T^n\}, \tag{3}$$

and every asymmetric TSP via the linear programming problem

$$\min\{c^T x \mid x \in P_T^n\}. \tag{4}$$

The monotone polytopes $\tilde{Q}_T^n$ and $\tilde{P}_T^n$ can be used for these purposes as well, in the sense that, if the distance c_{ij} of every edge $\{i, j\}$ or arc (i, j) is replaced by the distance $\bar{c}_{ij} := M - c_{ij}$, where $M = \max\{|c_{ij}| : \{i, j\} \in E \quad ((i, j) \in A,$ respectively)$\} + 1$, then the resulting maximization problems over $\tilde{Q}_T^n$ and $\tilde{P}_T^n$ provide the same answers as (3) and (4), respectively.

2.3 Basic properties of $\tilde{Q}_T^n$ and $\tilde{P}_T^n$

If E is a finite set and $\mathscr{I}$ a nonempty system of subsets of E, then $\mathscr{I}$ is called *monotone* (or *subclusive*, or *lower comprehensive*, or *hereditary system*, or *independence system*) if $J \in \mathscr{I}$ and $I \subseteq J$ imply $I \in \mathscr{I}$. If $\mathscr{I} \subseteq 2^E$, then $\tilde{\mathscr{I}} = \{I \subseteq E \mid \exists J \in \mathscr{I} \text{ with } I \subseteq J\}$ is called the *monotonization* of $\mathscr{I}$. Monotonization often preserves important properties of the original system and, at the same time, makes a problem easier to analyze.

A polyhedron $P \subseteq \mathbb{R}_+^n$ (i.e. P is contained in the nonnegative orthant) is called *monotone* if $y \in P$ and $0 \leqslant x \leqslant y$ imply $x \in P$. Clearly, if $P_{\mathscr{I}} \subseteq \mathbb{R}^E$ is a polytope associated with a set of subsets on a finite set E, then the polytope $P_{\tilde{\mathscr{I}}} \subseteq \mathbb{R}^E$ associated with the monotonization $\tilde{\mathscr{I}}$ of $\mathscr{I}$ is a monotone polytope. This implies that the traveling salesman polytopes $\tilde{Q}_T^n$ and $\tilde{P}_T^n$ are monotone.

By going from a polytope to its monotonization, we enlarge the polytope 'below'. The advantage of this is that, if $E = \bigcup \mathscr{I}$, we get a full-dimensional polytope which is technically easier to handle. Moreover, a full-dimensional polytope has a unique complete and nonredundant inequality system describing it. This implies in particular that the problem of equivalence of inequalities is easy to solve. Thus, if the monotone polytope is still sufficiently closely related to the original problem, it is often preferable to study the monotone polytope. For the TSP, sufficient closeness is assured by Exercise 1. In the following we shall study the natural TSP-polytopes Q_T^n, P_T^n as well as their monotone versions, $\tilde{Q}_T^n$, $\tilde{P}_T^n$.

Proposition 1   *Let E be a finite set, let $\mathscr{I}$ be an independence system on E, and let $F = E - \bigcup \mathscr{I}$. Then the dimension of $P_{\mathscr{I}}$ is $|E| - |F|$.*

Proof $P_{\mathscr{I}}$ is contained in $\{x \in \mathbb{R}^E \mid x_f = 0, f \in F\}$ and thus $\dim(P_{\mathscr{I}}) \leqslant |E| - |F|$ holds. On the other hand, $P_{\mathscr{I}}$ contains the zero vector and the unit vector u_e for all $e \in E - F$. Hence, $P_{\mathscr{I}}$ contains $|E| - |F| + 1$ affinely independent vectors, and we are done. $\square$

Corollary 1
$$\dim(\tilde{Q}_T^n) = |E| = n(n-1)/2, \qquad \text{for } n \geqslant 3.$$
$$\dim(\tilde{P}_T^n) = |A| = n(n-1), \qquad \text{for } n \geqslant 2.$$

Every polytope $P_{\mathscr{I}}$, cf. (1), is contained in the unit hypercube; thus the hypercube constraints (from now on called *trivial inequalities*) $0 \leqslant x_e \leqslant 1$, $e \in E$, are valid inequalities for $P_{\mathscr{I}}$. In fact – except for the obvious case – the nonnegativity constraints always define facets of monotone polytopes.

Lemma 1 *Let $\mathcal{I}$ be an independence system on a finite set E and $P_{\mathcal{I}}$ be the corresponding polytope, then $x_e \geq 0$ defines a facet of $P_{\mathcal{I}}$ if and only if $e \in \bigcup \mathcal{I}$.*

Again, since $E = \bigcup \mathcal{I}$ holds in the TSP case, we obtain the following.

Corollary 2
(a) *For all edges $\{i, j\}$ in K_n, $x_{ij} \geq 0$ defines a facet of $\tilde{Q}_T^n, n \geq 3$.*
(b) *For all arcs (i, j) in D_n, $x_{ij} \geq 0$ defines a facet of $\tilde{P}_T^n, n \geq 2$.* □

Note that, above, a variable corresponding to an edge $\{i, j\}$ or an arc (i, j) should actually be written as $x_{\{i,j\}}$ or $x_{(i,j)}$. For notational convenience we drop the brackets and, in most cases, also the comma. We shall keep this notation in the following as well as in the next chapter. Thus in the symmetric case, the variables x_{ij} and x_{ji} are identical (but not in the asymmetric case).

The trivial inequalities $x_e \leq 1$ do not necessarily define facets, not even for monotone polytopes, i.e. here every problem has to be checked individually.

Proposition 2 *For every edge $\{i, j\}$ in K_n the inequality $x_{ij} \leq 1$ defines a facet of $\tilde{Q}_T^n, n \geq 3$.*

Proof For this proof we use the direct method suggested by Theorem 1(c). The $|E|$ edge sets $\{\{i, j\}\}$ and $\{\{i, j\}, \{p, q\}\}$, where $\{p, q\} \in E - \{i, j\}$, are obviously contained in $\mathcal{T}_n$. Their incidence vectors satisfy $x_{ij} \leq 1$ with equality and are linearly independent. Moreover, there is a set in $\mathcal{T}_n$ whose incidence vector does not satisfy $x_{ij} \leq 1$ with equality. Thus by Theorem 1, $x_{ij} \leq 1$ defines a facet of $\tilde{Q}_T^n$. □

In fact, it is easy to see that $\tilde{Q}_T^3$ equals the unit hypercube in $\mathbb{R}^3$ and $\tilde{P}_T^2$ equals the unit hypercube in $\mathbb{R}^2$ (see also Exercise 3). These are the only cases where the trivial inequalities are sufficient to describe a traveling salesman polytope.

2.4 Elementary properties of tours and related inequalities

The feasible solutions of combinatorial optimization problems are usually 'structured' in some way. From such structural properties, inequalities which are valid for the associated polytope can often be derived in a straightforward manner.

In the symmetric case, a tour has the property that every vertex lies on exactly two edges, and hence if S is a subset of a tour, then every vertex lies on at most two edges in S. Let $\delta(v)$ be the *star* (or cut) of v, i.e. the set of edges in K_n having v as one endpoint, then our foregoing observation implies that

$$x(\delta(v)) = 2 \qquad \text{for all } v \in V \tag{5}$$

is a system of n equations satisfied by all incidence vectors of tours. (Note that above and in the following $x(F)$ is used as an abbreviation of $\sum_{e \in F} x_e$ where F is an arc or edge set.) This implies that $Q_T^n \subseteq \{x \in \mathbb{R}^E \mid x$ satisfies

(5)}. Similarly, we obtain that every incidence vector of a subset of a tour satisfies the n inequalities

$$x(\delta(v)) \leq 2 \qquad \text{for all } v \in V. \tag{6}$$

Thus we have that $\tilde{Q}_T^n \subseteq \{x \in \mathbb{R}^E \mid x \text{ satisfies } (6)\}$.

In the asymmetric case we observe that every tour has the property that every vertex in D_n is the head of exactly one arc and the tail of exactly one arc. Let $\tilde{\delta}(v)$, $\vec{\delta}(v)$, respectively, denote the set of arcs having head v, and having tail v, respectively. Then the system

$$\begin{aligned} x(\tilde{\delta}(v)) &= 1 \qquad \text{for all } v \in V, \\ x(\vec{\delta}(v)) &= 1 \qquad \text{for all } v \in V, \end{aligned} \tag{7}$$

of $2n$ equations is satisfied by every vector in P_T^n, whereas every point in $\tilde{P}_T^n$ satisfies

$$\begin{aligned} x(\tilde{\delta}(v)) &\leq 1 \qquad \text{for all } v \in V, \\ x(\vec{\delta}(v)) &\leq 1 \qquad \text{for all } v \in V. \end{aligned} \tag{8}$$

This implies $P_T^n \subseteq \{x \in \mathbb{R}^A \mid x \text{ satisfies } (7)\}$ and $\tilde{P}_T^n \subseteq \{x \in \mathbb{R}^A \mid x \text{ satisfies } (8)\}$. The equations (5), (7) and the inequalities (6), (8) are called *degree constraints* since they restrict the possible degree (indegree, outdegree) of a vertex of the graph (digraph) in a feasible solution.

Note that the fact that a tour contains n edges (n arcs, respectively) gives no additional polyhedral information since this is implied by (5) (by (7), respectively).

A further obvious property of a tour is that it is a (directed) cycle. This means that a tour or a subset of a tour contains no cycle of length less than n. From this observation we can derive, for example in the symmetric case, that

$$x(C) \leq |C| - 1 \tag{9}$$

is a valid inequality for Q_T^n and $\tilde{Q}_T^n$, where C is the edge set of a cycle in K_n of length less than n. Such a cycle inequality (9) can be improved by the following observation. If $W \subseteq V$ is a set of vertices with $2 \leq |W| \leq n - 1$, then the set of edges $E(W)$ (i.e. the set of edges in K_n with both endpoints in W) intersects every tour in at most $|W| - 1$ edges, because every set of more than $|W| - 1$ edges contained in the induced subgraph $(W, E(W))$ contains at least one cycle. Consequently, the system of inequalities

$$x(E(W)) \leq |W| - 1 \qquad \text{for all } W \subseteq V, \qquad 2 \leq |W| \leq n - 1 \tag{10}$$

is satisfied by all points in Q_T^n and $\tilde{Q}_T^n$. The inequalities (10) are the well-known *subtour elimination constraints* introduced by Dantzig, Fulkerson & Johnson [1954]. Note that for $|W| = 2$, the inequality $x(E(W)) \leq 1$ is nothing but a trivial inequality $x_{ij} \leq 1$.

In the asymmetric case, for $W \subseteq V$ let $A(W)$ denote the set of arcs in D_n

having head and tail in W. The same observation as above implies that the *subtour elimination constraints*

$$x(A(W)) \leq |W| - 1 \qquad \text{for all } W \subseteq V, \qquad 2 \leq |W| \leq n - 1 \qquad (11)$$

are valid inequalities for P_T^n and $\tilde{P}_T^n$.

We shall study the equations and inequalities introduced above in more detail in a later section.

The equations and inequalities (5), (6), (7) and (8) can be used to show the following.

Lemma 2
(a) Q_T^n is a face of $\tilde{Q}_T^n$.
(b) P_T^n is a face of $\tilde{P}_T^n$.

This implies the following observation. (Why?)

Corollary 3 *Every inequality valid for $\tilde{Q}_T^n$ (resp. $\tilde{P}_T^n$) is also valid for Q_T^n (resp. P_T^n).*

Note that Corollary 3 implies that every complete linear description of $\tilde{Q}_T^n$ or $\tilde{P}_T^n$ yields a complete description of Q_T^n or P_T^n.

Exercises
1. Given a n-city symmetric (asymmetric) TSP with distance function c, prove that every optimum vertex solution of $\max\{\bar{c}^T x \mid x \in \tilde{Q}_T^n\}$ (of $\max\{\bar{c}^T x \mid x \in \tilde{P}_T^n\}$, respectively) corresponds to an optimum tour and vice versa (for the definition of $\bar{c}$ see the end of Section 2.2).
2. Prove Lemma 1. (*Hint:* see Hammer, Johnson & Peled [1975].)
3. Prove that for $n \geq 3$ no inequality $x_{ij} \leq 1$ defines a facet of $\tilde{P}_T^n$. (*Hint:* consider subtour elimination constraints (11) when $|W| = 2$.)
4. Prove Lemma 2.
5. Does every inequality which defines a facet of $\tilde{Q}_T^n$ (of $\tilde{P}_T^n$) also define a facet of Q_T^n (of P_T^n)? What about the other way around?

3 WELL-SOLVABLE COMBINATORIAL OPTIMIZATION PROBLEMS RELATED TO THE TSP

Solution methods for $\mathcal{NP}$-complete combinatorial optimization problems, such as branch and bound, are usually based on relaxations of the problem which are easy to solve. A relaxation in this case is another problem (often itself a combinatorial optimization problem) which has the property that every feasible solution of the original problem corresponds (in a unique way) to a feasible solution of the relaxed problem. As we shall see below, relaxations can also be used to obtain polyhedral information about the problem in question. We do not discuss in this section the several known special cases of the TSP which are well solved. For a discussion of these the reader is referred to Chapter 4.

3.1 The symmetric case

A *forest* in a graph $G = (V, E)$ is a set of edges containing no cycle; a *spanning tree* is a forest with $|V| - 1$ edges. It is well known that by adding an edge to a spanning tree, exactly one cycle is created. Thus, a spanning tree plus an edge is an edge set containing n edges and exactly one cycle. Hence, every tour is a spanning tree plus an edge.

Let us consider a slightly more special construction. Consider the complete graph $K_n = (V, E)$ and assume that the vertices are labeled $1, 2, \ldots, n$. Call an edge set S a *1-tree* (in K_n) if $|S \cap \delta(1)| = 2$ and $S \cap E(\{2, \ldots, n\})$ is a spanning tree in $K_n - \{1\}$. That is, a 1-tree is a set of n edges containing exactly one cycle which contains vertex 1. Thus every tour is a 1-tree. By calculating a minimum spanning tree on the vertices $2, \ldots, n$ and choosing the two shortest edges containing vertex 1, it is easy to find a minimum weight 1-tree in K_n. Hence the minimum 1-tree problem is an (often used and reasonable) relaxation of the symmetric TSP.

The *1-tree polytope* Q_{1T}^n is the convex hull of all incidence vectors of 1-trees in K_n, i.e.

$$Q_{1T}^n = \text{conv}\{x^S \subseteq \mathbb{R}^E \mid S \text{ is a 1-tree in } K_n\},$$

and clearly we have $Q_T^n \subseteq Q_{1T}^n$. Let $\tilde{\mathcal{I}}$ denote the set of all subsets of 1-trees in K_n and

$$\tilde{Q}_{1T}^n = \text{conv}\{x^S \in \mathbb{R}^E \mid S \in \tilde{\mathcal{I}}\},$$

then one can easily see that $(E, \tilde{\mathcal{I}})$ is a *matroid* (i.e. an independence system satisfying: $I, J \in \tilde{\mathcal{I}}, |I| < |J| \Rightarrow \exists e \in J - I$ such that $I \cup \{e\} \in \tilde{\mathcal{I}}$).

Edmonds [1971] has shown how a complete and nonredundant system describing a polytope associated with a matroid can be constructed; see also Giles [1975]. In the case of 1-trees in K_n, $n \geq 3$, such a system describing $\tilde{Q}_{1T}^n$ is the following:

$$0 \leq x_e \leq 1 \qquad \text{for all } e \in E, \tag{12}$$

$$x(\delta(1)) \leq 2, \tag{13}$$

$$x(E(W)) \leq |W| - 1 \qquad \text{for all } W \subseteq V, |W| \geq 3, 1 \notin W. \tag{14}$$

A complete and nonredundant system for Q_{1T}^n can be derived easily now (see Held & Karp [1970], and for general techniques similar to this one see Giles [1975] and Grötschel [1977a]):

$$0 \leq x_e \leq 1 \qquad \text{for all } e \in E, \tag{15}$$

$$x(\delta(1)) = 2, \tag{16}$$

$$x(E(\{2, \ldots, n\})) = n - 2, \tag{17}$$

$$x(E(W)) \leq |W| - 1 \qquad \text{for all } W \subseteq V, 3 \leq |W| \leq |V| - 2, 1 \notin W. \tag{18}$$

In other words, the vertices of the polyhedron given by (15), (16), (17), (18) are the incidence vectors of 1-trees in K_n. Note that the inequalities (14), (18) respectively, are nothing but subtour elimination constraints (10). Moreover, we know that the inequalities (12), (13), (14), ((15), (18), respectively) define facets of $\tilde{Q}_{1T}^n$ (of Q_{1T}^n, respectively) and that no two of these inequalities are equivalent.

A second interesting relaxation of the symmetric TSP is the 2-matching problem. A *2-matching* (*perfect 2-matching*) in a graph is a set of edges such that every vertex is contained in at most (exactly) two edges. Clearly, every tour (subset of a tour) is a perfect 2-matching (a 2-matching). Denote by Q_{2M}^n (by $\tilde{Q}_{2M}^n$, respectively) the *perfect 2-matching polytope* (the *2-matching polytope*, respectively) of K_n, where $n \geq 3$, i.e.

$$Q_{2M}^n = \text{conv}\{x^M \in \mathbb{R}^E \mid M \text{ is a perfect 2-matching in } K_n\},$$

$$\tilde{Q}_{2M}^n = \text{conv}\{x^M \in \mathbb{R}^E \mid M \text{ is a 2-matching in } K_n\}.$$

$\tilde{Q}_{2M}^n$ is the monotonization of Q_{2M}^n and $\tilde{Q}_T^n \subseteq \tilde{Q}_{2M}^n$ and $Q_T^n \subseteq Q_{2M}^n$ hold.

Edmonds [1965c] has given a result which includes a complete linear description of $\tilde{Q}_{2M}^n$ and Q_{2M}^n. From these descriptions, nonredundant characterizations of $\tilde{Q}_{2M}^n$ and Q_{2M}^n (for K_n only) were derived by Grötschel [1977b] and Grötschel [1977a], respectively. In order to show how the *2-matching inequalities* of Edmonds can be generalized further, we introduce them in a form different from the usual one.

Let $K_n = (V, E)$ be the complete graph on $n \geq 3$ vertices and assume that $H, T_1, T_2, \ldots, T_k \subseteq V, k \geq 1$, are vertex sets satisfying

$$|H \cap T_i| = 1, \qquad i = 1, \ldots, k,$$

$$|T_i - H| = 1, \qquad i = 1, \ldots, k,$$

then the *2-matching inequality*

$$x(E(H)) + \sum_{i=1}^{k} x(E(T_i)) \leq |H| + \left\lfloor \frac{k}{2} \right\rfloor \tag{19}$$

is valid for $\tilde{Q}_{2M}^n$ and Q_{2M}^n. It is easy to see that if there is no round-down in (19), i.e. if k is even, a 2-matching inequality is redundant with respect to Q_{2M}^n and $\tilde{Q}_{2M}^n$. Edmonds [1965c] has proved that the inequalities (19) with odd k yield a complete linear description. In fact, we have the following slightly stronger result.

Theorem 3 *The following system of inequalities is a complete and nonredundant characterization of the 2-matching polytope $\tilde{Q}_{2M}^n$, $n \geq 4$:*

$$0 \leq x_e \leq 1 \qquad\qquad\qquad \text{for all } e \in E, \tag{20}$$

$$x(\delta(x)) \leq 2 \qquad\qquad\qquad \text{for all } v \in V, \tag{21}$$

$$x(E(H)) + \sum_{i=1}^{k} x(E(T_i)) \leq |H| + \frac{k-1}{2} \qquad \text{for all } H, T_1, \ldots, T_k \subseteq V,$$

$$\tag{22}$$

satisfying
(a) $|H \cap T_i| = 1$, $i = 1, \ldots, k$,
(b) $|T_i - H| = 1$, $i = 1, \ldots, k$,
(c) $T_i \cap T_j = 0$, $1 \leq i < j \leq k$,
(d) $k \geq 3$ *and odd, or* $k = 1$ *and* $|H| \geq 4$.

The polytope Q^3_{2M} is the unit hypercube in $\mathbb{R}^3$.

In the case of perfect 2-matchings the inequalities (21) must be stated as equations. Then one can show the following result.

Lemma 3 *Let* $H, T_1, \ldots, T_k \subseteq V$ *and* $H', T'_1, \ldots, T'_{k'}$ *be two different systems of vertex sets satisfying* (22)(a), ..., (d). *Then the 2-matching inequalities* (22) *corresponding to* $H, T_1, \ldots, T_k$ *and* $H', T'_1, \ldots, T'_{k'}$ *are equivalent with respect to* Q^n_{2M} *if and only if*
(a) $k = k'$,
(b) *for every* $i \in \{1, \ldots, k\}$ *there is a* $j \in \{1, \ldots, k'\}$ *with* $T_i = T'_j$,
(c) $H' = V - H$.

The degree equations $x(\delta(v)) = 2$, $v \in V$, form a minimal equation system for Q^n_{2M} and the rank of the matrix corresponding to these equations is n. In fact, one can prove that the degree equations determine the affine hull of Q^n_{2M} [Grötschel 1977a]. Combining this observation with Theorem 3 and Lemma 3, one can show the following result.

Theorem 4 *Let* Q^n_{2M} *be the perfect 2-matching polytope for* $K_n = (V, E)$, $n \geq 5$. *Then*

$$\dim Q^n_{2M} = |E| - n.$$

Let $\mathcal{V}$ *be any set of subsets of* V *with* $W \in \mathcal{V}$ *if and only if* $V - W \notin \mathcal{V}$. *Then the following system of equations and inequalities is a complete and nonredundant description of* Q^n_{2M}:

$$0 \leq x_e \leq 1 \qquad \text{for all } e \in E, \tag{23}$$

$$x(\delta(v)) = 2 \qquad \text{for all } v \in V, \tag{24}$$

$$x(E(H)) + \sum_{i=1}^{k} x(E(T_i)) \leq |H| + \frac{k-1}{2} \tag{25}$$

for all $H, T_1, \ldots, T_k \subseteq V$ *satisfying* (a), (b), (c) *of* (22) *and*
(d') $(k \geq 3$ *and* k *odd*) *or* $(k = 1$ *and* $4 \leq |H| \leq n - 4)$,
(e) $H \in \mathcal{V}$.

A consequence of the results of this section is that

$$\tilde{Q}^n_T \subseteq \tilde{Q}^n_{1T} \cap \tilde{Q}^n_{2M},$$

$$Q^n_T \subseteq Q^n_{1T} \cap Q^n_{2M}$$

hold, and thus, every incidence vector of a tour satisfies (15), (16), (17), (18)

and (23), (24), (25); and every incidence vector of a subset of a tour satisfies
(12), (13), (14) and (20), (21), (22). We will see in Chapter 9 that it is
possible to optimize over $Q_{1T}^n \cap Q_{2M}^n$ in polynomial time and that excellent
lower bounds for the length of the shortest tour can be obtained this way.

A $\{0, 2\}$-*matching* is an assignment of the integers $0, 2$ to the edges of a
graph G such that for every vertex the sum of the integers on the incident edges is at most 2. The paper by Cornuéjols & Pulleyblank [1982]
contains a study of the polytope $P(G)$ which is the convex hull of the
$\{0, 2\}$-matchings and tours in G and its relation to Q_T^n. In fact, they show
among other things that for n odd, Q_T^n is a face of $P(K_n)$ and for any facet F
of Q_T^n there is a unique facet of $P(K_n)$ whose intersection with Q_T^n is exactly
F. Recently, Hartvigsen [1984] investigated perfect 2-matchings without
triangles and $\{0, 2\}$-matching without pentagons, but complete characterizations of the associated polytopes could not be obtained.

3.2 The asymmetric case

The most common relaxation of the asymmetric TSP is the assignment
problem. An *assignment* B in a complete digraph $D_n = (V, A)$ is a set of arcs
such that every vertex of D_n is the head and the tail of exactly one arc of B.
In other words, B is a set of disjoint directed cycles in D_n such that every
vertex is on a cycle. The *assignment polytope* P_A^n (on D_n) is the convex hull
of all incidence vectors of assignments in D_n. There is of course a monotone
version $\tilde{P}_A^n$ which is the convex hull of all incidence vectors of subsets of
assignments in D_n and clearly we have $P_T^n \subseteq P_A^n$ and $\tilde{P}_T^n \subseteq \tilde{P}_A^n$. The following
result has been proved (in different contexts) by various people and usually
is associated with the names of Birkhoff and Von Neumann.

Theorem 5 *Let $n \geq 2$ and $D_n = (V, A)$ be the complete digraph on n vertices.
Then*

$$P_A^n = \{x \in \mathbb{R}^A \mid x \text{ satisfies (7) and } x \geq 0\},$$
$$\tilde{P}_A^n = \{x \in \mathbb{R}^A \mid x \text{ satisfies (8) and } x \geq 0\}.$$

Note that in the assignment problem usually loops (i, i), $i = 1, \ldots, n$, are
allowed. In other words, the set of assignments corresponds to the set of all
permutations of the numbers $1, \ldots, n$. Since loops are of no interest for the
TSP, we consider a slightly different definition; our assignments correspond
to the set of permutations of $\{1, \ldots, n\}$ leaving no element fixed.

Theorem 5 is implied by the fact that the matrix corresponding to the
equation system (7) is *totally unimodular*, i.e. every square submatrix has
determinant $+1$, 0 or -1. It is nice to know that all vertices of the polyhedra
defined by (7) (respectively (8)) and the nonnegativity conditions are integral, but we do not get any new polyhedral information for the asymmetric
traveling salesman polytope from this fact.

It is easy to see that the rank of the $(2n, n^2 - n)$-matrix given by (7) is
$2n - 1$ and that each row can be written as a linear combination of the

$2n-1$ other rows, for $n \geqslant 3$. This implies that $\dim(P_A^n) \leqslant |A| - 2n + 1$, and one can show the following.

Proposition 3 $\dim(P_A^n) = |A| - 2|V| + 1 = n^2 - 3n + 1, n \geqslant 3$.

We now want to consider a different approach which resembles the 1-tree relaxation in the symmetric case. To get a convenient description we have to reformulate the asymmetric TSP slightly.

Let $D_n = (V, A)$ be the complete digraph on the vertices $\{1, \ldots, n\}$. Denote by $D_n' = (V', A')$ the digraph on the vertices $\{1, \ldots, n, n+1\}$ defined in the following way

$$A' := \{(i, j) \mid i, j \in \{2, \ldots, n\}, i \neq j\} \cup \{(1, j) \mid j \in \{2, \ldots, n\}\}$$

$$\cup \{(i, n+1) \mid i \in \{2, \ldots, n\}\}.$$

D_n' can be viewed as follows. We take D_n, add a new vertex $n+1$, take all those arcs in D_n going into vertex 1 and let them go into vertex $n+1$. Thus D_n' has the same number of arcs as D_n, and every tour in D_n corresponds to a directed Hamiltonian path in D_n' from 1 to $n+1$, and vice versa.

Let $\mathcal{I}_n$ be the set of all directed Hamiltonian paths from 1 to $n+1$ in D_n' and $\tilde{\mathcal{I}}_n$ be its monotonization. Then it is easy to see that $\mathcal{I}_n = \mathcal{T}_n$ and $\tilde{\mathcal{I}}_n = \tilde{\mathcal{T}}_n$ (with the obvious reinterpretation of arcs) and hence that $P_T^n(\tilde{P}_T^n)$ is the convex hull of all incidence vectors of (subsets of) directed Hamiltonian paths from 1 to $n+1$ in D_n'.

Let us define the following independence systems on A':

$$\vec{\mathcal{I}}_n := \{B \subseteq A' \mid |B \cap \vec{\delta}(v)| \leqslant 1 \text{ for all } v \in \{1, \ldots, n\}\},$$

$$\tilde{\mathcal{I}}_n := \{B \subseteq A' \mid |B \cap \tilde{\delta}(v)| \leqslant 1 \text{ for all } v \in \{2, \ldots, n+1\}\},$$

$$\mathcal{I}_n^F := \{B \subseteq A' \mid B \text{ contains no cycle (in the undirected sense)}\}.$$

It is well known and an easy exercise to show that $(A', \vec{\mathcal{I}}_n)$, $(A', \tilde{\mathcal{I}}_n)$ and $(A', \mathcal{I}_n^F)$ are matroids on A'. Moreover, we have the following result.

Lemma 4 $\mathcal{I}_n = \vec{\mathcal{I}}_n \cap \tilde{\mathcal{I}}_n \cup \mathcal{I}_n^F$ and $\mathcal{I}_n$ is the intersection of the bases (of A') of $\vec{\mathcal{I}}_n, \tilde{\mathcal{I}}_n$ and $\mathcal{I}_n^F$.

Proof   Left as an exercise for the reader.

Lemma 4 justifies the statement that the asymmetric can be viewed as the intersection of three matroids.

We know from a result of Edmonds [1970] how a linear description of the polytope associated with the intersection of two matroids can be obtained. (This result does not extend to the intersection of three or more matroids!) Thus we are able to give complete and nonredundant characterizations of the polytopes corresponding to the independence systems $\vec{\mathcal{I}}_n \cap \tilde{\mathcal{I}}_n$, $\vec{\mathcal{I}}_n \cap \mathcal{I}_n^F$, $\tilde{\mathcal{I}}_n \cap \mathcal{I}_n^F$ (respectively their bases). The last two have been investigated in detail [Giles, 1975; Grötschel, 1977a].

As a matter of fact, the polytope associated with $\vec{\mathcal{I}}_n \cap \tilde{\mathcal{I}}_n$ is the polytope

$\tilde{P}_A^n$; the polytope associated with the bases (of A') of $\tilde{\mathscr{I}}_n \cap \tilde{\mathscr{I}}_n$ is the assignment polytope P_A^n.

An arc set in A' containing no cycle (in the undirected sense) and in which every vertex is the head (tail) of at most one arc is called a *branching* (*antibranching*). A branching (antibranching) in D_n' with n arcs is called *arborescence* (*antiarborescence*). Thus $\tilde{\mathscr{I}}_n \cap \mathscr{I}_n^F$ ($\tilde{\mathscr{I}}_n \cap \mathscr{I}_n^F$) is the set of branchings (antibranchings) in D_n', and the bases (of A') of $\tilde{\mathscr{I}}_n \cap \mathscr{I}_n^F$ ($\tilde{\mathscr{I}}_n \cap \mathscr{I}_n^F$) are exactly the arborescences (antiarborescences) in D_n'. Let P_B^n (P_B^n) denote the convex hull of the incidence vectors of the arborescences (antiarborescences) in D_n', and $\tilde{P}_B^n$ ($\tilde{P}_B^n$) the convex hull of the incidence vectors of branchings (antibranchings) in D_n'. We clearly have $P_T^n \subseteq P_B^n \cap P_B^n$ and $\tilde{P}_T^n \subseteq \tilde{P}_B^n \cap \tilde{P}_B^n$. These polytopes can be described as follows.

Theorem 6

$$\tilde{P}_B^n = \{x \in \mathbb{R}^{A'} \mid x_{ij} \geq 0 \qquad\qquad \text{for all } (i, j) \in A', \tag{26}$$

$$x(\tilde{\delta}(v)) \leq 1 \qquad \text{for all } v \in \{2, \ldots, n+1\}, \tag{27}$$

$$x(A(W)) \leq |W| - 1 \text{ for all } W \subseteq V', |W| \geq 2,$$
$$1, n+1 \notin W\}, \tag{28}$$

$$\tilde{P}_B^n = \{x \in \mathbb{R}^{A'} \mid x(\tilde{\delta}(v)) \leq 1 \text{ for all } v \in \{1, \ldots, n\}$$
$$\text{and } x \text{ satisfies (26) and (28)}\}, \tag{29}$$

$$P_B^n = \{x \in \mathbb{R}^{A'} \mid x(\tilde{\delta}(v)) = 1 \text{ for all } v \in \{2, \ldots, n+1\}$$
$$\text{and } x \text{ satisfies (26) and (28)}\}, \tag{30}$$

$$P_B^n = \{x \in \mathbb{R}^{A'} \mid x(\tilde{\delta}(v)) = 1 \text{ for all } v \in \{1, \ldots, n\}$$
$$\text{and } x \text{ satisfies (26) and (28)}\}. \tag{31}$$

Moreover, all these linear descriptions are nonredundant.

Note that (28) are just subtour elimination constraints, so we did not really get any new polyhedral information about the TSP. But on the other hand, it is interesting to see that certain degree constraints plus certain subtour elimination constraints define integral polyhedra. (The reinterpretation of the polyhedra $\tilde{P}_B$, $\tilde{P}_B$, etc., with respect to the complete digraph D_n is obvious.)

Since the assignment, branching and antibranching problem are solvable in polynomial time, we can optimize over $P_B^n \cap P_B^n$ and $\tilde{P}_B^n \cap \tilde{P}_B^n$ in polynomial time; cf. Chapter 9.

Exercises

6. Prove Lemma 3. (*Hint*: see Grötschel & Pulleyblank [1985] for the 'only if' part.)

7. Find complete and nonredundant systems of equations and inequalities

describing Q_{2M}^3 and Q_{2M}^4. (Note that for $n = 3$, 4 the system (23), (24), (25) is complete for Q_{2M}^n, but redundant.)

8. It is also quite easy to describe the vertices of the polytope

$$\bar{Q}_{2M}^n := \{x \in \mathbb{R}^E \mid x \text{ satisfies (23) and (24)}\}.$$

Prove that the vertices of $\bar{Q}_{2M}^n$ are either incidence vectors of perfect 2-matchings or fractional vertices whose components are 0, 1 or $\frac{1}{2}$. Moreover, show that the edges corresponding to $\frac{1}{2}$-components of fractional vertices of $\bar{Q}_{2M}^n$ form an even number of disjoint cycles of odd length. (*Hint*: see Grötschel [1977a].)

9. Prove Lemma 4.

10. Find a representation of the symmetric TSP (i.e. of $\tilde{\mathcal{S}}_n$) as the intersection of matroids. (As a research problem, try to find the minimal number of matroids that is sufficient.)

4   THE SYMMETRIC TRAVELING SALESMAN POLYTOPES

We shall now study those properties of the traveling salesman polytopes $\tilde{Q}_T^n$ and Q_T^n which cannot be derived from general results about combinatorial polyhedra or from the relaxations introduced in Section 3.1. In particular, we shall introduce all classes of facets of Q_T^n and $\tilde{Q}_T^n$ which are known at present (to our knowledge).

The results are not presented in chronological order, rather in an order that minimizes space. The presentation is based on several papers [Grötschel, 1977a, 1980a; Grötschel & Padberg, 1974, 1975a, 1978, 1979a, 1979b; Grötschel & Pulleyblank, 1985; Maurras, 1975, 1976; Papadimitriou & Yannakakis, 1984], from which most of the results are taken. Research on Q_T^n (and P_T^n) was also very active in the mid-1950s. A summary of these developments is given by Gomory [1966] and Grötschel [1977a].

4.1   Some properties of Q_T^n, relations to $\tilde{Q}_T^n$

We shall first investigate the dimension of Q_T^n and the trivial inequalities. Then we shall study some interesting relations between Q_T^n and $\tilde{Q}_T^n$ and state a general procedure by which, from each inequality defining a facet of Q_T^n, an inequality defining a facet of $\tilde{Q}_T^n$ can be obtained.

From Theorem 4 we know that $\dim(Q_{2M}^n) = |E| - n$, hence $\dim(Q_T^n) \leq |E| - n$ since $Q_T^n \subseteq Q_{2M}^n$. We shall now prove that the dimensions of Q_{2M}^n and Q_T^n are equal. To give applications of the two proof techniques introduced in Section 1 (cf. the discussion after Theorem 1), we outline two proofs, each based on a different technique.

Theorem 7   *The dimension of Q_T^n equals*

$$d_n := |E| - |V| = \tfrac{1}{2}n(n-3) \qquad \text{for all } n \geq 3.$$

First proof [Grötschel & Padberg, 1975a, 1979a]   We first have to state a well known graph-theoretical lemma.

Lemma 5   *Let $K_n = (V, E)$ be the complete graph on n vertices, and let k denote any integer.*
(i) *If $|V| = 2k + 1$, then there exist k edge-disjoint tours T_i such that $E = \bigcup_{i=1}^{k} T_i$.*
(ii) *If $|V| = 2k$, then there exist $k - 1$ edge-disjoint tours T_i and a perfect 1-matching M edge-disjoint from any T_i such that $E = M \cup \bigcup_{i=1}^{k-1} T_i$.*

We now show that Q_T^n contains $d_n + 1$ linearly independent tours. For $n = 3$ the claim is trivially true.

(a) Assume that $n = 2k + 2$ with $k \geq 1$ and integer. The subgraph $K_{n-1} = (V', E')$ of K_n induced by the $n - 1$ first vertices is again complete and by the lemma, its edge set is the union of k edge-disjoint tours τ_i of length $n - 1$. From each $(n-1)$-tour τ_i we construct $n - 1$ tours τ_{ij} of length n by replacing, one at a time, each edge $\{u, v\} \in \tau_i$ by the path $[u, n, v]$. The incidence matrix of the tours τ_{ij} for $j = 1, \ldots, n - 1$ (rows) versus the edges of K_n (columns) contains the submatrix $E - I$, where E is the $(n-1) \times (n-1)$ matrix of all ones and I is the $(n-1) \times (n-1)$ identity matrix. Furthermore, we obtain a total of $k(n-1) = d_n + 1$ tours. Since the tours τ_i of length $n - 1$ are edge-disjoint, the incidence matrix of all $d_n + 1$ tours τ_{ij} contains a $(d_n + 1) \times (d_n + 1)$ submatrix N which is block-diagonal and whose diagonal blocks are all equal to $E - I$ after a suitable arrangement of the rows and columns. Since $E - I$ is nonsingular, it follows that N is nonsingular and consequently, Theorem 7 holds if $n = 2k + 2$.

(b) Assume that $n = 2k + 1$ with $k \geq 2$ and integer. We proceed as in the case (a) and construct $(k - 1)(n - 1)$ linearly independent tours from the $k - 1$ tours of length $n - 1$. The perfect matching in K_{n-1} is completed arbitrarily to an $(n - 1)$-tour in K_{n-1} and subsequently used to construct k tours of length n by replacing, one at a time, each edge $\{u, v\} \in M$ by the path $[u, n, v]$. In this way we obtain a total of $d_n + 1$ tours whose incidence matrix contains a $(d_n + 1) \times (d_n + 1)$ block-triangular matrix N with $k - 1$ blocks $E - I$ of size $(n - 1) \times (n - 1)$ and an additional block $E' - I'$ of size $k \times k$. $\square$

Second proof [Maurras, 1975]   We know that $Q_T^n \subseteq \{x \in \mathbb{R}^E \mid x(\delta(i)) = 2, i = 1, \ldots, n\}$ and that the matrix corresponding to these n equations has rank n. To prove our claim, we have to show that for every hyperplane $H = \{x \mid a^T x = a_0\}$ containing Q_T^n, the normal vector a is a linear combination of the normal vectors of the known equation system. So suppose that $a^T x = a_0$, $a \neq 0$, is an equation satisfied by all $x \in Q_T^n$. We have to prove that there are λ_i, $i = 1, \ldots, n$, with $a^T x = \sum_{i=1}^{n} \lambda_i x(\delta(i))$.

The incidence vectors $x^{\delta(i)}$ have a very special structure which we will utilize. By adding appropriate multiples of the incidence vectors of $\delta(1)$, $\delta(2)$ and $\delta(3)$ to twice the negative of a, we get a vector which is 0 on the triangle $\{1, 2\}$, $\{2, 3\}$, $\{1, 3\}$. Namely, setting

$$\lambda_1 := a_{12} + a_{13} - a_{23},$$
$$\lambda_2 := a_{12} + a_{23} - a_{13},$$
$$\lambda_3 := a_{13} + a_{23} - a_{12}$$

and

$$a' := \lambda_1 x^{\delta(1)} + \lambda_2 x^{\delta(2)} + \lambda_3 x^{\delta(3)} - 2a,$$

we obtain $a'_{12} = a'_{13} = a'_{23} = 0$. Now we set $\lambda_i := -a'_{1i}$, $i = 4, \ldots, n$, and define $b := a' + \sum_{i=4}^{n} \lambda_i x^{\delta(i)}$. The definition clearly implies that $b_{1i} = 0$, $i = 2, \ldots, n$, and that $b_{23} = 0$. The construction above works because of the following reason. One can show that the (n, n)-matrix M having the n vectors $x^{\delta(i)}$ as rows and consisting of the columns corresponding to the edges $S := \{\{1, i\} \mid i = 2, \ldots, n\} \cup \{\{2, 3\}\}$ is nonsingular. The λ_i constructed above are the unique solutions of $M^T x = 2\bar{a}$, where $\bar{a}$ arises from a by deleting all components except for those belonging to S. (For further details, see the remarks after Theorem 9, and for another application of this technique, see the proof of Theorem 11.)

We have now used up our degrees of freedom. If we can show that the vector b constructed above equals 0 then we are done, since in this case,

$$a = \frac{1}{2} \sum_{i=1}^{n} \lambda_i x^{\delta(i)}.$$

But as we shall see, this is quite easy.

Let $i \in \{4, \ldots, n\}$ be any vertex and P_{i3} be any path from i to 3 going through all vertices in $\{3, \ldots, n\}$. Define the following tours: $\tau_1 := P_{i3} \cup \{\{1, i\}, \{1, 2\}, \{2, 3\}\}$ and $\tau_2 := P_{i3} \cup \{\{2, i\}, \{1, 2\}, \{1, 3\}\}$. If x^{τ_i} denotes the incidence vector of τ_i, then we have $(x^{\delta(j)})^T x^{\tau_i} = 2$ and $a^T x^{\tau_i} = a_0$. Since b is a linear combination of the vectors $x^{\delta(j)}$ and a, $b^T x^{\tau_i} = b_0$ for some constant b_0. Therefore, $0 = b^T x^{\tau_1} - b^T x^{\tau_2} = b_{1i} + b_{23} - b_{2i} - b_{13} = -b_{2i}$. This proves that $b_{2i} = 0$, $i = 1, 3, 4, \ldots, n$.

Similarly, we obtain $b_{3i} = 0$ for all $i \neq 3$, and by iterating this procedure we get $b_{ij} = 0$ for all $i \neq j$, which proves our claim. $\square$

The proof that the trivial inequalities $0 \leq x_{ij} \leq 1$ define facets of the monotone traveling salesman polytope $\tilde{Q}_T^n$ is trivial. The proof that these inequalities define facets of Q_T^n requires about the same amount of technical detail as the proof of Theorem 7. This illustrates also that lower-dimensional polyhedra are not as easy to handle as full-dimensional ones and why it is preferable (from a technical point of view) to deal with full-dimensional polyhedra.

Theorem 8 Let $K_n = (V, E)$ be the complete graph on n vertices.
(a) The inequalities $x_{ij} \leq 1$, $\{i, j\} \in E$, define facets of Q_T^n for all $n \geq 4$.
(b) The inequalities $x_{ij} \geq 0$, $\{i, j\} \in E$, define facets of Q_T^n for all $n \geq 5$.

Since it is somewhat easier to deal with $\tilde{Q}_T^n$ than with Q_T^n it would be nice to have a theorem which characterizes those facet-defining inequalities of $\tilde{Q}_T^n$ which also define facets of Q_T^n. Clearly, not all of the inequalities defining facets of $\tilde{Q}_T^n$ have this property. We shall see later that the degree constraints (6) define facets of $\tilde{Q}_T^n$, but they are satisfied with equality for all $x \in Q_T^n$. By comparing Corollary 2(a) and Proposition 2 with Theorem 8(b) and (a), one can see that there are even slight differences with respect to the trivial inequalities. This could be explained as an irregularity of low dimensions, but it has to be taken into account. Anyway, a reasonable result of the desired type is not known. Let us formulate the problem in a somewhat more modest form.

Research problem *Find (reasonable) sufficient conditions which imply that an inequality defining a facet for $\tilde{Q}_T^n$ also defines a facet for Q_T^n.*

Since Q_T^n is a face of $\tilde{Q}_T^n$, we know that for every facet of Q_T^n there is at least one inequality defining it which also defines a facet of $\tilde{Q}_T^n$. But since we can add degree equations (5) to every facet-defining inequality of Q_T^n there are many inequalities defining a facet of Q_T^n which are not even valid with respect to $\tilde{Q}_T^n$. However, Grötschel & Pulleyblank [1985] describe a procedure by means of which every facet-defining inequality $a^T x \leq a_0$ of Q_T^n can be turned into an inequality which is equivalent to $a^T x \leq a_0$ with respect to Q_T^n and which defines a facet of $\tilde{Q}_T^n$. We shall briefly describe this method here.

For notational convenience, let us write

$$Ax = 2 \tag{32}$$

for the degree equations $x(\delta(i)) = 2$, $i = 1, \ldots, n$, and suppose that $a^T x \leq a_0$ defines a facet of Q_T^n.

If $a \geq 0$ holds, then $a^T x \leq a_0$ is valid for $\tilde{Q}_T^n$. (Why?) If a has negative coefficients, then we choose a $\lambda \in \mathbb{R}^n$ with sufficiently large coefficients (it should be clear how these have to be selected) such that $\bar{a}^T := a^T + \lambda^T A \geq 0$. Let $\bar{a}_0 := a_0 + \lambda^T 2$, then $\bar{a}^T x \leq \bar{a}_0$ is equivalent to $a^T x \leq a_0$ with respect to Q_T^n and valid for $\tilde{Q}_T^n$.

Let us assume therefore that the initial inequality $a^T x \leq a_0$ satisfies $a \geq 0$, and let $E^0(a)$ be the set of edges in K_n corresponding to a zero coefficient of a, i.e. $E^0(a) = \{\{i, j\} \in E \mid a_{ij} = 0\}$. Denote by $A_{E^0(a)}$ the submatrix of A (cf. (32)) consisting of all rows of A and the columns corresponding to the edges in $E^0(a)$. We then carry out the following computations in sequence.

Step 1. If the rows of $A_{E^0(a)}$ are linearly independent, go to Step 2. If not, find a $\lambda \in \mathbb{R}^n$ such that $\lambda^T A \neq 0$ and $\lambda^T A_{E^0(a)} = 0$ (clearly, such a λ exists).

Step 2. Set $\bar{a}^T := a^T - \mu \lambda^T A$, $\bar{a}_0 := a_0 - \mu \lambda^T 2$ where μ is an appropriately chosen number such that $\bar{a} \geq 0$ and $E^0(a) \subset E^0(\bar{a})$. Set $a := \bar{a}$, $a_0 := \bar{a}_0$ and go to Step 1.

Let us call the above procedure *reducing* the inequality $a^T x \leq a_0$. It is clear that after at most $|E|$ iterations we obtain an inequality, say $ax \leq a_0$, such that $A_{E^0(a)}$ has rank n, and $a \geq 0$. To normalize our procedure we add a final step.

Step 3. Scale $a^T x \leq a_0$ such that the smallest nonzero coefficient of a has value 1, and stop.

We call an inequality obtained by applying the above algorithm *support reduced*. One could also say that it is a normalized inequality with minimal support. Before stating the main result about the algorithm, we have to exclude a trivial case.

Lemma 6 *Let $a^T x \leq a_0$ be a support-reduced facet-inducing inequality for Q_T^n. Then $a^T x \leq a_0$ induces a trivial facet of Q_T^n if and only if*
(a) *$E - E^0(a) = \delta(v) - \{k\}$ for some $v \in V$ and $k \in \delta(v)$, and in this case $a_{ij} = 1$ for all $\{i, j\} \in \delta(v) - \{k\}$ and $a_0 = 2$; or*
(b) *$E^0(a) = \delta(v) \cup \{k\}$ for some $v \in V$ and $k \in E(V - \{v\})$, and in this case $a_{ij} = 1$ for all $\{i, j\} \in E - E^0(a)$ and $a_0 = n - 2$.*

The following result was proved by Grötschel & Pulleyblank [1985].

Theorem 9 *Let $a^T x \leq a_0$ be a support-reduced facet-inducing inequality for Q_T^n not of the form* (a) *or* (b) *of Lemma 6. Then $a^T x \leq a_0$ is facet-inducing for $\tilde{Q}_T^n$.*

As we shall see later, Theorem 9 will be quite helpful for obtaining facet-defining inequalities for $\tilde{Q}_T^n$.

A very important point is that the linear independence of the rows of $A_{E^0(a)}$ can be checked easily using graph-theoretical (or matroidal) methods. More precisely, the rows of $A_{E^0(a)}$ are linearly independent if and only if the edge set $E^0(a)$ is a basis of the real (matric) matroid $\mathcal{M}(K_n)$ of K_n, $n \geq 3$; and $E^0(a)$ is a basis of $\mathcal{M}(K_n)$ if and only if it is a maximal subset of E such that each component of $E^0(a)$ contains exactly one cycle of odd length and no cycle of even length; for details, see Grötschel & Pulleyblank [1985].

4.2 Clique tree inequalities

In this section we investigate a class of inequalities introduced by Grötschel & Pulleyblank [1985] that subsumes all the nontrivial inequalities valid for $\tilde{Q}_T^n$ introduced so far, and also subsumes the classes of inequalities studied by Chvátal [1973a] and Grötschel & Padberg [1979a, 1979b].

A *clique* in a graph $G = (V, E)$ is a set C of vertices such that any two vertices in C are adjacent and such that C is maximal with respect to this property. A set A of vertices in a connected graph G is called an *articulation set* if the graph obtained from G by removing A is disconnected.

A *clique tree* is a connected graph C composed of cliques which satisfy the following properties (in the following we shall always consider clique trees as subgraphs of K_n):

(1) The cliques are partitioned into two sets, the set of *handles* and the set of *teeth*.
(2) No two teeth intersect.
(3) No two handles intersect.
(4) Each tooth contains at least two and at most $n-2$ vertices and at least one vertex not belonging to any handle.
(5) The number of teeth that each handle intersects is odd and at least three.
(6) If a tooth T and a handle H have a nonempty intersection, then $H \cap T$ is an articulation set of the clique tree.

Figure 8.1 shows an example of a clique tree, where cliques are indicated by ellipse-shaped figures. Each ellipse containing a '∗' is a tooth. The '∗' indicates that there must be a vertex in the respective tooth which does not belong to any handle.

We call a clique tree *simple* if any handle and any tooth have at most one vertex in common.

Suppose we have a clique tree C with handles $H_1, H_2, \ldots, H_r$ and teeth $T_1, T_2, \ldots, T_s$. We show below that the following *clique tree inequality* is valid for Q_T^n and $\tilde{Q}_T^n$ (in fact it defines a facet):

$$\sum_{i=1}^{r} x(E(H_i)) + \sum_{j=1}^{s} x(E(T_j)) \leq \sum_{i=1}^{r} |H_i| + \sum_{j=1}^{s} (|T_j| - t_j) - \frac{s+1}{2} = s(C), \quad (33)$$

where for every tooth T_j the integer t_j denotes the number of handles which intersect T_j, $j = 1, \ldots, s$. The right-hand side $s(C)$ of (33) is called the *size* of C.

Note that in the case where there is a tooth T and a handle H with $|H \cap T| \geq 2$, the coefficients on the left-hand side of (33) are 0, 1 and 2. The inequality (33) is a 0–1 inequality only if the clique tree is simple. If W is the set of all vertices of a clique tree, then, for simple clique trees, inequality

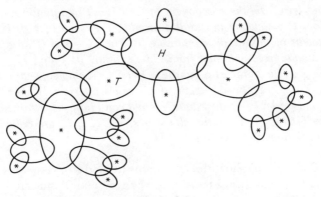

Figure 8.1

(33) can be written as

$$\sum_{i=1}^{r} x(E(H_i)) + \sum_{j=1}^{s} x(E(T_j)) \leq |W| - \frac{s+1}{2}.$$

We shall now consider various special cases of (33). A clique tree with only one handle H is called a *comb*, and the corresponding inequality

$$x(E(H)) + \sum_{j=1}^{s} x(E(T_j)) \leq |H| + \sum_{j=1}^{s} (|T_j| - 1) - \frac{s+1}{2} \qquad (34)$$

is called a *comb inequality*. These inequalities were introduced and studied by Grötschel & Padberg [1979a, 1979b].

Comb inequalities in turn are generalizations of inequalities introduced by Chvátal [1973a]. A comb is a *Chvátal* comb if every tooth has exactly one vertex in common with the handle, i.e. Chvátal combs are simple combs. The Chvátal comb inequality is the same as (34). Actually, Chvátal introduced a slightly larger class of inequalities (cf. Chapter 11), but all those not contained in our definition can be shown to be redundant.

The class of Chvátal combs generalizes Edmonds' 2-matching inequalities (22). Namely, the 2-matching inequalities (29) (except for those with $k = 1$) are exactly those Chvátal comb inequalities where every tooth contains exactly two vertices.

In addition, the class of clique tree inequalities also contains the subtour elimination constraints (10), except for $|W| = n - 1$. They are exactly those clique tree inequalities having a clique tree consisting of one tooth and no handle. Thus, in particular, the trivial inequalities $x_{ij} \leq 1$ are special clique tree inequalities.

We now want to prove that the clique tree inequalities (33) are valid for $\tilde{Q}_T^n$ (and thus for Q_T^n). For this we introduce the following two splitting operations.

(a) *Splitting a clique tree at a tooth and a handle.*   Let C be a clique tree and T a tooth of C. Let H be a handle of C intersecting T. Delete the vertices $H - T$ from C and let C'' be the component of $C - (H - T)$ containing T. Delete all vertices from C which are in handles meeting T but not in T or H. Let C' be the component of this graph containing T. Then C' and C'' are clique trees called the clique trees obtained from C by splitting at T and H.

(b) *Splitting a clique tree at a handle.*   Let C be a clique tree and H a handle of C. Let $T_1, \ldots, T_k$ be the teeth of C which intersect H. For every tooth $T_i, i \in \{1, \ldots, k\}$, let C_i be the clique tree not containing H obtained from C by splitting at T_i and H. Then the clique trees $C_1, \ldots, C_k$ are called the clique trees obtained from C by splitting at H.

Figures 8.2(a) and (b) show the operations (a) and (b), respectively, applied to the clique tree given in Figure 8.1, where H and T indicate the relevant tooth and handle.

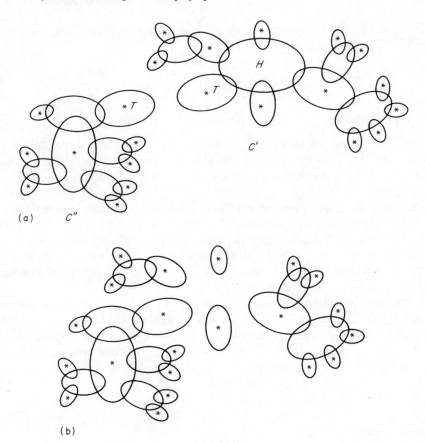

Figure 8.2

The following observation is immediate.

Lemma 7

(a) *Let C' and C'' be the clique trees obtained from C by splitting at tooth T and handle H (as in (a) above). Then*

$$s(C') + s(C'') = s(C) + |T| - 1.$$

(b) *Let C be a clique tree and H a handle of C intersecting k teeth. Let $C_1, \ldots, C_k$ be the clique trees obtained from C by splitting at handle H (as in (b) above). Then*

$$\sum_{i=1}^{k} s(C_i) = s(C) - |H| + \frac{k+1}{2}.$$

The proof of the validity of (33) is given by Grötschel & Pulleyblank [1985]. It is inductive and uses the fact that the subtour elimination constraints (10) are valid.

Theorem 10 *Let C be a clique tree in K_n with handles $H_1, \ldots, H_r$ and teeth $T_1, \ldots, T_s$. Then the clique tree inequality*

$$\sum_{i=1}^{r} x(E(H_i)) + \sum_{j=1}^{s} x(E(T_j)) \leq \sum_{i=1}^{r} |H_i| + \sum_{j=1}^{s} (|T_j| - t_j) - \frac{s+1}{2} = s(C)$$

is valid with respect to $\tilde{Q}_T^n$ (and hence with respect to Q_T^n).

Proof We prove the theorem by induction on the number of handles. If C has no handle, then the clique tree consists of just one tooth, and the clique tree inequality is a subtour elimination constraint. Thus there is nothing to prove.

Suppose the claim is true for all clique trees with r handles, and assume C is a clique tree with $r+1$ handles. Pick any handle H of C. Let $T_1, \ldots, T_k$ be the teeth of C intersecting H, and let $C_1, \ldots, C_k$ be the clique trees obtained from C by splitting at H. Every such clique tree has at most r handles. By construction C_i contains T_i, $i = 1, \ldots, k$. Let $a_i^T x \leq s(C_i)$ be the corresponding clique tree inequalities.

For every clique tree C_i, $i \in \{1, \ldots, k\}$, let $\bar{C}_i$ be the clique tree obtained from C_i after replacing T_i by $T_i - H$, and let $\bar{a}_i^T x \leq s(\bar{C}_i)$ be the corresponding clique tree inequality. (If a tooth T_i contains only two vertices, then $\bar{C}_i$ is not a clique tree, but the counting arguments used below remain valid.)

By Lemma 7 we have

$$\sum_{i=1}^{k} s(C_i) = s(C) - |H| + \frac{k+1}{2}$$

which implies

$$\sum_{i=1}^{k} s(\bar{C}_i) = s(C) - |H| - \sum_{i=1}^{k} |H \cap T_i| + \frac{k+1}{2}.$$

From this we obtain

$$2\left(\sum_{i=1}^{r} x(E(H_i)) + \sum_{j=1}^{s} x(E(T_j)) \right) \leq \sum_{i=1}^{k} (a_i^T x + \bar{a}_i^T x + x(E(H \cap T_i))) + \sum_{v \in H} x(\delta(v))$$

$$\leq \sum_{i=1}^{k} (s(C_i) + s(\bar{C}_i) + |H \cap T_i| - 1) + 2|H|$$

$$= 2s(C) + 1.$$

For every incidence vector of a subset of a tour, the left-hand side above is an even integer. So, dividing by 2 and rounding down the right-hand side we get the desired result. □

4.3 'Nice' facets of Q_T^n and $\tilde{Q}_T^n$

The clique tree inequalities (33) and all their special cases are in a certain intuitive sense 'nice', since they can be described easily by formulas, we have easy-to-state inductive definitions; for some special cases, good separation algorithms are known (cf. Chapter 9), and there is some hope that they may be handled efficiently in cutting plane procedures. (For some other 'bad' inequalities to be discussed in the next section no such hope exists at present.)

In this section we prove that subtour elimination constraints define facets of Q_T^n, and we indicate how to show that clique tree inequalities define facets.

Theorem 11 Let $n \geqslant 4$ and W be a vertex set in $K_n = (V, E)$ with $2 \leqslant |W| \leqslant n - 2$. Then the subtour elimination constraint $x(E(W)) \leqslant |W| - 1$ defines a facet of Q_T^n.

Proof Let us first assume that $n \geqslant 6$ and that $W = \{1, 2, \ldots, k\}$, $3 \leqslant k \leqslant n - 3$. For notational convenience we denote $x(E(W)) \leqslant |W| - 1$ by $a^T x \leqslant a_0$.

Suppose now that $b^T x \leqslant b_0$ is a valid inequality for Q_T^n satisfying $\{x \in Q_T^n \mid a^T x = a_0\} \subseteq \{x \in Q_T^n \mid b^T x = b_0\}$. If we can show that, for some $\alpha \geqslant 0$ and $\lambda \in \mathbb{R}^n$, $b^T = \alpha a^T + \lambda^T A$ then we are done by Theorem 1(d) (matrix A is defined in (32)).

The edge set $F := \{\{1, i\}, i = 2, \ldots, n\} \cup \{\{2, 3\}\}$ contains a spanning tree and one odd cycle but no even cycle, thus it is a basis of $\mathcal{M}(K_n)$, which means that the matrix A_F consisting of all rows of A and the columns corresponding to edges in F is nonsingular. Thus there exists a vector $\bar{\lambda} \in \mathbb{R}^n$ such that $\bar{b}^T := b^T + \bar{\lambda}^T A$ satisfies $\bar{b}_{1i} = a_{1i}$, $i = 2, \ldots, k$ and $\bar{b}_{23} = a_{23}$. Recalling that a is the incidence vector of $E(\{1, \ldots, k\})$, we may therefore assume that our initial vector b satisfies

$$b_{1i} = 1 \ (= a_{1i}), \qquad i = 2, \ldots, k,$$
$$b_{1i} = 0 \ (= a_{1i}), \qquad i = k + 1, \ldots, n,$$
$$b_{23} = 1 \ (= a_{23}).$$

Let $i \in \{4, \ldots, k\}$, for convenience say $i = k$, and consider the tours $\tau_1 = \langle 1, k, k - 1, \ldots, 4, 2, 3, k + 1, \ldots, n \rangle$ and $\tau_2 = \langle 1, 2, 4, \ldots, k - 1, k, 3, k + 1, \ldots, n \rangle$, then the incidence vectors x^{τ_1} and x^{τ_2} of τ_1 and τ_2 satisfy $a^T x = a_0$ and hence $b^T x = b_0$ with equality. This implies $0 = b_0 - b_0 = b^T x^{\tau_1} - b^T x^{\tau_2} = b_{1k} + b_{23} - b_{12} - b_{3k} = 1 - b_{3k}$. Thus $b_{3k} = 1$. By iterating this argument we obtain

$$b_{ij} = 1, \qquad 1 \leqslant i < j \leqslant k.$$

Let $i \in \{k + 1, \ldots, n\}$; say $i = n$, and consider the tours $\tau_3 = \langle 1, 2, \ldots, n \rangle$ and $\tau_4 = \langle 2, 1, 3, 4, \ldots, n \rangle$ whose incidence vectors satisfy $a^T x = a_0$ and consequently $b^T x = b_0$ as well. We obtain $0 = b^T x^{\tau_3} - b^T x^{\tau_4} = b_{23} + b_{1n} - b_{13} - b_{2n} = -b_{2n}$. Applying this construction repeatedly we obtain

$$b_{ij} = 0, \qquad i \in \{1, \ldots, k\}, \qquad j \in \{k + 1, \ldots, n\}.$$

Using a similar construction one can also show that there exists a number β

such that

$$b_{ij} = \beta, \qquad k+1 \leqslant i < j \leqslant n.$$

This implies that $b^T x = x(E(W)) + \beta x(E(V - W))$ and that $b_0 = |W| - 1 + \beta(|V - W| - 1)$. The incidence vector of the tour $\tau_5 = \langle 1, n, 2, \ldots, k, k+1, \ldots, n-1 \rangle$ satisfies $b^T x^{\tau_5} = |W| - 2 + \beta(|V - W| - 2)$. Since $b^T x \leqslant b_0$ is valid for Q_T^n we also have $b^T x^{\tau_5} \leqslant |W| - 1 + \beta(|V - W| - 1)$; hence $\beta \geqslant -1$ has to hold. From this we obtain the desired representation of b as

$$b^T = \alpha a^T + \lambda^T A$$

where $\alpha = 1 + \beta$, $\lambda_i = -\beta/2$ for $i = 1, \ldots, k$ and $\lambda_i = \beta/2$ for $i = k+1, \ldots, n$.

The case $|W| = 2$ follows from Theorem 8(a). The case $|W| = n - 2$ follows from Theorem 8(a) combined with Lemma 8(a). The cases $n = 4, 5$ are easy. $\square$

The proof given above implicitly contains part (a) of the following lemma.

Lemma 8 *Let $n \geqslant 4$.*
(a) *Suppose W and W' are different vertex sets in K_n with at least two and at most $n - 2$ vertices. Then the corresponding subtour elimination constraints are equivalent with respect to Q_T^n if and only if $W' = V - W$.*
(b) *Let $\delta(W)$, $W \subseteq V$, denote the set of edges in K_n with one endpoint in W and the other in $V - W$. For every $W \subseteq V$, $2 \leqslant |W| \leqslant n - 2$, the so-called loop constraint*

$$x(\delta(W)) \geqslant 2$$

is equivalent to $x(E(W)) \leqslant |W| - 1$ with respect to Q_T^n (and therefore defines a facet of Q_T^n).

The only existing proof that clique tree inequalities define facets of Q_T^n is quite involved. We give here an outline only of the basic proof technique. Grötschel & Padberg [1979a] have shown (by brute force) that the 2-matching inequality derived from the smallest comb (a comb with a handle of cardinality 3 and three teeth of cardinality 2) defines a facet of Q_T^n for all $n \geqslant 6$. Such a smallest comb is shown in Figure 8.3. The comb (or

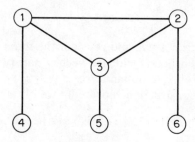

Figure 8.3

2-matching) inequality for the comb of Figure 8.3 is

$$x_{12} + x_{13} + x_{14} + x_{23} + x_{26} + x_{35} \leqslant 4.$$

Grötschel & Padberg [1979b] have established various lifting theorems which show how one can blow up a comb by adding new teeth, or enlarging a handle or a tooth such that the new comb inequality is a facet in case the original one was a facet. (In fact, the lifting theorems are more general.) Using the result that the smallest comb induces a facet, one can then derive that all comb inequalities define facets of Q_T^n. For completeness we state two examples of such lifting theorems. In these theorems $K_n = (V, E)$ is the complete graph on n vertices.

Theorem 12 *Let $a^T x \leqslant a_0$ define a facet of Q_T^n satisfying $a \geqslant 0$. Let C be a clique in the graph $G(a)$ induced by the edges $E(a) := \{\{i, j\} \in E \mid a_{ij} > 0\}$ with $|C| \geqslant 3$. Suppose that every vertex $v \in C$ is contained in one additional clique C_v of cardinality 2 in $G(a)$, say $C_v = \{v, v'\}$, and assume that for every $v \in C$, $a_{v'i} = 0$ for all $i \in V - C_v$ and that $a_{ij} = \alpha$ for every edge $\{i, j\} \in E(a)$ with $\{i, j\} \cap C \neq \emptyset$.*
(a) Now add four vertices $n+1, \ldots, n+4$ (two new teeth of size 2 each) and define a new inequality in the following way:

$$a_{ij}^* := a_{ij} \quad \text{for all } \{i, j\} \in E - E(C),$$
$$a_{ij}^* := \alpha \quad \text{for all } \{i, j\} \in E(C \cup \{n+1, n+2\}),$$
$$a_{n+1,n+3}^* := a_{n+2,n+4}^* = \alpha,$$
$$a_{ij}^* := 0 \quad \text{otherwise},$$
$$a_0^* := a_0 + 3\alpha.$$

Then $a^{*T} x \leqslant a_0^*$ defines a facet of Q_T^{n+4}.
(b) Add one vertex $n+1$ (to C) and set $a_0^* := a_0 + \alpha$, $a_{ij}^* := a_{ij}$ for all $\{i, j\} \in E$, $a_{i,n+1}^* := \alpha$ for all $i \in C$ and $a_{ij}^* := 0$ otherwise. Then, $a^{*T} x \leqslant a_0^*$ defines a facet of Q_T^{n+1}.

Theorem 13 *Let $a^T x \leqslant a_0$ define a facet of Q_T^n satisfying $a \geqslant 0$, and let C be a clique in the graph $G(a)$. Let $Z := \{v \in C \mid a_{vi} = 0 \text{ for all } i \in V - C\}$ and let $Y := \{v \in V - C \mid \exists w \in C - Z \text{ such that } a_{vw} = 0\}$ (if $C = Z$, then $Y := V - C$). Suppose one of the following conditions is satisfied:*
(i) $|Z| \geqslant 2$, $a_{ij} = \alpha$ for all $\{i, j\} \in E$ with $\{i, j\} \cap Z \neq \emptyset$ and $a_{ij} \geqslant \alpha$ for all $\{i, j\} \in E(C - Z)$; or
(ii) $|Z| = 1$, $|Y| \geqslant 2$ and $a_{ij} = \alpha$ for all $\{i, j\} \in E$ with $\{i, j\} \cap C \neq \emptyset$.
Set $a_0^* := a_0 + \alpha$, $a_{ij}^* := a_{ij}$ for all $\{i, j\} \in E$, $a_{i,n+1}^* := \alpha$ for all $i \in C$ and $a_{ij}^* := 0$ otherwise, then $a^{*T} x \leqslant a_0^*$ defines a facet of Q_T^{n+1}.

By employing some additional lifting theorems of the above type, it was shown by Grötschel & Padberg [1979b] that all comb inequalities define facets of Q_T^n.

Grötschel & Pulleyblank [1985] use this result to show by means of a technically involved double induction that all clique tree inequalities define facets of Q_T^n.

By combining the result of Exercise 15 and the fact that clique tree inequalities define facets of Q_T^n, Theorem 9 implies that all clique tree inequalities also define facets of the monotone polytope $\tilde{Q}_T^n$. Moreover, it was shown by Grötschel & Pulleyblank [1985] that among a well-defined large class of valid inequalities for Q_T^n (resp. $\tilde{Q}_T^n$), the clique tree inequalities are the only ones defining facets of Q_T^n (resp. $\tilde{Q}_T^n$).

Furthermore, except for some obvious cases, no two clique tree inequalities are equivalent with respect to Q_T^n. (In considering the exceptions, see Lemma 8(a) and also compare this to Lemma 3.)

Let us now summarize all the results discussed so far.

Theorem 14 *Let $K_n = (V, E)$ be the complete graph on $n \geq 6$ vertices and let $\mathcal{W}$ be a set of vertex sets in K_n such that for all $W \in \mathcal{W}$, $3 \leq |W| \leq n-3$, and $W \in \mathcal{W}$ if and only if $V - W \notin \mathcal{W}$. Then the following is a system of facet-defining inequalities for Q_T^n, no two of which are equivalent:*

(a) $x_{ij} \geq 0$ *for all $\{i, j\} \in E$,*
(b) $x_{ij} \leq 1$ *for all $\{i, j\} \in E$,*
(c) *subtour elimination constraints:*

$$x(E(W)) \leq |W| - 1 \qquad \text{for all } W \in \mathcal{W},$$

(d) *comb inequalities:*

$$x(E(H)) + \sum_{j=1}^{s} x(E(T_j)) \leq |H| + \sum_{j=1}^{s} (|T_j| - 1) - \frac{s+1}{2}$$

for all $H, T_1, \ldots, T_s \subseteq V$ satisfying
(d₁) $|H \cap T_j| \geq 1$, $j = 1, \ldots, s$,
(d₂) $|T_j - H| \geq 1$, $j = 1, \ldots, s$,
(d₃) $T_i \cap T_j = \varnothing$, $1 \leq i \leq j \leq s$,
(d₄) $s \geq 3$ *and odd*,
(d₅) $H \in \mathcal{W}$,
(e) *clique tree inequalities (with at least two handles):*

$$\sum_{i=1}^{r} x(E(H_i)) + \sum_{j=1}^{s} x(E(T_j)) \leq \sum_{i=1}^{r} |H_i| + \sum_{j=1}^{s} (|T_j| - t_j) - \frac{s+1}{2}$$

for all handles $H_1, \ldots, H_r, r \geq 2$, and teeth $T_1, \ldots, T_s$ satisfying the definition in Section 4.2.
Moreover, the degree equations

$$x(\delta(i)) = 2, \qquad i = 1, \ldots, n$$

form a minimal equation system for Q_T^n.

Theorem 15 *The following is a nonredundant system of facet-defining inequalities for $\tilde{Q}_T^n$, $n \geq 6$:*
(a) $x_{ij} \geq 0$ *for all $\{i, j\} \in E$,*

(b) *degree constraints:*

$$x(\delta(i)) \leqslant 2 \qquad \text{for all } i \in V,$$

(c) *subtour elimination constraints:*

$$x(E(W)) \leqslant |W| - 1 \qquad \text{for all } W \subseteq V, 2 \leqslant |W| \leqslant n - 1,$$

(d) *clique tree inequalities (with at least one handle):*

$$\sum_{i=1}^{r} x(E(H_i)) + \sum_{j=1}^{s} x(E(T_j)) \leqslant \sum_{i=1}^{r} |H_i| + \sum_{j=1}^{s} (|T_j| - t_j) - \frac{s+1}{2}$$

for all clique trees with at least one handle defined in Section 4.2.

By comparing the inequalities listed in Theorems 14 and 15 with those defining Q_{1T}^n, $\tilde{Q}_{1T}^n$ (cf. (12), ..., (18)), and Q_{2M}^n, $\tilde{Q}_{2M}^n$ (cf. Theorems 4 and 3), one can easily see which of the facet-defining inequalities for the 1-tree (resp. 2-matching) polytopes define facets of the symmetric traveling salesman polytopes. More precisely (cf. Grötschel [1977a]), the inequalities from (12), ..., (18) and Theorems 3 and 4 which are missing in Theorem 14 (in Theorem 15, respectively) are redundant with respect to Q_T^n (to $\tilde{Q}_T^n$, respectively). In particular, we can make the following remarks.

Remark 1
(a) *Every nonredundant system of facet-defining subtour elimination constraints (18) for Q_{1T}^n is a nonredundant system of facet-defining subtour elimination constraints for Q_T^n.*
(b) *Every facet-defining inequality for $\tilde{Q}_{1T}^n$ is also facet defining for $\tilde{Q}_T^n$.*
(c) *All facet-defining 2-matching constraints for $\tilde{Q}_{2M}^n$ except for those with $k = 1$ (one tooth) are facet-defining for $\tilde{Q}_T^n$.*
(d) *Q_T^n and Q_{2M}^n have the same affine hull and for every nonredundant complete system of inequalities and equations for Q_{2M}^n, the corresponding system without the 2-matching inequalities having $k = 1$ (one tooth) is a nonredundant facet-defining system for Q_T^n.*

4.4 'Bad' facets of Q_T^n and $\tilde{Q}_T^n$

We shall now discuss several classes of inequalities, termed 'bad', which define facets for Q_T^n or $\tilde{Q}_T^n$ and which are thus, by definition, required in any complete linear description of the respective polytopes. We do, however, have reason to believe that they are of little practical use in cutting plane algorithms for the TSP.

These inequalities are usually defined by certain properties which – unless $\mathcal{P} = \mathcal{NP}$ – cannot be checked in polynomial time. Some of these properties are not even known to be in $\mathcal{NP}$ or co-$\mathcal{NP}$. In some (intuitive) sense these inequalities provide a polyhedral explanation for the 'intractability' of the TSP (see Chapter 3 for a precise version of this statement).

Let $\tilde{\mathcal{S}}_n$ be the set of subsets of tours in $K_n = (V, E)$. As mentioned in Section 2, $\tilde{\mathcal{S}}_n$ is an independence system on the edge set E of K_n. With every subset $F \subseteq E$ we can associate a number $r(F)$ called *rank* of F as follows:

$$r(F) := \max\{|S| : S \subseteq F \text{ and } S \in \tilde{\mathcal{S}}_n\}.$$

A moment's thought shows that for every subset $F \subseteq E$ the inequality

$$x(F) \leq r(F)$$

is valid and supporting with respect to $\tilde{Q}_T^n$. This way of defining valid and supporting 0–1 inequalities is applicable to any other combinatorial optimization problem in an analogous manner. The inequalities of the type $x(F) \leq r(F)$ are usually called *rank inequalities*. As a matter of fact, all inequalities for the TSP encountered so far are rank inequalities except for those clique tree inequalities which contain a tooth and a handle meeting in more than one vertex.

It is of course not apparent how to compute the rank of a set F; in fact this is as hard as the TSP itself, and assuming the rank is known, it is not easy to decide whether or not a rank inequality defines a facet of the TSP. There are two obvious necessary conditions (valid for general independence systems and not only for the TSP) which we would like to mention.

A set $F \subseteq E$ is *closed* if $r(F) < r(G)$ for all G which strictly contain F, and F is called *inseparable* if there are no two disjoint nonempty subsets F_1, F_2 of F with $F = F_1 \cup F_2$ and $r(F) = r(F_1) + r(F_2)$.

Lemma 9 *If the inequality $x(F) \leq r(F)$ defines a facet of $\tilde{Q}_T^n$, then F is closed and inseparable.*

We next study some graphs whose edge sets give rise to rank inequalities defining facets of $\tilde{Q}_T^n$. If v is a vertex of a graph G, then $G - v$ denotes the graph obtained by removing v.

Let $G = (W, F)$ be a graph.

(a) G is called *Hamiltonian* if it contains a Hamiltonian cycle.

(b) G is called *semi-Hamiltonian* if it contains a Hamiltonian path.

(c) G is called *maximal non-Hamiltonian* (*maximal non-semi-Hamiltonian*) if G is non-Hamiltonian (not semi-Hamiltonian) but if the addition of any edge (not in G) to G makes the new graph Hamiltonian (semi-Hamiltonian).

(d) G is called *hypo-Hamiltonian* (*hypo-semi-Hamiltonian*) if G is non-Hamiltonian (non-semi-Hamiltonian) and $G - v$ is Hamiltonian (semi-Hamiltonian) for all $v \in W$.

(e) G is called *maximal hypo-Hamiltonian* (*maximal hypo-semi-Hamiltonian*) if G is hypo-Hamiltonian (hypo-semi-Hamiltonian) and maximal non-Hamiltonian (maximal non-semi-Hamiltonian).

For the history of hypo-Hamiltonian and hypo-semi-Hamiltonian graphs

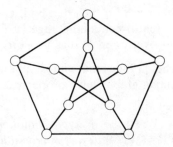

Figure 8.4

see Thomassen [1974, 1978] and Grötschel [1977a]. To mention some results, it is known that the smallest hypo-Hamiltonian graph has 10 vertices and is unique. This graph is the famous Petersen graph which is given in Figure 8.4. There are hypo-Hamiltonian graphs with n vertices for $n = 10, 13, \ldots, 16, 18$ and larger. There are no hypo-Hamiltonian graphs with 11 or 12 vertices and no such graph with 9 or fewer vertices. The only open case is $n = 17$.

Hypo-semi-Hamiltonian graphs of order n are known for $n = 34, 37$ and for each $n \geq 39$. One can show that there are no hypo-semi-Hamiltonian graphs with fewer than 12 vertices. All other cases are open.

It is obvious that for any non-Hamiltonian graph $G = (W, F)$ with k vertices, the inequality

$$x(F) \leq |W| - 1 \tag{35}$$

is valid for $\tilde{Q}_T^n$, $n \geq k$, and that in case G is maximal non-Hamiltonian the inequality is supporting. However, if $n > k$, then the subtour elimination constraint for W implies (35), i.e. $x(F) \leq x(E(W)) \leq |W| - 1$. So, (35) is a candidate for a facet only in the case $k = n$. Clearly, if $G = (W, F)$ is maximal non-Hamiltonian then F is closed, but F may be separable. (Consider the graph K_{n-1} plus an edge, say $\{n - 1, n\}$.)

Research problem *Characterize those maximal non-Hamiltonian graphs of order n for which (35) defines a facet of $\tilde{Q}_T^n$.*

By definition, all maximal hypo-Hamiltonian graphs are maximal non-Hamiltonian graphs. It is not even known whether all maximal hypo-Hamiltonian graphs define facets of $\tilde{Q}_T^n$, but there is a useful sufficient condition known.

Definition Let $G = (W, F)$ be a hypo-Hamiltonian (or hypo-semi-Hamiltonian) graph. A vertex $v \in W$ is said to have *property* Δ if for any two neighbors v_1, v_2 of v, one of the following conditions is satisfied:
(a) $G - v_1$ contains a Hamiltonian cycle (path) containing edge $\{v, v_2\}$.
(b) $G - v_2$ contains a Hamiltonian cycle (path) containing edge $\{v, v_1\}$.

(c) There exists a neighbor v_3 of v such that both $G - v_1$ and $G - v_2$ contain a Hamiltonian cycle (path) containing edge $\{v, v_3\}$.

G has *property* Δ if every vertex in W has property Δ.

It was shown by Grötschel [1980a] that almost all known hypo-Hamiltonian and hypo-semi-Hamiltonian graphs have property Δ. Moreover, the following result was proved.

Theorem 16 *Let* $G = (W, F)$ *be a hypo-Hamiltonian graph of order* n *having property* Δ. *Let* $G' = (W, F')$ *be any maximal hypo-Hamiltonian graph with* $F \subseteq F'$, *then*

$$x(F') \leqslant n - 1$$

defines a facet of $\tilde{Q}_T^n$ (*but not a facet of* $\tilde{Q}_T^k$, $k > n$).

Note that the hypo-Hamiltonian graphs of order n in Theorem 16 induce a kind of inequality which are peculiar to $\tilde{Q}_T^n$. All inequalities of the type $x(F) \leqslant r(F)$ encountered so far have the property that if they define a facet of $\tilde{Q}_T^n$ they also define a facet of $\tilde{Q}_T^k, k \geqslant n$. This is not the case for hypo-Hamiltonian inequalities.

To give an example, the Petersen graph is known to be a maximal hypo-Hamiltonian graph having property Δ. Thus, if F is the edge set of a Petersen graph in K_{10}, then $x(F) \leqslant 9$ defines a facet of $\tilde{Q}_T^{10}$. Maurras [1976] showed that this Petersen inequality also defines a facet of Q_T^{10}. Moreover, he proved that if the two vertices of an edge in the Petersen graph are replaced by a clique of size $k \geqslant 2$, then the corresponding inequality $x(F) \leqslant n + k - 3$ defines a facet of Q_T^{n+k-2}, $n \geqslant 10$. This is the only known case of such 'bad' inequalities which also define facets of Q_T^n.

Research problem *Which inequalities induced by maximal non-Hamiltonian graphs define facets of* Q_T^n?

Statements similar to the ones made about maximal non-Hamiltonian graphs can be made with respect to hypo-semi-Hamiltonian and maximal non-semi-Hamiltonian graphs. The main result of Grötschel [1980a] about this type of graphs is the following.

Theorem 17 *Let* $G = (W, F)$ *be a hypo-semi-Hamiltonian graph of order* n *having property* Δ, *and let* $G' = (W, F')$ *be a maximal hypo-semi-Hamiltonian graph with* $F \subseteq F'$; *then*

$$x(F') \leqslant n - 2$$

defines a facet of $\tilde{Q}_T^k$ *for all* $k \geqslant n$.

It should be noted that the number of nonisomorphic hypo-Hamiltonian (hypo-semi-Hamiltonian, respectively) graphs with property Δ is not at all small, i.e. that every possible maximal graph containing it and labeled to give a different subgraph of K_n defines a different facet of $\tilde{Q}_T^n$. Thus the number of such facet-defining inequalities is large in general.

On the other hand, for some small cases we have computed the number of tours whose incidence vectors satisfy the hypo-Hamiltonian (hypo-semi-Hamiltonian, respectively) inequalities with equality, and it turned out that these numbers are rather small compared to the number of tours whose incidence vectors satisfy the subtour elimination constraints, say, with equality. This is a more or less intuitive explanation of the fact that such inequalities were not needed to prove optimality in cutting plane procedures, cf. Chapter 9.

Papadimitriou & Yannakakis [1984] define a further class of bad facets. Call a vertex v of a graph a *supernode* if v is adjacent to every other vertex. Let $G = (W, F)$ be a graph of order n without a supernode. Construct a graph $G' = (W', F')$ with $3n$ vertices as follows. Replace every vertex $v \in W$ by three mutually adjacent vertices v_1, v_2, v_3. G' has the following edges: all edges $\{u_3, v_3\}$, two edges $\{u_3, v_1\}$, $\{v_3, u_1\}$ if $\{u, v\} \in F$ and an edge $\{u_3, v_2\}$ if all neighbors of v in G are also neighbors of u. Papadimitriou & Yannakakis [1984] prove the following results.

Theorem 18 *Let $G = (W, F)$ be a graph of order n without a supernode. If G is maximal non-Hamiltonian then $G' = (W', F')$ is maximal non-Hamiltonian. Moreover*
$$x(F') \leqslant 3n - 1$$
is a facet of $\tilde{Q}_T^{3n}$ if and only if G is maximal non-Hamiltonian.

So Theorem 18 shows how to modify a maximal non-Hamiltonian graph to make the corresponding inequality facet-inducing. In addition to Theorems 16 and 17, Theorem 18 gives a further class of bad facets of $\tilde{Q}_T^n$.

It is easy to see that none of the inequalities introduced in this section is equivalent to any of the inequalities described in Theorems 14 and 15. By adding all the facet-inducing hypo-Hamiltonian, hypo-semi-Hamiltonian inequalities, etc., to the systems in Theorems 14 and 15, we obtain better linear descriptions of Q_T^n (of $\tilde{Q}_T^n$, respectively) even though we have no claim (nor conjecture) as to the completeness of the linear system thus obtained.

4.5 Further remarks

We have already mentioned some open problems about Q_T^n and $\tilde{Q}_T^n$, which might be solvable with some effort. There are many more interesting questions which one could ask but most of them seem to be hopelessly difficult. Let us mention one of those.

Research problem *Characterize all (or some interesting) 0–1 inequalities which define facets of Q_T^n (resp. $\tilde{Q}_T^n$).*

The 0–1 inequalities are simply the rank inequalities with respect to the independence system $\mathscr{I}_n$ (cf. the beginning of Section 4.4).

The usual way to exhibit new classes of facet-inducing inequalities is to consider small examples, i.e. Q_T^n for small n, and to try to find a complete inequality system. If the system one has at hand is not complete, then this system must have some fractional solutions. By investigating the fractional solutions one may be able to obtain new valid inequalities which cut off fractional solutions and which might be the basic examples of a new class of interesting inequalities.

Let us therefore mention the values of n for which complete systems for Q_T^n and $\tilde{Q}_T^n$ are known, and compare these results to Theorems 14 and 15.

For $n = 3$, 4 and 5, it is trivial to see that $Q_T^n = Q_{2M}^n$, and hence complete and nonredundant systems for Q_T^n, $n = 3$, 4, 5, are known from Theorem 4 and Exercise 7.

The case $n = 6$ is the first where $Q_T^n \neq Q_{2M}^n$ and where subtour elimination constraints have to be used. It is not too hard to prove that the inequality system given in Theorem 14, i.e. trivial constraints, 2-matching inequalities and subtour elimination constraints, is complete and nonredundant for Q_T^6.

However, the three types of inequalities are not sufficient for Q_T^7. Here comb inequalities with teeth of size 3 have to be used. This follows from a result of Norman [1955] which is discussed in detail by Grötschel [1977a, pp. 144–145]. But still, the system of Theorem 14 is complete and non-redundant for Q_T^7.

No further completeness results about Q_T^n are known. We believe that the system of Theorem 14 is complete and nonredundant for Q_T^8 and Q_T^9, but we have no proof.

For $n = 10$, the Petersen graph inequalities (cf. Section 4.4) define facets, so the system of Theorem 14 is not complete for Q_T^{10}.

The first time where clique tree inequalities, which are not comb in-equalities, enter is the case $n = 11$. To give an example, consider the polytope $P \subseteq \mathbb{R}^{55}$ ($n = 11$) defined by the degree equations (5), the trivial inequalities in Theorem 8, the subtour elimination constraints (10) and the 2-matching inequalities (25); then P has the fractional vertex shown in Figure 8.5(a). If $P' \subseteq \mathbb{R}^{55}$ is the polytope obtained from P by adding the comb inequalities (34) then P' has the fractional vertex shown in Figure 8.5(b). We leave it as an exercise to the reader to find the comb and clique tree inequalities that are violated by the vertices depicted in Figures 8.5(a) and (b), respectively.

Another way to look at Q_T^n is from the subtour elimination point of view. Namely, for $n = 3$, 4, 5, Q_T^n is given by the degree equations and trivial inequalities (2-matching constraints are not needed, and for $n = 5$, subtour elimination constraints for $|W| = 3$ are equivalent to trivial inequalities.) So one may ask up to which n do the subtour elimination constraints of Theorem 11 (and trivial inequalities and degree equations) determine Q_T^n. In fact, subtour elimination constraints are not sufficient for Q_T^6. This has already been observed by Held & Karp [1970], but no polyhedral interpretation was given there. Held & Karp [1970] have shown that a Lagrangean relaxation method finds the optimum value of any minimization problem over the 1-tree polytope Q_{1T}^n intersected with the affine space defined by the degree equations (5). (Recall the complete description of Q_{1T}^n and Q_T^n given

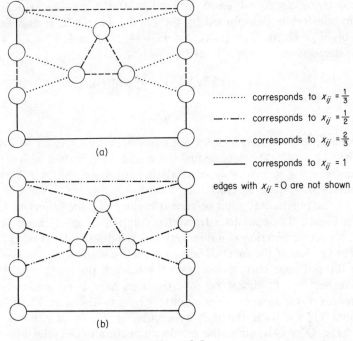

.... corresponds to $x_{ij} = \frac{1}{3}$

—··—·· corresponds to $x_{ij} = \frac{1}{2}$

————— corresponds to $x_{ij} = \frac{2}{3}$

————— corresponds to $x_{ij} = 1$

edges with $x_{ij} = 0$ are not shown

Figure 8.5

in (15), (16), (17) and also recall the close relationship between Q_{1T}^n and Q_T^n as was observed in Remark 1(a).) Held and Karp observed that if the objective function shown in Figure 8.6 is minimized, the optimal tour length is 4 while the relaxed problem mentioned above has an optimum value 3. (We are in the case $n = 6$.)

The edges in Figure 8.6 have the weight assigned to them as shown; all other edges of K_6 have a large positive weight. In fact, we may assume that all other edges have weight 2. Let us denote the $\{0, 1, 2\}$-valued objective function defined this way by $c^T x$.

We claim that $-c^T x \leqslant -4$ defines a facet of Q_T^6 which is equivalent to a 2-matching constraint. This can be seen as follows.

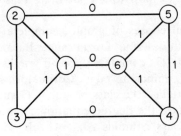

Figure 8.6

Denote by $a^T x \leq a_0 = 4$ (resp. $b^T x \leq b_0 = 4$) the two facet-defining 2-matching constraints determined by the handle $H = \{1, 2, 3\}$ and the teeth $T_1 = \{1, 6\}$, $T_2 = \{2, 5\}$, $T_3 = \{3, 4\}$, by $H' = \{4, 5, 6\}$ and $T_1' = T_1$, $T_2' = T_2$, $T_3' = T_3$, respectively. Then we get

$$-c^T x = a^T x + b^T x - \sum_{i=1}^{6} x(\delta(i)),$$

and

$$-4 = a_0 + b_0 - 12.$$

By Lemma 3, $a^T x \leq 4$ and $b^T x \leq 4$ are equivalent with respect to Q_{2M}^n, and since $\mathrm{aff}(Q_{2M}^n) = \mathrm{aff}(Q_T^n)$ these inequalities are also equivalent with respect to Q_T^n. Thus $c^T x \geq 4$ is a further equivalent version of the two 2-matching constraints with respect to Q_T^6.

So from the polyhedral point of view it is clear that the objective function shown in Figure 8.6 leads to a fractional solution of the relaxed problem, since an objective function is minimized which induces a facet of Q_T^n but no equivalent version of the facet-defining inequality is contained in the system defining the polytope corresponding to the relaxed problem.

With respect to $\tilde{Q}_T^n$ almost no investigations have been made about the completeness of the system of inequalities given in Theorem 15. It is trivial to see that $\tilde{Q}_T^3 = \tilde{Q}_{2M}^3$ is the unit hypercube in $\mathbb{R}^3$. In case $n = 4$, we do already have $\tilde{Q}_T^4 \neq \tilde{Q}_{2M}^4$ since the incidence vectors of 3-cycles are in $\tilde{Q}_{2M}^4$ but not in $\tilde{Q}_T^4$. It is shown by Grötschel [1977b] that $\tilde{Q}_T^4$ is given by the trivial inequalities, the degree inequalities and the four subtour elimination constraints (on vertex sets of cardinality 3), i.e. the system in Theorem 15 is complete and nonredundant for $n = 4$. We state our conjecture about 'small $\tilde{Q}_T^n$' in the following problem.

Research problem *Prove that the system of linear inequalities in Theorem 15 is complete (it is known to be nonredundant!) for $\tilde{Q}_T^n$ for $n = 5, \ldots, 9$.*

In this chapter we have discussed only the TSP defined on the complete graph K_n. One may as well study the polytope $Q_T(G) := \mathrm{conv}\{x^T \in \mathbb{R}^E \mid T$ is a Hamiltonian cycle in $G\}$ where $G = (V, E)$ is an arbitrary graph. (Similarly, $\tilde{Q}_T(G)$ can be defined.) Since the Hamiltonian graph problem is $\mathcal{NP}$-complete, it is $\mathcal{NP}$-complete to decide whether $Q_T(G)$ is nonempty. Therefore it seems quite hard to say anything reasonable about the facet structure of $Q_T(G)$.

However, for special classes of graphs, complete inequality systems for $Q_T(G)$ might be easy to describe. For instance, Barahona & Grötschel were able to characterize $Q_T(G)$ completely for all graphs G not contractible to the complete graph K_6 minus an edge. Cornuéjols, Naddef & Pulleyblank [1983] have recently studied the class of graphs G such that $Q_T(G)$ is given by the trivial inequalities, the degree equations, and one equation for each 3-edge cut-set. This class contains $K_{3,3}$, wheels, Halin graphs and some other graphs. More generally, we may ask the following question.

Research problem *What is the class of graphs G such that $Q_T(G)$ is determined by the system described in Theorem 14 or a subsystem thereof?*

Cornuéjols, Naddef & Pulleyblank [1983] moreover proved the following very interesting 3-cut set composition theorem for traveling salesman polytopes.

Theorem 19 *Let $G_1 = (V_1, E_1)$, resp. $G_2 = (V_2, E_2)$ be graphs each having a vertex of degree 3; say $i \in V_1$ lies on the edges $\{i, i_1\}$, $\{i, i_2\}$, $\{i, i_3\} \in E_1$ and $j \in V_2$ on the edges $\{j, j_1\}$, $\{j, j_2\}$, $\{j, j_3\} \in E_2$. Let $G = G_1 * G_2 = (V, E)$ be the graph defined as follows: $V = (V_1 \cup V_2) - \{i, j\}$, $E = ((E_1 \cup E_2) - \{\{i, i_k\}, \{j, j_k\} \mid k = 1, 2, 3\}) \cup \{\{i_1, j_1\}, \{i_2, j_2\}, \{i_3, j_3\}\}$. Then a complete system of equations and inequalities for $Q_T(G)$ is obtained by juxtaposing the inequalities and equations which define $Q_T(G_1)$ and $Q_T(G_2)$ and identifying $x_{ii_1} = x_{jj_1} = x_{i_1j_1}$, $x_{ii_2} = x_{jj_2} = x_{i_2j_2}$, and $x_{ii_3} = x_{jj_3} = x_{i_3j_3}$.*

Such investigations may lead to new classes of graphs for which the TSP is solvable in polynomial time. For instance, we shall show in Chapter 9 that we can optimize in polynomial time over the trivial inequalities, the subtour elimination constraints, the 2-matching constraints and the degree equations. Thus, the TSP is solvable in polynomial time for all graphs G for which $Q_T(G)$ is completely determined by these equations and inequalities. But which are these graphs? More modestly put, the problem is to find (large) classes of graphs for which $Q_T(G)$ can be described this way!

Another way to use the facet-inducing inequalities is the following. Clearly, if $G = (V, E)$ has n vertices, then every inequality valid for Q_T^n is also valid for $Q_T(G)$ (the variables corresponding to edges in K_n which are not in G have to be deleted, of course). Using Farkas' lemma (or equivalent theorems of the alternative) it is sometimes easy to show that a system of inequalities valid for $Q_T(G)$ (e.g. all known ones for Q_T^n) has no solution. This in turn implies that $Q_T(G)$ is empty and hence that G is not Hamiltonian. (This proof technique is for instance described by Chvátal [1973a]). We think that these remarks are quite important, since there are only few other (and not very powerful) methods known to show that a given graph is non-Hamiltonian. (For a sampling of other techniques, see Chapter 11.)

Exercises

11. (a) Prove that none of the inequalities $x_{ij} \geq 0$ defines a facet for Q_T^3 and Q_T^4.

(b) Prove that no two inequalities $x_{ij} \leq 1$ and $x_{pq} \leq 1$, $\{i, j\} \neq \{p, q\}$, are equivalent for Q_T^n, $n \geq 5$, but that when $n = 4$, $x_{ij} \leq 1$ and $x_{pq} \leq 1$ are equivalent if all vertices i, j, p, q are different.

(c) Prove that $Q_T^n = Q_{2M}^n$ for $n = 3, 4, 5$.

12. Prove Lemma 7.

13. Prove Lemma 8.

14. (a) Show that the 2-matching inequalities (22) with $k = 1$ are implied by the subtour elimination constraints.

(b) Use the fact that the smallest comb (cf. Figure 8.3) defines a facet of Q_T^n, $n \geq 6$, and Theorems 12 and 13 to show that all 2-matching inequalities (22) with $k \geq 3$ define facets of Q_T^n. (*Hint*: The handle of the comb corresponding to a 2-matching constraint should be used as the clique C in Theorems 12 and 13; see Grötschel & Padberg [1979a, 1979b].)

15. Prove that all clique tree inequalities (33) are support reduced (cf. the procedure preceding Lemma 6).

16. Prove Lemma 9.

17. (a) Find a comb inequality which is violated by the point $x \in \mathbb{R}^{55}$ shown in Figure 8.5(a).

(b) Find a clique tree inequality which is violated by the point $x \in \mathbb{R}^{55}$ shown in Figure 8.5(b).

18. Let $G = (V, E)$ be the graph consisting of the vertices $V = \{1, 2, \ldots, 8\}$ and the edges $E = \{\{1, 2\}, \{2, 3\}, \{3, 4\}, \{1, 4\}, \{1, 5\}, \{5, 6\}, \{6, 7\}, \{7, 8\}, \{5, 8\}, \{4, 8\}\}$. Clearly, $Q_T(G)$ is contained in the polyhedron Q given by

$$x(\delta(i)) = 2, \quad i = 1, \ldots, 8,$$

$$\left.\begin{array}{l} x(E\{1, 2, 3, 4\}) \leq 3 \\ x(E\{5, 6, 7, 8\}) \leq 3 \end{array}\right\} \quad (\textit{two subtour elimination constraints}),$$

$$x_{ij} \leq 1 \quad \text{for all } \{i, j\} \in E,$$

$$x_{ij} \geq 0 \quad \text{for all } \{i, j\} \in E.$$

Prove that $Q_T(G)$ is empty (i.e. G is not Hamiltonian) by showing that Q is empty. (*Hint*: Use Farkas' Lemma and exhibit a solution of the system dual to the system defining Q. Recall that Farkas' lemma states that either the primal system $Dx = d$, $Ax \leq b$, $x \geq 0$ or the dual system $u^T D + v^T A \geq 0$, $v \geq 0$, $u^T d + v^T b < 0$ has a solution, but never both.)

5 THE ASYMMETRIC TRAVELING SALESMAN POLYTOPES

The asymmetric traveling salesman polytopes P_T^n and $\tilde{P}_T^n$ have not received as much attention in the literature as the corresponding symmetric ones. Perhaps as a result, most computational studies of the asymmetric TSP utilize no more polyhedral information than is provided by the subtour elimination constraints. While asymmetric TSPs appear to be easier to solve than their symmetric counterparts of equal size, it is to be expected that the exploitation of other classes of facet-defining inequalities as well as of several other interesting properties of P_T^n and $\tilde{P}_T^n$ known to date, should push the problem-solving capabilities for the TSP beyond its current limits.

The results reported in this section are mainly due to Grötschel [1977a], Grötschel & Padberg [1974, 1975b, 1977], Grötschel & Wakabayashi [1981a, 1981b] and Padberg & Rao [1974]. In the following, $D_n = (V, A)$ denotes the complete digraph on n vertices.

5.1 Basic properties of P_T^n and $\tilde{P}_T^n$, sequential lifting

The asymmetric traveling salesman polytope P_T^n is contained in the assignment polytope P_A^n (cf. Theorem 5), and we know from Proposition 3 that $\dim(P_A^n) = |A| - 2|V| + 1$. Thus we have an upper bound for the dimension of P_T^n. In fact we have the following theorem.

Theorem 20 $\dim(P_T^n) = |A| - 2|V| + 1 = (n-1)^2 - n$, for $n \geqslant 3$.

The result above has been stated in two abstracts [Heller, 1953; Kuhn, 1955a]. A direct proof of Theorem 20 analogous to the first proof of Theorem 7 has been given by Grötschel & Padberg [1977]. It is not too difficult to give a proof of Theorem 20 paralleling the second proof of Theorem 7. From the $|E| - |V| + 1$ undirected tours constructed in the first proof of Theorem 7 we can obtain $|A| - 2|V| + 2$ directed tours by taking the two possible orientations of each undirected tour. In order to complete this approach we must show that the incidence vectors of these directed tours are linearly independent, and this is left as an exercise.

Since the subtour elimination constraints for $|W| = 2$, i.e. $x_{ij} + x_{ji} \leqslant 1$, are valid with respect to P_T^n (cf. (11)), it is obvious that the upper bounds $x_{ij} \leqslant 1$ do not define facets of P_T^n. However, the nonnegativity constraints do.

Proposition 4 Let $n \geqslant 5$, then $x_{ij} \geqslant 0$ defines a facet of P_T^n for all $(i, j) \in A$.

In Section 4.1 we discussed the relations between the symmetric traveling salesman polytopes Q_T^n and $\tilde{Q}_T^n$ and in particular stated Theorem 9, which shows how a facet-defining inequality for $\tilde{Q}_T^n$ can be derived from a facet-defining inequality for Q_T^n. S. Boyd [1984] has generalized Theorem 9 to polyhedra of independence systems arising from monotonization. And thus, by making a valid inequality for P_T^n nonnegative (by adding appropriate multiples of the equation system (7) of Section 2.4) and reducing its support, one can obtain facet-inducing inequalities for $\tilde{P}_T^n$ from facet-inducing inequalities for P_T^n, just as in the symmetric case.

We shall now introduce a technique, called *sequential lifting*, which leads to new facet-defining inequalities for $\tilde{P}_T^n$ and P_T^n. This technique is also applicable to the symmetric TSP but does not produce anything interesting there. The sequential lifting method will be described in a general framework.

Let $\mathscr{I}$ be an independence system (or monotone set system) on a set E, (cf. Section 2.3), and let $P_{\mathscr{I}}$ be the polytope associated with $\mathscr{I}$ (cf. (1)). For every subset $F \subseteq E$, $P_{\mathscr{I}}(F)$ denotes the polytope $\{x \in P_{\mathscr{I}} \mid x_e = 0 \text{ for all } e \in F\}$.

Theorem 21 (Sequential lifting theorem) Let $\mathscr{I}$ be an independence system on E, let $F \subseteq E$ and let $e \in F$. Suppose $\sum_{k \notin F} a_k x_k \leqslant a_0$ defines a facet of $P_{\mathscr{I}}(F)$ with $a_0 > 0$. Set

$$a_e := a_0 - \max\left\{ \sum_{k \notin F} a_k x_k^I \mid I \subseteq E - F, \{e\} \cup I \in \mathscr{I} \right\}.$$

Then $a_e x_e + \sum_{k \notin F} a_k x_k \leqslant a_0$ defines a facet of $P_{\mathscr{I}}(F - \{e\})$.

Theorem 21 was proved by Padberg [1975], who has found various generalizations which we do not discuss here.

The interesting feature of Theorem 21 is the following. Sometimes it is
easy to find a set F and an inequality $\sum_{k \notin F} a_k x_k \leq a_0$ such that this inequality
defines a facet of $P_{\mathcal{J}}(F)$. Now Theorem 21 tells us what the missing
coefficients of a (i.e. the coefficients a_e for all $e \in F$) have to look like such
that the extended inequality $\sum_{e \in E} a_e x_e \leq a_0$ defines a facet of $P_{\mathcal{J}}$. Since the
coefficient calculation is done sequentially, we may end up with different
facets of $P_{\mathcal{J}}$ depending on the order in which the coefficients are lifted.
However, it should be observed that the calculation of the new coefficients is
a hard problem in general. Only in rare cases the lifted coefficients can be
obtained easily.

Let us go back to the asymmetric TSP and let us consider the independence system $\tilde{\mathcal{J}}_n$ of subsets of tours contained in the complete digraph
$D_n = (V, A), n \geq 3$.

Proposition 5 *Let C be the arc set of a directed cycle in D_n, $n \geq 3$, of length
$k \leq n - 1$, and let $F := A - C$. Then the cycle inequality $x(C) \leq |C| - 1$ defines
a facet of $\tilde{P}_T^n(F)$.*

Proof Let $C_1, \ldots, C_k$ be the paths of length $k - 1$ obtained from C by
deleting one arc. Then the incidence vectors of these paths are contained in
$\tilde{P}_T^n(F)$ and satisfy $x(C) \leq |C| - 1$ with equality. Let M be the (k, k)-matrix
whose columns correspond to the arcs of C and whose rows correspond to
the incidence vectors $x^{C_i}, i = 1, \ldots, k$. By permuting rows and columns, M
can be transformed into the matrix $E_k - I_k$, where E_k is the (k, k)-matrix
whose components are all 1, and where I_k is the (k, k)-identity matrix.
$E_k - I_k$ is obviously nonsingular, and thus the k incidence vectors are
linearly independent, which proves that $x(C) \leq |C| - 1$ defines a facet of
$\tilde{P}_T^n(F)$. $\square$

Now Theorem 21 tells us that every such facet of $\tilde{P}_T^n(F)$ can be lifted to a
facet of $\tilde{P}_T^n$. In the analogous case for the symmetric TSP, the inequalities
obtained from cycle inequalities by lifting are the subtour elimination
constraints. This is not so in the asymmetric case.

It is clear that at every stage of the sequential lifting procedure, the lifting
coefficients are 0 for arcs which are not diagonals of C. In Exercise 21, the
reader is asked to show that the first time we lift a diagonal arc of a cycle we
obtain a coefficient 2. Afterwards we may get a 2, 1 or 0 depending on the
order of lifting. But note that in any case we obtain a facet of $\tilde{P}_T^n$ by
sequential lifting.

Corollary 4 *All inequalities obtained by lifting cycle inequalities $x(C) \leq
|C| - 1$, $2 \leq |C| \leq n - 1$, sequentially in any order define facets of $\tilde{P}_T^n$.*

The sequential lifting technique with respect to $\tilde{P}_T^n$ is discussed in detail by
Grötschel [1977a]. There is no formula known which describes all the

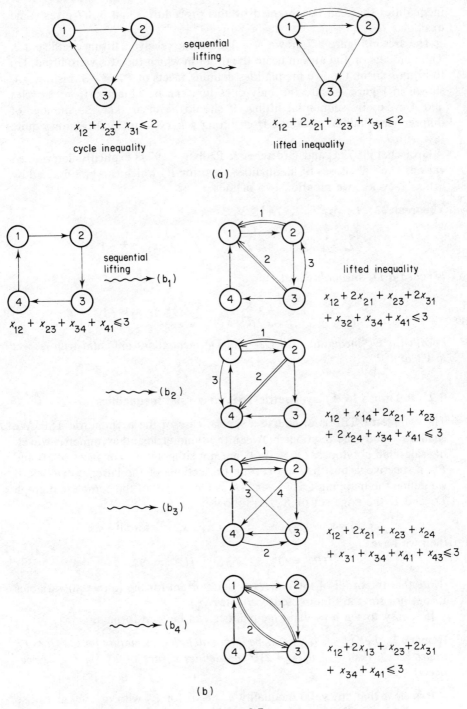

$$x_{12} + x_{23} + x_{31} \leqslant 2$$

cycle inequality

sequential lifting

$$x_{12} + 2x_{21} + x_{23} + x_{31} \leqslant 2$$

lifted inequality

(a)

sequential lifting

$$x_{12} + x_{23} + x_{34} + x_{41} \leqslant 3$$

(b₁)

lifted inequality

$$x_{12} + 2x_{21} + x_{23} + 2x_{31} + x_{32} + x_{34} + x_{41} \leqslant 3$$

(b₂)

$$x_{12} + x_{14} + 2x_{21} + x_{23} + 2x_{24} + x_{34} + x_{41} \leqslant 3$$

(b₃)

$$x_{12} + 2x_{21} + x_{23} + x_{24} + x_{31} + x_{34} + x_{41} + x_{43} \leqslant 3$$

(b₄)

$$x_{12} + 2x_{13} + x_{23} + 2x_{31} + x_{34} + x_{41} \leqslant 3$$

(b)

Figure 8.7

inequalities that can be obtained by this procedure. Figure 8.7 gives some examples.

The arcs in Figure 8.7 drawn as a double line receive a lifting coefficient 2. The numbers on the arcs indicate the order in which the arcs were lifted. Up to isomorphism, the five inequalities defining facets of $\tilde{P}_T^n$, $n \geq 3$, resp. $n \geq 4$, shown in Figure 8.7 are the only ones that can be obtained from 3-cycles and 4-cycles by sequential lifting. It should be clear that the number of different inequalities obtained from lifting a k-cycle inequality grows quite fast with k.

Grötschel [1977a] and Grötschel & Padberg [1977] explicitly determined various general classes of inequalities valid for $\tilde{P}_T^n$ which can be obtained by lifting k-cycles; we mention two of these.

Theorem 22 *Let* $\{i_1, i_2, \ldots, i_k\} \subseteq V$, $3 \leq k \leq n-1$, *then*

$$\sum_{j=1}^{k-1} x_{i_j i_{j+1}} + x_{i_k i_1} + 2 \sum_{j=2}^{k-1} x_{i_j i_1} + \sum_{j=3}^{k-1} \sum_{h=2}^{j-1} x_{i_j i_h} \leq k-1$$

is called a $\tilde{D}_k$-*inequality and*

$$\sum_{j=1}^{k-1} x_{i_j i_{j+1}} + x_{i_k i_1} + 2 \sum_{j=3}^{k} x_{i_1 i_j} + \sum_{j=4}^{k} \sum_{h=3}^{j-1} x_{i_j i_h} \leq k-1$$

is called a $\vec{D}_k$-*inequality. All* $\tilde{D}_k$- *and* $\vec{D}_k$-*inequalities are valid with respect to* $\tilde{P}_T^n$ *and* P_T^n.

5.2 Relations to the symmetric TSP, new valid inequalities

The symmetric TSP is of course a special case of the asymmetric TSP. We shall now study the relations between the symmetric and asymmetric traveling salesman polytopes. Q_T^n and $\tilde{Q}_T^n$ are not subpolytopes or faces of P_T^n and $\tilde{P}_T^n$, respectively, but they are certain projections of the latter polytopes. If we define the mapping $f: \mathbb{R}^A \rightarrow \mathbb{R}^E$ (A is the arc set of the complete digraph D_n and E the edge set of K_n) as follows:

$$f(x) = y, \qquad \text{where} \qquad y_{ij} = x_{ij} + x_{ji} \qquad \text{for all } i \neq j,$$

then we have

$$f(P_T^n) = Q_T^n, \qquad \text{and} \qquad f(\tilde{P}_T^n) = \tilde{Q}_T^n.$$

(Note that the order of the indices ij is important for the (directed) variables x_{ij} but not for the (undirected) variables y_{ij}.)

It is easy to see how valid inequalities can be transformed.

Remark 2 *Let* $\sum_{\{i,j\} \in E} a_{ij} y_{ij} \leq a_0$ *be a face-defining inequality for* Q_T^n *(for* $\tilde{Q}_T^n$, *respectively), then* $\sum_{i < j} a_{ij}(x_{ij} + x_{ji}) \leq a_0$ *defines a face of* P_T^n *(of* $\tilde{P}_T^n$, *respectively).*

It is clear that any valid inequality $a^T x \leq a_0$ for $\tilde{P}_T^n$ with $a_{ij} = a_{ji}$ gives rise to a valid inequality for $\tilde{Q}_T^n$. It is not obvious, however, how to treat valid inequalities $a^T x \leq a_0$ for P_T^n with $a_{ij} \neq a_{ji}$ for some $i \neq j$. A method to symmetrize such inequalities has been investigated by Heller [1956].

Remark 2, however, is important, since we know now that all the valid and facet-defining inequalities for Q_T^n and $\tilde{Q}_T^n$ give rise to valid inequalities for P_T^n and $\tilde{P}_T^n$. Thus we have that the following inequalities are valid for $\tilde{P}_T^n$:

- Subtour elimination constraints; cf. (10), (11).
- 2-matching inequalities; cf. (19).
- Comb inequalities; cf. (34).
- Clique tree inequalities; cf. (33).
- Hypo-Hamiltonian, hypo-semi-Hamiltonian, etc., inequalities; cf. Section 4.4.

An important question now is whether or not the directed versions of inequalities defining facets of Q_T^n (of $\tilde{Q}_T^n$) also define facets of P_T^n (of $\tilde{P}_T^n$). This seems plausible and has been verified – as we shall see – for subtour elimination constraints and some comb inequalities. It is, however, not true for the degree constraints (6) whose directed versions are the sums of two facet-defining directed degree constraints (8).

Moreover, certain directed comb inequalities induce facets of $\tilde{P}_T^n$ but not of P_T^n for small n (cf. the results reported in Section 5.3).

If $a^T y \leq a_0$, $a_0 > 0$, defines a facet of Q_T^n, say, then there are $\frac{1}{2} n(n-1) - n$ linearly independent incidence vectors of undirected tours satisfying the inequality with equality. By directing each of these tours in the two possible ways we obtain $n(n-1) - 2n$ directed tours whose incidence vectors satisfy the directed version of $a^T y \leq a_0$ with equality. It is not known under what conditions these incidence vectors are linearly independent. If they are, then these are not enough to prove that the directed version of the inequality defines a facet of P_T^n, since $\dim(P_T^n) = n(n-1) - 2n + 1$. We have to find one more tour whose incidence vector satisfies the inequality with equality and is linearly independent from the others.

Research problem *Find reasonable sufficient (and necessary) conditions which imply that the directed version of an inequality defining a facet of Q_T^n (of $\tilde{Q}_T^n$) also defines a facet of P_T^n (of $\tilde{P}_T^n$).*

There are, of course, valid inequalities for $\tilde{P}_T^n$ which are not symmetric. Interesting classes of such inequalities have been discussed by Grötschel [1977a] and Grötschel & Padberg [1977]. We shall now describe some of these.

Proposition 6 *Let W be a vertex set in $D_n = (V, A)$ with $2 \leq |W| = k \leq n-2$, let $w \in W$ and $p, q \in V - W$, then*

$$x(A(W)) + x_{pw} + x_{pq} + x_{wq} \leq k$$

is called a T_k-inequality and is valid with respect to $\tilde{P}_T^n$.

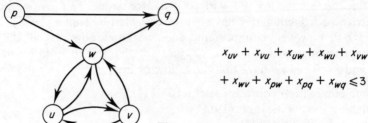

$$x_{uv} + x_{vu} + x_{uw} + x_{wu} + x_{vw}$$

$$+ x_{wv} + x_{pw} + x_{pq} + x_{wq} \leq 3$$

Figure 8.8

A T_3-inequality with $W = \{u, v, w\}$ and the corresponding digraph are shown in Figure 8.8.

T_k-inequalities can be generalized by attaching a source p and a sink q to a comb as follows.

Proposition 7 *Let H be a handle and $T_1, \ldots, T_s$ be teeth satisfying:* (a) $|H \cap T_i| \geq 1$, (b) $|T_i - H| \geq 1$, $i = 1, \ldots, s$; (c) $|T_i \cap T_j| = \emptyset$, $1 \leq i < j \leq s$; *and* (d) $s \geq 3$ *and s odd. Let $p, q \in V - (H \cup \bigcup_{i=1}^{s} T_i)$, then*

$$x(A(H)) + \sum_{i=1}^{s} x(A(T_i)) + \sum_{v \in H} (x_{pv} + x_{vq}) + x_{pq}$$

$$\leq |H| + \sum_{i=1}^{s} (|T_i| - 1) - \frac{s+1}{2} + 1 \ (=: s(C) + 1)$$

is called a C2-inequality and is valid with respect to $\tilde{P}_T^n$.

Proposition 8 *Let i_1, i_2, i_3 be three different vertices and let W_1, W_2 be subsets of V such that* (a) $W_1 \cap W_2 = \emptyset$, (b) $W_1 \cap \{i_1, i_2, i_3\} = \{i_1\}$, (c) $W_2 \cap \{i_1, i_2, i_3\} = \{i_2\}$, (d) $|W_j| \geq 2$, $j = 1, 2$. *Then*

$$x(A(W_1)) + x(A(W_2)) + \sum_{j \in W_2} x_{i_1 j} + x_{i_2 i_1} + x_{i_3 i_1} + x_{i_3 i_2} \leq |W_1| + |W_2| - 1$$

is called a C3-inequality and is valid with respect to $\tilde{P}_T^n$.

The arcs having positive coefficients in a C3-inequality are shown in Figure 8.9.

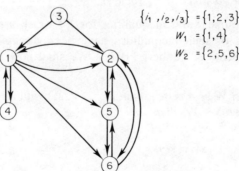

$$\{i_1, i_2, i_3\} = \{1, 2, 3\}$$
$$W_1 = \{1, 4\}$$
$$W_2 = \{2, 5, 6\}$$

Figure 8.9

Replacing 'cycle', 'path', 'edge' and 'graph' by 'directed cycle', 'directed path', 'arc' and 'digraph', we obtain the notions of maximal non-Hamiltonian, hypo-Hamiltonian and hypo-semi-Hamiltonian, etc., digraphs. Clearly, if $D = (V, B)$ is a maximal non-Hamiltonian subdigraph of D_n, then

$$x(B) \leqslant |V| - 1$$

is valid with respect to $\tilde{P}_T^n$; and similarly

$$x(B) \leqslant |V| - 2$$

is valid with respect to $\tilde{P}_T^n$ if $D = (V, B)$ is a maximal non-semi-Hamiltonian subdigraph of D_n. The remarks made about such kinds of inequalities in Section 4.4 with respect to the symmetric TSP apply – *mutatis mutandis* – also to the asymmetric TSP. In the asymmetric case there is an example of a maximal hypo-Hamiltonian digraph such that the corresponding inequality does not define a facet of $\tilde{P}_T^n$; cf. Grötschel & Wakabayashi [1981a], and see Exercise 22.

5.3   Facets of P_T^n and $\tilde{P}_T^n$

We now report which of the inequalities introduced in the foregoing sections are known to define facets of P_T^n or $\tilde{P}_T^n$. The results are not as complete as for the symmetric TSP, and many cases are still open. Unless otherwise mentioned, all results are from Grötschel [1977a] and Grötschel & Padberg [1977]. As usual, $D_n = (V, A)$ is the complete digraph on n vertices.

Theorem 23
(a) $\mathrm{aff}(P_T^n) = \mathrm{aff}(P_A^n) = \{x \in \mathbb{R}^A \mid x(\vec{\delta}(i)) = 1, i = 2, \ldots, n, x(\overleftarrow{\delta}(i)) = 1,$
  $i = 1, \ldots, n\}$, and $\dim(P_T^n) = |A| - 2|V| + 1$.
(b) *The nonnegativity constraints $x_{ij} \geqslant 0$ define facets of P_T^n for all $(i, j) \in A, n \geqslant 5$ (cf. Proposition 4 and Exercise 20).*
(c) *Let $n \geqslant 5$. (Exercise: How about the case $n = 3, 4$?)*
  (c$_1$) *The subtour elimination constraints*

$$x(A(W)) \leqslant |W| - 1$$

  define facets of P_T^n if $2 \leqslant |W| \leqslant n - 2$.
  (c$_2$) *Two different subtour elimination constraints $x(A(W)) \leqslant |W| - 1$ and $x(A(W')) \leqslant |W'| - 1$ are equivalent with respect to P_T^n if and only if $W' = V - W$.*
  (c$_3$) *For $W \subseteq V$, $2 \leqslant |W| \leqslant n - 2$, the loop constraints*

$$x(\overleftarrow{\delta}(W)) = x(\overleftarrow{\delta}(V - W)) \geqslant 1$$

  are equivalent to the subtour elimination constraints with respect to P_T^n.
(d) *The directed versions of the comb inequalities (34) are not known to define facets of P_T^n. In fact, the directed versions of the 2-matching inequalities*

(22) *with three teeth have been shown not to define facets of P_T^6 and P_T^7 by means of a computer program (cf. Grötschel [1977a]). Nothing is known about general (directed) clique tree inequalities.*

(e) *It is not known which of the C2-inequalities (cf. Proposition 7) define facets of P_T^n.*

(f) *Let $n \geqslant 4$, then a T_k-inequality (cf. Proposition 6) defines a facet of P_T^n if and only if $2 \leqslant k \leqslant n-2$ and $k \neq n-3$. If $n \geqslant 5$, $k \neq n-1$, then two different facet-defining T_k-inequalities define different facets of P_T^n. In case $n = 4$, the 24 different T_2-inequalities define six different facets only.*

(g) *C3-inequalities (Proposition 8) define facets of P_T^n if $|W_1| + |W_2| = n - 1$. All other cases are open.*

(h) *For $k \leqslant n-1$ the $\vec{D}_k$- and $\bar{D}_k$-inequalities (cf. Theorem 22) define facets of P_T^n in case $k = 3$ or $k = 4$. All other cases are open.*

There are a few other inequalities known which define facets of P_T^n, e.g. the inequality corresponding to the digraph shown in Figure 8.7(b_4) for $n \geqslant 5$ (this is an E_4-inequality considered by Grötschel & Padberg [1977]) or some hypo-Hamiltonian inequalities for small n; cf. Grötschel & Wakabayashi [1981a]. But there are no further large classes of facet-defining inequalities known.

By comparing Theorem 23 with the 'nice' relatives of P_T^n described in Theorem 7, we can conclude the following.

Corollary 5 *Let $n \geqslant 5$, then except for the subtour elimination constraint $x(A(W)) \leqslant n - 2$, $W = \{2, \ldots, n\}$, each inequality of the complete and non-redundant system of inequalities (26) and (28) defining the facets of the arborescence polytope P_B^n and of the antiarborescence polytope $P_{\bar{B}}^n$ on D_n', respectively, also defines a facet of P_T^n. Moreover, this system of inequalities is nonredundant with respect to P_T^n.*

The relation of the assignment polytope P_A^n to P_T^n is obvious.

Not much is known about the completeness of the system defined above for P_T^n, n small. Clearly $P_T^3 = P_A^3$, i.e. the case $n = 3$ is trivial.

The case $n = 4$ seems to be an odd case. Neither the nonnegativity constraints nor the subtour elimination constraints define facets of P_T^4. P_T^4 obviously has six vertices, and is of dimension 5 by Theorem 20. Thus the six incidence vectors of tours form a set of linearly independent points. This implies that every five-element subset of the vertices spans a facet of P_T^4, and hence that P_T^4 has six facets. Recall that the T_2-inequalities (Proposition 6) have the form $x_{i_1 i_2} + x_{i_2 i_1} + x_{i_3 i_1} + x_{i_1 i_4} \leqslant 2$. Thus there are 24 inequalities of this type. It was shown by Grötschel [1977a] that these inequalities define facets of P_T^4 but only six different ones. Hence a system of six T_2-inequalities plus degree equations suffices for a complete and nonredundant description of P_T^4. Such a system describing P_T^4 completely and nonredundantly is given in Table 8.1.

Table 8.1

12	13	14	21	23	24	31	32	34	41	42	43	
1	1	1										= 1
			1	1	1							= 1
						1	1	1				= 1
									1	1	1	= 1
1							1			1		= 1
	1			1							1	= 1
		1			1			1				= 1
1	1			1	1					1		≤ 2
1	1						1	1		1		≤ 2
	1	1	1	1					1			≤ 2
			1	1		1			1		1	≤ 2
1			1			1	1			1		≤ 2
			1		1	1	1				1	≤ 2

In an abstract, Heller gives a system of 224 equations and inequalities and claims that this completely describes P_T^5 [Heller, 1953]. In another abstract, Kuhn proves that this is wrong and gives a much larger system of 390 equations and inequalities which is claimed to be complete for P_T^5 [Kuhn, 1955a; Gomory, 1966].

Let us now turn to the monotone asymmetric traveling salesman polytope $\tilde{P}_T^n$ and review the results known about facet-defining inequalities. The results mentioned in the next theorem are from Grötschel [1977a].

Theorem 24

(a) *For all $n \geq 3$ all nonnegativity constraints $x_{ij} \geq 0$, $(i, j) \in A$, define facets of $\tilde{P}_T^n$.*

(b) *For all $n \geq 3$ the degree constraints $x(\bar{\delta}(v)) \leq 1$ and $x(\vec{\delta}(v)) \leq 1$, $v \in V$, define facets of $\tilde{P}_T^n$.*

(c) *For all $n \geq 3$ the subtour elimination constraints $x(A(W)) \leq |W| - 1$ define facets of $\tilde{P}_T^n$ if and only if $2 \leq |W| \leq n - 1$.*

(d) *All inequalities obtained from lifting cycle constraints $x(C) \leq |C| - 1$, $2 \leq |C| \leq n - 1$, sequentially (in any order) define facets of $\tilde{P}_T^n$. In particular, all $\hat{D}_k$- and $\check{D}_k$-inequalities, $3 \leq k \leq n - 1$, define facets of $\tilde{P}_T^n$.*

(e) *All directed versions of Chvátal comb inequalities (cf. (34)), such that the corresponding comb has three teeth, define facets of P_T^n for $n \geq 6$. All other cases are open.*

(f) *All T_k-inequalities, $2 \leq k \leq n - 2$, define facets of $\tilde{P}_T^n$, $n \geq 4$. No other C2-inequalities are known to define facets.*

(g) *The C3-inequalities from Proposition 8 define facets if $|W_2| = 2$ and $2 \leq |W_1| \leq n - 3$, $n \geq 5$. All other cases are open.*

Again we can compare Theorem 24 with the nice relatives of $\tilde{P}_T^n$ described in Theorem 6 (identifying vertex $n+1$ of D_n' with vertex 1 in D_n).

Corollary 6 *Let $n \geq 3$, then each of the inequalities* (26), (27), (28), (29) *(providing a complete and nonredundant system for $\tilde{P}_B^n$ and $\tilde{P}_B^n$, respectively) defines a facet of $\tilde{P}_T^n$. Moreover, the system of these inequalities is nonredundant with respect to $\tilde{P}_T^n$.*

Thus $\tilde{P}_T^n$ inherits all facets of $\tilde{P}_B^n$ and $\tilde{P}_B^n$, while P_T^n inherits all facets of P_B^n and P_B^n but one.

The proofs of the above results are quite complicated and use a rather involved technical machinery.

To close this section we would like to mention some 'bad' facets (cf. Section 4.4) of $\tilde{P}_T^n$ which were found by Grötschel & Wakabayashi [1981a, 1981b].

Clearly, replacing an edge $\{i, j\}$ of a hypo-Hamiltonian or hypo-semi-Hamiltonian graph by two arcs (i, j) and (j, i), one obtains a hypo-Hamiltonian or hypo-semi-Hamiltonian digraph. In fact, there are many more constructions of such digraphs. Hypo-Hamiltonian (hypo-semi-Hamiltonian) digraphs, for example, are known to exist for any order $n \geq 6$ $(n \geq 7)$.

We already know that there are maximal hypo-Hamiltonian digraphs which do not define facets of $\tilde{P}_T^n$; cf. Exercise 22. However, it was shown by Grötschel & Wakabayashi [1981a, 1981b] that almost all known maximal hypo-Hamiltonian and hypo-semi-Hamiltonian digraphs (and these are quite a lot) define facets of $\tilde{P}_T^n$. In particular, every polytope $\tilde{P}_T^n$, $n \geq 7$, has some hypo-Hamiltonian and hypo-semi-Hamiltonian facets. We give two examples.

The digraph $D = (V, B)$ shown in Figure 8.10 is maximal hypo-semi-

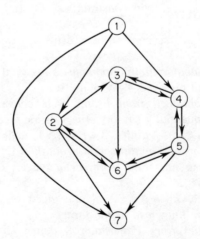

Figure 8.10

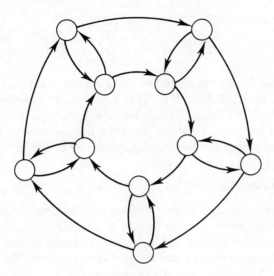

Figure 8.11

Hamiltonian and the inequality $x(B) \le 5$ defines a facet of $\tilde{P}_T^n$ for all $n \ge 7$.
In fact, $\tilde{P}_T^n$ has $5040 \binom{n}{7}$ facets of this type.

The digraph $D' = (V, B')$ shown in Figure 8.11 is hypo-Hamiltonian, but not maximal. D' has the property that every maximal hypo-Hamiltonian digraph $D = (V, B)$ with $B' \subseteq B$ defines a facet $x(B) \le 9$ of $\tilde{P}_T^{10}$, but not of $\tilde{P}_T^n$, $n \ne 10$.

Finally, we would like to mention a peculiar case. Consider the digraph D on the vertices $V = \{1, 2, \ldots, 6\}$ with arc set $B \cup C_1 \cup C_2 \cup \{(1, 3)\}$, where $B = \{(i, i+3), (i+3, i) \mid i = 1, 2, 3\}$, $C_1 = \{(1, 2), (2, 3), (3, 1)\}$, $C_2 = \{(4, 5), (5, 6), (6, 4)\}$. This digraph D is the digraph shown in Figure 8.12 without arc $(4, 6)$. D is hypo-Hamiltonian but not maximal. It was shown by

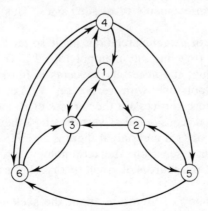

Figure 8.12

Grötschel & Wakabayashi [1981a] that the inequality

$$x(C_2) + 2x(B) + 3x(C_1) + 4x_{13} \leqslant 10$$

defines a facet of $\tilde{P}_T^6$. By sequential lifting, it is easy to see that the inequality also defines a facet of $\tilde{P}_T^n, n \geqslant 6$. This is a strange case where a hypo-Hamiltonian digraph induces a facet, but where the arcs in the corresponding inequality have to be weighted. So, even for $n = 6$ there are facets such that the corresponding inequalities have coefficients not just 0, 1 or 2.

5.4 Neighbor relations

Up to now we have looked at the traveling salesman polyhedra from a facet point of view, i.e., we have tried to find inequalities which define maximal faces, which are necessary in any complete description, and which can be used in linear programming based cutting plane procedures for the TSP.

There is another more combinatorial aspect, related to minimal faces, which could also be useful in linear programming approaches. Namely, the simplex method has the property that it starts at a vertex of a polytope P and (except for degenerate pivot steps) moves to vertices $v_2, v_3, \ldots, v_k$ of P such that two successive vertices v_i and v_{i+1}, $i = 1, \ldots, k-1$, are adjacent on P. Here *adjacency* means that v_i and v_{i+1} belong to a common face of dimension one of P, which is usually called an *edge* of P. If one could get handy descriptions of adjacency, one might be able to specialize the simplex method for certain polytopes in a combinatorial fashion and derive efficient algorithms this way.

There are quite a few interesting theoretical results known about adjacency of vertices on polytopes associated with combinatorial optimization problems (see Hausmann [1980] for an extensive survey), but up to now these results have not found algorithmic applications. Nevertheless, there is some hope that studies concerning adjacency may lead to new types of algorithms, or to improvements of existing ones. This area remains to be explored.

Almost all studies of neighbor relations made so far have been concerned with the asymmetric traveling salesman polytope P_T^n. To make the approach clear, we will introduce the necessary concepts in full generality.

Suppose P is a polytope with vertex set V. Let $G = (V, E)$ be the undirected graph whose vertices are the vertices of P. Two vertices of G are adjacent if and only if (considered as vertices of P) they are adjacent on P, i.e. $\{v, w\}$ is an edge of G if and only if there is an edge of P which contains v and w. (As one can see from the terminology, graphs associated with polyhedra are one of the sources of graph theory.) Let us call $G = (V, E)$ the *skeleton* of P.

There is a large body of literature about the skeletons of polytopes, in particular about the skeletons of 3-dimensional polytopes; see for example,

Grünbaum [1967] for related references. One may ask the following questions: Is the skeleton of a certain polytope Hamiltonian; what is its connectivity, etc.? Of particular importance are mutual characterizations of the following type. Is there a 'nice' graphical characterization of adjacency on P, or is there a 'nice' polyhedral characterization of adjacency in the skeleton G?

One important linear programming related parameter is the diameter of G and P. Let us define the *distance* of two vertices v and w of G, denoted by $\text{dist}(v, w)$, as the length of the shortest path from v to w in G. For instance, adjacent vertices have distance 1. The *diameter* of G, $\text{diam}(G)$, is the maximum distance of any pair of vertices of G, i.e.

$$\text{diam}(G) := \max_{u, v \in V} \{\text{dist}(v, w)\}.$$

If G is the skeleton of a polytope P, then $\text{diam}(G)$ is also called the *diameter* of P.

The polytope whose skeleton has probably been studied most intensively is the assignment polytope (see for instance Balinski & Russakoff [1974]; Hausmann [1980], Heller [1955, 1956] and Padberg & Rao [1974]). The polytope considered in these papers is not exactly our polytope P_A^n (cf. Theorem 5), but a slightly larger one which we will denote by $\bar{P}_A^n$ for convenience:

$$\bar{P}_A^n = \left\{ x \in \mathbb{R}^{n^2} \mid x_{ij} \geq 0, \, i, j = 1, \ldots, n; \, \sum_{i=1}^n x_{ij} = 1, \, j = 1, \ldots, n; \right.$$

$$\left. \sum_{i=1}^n x_{ij} = 1, \, i = 1, \ldots, n \right\}$$

In other words, in the assignment polytope $\bar{P}_A^n$, loops (i.e. assignments (i, i)) are allowed; which is not the case in P_A^n. The polytope P_A^n can be obtained from $\bar{P}_A^n$ by setting $x_{ii} = 0$, $i = 1, \ldots, n$. Each vertex of the assignment polytope $\bar{P}_A^n$ corresponds to a permutation of $\{1, \ldots, n\}$; or in graphical terms, each vertex corresponds to an arc set which is the union of directed cycles such that no two cycles have a vertex in common (here loops are considered as directed cycles of length 1).

Now let G_A^n denote the skeleton of $\bar{P}_A^n$. The following adjacency characterization for G_A^n and $\bar{P}_A^n$ is due to Balinski & Russakoff [1974].

A *directed trail* is a sequence $(v_1, v_2), (v_2, v_3), \ldots, (v_{k-1}, v_k)$ of distinct arcs, and is called *closed* if $v_1 = v_k$.

Theorem 25 *Let v, w be two different vertices of $\bar{P}_A^n$, $n \geq 3$, and let A_v and A_w denote the arc sets (unions of directed cycles) corresponding to v and w. Then v and w are adjacent on $\bar{P}_A^n$ if and only if $A_v \cup A_w$ is a closed directed trail.*

Another example of such an adjacency characterization – now permutation oriented – is due to Padberg & Rao [1974]. If v is a vertex of $\bar{P}^n_A$, then π_v denotes the permutation of $\{1, \ldots, n\}$ corresponding to v, and by '$\circ$' we denote the usual composition of permutations.

Theorem 26 *Let v, w be two different vertices of $\bar{P}^n_A$, $n \geq 3$, then v and w are adjacent on $\bar{P}^n_A$ if and only if there exists a permutation π such that $\pi_v = \pi_w \circ \pi$ holds and π consists of a single cyclic permutation of length greater than 1 and possibly some cycles of length 1.*

In algebra it is well known that given any permutation π, one can generate a sequence $\pi_0 = \pi, \pi_1, \ldots, \pi_{n!} = \pi$ of permutations such that all permutations $\pi_1, \ldots, \pi_{n!}$ are distinct and $\pi_{i+1} = \pi_i \circ \tau$, where τ is a transposition. By Theorem 26, π_{i+1} and π_i are adjacent; thus we can conclude the following result.

Theorem 27 *The skeleton G^n_A of $\bar{P}^n_A$ is Hamiltonian, $n \geq 3$.*

An interesting result of Heller [1955] is the following.

Theorem 28 *If v is the vertex of $\bar{P}^n_A$ corresponding to the identity permutation, then the set of neighbors of v on P^n_A is precisely the set of incidence vectors of tours.*

With respect to P^n_T, no good necessary and sufficient criteria for adjacency are known. The following sufficient condition was given by Murty [1969].

Theorem 29 *Let S and T be two different tours in D_n. Then the incidence vectors x^S and x^T are adjacent on P^n_T if there is no other tour R such that $S \cap T \subseteq R \subseteq S \cup T$.*

Murty claimed that this condition is also necessary, but this was shown to be wrong; see Rao [1976], who also gave sufficient conditions for adjacency on P^n_T other than Theorem 29. Coloring criteria for general 0–1-polytopes and their relationship to the adjacency of tours of the traveling salesman are extensively discussed by Hausmann [1980]; see also Balas & Padberg [1979]. These latter conditions are often helpful to prove adjacency in practice.

On the other hand, it is quite unlikely that a 'good' characterization of adjacency on P^n_T or Q^n_T can ever be found. Papadimitriou [1978] has proved that the question 'Are two given vertices of P^n_T, of Q^n_T respectively, nonadjacent?' is $\mathcal{NP}$-complete.

The following theorem – based on a further adjacency criterion – is one of the deepest adjacency results for P^n_T and quite surprising. It is due to Padberg & Rao [1974].

Theorem 30 *The diameter of P^n_T is equal to 2 for $n \geq 6$, and equal to 1 for $3 \leq n \leq 5$.*

Geometrically interpreted, Theorem 30 states the following. Suppose two persons A and B are sitting on vertices of P^n_T. Person A wants to walk to person B, where walking is done by making a step from one vertex to an adjacent vertex (along an edge of the polytope). Then it is possible for A to reach B in at most two steps.

This does not mean, however, that the simplex method could get from a given basic solution to an optimal basic solution in two pivot steps by some proper column-and-row selection rule. Indeed, quite a large number of degenerate pivots (corresponding to one and the same vertex) may be required to get from one vertex to an optimal one. But Padberg & Rao [1974] have also shown that – if columns and rows are chosen properly – the number of necessary pivot steps is not too large.

Theorem 31 *Let v_1, v_2 be two vertices of P_T^n and let B_1 denote a basis corresponding to v_1. Then there is a sequence of pivot operations such that starting from B_1, a basis corresponding to v_2 is reached after at most $2n-1$ steps.*

So if we knew how to select rows and columns properly we could solve TSPs in a few simplex steps. A direct consequence of Theorem 31 is that the famous Hirsch conjecture [Dantzig, 1963] holds for P_T^n.

To our knowledge, nothing similar is known with respect to Q_T^n. Thus we can close this section with a few research problems.

Research problems
(a) *Determine the diameter of Q_T^n. (Conjecture:* $\mathrm{diam}(Q_T^n)=2$.*)*
(b) *Is the skeleton of Q_T^n Hamiltonian?*
(c) *What are the diameters of $\tilde{Q}_T^n$ and $\tilde{P}_T^n$?*

Exercises
19. Prove that the incidence vectors of the $|A|-2|V|+2$ directed tours obtained as outlined in the text following Theorem 20 are linearly independent.
20. (a) Prove that the nonnegativity constraints define facets of P_T^3, but only two different ones.
(b) Prove that every nonnegativity constraint defines a face of P_T^4 which is the intersection of two unique facets of P_T^4.
21. Let C be a cycle of length $3 \leq k \leq n-1$ in D_n. Let (i, j) be a diagonal of C. Prove that the coefficient a_{ij} obtained for (i, j) by the formula of Theorem 21 is 2.
22. (a) Prove that the digraph $D = (V, B)$ shown in Figure 8.12 is a maximal hypo-Hamiltonian digraph.
(b) Prove that the hypo-Hamiltonian inequality $n(B) \leq 5$ corresponding to D does not define a facet of $\tilde{P}_T^6$. (In fact, the face defined by this inequality has dimension 28. To be a facet it should have dimension 29.)

The Traveling Salesman Problem
Edited by E. L. Lawler, J. K. Lenstra,
A. H. G. Rinnooy Kan, D. B. Shmoys
© 1985 John Wiley & Sons Ltd.

9

Polyhedral computations

M. W. Padberg
New York University

M. Grötschel
Universität Augsburg

1   EQUIVALENCE OF OPTIMIZATION AND FACET IDENTIFICATION

This chapter focuses on the computational aspects of the polyhedral theory developed in the preceding chapter for the TSP. While in the previous chapter we were concerned with the problem of *describing* facet-inducing linear inequalities for the traveling salesman polytopes, we turn now to the problem of algorithmically *finding* facet-inducing linear inequalities. That is, we address the problem that one encounters if one wants to use the theoretical results of the preceding chapter in a cutting plane algorithm for the TSP using linear programming techniques.

After some introductory remarks concerning the number of facet-inducing linear inequalities and their algorithmic implications for the resolution of large-scale TSPs we discuss briefly the *equivalence* of optimization and

The first author's work was partially supported by the Università di Pisa and by the Consiglio Nazionale delle Ricerche, Italy.

(algorithmic) facet identification, a result which is based on the polynomial-time ellipsoid method of Khachian [1979] for linear programming problems, and which – in retrospect – has provided the theoretical backbone for the 'facet hunt' which began in the early 1970s for difficult combinatorial optimization problems [Padberg 1971, 1973; Pulleyblank 1973; Trotter 1973]. Then exact algorithms for the identification of subtour elimination and 2-matching constraints are given, as well as heuristic identification algorithms for comb inequalities. Finally, computational experiments using the above results are summarized. We use the same notation as in the previous chapter.

1.1   The number of facets of TSP polytopes and algorithmic implications

Except for the cases mentioned in Chapter 8, the exact numbers of facets of the traveling salesman polytopes are not known. One can, however, readily establish a (rather weak) upper bound on the number of facets for these polytopes. For instance, the polytope Q_T^n has at most

$$\binom{\frac{1}{2}(n-1)!}{\frac{1}{2}n(n-3)}$$

different facets. The bound is obtained by observing that there are $\frac{1}{2}(n-1)!$ different vertices (tours) of Q_T^n and that among those, possibly, any subset of $\frac{1}{2}n(n-3)$ vertices is linearly independent and thus generates a facet. However, the above bound is rather weak as some facets of Q_T^n contain considerably more than the minimum number of $\frac{1}{2}n(n-3)$ linearly independent tours needed in order to obtain a facet. In particular, one proves readily the following result.

Lemma 1   *Given an n-city symmetric TSP and a subtour elimination constraint $x(E(W)) \leqslant |W| - 1$, there are exactly $\frac{1}{2}w!(n-w)!$ tours satisfying $x(E(W)) = |W| - 1$, where $w = |W|$, and $2 \leqslant w \leqslant n - 2$.*

For the polytope P_T^n of the asymmetric TSP, one obtains similar statements quite easily.

Since the bound given above is rather weak, it is interesting to calculate the number of known different facets of the traveling salesman polytopes. We have done this for the polytope Q_T^n and the facets described in Theorem 14 of Chapter 8 for $n \leqslant 120$. The respective numbers are given in Table 9.1.

For Q_T^{120} the number of nonequivalent subtour elimination and comb constraints has been computed exactly. Including the nonnegativity constraints, this number is exactly

26792549076063489375554618994821987399578869037768
70780484651943295772470308627340156321170880759399
86913459296483643418942533445648036828825541887362
42799920969079258554704177287.

Table 9.1

No. of cities	No. of subtour elimination constraints cf. Theorem 14 (b) and (c) of Ch. 8	No. of comb constraints cf. Theorem 14 (d) of Ch. 8
6	25	60
7	56	2,100
8	119	42,840
9	246	667,800
10	501	8,843,940
15	16,368	1,993,711,339,620
20	0.5×10^6	1.5×10^{18}
30	0.5×10^9	1.5×10^{31}
40	0.5×10^{12}	1.5×10^{45}
50	0.5×10^{15}	10^{60}
120	0.6×10^{36}	2×10^{179}

The formulas to compute the respective numbers are given by Grötschel & Padberg [1979a]. We note that the numbers do not include the clique tree inequalities of Theorem 14(e) of Chapter 8, as at present we have no formula for the number of clique tree inequalities which are not comb inequalities. But, obviously, for reasonably large n there are many more possibilities to form clique tree inequalities than there are ways to form comb inequalities.

The simple story told by the above numbers is that, for the resolution of TSPs, linear programming techniques cannot be used in the *traditional* way which consists of listing explicitly all constraints over which we want to optimize. Ignoring for the moment the fact that we do not know a complete system of facet-inducing linear inequalities for the traveling salesman polytopes, it is already completely out of the question to *list* all *known* facet-inducing linear inequalities for the TSP and to solve the resulting linear program, because there are no computers available that are large enough to handle systems of linear inequalities of this size. In fact, there will never be such computers, since, for instance, the number of known facets of Q_T^{120} is about 10^{100} times the number of atoms of our universe. To abandon linear programming techniques for the resolution of TSPs on the basis of the above numbers – just because we cannot list and store all known facet-inducing linear inequalities – would be an equally erroneous conclusion to make, though a very common one, because historically, the exponential growth of the number of subtour elimination constraints is probably the reason why the seminal work by Dantzig, Fulkerson & Johnson [1954] has been ignored for such a long time. Indeed, in order to prove optimality of a vertex of Q_T^n, for example, all we really need is a *suitable* set of at most $\frac{1}{2}n(n-1)$ linear inequalities out of the immense universe of all possible facet-inducing linear inequalities.

Thus if we can prove optimality of a tour with respect to some set of at most $\frac{1}{2}n(n-1)$ facet-inducing linear inequalities, by the validity of these inequalities for Q_T^n, optimality of this tour with respect to Q_T^n follows *a fortiori*. And what is most interesting, these considerations remain correct for any combinatorial optimization problem when we wish to optimize a given linear objective function.

The inevitable conclusion is thus that *suitable* constraints for the TSP (as well as for other combinatorial optimization problems with a linear objective function) must be generated 'on the fly', i.e. as computation progresses, if one wants to employ linear programming techniques in the resolution of large scale TSPs or any other hard combinatorial optimization problem. This idea for the TSP, which was implemented by Dantzig, Fulkerson & Johnson [1954], gave rise to the cutting plane approach to integer programming and has led to the famous algorithmic proof of finite solvability of integer programming problems by Gomory [1963]. However, the cutting planes considered by Gomory – while guaranteeing finite convergence of the procedure – in general do not belong to a system of facet-inducing linear inequalities. As a result, convergence tends to be slow and, more importantly from a computational point of view, because of the great number of the nonzero coefficients of the cutting planes which have to be stored during the calculation, storage requirements simply explode.

It therefore appeared necessary to consider mathematically proven *good* cutting planes, namely facet-inducing linear inequalities, if the cutting plane idea was useful at all in actual computation. Every facet-inducing linear inequality belongs to a minimal system of linear inequalities describing the convex hull of the solution set of an integer program (cf. Section 1 of Chapter 8). Facet-inducing inequalities are the strongest possible valid cutting planes and hence the most useful cutting planes in linear programming based calculations, while arbitrary valid inequalities need not necessarily be considered in the solution of integer programming problems and thus should be avoided.

The problem we want to solve in an iterative procedure for the resolution of TSPs (or, likewise, for any other combinatorial optimization problem with linear objective function) using linear programming techniques, can be formulated in general terms as follows. As in Section 2.1 of Chapter 8, let E be a finite ground set and $\mathscr{I}$ be a nonempty set of subsets of E, and let

$$P_{\mathscr{I}} := \operatorname{conv}\{x^F \in \mathbb{R}^E \mid F \in \mathscr{I}\}$$

be the polytope given by the convex hull of the incidence vectors x^F of the elements of $\mathscr{I}$.

Facet identification problem   *Given a point $\bar{x} \in \mathbb{R}^E$ and a polytope $P_{\mathscr{I}}$, find a facet-inducing linear inequality $f^T x \leqslant f_0$ for $P_{\mathscr{I}}$ which is violated by $\bar{x}$, i.e. such that $f^T \bar{x} > f_0$, or prove that no such inequality exists, i.e. that $\bar{x} \in P_{\mathscr{I}}$.*

We can now state a general procedure for the resolution of combinatorial optimization problems using linear programming calculations which we could call a (dual) cutting plane procedure, but which we prefer to call a *relaxation* procedure because what one solves is indeed a sequence of relaxations of the underlying combinatorial problem.

Relaxation method for combinatorial problems

Step 1. (*Initialization*) Let (LP_0) be a valid linear programming relaxation of the combinatorial problem under consideration; set $k = 0$.

Step 2. (*LP solver*) Solve (LP_k); let x^k be an optimal solution to (LP_k).

Step 3. (*Facet identification*). Solve the facet identification problem for x^k and the polytope $P_{\mathcal{I}}$.

    Step 3.1. If one or more violated facet-inducing linear inequalities for $P_{\mathcal{I}}$ are found, define (LP_{k+1}) to be (LP_k) amended by the violated facet-inducing inequalities, set $k = k + 1$ and go to Step 2.

    Step 3.2. If a violated facet-inducing linear inequality does not exist, stop.

If a *finite* method for solving the linear programs is used in Step 2, the finiteness of the above method follows from the finiteness of the number of facet-inducing linear inequalities which 'in principle' can simply be listed and checked off one by one.

In an iterative procedure for the symmetric TSP, for instance, we can thus start with a linear programming relaxation of the problem where the objective function is specified by the given distance function c and the constraint set is initially empty or is the one given by the constraints

$$
\begin{aligned}
Ax &= \mathbf{2}, \\
0 \leqslant x_e \leqslant 1 \quad &\text{for all } e \in E,
\end{aligned}
\tag{1}
$$

where A is the vertex–edge incidence matrix of the complete undirected graph having n vertices. Now one proves readily the following result.

Lemma 2 *If the simplex method is used in Step 2 of the relaxation method, then an incidence vector $\bar{x}$ corresponding to an optimal tour is obtained in a finite number of iterations provided that a complete system of facet-inducing linear inequalities for Q_T^n is known.*

Of course, the obvious trouble with the relaxation method is that we do not know all the facet-inducing inequalities of Q_T^n or, more generally, of an arbitrary polytope $P_{\mathcal{I}}$. As a consequence we have to resort to branch and bound (or to some other enumerative technique) at some point during the calculation.

Surprising as it may seem, this idea works well in computational practice. The pertinent computational results for the TSP are summarized in Section 4 of this chapter. It should also be noted that the above approach has yielded good computational results for the optimization of sparse large-scale 0–1 linear programming problems having no special structure [Crowder, Johnson & Padberg, 1983], as well as for some other combinatorial optimization problems [Barahona & Maccioni, 1982; Grötschel, Jünger & Reinelt, 1984].

A less obvious drawback of the relaxation method is the following one. Even if a complete list of facet-inducing inequalities is known (for the TSP or any other combinatorial optimization problem with linear objective function), it is not obvious that the facet identification problem can be solved efficiently. Of course, it can evidently be solved *enumeratively* by listing all facet-inducing inequalities and checking them one by one for violation by the given point $\bar{x}$. But in most cases, even for polynomially solvable problems, the number of facets is exponential in the problem data (see Section 3 of Chapter 8); thus – disregarding possible difficulties with Step 2 – the linear programming based algorithm would be bad because Step 3 requires exponential time.

Thus, the question is: Under what conditions can the facet identification problem be solved by a good algorithm? The next two sections of this chapter give a satisfactory general answer to this fundamental question. We note for completeness that the facet identification problem has been solved by means of good algorithms for the b-matching problem with and without upper bounds by Padberg & Rao [1982], for the spanning tree problem by Padberg & Wolsey [1983], and for the matroid optimization problem by Cunningham [1984].

1.2 The ellipsoid method for linear programs

To discuss the fundamental relationship between optimization and facet identification we first review briefly the ellipsoid method for linear programs as developed by Khachian [1979]. (For a recent survey on computational aspects of the method we refer the reader to Bland, Goldfarb & Todd [1981] or Schrader [1982].) In the next section we discuss some of the theoretical consequences that this polynomially bounded algorithm for linear programming problems has for combinatorial optimization problems like the TSP. The material of this section and the next one is based on papers by Grötschel, Lovász & Schrijver [1981], Karp & Papadimitriou [1982] and Padberg & Rao [1985], though we will follow most closely the last paper.

To state the ellipsoid method for linear programs, we consider the linear program

$$\max\left\{\sum_{j=1}^{n} c_j x_j \ \middle|\ Ax \leq b\right\} \tag{2}$$

and denote the ith row of (A, b) as (a^i, b_i) for $i = 1, \ldots, m$. We assume that all data are *integers*, i.e. rational data are converted to integers by appropriate scaling, and, for simplicity, that A has full column rank which is the case, for example, if the nonnegativity constraints $x_j \geq 0$ for $j = 1, \ldots, n$ are among the constraints of (2). Let P denote the feasible set of (2) and suppose that we want to maximize $c^T x$ over the set

$$S = P \cap \left\{ x \in \mathbb{R}^n \;\middle|\; \sum_{j=1}^{n} x_j^2 \leq u^2 \right\},$$

where u is some positive number chosen to be large enough such that S contains all *basic* solutions to $Ax \leq b$. We define

$$z_L = -1 + u \sum_{j=1}^{n} \min\{0, c_j\},$$

$$\bar{c} = 1 + \max\{|c_j|, j = 1, \ldots, n\},$$

$$h \geq 2\bar{c} n^2 \Delta_A, \qquad h \text{ integer},$$

$$t = 4n^2 \lceil \log_2 h^2 u n^{-1/2} \rceil,$$

$$R = 16n \lceil \log_2 h u^{1/2} \rceil,$$

where $\Delta_A \geq 2$ is an integral upper bound on the absolute values of the determinants of the submatrices of the matrix A.

The following algorithm, ALG1(u, h), is one version of the ellipsoid method with approximate arithmetic for linear programs with integer data.

The ellipsoid method for linear programs ALG1(u, h)

Step 1. (*Initialization*) Set $x_j^0 = 0$ for $j = 1, \ldots, n$; $Q_0 = u I_n$ where I_n is the $n \times n$ identity matrix; $\bar{z} = z_L$, $k = 0$.

Step 2. (*Constraint identification*) If $a^i x^k \leq b_i + 1/h$ for all $i = 1, \ldots, m$, go to Step 3. Else let j be any index with $a^i x^k > b_i + 1/h$. Set $r = a^i$ and go to Step 4.

Step 3. (*Objective function as a constraint*) If $cx^k > \bar{z}$, replace $\bar{z}$ by cx^k and set $\bar{x} = x^k$. Set $r = -c$.

Step 4. (*Updating*) If $k = t$, go to Step 5. Else set

$$x^{k+1} = x^k - Q_k Q_k^T r^T / ((n+1) \|r Q_k\|),$$

$$Q_{k+1} \approx 2^{1/8n^2} (n/\sqrt{n^2 - 1}) Q_k \left(I_n - \left(1 - \sqrt{\frac{n-1}{n+1}}\right) Q_k^T r^T r Q_k / \|r Q_k\| \right),$$

where $\approx$ means that for each component the computation is carried out with a precision of R binary positions after the point. Set $k = k + 1$ and go to Step 2.

Step 5. (*Termination*) If $\bar{z} = z_L$, stop; the problem has no feasible solution. Else stop; $\bar{x}$ approximately solves the linear programming problem.

The algorithm ALG1(u, h) thus executes t iterations and, apart from the space requirements for storing the constraints of (2), it requires $O(n^2 R)$ bits of workspace. Both the running time and the workspace requirements are bounded by a polynomial function of n, $\log_2 h$ and $\log_2 u$. The parameters u

and h can assume different values, and the implications of different parameter settings are discussed next.

Let $D \geqslant 2$ be an integral upper bound on the absolute value of a determinant of a submatrix of (A, b). Then, if $\bar{x}$ is a basic solution to $Ax \leqslant b$, we have $|\bar{x}_j| \leqslant D$ for all $j = 1, \ldots, n$, and furthermore, $D \geqslant \Delta_A$ holds. Running the algorithm $ALG1(u, h)$ with the parameters

$$u = 2n^{3/2}\bar{c}D^3, \qquad h = 2n^2\bar{c}\Delta_A^2,$$

one can prove that (2) has an unbounded optimum solution if and only if the algorithm terminates with an objective function value $\bar{z} \geqslant n\bar{c}D$. This follows because we assume integrality of the data and because the initial ellipsoid contains all points $x \in \mathbb{R}^n$ satisfying

$$-2n\bar{c}D^3 \leqslant x_j \leqslant 2n\bar{c}D^3 \qquad \text{for } j = 1, \ldots, n.$$

If we conclude infeasibility or unboundedness, we have solved (2). Else, we run $ALG1(u, h)$ a second time with the additional upper and lower bounds $|x_j| \leqslant D$ for $j = 1, \ldots, n$, and the following parameters:

$$u = \sqrt{n}(D + 1), \qquad h = 2n^2\bar{c}\Delta_A^3.$$

Assuming for simplicity that (2) has a unique optimum over the feasible set of (2) – alternatively, we perturb the objective function of (2) slightly, as in Exercise 6 below – one can prove that we get an optimal solution to (2) which is basic to the system of linear inequalities $Ax \leqslant b$, $-D \leqslant x_j \leqslant D$ for $j = 1, \ldots, n$ by rounding the final trial solution $\bar{x}$ obtained from $ALG1(u, h)$ using the method of continued fractions. If the optimal solution x obtained this way satisfies $-D < x_j < D$ for all $j = 1, \ldots, n$, then we are done. Else, because of the perturbation device mentioned above, the optimum of the perturbed objective function may have become unbounded over the constraint set $Ax \leqslant b$ of (2) even though the original objective function is bounded, i.e. some of the components of the solution x may be equal to $\pm D$. However, one can show that starting from the solution x obtained by $ALG1(u, h)$, one can find an optimal basic solution to (2) with a computational effort which remains polynomially bounded in the desired parameters. Thus by running the ellipsoid method $ALG1(u, h)$ at most twice we can *solve* the linear program (2).

Theorem 1 *There exists an algorithm based on the ellipsoid method $ALG1(u, h)$ which determines infeasibility or unboundedness of (2) or finds an optimal basic solution to (2) and whose time and workspace requirements depend linearly on the number m of constraints of (2) and polynomially upon the problem parameters n, $\log_2 \bar{c}$ and $\log_2 D$.*

The length L of the input data of (2) for a binary computer is at least

$$L = 1 + \log_2(mn) + \sum_{i=1}^{m} \log_2(|b_i| + 1) + \sum_{j=1}^{n} \log_2(|c_j| + 1) + \sum_{i,j} \log_2(|a_{ij}| + 1).$$

Using Hadamard's inequality (cf. Marcus & Minc [1964]) to estimate D, it can be shown that L is bounded from below by a polynomial function of the parameters $m, n, \log_2 \bar{c}$ and $\log_2 D$ of Theorem 1. Thus the theorem implies the existence of a polynomial algorithm for (2) in the usual sense of the definition of polynomiality of algorithms [Garey & Johnson, 1979].

1.3 Facet identification and optimization

The fact that the ellipsoid method for linear programs does *not* depend on the input length L of (2), but rather upon the parameters specified in Theorem 1, makes it a possible instrument for answering the fundamental question raised in Section 1.1 concerning the relationship between optimization and facet identification. As pointed out earlier, the linear programming formulation of most combinatorial problems involves a number m of constraints which depends exponentially upon the number n of variables, thus producing linear programs of the form (2) whose length L grows exponentially with n, as in the case of the TSP. The parameters other than m appearing in Theorem 1, however, can be estimated using n and the largest absolute value of the numbers of the data of (2), and are thus independent of the actual number of constraints. In order to (theoretically) successfully apply the ellipsoid method to combinatorial optimization problems, we must thus be able to

 (i) remove the explicit dependence on the number m of constraints of the linear programming formulation of the combinatorial problem; and
(ii) prove that the coefficients of the linear programming formulation of the combinatorial problem remain reasonably small.

If both difficulties can be removed, we can prove the existence of polynomial algorithms for combinatorial optimization problems, under the assumption that complete inequality systems for the associated polytopes are known. As we shall see, the second problem (ii) is a minor one, while the first one is indeed equivalent to the solvability of a combinatorial optimization problem by a good algorithm.

Consider now the combinatorial optimization problem

$$\max\{p^T x \mid x \in P_{\mathscr{G}}\} \tag{3}$$

where $p \in \mathbb{R}^E$ is a vector with integer components p_j for $j = 1, \ldots, |E|$ and $P_{\mathscr{G}}$ is defined in Section 1.1. For notational simplicity denote $n = |E|$. Let $r \leqslant n$ denote the dimension of $P_{\mathscr{G}}$. In this section only, we shall call any valid inequality which is satisfied by *at least* r affinely independent 0–1 points of $P_{\mathscr{G}}$ a *facet* of $P_{\mathscr{G}}$. This definition differs slightly from our earlier one where *at least* is replaced by *exactly*. It is more convenient to work here with this definition because it means that we need not distinguish between the equations and inequalities which define $P_{\mathscr{G}}$ (cf. Section 1 of Chapter 8).

We will assume without loss of generality that $P_{\mathscr{G}}$ is nonempty. If we let

$z_U \geqslant 0$ (z_L, respectively) denote a proper upper (lower, respectively) bound on the linear form $p^T x$ over $0 \leqslant x_e \leqslant 1$ for all $e \in E$, we can introduce a new 0–1 variable x_{n+1} having an objective function coefficient $p_{n+1} = z_L - z_U$. (Remember: $n = |E|$.) If we modify E by adjoining a new element $n + 1$ and changing $\mathcal{I}$ by declaring all incidence vectors $(x^F, 0)$ with $F \in \mathcal{I}$ and the vector $(0, 1)$ *feasible* where 0 is the vector with n components equal to 0, the problem in $n + 1$ variables always has a feasible solution. The original problem is feasible if and only if the objective function value over the problem in $n + 1$ variables is greater than z_L. Increasing the dimension of the problem by one does not change the question we are addressing in any significant way.

As we know (for instance, from Weyl [1935]), we can describe $P_{\mathcal{I}}$ by a system of linear inequalities. More precisely, one can prove the following theorem.

Theorem 2   *There exists a system of facet-defining linear inequalities for $P_{\mathcal{I}}$ such that the absolute value of each component is an integer less than or equal to*

$$\Xi = n^{n/2}.$$

It follows from Theorem 2 that for a suitably chosen system of facet-defining inequalities for $P_{\mathcal{I}}$, the logarithm (base 2) of the absolute value of a nonzero coefficient is bounded by a polynomial in the number of variables n and this answers problem (ii) above completely.

We will thus use the term *facet-defining inequality for $P_{\mathcal{I}}$* to mean only facet-defining inequalities with integer coefficients whose absolute values are less than or equal to Ξ.

Denote by $Ax \leqslant b$ a complete system of facet-defining inequalities for the polytope $P_{\mathcal{I}}$. Then problem (3) is equivalent to the linear program

$$\max\left\{ \sum_{j=1}^{n} p_j x_j \,\middle|\, Ax \leqslant b \right\}.$$

In order to get a unique optimum solution to this linear program, perturb the objective functions coefficients as follows:

$$c_j = 2^n p_j + 2^{n-j}, \qquad \text{for } j = 1, \dots, n,$$

and consider the corresponding linear program with integer data,

$$\max\left\{ \sum_{j=1}^{n} c_j x_j \,\middle|\, Ax \leqslant b \right\}. \tag{4}$$

Let $\Delta_A \geqslant 2$ be an integral upper bound on the absolute value of a determinant of a submatrix of A. With the above convention it follows from Hadamard's inequality that

$$\Delta_A \leqslant n^{n/2} \Xi^n = n^{(n^2+n)/2}$$

holds. Let z_L be a proper lower bound on the optimum value of (4) and let $\bar{p} = 1 + \max\{|p_j|, j = 1, \ldots, n\}$.

It then follows by choosing the parameters

$$u = 2\sqrt{n}, \qquad h = \bar{p}n^2 2^{n+2}\Delta_A$$

that the ellipsoid method ALG1(u, h) finds an approximate optimal solution $\bar{x}$ to (4) in time and workspace requirements which depend polynomially on n, $\log_2 \bar{p}$ and linearly on m, the number of constraints of (4). Moreover, the approximate solution $\bar{x}$ to (4) can be rounded to an optimal integer solution x^* to (3) by setting $x_j^* = \lfloor x_j + 0.5 \rfloor$ for $j = 1, \ldots, n$.

As discussed previously, the dependence on the number m of constraints of (4) is linear. It is clear that the entire computational effort for the solution of (4) is bounded by a polynomial function of n and $\log_2 \bar{p}$ if the constraint identification in Step 2 of the ellipsoid algorithm can be carried out by some *subroutine* whose computational effort is bounded by a polynomial function of n and $\log_2 \bar{p}$. The constraint identification step, however, is exactly the facet identification problem – except that we permit a small error given by the term $1/h$ in the respective constraints. The vector $\bar{x}$ for which the facet identification has to be carried out is a *rational* vector whose components require $O(R)$ bits in the binary representation, where R is the required precision of the algorithm and R is a polynomial function in the above parameters. Thus if the facet identification problem can be solved for a rational vector $\bar{x}$ and the polytope $P_{\mathcal{I}}$ by an algorithm whose running time and workspace requirements depend polynomially upon n, $\log_2 \bar{p}$ and the length of the binary encoding of $\bar{x}$, then it follows that (3) can be optimized by an algorithm which is polynomial in the desired parameters, i.e. we can resolve problem (i) introduced above.

The preceding discussion partially settles the question concerning the relationship between facet identification and optimization. It is a most interesting fact – whose proof is too technical to be discussed here – that the above statement can be reversed as well.

Theorem 3 *The combinatorial optimization problem* (3) *can be solved by a polynomial algorithm for any integer vector p if and only if the facet identification problem can be solved by a polynomial algorithm for any rational vector $\bar{x}$.*

Thus Theorem 3 can be used to prove the existence of good algorithms for (3) by exhibiting good algorithms for the facet identification problem, and vice versa. For instance, the above theorem implies the existence of a good algorithm for the facet identification problem of the vertex packing problem in claw-free graphs because there is a polynomial algorithm for such problems [Minty, 1980]. Yet preliminary studies of the associated polytope by Giles & Trotter [1981] have shown how complex this polytope is, while leaving the facet identification problem unanswered. Its solution remains an

interesting challenge. On the other hand, the facet identification problem
has been resolved satisfactorily for the b-matching problem, the spanning
tree problem and the matroid optimization problem, thus yielding polynomial algorithms for these problems which are different from the previously
known ones. As we shall see, this has interesting implications for the TSP.

While our discussion here has concentrated on finding facets of the
underlying polytope $P_{\mathcal{g}}$, it is clear from the discussion that we need not
restrict ourselves to facet-defining inequalities. Two properties, however, are
crucial to the argument, namely: (i) the totality of the linear constraints
considered must define the polytope $P_{\mathcal{g}}$ (or do so at least locally for some
optimizing point of $P_{\mathcal{g}}$), and (ii) the length of the coefficients of the linear
constraints *must not* grow exponentially in the problem parameters. Thus
any set of *valid* linear inequalities satisfying (i) and (ii) permit us to arrive at
the same conclusion. Using this fact, Grötschel, Lovász & Schrijver [1981]
have derived polynomial algorithms for various problems on perfect graphs.
It is therefore worthwhile to keep in mind that *for theoretical purposes* it
suffices to work with linear inequalities that do the job. However, as the
experience with earlier cutting plane methods has demonstrated, practical
computational considerations suggest that best possible linear inequalities,
facet-defining linear inequalities, should be used because the latter are the
tightest constraints possible and typically have the additional advantage of
sparsity of the nonzero coefficients, thus permitting storage requirements to
be kept at a minimum.

1.4   General computational considerations

The polynomial-time ellipsoid method for linear programs has permitted us
to answer the fundamental question concerning the relationship between
optimization and facet identification, thus putting linear programming
techniques for the solution of combinatorial optimization problems on a
sound theoretical basis.

However, given the current state of the development of the ellipsoid
method, it is an undisputed fact that the simplex method is superior in
numerical computation. Part of the reason for this statement rests with the
fact that the polynomial bound applies to the worst-case situation. Practical
problems arising in combinatorial problem solving hardly qualify for the
attribute 'worst-case'. Furthermore, the analysis of algorithms is an asymptotic theory, and therefore, is concerned with the behavior of algorithms for
large problem sizes. More importantly, sparsity of the constraint matrix,
special structure of the constraint matrix, the possibility of using heuristically
obtained solutions to speed up convergence, and so forth, are approaches
which by now, 35 years after the invention of the simplex method, are
integrated to a very large degree into existing software for the solution of
linear programming problems. Mathematical programming software products, such as CDC's code APEX, IBM's software system MPSX-MIP/370,

Ketron's MPSIII, SCICON's code SCICONIX, Sperry Univac's FMPS, etc.,
are all highly developed products, and are the outcome of years of effort
that combined the skills of many mathematicians, computer scientists and
computer programmers. It is therefore not only natural but also advisable
to use such software systems as building blocks for the practical solution of
difficult combinatorial optimization problems. More precisely, in Step 2 of
the relaxation method for combinatorial optimization problems we propose
to use the *most efficient* linear programming solver that is available.

This implies in particular that we favor a *dual* cutting plane approach
over the *primal* cutting plane approach, though this is partly due to the fact
that a primal cutting plane approach requires a different set of linear
programming tools than are available. (For the terminology we refer the
reader to Garfinkel & Nemhauser [1972].) The intuitive appeal of a primal
cutting-plane procedure stems from the fact that for many practical combinatorial optimization problems, heuristics can be used to find a good or
sometimes even, unknowingly, an optimal solution to the problem at hand.
In an attempt to *prove optimality* of the heuristically obtained solution x, one
can therefore start the linear programming calculations at the extreme point
x of $P_{\mathcal{G}}$ obtained heuristically, and iterate by cutting off adjacent fractional
solutions by hyperplanes which contain x, until either optimality of x is
proven or a better adjacent integer solution is found. In the latter case, one
restarts the whole procedure at the new integer solution. If a complete list of
facet-inducing linear inequalities is known, the procedure can be implemented, for example, in the framework of a modified simplex method,
and one need only solve the following facet identification problem.

Primal facet identification problem *Given a point $\hat{x} \in \mathbb{R}^E$ and an extreme
point $x^* \in \mathbb{R}^E$ of the polytope $P_{\mathcal{G}}$, find a facet-inducing linear inequality
$f^T x \leq f_0$ for $P_{\mathcal{G}}$ such that $f^T \hat{x} > f_0$ and $f^T x^* = f_0$ hold, or prove that no such
inequality exists.*

We note that for the cases where the facet identification problem has been
solved by exact algorithms, the same methods apply to answer the primal
facet identification problem (see Exercise 7).

In a computational study [Padberg & Hong, 1980] a primal cutting
plane approach was employed and this required the writing of a simplex
code of their own. In more computational studies [Grötschel, 1977a, 1980b;
Crowder & Padberg, 1980; Crowder, Johnson & Padberg, 1983] a dual
cutting plane approach was adopted and IBM's system MPSX/370 was used
to solve the linear programs. Based on this experience we prefer the dual
cutting plane approach, last but not least since the dual approach permits
one to treat the linear programming routine as a 'black box' in combinatorial problem solving.

This leaves the question of how to solve the facet identification problem.
In order to make the solution of this problem operational we distinguish

different types or classes of facet-inducing linear inequalities. The subtour elimination constraints form a first class of facets of the TSP, the 2-matching constraints a second class, the comb constraints a third class, and so forth. The reason that we make such a distinction is not because of the chronological order in which these classes of facet-inducing inequalities were found, but rather, as we shall see, *different algorithms* are needed to solve the facet identification problem for these different classes of facet-inducing inequalities. This means that Step 3 of the relaxation method for combinatorial optimization problems must be thought of as a whole set of different subroutines which are called upon when needed. Thus we could dub the whole preceding a *multi-algorithmic approach* to combinatorial problem solving.

It is clear that the basic scheme of the procedure is rather simple to implement. For, regardless of the *number* of subroutines required in Step 3 of the relaxation method, once the data structures are set up for a single subroutine to do the facet identification, we simply add more and more subroutines as our knowledge of exact (or heuristic) solution procedures for the identification of different types of facets increases. Furthermore, since the basic outline is the same for any combinatorial optimization problem, we can use the same main routine for quite different combinatorial optimization problems simply by exchanging the subroutines used for the facet identification phase.

Since currently available linear programming software permits the user to revise the linear program by generating, for instance, new constraints, the implementation of the above ideas is feasible with almost any software system. However, it appears that there are inefficiencies in the present-day codes concerning the addition of new constraints. These inefficiencies do not prohibit the implementation, but it appears that software systems especially designed to handle constraint generation would enhance the performance. Most linear programming software systems were designed originally with a fixed number of rows in mind, where the addition of new rows was the exception rather than the rule, as is the case here.

Exercises

1. Prove Lemma 1.
2. Given any linear program (LP) with p nonnegative variables and q linear constraints having a finite optimum solution, prove that there exists a linear program (LP*) with (at most) p linear constraints obtained from (LP) by dropping (at least) q of the $p+q$ linear constraints of (LP) such that every optimal solution to (LP) is also an optimal solution to (LP*). Moreover, every optimal basic solution to (LP*) is also an optimal basic solution to (LP).
3. Prove Lemma 2.
4. Prove the more general statement analogous to Lemma 2 for an arbitrary

polytope P_g associated with any combinatorial optimization problem having a linear objective function (cf. Section 2.1 of Chapter 8).

5. (a) Prove that there exists a system of facet-defining inequalities for the traveling salesman polytope Q_T^n such that each coefficient is a nonnegative number less than or equal to $n^{n(n-3)/4}$. (b) Prove Theorem 2 if $\dim(P_g) = n$ and $\mathscr{I}$ is an independence system. (*Hint:* Give an extreme point characterization of the facet-defining inequalities of Q_T^n (P_g, respectively). Then use Cramer's rule and Hadamard's inequality.)

6. Prove that (4) has a unique optimum solution and that the optimum solution to (4) is optimum for (3).

7. (a) Show that the primal facet-identification problem can be reduced to solving the facet-identification problem for some point $\bar{x} = (1 - \mu)x^* + \mu\hat{x}$ where $0 < \mu \leq 1$. (b) Using the notation of Section 1.3 and assuming that $\hat{x} \in \mathbb{R}^E$ has rational components, give a formula for a value μ of part (a) that works.

2 IDENTIFICATION OF SUBTOUR ELIMINATION CONSTRAINTS

When restricted to subtour elimination constraints, the facet-identification problem can be formulated in the case of the TSP as follows, where $G = (V, E)$ is the complete graph on n vertices.

Subtour problem *Given a point $\bar{x} \in \mathbb{R}^E$ satisfying $0 \leq \bar{x}_e \leq 1$ for all $e \in E$, find a set $W \subseteq V$, $2 \leq |W| \leq n - 1$, such that $\bar{x}(E(W)) > |W| - 1$ holds, or prove that no such $W \subseteq V$ exists.*

Note that we have assumed for simplicity that the point $\bar{x} \in \mathbb{R}^E$ satisfies $0 \leq \bar{x}_e \leq 1$ for all $e \in E$ because there are only $2|E|$ such constraints and thus they can be checked in time polynomial in $|E|$.

In the asymmetric case we have the same problem except that E is replaced by A throughout in the subtour problem. Using the mapping $f(y) = x$ defined in Section 5.2 of Chapter 8, one reduces the problem of finding a violated subtour elimination constraint for the asymmetric TSP to the subtour problem by replacing each pair of arcs (i, j) and (j, i) by the (undirected) edge $e = \{i, j\}$ and giving this edge the weight $\bar{\bar{x}}_e = \bar{x}_{ij} + \bar{x}_{ji}$.

Lemma 3 *Let $\bar{x} \in \mathbb{R}^A$ be given and let $\bar{\bar{x}} \in \mathbb{R}^E$ be obtained by the above symmetrization.*

(a) *There exists a subtour elimination constraint for P_T^n which is violated by $\bar{x}$ if and only if there exists a subtour elimination constraint for Q_T^n which is violated by $\bar{\bar{x}}$.*

(b) *If $\bar{x} \in \mathbb{R}^A$ satisfies $x(\vec{\delta}(v)) = x(\vec{\delta}(v)) = 1$ for all $v \in V$, then $\bar{\bar{x}}(\delta(v)) = 2$ holds for all $v \in V$.*

(c) *Let $\hat{x} \in \mathbb{R}^E$ satisfy (1) and let $x^* \in \mathbb{R}^E$ be the incidence vector of a tour, i.e. x^* is an extreme point of Q_T^n. Then there exists a set $W \subseteq V$ with $2 \leq |W| \leq n - 1$ such that $\hat{x}(E(W)) > |W| - 1$ and $x^*(E(W)) = |W| - 1$ hold if and only if*

there exists $W \subseteq V$ *with* $2 \leq |W| \leq n-1$ *such that* $\bar{x}(E(W)) > |W| - 1$ *holds,*
where $\bar{x} = \frac{1}{2}\hat{x} + \frac{1}{2}x^*$.

Thus we need to consider only the case of the symmetric TSP.

As part (c) of Lemma 3 shows, the primal facet identification problem when restricted to subtour elimination constraints, can be reduced to the subtour problem as well. Exercise 9 extends the above symmetrization technique to constraints other than subtour elimination constraints.

The facet identification problem for the 1-tree polytope Q_{1T}^n and its monotonization $\tilde{Q}_{1T}^n$ (cf. Section 3.1 of Chapter 8) is closely related to the foregoing and can be broken into two parts. First, there are only polynomially many constraints involving the special vertex 1 of the underlying graph. Thus they can be checked in polynomial time. Second, the exponentially many constraints (14) of Section 3.1 of Chapter 8 do not involve the special vertex 1. We can thus delete vertex 1 and all edges incident to it. The facet identification problem for Q_{1T}^n and $\tilde{Q}_{1T}^n$, respectively, then becomes precisely the subtour problem on the smaller graph *except* that W is permitted to equal the full vertex set of the smaller graph. In terms of the subtour problem, this means that the cardinality restriction $|W| \leq n-1$ must be dropped to deal with this case. Furthermore, in the case of the branching polytope $\tilde{P}_B^n$, the antibranching polytope $\tilde{P}_B^n$, the arborescence polytope P_B^n and the antiarborescence polytope P_B^n (cf. Section 3.2 of Chapter 8), one proceeds likewise by dropping the two special vertices 1 and $n+1$ and using the symmetrization technique described above. In this way, the facet identification problem for the exponentially many constraints (28) of Chapter 8 becomes precisely the problem we have just discussed.

We discuss in Section 2.1 a *heuristic* procedure for the solution of the subtour problem and its variant as necessary for the 1-tree polytope. In many cases this heuristic solves the problem. Moreover, if it does not solve it, then it frequently brings about a reduction in the *size* of the problem which has to be solved by an exact algorithm. In Section 2.2 we state *exact* algorithms for the identification of subtour elimination constraints: The first one deals with the specific case of the symmetric TSP; that is, we assume that the point $\bar{x} \in \mathbb{R}^E$ of the subtour problem satisfies the equations of (1). In particular, here we are looking for a *nonempty proper* subset $W \subset V$ which does the job, or we want to prove that no such subset exists. The second algorithm addresses the problem for the 1-tree polytope where the point $\bar{x} \in \mathbb{R}^E$ need not satisfy the equations of (1) and where we are looking for a *nonempty* set $W \subseteq V$ which does the job. In this case, however, W may be equal to V.

2.1 A heuristic for subtour elimination constraints

Let $\bar{x} \in \mathbb{R}^E$ satisfy $\bar{x}_e \geq 0$ for all $e \in E$. Interpret $\bar{x}_e$ as the *weight* of edge e. Edges having a weight of 0 are of no interest to us here and we denote by $G(\bar{x}) = (V, E(\bar{x}))$ the partial graph of $G = (V, E)$ induced by the edges $e \in E$ having $\bar{x}_e > 0$.

Lemma 4 (a) *Suppose that the point* $\bar{x} \in \mathbb{R}^E$ *satisfies* (1). *Then the vertex set of every connected component of* $G(\bar{x})$ *defines a violated subtour elimination constraint if the graph* $G(\bar{x})$ *is disconnected.*
(b) *Suppose that the point* $\bar{x} \in \mathbb{R}^E$ *does not satisfy* (1). *There exists a nonempty set of* $W \subseteq V$ *such that* $\bar{x}(E(W)) > |W| - 1$, *if and only if there exists a nonempty set* W^*, *where* W^* *is contained in a connected component of* $G(\bar{x})$, *such that* $\bar{x}(E(W^*)) > |W^*| - 1$.

Thus we can assume that $G(\bar{x})$ is connected. Let $e \in E$ be any edge of $G(\bar{x})$ such that $\bar{x}_e \geq 1$. (We note that if $\bar{x}_e > 1$ holds for an edge $e = \{i, j\}$, then the set $W = \{i, j\}$ solves the subtour problem.) Clearly, edges with value 1 or bigger play a special role because of the form of the constraints $x(E(W)) \leq |W| - 1$. Indeed, we can shrink such edges away, thus reducing the size of the hard part of the subtour problem. To do so we carry out the following steps in sequence.

Shrinking an edge $e = \{i, j\}$ *of* $G(\bar{x})$

Step 1. Replace vertices i and j by a single vertex i_1.
Step 2. Every pair of edges $e = \{i, k\}$ and $e' = \{j, k\}$ is replaced by a single edge $e^* = \{i_1, k\}$ with weight $\bar{x}_{e*}' = \bar{x}_e + \bar{x}_{e'}$.
Step 3. All other edges $\{i, l\}$ and $\{j, h\}$ of G, respectively, are replaced by the edges $\{i_1, l\}$ and $\{i_1, h\}$, respectively, and keep their old weights.

Denote by $G' = (V', E')$ the graph obtained from $G = (V, E)$ by shrinking edge e. Let $\bar{x}' \in \mathbb{R}^{E'}$ be the vector of weights that results from steps 2 and 3, and call $G(\bar{x}') = (V', E'(\bar{x}'))$ the partial graph induced by the edges $e \in E'$ having $x_e' > 0$.
    It follows that $G(\bar{x}')$ is connected if $G(\bar{x})$ is connected. More importantly, one can prove the following lemma.

Lemma 5   *There exists* $W \subseteq V$, $W \neq \{i, j\}$, *such that* $\bar{x}(E(W)) > |W| - 1$ *holds, if and only if there exists a set* $W^* \subseteq V'$ *such that* $\bar{x}'(E'(W^*)) > |W^*| - 1$ *holds when an edge* $e = \{i, j\}$ *with* $\bar{x}_e \geq 1$ *is shrunk.*

Thus the shrinking operation suggests the following reduction procedure for the solution of the subtour problem.

A heuristic for the identification of subtour elimination constraints

Step 1. Given $\bar{x} \in \mathbb{R}^E$, $\bar{x} \geq 0$, set up the graph $G(\bar{x}) = (V, E(\bar{x}))$.
Step 2. If $\bar{x}_e < 1$ holds for all $e \in E(\bar{x})$ or if $|V| = 1$ holds, stop. If for some $e \in E(\bar{x})$, $\bar{x}_e > 1$ holds, stop: The set of original vertices corresponding to the vertices of edge e defines a set W such that $x(E(W)) > |W| - 1$ holds. Else let $e \in E(\bar{x})$ be such that $\bar{x}_e = 1$.
Step 3. Shrink edge e to get a new weight vector $\bar{x}'$ and the graph $G(\bar{x}')$. Replace $\bar{x}$ by $\bar{x}'$, $G(\bar{x})$ by $G(\bar{x}')$, and go to Step 2.

Using Lemma 5 one proves readily the following properties of the shrinking heuristic.

Lemma 6   *Given a graph $G = (V, E)$ and a point $\bar{x} \in \mathbb{R}^E$ satisfying $0 \leqslant \bar{x}_e \leqslant 1$ for all $e \in E$, denote by $G^0 = (V^0, E^0)$ the graph obtained by applying the shrinking heuristic to G and let x^0 be the vector of the respective edge weights.*
(a) If $|V^0| = 1$, then there does not exist a nonempty subset $W \subseteq V$ such that $\bar{x}(E(W)) > |W| - 1$ holds.
(b) If $|V^0| = 2$, then there does not exist a nonempty proper subset $W \subseteq V$ such that $\bar{x}(E(W)) > |W| - 1$ holds.
(c) If $|V^0| \geqslant 3$ and there exists a nonempty (a nonempty and proper, respectively) subset $W \subseteq V$ such that $\bar{x}(E(W)) > |W| - 1$ holds, then there exists a nonempty (a nonempty and proper, respectively) subset $W^* \subseteq V^0$ such that $x^0(E^0(W^*)) > |W^*| - 1$. In other words, there exists a subtour elimination constraint violated by $\bar{x}$ in the original graph G if and only if there exists a subtour elimination constraint violated by x^0 in the reduced graph G^0.

The shrinking heuristic for the identification of violated subtour elimination constraints has been considered by Crowder & Padberg [1980] and was found to be very effective. A similar procedure was used by Land [1979]. Moreover, if the calculations of this algorithm are carefully implemented, then the algorithm requires a total computational effort which is polynomially bounded. We leave the calculation of the polynomial bound as an exercise to the reader. If several violated subtour elimination constraints are found, then it is advisable to generate all of them except, of course, equivalent ones. To minimize storage requirements one should store the subtour elimination constraint on $V - W$ rather than the one on W if $|W| > \lceil n/2 \rceil$.

We note for completeness that Padberg & Hong [1980] have given two further heuristics which (sometimes) solve the *primal* facet identification problem when restricted to subtour elimination constraints. The procedures are simple to program and have been found effective in actual computation. However, they are geared to the primal cutting plane approach to the TSP, and the reader is referred to Padberg & Hong [1980, Section 4.1] for details. One verifies readily that there are at most polynomially many possible subtour constraints for the primal facet identification problem, and thus one can effectively enumerate all possibilities.

2.2 A polynomial algorithm for subtour elimination constraints

The shrinking heuristic does not always solve the subtour problem. Because of the properties described in Lemma 6(c), however, the heuristic can always be carried out prior to the execution of an exact algorithm. It should always be carried out prior to any further calculation because of the reduction in problem size that is generally achieved.

The solution of the subtour problem is more difficult than it may appear.

To give a complete answer we first treat the case where $\bar{x} \in \mathbb{R}^E$ satisfies (1) and then discuss the general case of arbitrary $\bar{x} \in \mathbb{R}^E$, because it is of interest if we want to optimize over the 1-tree polytope Q_{1T}^n or its monotonization $\tilde{Q}_{1T}^n$ introduced in Section 3.1 of Chapter 8. In both cases, however, we may assume that $\bar{x} \in \mathbb{R}^E$ satisfies $0 \leq \bar{x}_e < 1$ for all $e \in E$, i.e. that the heuristic has been applied already. If $\bar{x} \in \mathbb{R}^E$ satisfies (1), then by summing over all vertices in some set $W \subseteq V$ we get

$$2\bar{x}(E(W)) + \bar{x}(\{W : V - W\}) = 2\,|W|$$

where

$$\{W : V - W\} = \{e \in E \mid e \text{ has exactly one end in } W\}$$

is the *cut-set* defined by W. The expression $\bar{x}(\{W : V - W\})$ is the *capacity* of the cut-set and we abbreviate it by $\bar{x}(W : V - W)$. One can show that the subtour problem is equivalent to the following cut problem.

Cut problem   *Given $\bar{x} \in \mathbb{R}^E$ satisfying $0 \leq \bar{x}_e < 1$ for all $e \in E$ and the equations* (1), *find a nonempty proper subset W of V such that $\bar{x}(W : V - W) < 2$ holds, or prove that no such $W \subseteq V$ exists.*

Consequently, what we are interested in is finding a *minimum capacity cut-set* in the graph $G(\bar{x})$ where the capacities are given by the weights $\bar{x}_e$, $e \in E$. If the minimum cut-set in $G(\bar{x})$ has a capacity which is greater than or equal to 2, then we conclude that there exists no subtour elimination constraint that is violated by $\bar{x}$. Else a vertex set W given by a minimum capacity cut-set defines a violated subtour elimination constraint. The determination of a minimum capacity cut-set in an undirected graph can be carried out by an algorithm given by Gomory & Hu [1961] which we discuss next.

Let $u \neq v \in V$ be any two vertices of G and consider the problem of finding a minimum cut-set:

$$\min\{\bar{x}(W : V - W) \mid W \subseteq V, u \in W, v \in V - W\}$$

separating vertices u and v or, for short, the problem of finding a minimum (u, v)-cut in G. Due to the famous maximum flow–minimum cut theorem (see e.g. Ford & Fulkerson [1962] or Lawler [1976]), the calculation of a minimum (u, v)-cut can be carried out by calculating the maximum flow from u to v (or from v to u, as the underlying graph is symmetric). Thus, considering all possible pairs of vertices of G, we can find the *minimum minimorum* among all cuts $\{W : V - W\}$ satisfying $W \neq \varnothing$ and $V - W \neq \varnothing$ (i.e. a minimum cut-set in the graph G) with $\frac{1}{2}|V|(|V| - 1)$ maximum flow calculations. The Gomory & Hu algorithm reduces this computation to at most $|V| - 1$ maximum flow calculations.

We state their algorithm in a somewhat more general form which is due to Hu [1969, p. 139] to solve the problem

$$\min\{\min\{\bar{x}(W : V - W) \mid W \subseteq V, u \in W, v \in V - W\} \mid u \neq v, u \in N, v \in N\}$$

where $N \subseteq V$ is a set of specified vertices of V called *terminal vertices* of the graph G.

Minimum cut algorithm

Input: An undirected connected graph $G = (V, E)$ with capacities $\bar{x}_e \geq 0$ for all $e \in E$ and a subset $N \subseteq V$ of terminal vertices.

Step 0. (*Initialize*) $L = \{0\}$, $G^0 = G$, $N^0 = N$, G_T has one vertex corresponding to G^0.

Step 1. If $L = \varnothing$, stop. Else let $l = \min\{j \mid j \in L\}$, $t = \max\{j \mid j \in L\}$.

Step 2. If $|N^l| \leq 1$, replace L by $L - \{l\}$ and go to Step 1. Else choose $u \neq v$, $u \in N^l$, $v \in N^l$.

Step 3. Calculate a minimum capacity (u, v)-cut-set $\{M : V^l - M\}$ using a maximum flow algorithm (V^l is the vertex set of G^l) and let v^l be its capacity.

Step 4. Create a new graph G^{t+1} (and a new graph G^{t+2}, respectively) by shrinking all edges of G^l in $V^l - M$ (in M, respectively) using the procedure given above, thus getting a new pseudo-vertex in each new graph. Let N^{t+1} (N^{t+2}, respectively) be the terminal vertices that G^{t+1} (G^{t+2}, respectively) inherit from G^l excepting those contained in the pseudo-vertices. Replace L by $L \cup \{t+1, t+2\} - \{l\}$

Step 5. Split the vertex of G_T corresponding to G^l into two vertices corresponding to G^{t+1} and G^{t+2}, respectively, and connect them by an edge with weight v^l. Connect a former neighbor G^j of G^l to G^{t+1} if $N^j \subseteq M$ (where M is considered as a subset of V), to G^{t+2} otherwise, and keep the old edge weights. Go to Step 1.

The output of the algorithm is a tree G_T whose edges have weights corresponding to certain (minimum) cut-sets in G and whose vertices correspond to subsets of the original graph G containing exactly one terminal vertex. The graph G_T is called the *cut tree* of G.

While Exercise 15 captures the more obvious aspects of the algorithm the next theorem, from Hu [1969, p. 138], asserts far more.

Theorem 4 *The capacity of a minimum (u, v)-cut separating any two terminal vertices u and v of the graph G is equal to the minimum of the weights of the edges in the unique path of the cut tree G_T connecting the two vertices of G_T containing u and v.*

Picking any edge of G_T with minimum weight and deleting it from G_T, we get two subtrees G_T^1 and G_T^2 of G_T. Let M be the set of vertices of G that correspond to the vertices of G_T^1. Then by Theorem 4 the cut-set $\{M : V - M\}$ is a cut-set which is minimum among all cut-sets separating any two terminal vertices of G and thus, in particular, a minimum cut-set of G if $N = V$ holds.

We consider now the case where the point $\bar{x} \in \mathbb{R}^E$ of the subtour problem does not satisfy the equations (1). More precisely, we are interested in deciding whether or not $\bar{x}$ satisfies the system of inequalities

$$x(E(W)) \leq |W| - 1 \qquad \text{for all } \varnothing \neq W \subseteq V,$$
$$x \geq 0, \tag{5}$$

which is known to have as extreme points the incidence vectors of trees and forests of the graph G [Edmonds, 1970]. The inequalities (5) occur in the definition of the 1-tree polytope Q_{1T}, and since there are exponentially many constraints in (5), the solution of the subtour problem in this case is by no means obvious; nor does it follow from the previous arguments. Since we no longer have the constraints (1), we cannot transform the problem into the cut problem. However, as Lemma 4(b) and Lemma 6 show, the application of the shrinking heuristic is justified in this case as well, thereby reducing the problem size.

To solve the general case of the subtour problem we define a capacitated network G^* using $G = (V, E)$ and the weights (capacities) $\bar{x}_e$, $e \in E$, as follows.

Construction of the capacitated network G^*

Step 1. Every (undirected) edge $e = \{u, v\}$ of G is replaced by a pair of arcs, (u, v) and (v, u) with capacities $c_{uv} = c_{vu} = \frac{1}{2}\bar{x}_e$.

Step 2. A source labeled 0 with arcs $(0, v)$ and capacities $c_{0v} = \max\{\frac{1}{2}b_v - 1, 0\}$ and a sink labeled $n+1$ with arcs $(v, n+1)$ and capacities $c_{v,n+1} = \max\{1 - \frac{1}{2}b_v, 0\}$ are adjoined to G, where $b_v = \bar{x}(\delta(v))$ for all $v \in V$ and $n = |V|$.

Now one calculates

$$c(W \cup \{0\} : V \cup \{n+1\} - W) = |W| - \bar{x}(E(W)) + \sum_{v \in V} \max\{\tfrac{1}{2}b_v - 1, 0\},$$

and since the last term in the equation is independent of W we have proven the following result [Padberg & Wolsey, 1983].

Theorem 5 *The minimization problem* $\min\{|W| - \bar{x}(E(W)) \mid W \subseteq V, W \neq \varnothing\}$ *is equivalent to the problem of finding a minimum* $(0, n+1)$-*cut in* G^* *satisfying* $W \neq \varnothing$, *i.e. to the problem*

$$\min\{c(W \cup \{0\} : V \cup \{n+1\} - W) \mid W \subseteq V, W \neq \varnothing\}. \tag{6}$$

Note that in problem (6) we do not require that W be a proper subset of V, as was the case in the cut problem. However, the restriction that $W \neq \varnothing$ implies that a single maximum-flow computation does not suffice. To satisfy the condition $W \neq \varnothing$, we solve $n - 2$ maximum flow problems with capacities as defined before except that for the kth problem we set $c_{0,k} = +\infty$, and if $k \geq 2$ holds, we set $c_{v,n+1} = +\infty$ for $v = 1, \ldots, k-1$, where k assumes the values $1, 2, \ldots, n-2$. We record the cut-set that is minimum over the $n-2$ iterations; the resulting vertex set W solves the subtour problem without the restriction $|W| \leqslant n-1$ in the general case.

It is perhaps worth noting that the construction underlying Theorem 5 can be modified to suit also the case where the point $\bar{x} \in \mathbb{R}^E$ satisfies the equations (1) and where we are interested in satisfying the restriction that W be a proper subset of V. In this case the minimum of (6) is obviously 0. To accommodate the condition $W \neq V$, since (1) holds, we can simply define the arc capacity $c_{n,n+1}$ to be $+\infty$ in all of the $n-2$ maximum flow calculations and proceed as previously.

Thus, we have given two procedures for solving the subtour problem but the second one, while applicable to a more general situation than is the case of the TSP, requires the same computational effort as the first one. The minimum cut algorithm will be used again in the next section. Because the maximum flow calculation can be carried out in $O(n^3)$ steps, we have proven the following result.

Theorem 6 *The identification of subtour elimination constraints can be carried out by a polynomial algorithm requiring at most $O(n^4)$ steps.*

Note that Theorem 6 (together with the ellipsoid method) implies that we can optimize in polynomial time over the 1-tree polytope Q_{1T}^n and the monotone 1-tree polytope $\tilde{Q}_{1T}^n$ (see (12) to (18) of Chapter 8). (Of course this can be done with the greedy algorithm in a much simpler way.)

Moreover, using Exercise 9 we can conclude that the identification problem for subtour elimination constraints can be carried out in polynomial time for the asymmetric case as well. So, Theorem 6, Exercise 9 and the ellipsoid method yield polynomial algorithms for optimizing linear objective functions over the branching polytope $\tilde{P}_B^n$, the antibranching polytope $\tilde{P}_B^n$, the arborescence polytope P_B^n, and the antiarborescence polytope P_B^n (see (26) to (31) of Chapter 8); in other words, we obtain new polynomial alternatives to the algorithm in Edmonds [1967].

Exercises
8. Prove Lemma 3.
9. Let $a^T x \leqslant a_0$ be an inequality valid for P_T^n with $a_{ij} = a_{ji}$, $1 \leqslant i, j \leqslant n$, and let $b \in \mathbb{R}^E$ be the vector defined by $b_{ij} = a_{ij}$, $1 \leqslant i, j \leqslant n$. Then $b^T x \leqslant a_0$ is valid for Q_T^n. Moreover, if $\bar{x} \in \mathbb{R}^A$ and $\bar{\bar{x}} = f(\bar{x}) \in \mathbb{R}^E$ is the symmetrized version of $\bar{x}$, then $\bar{x}$ violates $a^T x \leqslant a_0$ if and only if $\bar{\bar{x}}$ violates $b^T x \leqslant a_0$.
10. Prove Lemma 4.
11. Prove Lemma 5.
12. Apply the shrinking heuristic to the graph of Figure 9.1.
13. Prove Lemma 6.
14. (a) Apply the shrinking heuristic to the graph $G(\bar{x})$ of Figure 9.2.

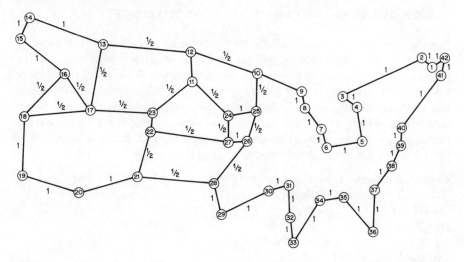

Figure 9.1   Fractional solution of the 42-city problem by Dantzig, Fulkerson & Johnson [1954]

(b) Find a violated subtour elimination constraint in the reduced graph by inspection.

15. (a) Prove that Step 3 of the minimum cut algorithm is carried out exactly $|N|-1$ times.

(b) Prove that the graph G_T constructed by the minimum cut algorithm is a tree.

16. Apply the minimum cut algorithm to the graph obtained from Exercise 14(a).

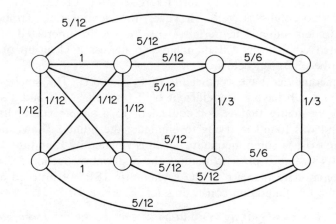

Figure 9.2   Graph for Exercise 14

3 IDENTIFICATION OF CLIQUE TREE INEQUALITIES

For the case of the general clique tree inequalities, the facet identification problem is not solved to date nor do we know any (nontrivial) heuristic for it. (For an introduction to clique tree inequalities see Section 4.2 of Chapter 8.) However, the problem of identifying any violated 2-matching constraint has been completely solved, and there is a reasonable heuristic for comb constraints. When restricted to comb constraints, the facet identification problem can be formulated in the symmetric case as follows, where $G = (V, E)$ is the complete graph having n vertices.

Comb problem *Given a point $\bar{x} \in \mathbb{R}^E$ satisfying (1), find sets H, $T_1, \ldots, T_k \subseteq V$ with the properties*
(a) $|H \cap T_i| \geqslant 1$, $\quad i = 1, \ldots, k$,
(b) $|T_i - H| \geqslant 1$, $\quad i = 1, \ldots, k$,
(c) $T_i \cap T_j = \varnothing$, $\quad 1 \leqslant i < j \leqslant k$,
(d) $k \geqslant 1$ and k odd,
such that $\bar{x}(E(H)) + \sum_{i=1}^{k} \bar{x}(E(T_i)) > |H| + \sum_{i=1}^{k} (|T_i| - 1) - \lceil k/2 \rceil$; or prove that no such sets H, $T_1, \ldots, T_k \subseteq V$ exist.

As in Chapter 8, we call a collection of subsets H, $T_1, \ldots, T_k \subseteq V$ satisfying properties (a), (b), (c), (d) a *comb* in G and abbreviate it by its edge set $C = E(H) \cup \bigcup_{i=1}^{k} E(T_i)$. The quantity

$$s(C) := |H| + \sum_{i=1}^{k} (|T_i| - 1) - \left\lceil \frac{k}{2} \right\rceil$$

is the *size* of the comb C. By slight abuse of notation we shall write

$$x(C) \leqslant s(C)$$

to denote a comb inequality. Note that in contrast to the definition given in Chapter 8, we permit here $k = 1$. Combs with $k = 1$ are dominated by subtour elimination constraints (cf. Exercise 14(a) of Chapter 8 which carries over to combs as well). However, for identification purposes it is more convenient initially to permit $k = 1$. As we are interested in finding undominated combs, we will then have to discuss a clean-up procedure which will be discussed below.

Comb inequalities have coefficients of 0, 1 and 2. The smallest graph admitting a comb having a coefficient of 2 (as well as 0's and 1's) in the associated inequality that is not equivalent to a simple comb, has $n = 8$ vertices and was found in trying to eliminate the point $\bar{x}$ shown in Figure 9.3. (There exists a comb inequality which is violated by $\bar{x}$, and the reader is asked to try to find it prior to reading the material of Section 3.3.)

To accommodate the case of the asymmetric TSP, we proceed as in the case of subtour elimination constraints (cf. Exercise 9).

Lemma 7 *Let $\hat{x} \in \mathbb{R}^E$ satisfy (1) and let $x^* \in \mathbb{R}^E$ be the incidence vector of a tour, i.e. x^* is an extreme point of Q_T^n. Then there exists a comb C such that*

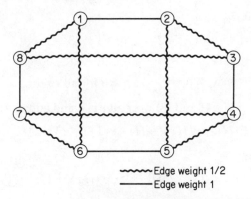

Figure 9.3   Graph illustrating comb constraints

$x^*(C) = s(C)$ and $\hat{x}(C) > s(C)$ hold if and only if there exists a comb C such that $\tilde{x}(C) > s(C)$ holds where $\tilde{x} = (n - 1/n)x^* + (1/n)\hat{x}$.

Thus the primal facet identification problem, when restricted to comb constraints, can be reduced to the comb problem.

3.1   A polynomial algorithm for 2-matching constraints

In the case of 2-matching constraints we have equality in properties (a) and (b) and therefore the problem can be reformulated as follows:

2-Matching problem   *Given a point $\tilde{x} \in \mathbb{R}^E$ satisfying* (1), *find a set $H \subseteq V$ and a set T of edges $e_1, \ldots, e_{|T|}$ in E with the properties*
(a) *e_i has one endpoint in H, $i = 1, \ldots, |T|$,*
(b) *$e_i \cap e_j = \varnothing$, $1 \leqslant i < j \leqslant |T|$,*
(c) *$|T|$ odd,*
such that $\tilde{x}(E(H)) + \tilde{x}(T) > |H| + \lfloor \frac{1}{2}|T| \rfloor$; or prove that no such sets $H \subseteq V$ and $T \subseteq E$ exist.

Formulated this way, the problem looks rather difficult to solve, and in order to tackle it we will make use of the assumption that the point $\tilde{x} \in \mathbb{R}^E$ satisfies (1). Indeed, unlike the case of the subtour elimination constraints, we do not know how to solve the above problem in the general case.

Remark 1   We note that the 2-matching problem for a point $\tilde{x} \in \mathbb{R}^E$ satisfying $Ax \leqslant 2$ rather than $Ax = 2$ in (1) can be reduced to the equality case by introducing a dummy vertex to the graph $G = (V, E)$ to absorb the slack in the inequalities [Padberg & Rao, 1982].

Introducing slack variables for the upper bounds of (1), we can write the system (1) as follows:

$$x(\delta(v)) = 2 \qquad \text{for all } v \in V, \tag{7}$$

$$x_e + t_e = 1 \qquad \text{for all } e \in E, \tag{8}$$

$$x_e \geqslant 0, \qquad t_e \geqslant 0 \text{ for all } e \in E.$$

Adding (7) over all $v \in H$ and (8) over all $e \in T$ and adding together yields

$$2x(E(H)) + x(H : V - H) + x(T) + t(T) = 2|H| + |T|,$$

and consequently

$$2(x(E(H)) + x(T)) = 2|H| + |T| - x(H : V - H) - t(T) + x(T).$$

It follows that

$$\bar{x}(E(H)) + \bar{x}(T) > |H| + \lfloor \tfrac{1}{2}|T| \rfloor \tag{9}$$

holds if and only if

$$\bar{x}(H : V - H) - \bar{x}(T) + \sum_{e \in T} (1 - \bar{x}_e) < 1 \tag{10}$$

holds. Now $T \subseteq \{H : V - H\}$ holds and thus *all* edges of the cut-set $\{H : V - H\}$ appear in (10) *exactly once*, except that the edges in T appear as variables that are complemented into their upper bounds. As in the case of the subtour elimination constraints, when the 2-matching constraints are brought into the form (10), the comb problem reduces to some kind of minimum cut problem with the additional feature that for some odd subset of its edges we need to complement the variables.

To find suitable sets H and T, we recall a standard device to transform a 2-matching problem in 0–1 variables into a matching problem without upper bounds on a larger graph with two classes of vertices labeled 1 and 2. Split each edge of G into three edges by inserting into an edge $e = \{i, j\}$ two vertices i_1 and i_2, with vertex label 1, and define $\bar{x}_{i,i_1} = \bar{x}_{i_2,j} = \bar{x}_e$ and $\bar{x}_{i_1,i_2} = 1 - \bar{x}_e$ to be the new weights. Doing so for all edges, one gets a new vector $\bar{x}$ of weights and a new graph G' with a vertex set $V' = V \cup V_*$ such that

$$\bar{x}(\delta(v)) = 2 \qquad \text{for all } v \in V$$

$$\bar{x}(\delta(v)) = 1 \qquad \text{for all } v \in V_*.$$

Clearly, G' has an even number of vertices with vertex label 1 and some other number of vertices (the original ones) with vertex label 2. Call the vertices with a vertex label 1 *odd* vertices and the other ones *even* vertices. By making the same transformation that brought us to (10) and ignoring for the moment the requirement (b) of the 2-matching problem, it follows that we want to find in G' a cut-set containing an odd number of odd vertices and having a capacity of less than 1.

Rather than splitting each edge into three edges, it suffices to split each edge into two edges, and this is important, since we want to keep the problem size as small as possible.

Labeling procedure constructing $G^*(\bar{x})$ from $G(\bar{x})$

Input: The graph $G(\bar{x})$ as defined in Section 2.1. All vertices of $G(\bar{x})$ are labeled even.

Step 1. Pick any edge $e \in E(\bar{x})$.

Step 2. Let $e = \{u, v\}$ and replace e by two edges $\{u, i_e\}$ and $\{i_e, v\}$ where i_e is a new vertex. Vertex i_e is labeled odd. Vertex u gets a new label which is odd if its old label is even and which is even if its old label is odd. Vertex v retains its old label. The edge $\{u, i_e\}$ gets the weight $1 - \bar{x}_e$ and edge $\{i_e, v\}$ gets the weight $\bar{x}_e$. Mark edge e as having been scanned.

Step 3. If all edges of $G(\bar{x})$ have been scanned, stop. Else pick any unscanned edge $e \in E(\bar{x})$ and go to Step 2.

As we shall see later, the number of vertices labeled odd in the above procedure determines the number of times a maximum flow algorithm has to be run in order to check whether all 2-matching constraints are satisfied. Thus, it is important to pick edges in Step 3 and their endpoints in Step 2 in such a way that the final number of vertices labeled odd is a minimum. In fact, there are (fast) labeling techniques which guarantee that for a connected graph $G(\bar{x})$ the number of old vertices in $G^*(\bar{x})$ (i.e. those from $G(\bar{x})$) labeled odd is zero or one. The latter case necessarily occurs if the number of edges of $G(\bar{x})$ is odd.

Denote by $\tilde{V} = V \cup V_E$ the vertex set of $G^*(\bar{x})$, where $V_E = \{i_e \mid e \in E(\bar{x})\}$ is the set of newly introduced vertices. Note that to every edge $e \in E(\bar{x})$ there corresponds a *unique* new vertex $i_e \in V_E$. Denote by F the edge set of $G^*(\bar{x})$ and let $\bar{y}_f$ for $f \in F$ be the weight (or the *capacity*) of edge f. We claim that $G^*(\bar{x})$ has an even number of vertices which are labeled odd, and leave the proof to the reader.

A cut-set $\{U : \tilde{V} - U\}$ of $G^*(\bar{x})$ is called *odd* if U contains an odd number of odd labeled vertices (and any number of even labeled vertices). A *minimum odd cut-set* is an odd cut-set having a minimum capacity among all odd cut-sets.

Lemma 8 *Let $H \subseteq V$ and $T \subseteq \{H : V - H\}$ be such that $H \neq \varnothing$ and $|T|$ is odd. Define*

$$H_1 = \{i_e \in V_E \mid e \in E(H), e \in E(\bar{x})\},$$
$$U_1 = \{i_e \in V_E \mid e \in \{H : V - H\}, e \in E(\bar{x})\}.$$

Partition U_1 into four disjoint sets:

$$U_{11} = \{i_e \in U_1 \mid e \notin T, \bar{y}_{ki_e} = 1 - \bar{x}_e \text{ for some } k \in H\},$$
$$U_{12} = \{i_e \in U_1 \mid e \notin T, \bar{y}_{ki_e} = \bar{x}_e \text{ for some } k \in H\},$$
$$U_{13} = \{i_e \in U_1 \mid e \in T, \bar{y}_{ki_e} = 1 - \bar{x}_e \text{ for some } k \in H\},$$
$$U_{14} = \{i_e \in U_1 \mid e \in T, \bar{y}_{ki_e} = \bar{x}_e \text{ for some } k \in H\},$$

and define $U = H \cup H_1 \cup U_{11} \cup U_{14}$. *Then*

(a) *U has an odd number of odd labeled vertices;*

(b) $\bar{y}(U:\tilde{V}-U) = \bar{x}(H:V-H) - \bar{x}(T) + \sum_{e\in T}(1-\bar{x}_e)$.

Thus we know how to construct an odd cut-set in $G^*(\bar{x})$ from a pair of sets $H \subseteq V$ and $T \subseteq \{H:V-H\}$ that define a 2-matching constraint.

The next theorem, which is given in a more general form by Padberg & Rao [1982], gives an equivalent formulation of the comb problem when one temporarily ignores condition (b) of the 2-matching problem.

Theorem 7   *Given a point $\bar{x} \in \mathbb{R}^E$ satisfying* (1) *there exist $H \subseteq V$ and $T \subseteq \{H:V-H\}$ with $|T|$ odd such that* (9) *holds if and only if the capacity of a minimum odd cut-set in $G^*(\bar{x})$ is less than 1. Furthermore, if $\{U:\tilde{V}-U\}$ is a minimum odd cut-set with capacity less than 1, then $H = U \cap V$ and T, where*

$$T = \{e \in E(\bar{x}) \mid \exists f \in \{U:\tilde{V}-U\} \text{ such that } f = \{i_e, j\}$$

$$\text{for some } j \in V \text{ and } \bar{y}_f = 1 - \bar{x}_e\}, \tag{11}$$

satisfy (9) *and $|T|$ is an odd number.*

Before stating an algorithm to solve the minimum odd cut-set problem in the labeled graph $G^*(\bar{x})$, we first show how we can alter a minimum odd cut-set of capacity less than 1 so as to satisfy the above mentioned property (b). If $|T| = 1$ holds for the set T defined in (11), then (b) is satisfied and the comb problem is solved.

Remark 2   By Remark 1(b) at the end of Section 4.3 in Chapter 8, a 2-matching constraint with $|T| = 1$ is dominated by a subtour elimination constraint with respect to Q_T^n. Thus if the calculation of a minimum odd cut-set yields a cut with capacity less than 1 and a set T with $|T| = 1$ we find a violated subtour elimination constraint which in numerical calculations for TSPs should be stored, rather than the dominated 2-matching constraint, because in this case the latter does not define a facet.

Thus we can assume without loss of generality that $|T| \geqslant 3$ holds. One establishes the following claim.

Lemma 9   *If the capacity of a minimum odd cut-set in $G^*(\bar{x})$ is less than 1 and $|T| \geqslant 3$ holds for the pair H, T defined in Theorem 7, then $|H| \geqslant 3$ holds.*

Consequently, to satisfy property (b) of the 2-matching conditions we can assume that both $|H| \geqslant 3$ and $|T| \geqslant 3$ hold in Theorem 7. Suppose now without loss of generality that $e_k \cap e_{k-1} \neq \varnothing$ where $k = |T|$. Let $e_k = \{u, v\}$ and $e_{k-1} = \{u, w\}$. If $u \notin H$, we define $H' = H \cup \{u, v, w\}$ and $T' = T - \{e_k, e_{k-1}\}$. If $u \in H$, we define $H' = H - \{u\}$ and T' as before.

Lemma 10   *Suppose the capacity of a minimum odd cut-set in $G^*(\bar{x})$ is less than 1 and that the pair H, T obtained from Theorem 7 violates property (b).*

Then the pair H', T' constructed above defines a minimum odd cut-set in $G^*(\bar{x})$ via the construction of Lemma 8.

If the pair H', T' thus obtained continues to violate (b) we reapply the above construction and in at most $\lfloor\frac{1}{2}|T|\rfloor$ steps we stop with a pair H', T' such that all of the 2-matching properties (a), (b), (c) and (9) hold. The exercise of satisfying (b) is necessary since we are interested in generating *facets* of Q_T^n rather than valid inequalities.

As the above construction shows, the process of converting a minimum odd cut-set in $G^*(\bar{x})$ to a pair H, T defining a facet-inducing linear inequality for Q_T^n can be done in polynomial time. The question is whether we can find a minimum odd cut-set in $G^*(\bar{x})$. This is indeed the case and can be done by the following modification from Padberg & Rao [1982] of the minimum cut algorithm given by Gomory & Hu [1961].

Minimum odd cut algorithm

Input: An undirected connected graph $G = (V, E)$ with capacities $\bar{x}_e \geqslant 0$ for all $e \in E$ and a subset $N \subseteq V$ of vertices labeled odd having an even cardinality $|N|$.

Step 1. Using the minimum cut algorithm with N being the terminal vertices, compute the cut tree $G_T = (N_T, F_T)$ and let d_f be the weight of edge $f \in F_T$. Initialize $L = \{0\}$ and $G_T^0 = G_T$, $N_T^0 = N_T$, $F_T^0 = F_T$, $\bar{c} = +\infty$.

Step 2. If $L = \varnothing$, stop. Else let $l = \min\{j \mid j \in L\}$, $t = \max\{j \mid j \in L\}$.

Step 3. Find $h \in F_T^l$ such that

$$d_h = \min\{d_f \mid f \in F_T^l\}$$

holds and denote by $G_T^{t+i} = (N_T^{t+i}, F_T^{t+i})$ the two subtrees obtained from G_T^l by removing edge h from G_T^l where $i = 1, 2$.

Step 3.1. If $|N_T^{t+1}|$ is odd and $d_h < \bar{c}$, replace $\bar{c}$ by d_h, replace L by $L - \{l\}$; set $f^* = h$ and go to Step 2.

Step 3.2. If $|N_T^{t+1}|$ is odd and $d_h \geqslant \bar{c}$, replace L by $L - \{l\}$ and go to Step 2.

Step 3.3. If $|N_T^{t+1}|$ is even, replace L by $L \cup \{t+1, t+2\} - \{l\}$ and go to Step 2.

The output of the algorithm is an edge f^* of the cut tree G_T having the property that it is an edge with smallest weight among those edges whose removal decomposes G_T into two subtrees each having an odd number of odd labeled vertices. Thus the vertex set of any one of the two subtrees of G_T found in this way defines the vertex set of a minimum odd cut-set in G. Furthermore, the value of $\bar{c}$ at the end of the calculation is the capacity of a minimum odd cut set. The algorithm iterates at most $|N_T| - 1$ times and requires one minimum cut calculation.

Theorem 8 *The identification of 2-matching constraints can be carried out by a polynomial algorithm requiring at most $O((n + m)^4)$ steps, where $n = |V|$ and $m = |E(\bar{x})|$.*

Proof   The set-up of the labeled graph $G^*(\bar{x})$ requires the scanning of each edge of the graph $G(\bar{x})$ and can be done in time linear in $m = |E(\bar{x})|$. The 'cleaning up' of the pair H, T obtained by Theorem 7 to satisfy condition (b) of the 2-matching problem can be done in time linear in $n = |V|$. The execution of the minimum odd cut algorithm requires at most $n + m$ steps since $G^*(\bar{x})$ has at most $n + m$ odd vertices. Thus the entire computation is dominated by the calculation of the cut tree G_T using the minimum cut algorithm in Step 1 above, and thus the claim is proved.   □

From Theorems 5 and 7, the following result now follows by the same line of reasoning that preceded Theorem 3.

Theorem 9   *There exists a polynomial algorithm to solve the optimization problem*

$$\min\{c^T x \mid x \in Q_{1T}^n \cap Q_{2M}^n\},$$

where Q_{1T}^n is the 1-tree polytope and Q_{2M}^n is the perfect 2-matching polytope (cf. Section 3 of Chapter 8).

By Remark 1, it follows that Theorem 9 remains true if we replace Q_{1T}^n and Q_{2M}^n by their monotonizations $\tilde{Q}_{1T}^n$ and $\tilde{Q}_{2M}^n$, respectively. Since the traveling salesman polytope Q_T^n is contained in the intersection of the 1-tree polytope with the perfect 2-matching polytope, we are thus guaranteed to find better lower bounds on the optimal tour length in polynomial time than was previously the case when the 1-tree relaxation and the 2-matching relaxation (but not the intersection of the two) could be solved in polynomial time.

As a recommendation for the implementation of the algorithm, we note that *all* odd cut-sets with capacity less than 1 in $G^*(\bar{x})$ define violated 2-matching constraints. Thus having calculated the cut-tree G_T for $G^*(\bar{x})$, one should generate and store *all* nonequivalent 2-matching constraints that are obtained by breaking the cut tree into two subtrees each having an odd number of vertices if an edge of G_T with weight less than 1 is removed. To minimize space one stores, of course, the smaller one of the two equivalent ones that result from the removal of a single edge.

3.2   Heuristics for 2-matching constraints

The reader who *actually* carried out Exercise 18 will be relieved to learn that the *size* of the problem necessary to solve the comb problem can generally be reduced substantially. In this section we state two procedures, one of which is in the spirit of the shrinking heuristic for the subtour elimination constraints which should *always* be applied before using the exact algorithm. The second one is an easy-to-implement straight heuristic (no claim to generality), which, however, was used with success in the computational study by Padberg & Hong [1980].

Let $G(\bar{x})$ be the graph defined in Section 2.1 and consider any path P connecting two vertices a and b such that every edge e of the path P has an weight $\bar{x}_e = 1$. Let a and b be such that both a and b are incident to edges which have fractional weights $0 < \bar{x}_e < 1$, i.e. the path P is a maximal path of edges having weights of 1. Let us call such a path a 1-*path* in $G(\bar{x})$. Now we delete all vertices of the 1-path except the two end vertices a and b and delete all edges of the path. We label the vertices a and b odd. We continue to do so until all 1-paths are removed. We call the graph that results from this construction G_1 and label all unlabeled vertices of G_1 even. Note that all edges of G_1 have weight less than 1.

Lemma 11   *There exists a minimum odd cut-set with capacity less than 1 in the labeled graph $G^*(\bar{x})$ if and only if there exists a minimum odd cut-set with capacity less than 1 in the graph G_1^* obtained by applying the labeling procedure with the graph G_1 constructed above as input.*

Furthermore, it is clear how to construct from an odd cut-set with capacity less than 1 in G_1^*, an odd cut-set with capacity less than 1 in $G^*(\bar{x})$: if for any removed 1-path the respective two endpoints a and b are on the same side of the cut, then all vertices of the path (including the ones that correspond to the edges of the path) are put on the same side of the cut as the endpoints. If the endpoints a and b are on different sides of the cut, then all vertices of the path other than vertex a (including the ones that correspond to the edges of the path) are put on the same side of the cut as vertex b.

Consider next the graph G_1. An *alternating path* of vertices $v_1, \ldots, v_k$ of G_1 is a path having at least three vertices such that vertices v_i for $i = 2, \ldots, k-1$ are labeled odd in G_1. By construction, the weights of successive edges of an alternating path assume values α and $1 - \alpha$, respectively, where $0 < \alpha < 1$. We permit the case $v_1 = v_k$ and v_1 or v_k may be labeled even or odd. As was the case with paths given by edges having weights of 1, we consider only alternating paths which are maximal with respect to their defining properties.

Shrinking alternating paths of the graph G_1

Input: The labeled graph G_1 constructed above and an alternating path of vertices $v_1, \ldots, v_k$.

Step 1. If $v_1 \neq v_k$, go to Step 2. Else shrink the cycle to a single vertex which retains the old label of v_1 if k is odd and which gets the opposite label to the old label of v_1 if k is even.

Step 2. Let $\alpha = \bar{x}_{v_1,v_2}$ be the weight of the first edge in the path and shrink the path with vertices $v_1, \ldots, v_k$ to a path having three vertices v_1, v_2', v_k by introducing a new vertex v_2' which is labeled odd. Define edge weights $\bar{x}_{v_1,v_2'} = \alpha$ and $\bar{x}_{v_2',v_k} = 1 - \alpha$. Vertex v_1 retains its old label. Vertex v_k retains its old label if k is odd. Otherwise v_k is labeled odd if its old label is even, and even otherwise.

The validation of the shrinking procedure is left to the reader. (*Hint:* Consider the graph that results if the labeling procedure is applied. Then argue the obvious simplifications that are possible if one looks for an odd cut-set with capacity less than 1.) We now can state a heuristic which uses the two shrinking operations described above.

A heuristic for 2-matching constraints

Input: The graph $G(\bar{x})$ defined in Section 2.1.
Step 1. Shrink all 1-paths in $G(\bar{x})$ to get the labeled graph G_1 described above.
Step 2. If no alternating paths in G_1 exist, stop. Else shrink all alternating paths in G_1 using the above shrinking procedure in any order.

Denote by $G_R = (V_R, E_R)$ the graph obtained by applying the heuristic for 2-matching constraints and let $\bar{x}^R$ be the vector of edge weights of G_R.

Lemma 12

(a) G_R has an even number of odd vertices.
(b) *If G_R has only even labeled vertices, then the point $\bar{x}$ satisfies all 2-matching constraints.*
(c) *If G_R has an isolated odd labeled vertex, then the vertex set of $G(\bar{x})$ corresponding to that vertex defines a set H and the edges connecting H to $V - H$ define a set T such that (9) holds, i.e. they define a 2-matching constraint which is violated by the point $\bar{x}$.*
(d) *There exists a minimum odd cut-set with capacity less than 1 in $G^*(\bar{x})$ if and only if there exists a minimum odd cut-set with capacity less than 1 in the graph G_R^* obtained by applying the labeling procedure with the graph G_R as input, using, however, in Step 1 only edges $e \in E(\bar{x}) \cap E_R$.*
(e) *The construction of an odd cut-set of capacity less than 1 in $G^*(\bar{x})$ from such a cut-set in G_R^* can be done in a manner analogous to the remarks made after Lemma 11.*

In other words, the 2-matching heuristic does about the same for 2-matching constraints as the shrinking heuristic does for subtour elimination constraints. However, the latter changes the graph in a more fundamental way by adding edges and can thus be expected to bring about a stronger reduction of the size of the graph $G(\bar{x})$.

While the above heuristic has still to be tested in actual computation, the following one has been used with success for the primal facet-identification problem by Padberg & Hong [1980]. It can, however, be adapted easily for the comb problem as well. This second heuristic is essentially enumerative and is derived from the following consideration: Suppose the point $\bar{x}$ for which the comb problem has to be solved is an extreme point of the feasible set of (1) which is *adjacent* to some 0–1 extreme point of the same set. Then there always exists a 2-matching constraint which is violated by $\bar{x}$ and satisfied by x^* at equality, i.e. there exists a 2-matching constraint which answers the first part of the primal facet identification problem. The reason is that the partial graph $G_F = (V_F, E_F)$ induced by the edges $e \in E$ with $0 < \bar{x}_e < 1$ consists of an even number of disjoint odd cycles (cf. Exercise 8 of Chapter 8). Every odd cycle has an odd number of edges e incident to it which satisfy $\bar{x}_e = 1$. Consequently, choosing H to be the vertex set of an odd cycle in G_F and T to be the collection of edges incident to it and having $\bar{x}_e = 1$, we obtain an even number of 2-matching constraints such that (9) holds and which solve the primal problem.

To generalize this construction, we first determine for a point $\bar{x} \in \mathbb{R}^E$ satisfying (1) the graph $G_F = (V_F, E_F)$. (Note that G_F is different from the graph $G(\bar{x})$ used otherwise.) By tedious but elementary considerations one can show that not only different connected components, but under certain circumstances, also the blocks of G_F play a role in determining a 2-matching constraint. To this end we use an algorithm by Paton [1971] to determine all blocks and cut vertices of G_F. (A *cut vertex* of G_F is a vertex whose removal increases the number of connected components of G_F by at least one.) The resulting blocks with at least three vertices are then used as candidate sets for the set H in the 2-matching constraint. For each set H we identify a set of edges T satisfying (a), (b) and (c) of the 2-matching problem such that their total weight is as large as possible. Then the resulting 2-matching constraint is checked to see if it is satisfied at equality by x^* and cuts off $\bar{x}$. The heuristic attempts to perform the constraint generation starting with the smallest cardinality candidate set H.

Even though this procedure does not guarantee a solution to the primal facet-identification problem, it has been found to be very effective in identifying 2-matching constraints. In judging the computational work involved, it should be kept in mind that the graph G_F is extremely sparse and generally has only a very small number of vertices. Furthermore, lengthy considerations show that one can always cut off points $\bar{x}$ which are such that the face of minimum dimension of the feasible set of (1) containing both x^* and $\bar{x}$ has dimension two.

The second heuristic is best illustrated by an example and we ignore the aspect of the primal facet-identification problem. Consider the graph $G(\bar{x})$ of Figure 9.4. The graph induced by the fractional edges has two connected

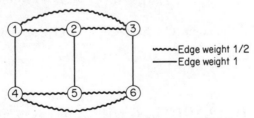

Figure 9.4   Graph illustrating the heuristics

components and the second heuristic finds the 2-matching constraint with $H = \{1, 2, 3\}$ and $T = \{\{1, 4\}, \{2, 5\}, \{3, 6\}\}$ which solves the comb problem. Of course, the heuristic given above also finds the same constraint.

If either the first or the second heuristic is applied to the graph of Figure 9.1, no violated 2-matching constraint is found. In contrast to the first 2-matching heuristic, however, the second heuristic does not permit us to conclude that the point $\bar{x}$ depicted in Figure 9.1 satisfies all 2-matching constraints.

3.3 A heuristic for comb constraints

For comb constraints we have at present only a heuristic procedure whose effectiveness remains to be tested in numerical calculations. It will, however, be seen to be useful in the sense that it permits us for instance to identify a comb constraint to cut off the fractional solution of Figure 9.1, thereby giving a list of facet-inducing linear inequalities which permit the solution of this well-known instance of the TSP entirely by the linear programming means described in this chapter.

Like the first 2-matching heuristic, our heuristic procedure for comb constraints is tailored to the TSP, i.e. we assume that the point $\bar{x} \in \mathbb{R}^E$ which we want to cut off satisfies (1) as well as all subtour elimination constraints. As in the case of the 2-matching constraints we do not know how to solve the general case.

One can derive a generalization of (10) for general comb constraints by summing the equations

$$x(\delta(v)) = 2 \qquad \text{for all } v \in V,$$
$$x(E(W)) + t_W = |W| - 1 \qquad \text{for all } \varnothing \neq W \subset V,$$
$$x_e \geqslant 0, \; t_W \geqslant 0$$

over all vertices v in the set H of a comb and adding to it all equations for $W = T_i$, $T_i \cap H$ and $T_i - H$, respectively, where $i = 1, \ldots, k$. For odd k this yields

$$2x(E(H)) + x(H : V - H) + \sum_{i=1}^{k} (x(E(T_i)) + x(E(T_i \cap H)) + x(E(T_i - H)))$$

$$+ \sum_{i=1}^{k} (t_{T_i} + t_{H \cap T_i} + t_{T_i - H}) = 2s(C) + 1.$$

Consequently, for the comb $C = E(H) \cup \bigcup_{i=1}^{k} E(T_i)$ we have that

$$\bar{x}(C) > s(C) \tag{12}$$

holds if and only if

$$\bar{x}(H : V - H) - \sum_{i=1}^{k} \bar{x}(H \cap T_i : T_i - H) + \sum_{i=1}^{k} (t_{T_i} + t_{H \cap T_i} + t_{T_i - H}) < 1 \tag{13}$$

holds. The inequality (13) imposes restrictions on the total slack of the subtour elimination constraints, but a graphical interpretation as in the special case where $|T_i| = 2$ for $i = 1, \ldots, k$, does not appear to be easy, especially in view of the exponentially many subtour elimination constraints. Despite that fact, we *conjecture* that there exists a polynomial algorithm for the resolution of the comb problem.

The basic idea of our heuristic for comb constraints is to reduce the problem to the 2-matching problem in a smaller graph obtained by shrinking certain parts of $G(\bar{x})$ into pseudo-vertices using the first shrinking procedure (Section 2).

We have seen that in the subtour elimination case all edges with weight 1 could be shrunk away in any order without loosing the relevant properties of the graph. In the 2-matching case, however, this is not possible. In order to show this, the reader is referred to Exercise 27(b), which gives appropriate examples. But there are other properties that violated combs must satisfy, and these are summarized in the following three lemmas.

Lemma 13 *Suppose that $\bar{x} \in \mathbb{R}^E$ satisfies (1) and that $\bar{x}(E(W)) \leq |W| - 1$ for all proper nonempty subsets W of V. Let G_1 be obtained from $G(\bar{x})$ by shrinking all 1-paths in $G(\bar{x})$ (cf. Section 3.2) to 1-paths having exactly one edge. Then there exists a violated comb in $G(\bar{x})$ if and only if there exists a violated comb in G_1.*

Lemma 14 *Suppose that $\bar{x} \in \mathbb{R}^E$ satisfies (1) and that $\bar{x}(E(W)) \leq |W| - 1$ for all proper nonempty subsets W of V.*
(a) *If there exists a comb with sets $H, T_1, \ldots, T_k \subseteq V$ such that $k \geq 3$ and (12) hold, then $\bar{x}(E(H)) < |H| - 1$.*
(b) *If $\bar{x} \in \mathbb{R}^E_+$ satisfies $\bar{x}(E(W)) \leq |W| - 1.5$ for all proper nonempty subsets $W \subseteq V$, then there exists no comb C such that (12) holds.*
(c) *If (12) holds for some comb C with sets $H, T_1, \ldots, T_k \subseteq V$, then $\bar{x}(T_i \cap H : T_i - H) > 0$ and $\bar{x}(E(T_i)) > |T_i| - 2$ for $i = 1, \ldots, k$.*
(d) *If $e = \{u, v\}$ is such that $\bar{x}_e = 1$ and there exists a comb which is violated by $\bar{x}$, then there exists a violated comb with sets $H, T_1, \ldots, T_k \subseteq V$ such that either $\{u, v\} \in H - \bigcup_{i=1}^{k} T_i$ or $\{u, v\} \in T_i$ for exactly one $i \in \{1, \ldots, k\}$.*

Lemma 15 *Suppose that $\bar{x} \in \mathbb{R}^E$ satisfies (1) and that $\bar{x}(E(W)) \leq |W| - 1$ for all proper nonempty subsets W of V. Let G_1 be obtained from $G(\bar{x})$ by shrinking all 1-paths in $G(\bar{x})$ to 1-paths having exactly one edge. Let $W \subseteq V$ be such that $\bar{x}(E(W)) = |W| - 1$ and either $|V| \geq 7$, $|W| = 3$ and $\bar{x}_{uv} = 1$ for u, $v \in W$, or $|V| \geq 8$, $|W| = 4$ and $\bar{x}_{uv} = \bar{x}_{rs} = 1$ where $W = \{r, s, u, v\}$. Let G^* denote the graph obtained from G_1 by shrinking vertices u and v to a single pseudo-vertex using the shrinking procedure from Section 2, and in the case where $|W| = 4$, by shrinking vertices r and s to a single pseudo-vertex using this procedure as well. Then there exists a violated comb in G_1 if there exists a violated comb in G^*.*

The preceding considerations give rise to the following heuristic for the identification of comb constraints. We will assume that the point $x \in \mathbb{R}^E$ satisfies all subtour elimination and 2-matching constraints.

A heuristic for comb constraints

Input: The graph $G(\bar{x})$ as defined in Section 2.1.

Step 1. Shrink all 1-paths in $G(\bar{x})$ as in Lemma 13 and replace $G(\bar{x})$ by the shrunk graph.

Step 2. Find a subset $W \subseteq V$ with $|W| \leq \lceil n/2 \rceil$ such that $\bar{x}(E(W)) = |W| - 1$ holds (choose $|W|$ as large as possible). If no such set W exists, stop.

Step 3. Find a proper subset $U \subseteq W$ such that $\bar{x}(E(U)) = |U| - 1$ holds (again choose $|U|$ as large as possible). If no such U exists, set $U = \varnothing$.

Step 4. Shrink all edges in $E(U)$ and all edges in $E(W - U)$, respectively, to single pseudo-vertices using the shrinking procedure from Section 2 and solve the 2-matching problem in the reduced graph.

    Step 4.1. If a violated 2-matching constraint is found, expand it to the original graph $G(\bar{x})$ and stop; the constraint thus found solves the comb problem.

    Step 4.2. If no violated 2-matching constraint exists go to Step 5.

Step 5. Replace $G(\bar{x})$ by the shrunk graph. If the graph has fewer than seven vertices, stop. Else go to Step 1.

To illustrate the heuristic, consider the graph in Figure 9.1. Carrying out Step 1, we obtain the graph of Figure 9.5.

Now $n = 15$ and the largest subset of vertices given by Step 2 is $W = \{10, 11, 12, 24, 25, 26, 27, 28\}$, and Step 3 yields $U = \{10, 24, 25, 26, 27, 28\}$. We shrink $G(\bar{x})$ using the shrinking procedure and obtain the graph of Figure 9.6.

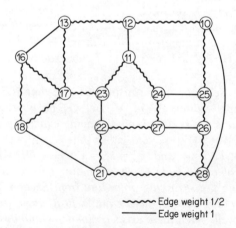

~~~~~~ Edge weight 1/2
———— Edge weight 1

Figure 9.5   Shrunk graph from Figure 9.1

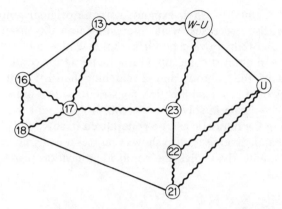

Figure 9.6   Shrunk graph from Figure 9.5

Now applying the heuristic for 2-matching constraints, we find that the comb with

$$H = \{1, 2, \ldots, 10, 21, 22, 24, 25, \ldots, 42\},$$
$$T_1 = \{20, 21\},$$
$$T_2 = \{22, 23\},$$
$$T_3 = \{1, 2, \ldots, 12, 24, 25, \ldots, 42\}$$

is violated by the point $\bar{x} \in \mathbb{R}^{862}$ depicted in Figure 9.1. (Note that this comb constraint was expanded from the 2-matching constraint determined by $\bar{H} = \{U, 21, 22\}$, $\bar{T}_1 = \{18, 21\}$, $\bar{T}_2 = \{22, 23\}$, $\bar{T}_3 = \{W - U, U\}$.) Of course, the comb with

$$H' = \{11, \ldots, 20, 23\}$$

and $T'_1 = T_1$, $T'_2 = T_2$, $T'_3 = T_3$ is equivalent to the former, requires less storage space and thus should be stored in actual numerical calculations.

We have recomputed the 42-city problem of Dantzig, Fulkerson & Johnson [1954] using a code currently under development in Augsburg, in which the solution methods for the identification of subtour elimination constraints described in Section 2.2 and for the identification of 2-matching constraints described in Section 3.1 are implemented. It turns out that the solution found by Dantzig *et al.* shown in Figure 9.1 is an optimum solution (of length 698) over the polytope given by the degree equation, the upper and lower bounds on the edges, the subtour elimination constraints and the 2-matching constraints. If the comb inequality found by the heuristic described above is added, the resulting linear system has a tour (of length 699) as an optimum solution. Thus the 42-city problem can be solved with the cutting plane generation techniques known at present without recourse to branch and bound.

We leave it as an exercise for the reader to prove that any violated 2-matching constraint obtained in Step 4.1 of the above heuristic yields a

violated comb inequality when expanded to the original graph $G(\bar{x})$. The
idea of the heuristic reverses in an interesting way the proof ideas of the
various lifting theorems proved by Grötschel & Padberg [1979b]. While we
have not yet been able to come up with a heuristic for combs which shares
the properties of the subtour and 2-matching heuristics, it appears that
nested families of subtour elimination constraints which are satisfied by the
point $\bar{x} \in \mathbb{R}^E$ play a role in solving the comb problem and that, possibly, the
ideas underlying the heuristic can be generalized to solve the comb problem.
On the other hand, Exercise 30(b) shows that it is a *heuristic* procedure; that
is, it is not guaranteed to solve the comb identification problem.

Exercises

17. Prove Lemma 7.
18. Apply the labeled graph construction to the graph of Figure 9.1.
19. Prove Lemma 8.
20. Prove Lemma 9.
21. Prove Lemma 10.
22. Prove Lemma 11.
23. Prove Lemma 12.
24. Apply the 2-matching heuristic to the graph of Figure 9.1.
25. As was mentioned in this section, although we have a polynomial
algorithm to solve the 2-matching problem under the condition that $\bar{x} \in \mathbb{R}^E$
satisfies (1), no such algorithm is known without this additional assumption.
Thus it would be of interest to consider the following *open problems*.
(a) What are the extreme points of the linear system

$$x(E(H)) + x(T) \leq |H| + \lfloor \tfrac{1}{2}|T| \rfloor \qquad \text{for all } T \in \mathcal{T}_H \text{ and } H \in \mathcal{G},$$

$$x_e \geq 0 \qquad\qquad \text{for all } e \in E,$$

where $\mathcal{G}$ is a family of subsets $H \subseteq V$ with the property that $H \in \mathcal{G}$ if and
only if $V - H \notin \mathcal{G}$ (or $\mathcal{G} = 2^E$) and for $H \in \mathcal{G}$ the family $\mathcal{T}_H$ is the collection of
sets T of edges of E satisfying (a), (b) and (c) of the 2-matching problem?
(b) Solve the 2-matching problem for an arbitrary point $\bar{x} \in \mathbb{R}^E$, i.e. the
problem of testing feasibility or finding a violated inequality for the inequality system of part (a).
26. Analogously to Exercise 25, we formulate the following *research
problem*.
(a) What are the extreme points of the linear system

$$x(C) \leq s(C) \qquad \text{for all combs } C \in \mathcal{C},$$

$$0 \leq x_e \leq 1 \qquad \text{for all } e \in E,$$

where $\mathcal{C}$ is the family of all combs in the undirected complete graph?
(b) Solve the comb problem for an arbitrary point $\bar{x} \in \mathbb{R}^E$, i.e. the problem of
testing feasibility or finding a violated inequality for the inequality system of
part (a).

(c) Solve the comb problem for a point $\bar{x} \in \mathbb{R}^E$ satisfying $\bar{x} \in Q_{1T}^n \cap Q_{2M}^n$.

27. (a) Prove Lemma 13.

(b) Using the graph $G(\bar{x})$ of Figure 9.3, show that if the edges $\{1, 2\}$ and $\{5, 6\}$ are shrunk using the shrinking procedure of Section 2, then the resulting weight vector violates a 2-matching constraint. However, if the edges $\{1, 2\}$ and $\{3, 4\}$ are shrunk using this procedure, then the resulting weight vector is a convex combination of incidence vectors of 2-matchings (in the smaller graph).

28. Prove Lemma 14.

29. Prove Lemma 15.

30. (a) Apply the comb heuristic to the graph of Figure 9.3.

(b) Apply the comb heuristic to the graph of Figure 8.5(a) of Chapter 8.

31. (*Research problem*) Consider the following possible extension of Lemma 14(d). Prove or disprove: If $W \subseteq V$ satisfies $\bar{x}(E(W)) = |W| - 1$ and $\bar{x}(E(W^*)) < |W^*| - 1$ for all proper subsets W^* of W with $|W^*| \geq 2$ and if there exists a comb which is violated by $\bar{x}$, then there exists a violated comb with sets $H, T_1, \ldots, T_k \subseteq V$ such that either $W \subseteq H - \bigcup_{i=1}^k T_i$ or $W \subseteq T_i$ for exactly one $i \in \{1, \ldots, k\}$.

32. (*Research problem*) Suppose $\varnothing \neq W \subseteq V$ and $\varnothing \neq U \subseteq V$ satisfy $U \cap W = \varnothing$ and both U and W satisfy the assumptions of Exercise 31 above. Furthermore, suppose that $\bar{x}(E(U \cup W)) = |U \cup W| - 1$ holds. Let G^* denote the graph obtained from G_1 by shrinking all edges in $E(U)$ and in $E(W)$, and assume that G^* has at least six vertices. Find conditions on U and W under which the following statement is true: there exists a violated comb in G_1 if and only if there exists a violated comb in G^*.

4 COMPUTATIONAL EXPERIMENTS

This is the *show and tell* section of our two-part survey of polyhedral aspects of TSPs. The objective of *optimization* is to solve actual problem instances and thus the ultimate test of a mathematical theory for such problems is whether or not it aides the numerical aspect of problem solving. While the story is by no means told, we give here an account of what has been done to date in terms of applying the polyhedral theory for the TSP to numerical problem solving. This includes the solution to optimality of the largest *symmetric* TSP known to have been solved, but does not include any experiments on the asymmetric TSP, as we are not aware of any computational study that uses the theoretical results of Section 5 of Chapter 8 in a consistent way.

As a result, we restrict our presentation to a brief summary of four papers [Crowder & Padberg, 1980; Grötschel, 1977a, 1980b; Padberg & Hong, 1980]. There are, however, several other studies under way which utilize polyhedral information in the actual solution of symmetric TSPs such as the solution of a 125-city problem done by students of Professor W. R. Pulleyblank at the University of Grenoble (France) and the solution of a

68-city problem done by students of Professor L. Wolsey at the Catholic University of Louvain-la-Neuve (Belgium).

Related studies concerning the use of cutting planes in the solution of symmetric TSPs have been carried out recently [Land, 1979; Miliotis, 1976, 1978; Fleischmann, 1981, 1982], and earlier [Hong, 1972]. While these studies reported good results for medium sized TSPs, their methodology does not focus on testing the polyhedral theory developed here, which is the intent of our brief survey.

For an application of polyhedral theory to the solution of large scale 0–1 programming problems having no special structure such as implied by the TSP, the reader is referred to the paper by Crowder, Johnson & Padberg [1983], where computation has confirmed the hypothesis that facet-inducing linear inequalities are an indispensable tool in the numerical solution of hard combinatorial optimization problems in addition to the TSP; see also Grötschel, Jünger & Reinelt [1984] and Barahona & Maccioni [1982].

4.1   Solution of a 120-city problem

The first instance of a symmetric TSP that was solved using only (a subset of the) clique tree inequalities as defined in Section 4.2 of Chapter 8 (namely subtour elimination, 2-matching and comb constraints) is a 120-city problem given by the data in the *Deutscher Generalatlas* (Mairs Geographischer Verlag, Stuttgart, 1967–68). Grötschel [1977a, 1980b] did not need to resort to branch and bound or other enumerative methods in order to obtain an optimal tour, i.e. the relaxation method for combinatorial optimization problems was used and nothing else.

To implement the procedure, the facet identification step (Step 3) of the procedure was carried out *visually*, i.e. the optimal solutions x^k of the linear programming relaxation obtained in Step 2 were plotted and suitable violated constraints from among those which define facets of Q_T^{120} were chosen by inspection. Thus this implementation is very much in the spirit of the work in Dantzig, Fulkerson & Johnson [1954], except that a better understanding of the underlying theory of the polyhedral aspects of TSPs was available, i.e. more facet-inducing linear inequalities were known, and better computers and better linear programming software could be used. Furthermore, rather than using 'pegs and strings' in order to obtain a heuristic solution to the problem as was done by Dantzig, Fulkerson & Johnson [1954], computer programs were used to find a round trip of length 7011 km which was rather close to the optimal tour of length 6942 km for this particular problem.

In order to find and to prove the optimality of the tour shown in Figure 9.7, thirteen iterations of the relaxation method were necessary. In this process only 96 subtour elimination and comb constraints of the total universe of 10^{179} such constraints were generated to establish optimality of

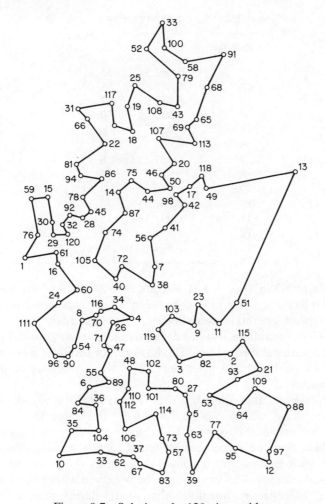

Figure 9.7   Solution of a 120-city problem

the tour (cf. Exercise 2). More precisely,

  36 subtour elimination constraints,
  25 2-matching constraints and
  35 (other) comb constraints

were needed to find and to prove optimality of the tour displayed in Figure 9.7. Table 9.2 gives the results of the thirteen iterations.

In Table 9.2, z_{LP} is the optimal objective function value of (LP_k) and $\#c$ is the number of constraints identified visually to chop off the optimal solution x^k of (LP_k) in the relaxation method for combinatorial optimization problems when applied to this particular problem, where $k = 1, \ldots, 13$.

The CPU times needed for the solution of the thirteen linear programs

Table 9.2   120-city problem

Run no.	z_{LP}	#c
1	6,662.5	13
2	6,883.5	15
3	6,912.5	7
4	6,918.75	9
5	6,928	6
6	6,935.3	9
7	6,937.222	8
8	6,939.5	5
9	6,940.383	4
10	6,940.816	12
11	6,941.184	5
12	6,941.5	3
13	6,942	0

using IBM's MPSX/370 on the IBM computer 370/168 of the Rechenzen-trum der Universität Bonn ranged between 30 seconds and 2 minutes, the number of pivot operations was between 100 and 1,000, and both CPU times and pivot operations increased slightly but not monotonically with the number of additional inequalities. The last run, for instance, was executed in 1.76 CPU minutes and 714 pivot operations were necessary to obtain the optimal solution.

Table 9.2 shows that the objective function values z_{LP} of the linear programs increase monotonically. Moreover, the gains in the objective function value are much larger in the beginning than in the later iterations. This is a behavior one should expect based on the existing computational experience with general cutting plane procedures (Gomory cuts, etc.). In these methods usually a 'tailing off' can be observed where no or almost no increase in the objective function value occurs during quite a number of iterations. This is due partly to the possibility of alternate optima of the relaxed problems which the Gomory (or other) cuts do not take care of. This behavior has been observed much less frequently when facet-incuding inequalities are added, as in the TSP example we discuss.

There is a further – one may say philosophical or tactical – difference between the two approaches. A traditional cutting plane procedure is a mechanism which creates a cutting plane that cuts off x^k whenever x^k is fractional. The cutting planes obtained this way are not taken from a class of inequalities defined beforehand and need not even be supporting hyper-planes of the underlying integer polytope (see Padberg [1973] for a relevant example), though for those cutting plane generation schemes for which finiteness has been established all facets will be generated after a finite number of iterations. The (empirically observed) trouble with these proce-dures is that often the cutting planes generated in the beginning are quite weak and that it takes some time to get a good approximation of the underlying integral polytope. Thus the empirical convergence is rather slow.

In contrast to this, in the approach described here, we use only cutting planes from well-defined classes of facet-defining inequalities. The approach is very problem-specific and uses the structural properties of the underlying combinatorial optimization problem. For points x^k not in Q_T^n we only generate cutting planes from the classes of inequalities we intend to consider (subtour elimination constraints, 2-matching constraints, etc.). We know from our theoretical investigations that these are in a precise sense best possible cutting planes and that they are not 'far away' from Q_T^n (which could be the case with Gomory-cuts). Moreover, we do not continue forever which, in principle, might be possible with 'general cuts'. We only check the facet-defining inequalities in specific classes and if a cutting plane for x^k from these classes ceases to exist we give up and default to branch and bound. Our computational experience has shown that not too many iterations are needed to reach this point and that the final branch and bound step can be finished very quickly. Moreover, we also recommend that branch and bound should only be used after the classes of facet-defining cutting planes are exhausted. This recommendation may be a surprise but its usefulness is also backed by other computational experiments like the ones reported by Crowder, Johnson & Padberg [1983] and Grötschel, Jünger & Reinelt [1985].

4.2 Computation of lower bounds for 74 TSPs

This section is based on the work of Padberg & Hong [1980] where a sample of 74 symmetric TSPs was used to assess the computational value of facet-inducing linear inequalities for the solution of TSPs. We note that out of the total 74 problems, only 54 were solved (to optimality), but in all cases excellent lower bounds were obtained.

To compute the lower bounds a *primal* cutting-plane procedure was implemented rather than the relaxation method. As explained in Section 1.4, subsequent computational experience has convinced us that there is no reason to prefer a primal approach. Indeed, it would have been simpler to implement the relaxation method, since this would have avoided the necessity of writing a simplex code of its own.

All problems were first run with the heuristic of Lin & Kernighan [1973]. As it turned out, this carefully designed heuristic found excellent, often optimal solutions.

The core of the linear programming procedure is the primal simplex algorithm with bounded variables. The program is started by reading in the distance table of the problem, or the coordinates of the n points in the case of Euclidean TSPs and, in most cases, the heuristic solution obtained earlier. This starting solution is then used to initialize the linear programming problem

$$\min\{c^T x \mid Ax = \mathbf{2}, 0 \leqslant x \leqslant \mathbf{1}\} \tag{14}$$

where c^T is the vector with $m = n(n-1)/2$ components given by the edge distances, A is the $n \times m$ incidence matrix of the complete graph having n vertices, **2** is the vector with n components equal to 2, and **1** is the vector with m components equal to 1. The program then proceeds by adjoining cuts (i.e. additional constraints) in the *primal* fashion: If the next feasible solution to the current linear program is the incidence vector of a tour, a usual pivot is carried out. (This includes the case of degeneracy, where the *next* feasible solution is identical to the current one.) Otherwise, the next feasible solution must be chopped off by some cutting plane which is satisfied by the current solution at equality. Subroutines are called which attempt to identify suitable subtour elimination, 2-matching and comb constraints. If suitable constraints are identified, the current linear program is enlarged by adjoining those cuts and a pivot is executed on the enlarged problem. At this point one has a *tighter* linear programming relaxation of the TSP than the one given by (14), since *all* tours satisfy the new constraints but a portion of the feasible space of (14) is chopped off. One can iterate this procedure and since there are only finitely many subtour elimination and comb constraints, termination is guaranteed. If the program halts by displaying optimality of the current linear programming problem, the optimality of an incidence vector of a *tour* has been proved, and the TSP in question has been solved. (This was the case in 54 of 74 sample problems.) Otherwise, the program, which is called *TSP code*, eventually encounters the situation where a suitable constraint cannot be found. One has no choice but to default, i.e. to solve the current *linear* program to optimality and thereby get a lower bound on the minimum tour length. (The alternative to use branch and bound is described in the next section.)

The overall objective of the computational study was to validate empirically the usefulness of facet-inducing inequalities in the solution of TSPs. In order to evaluate the value of facet-inducing inequalities towards the goal of proving optimality, one proceeds as follows: Given a heuristically obtained solution, the 2-matching problem is solved as a *linear* program, i.e. the constraints are given by the system (1) (without the integrality stipulation). Using the same solution as a starting solution, the problem is run a second time generating facet-inducing inequalities. The second run either terminates with an optimal tour or, in case a suitable new constraint is not found, defaults to solving the by now enlarged linear programming problem. This gives two values: VALUE1 is the objective function value without cuts (problem (14)) and VALUE2 is the objective function value with cuts. If TOUR denotes the minimum length tour of the problem, then the following ratio is a good proxy for measuring the added value of the additional work:

$$\text{RATIO} = (\text{VALUE2} - \text{VALUE1})/(\text{TOUR} - \text{VALUE1}).$$

The value of RATIO can vary between 0 and 1, where 0 indicates that the additional cuts did not strengthen the lower bound, and 1 indicates that the additional cuts were sufficient to solve the problem to optimality. The measure RATIO is invariant under any scaling and translating of the data. It is a *conservative* measure, since only an upper bound on TOUR maybe known. In this case, the value of the additional cuts is not overestimated. Since the choice of the *starting solution* is known to greatly affect the performance of simplex methods, the same starting solution was used in the computation of both VALUE1 and VALUE2. Due to this choice it is to some extent meaningful to evaluate the trade-off between added value and additional work also in terms of increased CPU times and increased number of pivots. Finally, all CPU times reported include the entire set-up of the problem, and in particular, a very costly ordering of all edges of the complete graph with respect to the reduced cost of an initial basis which is set up with reference to the starting solution. (This feature of the program was dropped for the largest sample problem having 318 cities.)

55 Randomly generated Euclidean TSPs

To generate the problems for this part of the computational study the pseudo-random number generator of Lin & Kernighan [1973] was used which generates coordinates x_i and y_i with values between 1 and 1,000 for $i = 1, \ldots, n$. Due to the fact that coordinates are generated as pairs, the same random seed for $n + m$ cities produces a graph that is properly contained in the graph on the first n cities, thus making it possible to study how increasing n affects the added value of the facet-inducing inequalities. Ten different problems were run for $n = 15, 30, 45, 60$ and 75, respectively using ten different seeds for the random number generator. Furthermore, five Euclidean problems with $n = 100$ due to Krolak, Felts & Marble [1971] were included in this statistical part of the study, though they are different from the other ones.

Table 9.3 contains all the relevant statistics for this part of the study. The entries in Table 9.3 were obtained by averaging the respective individual figures and their mean μ is given with the standard deviation σ. The top row of Table 9.3 contains the value RATIO. As it is to be expected, RATIO declines with increasing n. TOUR is the tour length obtained by the heuristic.

The bottom line of Table 9.3 (OPTIM) specifies the number of times the linear program terminated by proving optimality of the heuristically obtained tour. GAP1 measures the average difference between TOUR and the objective function value of the (initial) linear program (14). GAP2 is the crucial measure in evaluating the constraint-generation procedure. It is the difference between TOUR and the objective function value of the amended linear program. For example, when $n = 100$ GAP2 averaged 120, and thus an average lower bound of 21,387 was shown for tours with mean length 21,507. Note that RATIO is then just $(GAP1 - GAP2)/GAP1$. PIVOT2 is the average of the total number of pivot operations carried out by the

Table 9.3   55 Euclidean TSPs

n		15	30	45	60	75	100
RATIO	μ	1.0	0.99	0.93	0.92	0.88	0.92
	σ	0.0	0.03	0.11	0.10	0.09	0.02
TOUR	μ	3,555	4,738	5,566	6,297	6,878	21,507
	σ	383	314	224	181	224	525
GAP1	μ	224	352	379	452	387	1507
	σ	121	100	149	133	93	313
GAP2	μ	0.0	5	24	38	50	120
	σ	0.0	15	57	44	44	43
PIVOT2	μ	11	34	47	76	87	167
	σ	2	7	13	30	23	40
Δ PIVOT	μ	2	13	17	36	37	97
	σ	2	5	12	29	22	38
TIME2*	μ	0.33	1.37	4.46	14.47	30.52	108.74
	σ	0.03	0.26	1.27	6.82	10.81	39.97
Δ TIME*	μ	0.07	0.46	1.39	6.25	11.64	50.4
	σ	0.03	0.23	1.23	6.63	10.63	31.7
CUTS	μ	3	12	15	26	28	72
	σ	2	5	8	13	12	18
OPTIM		10	9	5	4	3	0

* Seconds, IBM 370/168 MVS

constraint-generating program. Δ PIVOT is the average increment of the pivot count over what it takes to solve the initial linear program. Likewise, TIME2 specifies the total CPU time of the constraint-generating program, and Δ TIME the average increment over the respective times for the initial linear program. (The numbers in the rows labeled σ are the respective standard deviations for the sample problems.) Finally, CUTS is the average number of constraints that were generated and amended to the original linear program. Thus for 100-city problems the initial linear program has 100 rows and 4,950 variables, while at termination of the constraint-generation procedure the linear program increased on average to 172 rows and 5,022 variables, a truly modest increase given the complexity of the problem and the tightness of the bound obtained. For the individual figures for all of the sample problems, the reader is referred to the original paper [Padberg & Hong, 1980].

Traps for the traveling salesman

The heading for this section is taken from a talk by Papadimitriou & Steiglitz [1967]. Papadimitriou and Steiglitz demonstrated the difficulty that local search procedures for combinatorial problems (more precisely, exchange heuristics) can encounter [Papaditimitriou & Steiglitz, 1977]. They construct a class of non-Euclidean TSPs for which local search procedures find the optimum tour only if computational work tantamount to total enumeration is carried out. In fact, by choosing a cost parameter appropriately, the best solution found by a local search heuristic can be made 'arbitrarily bad'. More precisely, the edge weights of these graphs are 0, 1, M or $2M$, respectively, and there are

$$\frac{1}{32} n^2 + \frac{3}{4} n + 2$$

edges having weights 0 and 1. These test problems were run both with the program made available by Shen Lin and with the TSP code. The TSP code was run with its initial tour chosen both arbitrarily and as the result of the heuristic, as was done above. To get a representative picture, 11 problems ranging from $n = 40$ to $n = 120$ were executed. In all but one of the 22 runs an optimal tour was found. (The exception occurred for $n = 104$ and a randomly selected starting tour.) The complete details of this work are given by Padberg & Hong [1980].

Eight test problems from the literature

In order to permit a limited comparison of the performance of the constraint-generation procedure *vis-à-vis* other approaches a number of test problems that have been used by other researchers were solved. The results are summarized in Table 9.4.

The largest problem, LIN318, is a 318-city problem, and the data were published by Lin & Kernighan [1973]. The data come from an actual problem involving the routing of a numerically controlled drilling machine through three identical sets of 105 points each plus three outliers. As the drilling is done by a pulsed laser, drilling time is negligible and the problem

Table 9.4 Eight problems from the literature

	DAN42	GRO48	HEL48	TOM57	KROL70	GRO120	KNU121	LIN318
RATIO	1.0	0.95	1.0	0.95	0.98	0.99	0.76	0.96
TOUR	699	5046	11461	12955	675	6942	349	41349
GAP1	58	277	264	321-1/2	51-1/2	279-1/2	21	2583-1/2
GAP2	0	14-15/16	0	15	1-3/4	3-19/26	5-1/2	112-128/240
PIVOT2	37	83	38	61	120	243	74	578
Δ PIVOT	7	50	5	17	67	174	29	327
TIME2*	3.10	9.16	4.30	10.40	31.91	221.50	7.25	1751.46
Δ TIME	0.53	5.07	0.61	2.69	15.58	110.30	2.71	1080.66
CUTS	9	32	10	22	44	75	10	171

* Seconds, IBM-370/168 MVS

| REFERENCE | [Dantzig, Fulkerson & Johnson, 1964] | [Grötschel, 1977a (Shell's Roadaltas of Germany)] | [Held & Karp, 1970] | [Karg & Thompson, 1964] | [Krolak, Felts & Marble, 1971] | [Grötschel, 1977a] | [Knuth, 1976] | [Lin & Kernighan, 1973] |

becomes a standard TSP. The only exception from the standard form is that particular start and end points are to be used; the resulting Hamiltonian path problem can, however, easily be accommodated within the linear programming framework by assigning a negative distance to the particular arc. The distance table of the complete graph on 318 points (with the exception of one edge) was computed from the coordinates published by Lin & Kernighan [1973]. The coordinates are given in milli-inches and the usual single-precision square root function was used to calculate the distance. More precisely, one computes the distances by taking the square root of the sum of the squared differences, adding 0.5 to the resulting real number and by subsequently truncating it to its integer part. While the resulting total path length differed by approximately 10 milli-inches from the total path length that results from adding up the 317 individual real numbers, it was felt that this difference was small enough to justify the approximation. If the best solution published earlier is calculated this way, it is 41,871 milli-inches (rather than 41,883 milli-inches) and the best solution that was found after several runs by a changed TSP code has 41,349 milli-inches. It was thus 522 milli-inches shorter than the solution given in Lin & Kernighan [1973] and as Table 9.4 shows, it is at most $\frac{1}{4}$% off the shortest possible Hamiltonian path through the 318 points with distances as defined above.

The changes in the TSP code included a form of *sequential optimization* in order to accommodate the 50,403 variables over which the optimization has to be carried out. That is, a sparse subgraph of only *short* edges was explicitly considered in the optimization and upon termination, the *long* arcs were checked by a subroutine to see if they price out correctly. If not, then (automatically) a new round was initiated; that is, the constraint-generation program was called again.

The original paper [Padberg & Hong, 1980] contains additional details on the implementation and actual computer runs that we cannot reproduce here because of space limitations.

4.3 Solution of ten large-scale TSPs

The most surprising outcome of the computational study described in Section 4.2 is that only *very few additional facet-inducing inequalities* are needed in order to obtain excellent lower bounds on the minimum tour length, and in some cases, to prove optimality as well. The results obtained in the statistical part of the computational study are consistently at most $\frac{1}{2}$% off the optimal tour length and the standard deviations are consistently small as well. The test problems which proved insoluble for the local search procedure were solved to optimality without any difficulties. The results for the test problems from the literature including the – by today's standards – truly large-scale TSPs with 120 and 318 cities, respectively, generally outperformed the results that one might expect based on the statistical part of the study. In particular, the bound for the 120-city problem obtained this way indicates that the solution is within 0.04% of the optimum tour and the bound for the 318-city problem indicates that the solution is within 0.26% of the minimum length Hamiltonian path through the 318 points. With the resulting (remaining) gap between the best tour found and the bound obtained by the use of facet-incuding inequalities being so relatively small, it is entirely realistic to expect that any good branch and bound procedure will enable one to solve large-scale TSPs to optimality. This is what we will describe in this last section of our ongoing saga of the traveling salesman. The material of this section is based on the paper of Crowder & Padberg [1980].

Before using the output of the TSP code described in the previous section as input for a more intricate software system, several changes were carried out to improve the bounds of ten of the large-scale TSPs of the previous section. These changes concerned the identification of additional subtour elimination constraints and the determination of the *hard core* of the respective TSPs that remained to be optimized.

To this end a subroutine was written to fix nonbasic variables of the last LP optimum at either 0 or 1, using the available upper and lower bounds on the optimal objective function value. The basic idea for this *variable fixing* dates back to Dantzig, Fulkerson & Johnson [1954] and is described in detail in the original paper. This procedure is very effective; on average, the number of variables was reduced from $\binom{n}{2}$ by a *factor of 20*.

The ten problems selected from the previous study are shown in Table 9.5 with KRO124 through KRO128 being the five 100-city problems from Krolak, Felts & Marble [1971]. In this table, n is the number of cities and $m = n(n-1)/2$ is the number of variables (=number of edges of the graph). The only exception is KNU121 which is a supersparse problem having 121

Table 9.5   Ten large-scale TSPs

Problem	n	m	n_R	m_R	TIME*	RATIO	LPVALUE
GRO48	48	1,128	86	104	9	0.95	5,031.06
TOM57	57	1,596	89	91	7	0.98	12,948.5
KRO124	100	4,950	187	248	66	0.97	21,225.31
KRO125	100	4,950	170	446	122	0.91	21,978.00
KRO126	100	4,950	183	185	52	0.98	20,730.08
KRO127	100	4,950	192	220	114	0.97	21,257.48
KRO128	100	4,950	203	334	213	0.93	21,970.83
GRO120	120	7,140	199	239	149	0.97	6,934.89
KNU121	121	222	139	182	9	0.90	346.5
LIN318A	318	50,403	496	1,372	2,231	0.97	41,269.83
LIN318B	318	50,403	495	1,144	2,283	0.97	41,269.00
LIN318C	318	50,403	495	1,208	2,295	0.97	412,820.0

* Seconds, IBM 370/168 MVS

cities and only 222 edges. n_R is the number of rows after running the problem with the changed TSP code using the best available tour as a starting solution for the linear program, and m_R is the number of variables that were either basic at the final linear programming optimum or that could *not* be fixed at their respective non-basic value. TIME is the total execution time to obtain LPVALUE at termination. RATIO is the ratio described in Section 4.2. Three runs were made with LIN318, labeled A, B and C. The first was started with the suboptimal solution of length 41,349 obtained earlier, and the second one was started with the optimal tour of length 41,345 obtained after executing LIN318A with the software system described below. The third one has an additional factor of 10 in the data in order to increase the precision of the distance calculations.

Table 9.6 gives a breakdown of the facet-inducing linear inequalities that were generated in the respective runs with the (changed) TSP code to get the linear programs of Table 9.5. The fact that only few (general) comb inequalities were found by the program reflects our limited knowledge of this type of constraint at that time. (The heuristic for comb constraints presented in Section 3 is new and should produce better results.)

After the TSP code is run, the LP obtained has an optimal solution with fractional values. The final phase of the computation consists of several iterations. In each iteration, a branch and bound routine is used to find an optimal 0–1 solution to the current LP. If the 0–1 solution thus found is a tour, the calculation is stopped. Otherwise, subtour elimination constraints are identified by the program to cut off this 0–1 solution, and the next iteration is begun.

The results of this procedure are displayed in Table 9.7. The second and third columns display the problem size: n_R is the number of rows and m_R is

Table 9.6   Breakdown of constraints by type

Problem	Subtour	2-Matching	Comb	Total
GRO48	21	16	1	38
TOM57	16	16	0	32
KRO124	54	32	1	87
KRO125	40	28	2	70
KRO126	43	37	3	83
KRO127	55	36	1	92
KRO128	45	57	1	103
GRO120	51	28	0	79
KNU121	18	0	0	18
LIN318	157	20	0	177
Total	500	270	9	779
Percent	64.3	34.6	1.1	100

Table 9.7 Optimizing ten large-scale TSPs

Problem	n_R	m_R	MIP	NODES	TIME	Δn	NODES	TIME	Δn	NODES	TIME	TOTAL OPT TIME*	TOUR LENGTH
GRO48	86	104	1	17	2		18	3				5	5,046
TOM57	89	91	1	2	0		3	1				6	12,955
KRO124	187	248	1	8	2		15	7				13	21,282
KRO125	170	445	2	133	59	1	147	70	1	115	51	159	22,141
KRO126	183	185	1	5	1		5	2				9	20,749
KRO127	192	220	2	4	2	1	12	7	1	2	0	21	21,294
KRO128	203	334	1	6	5		22	11				24	22,068
GTO120	199	239	2	17	5	1	19	8	1	18	20	24	6,942
KNU121	139	182	3	14	1	1	25	2	1	15	23	16	349
LIN318A	496	1,372	3	22	50	5	22	52	1	35	81	319	41,345
LIN318B	495	1,144	2	41	123	4	41	125	1	54	129	321	41,345
LIN318C	495	1,208	2	188	349	4	188	359	1	150	368	818	413,589

* Seconds, IBM 370/168 MVS

the number of columns of the (pure) 0–1 problem to be optimized. The column labeled MIP gives the number of overall iterations necessary to come to a halt. The first of the two columns labeled NODES gives the number of nodes of the branch and bound tree generated to find the optimum 0–1 solution, and the second such column gives the total number of nodes generated to prove optimality.

Likewise, the first of the two columns labeled TIME gives the time spent in the branch and bound procedure to find the optimum 0–1 solution, whereas the second one gives the total time spent to prove optimality. (Thus in problem GRO48 it took 17 nodes and 2 seconds of CPU time to find the optimum and one additional node and an additional second to prove optimality.) The times have been rounded to the nearest second. In the column labeled TOTAL TIME is the CPU time required for all aspects of the procedure, both computational and bookkeeping. The last column of Table 9.7 gives the respective optimum tour lengths. If more than one iteration was required, the figure in the column labeled Δn indicates the number of new subtour elimination constraints generated. (Thus in the run LIN318A, after the first iteration, five subtour elimination constraints were violated by the 0–1 solution found and appended to the linear program which now is of size $501 \times 1,372$.) Using the previous optimal basis, the enlarged program is reoptimized.

The runs described in this section and the previous one were executed on the IBM 370/168, MVS/TSO at the IBM T. J. Watson Research Center in Yorktown Heights, N.Y. The software packages MPSX/370 and MIP/370 of the IBM Corporation were used for the linear programming and the branch and bound calculations, respectively, for the runs reported in this section.

A first glance at Table 9.7 shows that the computation times as well as the total branch and bound effort spent on optimizing the 0–1 linear programming problems are extremely low. To optimize the (previously unsolved) problem GRO48, a total of 18 nodes had to be generated and the entire execution time took 5 seconds of CPU time. The 'gap' between the linear program value of the corresponding TSP output and the optimal tour is 14.94, i.e. roughly 0.3% of the optimal tour length, and this fact together with the high cutting power of the facet-inducing subtour elimination and comb constraints (of which a total of 38 was generated) is responsible for the low computation time. The same can be said about virtually every other problem. The gap between the linear programming value LPVALUE and the optimum tour for KRO125 is the largest gap of these 100-city problems and its value RATIO (see Table 9.5) is one of the lowest ratios of the table. Why this is so, one can only guess; but it is clearly indicative of the comparatively longer time it took to solve KRO125. Still, only two iterations were required and (absolutely speaking) the total number of nodes in the respective branching trees is still very small. For the problems GRO120 and KNU121, the 0–1 solutions found at the end of the intermediate iterations always had the same objective function value as the optimal tour, so the additional iterations were needed to exclude these solutions with subtours.

LIN318A and LIN318B are both runs of the 318-city problem LIN318. The first run LIN318A was made with the output from the cutting plane method (TSP) using the suboptimal tour of length 41,349 found by Padberg & Hong [1980]. After three iterations, the program halted and the optimal tour of length 41,345 was found. Using Stirling's approximation formula for $n!$, the optimal tour displayed in Figure 9.8 is the (possibly unique) tour (having one arc fixed) from among 10^{655} tours that are possible among 318 points and have one arc fixed. Assuming that one could possibly enumerate 10^9 solutions (tours) per second on a computer it would thus take roughly 10^{639} years of computing to establish the optimality of this tour by exhaustive enumeration. Solving the TSP output to optimality took less than 6 minutes of CPU time. The run LIN318B was essentially made to validate the previous run; in a way, it was sort of a check of internal consistency. First, the TSP code was rerun with the optimal tour as the starting solution.

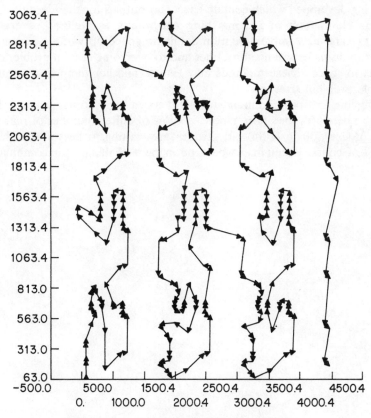

Figure 9.8   Solution of a 318-city problem

The results of this run are displayed in Table 9.7 in the row labeled LIN318B. As a result of the (slightly) smaller gap, the TSP code fixed more variables than previously and the problem generated had 495 rows and 1,144 variables. Again, within less than 6 minutes of CPU time, the optimal solution of length 41,345 was obtained and thus the optimal solution verified.

LIN318C is a run of LIN318 using a factor of 10 in the original coordinates. (Thus the distances are calculated on the basis of $(10x_i, 10y_i)$ rather than on the basis of (x_i, y_i) where $i = 1, \ldots, 318$.) This run was executed to test the issue of *precision* in the calculation of the Euclidean distances referred to in Section 4.2. While both the computation times and the number of nodes increased markedly with the increased number of digits to be processed, the last row of Table 9.7 exhibits substantial similarity to the run LIN318B. More importantly, increasing the precision in the distance table did not alter the optimal tour displayed in Figure 9.8.

The problem with 318 cities should not be the end of the story. The codes we have reported here have used only some of the heuristics described above. Currently, new linear programming based cutting plane procedures are being developed which contain exact subroutines for the identification of subtour elimination and 2-matching constraints as well as several new heuristics and new implementation details to speed up various communication procedures between subroutines and to overcome certain problems with respect to space. These methods may lead to another jump in the range of solvable problem sizes.

Designing and programming such TSP codes is by no means easy. But it seems to be worth the effort, since we know of quite a number of real-world TSPs of size 500 to 6,000 cities which are waiting to be solved. The real world – of course – remains to be a permanent challenge for combinatorial optimizers.

The Traveling Salesman Problem
Edited by E. L. Lawler, J. K. Lenstra,
A. H. G. Rinnooy Kan, D. B. Shmoys
© 1985 John Wiley & Sons Ltd.

10

Branch and bound methods

E. Balas
Carnegie-Mellon University, Pittsburgh

P. Toth
Università di Bologna

1 INTRODUCTION

The origins of the branch and bound idea go back to the work of Dantzig,
Fulkerson & Johnson [1954, 1959] on the TSP. The first full-fledged

The research of the first author was supported by Grant ECS-8205425 of the U.S. National
Science Foundation and by Contract N00014-75-C-0621 NR 047-048 with the U.S. Office of
Naval Research; and that of the second author by the Consiglio Nazionale delle Ricerche of
Italy.

attempt to solve TSPs by an enumerative approach is apparently due to
Eastman [1958]. Many such procedures have since been proposed. In a
sense the TSP has served as a testing ground for the development of solution
methods for discrete optimization, in that many procedures and devices
were first developed for the TSP and then, after successful testing, extended
to more general integer programs. The term 'branch and bound' itself was
coined by Little, Murty, Sweeney & Karel [1963] in conjunction with their
TSP algorithm.

Enumerative (branch and bound, implicit enumeration) methods solve a
discrete optimization problem by breaking up its feasible set into successively smaller subsets, calculating bounds on the objective function value
over each subset, and using them to discard certain subsets from further
consideration. The bounds are obtained by replacing the problem over a
given subset with an easier (relaxed) problem, such that the solution value of
the latter bounds that of the former. The procedure ends when each subset
has either produced a feasible solution, or has been shown to contain no
better solution than the one already in hand. The best solution found during
the procedure is a global optimum.

For any problem P, we denote by $v(P)$ the value of (an optimal solution
to) P. The essential ingredients of any branch and bound procedure for a
discrete optimization problem P of the form $\min\{f(x) \mid x \in S\}$ are:

(i) a relaxation of P, i.e. a problem R of the form $\min\{g(x) \mid x \in T\}$, such
    that $S \subseteq T$ and for every $x, y \in S$, $f(x) < f(y)$ implies $g(x) < g(y)$;
(ii) a branching or separation rule, i.e. a rule for breaking up the feasible
    set S_i of the current subproblem P_i into subsets $S_{i1}, \ldots, S_{iq}$, such that
    $\bigcup_{j=1}^{q} S_{ij} = S_i$;
(iii) a lower bounding procedure, i.e. a procedure for finding (or approxima-
    ting from below) $v(R_i)$ for the relaxation R_i of each subproblem P_i; and
(iv) a subproblem selection rule, i.e. a rule for choosing the next subprob-
    lem to be processed.

Additional ingredients, not always present but always useful when present, are:

(v) an upper bounding procedure, i.e. a heuristic for finding feasible
    solutions to P; and
(vi) a testing procedure, i.e., a procedure for using the logical implications
    of the constraints and bounds to fix the values of some variables
    (reduction, variable fixing) or to discard an entire subproblem (domi-
    nance tests).

For more information on enumerative methods in integer programming
see, for instance, Garfinkel & Nemhauser [1972, Ch. 4] and some surveys
[Balas, 1975; Balas & Guignard, 1979; Beale, 1979; Spielberg, 1979].

Since by far the most important ingredient above is (i), we will classify the
branch and bound procedures for the TSP according to the relaxation that
they use.

The integer programming formulation of the TSP that we will refer to when discussing the various solution methods is defined on a complete directed graph $G = (V, A)$ on n vertices, with vertex set $V = \{1, \ldots, n\}$, arc set $A = \{(i, j) \mid i, j = 1, \ldots, n\}$ and nonnegative costs c_{ij} associated with the arcs. The fact that G is complete involves no restriction, since arcs that one wishes to ignore can be assigned the cost $c_{ij} = \infty$. In all cases $c_{ii} = \infty$, for all $i \in V$. The TSP can be formulated, following Dantzig, Fulkerson & Johnson [1954], as the problem of minimizing

$$\sum_{i \in V} \sum_{j \in V} c_{ij} x_{ij} \tag{1}$$

subject to

$$\sum_{j \in V} x_{ij} = 1, \quad i \in V,$$

$$\sum_{i \in V} x_{ij} = 1, \quad j \in V, \tag{2}$$

$$\sum_{i \in S} \sum_{j \in S} x_{ij} \leq |S| - 1, \quad \text{for all } S \subset V, S \neq \emptyset, \tag{3}$$

$$x_{ij} = 0 \text{ or } 1, \quad i, j \in V, \tag{4}$$

where $x_{ij} = 1$ if arc (i, j) is in the solution, $x_{ij} = 0$ otherwise.

The subtour elimination inequalities (3) can also be written as

$$\sum_{i \in S} \sum_{j \in V-S} x_{ij} \geq 1, \quad \text{for all } S \subset V, S \neq \emptyset. \tag{5}$$

A very important special case is the symmetric TSP, in which $c_{ij} = c_{ji}$, for all i, j. The symmetric TSP can be defined on a complete undirected graph $G = (V, E)$ on n vertices, with vertex set V, edge set E and arbitrary costs c_{ij}. It can be stated as the problem of minimizing

$$\sum_{i \in V} \sum_{j > i} c_{ij} x_{ij} \tag{6}$$

subject to

$$\sum_{j < i} x_{ji} + \sum_{j > i} x_{ij} = 2, \quad i \in V, \tag{7}$$

$$\sum_{i \in S} \sum_{\substack{j \in S \\ j > i}} x_{ij} \leq |S| - 1, \quad \text{for all } S \subset V, S \neq \emptyset, \tag{8}$$

$$x_{ij} = 0 \text{ or } 1, \quad i, j \in V, j > i, \tag{9}$$

where the subtour elimination inequalities (8) can also be written as

$$\sum_{i \in S} \sum_{\substack{j \in V-S \\ j > i}} x_{ij} + \sum_{i \in V-S} \sum_{\substack{j \in S \\ j > i}} x_{ij} \geq 2, \quad \text{for all } S \subset V, S \neq \emptyset. \tag{10}$$

Next we outline two versions of a branch and bound procedure for the TSP. Prior to using any of these versions, a relaxation R of the TSP must be chosen. Both versions carry at all times a list of active subproblems. They differ in that version 1 solves a (relaxed) subproblem R_k only when node k is selected and taken off the list, while version 2 solves each (relaxed) subproblem as soon as it is created, i.e. before it is placed on the list. Although the branch and bound procedures used in practice differ among themselves in many details, nevertheless all of them can be viewed as variants of one of these two versions.

Branch and bound method for the TSP

Version 1

Step 1. (*Initialization*) Put TSP on the list (of active subproblems). Initialize the upper bound at $U = \infty$

Step 2. (*Subproblem selection*) If the list is empty, stop: the tour associated with U is optimal (or, if $U = \infty$, TSP has no solution). Otherwise choose a subproblem TSP_i according to the subproblem selection rule and remove TSP_i from the list.

Step 3. (*Lower bounding*) Solve the relaxation R_i of TSP_i or bound $v(R_i)$ from below, and let L_i be the value obtained.
   If $L_i \geq U$, return to Step 2.
   If $L_i < U$ and the solution defines a tour for TSP, store it in place of the previous best tour, set $U \leftarrow L_i$, and go to Step 5.
   (Now, $L_i < U$ and the solution does not define a tour.)

Step 4. (*Upper bounding: optional*) Use a heuristic to find a tour for TSP. If a better tour is found than the current best, store it in place of the latter and update U.

Step 5. (*Reduction: optional*) Remove from the graph of TSP_i all the arcs whose inclusion in a tour would raise its value above U.

Step 6. (*Branching*) Apply the branching rule to TSP_i, i.e. generate new subproblems $TSP_{i1}, \ldots, TSP_{iq}$, place them on the list, and go to Step 2.

Version 2

Step 1. (*Initialization*) As in version 1, but solve R before putting TSP on the list.

Step 2. (*Subproblem selection*) Same as in version 1.

Step 3. (*Upper bounding: optional*) Same as Step 4 of version 1.

Step 4. (*Reduction: optional*) Same as Step 5 of version 1.

Step 5. (*Branching*) Use the branching rule to define the set of subproblems $TSP_{i1}, \ldots, TSP_{iq}$ to be generated from the current subproblem TSP_i.

Step 6. (*Lower bounding*) If all the subproblems to be generated from TSP_i according to the branching rule have already been generated, go to Step 2. Otherwise generate the next subproblem TSP_{ij} defined by the branching rule, solve the relaxation R_{ij} of TSP_{ij} or bound $v(R_{ij})$ from below, and let L_{ij} be the value obtained.

If $L_{ij} \geqslant U$, repeat Step 6.

If $L_{ij} < U$ and the solution defines a tour for TSP, store it in place of the previous best tour, set $U \leftarrow L_{ij}$, and repeat Step 6.

If $L_{ij} < U$ and the solution does not define a tour, place TSP_{ij} on the list and repeat Step 6.

In both versions, the procedure can be represented by a rooted tree (search tree or branch and bound tree) whose nodes correspond to the subproblems generated, with the root node corresponding to the original problem, and the successor nodes of a given node i associated with TSP_i corresponding to the subproblems $TSP_{i1}, \ldots, TSP_{iq}$ defined by the branching rule.

It is easy to see that under very mild assumptions on the branching rule and the relaxation used, both versions of the above procedure are finite (see Exercise 1).

Next we discuss various specializations of the procedure outlined above, classified according to the relaxation that they use. When assessing and comparing the various relaxations, one should keep in mind that a 'good' relaxation is one that: (i) gives a strong lower bound, i.e. yields a small difference $v(TSP) - v(R)$; and (ii) is easy to solve. Naturally, these are often conflicting goals, and one has to weigh the tradeoffs.

Exercise

1. Show that, if the relaxation R of the TSP used in the branch and bound procedure (either version) has a finite solution set and the branching rule is such that at every node i of the search tree at least one solution to the relaxed problem R_i becomes infeasible for all the successor problems $R_{i1}, \ldots, R_{iq}$, then the procedure is finite. For the rooted tree representation of the branch and bound procedure, what is the maximum depth of the tree, i.e., the maximum length of a path joining any node to the root, if each successor problem TSP_{ij} of TSP_i is generated by deleting some arc? Give a bound on the number of nodes of the rooted tree.

2 RELAXATION I: THE ASSIGNMENT PROBLEM WITH THE TSP COST FUNCTION

The most straightforward relaxation of the TSP, and historically the first one to have been used, is the problem obtained from the integer programming formulation (1), (2), (3), (4) by removing the constraints (3), i.e. the assignment problem (AP) with the same cost function as TSP. It was used, among others, by Eastman [1958], Little, Murty, Sweeney & Karel [1963], Shapiro [1966], Bellmore & Malone [1971], Smith, Srinivasan & Thompson [1977] and Carpaneto & Toth [1980].

An assignment (i.e., a solution to AP) is a union of directed cycles, hence either a tour, or a collection of subtours. There are $n!$ distinct assignments, of which $(n-1)!$ are tours. Thus on the average one in every n assignments is a tour. Furthermore, in the current context only those assignments are of interest that contain no diagonal elements (i.e., satisfy $x_{ii} = 0$, $i = 1, \ldots, n$), and their number is $n!/e$ rounded to the nearest integer, i.e. $\lfloor n!/e + 1/2 \rfloor$ (see, for example, Hall [1967, p. 10]). Thus on the average, one in every n/e 'diagonal-free' assignments is a tour. This relatively high frequency of tours among assignments suggests that $v(\mathrm{AP})$ is likely to be a pretty strong bound on $v(\mathrm{TSP})$, and computational experience with AP-based solution methods supports such a view. To test how good this bound actually is for randomly generated problems, we performed the following experiment. We generated 400 problems with $50 \leqslant n \leqslant 250$, with the costs independently drawn from a uniform distribution of the integers over the intervals $[1, 100]$ and $[1, 1000]$, and solved both the AP and the TSP. We found that on the average $v(\mathrm{AP})$ was 99.2% of $v(\mathrm{TSP})$. Furthermore, we found the bound to improve with problem size, in that for the problems with $50 \leqslant n \leqslant 150$ and $150 \leqslant n \leqslant 250$ the outcomes were 98.8% and 99.6%, respectively.

The AP can be solved by the Hungarian method in at most $O(n^3)$ steps [Kuhn, 1955b; Christofides, 1975; Lawler, 1976]. The assignment problems AP_i to be solved at every node of the search tree differ from the initial assignment problem AP in that some arcs are excluded (forbidden) from, while other arcs are included (forced) into the solution. These modifications do not present any difficulty. Since the Hungarian method provides at every iteration a lower bound on $v(\mathrm{AP})$, the process of solving a subproblem can be stopped whenever the lower bound meets the upper bound U. More importantly, in the typical case (see the branching rules below), the assignment problem AP_j to be solved at node j of the search tree differs from the problem AP_i solved at the parent node i only in that a certain arc belonging to the optimal solution of AP_i is excluded from the solution of AP_j, and possibly some other arcs are required to maintain the same position (in or out) with respect to the solution of AP_j that they have with respect to that of AP_i. Whenever this is the case, the problem AP_j can be solved by the Hungarian method starting from the optimal solution of the problem at the parent node (or at a brother node) in at most $O(n^2)$ steps (see Exercise 2 or Bellmore & Malone [1971]). For an efficient implementation of this version of the Hungarian method, which uses on the average considerably less than $O(n^2)$ steps, see Carpaneto & Toth [1980]. The primal simplex method for the assignment problem has also been used in a parametric version to solve efficiently this sequence of interrelated assignment problems by Smith, Srinivasan & Thompson [1977].

This lower bound $v(\mathrm{AP})$ can be slightly improved by the addition of a penalty. This can be calculated as the minimal increase in the objective function caused either by a first simplex pivot that eliminates some arc from the solution, or by a first iteration of the Hungarian method that accomplishes the same thing. Furthermore, the arc to be included in the solution by the pivot can be restricted to a cutset defined by some subtour of the AP solution. Computational experience indicates, however, that the impact of such a penalty tends to decrease with problem size and is negligible for anything but small problems. In the computational experiment involving the 400 randomly generated problems that we ran, the addition of a penalty to $v(AP)$ raised the value of the lower bound on the average by 0.03%, from 99.2% to 99.23% of $v(TSP)$.

2.1 Branching rules

Several branching rules have been used in conjunction with the AP relaxation of the TSP. In assessing the advantages and disadvantages of these rules one should keep in mind that the ultimate goal is to solve the TSP by solving as few subproblems as possible. Thus a 'good' branching rule is one that (a) generates few successors of a node of the search tree, and (b) generates strongly constrained subproblems, i.e. excludes many solutions from each subproblem. Again, these criteria are usually conflicting and the merits of the various rules depend on the tradeoffs.

We will discuss the various branching rules in terms of sets of arcs E_k and I_k excluded from and included in the solution of subproblem k. Here the symbol k is in general a string, a notation that indicates the ancestry of each subproblem (thus if $k = (pqr)$, then subproblem k is the rth successor of (pq), which in turn is the qth successor of p). In terms of the variables x_{ij}, the interpretation of the sets E_k and I_k is that subproblem k is defined by the conditions

$$x_{ij} = \begin{cases} 0, & (i,j) \in E_k, \\ 1, & (i,j) \in I_k, \end{cases} \tag{11}$$

in addition to (1), (2), (3), (4). Thus the relaxation of subproblem k is given by (11) in addition to (1), (2), (4).

Branching rule 1 [Little, Murty, Sweeney & Karel, 1963] *Given the current relaxed subproblem* AP_k *and its reduced costs* $\bar{c}_{ij} = c_{ij} - u_i - v_j$, *where* u_i *and* v_j *are optimal dual variables, for every arc* (i, j) *such that* $\bar{c}_{ij} = 0$ *define the penalty*

$$p_{ij} = \min\{\bar{c}_{ih} : h \in V - \{j\}\} + \min\{\bar{c}_{hj} : h \in V - \{i\}\}$$

and choose $(r, s) \in A - E_k \cup I_k$ *such that*

$$p_{rs} = \max\{p_{ij} : \bar{c}_{ij} = 0\}.$$

Then generate two successors of node k, *nodes* $k1$ *and* $k2$, *by defining*

$$E_{k1} = E_k \cup \{(r, s)\}, \qquad I_{k1} = I_k$$

and

$$E_{k2} = E_k, \qquad I_{k2} = I_k \cup \{(r, s)\}.$$

This rule does not use the special structure of the TSP (indeed, it applies to any integer program), and has the disadvantage that it leaves the optimal solution to AP_k feasible for AP_{k2}.

The following rules are based on disjunctions derived from the subtour elimination inequalities (3) or (5).

Branching rule 2 [Eastman, 1958; Shapiro, 1966] *Let x^k be the optimal solution to the current relaxed subproblem AP_k, and let $A_S = \{(i_1, i_2), \ldots, (i_t, i_1)\}$ be the arc set of a minimum cardinality subtour of x^k, involving the vertex set $S = \{i_1, \ldots, i_t\}$. Constraint (3) for S implies the inequality*

$$\sum_{(i,j) \in A_S} x_{ij} \leq |S| - 1. \tag{3'}$$

Without loss of generality, assume $A_S - I_k = \{(i_1, i_2), \ldots, (i_s, i_{s+1})\}$, with $s \leq t$. Then (3') implies

$$x_{i_1 i_2} = 0 \vee \ldots \vee x_{i_s i_{s+1}} = 0 \tag{12}$$

(where $s + 1$ is to be taken modulo t).

  Generate s successors of node k, defined by

$$\left. \begin{array}{l} E_{kr} = E_k \cup \{(i_r, i_{r+1})\} \\ I_{kr} = I_k \end{array} \right\} \; r = 1, \ldots, s. \tag{13}$$

Now x^k is clearly infeasible for all AP_{kr}, $r = 1, \ldots, s$, and the choice of a shortest subtour for branching keeps the number of successor nodes small. However, the disjunction (12) does not define a partition of the feasible set of AP_k, and thus different successors of AP_k may have solutions in common. This shortcoming is remedied by the next rule, which differs from branching rule 2 only in that it strengthens the disjunction (12) to one that defines a partition.

Branching rule 3 [Murty, 1968; Bellmore & Malone, 1971; Smith, Srinivasan & Thompson, 1977] *The disjunction (12) can be strengthened to*

$$(x_{i_1 i_2} = 0) \vee (x_{i_1 i_2} = 1, x_{i_2 i_3} = 0) \vee \ldots \vee (x_{i_1 i_2} = \ldots = x_{i_{s-1} i_s} = 1, x_{i_s i_{s+1}} = 0),$$

and accordingly (13) can be replaced by

$$\left. \begin{array}{l} E_{kr} = E_k \cup \{(i_r, i_{r+1})\} \\ I_{kr} = I_k \cup \{(i_1, i_2), \ldots, (i_{r-1}, i_r)\} \end{array} \right\} \; r = 1, \ldots, s.$$

A slightly different version of rule 3 (as well as of rule 2) is to replace the arc set A_S of a minimum cardinality subtour with that of a subtour with a minimum number of free arcs. This rule is used by Carpaneto & Toth [1980].

Branching rule 4 [Bellmore & Malone, 1971] *Let x^k and S be as before. Constraint (5) implies the disjunction*

$$(x_{i_1 j} = 0, j \in S) \vee (x_{i_2 j} = 0, j \in S) \vee \ldots \vee (x_{i_t j} = 0, j \in S). \tag{14}$$

Generate t successors of node k, defined by

$$\left. \begin{array}{l} E_{kr} = E_k \cup \{(i_r, j) : j \in S\} \\ I_{kr} = I_k \end{array} \right\} \; r = 1, \ldots, t. \tag{15}$$

As in the case of rule 2, rule 4 makes x^k infeasible for all successor problems of AP_k, but again (14) does not partition the feasible set of AP_k. This is remedied by the next rule, which differs from rule 4 only in that it defines a partition.

Branching rule 5 [Garfinkel, 1973] *The disjunction (14) can be strengthened to*

$$(x_{i,j} = 0, j \in S) \vee (x_{i,j} = 0, j \in V - S; x_{i_2 j} = 0, j \in S) \vee \ldots$$
$$\vee (x_{i,j} = 0, j \in V - S, r = 1, \ldots, t - 1; x_{i,j} = 0, j \in S)$$

and accordingly (15) can be replaced by

$$E_{kr} = E_k \cup \{(i_r, j) : j \in S\} \cup \{(i_q, j) : q = 1, \ldots, r - 1, j \in V - S\},$$
$$I_{kr} = I_k.$$

The two branching rules 2 and 4 (or their strengthened variants, rules 3 and 5), based on the subtour elimination constraints (3') and (5), respectively, generate the same number of successors of a given node k. However, the rule based on inequality (5) generates more tightly constrained subproblems, i.e., excludes a greater number of assignments from the feasible set of each successor problem, than the rule based on inequality (3'). Indeed, with $|S| = k$, we have the following result.

Theorem 1 [Bellmore & Malone, 1971] *Each inequality (3') eliminates* $\lfloor (n - k)!/e + 1/2 \rfloor$ *diagonal-free assignments, whereas each inequality (5) eliminates* $\lfloor (n - k)!/e + 1/2 \rfloor \cdot \lfloor k!/e + 1/2 \rfloor$ *diagonal-free assignments.*

Proof Each inequality (3') eliminates those diagonal-free assignments that contain the subtour with arc set A_S. There are as many such assignments as there are diagonal-free assignments in the complete graph defined on vertex set $V - S$, and the number of these is $(n - k)!/e$ rounded to the nearest integer, i.e., $\lfloor (n - k)!/e + 1/2 \rfloor$ (see Section 2).

On the other hand, each inequality (5) eliminates those diagonal-free assignments consisting of the union of two such assignments, one in the complete graph defined on S, the other in the complete graph defined on $V - S$. Since the number of the latter is $\lfloor (n - k)!/e + 1/2 \rfloor$ and that of the former is $\lfloor k!/e + 1/2 \rfloor$, the number of diagonal-free assignments eliminated by each inequality (5) is as stated in the theorem. $\square$

Nevertheless, both Smith, Srinivasan & Thompson [1977] and Carpaneto & Toth [1980] found the respective implementations of branching rule 3 to be more efficient than rules 4 and 5, both in terms of total computing time and number of nodes generated. We have no good explanation for this.

2.2   Other features

The subproblem selection rule used by many branch and bound algorithms is the one known as 'depth first' or LIFO (Last In First Out). It amounts to choosing one of the nodes generated at the last branching step (in order, for instance, of nondecreasing penalties, as Smith, Srinivasan & Thompson do [1977]), and when no more such nodes exist, backtracking to the parent node and applying the same rule to its brother nodes. This rule has the advantage of modest storage requirements and easy bookkeeping. Its disadvantage is that possible erroneous decisions (with respect to arc exclusion or inclusion) made early on cannot be corrected until late in the procedure.

The alternative extreme is known as the 'breadth first' rule, which amounts to always choosing the node with the best lower bound. This rule has the desirable feature of keeping the size of the search tree as small as possible (see Exercise 3), but on the other hand requires considerable storage space. In order to keep simple the passage from one subproblem to the next one, this rule must be embedded in a procedure patterned after version 2 of the outline in the introduction to this chapter, which solves each assignment problem as soon as the corresponding node is generated, and places on the list only those subproblems TSP_{ij} with $L_{ij} < U$. The procedure of Carpaneto & Toth [1980] uses this rule, and it chooses the subproblems to be processed (successors of a given node) in the order defined by the arc adjacencies in the subtour that serves as a basis for the branching.

As mentioned earlier, the high frequency of tours among assignments makes AP a relatively strong relaxation of TSP, which in the case of random (asymmetric) costs provides an excellent lower bound on $v(TSP)$. However, in the case of the symmetric TSP, the bound given by the optimal AP solution is substantially weaker. An experiment that we ran on 140 problems with $40 \leq n \leq 100$ and with symmetric costs independently drawn from a uniform distribution of the integers in the interval [1, 1000], showed $v(AP)$ to be on the average 82% of $v(TSP)$, while the addition of a penalty raised the bound to 85%. The explanation of the relative weakness of this bound is straightforward: in the symmetric case, there is a tendency towards a certain symmetry also in the solution, to the effect that if $x_{ij} = 1$, then (since $c_{ij} = c_{ji}$) one tends to have $x_{ji} = 1$ too; and thus the optimal AP solution usually contains many subtours of length 2, irrespective of the size of n. Thus, as a rule, a much larger number of subtours has to be eliminated before finding an optimal tour in the symmetric case than in the asymmetric one. This makes the AP a poor relaxation for the symmetric TSP.

Exercises

2. Let $x^* = (x_{ij})$ be an optimal solution to the assignment problem AP, and let AP_1 be the assignment problem obtained from AP by adding the

constraint $x_{i_0 j_0} = 0$ for some (i_0, j_0) such that $x^*_{i_0 j_0} = 1$. Describe a version of the Hungarian method that starts with x^* and finds an optimal solution to AP_1 in $O(n^2)$ steps. (*Hint*: show that only one labeling is required.)

3. Show that the 'breadth first' rule of always choosing the node with the best lower bound produces a search tree with a minimum number of nodes, if (i) every node selection is uniquely determined, i.e., there are no ties for the best lower bound; and (ii) the branching and bounding at any given node is done only on the basis of information generated on the path from the root of the tree to the given node. Construct examples to show that neither (i) nor (ii) is sufficient by itself [Fox, Lenstra, Rinnooy Kan & Schrage, 1978]. Assuming that conditions (i) and (ii) are not satisfied, describe a subproblem selection rule that combines some of the advantages of 'breadth first' with some of those of 'depth first' [Forrest, Hirst & Tomlin, 1974; Balas, 1975].

3 RELAXATION II: THE 1-TREE PROBLEM WITH LAGRANGEAN OBJECTIVE FUNCTION

This relaxation was first successfully used for the symmetric TSP by Held & Karp [1970, 1971] and Christofides [1970] and subsequently by Helbig, Hansen & Krarup [1974], Smith & Thompson [1977], Volgenant & Jonker [1982] and Gavish & Srikanth [1983].

Consider the symmetric TSP and the complete undirected graph $G = (V, E)$ associated with it. The problem of finding a connected spanning subgraph H of G with n edges that minimizes the cost function (6) is obviously a relaxation of the symmetric TSP. Such a subgraph H consists of a spanning tree of G, plus an extra edge. We may further restrict H to the class $\mathcal{T}$ of subgraphs of the above type in which some arbitrary vertex of G, say vertex 1, has degree 2 and is contained in the unique cycle of H. For lack of a better term, the subgraphs of this class $\mathcal{T}$ are called 1-trees. To see that finding a 1-tree that minimizes (6) is a relaxation of the TSP, it suffices to realize that the constraint set defining the family $\mathcal{T}$ is (9) and

$$\sum_{\substack{i \in S \\ }} \sum_{\substack{j \in V'-S \\ j>i}} x_{ij} + \sum_{\substack{i \in V'-S \\ }} \sum_{\substack{j \in S \\ j>i}} x_{ij} \geq 1, \quad \text{for all } S \subset V' = V - \{1\}, S \neq \varnothing, \quad (16)$$

$$\sum_{i \in V} \sum_{j>i} x_{ij} = n, \quad (17)$$

$$\sum_{j \in V} x_{1j} = 2. \quad (18)$$

Here (16) is a weakening of (10); (17) is the sum of all equations (7) divided by 2; and (18) is the first equation (7).

The minimum cost 1-tree problem is easily seen to be decomposable into two independent problems:

(α) to find a minimum cost spanning tree in $G - \{1\}$; and
(β) to find two smallest cost edges among those incident in G with vertex 1.

The $n-2$ edges of the spanning tree found under (α), together with the two edges found under (β), form a minimum cost 1-tree in G.

Solving problem (β) requires $O(n)$ comparisons, whereas problem (α) can be efficiently solved by the algorithms of Dijkstra [1959] and Prim [1957] of complexity $O(n^2)$, or by the algorithm of Kruskal [1956] of complexity $O(|E| \log |E|)$. Since the $\log |E|$ in the last expression comes from sorting the edges, a sequence of subprobems that requires only minor re-sorting of the edges between two members of the sequence can be more efficiently solved by Kruskal's procedure than by the other two.

The number of 1-trees in the complete undirected graph G on n vertices can be calculated as follows: the number of distinct spanning trees in $G-\{1\}$ is $(n-1)^{n-3}$ (Cayley's formula), and from each spanning tree one can get $\binom{n-1}{2}$ distinct 1-trees by inserting two edges joining vertex 1 to the tree. Thus the number of 1-trees in G is $\frac{1}{2}(n-2)(n-1)^{n-2}$, which is much higher than the number of solutions to the AP. Since G has $(n-1)!$ tours, on average the number of tours among the 1-trees of a complete undirected graph is one in every $\frac{1}{2}(n-2)(n-1)^{n-3}/(n-2)!$, and hence the minimum-cost 1-tree problem with the same objective function as the TSP is a rather weak relaxation of the TSP. In the above mentioned computational experiment on 140 randomly generated symmetric problems, we also solved the corresponding 1-tree problems and found the value of an optimal 1-tree to be on the average only 63% of $v(\text{TSP})$. However, this relaxation can be strengthened considerably by taking the equations (7) into the objective function in a Lagrangean fashion, and then maximizing the Lagrangean as a function of the multipliers.

The problem

$$L(\lambda) = \min_{x \in X(\mathcal{T})} \left\{ \sum_{i \in V} \sum_{j>i} c_{ij}x_{ij} + \sum_{i \in V} \lambda_i \left(\sum_{j<i} x_{ji} + \sum_{j>i} x_{ij} - 2 \right) \right\}$$
$$= \min_{x \in X(\mathcal{T})} \left\{ \sum_{i \in V} \sum_{j>i} (c_{ij} + \lambda_i + \lambda_j)x_{ij} \right\} - 2 \sum_{i \in V} \lambda_i, \tag{19}$$

where λ is any n-vector and $X(\mathcal{T})$ is the set of incidence vectors of 1-trees in G, i.e., the set defined by (9), (16), (17), (18), is a *Lagrangean relaxation* of the TSP. From the last expression in (19) and the fact that $X(\mathcal{T})$ contains all tours, it is easy to see that for any λ, $L(\lambda) \leq v(\text{TSP})$. (For surveys of Lagrangean relaxation in a more general context see Geoffrion [1974], Fisher [1981] and Shapiro [1979].) The strongest Lagrangean relaxation is obviously given by $\lambda = \bar{\lambda}$ such that

$$L(\bar{\lambda}) = \max_{\lambda} \{L(\lambda)\}. \tag{20}$$

Problem (20) is sometimes called a *Lagrangean dual* of the TSP.

Now (20) is a much stronger relaxation than the 1-tree problem with the TSP cost function. Indeed, computational experience with randomly generated problems has produced on the average values of $L(\bar{\lambda})$ of about 99% of $v(\text{TSP})$ according to Christofides [1979, p. 134] and of about 99.7% of $v(\text{TSP})$ according to Volgenant & Jonker [1982].

However, solving (20) is a lot more difficult than solving a 1-tree problem. The objective function of (20), i.e. the function $L(\lambda)$ of (19), is piecewise linear and concave in λ. Thus $L(\lambda)$ is not everywhere differentiable. Held & Karp [1971], who first used (20) as a relaxation of the TSP, tried several methods and found that an iterative procedure akin to the relaxation method of Agmon [1954] and Motzkin & Schoenberg [1954] was the best-suited approach for this type of problem. The method, which turned out to have been theoretically studied in the Soviet literature (see Poljak [1967] and others) became the object of extensive investigations in the Western literature under the name of *subgradient optimization*, as a result of its successful use in conjunction with the TSP (for surveys of subgradient optimization in a more general context see Held, Wolfe & Crowder [1974] or Sandi [1979]).

The subgradient optimization method for solving (20) starts with some arbitrary $\lambda = \lambda^0$ (say the zero vector) and at iteration k updates λ^k as follows. Find $L(\lambda^k)$, i.e. solve problem (19) for $\lambda = \lambda^k$. Let $H(\lambda^k)$ be the optimal 1-tree found. If $H(\lambda^k)$ is a tour, or if $v(H(\lambda^k)) \geq U$, stop. Otherwise, for $i \in V$, let d_i be the degree of vertex i in $H(\lambda^k)$. Then the n-vector with components $d_i^k - 2$, $i \in V$, is a subgradient of $L(\lambda)$ at λ^k (see Exercise 4). Set

$$\lambda_i^{k+1} = \lambda_i^k + t^k(d_i^k - 2), \qquad i \in V, \tag{21}$$

where t^k is the 'step length' defined by

$$t^k = \alpha(U - L(\lambda^k))/\sum_{i \in V} (d_i^k - 2)^2 \tag{22}$$

with $0 < \alpha \leq 2$. Then set $k \leftarrow k + 1$ and repeat the procedure.

It can be shown (see any of the surveys mentioned above) that the method converges if $\sum_{k=1}^{\infty} t^k = \infty$ and $\lim_{k \to \infty} t^k = 0$. These conditions are satisfied if one starts with $\alpha = 2$ and periodically reduces α by some factor.

Example 1

Consider the eight-city symmetric TSP whose graph is shown in Figure 10.1 (only arcs with finite cost are present). Initially $U = 25$, $\alpha = 2$, $\lambda_i^0 = 0$ for $i = 1, \ldots, 8$. The optimal 1-tree, shown in heavy lines in Figure 10.1, has a weight of $L(\lambda^0) = 21$. At iteration 0 we have:

$$d_i^0 = (2, 2, 4, 1, 1, 3, 2, 1);$$
$$t^0 = 2(25 - 21)/8 = 1;$$
$$\lambda_i^1 = (0, 0, 2, -1, -1, 1, 0, -1).$$

The updated arc costs $(c_{ij} + \lambda_i^1 + \lambda_j^1)$ and the corresponding optimal 1-tree, having a weight of $L(\lambda^1) = 24$, are shown in Figure 10.2.

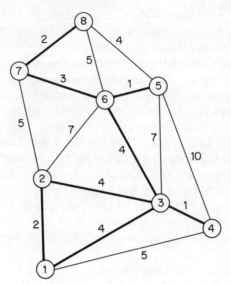

Figure 10.1   Initial graph $G = (V, E)$

We have $d_i^1 = 2$ for $i = 1, \ldots, 8$; thus a tour has been found and the procedure stops.

Held & Karp [1971] point out that if λ^0 is taken to be, instead of 0, the vector defined by

$$\lambda_i^0 = -(u_i + v_i)/2, \qquad i \in V,$$

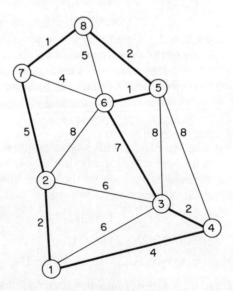

Figure 10.2   Updated graph $G = (V, E)$

where (u, v) is an optimal solution to the dual of the assignment problem with costs $c_{ij} = c_{ji}$, for all i, j, then one always has $v(H(\lambda^0)) \geqslant v(AP)$. Indeed, for this choice of λ^0 one has,

$$
\begin{aligned}
L(\lambda^0) &= \min_{x \in X(\mathcal{T})} \left\{ \sum_{i \in V} \sum_{j > i} (c_{ij} + \lambda_i^0 + \lambda_j^0) x_{ij} \right\} - 2 \sum_{i \in V} \lambda_i^0 \\
&= \min_{x \in (\mathcal{T})} \left\{ \sum_{i \in V} \sum_{j > i} \tfrac{1}{2} [(c_{ij} - u_i - v_j) x_{ij} + (c_{ji} - u_j - v_i)] \right\} + \sum_{i \in V} (u_i + v_i) \\
&\geqslant v(AP),
\end{aligned}
$$

since $v(AP) = \sum_{i \in V} (u_i + v_i)$ and $c_{ij} - u_i - v_j \geqslant 0$, for all i, j. This kind of initialization requires of course that one solves AP prior to addressing problem (20).

Helbig, Hansen & Krarup [1974], Smith & Thompson [1977] and Gavish & Srikanth [1983] distinguish between the application of the subgradient procedure at the root node of the search tree and at subsequent nodes, by using different starting vectors λ^0 and different stopping rules.

Volgenant & Jonker [1982] use an updating formula for λ^k and an expression for t^k different from (21) and (22), respectively. Namely, they take t^k to be a positive scalar decreasing according to a series with a constant second-order difference, i.e.

$$
t^{k+1} - 2t^t + t^{k-1} = \text{constant},
$$

and define λ^{k+1} by setting, for $i \in V$,

$$
\lambda^{k+1} = \begin{cases} \lambda_i^k & \text{if } d_i^k = 2, \\ \lambda_i^k + 0.6 t^k (d_i^k - 2) + 0.4 t^k (d_i^{k-1} - 2) & \text{otherwise.} \end{cases}
$$

It should be mentioned that none of the versions of this subgradient optimization method can be guaranteed to solve (20) in polynomial time with a prespecified degree of accuracy. However, the stopping rules are such that after a certain number of iterations the procedure terminates with an approximation to an optimal λ, which gives a (usually good) lower bound on $L(\bar{\lambda})$.

3.1 Branching rules

Branching rule 6 [Held & Karp, 1971] *At node k, let the free edges of the current 1-tree (i.e. those in $E - E_k \cup I_k$) be ordered according to nonincreasing penalties, and let the first q elements of this ordered set be $J = \{\{i_1, j_1\}, \ldots, \{i_q, j_q\}\}$, where q will be specified below. Define q new nodes, $k1, \ldots, kq$, by*

$$
\begin{aligned}
I_{kr} &= I_k \cup \{\{i_h, j_h\} : h = 1, \ldots, r-1\}, & r &= 1, \ldots, q, \\
E_{kr} &= E_k \cup \{\{i_r, j_r\}\}, & r &= 1, \ldots, q-1, \\
E_{kq} &= E_k \cup \{\{i, j\} \notin I_{kq} : i = p \text{ or } j = p\}.
\end{aligned}
$$

Here $p \in V$ is such that I_k contains at most one edge incident with p, while I_{kq} contains two such edges; and q is the smallest subscript of an edge in J for which a vertex with the properties of p exists.

This rule partitions the feasible set, and makes the current 1-tree infeasible for each of the new subproblems generated, but the number q of the new subproblems is often larger than necessary.

Branching rule 7 [Smith & Thompson, 1977] *Choose a vertex i of G whose degree in the current 1-tree is not 2, and a maximum cost edge $\{i, j\}$ in the 1-tree. Then generate new subproblems defined by*

$$
\begin{aligned}
E_{k1} &= E_k \cup \{\{i, j\}\}, & I_{k1} &= I_k, \\
E_{k2} &= E_k, & I_{k2} &= I_k \cup \{\{i, j\}\}.
\end{aligned}
\tag{23}
$$

This rule generates only two successors of each node k of the search tree, but the minimum 1-tree in subproblem k remains feasible for subproblem $k2$.

Branching rule 8 [Volgenant & Jonker, 1982] *Choose a vertex i whose degree in the current 1-tree exceeds 2, and two free edges $\{i, j_1\}$, $\{i, j_2\}$ in the 1-tree (such edges exist; otherwise I_k contains two edges incident with i and the remaining edges incident with i belong to or should belong to E_k). Generate three new subproblems by*

$$
\begin{aligned}
E_{k1} &= E_k \cup \{\{i, j\} : j \notin \{j_1, j_2\}\}, & I_{k1} &= I_k \cup \{\{i, j_1\}, \{i, j_2\}\}, \\
E_{k2} &= E_k \cup \{\{i, j_2\}\}, & I_{k2} &= I_k \cup \{\{i, j_1\}\}, \\
E_{k3} &= E_k \cup \{\{i, j_1\}\}, & I_{k3} &= I_k.
\end{aligned}
$$

If i is incident with an edge in I_k, then node $k1$ is not generated.

This rule also partitions the feasible set and makes the 1-tree at node k infeasible for each of the successor nodes, while the number of successors of each node is at most three.

Branching rule 9 [Gavish & Srikanth, 1983] *Choose an edge $\{i, j\}$ of the current 1-tree such that the penalty for setting $x_{ij} = 1$ is maximal (with auxiliary rules for breaking ties), and generate two new subproblems defined by (23).*

3.2 Other features

Held & Karp [1971], Smith & Thompson [1977] and Gavish & Srikanth [1983] use a depth first subproblem selection rule, while Volgenant & Jonker [1982] implement both a depth first and a breadth first rule, with computational results that indicate a slight advantage for the depth first rule (in their implementation).

Gavish & Srikanth [1983] use a tour-building heuristic as an upper bounding device. Their procedure starts with a partial solution obtained from the current 1-tree by removing all edges incident with vertices of degree greater than 2, and proceeds to connect the resulting paths into a tour. The latter is then improved by the interchange heuristic of Lin & Kernighan [1973]. They also make extensive use of reduction procedures to fix variables at 0 or 1. These procedures examine the implications of forcing a given variable to 0 or to 1 by way of sensitivity analysis, and fix the variable at one of the two values whenever the alternative would drive the cost of a tour above the current upper bound. Executing the main procedure once (for all the variables) requires $O(n^2)$ steps, and usually a few applications lead to the removal of a very high proportion of all the edges.

3.3 Extension to the asymmetric TSP

The basic ideas of the 1-tree relaxation of the symmetric TSP carry over to the asymmetric case [Held & Karp, 1970], in that the 1-tree in an undirected graph can be replaced by a 1-arborescence in the directed graph $G = (V, A)$, defined as an arborescence (directed tree) rooted at vertex 1, plus an arc $(i, 1)$ joining some vertex $i \in V - \{1\}$ to vertex 1. The constraints defining a 1-arborescence, namely (4) and

$$\sum_{i \in S} \sum_{j \in V-S} x_{ij} \geq 1, \qquad \text{for all } S \subset V: 1 \in S,$$

$$\sum_{i \in V} \sum_{j \in V} x_{ij} = n,$$

$$\sum_{i \in V} x_{i1} = 1,$$

are easily seen to be a relaxation of the constraint set (2), (4), (5) of the TSP.

The problem of finding a minimum cost 1-arborescence can again be decomposed into two independent problems, namely (α) finding a minimum cost arborescence in G rooted at vertex 1, and (β) finding a minimum cost arc $(i, 1)$ in G. Problem (α) can be solved by the polynomial-time algorithms of Edmonds [1967] or Fulkerson [1974], or by the $O(n^2)$ time algorithm of Tarjan [1977].

To obtain the Lagrangean version of the 1-arborescence relaxation, one forms the function

$$L(\lambda) = \min_{x \in X(\mathscr{A})} \left\{ \sum_{i \in V} \sum_{j \in V} c_{ij} x_{ij} + \sum_{i \in V} \lambda_i \left(\sum_{j \in V} x_{ij} - 1 \right) \right\}$$

$$= \min_{x \in X(\mathscr{A})} \left\{ \sum_{i \in V} \sum_{j \in V} (c_{ij} + \lambda_i) x_{ij} \right\} - \sum_{i \in V} \lambda_i,$$

where $X(\mathscr{A})$ is the set of incidence vectors of $\mathscr{A}$, the family of 1-arborescences in G. Again, the strongest lower bound on $v(\text{TSP})$ is of course given by $\lambda = \bar{\lambda}$ such that

$$L(\bar{\lambda}) = \max_{\lambda} \{L(\lambda)\}, \tag{24}$$

and subgradient optimization can be used to solve problem (24). However, computational experience with this relaxation [Smith, 1975] shows it to be inferior (for asymmetric problems) to the AP relaxation, even when the latter uses the original objective function of the TSP.

Exercise

4. A subgradient of a convex function $f(x)$ at $x = x^k$ is a vector s such that

$$f(x) - f(x^k) \geq s(x - x^k), \qquad \text{for all } x,$$

and the subdifferential of $f(x)$ at x^k is the set of all subgradients of $f(x)$ at $x = x^k$.

Let $\mathcal{T}$ be the family of 1-trees in $G = (V, E)$, and let $X(\mathcal{T})$ denote the set of incidence vectors of 1-trees. Show that, if $H(\lambda^k)$ is a 1-tree whose incidence vector x^k minimizes the function

$$\sum_{i \in V} \sum_{j > i} (c_{ij} + \lambda_i^k + \lambda_j^k) x_{ij}$$

on $X(\mathcal{T})$, and d_i^k is the degree of vertex i in $H(\lambda^k)$, then the n-vector whose components are $d_i^k - 2$, $i \in V$, is a subgradient of $L(\lambda)$ at λ^k. Identify the subdifferential of $L(\lambda)$ at λ^k.

4 RELAXATION III: THE ASSIGNMENT PROBLEM WITH LAGRANGEAN OBJECTIVE FUNCTION

This relaxation was used for the asymmetric TSP by Balas & Christofides [1981]. It is a considerable strengthening of the relaxation consisting of the AP with the original cost function, involving a significant computational effort, which however seems amply justified by the computational results that show this approach to be the fastest currently available method for this class of problems.

Consider the asymmetric TSP defined on the complete directed graph $G = (V, A)$, in the integer programming formulation (1), (2), (4), plus the subtour elimination constraints. The latter can be written either as (3) or as (5), but for reasons to be explained later, we include *both* (3) and (5), as well as some positive linear combinations of such inequalities, and write the resulting set of subtour elimination inequalities in the generic form

$$\sum_{i \in V} \sum_{j \in V} a_{ij}^t x_{ij} \geq a_0^t, \qquad t \in T. \tag{25}$$

Thus our integer programming formulation of the TSP consists of (1), (2), (4) and (25). To construct a Lagrangean relaxation of TSP, we denote by X the feasible set of AP, and associate a multiplier w_t, $t \in T$, with every inequality in the system (25). We then have

$$L(w) = \min_{x \in X} \left\{ \sum_{i \in V} \sum_{j \in V} c_{ij} x_{ij} - \sum_{t \in T} w_t \left(\sum_{i \in V} \sum_{j \in V} a_{ij}^t x_{ij} - a_0^t \right) \right\}$$

$$= \min_{x \in X} \left\{ \sum_{i \in V} \sum_{j \in V} \left(c_{ij} - \sum_{t \in T} w_t a_{ij}^t \right) x_{ij} \right\} + \sum_{t \in T} w_t a_0^t, \tag{26}$$

where $w = (w_t)$. Clearly, the strongest such relaxation is given by $w = \bar{w}$ such that

$$L(\bar{w}) = \max_{w \geq 0} \{L(w)\}. \tag{27}$$

The Lagrangean dual (27) of the TSP could be solved by subgradient optimization, as in the case of the 1-tree relaxation of the symmetric TSP. However, in this case the vector w of multipliers has an exponential number of components, and until an efficient way is found to identify the components that need to be changed at every iteration, such a procedure seems computationally expensive. Therefore, (27) is replaced by the 'restricted' Lagrangean dual

$$\max_{w \in W} \{L(w)\}, \tag{28}$$

where

$$W = \left\{ w \;\middle|\; w \geq 0 \text{ and there exists } u, v \in \mathbb{R}^n \text{ such that} \right.$$

$$\left. u_i + v_j + \sum_{t \in T} w_t a_{ij}^t = c_{ij} \text{ if } \bar{x}_{ij} = 1; \; \leq c_{ij} \text{ if } \bar{x}_{ij} = 0 \right\}$$

and $\bar{x}$ is the optimal solution found for the AP.

In other words, (28) restricts the multipliers w_t to values that, together with appropriate values u_i, v_j, form a feasible solution to the dual of the linear program given by (1), (2), (25) and $x_{ij} \geq 0$, $i, j \in V$. This may cause the value of (28) to be less than that of (27), but it leaves the optimal solution $\bar{x}$ to AP also optimal for the objective function (26). Thus (28) can be solved without changing $\bar{x}$. While no good method is known for the exact solution of (28), there is a polynomially bounded sequential noniterative approximation procedure [Balas & Christofides, 1981], which yields multipliers $\hat{w}_t$ such that $L(\hat{w})$ typically comes close to $v(\text{TSP})$: for randomly generated asymmetric TSPs, $L(\hat{w})$ was found to be on the average 99.5% of $v(\text{TSP})$ [Christofides, 1979, pp. 139–140].

The procedure starts by solving AP for the costs c_{ij}, for all i, j, and taking u_i, v_j to be the components of the optimal solution to the dual of AP. It then assigns values to the multipliers w_t sequentially, without changing the values assigned earlier. We say that an inequality (25) *admits a positive multiplier* if there exists a $w_t > 0$ which, together with the multipliers already chosen, satisfies the constraints of W. At any stage, $v(\text{TSP})$ is bounded from below by

$$\sum_{i \in V} u_i + \sum_{j \in V} v_j + \sum_{t \in T} w_t a_t^0, \tag{29}$$

since (u, v, w) is a feasible solution to the dual of the linear program defined by (1), (2), (25) and $x_{ij} \geq 0$, for all i, j.

The bounding procedure successively identifies valid inequalities that

(i) are violated by the AP solution $\bar{x}$, and
(ii) admit a positive multiplier.

Such inequalities are included in $L(w)$ in the order in which they are found, with the largest possible multiplier w_t. The inclusion of each new inequality strengthens the lower bound $L(w)$. We denote by $\bar{c}_{ij}$ the reduced costs defined by the optimal dual variables u_i, v_j and the multipliers w_t, i.e., $\bar{c}_{ij} = c_{ij} - u_i - v_j - \sum_{t \in T} w_t a_{ij}^t$.

At any given stage, the admissible graph $G_0 = (V, A_0)$ is the spanning subgraph of G containing those arcs with zero reduced cost, i.e.

$$A_0 = \left\{ (i, j) \in A \;\middle|\; u_i + v_j + \sum_{t \in T} w_t a_{ij}^t = c_{ij} \right\},$$

where T is the index set of the inequalities included so far in $L(w)$. The inclusion of each new inequality into the Lagrangean function adds at least one new arc to the set A_0. Furthermore, as long as G_0 is not strongly connected, the procedure is guaranteed to find a valid inequality satisfying (i) and (ii). Thus the number of arcs in A_0 steadily grows; and when no more inequalities can be found that satisfy (i) and (ii), G_0 is strongly connected. Finally, if at some point G_0 becomes Hamiltonian and a tour H is found in G_0 whose incidence vector satisfies (25) with equality for all $t \in T$ such that $w_t > 0$, then H is an optimal solution to TSP (see Exercise 5).

Three types of inequalities, indexed by T_1, T_2 and T_3, are used in three noniterative bounding procedures applied in sequence. We will denote the three components of w corresponding to these three inequality classes, by $\lambda = (\lambda_i)_{i \in T_1}$, $\mu = (\mu_i)_{i \in T_2}$ and $\nu = (\nu_i)_{i \in T_3}$, respectively.

4.1 Bounding procedure 1

This procedure uses the inequalities (5) satisfying conditions (i) and (ii). For any $S \subseteq V$, the set of arcs $(S, V - S) = \{(i, j) \in A \mid i \in S, j \in V - S\}$ is called a *directed cutset*. The inequalities (5) corresponding to the vertex sets S_t, $t \in T$, can be represented in terms of the directed cutsets $K_t = (S_t, V - S_t)$, as

$$\sum_{(i,j) \in K_t} x_{ij} \geq 1, \qquad t \in T_1. \tag{30}$$

At any stage of the procedure, the inequality corresponding to cutset K_t is easily seen to satisfy conditions (i) and (ii) if and only if

$$K_t \cap A_0 = \varnothing. \tag{31}$$

To find a cutset K_t satisfying (31), one chooses a vertex $i \in V$ and forms its *reachable set* $R(i) = \{j \in V \mid \text{there is a directed path from } i \text{ to } j\}$ in G_0. If $R(i) = V$, there is no cutset K_t with $i \in S_t$ satisfying (31), so one chooses another vertex. If $R(i) \neq V$ for some $i \in V$, then $K_t = (R(i), V - R(i))$ satisfies (31), and the largest value that one can assign to the corresponding multiplier λ_t without violating the constraints of W is $\bar{\lambda}_t = \min_{(i,j) \in K_t} \{\bar{c}_{ij}\}$. Thus the inequality (30) corresponding to K_t is included in $L(w)$ by setting the reduced costs to $\bar{c}_{ij} \leftarrow \bar{c}_{ij} - \lambda_t$, $(i, j) \in K_t$, $\bar{c}_{ij} \leftarrow \bar{c}_{ij}$ otherwise. This adds to A_0

all arcs for which the minimum in the definition of $\bar{\lambda}_t$ is attained. The search is then started again for a new cutset; and the procedure ends when the reachable set of every vertex is V. At that stage G_0 is strongly connected, and $K \cap A_0 \neq \varnothing$ for all directed cutsets K in G. Also, from (29) and the fact that $a_0^t = 1$, for all $t \in T_1$, it follows that procedure 1 improves the lower bound on $v(\text{TSP})$ by $\sum_t \lambda_t$, i.e., at the end of procedure 1 the lower bound is

$$B_1 = v(\text{AP}) + \sum_{t \in T_1} \lambda_t.$$

One can show that bounding procedure 1 generates at most $(h-1)(h+2)/2$ cutsets, where h is the number of subtours in $\bar{x}$ (see Exercise 6). The computational effort required to find a cutset satisfying (31), or showing that none exists, is $O(n\,|A|)$.

Example 2

Consider the eight-city TSP whose cost matrix is shown in Table 10.1.

Table 10.1

	1	2	3	4	5	6	7	8
1	–	2	11	10	8	7	6	5
2	6	–	1	8	8	4	6	7
3	5	12	–	11	8	12	3	11
4	11	9	10	–	1	9	8	10
5	11	11	9	4	–	2	10	9
6	12	8	5	2	11	–	11	9
7	10	11	12	10	9	12	–	3
8	7	10	10	10	6	3	1	–

Table 10.2

	1	2	3	4	5	6	7	8	
1	–	[0]	9	8	6	5	4	3	2
2	3	–	[0]	7	7	3	5	6	1
3	[0]	9	–	8	5	9	0	8	3
4	8	8	9	–	[0]	8	7	9	1
5	7	9	7	2	–	[0]	8	7	2
6	8	6	3	[0]	9	–	9	7	2
7	5	8	9	7	6	9	–	[0]	3
8	4	9	9	9	5	2	[0]	–	1
	2	0	0	0	0	0	0	0	

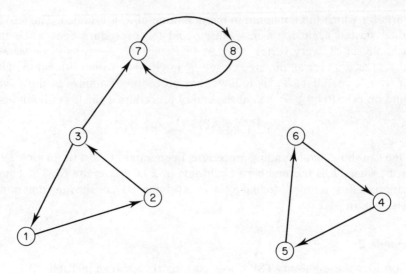

Figure 10.3   Graph G_0 defined by the optimal assignment

Table 10.2 shows the optimal solution $\bar{x}$ to AP ($\bar{x}_{ij} = 1$ for (i, j) boxed in, $\bar{x}_{ij} = 0$ otherwise), the optimal solution $(\bar{u}, \bar{v})$ to the dual of AP (the numbers on the rim), and the reduced costs $\bar{c}_{ij}$. The solution value is 17. The corresponding admissible graph G_0 is shown in Figure 10.3.

Bounding procedure 1. Cutset $K_1 = (\{1, 2, 3, 7, 8\}, \{4, 5, 6\})$ admits $\lambda_1 = \bar{c}_{8,6} = 2$, and cutset $K_2 = (\{4, 5, 6\}, \{1, 2, 3, 7, 8\})$ admits $\lambda_2 = \bar{c}_{6,3} = 3$. The lower bound becomes $17 + 2 + 3 = 22$. The new reduced cost matrix is shown in Table 10.3 and the corresponding admissible graph G_0 in Figure 10.4. Note that G_0 of Figure 10.4 is strongly connected.

Table 10.3

	1	2	3	4	5	6	7	8
1	–	[0]	9	6	4	3	4	3
2	3	–	[0]	5	5	1	5	6
3	[0]	9	–	6	3	7	0	8
4	5	5	6	–	[0]	8	4	6
5	4	6	4	2	–	[0]	5	4
6	5	3	0	[0]	9	–	6	4
7	5	8	9	5	4	7	–	[0]
8	4	9	9	7	3	0	[0]	–

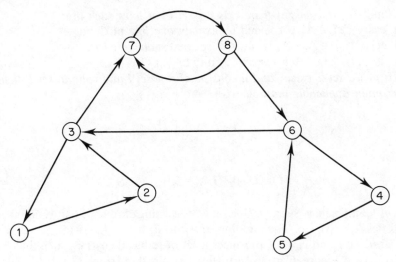

Figure 10.4   Graph G_0 after bounding procedure 1

4.2   Bounding procedure 2

This procedure uses the inequalities (3) that satisfy conditions (i) and (ii), i.e.
are violated by $\bar{x}$ and admit a positive multiplier. To write these inequalities
in the general form (25), we restate them as

$$- \sum_{i \in S_t} \sum_{j \in S_t} x_{ij} \geq 1 - |S_t|, \qquad t \in T_2. \tag{32}$$

The subtour elimination inequalities (3) (or (32)) are known to be equivalent to (5) (or (30)). Nevertheless, an inequality (32) may admit a positive
multiplier when the corresponding inequality (30) does not, and vice versa.

If $S_1, \ldots, S_h$ are the vertex sets of the h subtours of $\bar{x}$, every inequality
(32) defined by S_t, $t = 1, \ldots, h$, is violated by $\bar{x}$; but a positive multiplier μ_t
can be applied without violating the condition that $\bar{x}_{ij} = 1$ implies $\bar{c}_{ij} = 0$,
only by changing the values of some u_i and v_j, and this in turn can only be
done if a certain condition is satisfied. Roughly speaking, we have to find a
set of rows I and columns J such that, by adding to each u_i, $i \in I$, and v_j, $j \in J$,
the same amount $\mu_t > 0$ that is being added to $\bar{c}_{ij}$, $(i, j) \in (S_t, S_t)$, we obtain a
new set of reduced costs $\bar{c}'_{ij}$ such that $\bar{c}'_{ij} \geq 0$ for all (i, j), and $\bar{c}'_{ij} = 0$ for all
those (i, j) such that $\bar{x}_{ij} = 1$. The condition for this is best expressed in terms
of the assignment tableau of the Hungarian algorithm whose rows and
columns are called *lines*, and whose row/column intersections are called
cells. Cells correspond to arcs of G and are denoted the same way.

Let S_t be the vertex set of a subtour of $\bar{x}$, and

$$A_t = \{(i, j) \in A_0 \mid i, j \in S_t\}, \qquad A'_t = \{(i, j) \in A_t \mid \bar{x}_{ij} = 1\}.$$

Theorem 2 [Balas & Christofides, 1981]   *Inequality (32) admits a positive*

multiplier if and only if there exists a set C of lines such that
(α) *every $(i, j) \in A'_t$ is covered by exactly one line in C,*
(β) *every $(i, j) \in A_t - A'_t$ is covered by at most one line in C,*
(γ) *no $(i, j) \in A_0 - A_t$ is covered by any line in C.*

If such a set C exists, and it consists of row set I and column set J, then the maximum applicable multiplier is

$$\mu_t = \min_{(i,j) \in M} \{\bar{c}_{ij}\},$$

where

$$M = (I, J) \cup (I, V - S_t) \cup (V - S_t, J).$$

Proof Sufficiency. Suppose line set C, consisting of row set I and column set J, satisfies (α), (β), (γ). Then adding $\mu_t > 0$ to $\bar{c}_{ij}$ for all $(i, j) \in (S_t, S_t)$, as well as to all u_i, $i \in I$ and v_j, $j \in J$, produces a set of reduced costs $\bar{c}'_{ij}$ such that $\bar{c}'_{ij} = 0$ for $(i, j) \in A'_t$, since $C = I \cup J$ satisfies (α). Further, since C satisfies (β) and (γ), $\bar{c}'_{ij} \geq \bar{c}_{ij} = 0$ for all $(i, j) \in A_t - A'_t$, and $\bar{c}'_{ij} = \bar{c}_{ij} = 0$ for all $(i, j) \in A_0 - A_t$. The only reduced costs that are diminished as a result of the above changes, are those corresponding to arcs in one of the three sets (I, J), $(I, V - S_t)$, $(V - S_t, J)$ whose union is the set M of the theorem. Hence setting μ_t equal to the minimum reduced cost over M provides a positive multiplier that can be applied to the arcs in (S_t, S_t).

Necessity. Suppose a multiplier $\mu > 0$ can be applied to the arc set (S_t, S_t). In order to prevent the $\bar{c}_{ij}$ for $(i, j) \in A'_t$ from becoming positive, one must increase $u_i + v_j$ by μ for all $(i, j) \in A'_t$. If this can be done, it can be done by adding μ to u_i or v_j (but not to both) for $(i, j) \in A'_t$; and the corresponding index sets I and J form a set $C = I \cup J$ that satisfies (α). Let $\mathscr{C}$ be the collection of all sets C obtained in this way. Now take any $C \in \mathscr{C}$. If C violates (β), then $\bar{c}'_{ij} = \bar{c}_{ij} + \mu - 2\mu < \bar{c}_{ij} = 0$ for some $(i, j) \in A_t - A'_t$, and if it violates (γ), then $\bar{c}'_{ij} < \bar{c}_{ij} = 0$ for some $(i, j) \in A_0 - A_t$. Since by assumption $\mu > 0$ can be applied to (S_t, S_t), there exists at least one set $C \in \mathscr{C}$ that satisfies both (β) and (γ). $\square$

To check whether for a given subtour vertex set S_t there exists a set of lines C satisfying conditions (α), (β), (γ), we proceed as follows.

First we construct a set R^- of rows that cannot belong to C, and a set K^+ of columns that must belong to C, if conditions (α), (β), (γ) are to be satisfied. To do this, we start with $K^+ = \varnothing$ and in view of (γ), put into R^- all rows i in which there exists a cell $(i, j) \in A_0$ with $j \in V - S_t$. Then we apply recursively the following two steps, until no more additions can be made to either set:

If a row i was put into R^-, then to satisfy (α) we put into K^+ the column j such that $(i, j) \in A'_t$.

If a column j was put into K^+, then to satisfy (β) we put into R^- every row h such that $(h, j) \in A_t$.

To state the procedure formally, we set $K_0^+ = \varnothing$,

$$R_0^- = \{i \in S_t \mid \exists (i, j) \in A_0 \text{ with } j \in V - S_t\},$$

and define recursively for $r = 1, \ldots, r_*$,

$$K_r^+ = K_{r-1}^+ \cup \{j \in S_t \mid \exists (i, j) \in A_t' \text{ with } i \in R_{r-1}^-\},$$
$$R_r^- = R_{r-1}^- \cup \{i \in S_t \mid \exists (i, j) \in A_t \text{ with } j \in K_r^+\}.$$

Here r_* is the smallest r for which $K_r^+ = K_{r-1}^+$ or $R_r^- = R_{r-1}^-$.

Next we define a set of columns that cannot belong to C if (α), (β) and (γ) are to hold, namely

$$K_0^- = \{j \in S_t \mid \exists (i, j) \in A_0 \text{ with } i \in V - S_t\}.$$

Now if $K_0^- \cap K_{r_*}^+ \neq \varnothing$, then some column that cannot belong to C, must belong to C for (α), (β) and (γ) to hold; hence there exists no set C of lines · satisfying (α), (β), (γ), and no positive multiplier can be applied to the inequality (32) corresponding to S_t.

If $K_0^- \cap K_{r_*}^+ = \varnothing$, then the set of lines $C = I \cup J$, where $I = S_t - R_{r_*}^-$ and $J = K_{r_*}^+$, satisfies conditions (α), (β) and (γ). Indeed, let $(i, j) \in A_t$. If $j \in K_{r_*}^+$, then $i \in R_{r_*}^-$, hence (i, j) is covered at most once. Now let $(i, j) \in A_t'$. If $j \in K_{r_*}^+$, $j \in C$; and if $j \notin K_{r_*}^+$, then $i \notin R_{r_*}^-$, hence $i \in C$; i.e., in both cases (i, j) is covered. Finally, if $(i, j) \in A_0 - A_t$, then either $i \in R_{r_*}^-$ or $j \in K_{r_*}^-$, hence $i \notin C$, $j \notin C$ and (i, j) is not covered. Thus C is as required. In this case we include the inequality (32) corresponding to S_t into $L(w)$ with the multiplier $\mu_t > 0$ defined in Theorem 2, and set the reduced costs to $\bar{c}_{ij} \leftarrow \bar{c}_{ij} - \mu_t$, $(i, j) \in M$, $\bar{c}_{ij} \leftarrow \bar{c}_{ij}$ otherwise. (Here M is the set defined in Theorem 2.)

In both cases, we then choose another subtour, until all subtours have been examined. If h is again the number of subtours, bounding procedure 2 requires $O(h |A|)$ steps. It can be shown (see Exercise 7) that this procedure improves the lower bound on $v(\text{TSP})$ by $\sum_t \mu_t$, i.e., at the end of procedure 2 the lower bound is

$$B_2 = v(\text{AP}) + \sum_{t \in T_1} \lambda_t + \sum_{t \in T_2} \mu_t.$$

Example 2 (continued)

Bounding procedure 2. The subtours of $\bar{x}$ are $(1, 2, 3)$, $(4, 5, 6)$ and $(7, 8)$ (see Table 10.3 and Figure 10.4).

For $S_1 = \{1, 2, 3\}$, we have $R_0^- = \{3\}$, $K_1^+ = \{1\}$; $K_0^- = \{3\}$, and $K_0^- \cap K_1^+ = \varnothing$. Thus $C = I \cup J$, where $I = \{1, 2\}$, $J = \{1\}$, and $\mu_1 = \bar{c}_{2,6} = 1$. For $S_2 = \{4, 5, 6\}$, we have $R_0^- = \{6\}$, $K_1^+ = \{4\}$; $K_0^- = \{6\}$, and since $K_0^- \cap K_1^+ = \varnothing$, $C = I \cup J$, with $I = \{4, 5\}$, $J = \{4\}$, and $\mu_2 = \bar{c}_{5,4} = 2$. Finally, for $S_3 = \{7, 8\}$, $R_0 = \{8\}$, $K_1^+ = \{7\}$; $K_0^- = \{7\}$, and since $K_1^+ \cap K_0^- = \{7\} \neq \varnothing$, the inequality corresponding to subtour $(7, 8)$ does not admit a positive multiplier.

The lower bound becomes $B_2 = B_1 + \mu_1 + \mu_2 = 22 + 1 + 2 = 25$. The new

Table 10.4

	1	2	3	4	5	6	7	8
1	–	[0]	9	3	3	2	3	2
2	2	–	[0]	2	4	0	4	5
3	[0]	9	–	4	3	7	0	8
4	2	3	4	–	[0]	8	2	4
5	1	4	2	0	–	[0]	3	2
6	4	3	0	[0]	9	–	6	4
7	4	8	9	3	4	7	–	[0]
8	3	9	9	5	3	0	[0]	–

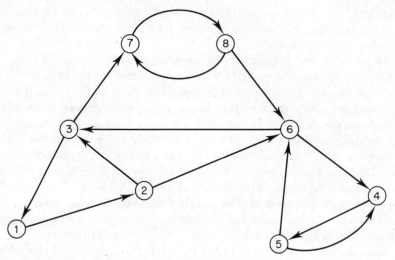

Figure 10.5   Graph G_0 after bounding procedure 2

reduced costs are shown in Table 10.4, and the corresponding admissible graph G_0 in Figure 10.5.

4.3   Bounding procedure 3

The class of inequalities used in this procedure is defined as follows. Suppose G_0 has an *articulation point*, i.e. a vertex k such that $G_0 - \{k\}$ has more than one component. Let one of the components have vertex set S_t, and put $W_t = V - S_t \cup \{k\}$. Then every tour contains an arc of at least one of the cutsets $K'_t = (S_t, W_t)$ and $K''_t = (W_t, S_t)$, hence the incidence vector x of any tour satisfies the inequality

$$\sum_{(i,j) \in K'_t \cup K''_t} x_{ij} \geq 1. \tag{33}$$

Furthermore, (33) satisfies condition (i), i.e. it is violated by the AP solution.

Bounding procedure 3 uses those inequalities (33) that also satisfy condition (ii). Although every inequality (33) is the combination of some inequalities (3) and equations (2) (see Exercise 8), nevertheless it is possible to find inequalities (33) that satisfy condition (ii), i.e., that admit a positive multiplier, when no inequality (3) (i.e., (32)) satisfies it. Indeed, it is not hard to see that if k is an articulation point of G_0 and S_t is the vertex set of one of the components of $G_0 - \{k\}$, then $K_t' \cap A_0 = K_t'' \cap A_0 = \emptyset$ and a positive multiplier given by

$$\nu_t = \min_{(i,j) \in K_t' \cup K_t''} \{\bar{c}_{ij}\} \qquad (34)$$

can be applied to the arc set $K_t' \cap K_t''$. On the other hand, if G_0 has no articulation point, then for any choice of the vertex k, the minimum in (34) is 0 and thus no inequality (33) admits a positive multiplier.

Thus bounding procedure 3 checks for every $i \in V$ whether it is an articulation point, and if so, it takes the corresponding inequality (33) into $L(w)$ with the multiplier ν_t given by (34). This is done by setting $\bar{c}_{ij} \leftarrow \bar{c}_{ij} - \nu_t$, $(i, j) \in K_t' \cup K_t''$, $\bar{c}_{ij} \leftarrow \bar{c}_{ij}$ otherwise. Since G_0 has n vertices and testing for connectivity requires $O(|A|)$ steps, bounding procedure 3 requires $O(n\,|A|)$ steps.

In view of the bound B_2 and the fact that (33) has a right-hand side of 1, at the end of bounding procedure 3 one has the following lower bound on v(TSP):

$$B_3 = v(\text{AP}) + \sum_{t \in T_1} \lambda_t + \sum_{t \in T_2} \mu_t + \sum_{t \in T_3} \nu_t.$$

Example 2 (continued)

Vertex 6 is an articulation point of G_0 (see Figure 10.5). The corresponding cutsets are $K_1' = (\{4, 5\}, \{1, 2, 3, 7, 8\})$ and $K_1'' = (\{1, 2, 3, 7, 8\}, \{4, 5\})$, and the arc set $K_1' \cup K_1''$ admits the multiplier $\nu_1 = \bar{c}_{5,1} = 1$. There is no other articulation point, and the procedure stops with the lower bound $B_3 = B_2 + \nu_1 = 25 + 1 = 26$. The new reduced costs are shown in Table 10.5, and the corresponding G_0 in Figure 10.6.

Table 10.5

	1	2	3	4	5	6	7	8
1	–	⬚0	9	2	2	2	3	2
2	2	–	⬚0	1	3	0	4	5
3	⬚0	9	–	3	2	7	0	8
4	1	2	3	–	⬚0	8	1	3
5	0	3	1	0	–	⬚0	2	1
6	4	3	0	⬚0	9	–	6	4
7	4	8	9	2	3	7	–	⬚0
8	3	9	9	4	2	0	⬚0	–

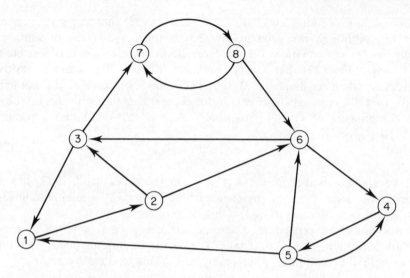

Figure 10.6   Graph G_0 after bounding procedure 3

4.4   Additional bounding procedures

At the end of bounding procedure 3, G_0 is strongly connected and without articulation points. At that stage an attempt is made to find a tour in G_0. For that purpose a specialized implicit enumeration technique is applied, with a cut-off rule. If a tour $\hat{H}$ is found whose incidence vector $\bar{x}$ satisfies with equality all those inequalities (25) such that $w_t > 0$, then $\hat{H}$ is optimal for the current subproblem (this follows from elementary Lagrangean theory).

Example 2 (continued)

The following tour can be identified by inspection in G_0 of Figure 10.6: $H = \{(1, 2),\ (2, 3),\ (3, 7),\ (7, 8),\ (8, 6),\ (6, 4),\ (4, 5),\ (5, 1)\}$. The tour H contains exactly one arc of each cutset associated with a positive λ_t, namely arc $(8, 6)$ of $K_1 = (\{1, 2, 3, 7, 8\}, \{4, 5, 6\})$, and arc $(5, 1)$ of $K_2 = (\{4, 5, 6\}, \{1, 2, 3, 7, 8\})$. Thus the incidence vector of H satisfies with equality the two inequalities (30) corresponding to K_1 and K_2, as required. Further, H contains exactly $|S_1| - 1 = 2$ arcs of the subtour with vertex set $S_1 = \{1, 2, 3\}$, namely, $(1, 2)$ and $(2, 3)$; and exactly $|S_2| - 1 = 2$ arcs of the subtour with vertex set $S_2 = \{4, 5, 6\}$, namely $(6, 4)$ and $(4, 5)$. Thus the complementarity condition is also satisfied for the two inequalities (32) corresponding to S_1 and S_2. Finally, it contains exactly one arc of the set $K_1' \cup K_1''$, where $K_1' = (\{4, 5\}, \{1, 2, 3, 7, 8\})$, $K_1'' = (\{1, 2, 3, 7, 8\}, \{4, 5\})$, namely $(5, 1)$: so the complementarity condition also holds for the inequality (33) corresponding to $K_1' \cup K_1''$. In conclusion, H is optimal, and its value is 26, equal to B_3

If, after bounding procedure 3, a tour $\hat{H}$ is found such that $\hat{x}$ violates this complementarity condition for some $t \in T$, then attempts are made to replace those inequalities (25) that are 'out of kilter', i.e., for which the complementarity condition is violated, by 'in kilter' inequalities (of the same type), i.e., inequalities that are tight for $\hat{x}$ and thus admit positive multipliers satisfying the complementarity condition. These attempts consist of a sequence of three additional bounding procedures, called 4, 5 and 6, one for each type of inequality (30), (32) and (33), respectively. Bounding procedure 4 takes in turn each inequality (30) which has a positive multiplier λ_t and yet is slack for $\hat{x}$, and performs an exhaustive search for other inequalities of type (30) that could replace the inequality in question (with new multipliers) and which are tight for $\hat{x}$. If the search is successful, the in-kilter inequalities with their new multipliers replace the out-of-kilter inequality, and one proceeds to the next out-of-kilter inequality of type (30). Procedures 5 and 6 perform the same function for out-of-kilter inequalities of type (32) and (33), respectively. These procedures are described in detail by Balas & Christofides [1981]. When procedures 4, 5 and 6 are not successful in replacing all out-of-kilter inequalities (and thus proving $\hat{H}$ to be an optimal tour), they nevertheless strengthen the lower bound on $v(\text{TSP})$.

Each of the six bounding procedures is polynomially bounded. The (worst-case) bound is $O(n^4)$ for procedure 1, $O(n^3)$ for each of the other procedures. The mean times are considerably shorter, and on the average procedure 2 (the only one that changes the dual variables u_i, v_j) takes the longest. The general algorithm of course remains valid if any subset of the six bounding procedures is used in place of the full set, but computational testing indicates that using all six procedures is more efficient (i.e. results in smaller search trees and shorter overall computing times) than using any proper subset.

4.5   Branching rules and other features

Before branching, all arcs (i, j) such that $\bar{c}_{ij} \geqslant U - L(w)$ are deleted from G. This 'reduction' has removed on a set of 120 randomly generated problems on the average 96–97% of the arcs in problems with up to 150 vertices, and 98% in problems with 175 to 325 vertices [Balas & Christofides, 1981].

The AP relaxation with Lagrangean objective function can of course be used with any of the branching rules 1 to 5 described in the context of the AP relaxation with objective function (1). Balas & Christofides [1981] use two rules intermittently, namely rule 3 (partitioning on the basis of a subtour elimination inequality (3)) and another rule based on a disjunction from a conditional bound, introduced earlier in the context of set covering [Balas, 1980]. This latter rule is motivated by the following considerations.

Let $\hat{H}$ be the current tour and $\hat{x}$ its incidence matrix. Remove from $L(w)$ all those inequalities (25) that are slack while the associated multiplier is positive. Let $\hat{c}_{ij}$ be the reduced costs, and $L(\hat{w})$ the lower bound, resulting from this removal.

Theorem 3   *Let $S \subseteq \hat{H}$, $S = \{(i_1, j_1), \ldots, (i_p, j_p)\}$ be such that*

$$\sum_{r=1}^{p} \hat{c}_{i,j_r} \geq U - L(\hat{w}), \tag{35}$$

and let the arc sets $Q_r \subseteq A$, $r = 1, \ldots, p$, satisfy

$$\sum_{r \mid (i,j) \in Q_r} \hat{c}_{i,j_r} \leq \hat{c}_{ij}, \qquad (i, j) \in A. \tag{36}$$

Then every solution x to the TSP such that $cx < U$ satisfies the disjunction

$$\bigvee_{r=1}^{p} (x_{ij} = 0, (i, j) \in Q_r). \tag{37}$$

Proof $L(\hat{w})$ is the value of a feasible solution to the dual of the linear program LP defined by (1), (2), $x_{ij} \geq 0$, $(i, j) \in A$, and those inequalities (25) with a positive multiplier. Now let x be a feasible solution to LP that violates (37). Then x satisfies

$$\sum_{(i,j) \in Q_r} x_{ij} \geq 1, \qquad r = 1, \ldots, p. \tag{38}$$

Let LP_+ be the linear program obtained by adding to LP the constraints (38). From (36), if we assign the values $\hat{c}_{i,j_r}$, $r = 1, \ldots, p$, to the dual variables associated with the inequalities (38), we obtain a feasible solution to the dual of LP_+. But then the objective function value of this solution is $L(\hat{w}) + \sum_{r=1}^{p} \hat{c}_{i,j_r}$, and hence from (35)

$$cx \geq L(\hat{w}) + \sum_{r=1}^{p} \hat{c}_{i,j_r} \geq U.$$

Thus every solution x to the TSP such that $cx < U$ satisfies (37). $\square$

The branching rule can now be stated as follows.

Branching rule 10   *Choose a minimum cardinality set*

$$S \subseteq \hat{H}, \qquad S = \{(i_1, j_1), \ldots, (i_p, j_p)\},$$

satisfying (35). Next construct a $p \times |A|$ 0–1 matrix $D = (d_{ij}^r)$ (where r is the row index and (i, j) the column index), with as many 1's in each column as possible, subject to the condition (36) and $(i_r, j_r) \in Q_r$, $r = 1, \ldots, p$, where

$$Q_r = \{(i, j) \in A \mid d_{ij}^r = 1\}.$$

Generate the p new subproblems defined by the disjunction (37), where the rth subproblem is given by

$$\left. \begin{array}{l} E_{k+r} = E_k \cup Q_r \\ I_{k+r} = I_k \end{array} \right\} r = 1, \ldots, p.$$

Branching rule 10 is used intermittently with rule 3 because at different nodes the ranking of the two rules (in terms of strength) may be different. The choice is based on certain indicators of relative strength.

As to subproblem selection, the Balas–Christofides algorithm uses a mixture of depth first and breadth first: a successor of the current node is selected whenever available; otherwise the algorithm chooses a node k that minimizes the function

$$E(k) = (L(w)_k - v(\mathrm{AP})) \frac{s(k)-1}{|s(0)-s(k)|},$$

where $L(w)_k$ is the value of $L(w)$ at node k, $v(\mathrm{AP})$ is the value of the initial AP, while $s(0)$ and $s(k)$ are the number of subtours in the solutions to the initial AP and the one at node k, respectively.

Exercises
5. Let $G_0 = (V, A_0)$ be the admissible graph with respect to (u, v, w), and let $\hat{x}$ be the incidence vector of a tour $H(\hat{x})$ in G_0. Show that $H(\hat{x})$ is an optimal tour in G if $\hat{x}$ satisfies inequality (25) with equality for all $t \in T$ such that $w_t > 0$. Is this sufficient condition also necessary? (*Hint*: Use the optimality conditions for the linear program defined by (1), (2), (25) and $x_{ij} \geq 0$, for all i, j, and its dual.)
6. Show that bounding procedure 1 generates at most $(h-1)(h+2)/2$ cut-sets, where h is the number of subtours in the optimal solution $\bar{x}$ to AP. (*Hint*: Use the following facts: (i) any vertex of a strongly connected component, hence of a subtour, is reachable from any other vertex; (ii) every directed cutset that is generated adds to A_0 at least one new arc joining some subtour to some other subtour; and (iii) when two subtours are joined by arcs in both directions, they form a strongly connected component.)
7. Show that, if B_1 is the lower bound on $v(\mathrm{TSP})$ obtained by bounding procedure 1, the lower bound generated by bounding procedure 2 is

$$B_2 = B_1 + \sum_{t \in T_2} \mu_t.$$

(*Hint*: Use the fact that if the cost of each arc in the set $\bigcup_{t \in T_2} (S_t, S_t)$ is increased by μ_t, then the value of the solution $\bar{x}$ (and hence of the solution (u, v) to the dual of AP obtained at the end of procedure 2) is $v(\mathrm{AP}) + \sum_{t \in T_2} |S_t| \mu_t$.)
8. Let k be an articulation point of the admissible graph G_0, let S_t be the vertex set of one of the components of $G_0 - \{k\}$, and consider the two directed cutsets

$$K'_t = \{S_t, V - S_t \cup \{k\}\}, \qquad K''_t = \{V - S_t \cup \{k\}, S_t\}.$$

Show that the inequality

$$\sum_{(i,j) \in K'_t \cup K''_t} x_j \geq 1$$

is the sum of the inequality (5) for $S = S_t \cup \{k\}$, the inequality (3) for $S = S_t$, and the equation (2) for all $i \in S_t$ and $j \in S_t$.

5 OTHER RELAXATIONS

For the same reasons as in the case of the AP relaxation with the original objective function, the AP relaxation with the Lagrangean objective function is inefficient (weak) in the case of the symmetric TSP. Limited computational experience indicates that on the average the bound $L(w)$ attains about 96% of v(TSP), which compares unfavorably with the bound obtained from the 1-tree relaxation.

On the other hand, the main reason for the weak performance of AP-based relaxations in the case of symmetric problems, namely the high frequency of subtours of length 2 in the optimal AP solution, can be eliminated if AP is replaced by the 2-matching problem in the undirected graph $G = (V, E)$.

5.1 The 2-matching relaxation

The problem of minimizing the function (6) subject to constraints (7) and (9) is known in the literature as the 2-*matching problem*, and is obviously a relaxation of the TSP. Bellmore & Malone [1971] have used it for the symmetric TSP in a way that parallels their use of the AP-relaxation for the asymmetric TSP. A 2-matching is either a tour or a collection of subtours, and the branching rules 2 to 5 based on the subtour elimination inequalities (3) and (5) for the asymmetric TSP have their exact parallels in branching rules based on the subtour elimination inequalities (8) and (10) for the symmetric TSP.

The objective function (6) can be replaced, just as in the case of the AP relaxation, with a Lagrangean function using the inequalities (8) and/or (10). The Lagrangean dual of the TSP formulated in this way is as hard to solve exactly as in the asymmetric case, but it can be approximated by a procedure similar to the one used by Balas & Christofides [1981] with the AP-relaxation. Further facet-defining inequalities, beyond (8) and (10), due to Grötschel & Padberg [1979a,b], can be used to enrich the set drawn upon in constructing the Lagrangean function.

Although the 2-matching problem is polynomially solvable [Edmonds, 1965c], the main impediment in the development of an efficient branch and bound procedure based on the 2-matching relaxation has so far been the absence of a good implementation of a weighted 2-matching algorithm. However, as this difficulty is likely to be overcome soon, the 2-matching relaxation with a Lagrangean objective function will in all likelihood provide bounds for the symmetric TSP comparable to those obtained from the 1-tree relaxation.

5.2 The n-path relaxation

The problem of minimizing (1) subject to the constraint that the solution x be the incidence matrix of a directed n-path starting and ending at a fixed vertex v (where 'path' is used in the sense of walk, i.e., with possible repetition of vertices, and n denotes the length of the path) is clearly a relaxation of the TSP. An analogous relaxation of the symmetric TSP can be formulated in terms of n-paths in the associated undirected graph. Furthermore, the constraints (2) in the asymmetric case, or (7) in the symmetric case, can be used to replace the objective functions (1) or (6), respectively, by a Lagrangean function of the same type as the one used with the 1-arborescence and 1-tree relaxations. This family of relaxations of the TSP was introduced by Houck, Picard, Queyranne & Vemuganti [1980]. The (directed or undirected) n-path problems involved in this relaxation can be solved by a dynamic programming recursion in $O(n^3)$ steps. Computational experience with this approach [Christofides, 1979, p. 142] seems to indicate that the quality of the bound obtained is comparable to the one obtained from the 1-arborescence relaxation in the asymmetric case, but slightly weaker than the bound obtained from the 1-tree relaxation in the symmetric case. Since solving the 1-tree and 1-arborescence problems is computationally cheaper than solving the corresponding n-path problems, this latter relaxation seems to be dominated (for the case of the 'pure' TSP) by the 1-tree or 1-arborescence relaxation. However, the n-path relaxation can easily accommodate extra conditions which the 1-tree and 1-arborescence relaxations cannot and which often occur in prolems closely related to the TSP, such as problems arising in vehicle routing (see Chapter 12) and other practical contexts.

A substantial generalization of the n-path relaxation, due to Christofides, Mingozzi & Toth [1981a] and called state-space relaxation, has the same desirable characteristics of being able to easily accommodate side constraints.

5.3 The linear program with cutting planes as a relaxation

Excellent computational results have been obtained recently by Crowder & Padberg [1980] for the symmetric TSP by a cutting plane/branch and bound approach. It applies the primal simplex method to the linear program defined by (6), (7), $x_{ij} \geqslant 0$, for all i, j, and an unspecified subset of the inequalities defining the convex hull of incidence vectors of tours, generated as needed to avoid fractional pivots. The procedure uses mostly inequalities of the form (10), but also other facet-inducing inequalities from among those introduced by Grötschel & Padberg [1979a,b]. When the search for the next inequality needed for an integer pivot fails, the procedure branches. The main feature of this approach is the identification of appropriate inequalities to be added to the linear program at each step, and it is reviewed in Chapter 9 on cutting plane methods.

Exercise

9. Formulate the n-path relaxation of the TSP for both the asymmetric and the symmetric cases, with a Lagrangean function involving the equations (2) (in the asymmetric case) or (7) (in the symmetric case). Give some examples of side constraints, i.e., extra conditions, that this relaxation of the TSP can accommodate but the 1-arborescence or 1-tree relaxations can not.

6   PERFORMANCE OF STATE-OF-THE-ART COMPUTER CODES

In this section we review the performance of some state-of-the-art branch and bound codes for the TSP, by comparing and analyzing the computational results reported by the authors of these codes.

6.1   The asymmetric TSP

The three fastest currently available computer codes for the asymmetric TSP seem to be those of Balas & Christofides [1981], Carpaneto & Toth [1980] and Smith, Srinivasan & Thompson [1977], to be designated in the following by BC, CT and SST, respectively. The main characteristics of these codes are summarized in Table 10.6. Table 10.7 describes the computational results reported by the authors of the codes. Each of the codes was run on a set of (different) asymmetric TSPs whose costs were independently

Table 10.6   Summary description of three codes for the asymmetric TSP

	SST	CT	BC
Relaxation	AP with TSP objective	AP with TSP objective	AP with Lagrangean objective
Lower bounding	$v(AP)$, obtained by parametric simplex method, plus penalty	$v(AP)$, obtained by Hungarian method (post- optimizing version)	lower bound on Lagrangean, obtained by approximation procedures
Branching rule	3	3	3 and 10
Subproblem selection	depth first	breadth first	depth first upon forward step, breadth first upon back- tracking
Upper bound- ing	no special procedure	no special procedure	tour-finding heuristic
Variable fixing	no	no	yes

Table 10.7   Computational results on randomly generated asymmetric TSPs

n	Nodes of the search tree			Computing time (seconds)		
	SST[1]	CT[2]	BC[2]	SST[3]	CT[4]	BC[5]
40	26	27	—	2.9	0.9	—
50	11	—	12	1.7	—	0.2
60	39	24	—	9.3	2.2	—
70	32	—	—	8.5	—	—
75	—	—	27	—	—	0.3
80	32	42	—	13.8	6.6	—
90	82	—	—	42.0	—	—
100	87	56	39	53.0	10.4	0.7
110	24	—	—	22.3	—	—
120	65	61	—	62.9	16.2	—
125	—	—	43	—	—	1.1
130	97	—	—	110.1	—	—
140	130	57	—	165.2	18.7	—
150	50	—	46	65.3	—	2.0
160	70	73	—	108.5	32.8	—
170	98	—	—	169.8	—	—
175	—	—	58	—	—	4.2
180	215	69	—	441.4	28.8	—
200	—	58	63	—	35.7	6.1
220	—	43	—	—	46.7	—
225	—	—	84	—	—	10.4
240	—	63	—	—	53.4	—
250	—	—	89	—	—	13.7
275	—	—	106	—	—	21.7
300	—	—	124	—	—	38.4
325	—	—	142	—	—	49.7

[1] Number of nodes that were explored; [2] total number of nodes; [3] UNIVAC 1108; [4] CDC 6600; [5] CDC 7600.

drawn from a uniform distribution of the integers in the interval [1,1000]. The entries of the table represent averages for five problems (SST), twenty problems (CT) and ten problems (BC), respectively, in each class. The number of nodes in the SST column is not strictly comparable with that in the CT and BC columns, since it is based on counting only those nodes that were selected for branching and processed. Also, the computing times are not strictly comparable without a correction, since the CDC 7600 is about three times faster than the UNIVAC 1108 and the CDC 6600 (*Computer Review*, GML Corporation, Lexington, MA, 1979). The picture that emerges, however, by comparing the figures *within* each column, for any of these three codes, is a pattern of growth in computational effort with problem size, that seems rather modest for a problem usually viewed as 'notoriously intractable'. We will discuss the functional relationship between problem size and computational effort in some detail further below.

For problems in the range $40 \leqslant n \leqslant 180$, the number of nodes generated by the BC algorithm is considerably smaller than the corresponding numbers for the other two algorithms, although CT uses a 'breadth first' branching strategy, meant to minimize the number of nodes generated, at the cost of increased storage requirements. The reason for this is that the Lagrangean bounding function used by BC changes the ranking of tours among the assignments, removing from consideration many assignment problems whose value in terms of the original objective function is higher than that of the optimal TSP, and which therefore must be processed by the CT algorithm. On the other hand, in the range $200 \leqslant n \leqslant 240$, BC seems to generate more nodes than CT; the reason for this may be that at this point the advantage of the 'breadth first' strategy used by CT outweighs that of the stronger bounding procedures used by BC. This seems to suggest that an algorithm based on the Lagrangean bounding procedures of BC, but using the 'breadth first' node selection strategy of CT, will generate fewer nodes for any problem size, than either the CT or the BC algorithms. This is undoubtedly true, but notice that at the current state of the art, the limiting factor in the use of both algorithms is *not* computing time (which has never exceeded 1.5 minutes for any problem), but (in core) storage space.

6.2 The symmetric TSP

The fastest currently available branch and bound codes for the symmetric TSP seem to be those of Smith & Thompson [1977], Volgenant & Jonker

Table 10.8 Summary description of three codes for the symmetric TSP

	ST	VJ	GS
Relaxation	1-tree with Lagrangean objective	1-tree with Lagrangean objective	1-tree with Lagrangean objective
Lower bounding	subgradient optimization	subgradient optimization with convex combination of subgradients	subgradient optimization
Branching rule	7	8	9
Subproblem selection	depth first	depth first	depth first
Upper bounding	no special procedure	no special procedure	special heuristic
Variable fixing	no	yes	yes

Table 10.9 Computational results on randomly generated symmetric TSPs

n	Nodes of the search tree			Subgradient iterations			Computing time (seconds)		
	ST[1]	VJ[2]	GS[2]	ST	VJ	GS[2]	ST[3]	VJ[4]	GS
50	17			526			22.1		
60	15			572	352	383	34.1	4.7	31.6[5]
70	19			760			61.6		
80	15			764	702	384	83.0	15.5	57.6[5]
100					1664	416		53.2	79.3[5]
150						818			42.5[6]

[1] Number of nodes explored; [2] not reported; [3] UNIVAC 1108; [4] CYBER 750; [5] HP3000/64; [6] IBM 3032.

[1982] and Gavish & Srikanth [1983], to be designated in the following by ST, VJ and GS, respectively. Table 10.8 summarizes their main characteristics, while Table 10.9 reports on their computational performance.

Again, each of the codes was run by their respective authors on a set of (different) symmetric TSPs whose costs were independently drawn from a uniform distribution of the integers in the interval [1, 1000]. The entries of the table represent averages for fifteen problems for ST and VJ (except for $n = 80$, where the entry for ST is the average for five problems only), and for ten problems for GS. The CYBER 750 is about three times faster than the UNIVAC 1108, and about 1.2 times faster than the IBM 3032. The speed of the HP3000/64 is, according to GS, about one-seventh of the IBM 3032.

The codes were also tested on randomly generated symmetric Euclidean TSPs, which required for each code a greater computational effort (e.g., for $n = 60$ the average number of subgradient iterations was 3049 for ST and 1034 for VJ).

6.3 Average performance as a function of problem size

The TSP is well known to be $\mathcal{NP}$-complete, hence in all likelihood there is no polynomial-time TSP algorithm, i.e. no algorithm guaranteed to solve every instance of the TSP in a number of steps polynomial in n. However, this statement refers to the worst-case behavior of algorithms and does not exclude the existence of algorithms whose performance, though exponential in the worst case, is on the average polynomial in n. To make the colloquial term 'on the average' more precise, assume the costs c_{ij} of the TSP are random numbers drawn independently from a uniform distribution over the unit interval. Whether the expected time required to solve such a problem is an exponential or polynomial function of n, is at present an open question, on which the opinion of experts is divided [Bellmore & Malone, 1971; Lenstra & Rinnooy Kan, 1978].

While the theoretical issue remains unsolved, it is not irrelevant to examine from this point of view the empirical performance of some of the more efficient algorithms on randomly generated TSPs. In a recent study [Balas, McGuire & Toth, 1983], three different approximating curves were fitted to the data of Table 10.7 for each of the three codes SST, CT and BC for the asymmetric TSP, in an attempt to determine which of the three types of functions describes best the behavior of each algorithm. The data of Table 10.7 were corrected for the difference in speed between the CDC 7600 and the other two computers by multiplying by 3 the computing times reported for the Balas–Christofides code. The functions examined were:

$$f(n) = \alpha n^\beta \qquad \text{(polynomial)},$$
$$f(n) = \alpha n^{\beta \log n} \qquad \text{(superpolynomial)}.$$
$$f(n) = \alpha e^{\beta n} \qquad \text{(exponential)},$$

where log stands for the natural logarithm and e for its base.

Each of the three functions was expressed in logarithmic form, and a simple regression of $\log f(n)$ was run on $\log n$ (in the case of the polynomial function), on $\log^2 n$ (in the case of the superpolynomial function), and on n (in the case of the exponential function), in order to find the best fitting values of α and β for each case. The outcome is shown in Tables 10.10, 10.11 and 10.12.

Table 10.10   Statistical analysis of the Smith–Srinivasan–Thompson algorithm: $40 \leqslant n \leqslant 180$

Type of function	Best fit	Standard error of estimation	Coefficient of determination
Polynomial	$1.13 \times 10^{-5} \times n^{3.243}$	0.513	0.895
Superpolynomial	$0.152 \times 10^{-1} \times n^{0.361 \log n}$	0.511	0.896
Exponential	$0.92 \times e^{0.0331n}$	0.575	0.868

Table 10.11   Statistical analysis of the Carpaneto–Toth algorithm: $40 \leqslant n \leqslant 240$

Type of function	Best fit	Standard error of estimation	Coefficient of determination
Polynomial	$0.27 \times 10^{-3} \times n^{2.256}$	0.198	0.977
Superpolynomial	$0.37 \times 10^{-1} \times n^{0.241 \log n}$	0.260	0.960
Exponential	$0.45 \times e^{0.014n}$	0.346	0.929

Table 10.12   Statistical analysis of the Balas–Christofides algorithm: $50 \leqslant n \leqslant 325$

Type of function	Best fit	Standard error of estimation	Coefficient of determination
Polynomial	$0.5 \times 10^{-6} \times n^{3.114}$	0.361	0.962
Superpolynomial	$0.87 \times 10^{-3} \times n^{0.320\log n}$	0.260	0.980
Exponential	$0.85 \times 10^{-1} \times e^{0.0205n}$	0.199	0.989

These results suggest that in the limited range of n for which the algorithms were tested ($40 \leqslant n \leqslant 180$ for SST, $40 \leqslant n \leqslant 240$ for CT, and $50 \leqslant n \leqslant 325$ for BC), their behavior can be almost equally well described by any of the three types of functions considered. Although the rankings given by the coefficient of determination seem to be polynomial/superpolynomial/exponential for SST and CT, versus exponential/superpolynomial/polynomial for BC, the differences between the coefficients of determination for the three function types are too small in comparison to the differences between the same coefficients for the different algorithms, in order to attach much significance to these rankings. Further caution and reservations are in order because of the considerable differences in the range of n over which the three codes were tested.

In an attempt to obtain a more meaningful ranking of the three types of approximation curves, the range of n for each of the three algorithms was then broken up into two approximately equal parts, and the same three function types were fitted separately to the data in the lower half and in the upper half of the range of n. The results, shown in Tables 10.13, 10.14 and

Table 10.13   The Smith–Srinivasan–Thompson algorithm, with splitting of the range of n

Type of function	Best fit	Standard error of estimation	Coefficient of determination
	$40 \leqslant n \leqslant 110$		
Polynomial	$0.3 \times 10^{-5} \times n^{3.578}$	0.528	0.827
Superpoly-nomial	$0.46 \times 10^{-2} \times n^{0.434\log n}$	0.505	0.841
Exponential	$0.21 \times e^{0.0554}$	0.455	0.871
	$120 \leqslant n \leqslant 180$		
Polynomial	$0.12 \times 10^{-4} \times n^{3.243}$	0.5183	0.400
Superpoly-nomial	$0.36 \times 10^{-1} \times n^{0.327\log n}$	0.5155	0.406
Exponential	$4.45 \times e^{0.0225n}$	0.5041	0.432

Table 10.14   The Carpaneto–Toth algorithm, with splitting of the range of n

Type of function	Best fit	Standard error of estimation	Coefficient of determination
	$40 \leqslant n \leqslant 120$		
Polynomial	$0.42 \times 10^{-4} \times n^{2.693}$	0.133	0.987
Superpoly-nomial	$0.12 \times 10^{-1} \times n^{0.318 \log n}$	0.141	0.986
Exponential	$0.25 \times e^{0.0364 n}$	0.257	0.952
	$140 \leqslant n \leqslant 240$		
Polynomial	$0.22 \times 10^{-1} \times n^{1.407}$	0.139	0.704
Superpoly-nomial	$0.9 \times n^{0.134 \log n}$	0.137	0.715
Exponential	$8.9 \times e^{0.0073 n}$	0.127	0.755

Table 10.15   The Balas–Christofides algorithm, with splitting of the range of n

Type of function	Best fit	Standard error of estimation	Coefficient of determination
	$50 \leqslant n \leqslant 175$		
Polynomial	$0.12 \times 10^{-4} \times n^{2.407}$	0.288	0.937
Superpoly-nomial	$0.26 \times 10^{-2} \times n^{0.267 \log n}$	0.242	0.956
Exponential	$0.54 \times 10^{-1} \times e^{0.0245 n}$	0.120	0.989
	$200 \leqslant n \leqslant 325$		
Polynomial	$0.49 \times 10^{-9} \times n^{4.379}$	0.100	0.984
Superpoly-nomial	$0.90 \times 10^{-4} \times n^{0.395 \log n}$	0.095	0.986
Exponential	$0.208 \times e^{0.0170 n}$	0.087	0.988

10.15, yield the same rankings as before for the lower half of the range of n, but almost completely reverse the rankings for the upper half of the range: ignoring differences of less than 0.01 in the coefficient of determination, the exponential function ranks first over this range for both the SST and CT algorithms, with the polynomial and superpolynomial functions tied for second place; whereas for the BC algorithm, all three functions are now tied. To the cautionary note voiced earlier, we should now add the fact that the coefficient of determination for this range of n (i.e., the upper half) is considerably weaker for SST (0.40–0.43) and CT (0.70–0.75) than for the full range of n, while for BC it is about the same, i.e., rather strong (0.98–0.99). The findings listed above are supported by additional statistical evidence, for which, as well as for the methodological details of the analysis, the reader is referred to Balas, McGuire & Toth [1983].

The conclusions that we draw from this statistical analysis are as follows.

First, over the limited range of n for which data are available, the performance of the three algorithms analyzed can be described almost equally well by each of the three function types considered: polynomial, superpolynomial and exponential. Second, while the best fitting polynomial functions are of a moderate degree (ranging between 1.4 and 4.4), the best fitting exponential functions have a base very close to 1 (ranging between $e^{0.046} = 1.079$ and $e^{0.007} = 1.012$). Note that an exponential function of this type is very different from the function e^n. While the value of the latter increases more than twice whenever the variable goes from n to $n+1$, the value of 1.012^n increases only by 1.2 percent when the variable goes from n to $n+1$.

The Traveling Salesman Problem
Edited by E. L. Lawler, J. K. Lenstra,
A. H. G. Rinnooy Kan, D. B. Shmoys
© 1985 John Wiley & Sons Ltd.

11

Hamiltonian cycles

V. Chvátal

McGill University, Montreal

1 INTRODUCTION

We assume that the reader is familiar with the essentials of graph theory (see Berge [1973], Bondy & Murty [1976], Harary [1969], Wilson [1972]) and with the essentials of $\mathcal{NP}$-completeness (see Garey & Johnson [1979] or Chapter 3 of this book). All our graphs are finite, undirected, without loops or multiple edges and with at least three vertices; throughout, we reserve the letter n for the number of vertices and the letter m for the number of edges of a graph G.

A *Hamiltonian cycle* in a graph is a cycle passing through all the vertices of this graph; a graph is called *Hamiltonian* if it has at least one Hamiltonian cycle. These terms derive from W. R. Hamilton's invention of what he called 'The Icosian Game', a set of puzzles related to various paths and cycles in the graph shown in Figure 11.1. In one version of this game, the twenty vertices represented twenty important places, from Brussels to Zanzibar, and the player was required to trace a 'voyage round the world' represented by a cycle passing through all the vertices.

Nevertheless, Hamiltonian cycles were studied before Hamilton, by the same T. P. Kirkman who studied Steiner triple systems before Steiner. In one of his papers [Kirkman, 1856], he gave the example of a 3-connected planar non-Hamiltonian graph shown in Figure 11.2. (A generalization of

The author wishes to thank Jean-Claude Bermond, Bob Bixby, David Johnson and Linda Lesniak-Foster for their helpful comments on the first draft of this chapter, and Dick Karp for his permission to include one of his unpublished gems in Section 4.

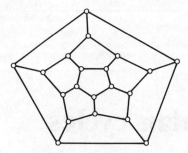

Figure 11.1

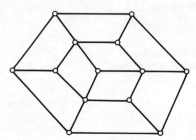

Figure 11.2

this example is left for Exercise 1.) More on the history of the subject is given by Biggs, Lloyd & Wilson [1976].

The aim of this chapter is to highlight some of the ideas used in the study of Hamiltonian graphs.

Exercise
1. A graph is called *bipartite* if its vertices can be colored red and blue in such a way that the two endpoints of each edge have distinct colors. Prove that every bipartite graph with an odd number of vertices is non-Hamiltonian.

2 WHICH GRAPHS ARE NON-HAMILTONIAN?

Sometimes there is an easily verifiable proof of the fact that a particular graph is non-Hamiltonian. (To put it differently, several classes of non-Hamiltonian graphs belong to $\mathcal{NP}$. Or, in the earlier terminology of Edmonds [1965a], there is a good characterization of certain non-Hamiltonian graphs.) For instance, consider the graph G shown in Figure 11.3. When the three vertices marked by stars are removed from G, the rest of the graph breaks down into four connected components. That could not happen if G contained a Hamiltonian cycle C: after the removal of the three starred vertices, the rest of C would hold the rest of G together in at most three

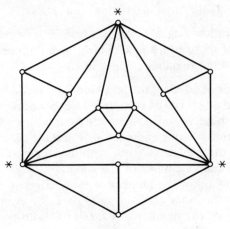

Figure 11.3

connected components. Hence G is non-Hamiltonian. More generally,

> if G contains a nonempty set S of vertices
> whose deletion breaks the rest of the graph
> into more than $|S|$ connected components
> then G is non-Hamiltonian.   (1)

Following Chvátal [1973b], we shall call a graph G *1-tough* if, for each nonempty set S of vertices in G, the graph $G - S$ resulting from G by the removal of S consists of at most $|S|$ connected components. (In Section 6, we shall introduce the more general concept of t-tough graphs.) In this terminology, (1) can be stated as follows:

> if G is not 1-tough then G is non-Hamiltonian.   (2)

The converse of (2) does not hold: the non-Hamiltonian graph shown in Figure 11.4 is 1-tough.

A different kind of a proof that a particular graph G does not contain a Hamiltonian cycle C relies on partitioning the set of vertices of G into

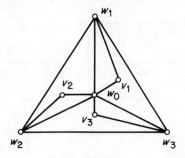

Figure 11.4

disjoint sets R, S, T and then estimating from above:

(i) the number of those edges in C which have at least one endpoint in S;
(ii) the number of those edges in C which have both endpoints in T;
(iii) the number of the remaining edges in C.

Clearly, the number of edges of the first kind is bounded from above by $2|S|$ and the number of edges of the second kind is bounded from above by the number $m(T)$ of those edges in G which have both endpoints in T. Each edge of the third kind has one endpoint in R and the other endpoint in R or T. The number of these edges is $\sum m_Q$, with the summation running through all the connected components Q of the subgraph of G induced by R and with each m_Q standing for the number of those edges in C which have one endpoint in Q and the other endpoint in Q or T. To estimate m_Q, note that $2|Q|$ is at least twice the number of edges in C with both endpoints in Q plus the number of edges in C with one endpoint in Q and the other endpoint in T. Since the number of edges in C with one endpoint in Q and the other endpoint in T is at most the number $m(Q, T)$ of edges in G with one endpoint in Q and the other endpoint in T, it follows that $2m_Q \leqslant 2|Q| + m(Q, T)$. Thus m_Q, being an integer, is at most $|Q| + \lfloor m(Q, T)/2 \rfloor$ and the number of edges of the third kind is at most

$$\sum_Q (|Q| + \lfloor m(Q, T)/2 \rfloor) = |R| + \sum_Q \lfloor m(Q, T)/2 \rfloor.$$

For instance, consider the graph G shown in Figure 11.5 with each vertex labeled by the subset to which it belongs. Here, the number of edges of the first kind is at most $2|S| = 4$ and the number of edges of the second kind is at most $m(T) = 1$. The subgraph of G induced by R consists of two connected components Q, each with $m(Q, T) = 3$. Hence the number of edges of the third kind is at most $|R| + 2\lfloor 3/2 \rfloor = 6 + 2 = 8$. Altogether, the Hamiltonian cycle C can have no more than $4 + 1 + 8 = 13$ edges. On the other hand, C must have precisely fourteen edges as G has precisely

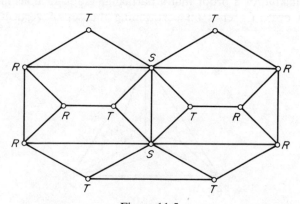

Figure 11.5

fourteen vertices. This contradiction shows that G is non-Hamiltonian; more generally, G is non-Hamiltonian whenever

$$2\,|S| + m(T) + |R| + \sum \lfloor m(Q,\,T)/2 \rfloor < n. \tag{3}$$

(For a stronger statement, which includes (1) as a special case, see Exercise 2.) Incidentally, note that the only property of C used in this argument is the fact that each vertex of G is the endpoint of precisely two edges of C; graphs C with this property are called *2-factors* of G. (Trivially, each of them consists of disjoint cycles which together cover all the vertices of G.) Thus the existence of a partition R, S, T satisfying (3) is sufficient for the nonexistence of a 2-factor of G. A special case of the beautiful 'f-factor theorem' due to Tutte [1952] asserts that the existence of such a partition is also necessary for the nonexistence of a 2-factor of G. In fact, the problem of finding a 2-factor in G can be reduced to the problem of finding a perfect matching in another graph easily constructible from G [Tutte, 1954]. Combined with the efficient algorithm for finding a largest matching in a graph [Edmonds, 1965a], this trick yields an efficient algorithm which, given any graph G, finds either a 2-factor in G or a partition satisfying (3).

Another well-solved problem related to the problem of recognizing Hamiltonian graphs concerns cycles passing through arbitrarily prescribed triples of vertices. A graph is called k-*cyclable* if every k of its vertices lie on a common cycle. Thus a graph is Hamiltonian if and only if it is n-cyclable; every k-cyclable graph is $(k-1)$-cyclable. A classical theorem due to Menger [1927] implies that a graph is not 2-cyclable if and only if it can be disconnected by the removal of a single vertex. A graph is called k-*connected* if it cannot be disconnected by the removal of fewer than k vertices. In this terminology, the above result states that a graph is 2-cyclable if and only if it is 2-connected. It turns out that every k-connected graph $(k \geqslant 2)$ is k-cyclable [Dirac, 1960] (see Exercise 4). Watkins & Mesner [1967] characterized those 2-connected graphs which are not 3-cyclable. The structure of every such graph follows one of three simple patterns. The first of these patterns is illustrated in Figure 11.6: graphs of this kind can be broken into at least three components by a removal of two vertices. (If a vertex v_i belongs to the ith component then there is no cycle passing through v_1, v_2, v_3.) The second pattern is illustrated in Figure 11.4. Graphs of this kind can be pasted together from disjoint graphs A_1, A_2, A_3,

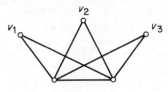

Figure 11.6

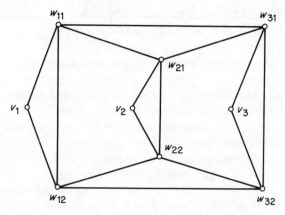

Figure 11.7

B with two distinguished vertices w_0, w_i in each A_i, and four distinguished vertices w_0, w_1, w_2, w_3 in B: as long as each A_i includes a vertex v_i distinct from w_0 and w_i, the graph obtained by identifying vertices with the same labels is not 3-cyclable. (There is no cycle passing through v_1, v_2, v_3.) The third pattern is illustrated in Figure 11.7. Graphs of this kind can be pasted together from disjoint graphs A_1, A_2, A_3, B_1, B_2 with two distinguished vertices w_{i1}, w_{i2} in each A_i, and three distinguished vertices w_{1j}, w_{2j}, w_{3j} in each B_j: as long as each A_i includes a vertex v_i distinct from w_{i1} and w_{i2}, the graph obtained by identifying vertices with the same labels is not 3-cyclable. (There is no cycle passing through v_1, v_2, v_3.)

To summarize, three of the easily verifiable ways to justify the claim that a particular graph G is non-Hamiltonian are as follows:

(i) show that G is not 1-tough by exhibiting an appropriate set S of vertices;
(ii) show that G has no 2-factor by exhibiting an appropriate partition R, S, T;
(iii) show that G is not 3-cyclable by exhibiting appropriate subgraphs A_1, A_2, A_3, B or A_1, A_2, A_3, B_1, B_2.

An attempt to find their common generalization led to the concept of a *weakly Hamiltonian* graph [Chvátal, 1973a]. The starting point is the observation that the characteristic function x of a Hamiltonian cycle C, defined as the assignment of numbers $x(e)$ to edges of G such that

$$x(e) = \begin{cases} 1 & \text{if } e \in C, \\ 0 & \text{if } e \notin C, \end{cases}$$

satisfies a number of easily described linear constraints. Trivially, $0 \leq x(e) \leq 1$ for all e. The fact that each vertex v of G is the endpoint of precisely two edges in C implies that $\sum x(e) = 2$ with the summation running through all the edges having v for an endpoint. The fact that each proper subgraph of C

is acyclic implies that $\sum x(e) \leqslant |S| - 1$ with the summation running through all the edges having both endpoints in a set S of fewer than n vertices. Finally, each subgraph of G with a certain comb-like structure gives rise to an additional linear inequality. More precisely, a *k-comb* is a graph obtained from disjoint graphs $A_1, A_2, \ldots, A_k, B$ with a distinguished vertex w_i and at least one additional vertex in each A_i and distinguished vertices $w_1, w_2, \ldots, w_k$ in B by identifying vertices with the same labels. (This definition is less general than the one given by Chvátal [1973a] but it yields the same results; see also Chapter 8.) It is not difficult to verify (see Exercise 6) that the characteristic function x of any Hamiltonian cycle satisfies the *comb inequality*

$$\sum x(e) \leqslant s - \lceil k/2 \rceil \tag{4}$$

with the summation running through all the edges of a k-comb with s vertices. (Here, as usual, $\lceil t \rceil$ stands for t rounded up to the nearest integer.) A graph is called *weakly Hamiltonian* if the system of all the linear constraints specified above (two bounds for each edge, one equation for each vertex, one inequality for each set of fewer than n vertices and one inequality for each comb) has at least one solution. Trivially, every Hamiltonian graph is weakly Hamiltonian; to put it differently,

if G is not weakly Hamiltonian then G is not Hamiltonian. (5)

The 'one–two–three theorem' proved by Chvátal [1973a] states that every weakly Hamiltonian graph is 1-tough, has a 2-factor and is 3-cyclable. (A proof is left for Exercise 8.) Thus (5) is a common generalization of the three conditions stating that

if G is not 1-tough then G is not Hamiltonian,
if G has no 2-factor then G is not Hamiltonian,
if G is not 3-cyclable then G is not Hamiltonian;

furthermore, there is *always* an easily verifiable proof of the fact that a particular graph is not weakly Hamiltonian. (The last statement follows from the duality theory of linear programming; see for instance, Chvátal [1983]. A discussion of the technical details would exceed the scope of this exposition.)

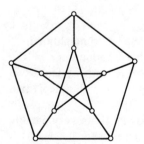

Figure 11.8

However, the converse of (5) does not hold: many non-Hamiltonian graphs are weakly Hamiltonian. One of them, the notorious Petersen graph, is shown in Figure 11.8. There seems to be little hope for a good characterization of all non-Hamiltonian graphs: as proved by Karp, Lawler and Tarjan, the problem of recognizing Hamiltonian graphs is $\mathcal{NP}$-complete (see Chapter 3 of this book).

Exercises

2. Let the set V of vertices of a graph G be partitioned into sets R, S, T such that, with $m(Q, T)$ as in (3) and with $k(T)$ standing for the number of connected components of the graph obtained from G by a removal of R and S,

$$|S| - k(T) + \sum \lfloor m(Q, T)/2 \rfloor < 0$$

and $T \neq V$. Prove that G is non-Hamiltonian. (*Hint*: Observe that at most $|T| - k(T)$ edges of a Hamiltonian cycle have both endpoints in T.)
3. Show that Exercise 2 provides a common generalization of the observations that (i) every Hamiltonian graph is 1-tough and (ii) every Hamiltonian graph has a 2-factor. (*Hint*: First try $R = \varnothing$ and then observe that $m(T) \geq |T| - k(T)$.)
4. [Dirac, 1960]. In its full generality, Menger's theorem states that the smallest size of a set S separating vertices u and v in a graph G (in the sense that u and v belong to distinct components of the graph obtained from G by a removal of S) equals the largest number of paths between u and v, every two of which share only the vertices u and v. Use this fact to prove that every k-connected graph is k-cyclable whenever $k \geq 2$. (*Hint*: Given a graph G with a cycle C and a vertex $u \notin C$, apply Menger's theorem to the graph obtained from G by adding an extra vertex v and making v adjacent to all vertices of C.)
5. Show that, for every k, there is a k-connected graph which is not $(k + 1)$-cyclable. (*Hint*: Generalize the example in Figure 11.6.)
6. Prove that the characteristic function x of any Hamiltonian cycle satisfies the comb inequality (4). (*Hint*: Observe that

$$2 \sum x(e) \leq 2|B| + \sum_{i=1}^{k} (|A_i| - 1) + \sum_{i=1}^{k} (|A_i| - 2).)$$

7. Prove: If a graph admits a partition satisfying (3) then it admits a partition satisfying (3) in which every $v \in R$ has at most one neighbor in T and every $w \in T$ has at most one neighbor in each component Q of the subgraph induced by R. (*Hint*: Show that every $v \in R$ with at least two neighbors in T can be transferred to S and that every $w \in T$ with at least two neighbors in some Q can be transferred to R.)
8. Prove the 'one–two–three theorem'. (*Hint*: In proving that every weakly Hamiltonian graph has a 2-factor, use the result of Exercise 7.)

3 WHICH GRAPHS ARE HAMILTONIAN?

Trivially, all complete graphs are Hamiltonian; a natural extension of this observation states that all graphs with n vertices and some sufficiently large number $f(n)$ of edges are Hamiltonian. Unfortunately, $f(n)$ must be nearly as large as the number of edges in a complete graph with n vertices: a non-Hamiltonian graph with n vertices and $1+(n-1)(n-2)/2$ edges can be obtained from the complete graph H on $n-1$ vertices by adding an extra vertex and making it adjacent to a single vertex in H. (In fact, this graph has the largest number of edges among all the non-Hamiltonian graphs with n vertices; a proof is left for Exercise 9.) Thus the presence of a Hamiltonian cycle is not guaranteed by the mere presence of a large number of edges (unless this number is greater than $1+(n-1)(n-2)/2$). Nevertheless, if a large number of edges are distributed throughout G in a reasonably even way, then G must be Hamiltonian: a theorem due to Dirac [1952] asserts that a graph with n vertices is Hamiltonian whenever each of its vertices is the endpoint of at least $n/2$ edges.

Note that the only information about the structure of G needed to verify the hypothesis of Dirac's theorem is the *degree* $d_G(v)$ of each vertex v, defined as the number of edges in G having v for an endpoint. More generally, one may ask which sequences $d_1, d_2, \ldots, d_n$ of positive integers less than n have the property that every graph G with vertices $v_1, v_2, \ldots, v_n$ such that $d_G(v_i) = d_i$ for all i is Hamiltonian; we shall call such sequences *forcibly Hamiltonian*. A large class of forcibly Hamiltonian sequences has been characterized by Chvátal [1972]: a sequence $d_1, d_2, \ldots, d_n$ is forcibly Hamiltonian whenever

> there is no k such that $0 < k < n/2$, at least k of the numbers d_i are at most k and at least $n-k$ of them are less than $n-k$. $\qquad$ (6)

In a sense which we are about to explain, this is the best theorem of its kind. More precisely, let us say that a sequence $d_1^*, d_2^*, \ldots, d_n^*$ *majorizes* a sequence $d_1, d_2, \ldots, d_n$ if $d_i^* \geq d_i$ for all i. A set S of sequences of length n will be called an *ideal* if, with each sequence d belonging to S, all the sequences which majorize d belong to S. Somewhat unexpectedly, the set of all the forcibly Hamiltonian sequences of length n fails to be an ideal whenever $n \geq 5$: the sequence with $d_1 = d_2 = 2$, $d_3 = \ldots = d_n = n-3$ is forcibly Hamiltonian (Exercise 10) and yet it is majorized by the sequence with $d_1^* = d_2^* = 2$, $d_3^* = \ldots = d_{n-2}^* = n-3$, $d_{n-1}^* = d_n^* = n-1$, which is not forcibly Hamiltonian. Dirac's theorem characterizes an ideal contained in the set of forcibly Hamiltonian sequences of length n, and so do its subsequent improvements [Pósa, 1962; Bondy, 1969]. Since the union of ideals is again an ideal, there is *the* largest ideal contained in the set of forcibly Hamiltonian sequences of length n. We claim that this ideal is characterized by condition (6). To put it differently,

> every sequence $d_1, d_2, \ldots, d_n$ satisfying (6)
> is forcibly Hamiltonian, $\qquad$ (7)

and

for every sequence $d_1, d_2, \ldots, d_n$ violating (6) there is a
non-Hamiltonian graph H with vertices $v_1, v_2, \ldots, v_n$ (8)
such that $d_H(v_i) \geqslant d_i$ for all i.

Claim (8) is easy to justify: if a sequence $d_1, d_2, \ldots, d_n$ violates (6) then
(after a suitable permutation of its terms) it is majorized by the sequence
$d_1^*, d_2^*, \ldots, d_n^*$ such that

$$d_i^* = \begin{cases} k & \text{for } 1 \leqslant i \leqslant k, \\ n-k-1 & \text{for } k < i \leqslant n-k, \\ n-1 & \text{for } n-k < i \leqslant n. \end{cases}$$

The non-Hamiltonian graph H with vertices $v_1, v_2, \ldots, v_n$ such that
$d_H(v_i) = d_i^*$ for all i can be obtained by joining v_i to v_j ($i < j$) if and only if
$i > k$ or $j > n-k$ or both. Since the removal of the k vertices v_j with
$j > n-k$ breaks the rest of H into $k+1$ components, H is not even 1-tough.

The original proof of (7) was nonconstructive; an attempt to find a
constructive proof led to a simple algorithm for finding Hamiltonian cycles
[Bondy & Chvátal, 1976]. This algorithm exploits a lemma due to Ore
[1960], concerning the relationship between G and $G+\{u, v\}$, the graph
obtained from G when previously nonadjacent vertices u and v are joined
by a new edge $\{u, v\}$:

If $G+\{u, v\}$ is Hamiltonian and $d_G(u)+d_G(v) \geqslant n$,
then G is Hamiltonian.

The proof is quite easy. Consider a Hamiltonian cycle C in $G+\{u, v\}$. If C
does not include the edge $\{u, v\}$ then there is nothing to prove; else G
contains a Hamiltonian path $(w_1, w_2, \ldots, w_n)$ with $w_1 = u$ and $w_n = v$. Now
it suffices to find a 'crossover' consisting of edges $\{u, w_{j+1}\}$ and $\{w_j, v\}$ for
some subscript j: then, as illustrated in Figure 11.9, a Hamiltonian cycle in
G is $(w_1, w_{j+1}, w_{j+2}, \ldots, w_n, w_j, w_{j-1}, \ldots, w_1)$. To prove the existence of
such a crossover, consider the set S of those subscripts j for which u is
adjacent to w_{j+1} and the set T of those subscripts j for which v is adjacent to
w_j. Clearly, S and T are subsets of the set of $n-1$ subscripts $1, 2, \ldots, n-1$.
Since $|S| = d_G(u), |T| = d_G(v)$ and $d_G(u)+d_G(v) \geqslant n$, there must be a sub-
script common to S and T, and so there must be a crossover.

The algorithm suggested by Ore's lemma is as follows.

Step 1. Mark all the edges of G by zeros and set $H = G, k = 1$.
Step 2. If H contains nonadjacent vertices u, v such that $d_H(u)+d_H(v) \geqslant n$,
then go to Step 3; otherwise go to Step 4.

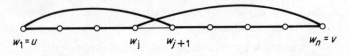

$w_1 = u$ w_j w_{j+1} $w_n = v$

Figure 11.9

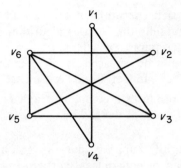

Figure 11.10

Step 3. Replace H by $H+\{u, v\}$, mark the edge $\{u, v\}$ by k, replace k by $k+1$ and return to Step 2.

Step 4. If a Hamiltonian cycle C in H is readily available then go to Step 5; otherwise give up.

Step 5. Let k be the largest mark appearing on an edge of C. If $k = 0$ then stop; otherwise proceed to Step 6.

Step 6. Some crossover yields a Hamiltonian cycle C^* with all the edges marked by less than k. Replace C by C^* and return to Step 5.

For illustration, let us apply this algorithm to the graph G shown in Figure 11.10. Repeated applications of Steps 2 and 3 lead to

> adding the edge $\{v_1, v_6\}$ and marking it by 1,
> adding the edge $\{v_1, v_5\}$ and marking it by 2,
> adding the edge $\{v_1, v_2\}$ and marking it by 3,
> adding the edge $\{v_2, v_3\}$ and marking it by 4,
> adding the edge $\{v_2, v_4\}$ and marking it by 5,
> adding the edge $\{v_3, v_4\}$ and marking it by 6,
> adding the edge $\{v_4, v_5\}$ and marking it by 7.

At this moment, the graph H becomes complete, and so a Hamiltonian cycle in H is readily available: in Step 4, we may let C stand for the cycle $(v_1, v_2, v_3, v_4, v_5, v_6, v_1)$. Now repeated applications of Steps 5 and 6 lead

> from the cycle $(v_1, v_2, v_3, v_4, v_5, v_6, v_1)$ with $k = 7$
> to the cycle $(v_1, v_4, v_3, v_2, v_5, v_6, v_1)$ with $k = 6$
> to the cycle $(v_1, v_4, v_2, v_3, v_5, v_6, v_1)$ with $k = 5$
> to the cycle $(v_1, v_4, v_6, v_5, v_3, v_2, v_1)$ with $k = 4$
> to the cycle $(v_1, v_4, v_6, v_3, v_5, v_2, v_1)$ with $k = 3$
> to the cycle $(v_1, v_4, v_6, v_2, v_5, v_3, v_1)$ with $k = 0$.

In general, the loop consisting of Steps 2 and 3 is executed $O(n^2)$ times and so is the loop consisting of Steps 5 and 6. Each execution of the first loop can be implemented in $O(n)$ steps if a pool of the edges $\{u, v\}$ satisfying $d_H(u) + d_H(v) \geqslant n$ is updated after each iteration (the setup time for this pool is only $O(n^2)$); each execution of the second loop takes only $O(n)$ steps. Thus the total running time of this algorithm comes to $O(n^3)$.

The rather ambiguous phrase 'if a Hamiltonian cycle C in H is readily available' in Step 4 could be replaced by 'if H is complete then take any Hamiltonian cycle C in H'. In fact, Bondy & Chvátal [1976] proved that

> the algorithm produces a complete graph H whenever the
> sequence $d_1, d_2, \ldots, d_n$ defined by $d_i = d_G(v_i)$ satisfies   (9)
> condition (6).

The proof is not difficult. Suppose that the graph H delivered by the algorithm contains a pair of nonadjacent vertices u and v. Choose this pair in such a way that $d_H(u) + d_H(v)$ is maximized and $d_H(u) \leq d_H(v)$; then set $k = d_H(u)$. Since $d_H(u) + d_H(v) < n$, we have $k < n/2$. Furthermore, each vertex w distinct from v and nonadjacent to v has $d_H(w) \leq d_H(u) = k$; the number $n - 1 - d_H(v)$ of such vertices is at least $d_H(u) = k$. Finally, each vertex w nonadjacent to u has $d_H(w) \leq d_H(v) < n - k$ and the number of such vertices, including u itself, is $n - d_H(u) = n - k$. Thus H, and therefore also G, contains at least k vertices of degree at most k and at least $n - k$ vertices of degree less than $n - k$.

Thus we have completed a proof of the theorem (7): given any graph G such that the sequence $d_1, d_2, \ldots, d_n$ defined by $d_i = d_G(v_i)$ satisfies (6), the algorithm will find a Hamiltonian cycle in G in only $O(n^3)$ steps. (An alternative algorithm with the same property has been designed by Bixby & Wang [1978].) As shown by the illustrative example, the algorithm may produce a complete graph H, and therefore find a Hamiltonian cycle in G, even if condition (6) is violated. Nevertheless, as proved by Clark, Entringer & Jackson [1980], the graph G must have at least $\lfloor (n+2)^2/8 \rfloor$ edges in order for H to be complete.

An efficient algorithm which is likely to find a Hamiltonian cycle even in a fairly sparse graph has been designed by Chvátal & Erdös [1972]; if this algorithm fails to find a Hamiltonian cycle then it points out a certain flaw in the structure of the graph. To be more precise, we need two definitions: a set of vertices in a graph is called *independent* if no two vertices in this set are adjacent; a set of vertices in a graph is called *disconnecting* if the graph becomes disconnected when this set is removed. If the algorithm fails to find a Hamiltonian cycle, then it finds an independent set S and a disconnecting set T such that $|S| > |T|$. The algorithm is based on a procedure which, given any non-Hamiltonian cycle C, finds either a longer cycle or the pair S, T. To describe the procedure, let us denote the successor (in a fixed cyclic order) of each vertex $v \in C$ by v^*. Consider an arbitrary component Q of the graph obtained from G by removing all the vertices in C, and let T stand for the set of those vertices $v \in C$ which have at least one neighbor in Q. If

> there are two vertices $v, w \in T$ such that v^* is adjacent to w^*,   (10)

then the longer cycle arises from C by removing the edges (v, v^*) and

(w, w^*), adding the edge (v^*, w^*) and adding a path which joins v to w via Q. (This trick works even if $v^* = w$.) On the other hand, if (10) fails to hold then consider the set T^* consisting of all the vertices v^* such that $v \in T$. Note that T and T^* are disjoint (otherwise (10) would hold for some $v \in T$ and $w = v^*$) and that T^* is independent (otherwise (10) would hold again). Since the neighbors of each $u \in Q$ are restricted to Q and T, the set T is disconnecting and any set S consisting of T^* and a single vertex in Q is independent. (To initialize, it suffices to find a cycle or a two-point independent set and a one-point disconnecting set. This can be done easily in $O(m)$ steps with m standing for the number of edges. The rest consists of fewer than n applications of the above procedure. Since the procedure can be implemented in $O(m)$ steps, the total running time of the algorithm is $O(mn)$.)

Note that we have obtained a sufficiency condition in terms of the *independence number* of G, defined as the largest size $\alpha(G)$ of an independent set in G, and the *connectivity* of G, defined as the smallest size $\kappa(G)$ of a disconnecting set in G (or as $n-1$ in case G is complete):

$$\text{if } \alpha(G) \leqslant \kappa(G) \text{ then } G \text{ is Hamiltonian.} \tag{11}$$

More precisely, the efficient algorithm described just above terminates by showing either that $\alpha(G) > \kappa(G)$ or that G is Hamiltonian. (Without such an algorithm, the appeal of the theorem (11) would be marred by the fact that its hypothesis may be difficult to check: see Exercise 11.) The inequality $\alpha(G) \leqslant \kappa(G)$ may be satisfied even if G has only $O(n^{3/2})$ edges (see Exercise 12); in the next section, we shall see that it is satisfied by an overwhelming majority of all graphs with n vertices and $2n^{3/2}\sqrt{\log n}$ edges. Incidentally, this hypothesis cannot be relaxed to $\alpha(G) \leqslant \kappa(G) + 1$ (see Exercise 13).

A related result involves the minimum degree $\delta(G)$ of a graph G. Clearly, $\kappa(G) \leqslant \delta(G)$ for all graphs G; a theorem due to Nash–Williams [1971] shows that the hypothesis $\alpha(G) \leqslant \kappa(G)$ in (11) can be relaxed to $\alpha(G) \leqslant \delta(G)$ whenever G is 2-connected and $\delta(G)$ is sufficiently large:

$$\begin{array}{l} \text{if } \alpha(G) \leqslant \delta(G), \ \kappa(G) \geqslant 2 \text{ and } \delta(G) \geqslant (n+2)/3 \\ \text{then } G \text{ is Hamiltonian.} \end{array} \tag{12}$$

A simplified proof of (12), due to Bondy [1980], is sketched in Exercises 14 to 17. The condition $\delta(G) \geqslant (n+2)/3$ cannot be relaxed to $\delta(G) \geqslant (n+1)/3$ (see Exercise 18).

There are many other theorems providing sufficient conditions for a graph to be Hamiltonian. We mention only one [Woodall, 1978]: if $\kappa(G) \geqslant 2$, $\delta(G) \geqslant (n+2)/3$, and if, for each nonempty set S of vertices in G, at least $(n+|S|-1)/3$ vertices have at least one neighbor in S, then G is Hamiltonian.

Exercises

9. Let G be a non-Hamiltonian graph with n vertices and a minimum degree at least d. Prove that the number of edges in G does not exceed

$$\frac{n(n-1)}{2} - \tfrac{1}{2}\min\left\{d(2n-3d-1), \left\lfloor\frac{n-1}{2}\right\rfloor\left(2n-3\left\lfloor\frac{n-1}{2}\right\rfloor-1\right)\right\}$$

and characterize graphs attaining this bound. (The special case $d = 1$ is due to Ore [1961] and Bondy [1972].) (*Hint:* Use (7) to show that G has at most

$$\frac{n(n-1)-k(2n-1)+3k^2}{2}$$

edges for some positive integer k such that $k < n/2$.)

10. [Nash–Williams, 1970]. Prove that the sequence $d_1, d_2, \ldots, d_n$ such that $d_i = 2$ for $i = 1, 2$ and $d_i = n-3$ for $i = 3, 4, \ldots, n$ is forcibly Hamiltonian, whenever $n \geqslant 4$. (*Hint:* In case $n \geqslant 6$, consider a graph G with vertices $v_1, v_2, \ldots, v_n$ such that $d_G(v_i) = d_i$ for all i. First observe that two vertices of degree $n-3$ must be nonadjacent. Then combine this observation with (9) to show that the Bondy–Chvátal algorithm applied to G will produce a complete graph H.)

11. Prove that recognizing graphs G such that $\alpha(G) > \kappa(G)$ is an $\mathcal{NP}$-complete problem. (*Hint:* Given a graph H and an integer k, consider the graph G obtained from H by adding $k+1$ pairwise adjacent vertices $w_0, w_1, \ldots, w_k$ and joining each w_i with $1 \leqslant i \leqslant k$ to all the vertices of G.)

12. Construct a graph G with k^2 vertices and $k(k-1)(k+2)/2$ edges such that $\alpha(G) = \kappa(G) = k$. (*Hint:* Begin with k disjoint complete graphs having k vertices each.)

13. Show that, for every positive integer k, there is a non-Hamiltonian graph G such that $\kappa(G) = k$ and $\alpha(G) = k+1$. (*Hint:* Replace 'non-Hamiltonian' by 'not 1-tough'.)

14. Consider a graph G containing a cycle $(u_1, u_2, \ldots, u_k, u_1)$ and a path $(u_1, v_1, v_2, \ldots, v_r, u_{t+1})$ such that $r \geqslant 1$ and $u_i \neq v_j$ for all i and j. Let x and y stand for the numbers of those vertices u_i with $1 \leqslant i \leqslant t$ which are adjacent to u_t and u_k, respectively. Prove: If $x + y > t$ then G contains a cycle with more than k vertices. (*Hint:* First show that, for some i with $1 \leqslant i < t$, the graph contains the edges $\{u_t, u_i\}$ and $\{u_k, u_{i+1}\}$.)

15. Let G, u_i and v_j be as in Exercise 16, except that now $r \geqslant 2$. Let x, y and z stand for the numbers of those vertices u_i with $t < i \leqslant k$ which are adjacent to u_t, u_k and v_2 respectively. Prove: If $x + y + z > k - t + 1$ then G contains a cycle with more than k vertices. (*Hint:* Let R stand for the set of all subscripts i with $t < i \leqslant k$ such that u_i is adjacent to v_2; let P stand for the set of all subscripts $i+1$ with $t < i \leqslant k$ such that u_i is adjacent to u_t; and let Q stand for the set of all subscripts $i+2$ with $t < i < k$ such that u_i is adjacent to u_k. First show that at least two of these three sets have a nonempty intersection.)

16. [Bondy, 1980]. Let G be a 2-connected graph such that, for some longest cycle C in G, some two vertices outside C are adjacent. Prove that G contains nonadjacent vertices u, v, w with $d_G(u) + d_G(v) + d_G(w) \leq n + 1$. (*Hint*: The vertices of C may be enumerated as $u_1, u_2, \ldots, u_k$ in such a way that there is a path $(u_1, v_1, \ldots, v_r, u_{t+1})$ with $r \geq 2$. No generality is lost by assuming that v_2 is adjacent to no u_i with $1 < i \leq t$. Since C is a longest cycle in G, the three vertices u_t, u_k, v_2 are nonadjacent and no two of them have a common neighbor outside C. The rest follows from Exercises 14 and 15.)

17. Prove (12). (*Hint*: Use the result of Exercise 16.)

18. Show that, for every positive integer k, there is a non-Hamiltonian graph G with $3k + 2$ vertices such that $\kappa(G) = 2$, $\alpha(G) = 3$ and $\delta(G) = k + 1$. (*Hint*: Replace 'non-Hamiltonian' by 'not 1-tough'.)

4 RANDOM GRAPHS

In the preceding section, we have seen examples of graphs having a very large number of edges and yet failing to be Hamiltonian. Nevertheless, such examples seem to be rather exceptional. Thus it is only natural to ask what is the probability that a randomly chosen graph with n (labeled) vertices and m edges is Hamiltonian. More generally, one may ask what is the probability that a randomly chosen graph with n vertices and m edges has some prescribed property. Clearly, the total number of graphs with vertices $w_1, w_2, \ldots, w_n$ and with m edges is precisely $\binom{n(n-1)/2}{m}$; if precisely N of these graphs have some property P then the probability that a randomly chosen one will have this property equals $N \Big/ \binom{n(n-1)/2}{m}$. Even when the number $N = N(n, m)$ is difficult to evaluate exactly, certain asymptotic results may be available: if, for a fixed function m of n,

$$\lim_{n \to \infty} \frac{N(n, m(n))}{\binom{n(n-1)/2}{m(n)}} = 1,$$

then it is said that *almost all* graphs with n vertices and $m(n)$ edges have the property P.

Erdös and Rényi, who founded the theory of random graphs, asked how fast $m(n)$ must grow in order to make almost all graphs with n vertices and $m(n)$ edges Hamiltonian. Three early results in this direction are as follows:

(i) Perepelica [1970] presented an efficient algorithm which, for some constant c, finds Hamiltonian cycles in almost all graphs with n vertices and $cn^{3/2}\sqrt{\log n}$ edges.

(ii) Chvátal and Erdös observed that the hypothesis $\alpha(G) \leq \kappa(G)$ of their theorem (11) is satisfied by almost all graphs with n vertices and

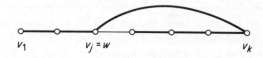

v_1 $v_j = w$ v_k

Figure 11.11

$2n^{3/2}\sqrt{\log n}$ edges. (The argument has remained unpublished; we leave it for Exercises 26 to 28.)

(iii) Wright [1973] gave a nonconstructive proof that almost all graphs with n vertices and $m(n)$ edges are Hamiltonian as long as $m(n)n^{-3/2} \to \infty$.

A decisive breakthrough in the methodology was made by Komlós & Szemerédi [1973]: they introduced a theme whose variations are used in proofs of all the subsequent results. Given a path $v_1, v_2, \ldots, v_k$ and a neighbor w of v_k, they construct a new path by one of two operations, depending on the location of w. If $w \neq v_j$ for all j, then the new path is simply $v_1, v_2, \ldots, v_k, w$; else it is $v_1, v_2, \ldots, v_j, v_k, v_{k-1}, \ldots, v_{j+1}$ with $v_j = w$. Following Karp, we shall refer to these two operations as *extension* and *rotation*, respectively; rotation is illustrated in Figure 11.11. (Rotations were used by Pósa [1962] in the proof of one of the precursors of (7).) Komlós and Szemerédi proceed to create a family of paths by repeated applications of extension and rotation, until they either find a Hamiltonian path that completes into a Hamiltonian cycle or else discover some unlikely flaw in the structure of the graph. The resulting theorem states that almost all graphs with n vertices and $2n \exp(\sqrt{\log n \log \log n})$ edges are Hamiltonian.

A decisive breakthrough in the results was made by Pósa [1976], who refined the analysis of the extension–rotation method to show that, for some constant c, almost all graphs with n vertices and $cn \log n$ edges are Hamiltonian. As we are about to note, this result is the best possible up to the value of c.

Next, Koršunov [1976] designed an efficient algorithm, using the extension–rotation method, to find Hamiltonian cycles in almost all graphs with n vertices and $3n \log n$ edges. (Pósa's proof is nearly but not quite algorithmic.) In addition, Koršunov stated that a more complex algorithm yields the following result: if

$$m(n) = \tfrac{1}{2}n \log n + \tfrac{1}{2}n \log \log n + nc(n) \tag{13}$$

with $c(n) \to \infty$, then almost all graphs with n vertices and $m(n)$ edges are Hamiltonian. (The paper appeared in a journal limiting the lengths of publications to at most four or five pages; this constraint prevented Koršunov from describing his argument in full.) To see that the latter result is best possible, one may appeal to one of the classical results of Erdös &

Rényi [1961]: if $f(n, m)$ is the probability that a randomly chosen graph with n vertices and m edges has no vertex of degree less than two, and if $m(n)$ is defined by (13), then

$$\lim_{n \to \infty} f(n, m(n)) = \begin{cases} 0 & \text{if } c(n) \to -\infty, \\ \exp(\exp(-2c)) & \text{if } c(n) \to c, \\ 1 & \text{if } c(n) \to \infty. \end{cases} \tag{14}$$

Finally, and independently of Koršunov, an even finer theorem was proved by Komlós & Szemerédi [1983]: if $g(n, m)$ is the probability that a randomly chosen graph with n vertices and m edges is Hamiltonian and if $m(n)$ is defined by (13), then g satisfies (14) in place of f. Thus, in a sense, most graphs are Hamiltonian if and only if they have no vertices of degree less than two; Komlós and Szemerédi pointed out the following way of making this statement precise. Let a graph G with vertices $w_1, w_2, \ldots, w_n$ be built edge by edge, with each new edge chosen at random and with equal probabilities among all the available candidates; let this process stop as soon as the degree of each w_i becomes at least two; now the probability that G is Hamiltonian approaches 1 as n tends to infinity. A proof of this theorem will appear in a forthcoming paper by Ajtai, Komlós and Szemerédi.

On the algorithmic side, Angluin & Valiant [1979] streamlined the extension–rotation method by storing of only a single path, rather than a family of paths, from a fixed starting vertex s to some other vertex. The resulting scheme is as follows.

The extension–rotation algorithm

Step 0. Let P stand for the path consisting of the single vertex s.

Step 1. Now you have a path P from s to some vertex x. If P is a Hamiltonian path and if s is adjacent to x then stop: a Hamiltonian cycle has been found.

Step 2. Choose a neighbor y of x; transform P by extension (if $y \notin P$) or rotation (if $y \in P$); return to Step 1.

This scheme embodies a class of algorithms differing from each other in the implementation of the 'choose' in Step 2; Angluin and Valiant choose y *at random* with uniform probabilities from the neighbors of x, and delete the edge $\{x, y\}$ from the graph immediately afterwards. (Of course, this policy may be implemented only as long as x retains at least one neighbor; if x has no neighbors left then the algorithm returns a failure message and stops.) A guarantee of performance of the resulting algorithm is as follows.

> For every positive a there are b and c with the following property: If $m \geq cn \log n$ then the extension–rotation algorithm, given a randomly chosen graph G with n vertices and m edges, finds a Hamiltonian cycle in G within $bn \log n$ iterations with probability $1 - O(n^{-a})$.

Note that this theorem involves two sources of randomness, one in the choice of input and the other in the algorithm; in addition, note that it implies Pósa's theorem instantly.

Angluin and Valiant's proof evolves from a simple observation on the classical 'coupon collector's problem'. This problem concerns sequences $x_1, x_2, x_3, \ldots$ whose terms are drawn from a finite set W at random in such a way that

$$\text{independently of the actual values of } x_1, x_2, \ldots, x_{i-1}, \quad \text{all elements of } W \text{ have an equal chance of becoming } x_i. \quad (15)$$

For definiteness, let us say that W has M elements. If $h(M, t)$ denotes the probability that at least one element of W is missing from the sequence $x_1, x_2, \ldots, x_t$, then clearly

$$h(M, t) \leqslant M\left(\frac{M-1}{M}\right)^t < Me^{-t/M},$$

and so

$$h(M, t) < M^{-a} \qquad \text{whenever} \qquad t \geqslant (a+1)M \log M. \quad (16)$$

(For more information on $h(M, t)$, see Feller [1968].) To relate this observation to the extension–rotation algorithm, consider the sequence $x_1, x_2, x_3, \ldots$ such that x_i is the value of x after the ith execution of Step 2; by definition, each x_i comes from the set W of vertices other than s. Of course, this sequence does not satisfy (15): if the current path is $v_1, v_2, \ldots, v_k$ (with $v_1 = s$ and $v_k = x_{i-1}$) and if $\{v_k, v_j\}$ has been deleted, then v_{j+1} has no chance at all of becoming x_i. Nevertheless, it can be argued that a long initial segment of the sequence comes at least close to satisfying (15). Taking this point of view, let us see what conclusions would follow if we could maintain the assumption that

$$\text{Step 2 gets executed at least } 2t \text{ times} \\ \text{and (15) holds for } i = 1, 2, \ldots, 2t, \quad (17) \\ \text{with } t = \lceil (a+1)(n-1)\log(n-1)\rceil.$$

Under this assumption, (16) guarantees that, with probability $1 - (n-1)^{-a}$, all elements of W appear in $x_1, x_2, \ldots, x_t$, and so a Hamiltonian path is found within the first t iterations. Next, (16) guarantees that, with probability $1 - (n-1)^{-a}$, all elements of W appear in $x_{t+1}, x_{t+2}, \ldots, x_{2t}$, and so Hamiltonian paths from s to all the vertices in W are found within the second t iterations. Finally, as s is adjacent to x_1, the Hamiltonian path from s to x_1 completes into a Hamiltonian cycle. Angluin and Valiant prove that this idealized model approximates closely enough to the actual behavior of their extension–rotation algorithm; the technical details of the proof get quite complicated.

R. M. Karp pointed out that (17) may be enforced with probability $1 - O(n^{-a})$ by changing (a) the way of generating the random input graph, and (b) the way of choosing the vertex y in Step 2. (A similar argument was developed independently by E. Shamir and D. E. Knuth.) Karp's beautifully simple proof yields a result analogous to the Angluin–Valiant theorem; we are going to describe its details.

As for (a), the input in Karp's algorithm is the graph $G(n, p)$ with vertices $v_1, v_2, \ldots, v_n$ in which any two vertices are adjacent with probability p independently of all the remaining adjacencies and nonadjacencies. To put it more formally, $G(n, p)$ is a random variable taking values in the set of all graphs with vertices $v_1, v_2, \ldots, v_n$; each graph with k edges occurs as the actual value of $G(n, p)$ with probability

$$\binom{\binom{n}{2}}{k} p^k (1-p)^{\binom{n}{2}-k}.$$

The definition of $G(n, p)$ is another popular way of formalizing the intuitive notion of a random graph with a specified density.

As for (b), Karp begins by preprocessing the input $G(n, p)$ to create, for each vertex x, a set $N(x)$ of neighbors of x such that, for each pair of distinct vertices x and y, the probability of $y \in N(x)$ is $p/2$ independently of all the remaining inclusions $y' \in N(x')$. To do so, one needs only set, for each edge (v_i, v_j) with $i < j$,

$$v_i \in N(v_j), v_j \in N(v_i) \qquad \text{with probability} \qquad p/4,$$
$$v_i \in N(v_j), v_j \notin N(v_i) \qquad \text{with probability} \qquad \tfrac{1}{2} - p/4,$$
$$v_i \notin N(v_j), v_j \in N(v_i) \qquad \text{with probability} \qquad \tfrac{1}{2} - p/4,$$
$$v_i \notin N(v_j), v_j \notin N(v_i) \qquad \text{with probability} \qquad p/4.$$

A certain subset $\text{OLD}(v)$ of each $N(v)$ is stored and updated throughout the run of the algorithm; this set consists of all the elements of $N(v)$ that have been chosen as y in previous executions of Step 2 with $x = v$. (In particular, each $\text{OLD}(v)$ is initially empty.) When it comes to choosing y in Step 2, Karp sets

$$C = \begin{cases} \text{OLD}(x) & \text{with probability} \quad \dfrac{|\text{OLD}(x)|}{n-1}, \\[2mm] N(x) - \text{OLD}(x) & \text{with probability} \quad 1 - \dfrac{|\text{OLD}(x)|}{n-1}, \end{cases}$$

and then he chooses y with equal probabilities from C. (If $C = N(x) - \text{OLD}(x)$ then y is added to $\text{OLD}(x)$.) It is easy to see that, as long as $N(x) - \text{OLD}(x)$ is nonempty, all vertices other than x have an equal chance of becoming y; in turn, it follows that all vertices in W (defined earlier as the set of vertices other than s) have an equal chance of becoming the new x.

The analogue of the Angluin–Valiant theorem goes as follows:

If a is positive and if $p \geqslant 15.95(a+1)\log n/(n-1)$, then Karp's extension–rotation algorithm finds a Hamiltonian cycle in $G(n, p)$ within $2(a+1)n \log n$ iterations with probability $1 - O(n^{-a})$.

To prove this theorem, we need only verify that (17) holds with probability $1 - O(n^{-a})$; the latter task reduces to showing that, with probability $1 - O(n^{-a})$, the inequality

$$|\text{OLD}(v)| < |N(v)|$$

persists for all vertices v throughout the first $2t$ iterations. (Here, as in (17), $t = \lceil (a+1)(n-1)\log(n-1) \rceil$.) For this purpose, consider an arbitrary but fixed vertex v; let $f(v)$ denote the probability that, at some time before the $2t$th execution of Step 2,

$$|\text{OLD}(v)| = |N(v)| \leq 0.271p(n-1),$$

but $|\text{OLD}(w)| < |N(w)|$ for all the remaining vertices w; let $g(v)$ denote the probability that, at some time before the $2t$th execution of Step 2,

$$|\text{OLD}(v)| = |N(v)| \geq 4.32(a+1)\log n$$

but $|\text{OLD}(w)| < N(w)|$ for all the remaining vertices w. Since $0.271p(n-1) \geq 4.32(a+1)\log n$, we need only prove that $f(v) = O(n^{-a-1})$ and $g(v) = O(n^{-a-1})$ for all v. These facts follow routinely from the inequalities

$$\sum_{i \leq 0.542pm} \binom{m}{i} p^i (1-p)^{m-i} < e^{-0.126pm} \tag{18}$$

and

$$\sum_{i \geq 2.16pm} \binom{m}{i} p^i (1-p)^{m-i} < e^{-pm/2}, \tag{19}$$

whose proofs are outlined in Exercises 19 to 21. (A more general standard bound on the tail of the binomial distribution is given in Exercise 20.) To prove that $f(v) = O(n^{-a-1})$, observe that the probability of $|N(v)| \leq 0.271p(n-1)$ is the left-hand side of (18) with $m = n-1$ and with $p/2$ in place of p. To prove that $g(v) = O(n^{-a-1})$, note that $t \leq (a+1)(n-1)\log n$ whenever $n-1 \geq 1/a$, in which case $g(v)$ is at most the left-hand side of (19) with $m = 2t$ and $p = 1/(n-1)$.

Just as Pósa's theorem is an instant corollary of Angluin and Valiant's theorem, the following theorem is an instant corollary of Karp's theorem:

> if $p \geq 15.96 \log n/(n-1)$ then $G(n, p)$ is Hamiltonian
> with probability $1 - o(1)$. $\tag{20}$

It is a routine matter to derive Pósa's theorem (with $c = 8$) from (20); we leave the details for Exercises 22 to 25.

Exercises

19. Prove that

$$\sum_{i \geq k} \binom{m}{i} p^i (1-p)^{m-i} \leq x^{-k}(px + (1-p))^m$$

whenever $x \geq 1$. (*Hint*: Expand $(px + (1-p))^m$ by the binomial formula.)

20. Prove that

$$\sum_{i \geq k} \binom{m}{i} p^i (1-p)^{m-i} \leq \left(\frac{pm}{k}\right)^k \left(\frac{m-pm}{m-k}\right)^{m-k}$$

whenever $k \geq pm$, and that

$$\sum_{i \leq k} \binom{m}{i} p^i (1-p)^{m-i} \leq \left(\frac{pm}{k}\right)^k \left(\frac{m-pm}{m-k}\right)^{m-k}$$

whenever $k \leq pm$. (*Hint*: The first inequality may be obtained by setting $x = k(1-p)/p(m-k)$ in Exercise 19; the second inequality follows from the first by the substitution $p \leftarrow 1-p$, $k \leftarrow m-k$, $i \leftarrow m-i$.)

21. Prove (18) and (19). (*Hint*: Note that $(m-pm)/(m-k) < \exp((k-pm)/(m-k))$; verify that

$$\left(\frac{1}{2.16}\right)^{2.16} e^{1.16} \doteq e^{-0.503} \quad \text{and} \quad \left(\frac{1}{0.542}\right)^{0.542} e^{-0.458} \doteq e^{-0.12603}.)$$

22. Prove: If $\varepsilon > 0$ and if $n^2 p(n) \to \infty$ then the probability of $G(n, p(n))$ having at least $(1+\varepsilon)n(n-1)p(n)/2$ edges is $o(1)$. (*Hint*: Use the first part of Exercise 20 with $m = n(n-1)/2$.)

23. A graph property is called *monotone* if it remains preserved whenever an edge is added to the graph. Consider an arbitrary but fixed monotone property; let $f(n, m)$ be the probability that a randomly chosen graph with vertices $v_1, v_2, \ldots, v_n$ and with m edges has this property. Prove that $f(n, m+1) \geq f(n, m)$. (*Hint*: Let N be the number of pairs (G_0, G_1) such that G_i is a graph with vertices $v_1, v_2, \ldots, v_n$ and with $m+i$ edges, and such that G_0 has the monotone property. Compare a formula for N in terms of n, m, and $f(n, m)$ with an upper bound on N in terms of n, m, and $f(n, m+1)$.)

24. Let $f(n, m)$ be defined as in the preceding exercise. Prove: If $n^2 p(n) \to \infty$, if $\varepsilon > 0$ and if $m(n) \geq (1+\varepsilon)n(n-1)p(n)/2$, then the probability of $G(n, p(n))$ having the property is at most $(1-o(1))f(n, m(n)) + o(1)$. (*Hint*: Use Exercises 22 and 23.)

25. Prove: If $m(n) \geq 8n \log n$ then almost all graphs with n vertices and $m(n)$ edges are Hamiltonian. (*Hint*: Use (20) and Exercise 24.)

26. Prove: If $m(n) \geq 10n \log n$ then almost all graphs with n vertices and $m(n)$ edges have no vertices of degree less than $m(n)/n$. (*Hint*: Set $p(n) = 1.5m(n)/n(n-1)$ and use the second part of Exercise 20 to show that the probability of $G(n, p(n))$ having a vertex of degree less than $0.5(n-1)p(n)$ is $1-o(1)$. Then use Exercise 24 with the property 'has no vertex of degree less than $0.5(n-1)p(n)$'.)

27. Prove: If $m(n) \geq 2n^{3/2}$ then almost all graphs with n vertices and $m(n)$ edges have $\kappa > m(n)/(2n)$. (*Hint*: Show that the number of graphs G with n vertices, m edges, $\kappa(G) \leq m/(2n)$ and $\delta(G) \geq m/n$ does not exceed

$$\sum_m \binom{\binom{n}{2} - |A||B|}{m},$$

with the summation running through all the partitions of the set of vertices into disjoint subsets A, B, C such that $|C| \le m/(2n)$, $|A| + |C| > m/n$, and $|B| + |C| > m/n$. Observe that

$$|A|\,|B| \ge \frac{m}{2n}\left(n - \frac{m}{n}\right) > \frac{m}{4},$$

and that the number of summands does not exceed 3^n. Finally, use the bounds

$$\frac{\binom{N-k}{m}}{\binom{N}{m}} \le \left(\frac{N-k}{N}\right)^m \le e^{-km/N},$$

valid whenever $k \ge 0$.)

28. Prove: Almost all graphs with n vertices and $m(n)$ edges have $\alpha < (2n^2 \log n)/m$. (*Hint:* Show that the number of graphs G with n vertices, m edges, and $\alpha(G) \le s$ does not exceed

$$\binom{n}{s}\binom{\binom{n}{2} - \binom{s}{2}}{m}.$$

Then use the bounds from the preceding hint and the trivial bound $\binom{n}{s} < n^s$.)

29. [Karp, 1983]. Consider the following variation on the extension–rotation algorithm: Initialize by letting each $N(v)$ consist of *all* the neighbors of v and by letting each $\mathrm{OLD}(v)$ be empty; in each execution of Step 2, choose y just as Karp does; then add y to $\mathrm{OLD}(x)$ *and* add x to $\mathrm{OLD}(y)$. One might argue that, in a randomly chosen graph with vertices $v_1, v_2, \ldots, v_n$ and with m edges, each vertex other than x can become y with probability $1/(n-1)$ as long as $N(x) - \mathrm{OLD}(x) \ne \varnothing$: since $\mathrm{OLD}(x)$ consists of all the vertices z such that the presence of the edge $\{x, z\}$ has been detected, all sets of $|N(x) - \mathrm{OLD}(x)|$ vertices disjoint from $\{x\} \cup \mathrm{OLD}(x)$ are equally likely to be $N(x) - \mathrm{OLD}(x)$. Where is the fallacy in this argument? (*Hint:* Consider the case of $n = m = 4$ with $s = v_1$; assume that $y = v_2$ has been chosen in the first execution of Step 2, that $y = v_3$ has been chosen in the second execution of Step 2, and that $N(v_3) - \mathrm{OLD}(v_3) \ne 0$ after the second execution of Step 2. Now the input G must be one of the following graphs:

G_1 with edges $\{v_1, v_2\}, \{v_2, v_3\}, \{v_3, v_1\}, \{v_3, v_4\}$,
G_2 with edges $\{v_1, v_2\}, \{v_2, v_3\}, \{v_3, v_1\}, \{v_1, v_4\}$,
G_3 with edges $\{v_1, v_2\}, \{v_2, v_3\}, \{v_3, v_1\}, \{v_2, v_4\}$,
G_4 with edges $\{v_1, v_2\}, \{v_2, v_3\}, \{v_3, v_4\}, \{v_1, v_4\}$,
G_5 with edges $\{v_1, v_2\}, \{v_2, v_3\}, \{v_3, v_4\}, \{v_2, v_4\}$.

If c_i denotes the probability that, given the input G_i, the two choices of y were as stipulated, then

$$c_1 = 1/2, \qquad c_2 = 1/3, \qquad c_3 = 1/4, \qquad c_4 = 1/2, \qquad c_5 = 1/2.$$

Hence the probabilities p_i of $G = G_i$ are

$$p_1 = 6/25, \qquad p_2 = 4/25, \qquad p_3 = 3/25, \qquad p_4 = 6/25, \qquad p_5 = 6/25.$$

It follows that the probabilities of v_1, v_2 and v_4 becoming y in the third execution of Step 2 are 4/15, 5/15 and 6/15, respectively.)

5 PLANAR GRAPHS

A graph is called *cubic* if each of its vertices has degree three. It was the four-color problem which stimulated interest in Hamiltonian planar graphs: if a planar cubic graph is Hamiltonian then it is easy to color its faces by four colors in such a way that adjacent faces always receive distinct colors. In 1880, P. G. Tait conjectured that every 3-connected planar cubic graph is Hamiltonian (see Biggs, Lloyd & Wilson [1976] for details). This conjecture remained open for more than sixty years, until the counterexample shown in Figure 11.12 was found [Tutte, 1946].

On the other hand, it was also proved that every 4-connected planar graph is Hamiltonian [Tutte, 1956]. The argument has been converted by Gouyou–Beauchamps [1982] into an algorithm which, given any 4-connected planar graph G with n vertices, finds a Hamiltonian cycle in G in only $O(n^3)$ steps.

The problem of recognizing Hamiltonian graphs does not get any easier when the input is restricted to planar graphs; as proved by Garey, Johnson & Tarjan [1976], the problem remains $\mathcal{NP}$-complete even if the input is restricted to 3-connected planar cubic graphs. (Akiyama, Nishizeki & Saito [1980] modified the argument to show that the problem remains $\mathcal{NP}$-complete when the input is restricted to cubic bipartite planar graphs; see also Chapter 3.) Nevertheless, Grinberg [1968] discovered a trick which sometimes simplifies the task of showing that a particular planar graph is

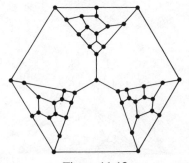

Figure 11.12

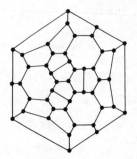

Figure 11.13

non-Hamiltonian: if, in a planar Hamiltonian graph with n vertices, precisely f_k faces are bounded by k edges ($k = 3, 4, \ldots$) then the system

$$\sum_{k=3}^{\infty} (k-2)x_k = n-2, \qquad 0 \leq x_k \leq f_k$$

has a solution in nonnegative integers x_k. The proof is easy: assume that there is a Hamiltonian cycle C and let x_k stand for the number of those faces bounded by k edges which lie inside C. If there are precisely i edges inside C then $\sum x_k = i+1$ and $\sum kx_k = 2i+n$, and the result follows. The use of this condition may be illustrated on the graph shown in Figure 11.13. Since the system

$$3x_5 + 6x_8 + 7x_9 = 44, \qquad 0 \leq x_5 \leq 21, \qquad 0 \leq x_8 \leq 3, \qquad 0 \leq x_9 \leq 1$$

has no integer solution (a proof is left for Exercise 30), the graph is non-Hamiltonian.

A planar graph is called a *triangulation* if each of its faces is bounded by three edges. Nishizeki [1980] constructed examples of non-Hamiltonian triangulations which are 1-tough; one such example is shown in Figure 11.14. More recently, Chvátal and Wigderson have independently shown that the problem of recognizing Hamiltonian graphs remains $\mathcal{NP}$-complete even if the input is restricted to triangulations; the details are left for Exercise 31.

On the other hand, Ewald [1973] found several conditions under which a

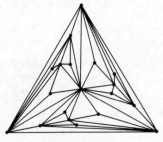

Figure 11.14

triangulation is Hamiltonian: for instance, this is the case whenever each vertex of the triangulation has degree at most six.

Exercises

30. Show that there are no integers x_5, x_8, x_9 such that

$$3x_5 + 6x_8 + 7x_9 = 44, \qquad 0 \leqslant x_5 \leqslant 21, \qquad 0 \leqslant x_8 \leqslant 3, \qquad 0 \leqslant x_9 \leqslant 1.$$

(*Hint*: Replace the equation by a congruence modulo 3.)

31. Given a cubic bipartite planar graph G, consider the triangulation H constructed as follows. Each red vertex of G which is the endpoint of edges e_1, e_2, e_3 gives rise to the graph shown in Figure 11.15(a). Each blue vertex of G which is the endpoint of edges f_1, f_2, f_3 gives rise to the graph shown in Figure 11.15(b). Vertices with the same labels are identified and then extra edges added until a triangulation H is obtained. Prove that H is Hamiltonian if and only if G is Hamiltonian.

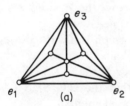 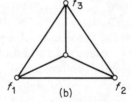

Figure 11.15

6 POWERS OF GRAPHS

The kth *power* G^k of a graph G is the graph with the same set of vertices as G, two vertices being adjacent in G^k if and only if they are joined by a path of at most k edges in G. G^3 is Hamiltonian whenever G is connected [Sekanina, 1960] (for a proof, see Exercise 32); an example of a connected graph G such that G^2 is non-Hamiltonian is shown in Figure 11.16.

Plummer and Nash–Williams conjectured, independently of each other, that G^2 is Hamiltonian whenever G is 2-connected; their conjecture has been proved [Fleischner, 1974]. The proof has been converted [Lau, 1980]

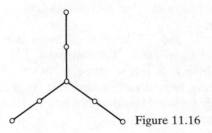

Figure 11.16

(see also Lau [1981]) into an algorithm which, given a 2-connected graph G with n vertices, finds a Hamiltonian cycle in G^2 in only $O(n^2)$ steps.

Since squares of 2-connected graphs are rather special graphs, one may ask which of their properties make them Hamiltonian. For instance, a graph is called *t-tough* if the deletion of an arbitrary set of s vertices leaves the rest of the graph either connected or else broken into no more than s/t components. It is easy to prove (see Exercise 33) that the square of a k-connected graph is always k-tough. Thus the conjecture of Chvátal [1973b] that every 2-tough graph is Hamiltonian would imply Fleischner's theorem.

It is an $\mathcal{NP}$-complete problem to recognize graphs whose squares are Hamiltonian [Underground, 1978] (see Exercise 34).

Exercises

32. Prove that, for every tree T and every choice of distinct vertices u, $v \in T$, there is a path from u to v in T^3 which passes through all the vertices. (*Hint*: Observe that the deletion of a suitable edge breaks T into disjoint trees T_u and T_v such that $u \in T_u$, $v \in T_v$. Now the desired result can be obtained by induction on the number of vertices.)

33. Prove that the square of a k-connected graph is always k-tough. (*Hint*: Let G be k-connected and let the deletion of a set S of vertices separate G^2 into connected components $G_1, G_2, \ldots, G_N$. Write $u \in S_i$ if $u \in S$ and if some edge of G joins u to G_i. Observe that the sets $S_1, S_2, \ldots, S_N$ are disjoint and that each of them has at least k elements.)

34. Prove that recognizing graphs G such that G^2 is Hamiltonian is an $\mathcal{NP}$-complete problem. (*Hint*: Given a graph H, consider the graph G obtained by adding vertices u_1, u_2 and edges $\{u, u_1\}, \{u_1, u_2\}$ for every vertex u of G.)

35. [Neumann, 1964; Harary & Schwenk, 1971]. Characterize those trees T for which T^2 is Hamiltonian. (*Hint*: Prove that a tree T does not contain the subtree of Figure 11.16 if and only if the tree obtained from T by deleting all the vertices of degree 1 is a path.)

36. [Parker & Rardin, 1984]. Let C be an $n \times n$ distance matrix that satisfies the triangle inequality; that is, $c_{ij} + c_{jk} \geqslant c_{ik}$ for all i, j, k. C represents the intercity distances for a TSP instance. If T is a tour, set $cost(T) = \max_{(i,j) \text{ traversed in } T}\{c_{ij}\}$; for the *bottleneck TSP*, the desired tour minimizes $cost(T)$. Denote the optimal tour T^*. Prove that, unless $\mathcal{P} = \mathcal{NP}$, for any fixed $\varepsilon > 0$, there does not exist a polynomial algorithm that always finds a tour T such that $cost(T)/cost(T^*) \leqslant 2 - \varepsilon$.

37. [Parker & Rardin, 1984]. Let $cost(T)$ and T^* be defined as in the previous exercise. Construct a polynomial algorithm for the bottleneck TSP with triangle inequality that produces a tour T such that $cost(T)/cost(T^*) \leqslant 2$. (Note how this compares with the result proved in Exercise 36!) (*Hint*: Use the algorithm of Lau [1980], which finds a Hamiltonian cycle in the square of a 2-connected graph, as a subroutine.)

7 CONCLUSION

This is a biased exposition, meant to introduce the reader to Hamiltonian graphs rather than to provide an extensive survey of their theory.

One of the glaring omissions is the subject of Hamiltonian cycles in directed graphs. This area (not related to the TSP quite as closely as its undirected counterpart) is rich in results and deserves a survey of its own. In fact, an excellent survey of the more general subject of cycles in directed graphs is available [Bermond & Thomassen, 1981].

Another subject not treated here concerns algorithms that, given an arbitrary graph G, either find a Hamiltonian cycle in G or establish its absence. (Of course, unless $\mathcal{P} = \mathcal{NP}$, the worst-case running time of such algorithms must be superpolynomial.) A class of such algorithms is based on a straightforward idea: Enumerate all the permutations of the n vertices and check each of them for inducing a Hamiltonian cycle. Several obvious shortcuts are available in this scheme. First, one may consider only those permutations whose first term is some prescribed vertex. Second, if the permutations are enumerated in the lexicographic order then many of the hopeless candidates may be bypassed at once. Finally, as the would-be Hamiltonian cycle is being built step by step, inclusion of certain edges forces exclusion of others; in turn, this may force inclusion of new edges, and the chain reaction may go on. Details, along with an encouraging report on experimental results, are given by Christofides [1975, Ch. 10].

Other topics not covered here may be found in several survey papers [Bermond 1979; Bondy 1978; Lesniak–Foster 1977; Nash–Williams 1975].

Research problems
1. How difficult is it to recognize 1-tough graphs?
2. How difficult is it to recognize forcibly Hamiltonian sequences? (Results extending beyond (7) have been obtained by Nash–Williams [1970].)
3. Prove or disprove: (i) every 2-tough graph is Hamiltonian; (ii) there is a constant t such that every t-tough graph is Hamiltonian.

The Traveling Salesman Problem
Edited by E. L. Lawler, J. K. Lenstra,
A. H. G. Rinnooy Kan, D. B. Shmoys
© 1985 John Wiley & Sons Ltd.

12

Vehicle routing

N. Christofides

Imperial College of Science and Technology, London

1 INTRODUCTION

We consider the distribution problem in which vehicles based at a central facility (depot) are required to visit – during a given time period – geographically dispersed customers in order to fulfill known customer requirements. The problem appears in a large number of practical situations concerning the distribution of commodities and is known by the generic name: the *vehicle routing problem* (VRP). The VRP is also known in the literature as the 'vehicle scheduling' [Clarke & Wright, 1964; Gaskell, 1967], 'truck dispatching' [Dantzig & Ramser, 1959; Christofides & Eilon, 1969; Krolak, Felts & Nelson, 1972] or simply 'delivery problem' [Hays, 1967], and appears frequently in situations not related to the delivery of goods. For example, the collection of mail from mail boxes or coins from

The author's work was partially supported by the SERC, England.

telephone boxes, house call tours by a doctor, salesman routing, preventive maintenance inspection tours, etc. [Stern & Dror, 1979] are all VRPs in which the 'delivery' operation may be a collection and/or delivery or neither, and in which the 'customer requirements' and 'vehicles' can take a variety of forms, some of which may not even be of a physical nature.

In view of the enormous number of practical situations which give rise to VRPs, one can only hope to study the basic problem which is at the core of all vehicle routing problems. We will call this core problem the *basic* VRP.

1.1   The basic VRP and its extensions

The customers are indexed $i = 2, \ldots, n$ and $i = 1$ refers to the depot. The vehicles are indexed $k = 1, \ldots, m$.

A customer i has a demand of q_i. The travel cost between customers i and j is c_{ij}. The capacity of vehicle k is Q_k. We will assume that all customers and vehicles are ordered in descending order of q_i and Q_k respectively.

The basic VRP is to route the vehicles (one route per vehicle, starting and finishing at the depot), so that all customers are supplied with their demands and the total travel cost is minimized. Figure 12.1 shows the shape of the solution to a VRP.

The basic VRP ignores a large number and variety of additional constraints and extensions that are often found in real-world problems. Some of

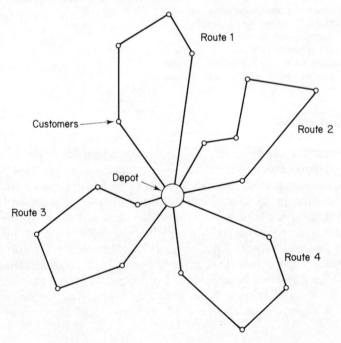

Figure 12.1   Shape of solution to the basic VRP

these constraints and extensions are [IBM, 1970; Christofides, Mingozzi & Toth, 1982]:

(i) Each vehicle can operate more than one route, provided the total time spent on these routes is less than a given time T (which is related to the operating period). Note that such a constraint – in common with many of the ones listed below – requires the knowledge of travel times (t_{ij}) between every pair of customers.

(ii) Each customer must be visited only at a time that lies in one of a given number of working *time windows* during the period.

(iii) The problem may involve both deliveries to and collections from customers. In addition, it may be possible to mix deliveries and collections on a single route, or alternatively, it may be required for a vehicle to first perform all the deliveries in the route before performing the collections. This latter case is often referred to as *backhauling*.

(iv) Just as in (ii) above (every customer has working time windows), vehicles (in fact their drivers) may also have working time windows during the period. The vehicle can then only operate during the specified time windows.

(v) Time-consuming activities other than the travel times (t_{ij}) mentioned above must also be considered. These include: unloading times (or loading times for the case of collections) at the customer premises; loading times of the vehicles at the depot – both for the first and for any subsequent routes (see (i)); queueing times of vehicles for loading at the depot if the number of available loading bays is limited; etc.

Although the constraints and extensions listed above are only a small fraction of those found in practice, they – and many others – do not change the essential nature of the basic VRP and can be incorporated in quite a number of the heuristic methods for solving the problem. On the other hand, there are some other practical considerations that also arise frequently, and which do not fit neatly into the basic VRP framework. Some of these aspects are discussed in the next section.

1.2 Some practical aspects of vehicle routing problems

Multiple depots

In companies with more than one depot, it is often the case that each depot is autonomous, with its own fleet of vehicles and its own geographical customer area to serve. In such cases, the company would simply face a number of similar single-depot vehicle routing problems. In other cases, however, depot operations are interdependent and vehicles leaving one depot may, after delivering to customers, end up at another depot, perhaps to load again and continue on a subsequent trip. In these cases each depot cannot be considered in isolation.

Level of customer service

The time period during which the customer requirements must be fulfilled is one of the most important parameters in a vehicle routing problem, and is a measure of the *service level*. Since customer ordering is a dynamic, non-periodic process, any attempt to define a vehicle routing problem for a given period must, by definition, be an approximation or an arbitrarily imposed order. Some of these approximations are as follows.

(a) *Typical period.* Consider the case when the customers are fixed and their demands are assumed to be typical in a given period. A customer that is expected to order once every t days is required to be visited T/t times during the period of T days, and these visits must be $t \pm \varepsilon$ days apart, for some small given value of ε. The fixed routes that are produced by solving the vehicle routing problem for the period are often made public so that each customer knows when to expect his deliveries. Clearly, problems of feasibility can arise in a real period that is not typical.

(b) *Cut-off time.* A frequently used *modus operandi* is to set a cut-off date for orders. Orders received in the previous T days are delivered in the following T days. The vehicle routing problem for a T-day period is then completely specified. However, with such a system, orders received during the current T-day period and which could (or perhaps should) have been delivered in the current period, are ignored until the next T-day period. The net result is that infeasibility problems (usually resolved by hiring extra vehicles) may arise in some periods.

(c) *Creeping customer priorities.* An often used alternative to defining a period, as in (a) or (b) above, is to allocate a priority to each customer according to the time interval remaining up to the date when the customer must be visited (say T days after receipt of the order). The smaller the time remaining, the higher the customer priority. At any one time the vehicle routing problem would then involve a complex objective of both routing costs and the priorities of the customers that are routed, in an attempt to maintain the customer service within a T-day maximum delay.

Multiple commodities

In some vehicle routing problems, the vehicles are compartmented so that different commodities are stored in segregated compartments. Each customer may require specified quantities of different types of commodity. Such problems appear in the distribution of gasoline fuel, refrigerated (or not) foods, etc., and involve – in addition to the routing aspect of vehicle routing problems – a knapsack or bin-packing aspect.

Different objectives

On some occasions the situation may arise when it is simply infeasible to solve the vehicle routing problem as given (see 'Level of customer service' above). In practice, this infeasibility is resolved by either (a) hiring more vehicles, and/or (b) postponing service to some customers beyond the established service level or into the next period. In these circumstances the objective may be to minimize:

(1) the number of extra vehicles hired; and/or
(2) the number (or sum of weights) of customers not served in the present period; and/or
(3) the total distance (or time) traveled.

In general, the objective in a vehicle routing problem may be a linear combination of objectives (1), (2) and (3) above.

2   FORMULATIONS OF THE BASIC VRP

The purpose of this section is not to give a comprehensive review of VRP formulations, which are many and varied [Golden, 1976; Gavish & Srikanth, 1979], but to present some formulations which have been used as a basis for solution methods.

2.1   Formulation 1 [Fisher & Jaikumar, 1978, 1981]

Let

$$x_{ijk} = \begin{cases} 1, & \text{if vehicle } k \text{ visits customer } j \text{ immediately} \\ & \text{after customer } i, \\ 0, & \text{otherwise,} \end{cases}$$

$$y_{ik} = \begin{cases} 1, & \text{if customer } i \text{ is visited by vehicle } k, \\ 0, & \text{otherwise.} \end{cases}$$

The basic VRP is then to minimize

$$\sum_{i,j} c_{ij} \sum_{k} x_{ijk} \tag{1}$$

subject to

$$\sum_{k} y_{ik} = \begin{cases} 1, & i = 2, \dots, n, \\ m, & i = 1, \end{cases} \tag{2}$$

$$\sum_{i} q_i y_{ij} \leqslant Q_k, \qquad\qquad k = 1, \dots, m, \tag{3}$$

$$\sum_{j} x_{ijk} = \sum_{j} x_{jik} = y_{ik}, \qquad i = 1, \dots, n, \qquad k = 1, \dots, m, \tag{4}$$

$$\sum_{i,j \in S} x_{ijk} \leqslant |S| - 1, \qquad \text{for all } S \subseteq \{2, \dots, n\}, \qquad k = 1, \dots, m, \tag{5}$$

$$y_{ik} \in \{0, 1\}, \qquad\qquad i = 1, \dots, n, \qquad k = 1, \dots, m, \tag{6a}$$

$$x_{ijk} \in \{0, 1\}, \qquad\qquad i, j = 1, \dots, n, \qquad k = 1, \dots, m. \tag{6b}$$

Constraints (2) ensure that every customer is allocated to some vehicle (except for the depot which is visited by all vehicles), constraints (3) are the vehicle capacity constraints, constraints (4) ensure that a vehicle which visits a customer also leaves that customer, and constraints (5) are the usual subtour elimination constraints for the TSP.

2.2 Formulation 2 [Christofides, Mingozzi & Toth, 1980]

Let all optimal feasible single routes for vehicle 1 in the VRP be indexed $r = 1, \ldots, \hat{r}$. Let the index set of customers in route r be M_r and the cost of the route (i.e. the cost of the optimal TSP solution through the customers of the route) be d_r. We will use $N_i = \{r \mid i \in M_r\}$.

We will assume that the routes are ordered in descending order of their load $K_r = \sum_{i \in M_r} q_i$ and use r_k as the smallest value of r such that $K_r \leq Q_k$. Define $r_{m+1} = \hat{r} + 1$. Let

$$y_r = \begin{cases} 1, & \text{if route } r \text{ is in the optimal VRP solution,} \\ 0, & \text{otherwise.} \end{cases}$$

The basic VRP is then to minimize

$$\sum_{r=1}^{\hat{r}} d_r y_r \tag{7}$$

subject to

$$\sum_{r \in N_i} y_r = 1, \qquad i = 2, \ldots, n, \tag{8}$$

$$\sum_{r=1}^{r_{k+1}-1} y_r \leq k, \qquad r_k \neq r_{k+1}, k = 1, \ldots, m, \tag{9}$$

$$\sum_{r=1}^{\hat{r}} y_r = m, \tag{10}$$

$$y_r \in \{0, 1\}, \qquad r = 1, \ldots, \hat{r}. \tag{11}$$

Constraints (8) ensure that every customer is visited, constraints (9) and (10) ensure that the m routes chosen for the solution are feasible to operate using the m vehicles.

2.3 Formulation 3 [Christofides, Mingozzi & Toth, 1981a]

The above two formulations are integer programming ones; we will now give a dynamic programming formulation of the basic VRP.

Let $N = \{2, \ldots, n\}$ be the set of customers. For any $T \subseteq N$, let $f(k, T)$ be the minimum cost of supplying the customers in T using only vehicles $1, \ldots, k$, let $v(T)$ be the minimum cost of a solution to the TSP defined by the depot and the customers in T, and let $q(T) = \sum_{i \in T} q_i$. The dynamic programming recursion is initialized for $k = 1$ by $f(1, T) = v(T)$ and defined for $k \geqslant 2$ by

$$f(k, T) = \min_{S \subset T} \{f(k-1, T-S) + v(S)\} \qquad (12)$$

subject to

$$q(T) - \sum_{h=1}^{k-1} Q_h \leqslant q(S) \leqslant Q_k, \qquad (13)$$

$$\frac{1}{m-k} q(N-T) \leqslant q(S) \leqslant \frac{1}{k} q(T). \qquad (14)$$

Here, $k = 2, \ldots, m$, except for the left-hand side of (14) for which $k \neq m$. The sets $T \subseteq N$ to be considered must satisfy

$$q(N) - \sum_{h=k+1}^{m} Q_h \leqslant q(T) \leqslant \sum_{h=1}^{k} Q_h. \qquad (15)$$

The restrictions on S and T are so as to avoid computation of $f(\cdot)$ and $v(\cdot)$ for sets that can only lead to load-infeasible completions. The right-hand side of constraint (13) is the capacity restriction on vehicle k, whereas the left-hand side of (13) is a capacity restriction on the first $k-1$ vehicles. We have imposed an (arbitrary) order on the routes so that a route with greater load is operated by a vehicle of greater capacity than another route with smaller load. The routes are then indexed by the index of the vehicle operating the route. Constraint (14) partly imposes this ordering by insisting that the load on route k is greater than the average load on the remaining $m-k$ routes, and less than the average load on the first $k-1$ routes.

Exercise

1. Consider an instance of the VRP with the depot at vertex 1 and six customers at vertices $2, \ldots, 7$. The symmetric distance matrix is shown in Table 12.1. There are two vehicles with capacities $Q_1 = Q_2 = 6$. The customer demands are $(q_2, \ldots, q_7) = (2, 3, 1, 1, 2, 1)$.

Generate all feasible routes to this problem. Write down the formulation of Section 2.2. Solve this model to optimality, by inspection.

Table 12.1   Distance matrix for a
VRP instance

	1	2	3	4	5	6	7
1	–						
2	28	–					
3	21	47	–				
4	14	36	26	–			
5	17	25	37	15	–		
6	18	20	30	31	29	–	
7	22	35	20	34	39	16	–

3 OPTIMIZATION ALGORITHMS FOR THE BASIC VRP

Optimization algorithms for solving the basic VRP are based on the formulations given in the previous section. As with any combinatorial problem, their success or failure is entirely dependent on the degree to which they exploit problem structure. We present here an approach based on Benders decomposition using formulation 1 of Section 2.1, and a branch and bound algorithm using bounds obtained from relaxations of formulation 2 and state-space relaxation of the recursion of formulation 3.

Before describing these algorithms we will first describe a well-solved case of the VRP.

3.1 A well-solved case of the VRP

Consider a VRP for which $Q_1 = Q_2 = \ldots = Q_m = Q$ and with $q_n + q_{n-1} + q_{n-2} > Q$. For such a problem, all routes contain one or two customers only. Form a graph $G = (N, E)$ with a set of vertices $N = \{2, \ldots, n\}$ and a set of edges $E = \{\{i, j\} \mid i, j \in N, q_i + q_j \leq Q\}$. Set the cost of edge $\{i, j\}$ equal to $c_{1i} + c_{ij} + c_{j1}$ and the penalty p_i of a vertex i to $2c_{1i}$. The solution of the generalized minimum cost matching problem on graph G provides a solution to the VRP. The *generalized matching problem* on a graph is to find a matching such that the sum of the costs of the arcs in the matching plus the sum of the penalties of the vertices that are unmatched is minimum [Christofides & Thornton, 1982].

In the graph G, the matching of vertex i to vertex j is interpreted as a route $(1, i, j, 1)$ in the VRP. A vertex i left unmatched is interpreted as a route $(1, i, 1)$. Note that if s arcs are in the matching then there are $n - s$ routes in the VRP. Thus, if it is required to have exactly m routes, s must be set to be $(n - m)$. Setting the cardinality of a matching does not lead to any additional computational problems.

It has been assumed here that the travel cost matrix is symmetric. Generalization to the asymmetric case is straightforward.

3.2 An algorithm based on Benders decomposition [Fisher & Jaikumar, 1978]

The problem defined by equations (1) to (6) in formulation 1 consists of two interlinked subproblems, namely, a *generalized assignment problem* defined by constraints (2), (3) and (6a), and a TSP (in fact m independent TSPs) defined by constraints (4), (5) and (6b). Formulation (1) can then be rewritten to bring out this structure, as the nonlinear generalized assignment problem of minimizing

$$\sum_k f_k(\mathbf{y}_k) \tag{16}$$

subject to

constraints (2), (3) and (6a),

where $\mathbf{y}_k$ is written for the vector $(y_{1k}, y_{2k}, \ldots, y_{nk})$ and $f_k(\mathbf{y}_k)$ is the cost of an optimal solution to the TSP defined by the customer set $\{i \mid y_{ik} = 1\}$ and the depot, for a given value of k. This function is given by

$$f_k(\mathbf{y}_k) = \min\left\{\sum_{i,j} c_{ij} x_{ijk}\right\} \tag{17}$$

subject to

constraints (4), (5) and (6b).

Obviously, $f_k(\mathbf{y}_k)$ is a very complicated function which cannot be written down explicitly. One possible approach is to construct (iteratively) a piecewise linear approximation of $f_k(\mathbf{y}_k)$ by applying Benders decomposition. Each time the generalized assignment problem – defined by (16), (2), (3) and (6a), with some approximation for $f_k(\mathbf{y}_k)$ – is solved to obtain $\mathbf{y}_k$, a lower linear support of $f_k(\mathbf{y}_k)$ is constructed. This support is derived by solving the m independent TSPs implied by (17), (4), (5) and (6b) for the given $\mathbf{y}_k$ and using the dual variables thus obtained. The Benders inequalities describing this lower support are then added to constraints (2), (3) and (6a) to form an extended generalized assignment problem. This problem is now resolved to obtain a new improved $\mathbf{y}_k$, which in turn leads to new TSPs, whose solution provides further Benders inequalities, and so on.

The procedure terminates when the value of the solution to the extended generalized assignment problem (which provides a lower bound to the value of the VRP) coincides with the sum of the values of the solutions to the TSPs (which provide an upper bound).

Although the overall picture painted above is very much that of a general Benders decomposition, a number of points have to be made.

The TSP subproblems

Since the TSP subproblems defined by (17), (4), (5) and (6b) are integer programs, dual variables cannot be obtained directly. This complication can be removed by replacing constraints (6b) with their linear counterpart

$$0 \leq x_{ijk} \leq 1, \qquad \text{for all } i, j, k,$$

together with as many linear inequalities of the form

$$\alpha_k \mathbf{x}_k + \beta_k \mathbf{y}_k \leq \gamma_k \tag{18}$$

as necessary to insure that x is naturally integer for any integer y.

Clearly, both the constraint sets (5) and (18) are very large and are best generated as and when required. Fisher & Jaikumar [1978] used Gomory cutting planes to impose integrality on the x, taking care that the constraints

of type (18) produced by these cutting planes are valid for all y_k. Constraints
(5) are generated as required in the standard way as for any TSP (cf. Chapter
9).

The generalized assignment master problem

The generalized assignment problem defined by (16), (2), (3) and (6a) is
extended – at some arbitrary iteration – by the addition of the Benders
constraints. This problem can be solved to optimality (although this is clearly
not necessary at every iteration) by using a branch and bound algorithm
using bounds obtained from the Lagrangean relaxation of constraints (2) and
the Benders constraints.

3.3   An algorithm based on set covering

The problem defined by (7) to (11) in formulation 2 is a set partitioning
problem with simple additional constraints. Any of the algorithms developed
for solving set covering or partitioning problems [Marsten, 1974; Balas &
Padberg, 1976; Christofides & Paixao, 1982] could be easily adapted to deal
with the above problem. However, a basic weakness with the above
approach – as an optimization procedure for the VRP – is the need to
enumerate all routes $r = 1, \ldots, \hat{r}$. Even for very moderate size problems –
other than for cases where there are only one or two customers per
route – this route generation step is a formidable task. An advantage of this
approach is that as the VRP becomes more and more constrained, the
number of routes that must be considered becomes smaller and smaller.

3.4   A branch and bound algorithm based on state-space relaxation
[Christofides, Mingozzi & Toth, 1980, 1981a]

As is the case with all branch and bound algorithms, their effectiveness is
entirely dependent on the quality of the bounds used to limit the tree
search. We will, therefore, first discuss the derivation of such bounds.

Minimum q-routes

Let W_k be the set of all possible loads (quantities) that could exist on a
route operated by vehicle k, i.e.

$$W_k = \left\{ q \mid \sum_i q_i \, \delta_i = q \leq Q_k, \, \delta_i \in \{0, 1\} \right\}.$$

Let the elements of W_k be ordered in ascending order. We will denote by
$q^{(l)}$ the value of the lth element of W_k and by $\lambda(q)$ that l for which $q^{(l)} = q$.
If $(i_1, i_2, \ldots, i_k)$ is a path (not necessarily simple), we will call $\sum_{h=1}^{k} q_{i_h}$ the
total load on that path.

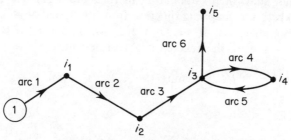

Figure 12.2 A q-path with a loop

Let $\phi_l(i)$ be the cost of the least cost path from the depot (vertex 1) to customer i with total load $q^{(l)}$. Figure 12.2 shows a possible such path called a q-path. It is not easy to impose the condition that no vertex on the path is visited more than once, but it is simple to impose the less stringent restriction that the path should not contain loops formed by three consecutive vertices (such as i_3, i_4, i_3 in Figure 12.2). Thus, we will henceforth refer to q-paths and their costs $\phi_l(i)$, implying that these paths are loopless.

Let $\psi_l(i)$ be the cost of the least cost route without loops, starting from the depot, passing through customer i and finishing back at the depot with a total load $q^{(l)}$. Such a route will be referred to as a *through q-route*. Figure 12.3 shows a through q-route.

Christofides, Mingozzi & Toth [1980] have shown how $\phi_l(i)$ and $\psi_l(i)$ can be computed for all $l = 1, \ldots, |W_1|$ and $i = 2, \ldots, n$ in time proportional to $|W_1|$ and n.

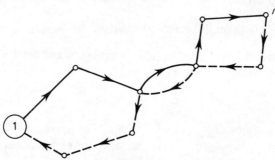

Figure 12.3 A through q-route via customer i

Bounds from state-space relaxation [Christofides, Mingozzi & Toth, 1980, 1981a]

Using the dynamic programming formulation of the basic VRP given by equations (12) to (15), we will use a state-space relaxation to compute lower bounds that will subsequently be used in a branch and bound algorithm for solving the VRP. The lower bounds derived in this way are, in general, of excellent quality.

The original state (k, T) appearing in recursion (12) will be relaxed to $(k, g(T))$ where g is a mapping function from the space of all subsets T to a lower-dimensional space. If we take $g(T) = q(T)$ for all $T \subseteq N$ and write $q(T) = t$, $q(S) = s$, then the relaxed problem becomes

$$f(k, t) = \min_{s < t}\{f(k - 1, t - s) + \bar{v}(s)\} \tag{12'}$$

subject to

$$t - \sum_{h=1}^{k-1} Q_h \le s \le Q_k, \tag{13'}$$

$$\frac{1}{m - k}(q(N) - t) \le s \le \frac{1}{k} t, \tag{14'}$$

$$q(N) - \sum_{h=k+1}^{m} Q_h \le t \le \sum_{h=1}^{k} Q_h, \tag{15'}$$

where $\bar{v}(s)$ is the minimum cost of a circuit, starting and finishing at the depot, with total load s.

A lower bound on $\bar{v}(s)$ is clearly either $\min_i\{\psi_l(i)\}$ or $\min_i\{\phi_l(i) + c_{i1}\}$, where $l = \lambda(s)$.

After one of the above substitutions is made for $\bar{v}(s)$ in (12'), the final value of the recursion, i.e. $f(m, q(N))$, is a lower bound to the VRP.

Another bound that can be obtained directly from (12) is as follows. Recursion (12) implies that the final solution to the VRP is given by

$$f(m, N) = v(S_1) + v(S_2) + \ldots + v(S_m) \tag{19}$$

for some subsets $S_1, \ldots, S_m$. Consider a subset S and let $l = \lambda(q(S))$. Then $\psi_l(i) \le v(S)$ for any $i \in S$ and, in general,

$$\sum_{i \in S} \alpha_i \psi_l(i) \le v(S)$$

for any $\alpha_i \ge 0$ subject to $\sum_{i \in S} \alpha_i = 1$. A choice of α_i which always guarantees the last equality is $\alpha_i = q_i/q^{(l)}$. Thus, an easy lower bound is obtained from (19) as

$$\sum_{i \in N} \min_{1 \le l \le |W_1|}\{q_i \psi_l(i)/q^{(l)}\}. \tag{20}$$

Other bounds from state-space relaxations were given by Christofides, Mingozzi & Toth [1980, 1981a]. Some of these bounds can also be derived by Lagrangean relaxation, starting from formulation 2 [Christofides, Mingozzi & Toth, 1980].

The bounds derived above from state-space relaxation can be improved by penalty methods (using subgradient optimization) in much the same way as bounds derived from Lagrangean relaxation.

Branching strategies

There are many branching rules that can be used in a branch and bound scheme using the bounds derived earlier. Possibly the simplest of these involves choosing an as yet unrouted customer to include in or exclude from the currently emerging route. The bound (e.g. that given by expression (20)) can be computed at every node of the branch and bound tree. When a route is completed, the customers in the route are sequenced optimally by solving the corresponding TSP. Note that additional constraints (e.g. delivery time windows) may require the use of a specialized TSP code [Christofides, Mingozzi & Toth, 1981b].

3.5 Computational comments

As far as the present author is aware, the largest VRP of any reasonable complexity that was solved optimally involved 53 customers and 8 vehicles. The problem was solved using the algorithm of Section 3.4. This problem involved – in addition to capacity constraints – constraints on the driving time, different capacity vehicles, unloading times, and a few (not very tight) customer delivery time windows. In this problem, it was possible to have up to 15 customers on a route.

Exercises

2. Consider the seven-city TSP whose symmetric distance matrix is given in Table 12.1 (see Exercise 1).
(a) Formulate the problem as a dynamic program and use the mapping function $g(T) = \sum_{i \in T} q_i$ (where T is any subset of cities and q_i is a nonnegative integer associated with city i) to produce a relaxed recursion.
(b) Use the vector $q = (0, 2, 3, 1, 1, 2, 1)$ to compute q-paths of length $\phi_l(i)$ based on city 1, and use them to obtain a TSP bound.
3. Consider the VRP defined in Exercise 1.
(a) Use the q-paths computed in Exercise 2 to compute $\bar{v}(s)$ $(s = 1, \ldots, 6)$ for the second term of equation (12').
(b) Use (12') to compute the lower bound $f(2, 10)$ to the VRP.
4. Consider the VRP defined in Exercise 1.
(a) Compute the through q-routes of length $\psi_l(i)$.
(b) Use these values to compute a lower bound to the VRP from expression (20). Compare this bound to the one obtained in Exercise 3.
5. Suppose that, in the VRP of Exercise 1, $Q_1 = 6$ and $Q_2 = 5$. Recompute the bounds from (12') and (20) and compare them with those obtained in Exercises 3 and 4.

4 HEURISTICS FOR THE BASIC VRP

A great deal of work has been done devising heuristics for the VRP, although much less effort has been spent comparing and drawing conclu-

sions. The possibilities for heuristics are virtually limitless and the purpose
of the present section is not to list them all, but simply to provide an outline
of some of the best known.

Heuristics can be classified in the following categories:

(1) constructive methods;
(2) two-phase methods;
(3) incomplete optimization methods.

4.1 Constructive methods

Constructive methods can be further classified according to:
(a) the criterion used to expand the routes,
and
(b) whether the routes are constructed sequentially or in parallel.

The savings algorithm [Clarke & Wright, 1964]

This heuristic is one of the earliest ones and is without doubt the most
widely known heuristic for the VRP. The algorithm proceeds as follows:

Step 1. Calculate the *saving* $s_{ij} = c_{1i} - c_{ij} + c_{j1}$ for all pairs of customers i and
j. Note that s_{ij} is the saving in cost that would result if the link (i, j)
is made to produce route $(1, i, j, 1)$ instead of supplying i and j on
two routes $(1, i, 1)$ and $(1, j, 1)$ (see Figure 12.4).

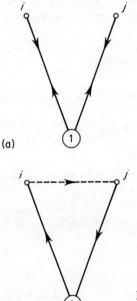

(a)

(b)

Figure 12.4 Saving of link (i, j). (a) Initial state.
(b) State after link (i, j) is made

Step 2. Order the savings in descending order.
Step 3. Starting at the top of the list, do the following.
Parallel version
Step 4. If making a given link results in a feasible route according to the constraints of the VRP, then append this link to the solution; if not, reject the link.
Step 5. Try the next link in the list and repeat Step 4 until no more links can be chosen.
Sequential version
Step 4. Find the first feasible link in the list which can be used to extend one of the two ends of the currently constructed route.
Step 5. If the route cannot be expanded further, terminate the route. Choose the first feasible link in the list to start a new route.
Step 6. Repeat Steps 4 and 5 until no more links can be chosen.

In both the sequential and parallel versions of this procedure, it is advisable to check the feasibility of the partial solution at every stage, to ensure that the available vehicles can operate the routes being formed. Otherwise, it is quite likely that at the end no feasible solution is found. Also note that the initial starting solution when every customer is on a separate route is infeasible. However, the possibility always exists at the end to leave unrouted some customers on single-customer routes.

Many modified definitions of savings have been proposed to achieve different results (see, e.g., Gaskell [1967] and Yellow [1970]). In particular, the original Clarke and Wright algorithm produces circumferential routes that were often objected to by schedulers. Golden, Magnanti & Nguyen [1977] substantially reduced the running time of the Clarke and Wright algorithm by sophisticated computer science methods.

Other constructive methods

Many other constructive methods exist which use criteria different from savings. We mention in particular the sequential tour building procedure of Mole & Jameson [1976], in which a criterion is used that can change the emphasis from giving preference to circumferential routes, to giving emphasis to radial shaped routes. This criterion contains parameters that are user controlled.

4.2 Two-phase methods

In two-phase methods, the first phase consists of clustering the customers by assigning them to vehicles, and the second phase routes these clusters.

The sweep algorithm [Gillett & Miller, 1974]

Both the first and second phases of this procedure are of a sequential nature. Assume that the VRP is Euclidean and that customers are located by their polar coordinates (r_i, θ_i) with the depot at $r_1 = 0$ and an arbitrary customer i^* at $\theta_{i^*} = 0$. (Other metrics can also be accommodated.) Reorder the customers such that $\theta_2 \leqslant \ldots \leqslant \theta_n$.

Phase I
Step 1. Choose an unused vehicle k.
Step 2. Starting from the unrouted customer i with smallest angle θ_i, include consecutive customers $i+1, i+2, \ldots$ in the route until the capacity constraint of the vehicle k is reached.
Step 3. If all customers are 'swept' or if all vehicles have been used go to Phase II, else return to Step 1.

Phase II
Step 4. Solve the TSP for every set of customers assigned to a vehicle to form the final routes.

Note that there are a number of possible variations of the sweep algorithm above. Different choices of the 'reference' customer i^* from which to measure the polar coordinate angles, lead to different final routes. The same is true with different rules used to choose the vehicle to consider next.

The two-phase method of Christofides, Mingozzi & Toth [1979]

The first phase of this heuristic consists of performing a number of clustering trials using a least cost insertion criterion with a user-controlled extra parameter that could produce different trials.

Phase I
Step 1. (*Sequential trial*) Choose an unrouted customer to be a *seed*. Choose a vehicle k to allocate to the emerging route.
Step 2. Enter unrouted customers into the emerging cluster, in increasing order of some insertion cost relative to the seed of the cluster, until the capacity limit of vehicle k is reached. If all customers are clustered, or all vehicles used, go to Step 3, else repeat from Step 1.
Step 3. (*Parallel trial*) Using the seeds chosen in the sequential trial, free all customers from their clusters.
Step 4. For every free customer, compute its insertion cost into a feasible cluster relative to the seed of the cluster. Consider all clusters and keep the best insertion for the customer.
Step 5. Of the free customers, allocate the one with minimum insertion cost to its corresponding cluster.
Step 6. Repeat Step 4 for any free customer whose previously best insertion is no longer feasible, and continue with Step 5 until no further feasible insertions are possible.

Phase II
Step 7. For both the above two clusterings formed sequentially and in parallel, solve the TSP for each cluster. Keep the best of the two as the VRP solution.

Once again, note that by making use of a user-controlled parameter in the measure of insertion cost, more than two trial clusterings can be produced.

The two-phase method of Fisher & Jaikumar [1981]

The first phase of this heuristic performs a parallel clustering by solving optimally a generalized assignment problem.

Phase I
Step 1. Choose m customers to be seeds of clusters and allocate a vehicle to each.
Step 2. For each customer i and for each cluster k, compute an insertion cost d_{ik} relative to the seed of the cluster.
Step 3. Solve the generalized assignment problem $\min\{\sum_{i,k} d_{ik} y_{ik} \mid (2), (3),$ (6a)\}.
Phase II
Step 4. Solve the TSP for every set of customers in the clusters implied by the y_{ik}.

Note that although the last two methods are similar, the latter heuristic solves the clustering phase optimally by using a fast algorithm for the generalized assignment problem [Fisher, Jaikumar & Van Wassenhove, 1979]. Thus, the objective $\sum_{i,k} d_{ik} y_{ik}$ can be considered as an easy-to-compute approximation to the objective in (16), and the whole method as a first iteration of the optimization method of Section 3.2. It is worthwhile to note here that all the problems and complications of the method discussed in Section 3.2 appear from the second iteration onwards and are, therefore, avoided by the above heuristic.

4.3 Incomplete optimization methods

The tree search algorithm described in Section 3.4, using the bound of expression (20), a depth first search, and a heuristic way of choosing the customer on which to branch, becomes a heuristic when terminated prematurely. It is worthwhile to note here that the branching rules which perform best when the method is prematurely terminated are not the same as those that perform best for the optimal solution of VRPs.

4.4 Computational comments

Computational tests on twelve Euclidean VRPs ranging in size from 50 to 200 customers have indicated the following results, as far as solution quality is concerned. The best heuristic on average (with a computing time limit of 120 seconds on a CDC 6600) is the incomplete tree search of Section 4.3.

The percentage average solution values over best for the other heuristics were: two-phase [Fisher & Jaikumar, 1981] 2.1%; two-phase [Christofides,

Mingozzi & Toth, 1979] 4.5%; sweep [Gillett & Miller, 1974] 4.8%; savings [Clarke & Wright 1964] 12.5%. The computing times were lowest for Fisher & Jaikumar and for Clarke & Wright, and worst for the incomplete tree search, the average time being 5 to 6 seconds for the fastest and 92 seconds for the slowest. The computational results for the heuristic of Fisher & Jaikumar were taken from their paper.

Exercises

6. Solve the VRP defined in Exercise 1 by both the sequential and the parallel version of the savings algorithm.

7. For the same VRP, apply a modified version of the sweep algorithm to obtain an approximate solution. (Note that the distance matrix in Table 12.1 is 'almost' Euclidean.)

8. For the same VRP, apply the two-phase method of Fisher and Jaikumar: Choose two seeds, solve the resulting generalized assignment problem by observation, and solve the TSP for each cluster to obtain an approximate solution.

Bibliography

A. ADRABIŃSKI, M.M. SYSLO (1983). Computational experiments with some approximation algorithms for the traveling salesman problem. *Zastos. Mat. 18*, 91-95. [*7*:1,3]

S. AGMON (1954). The relaxation method for linear inequalities. *Canad. J. Math. 6*, 383-392. [*10*:3]

A.V. AHO, J.E. HOPCROFT, J.D. ULLMAN (1974). *The Design and Analysis of Computer Algorithms*, Addison-Wesley, Reading, MA. [*3*:2,3,4; *5*:3]

T. AKIYAMA, T. NISHIZEKI, N. SAITO (1980). *NP*-Completeness of the Hamiltonian cycle problem for bipartite graphs. *J. Inform. Process. 3*, 73-76. [*11*:5]

S. AKL (1980). The minimal directed spanning subgraph for combinatorial optimization. *Austral. Comput. J. 12*, 132-136. [*7*:5]

D. ANGLUIN, L.G. VALIANT (1979). Fast probabilistic algorithms for Hamiltonian circuits and matchings. *J. Comput. System Sci. 18*, 155-193. [*11*:4]

K. ARIYAWANSA (1980). *Estimating Global Optima in NLP Using Structural Inference*, Presented at the ORSA/TIMS Joint National Meeting, Colorado Springs. [*7*:6]

E. BACH, M. LUBY, S. GOLDWASSER (1982). *Private Communication*. [*4*:4]

A. BACHEM, M. GRÖTSCHEL (1982). New aspects of polyhedral theory. B. KORTE (ed.). *Modern Applied Mathematics, Optimization and Operations Research*, North-Holland, Amsterdam, 51-106. [*8*:1]

B.S. BAKER, E.G. COFFMAN, JR., R.L. RIVEST (1980). Orthogonal packings in two dimensions. *SIAM J. Comput. 9*, 846-855. [*5*:7]

E. BALAS (1975). Bivalent programming by implicit enumeration. J. BELZER, A.G. HOLZMAN, A. KENT (eds.). *Encyclopedia of Computer Science and Technology 2*, Dekker, New York, 479-494. [*10*:1,2]

E. BALAS (1980). Cutting planes from conditional bounds: a new approach to set covering. *Math. Programming Stud. 12*, 19-36. [*10*:4]

E. BALAS, N. CHRISTOFIDES (1981). A restricted Lagrangean approach to the traveling salesman problem. *Math. Programming 21*, 19-46. [*10*:4,5,6]

E. BALAS, M. GUIGNARD (1979). Branch and bound/implicit enumeration. *Ann. Discrete Math. 5*, 185-191. [*10*:1]

E. BALAS, T.W. MCGUIRE, P. TOTH (1984). *Statistical Analysis of Some Traveling Salesman Algorithms*, Management science research report 501, Graduate School of

The citations of each publication are given between brackets, with chapters in *italic* and sections in roman.

The editors wish to thank Gerard Kindervater and Martin Savelsbergh for their help in compiling the bibliography and the Centre for Mathematics & Computer Science (CWI) in Amsterdam for the phototypesetting.

Industrial Administration, Carnegie-Mellon University, Pittsburgh, PA. [10:6]

E. BALAS, M.W. PADBERG (1976). Set partitioning: a survey. *SIAM Rev. 18*, 710-780. [12:3]

E. BALAS, M.W. PADBERG (1979). Adjacent vertices of the all 0-1 programming polytope. *RAIRO Rech. Opér. 13*, 3-12. [8:5]

M.L. BALINSKI, A. RUSSAKOFF (1974). On the assignment polytope. *SIAM Rev. 16*, 516-525. [8:5]

M. BALL, M. MAGAZINE (1981). The design and analysis of heuristics. *Networks 11*, 215-219. [7:1]

F. BARAHONA, E. MACCIONI (1982). On the exact ground states of three-dimensional Ising spin glasses. *J. Phys. A 15*, L611-L615. [9:1,4]

E.M.L. BEALE (1979). Branch and bound methods for mathematical programming systems. *Ann. Discrete Math. 5*, 201-219. [10:1]

J. BEARDWOOD, J.H. HALTON, J.M. HAMMERSLEY (1959). The shortest path through many points. *Proc. Cambridge Philos. Soc. 55*, 299-327. [1:7; 6:1,2; 7:6]

R.E. BELLMAN (1962). Dynamic programming treatment of the travelling salesman problem. *J. Assoc. Comput. Mach. 9*, 61-63. [1:7; 6:2]

R.E. BELLMAN, S.E. DREYFUS (1962). *Applied Dynamic Programming*, Princeton University Press, Princeton, NJ. [3:2]

M. BELLMORE, S. HONG (1974). Transformation of the multisalesmen problem to the standard traveling salesman problem. *J. Assoc. Comput. Mach. 21*, 500-504. [2:3]

M. BELLMORE, J.C. MALONE (1971). Pathology of traveling-salesman subtour-elimination algorithms. *Oper. Res. 19*, 278-307, 1766. [10:2,5,6]

M. BELLMORE, G.L. NEMHAUSER (1968). The traveling salesman problem: a survey. *Oper. Res.16*, 538-558.

X. BERENGUER (1979). A characterization of linear admissible transformations for the *m*-travelling salesmen problem. *European J. Oper. Res. 3*, 232-249. [4:2]

C. BERGE (1973). *Graphs and Hypergraphs*, North-Holland, Amsterdam. [11:1]

J.C. BERMOND (1979). Hamiltonian graphs. L.W. BEINEKE, R.J. WILSON (eds.). *Selected Topics in Graph Theory*, Academic Press, New York, 127-167. [11:7]

J.C. BERMOND, C. THOMASSEN (1981). Cycles in digraphs - a survey. *J. Graph Theory 5*, 1-43. [11:7]

N.L. BIGGS (1981). T.P. Kirkman, mathematician. *Bull. London Math. Soc. 13*, 97-120. [1:2]

N.L. BIGGS, E.K. LLOYD, R.J. WILSON (1976). *Graph Theory 1736-1936*, Clarendon Press, Oxford. [1:2; 11:1,5]

N.H. BINGHAM (1981). Tauberian theorems and the central limit theorem. *Ann. Probab. 9*, 221-231. [6:2]

G. BIRKHOFF (1946). Tres observaciones sobre el algebra lineal. *Rev. Univ. Nac. Tucuman Ser. A 5*, 147-151. [1:4]

R.E. BIXBY, D. WANG (1978). An algorithm for finding Hamiltonian circuits in certain graphs. *Math. Programming Stud. 8*, 35-49. [11:3]

R.G. BLAND, D. GOLDFARB, M.J. TODD (1981). The ellipsoid method: a survey. *Oper. Res. 29*, 1039-1091. [9:1]

C.G.E. BOENDER, A.H.G. RINNOOY KAN, G.T. TIMMER, L. STOUGIE (1982). A stochastic method for global optimization. *Math. Programming 22*, 125-140. [7:6]

J.A. BONDY (1969). Properties of graphs with constraints on degrees. *Studia Sci. Math. Hungar. 4*, 473-475. [11:3]

J.A. BONDY (1972). Variations on the Hamiltonian theme. *Canad. Math. Bull. 15*, 57-62. [11:3]

J.A. BONDY (1978). Hamilton cycles in graphs and digraphs. *Proc. Ninth Southeastern Conf. Combinatorics, Graph Theory and Computing*, Utilitas Mathematica, Winnipeg, 3-28. [11:7]

J.A. BONDY (1980). *Longest Paths and Cycles in Graphs of High Degree*, Research report

CORR 80-16, Department of Combinatorics and Optimization, University of Waterloo. [*11*:3]

J.A. BONDY, V. CHVÁTAL (1976). A method in graph theory. *Discrete Math. 15*, 111-135. [*11*:3]

J.A. BONDY, U.S.R. MURTY (1976). *Graph Theory with Applications,* MacMillan, London. [*Preface; 11*:1]

I. BOROSH, L.B. TREYBIG (1976). Bounds on positive integral solutions of linear diophantine equations. *Proc. Amer. Math. Soc. 55*, 299-304. [*3*:3]

S. BOYD (1984). *Private Communication.* [*8*:5]

M.W. BROWNE (1979). An approach to difficult problems. *The New York Times,* November 27, 1979. [*3*:5]

G. CARPANETO, P. TOTH (1980). Some new branching and bounding criteria for the asymmetric travelling salesman problem. *Management Sci. 26*, 736-743. [*10*:2,6]

N. CHRISTOFIDES (1970). The shortest Hamiltonian chain of a graph. *SIAM J. Appl. Math. 19*, 689-696. [*10*:3]

N. CHRISTOFIDES (1975). *Graph Theory - An Algorithmic Approach,* Academic Press, London. [*10*:2; *11*:7]

N. CHRISTOFIDES (1976). *Worst-Case Analysis of a New Heuristic for the Travelling Salesman Problem,* Report 388, Graduate School of Industrial Administration, Carnegie-Mellon University, Pittsburgh, PA. [*1*:7; *5*:3]

N. CHRISTOFIDES (1979). The travelling salesman problem. N. CHRISTOFIDES, A. MINGOZZI, P. TOTH, C. SANDI (eds.). *Combinatorial Optimization,* Wiley, Chichester, 131-149. [*10*:3,4,5]

N. CHRISTOFIDES, S. EILON (1969). An algorithm for the vehicle-dispatching problem. *Oper. Res. Quart. 20*, 309-318. [*12*:1]

N. CHRISTOFIDES, S. EILON (1972). Algorithms for large-scale travelling salesman problems. *Oper. Res. Quart. 23*, 511-518. [*7*:4]

N. CHRISTOFIDES, A. MINGOZZI, P. TOTH (1979). The vehicle routing problem. N. CHRISTOFIDES, A. MINGOZZI, P. TOTH, C. SANDI (eds.). *Combinatorial Optimization,* Wiley, Chichester, 315-338. [*12*:4]

N. CHRISTOFIDES, A. MINGOZZI, P. TOTH (1980). Exact algorithms for the vehicle routing problem based on spanning tree and shortest path relaxations. *Math. Programming 20*, 255-282. [*12*:2,3]

N. CHRISTOFIDES, A. MINGOZZI, P. TOTH (1981a). State-space relaxation procedures for the computation of bounds to routing problems. *Networks 11*, 145-164. [*10*:5; *12*:2,3]

N. CHRISTOFIDES, A. MINGOZZI, P. TOTH (1981b). *An Algorithm for the Time Constrained TSP,* Report IC-OR-81/12, Imperial College of Science and Technology, London. [*12*:3]

N. CHRISTOFIDES, A. MINGOZZI, P. TOTH (1982). *MOVER (Modeling and Optimisation of Vehicle Routing) - A Users Manual,* Imperial College of Science and Technology, London. [*12*:1]

N. CHRISTOFIDES, J. PAIXÁO (1982). *State-Space Relaxation Algorithms for the Set Covering Problem,* Report IC-OR-82/3, Imperial College of Science and Technology, London. [*12*:3]

N. CHRISTOFIDES, M. THORNTON (1982). *A Shortest Path Algorithm for Generalised Weighted Matchings,* Report IC-OR-82/2, Imperial College of Science and Technology, London. [*12*:3]

V. CHVÁTAL (1972). On Hamilton's ideals. *J. Combin. Theory 12*, 163-168. [*11*:3]

V. CHVÁTAL (1973a). Edmonds polytopes and weakly Hamiltonian graphs. *Math. Programming 5*, 29-40 [*1*:8; *3*:5; *8*:4; *11*:2]

V. CHVÁTAL (1973b). Tough graphs and Hamiltonian circuits. *Discrete Math. 5*, 215-228. [*11*:2,6]

V. CHVÁTAL (1979). A greedy heuristic for the set covering problem. *Math. Oper. Res. 4*, 233-235. [*5*:7]

V. CHVÁTAL (1983). *Linear Programming*, Freeman, San Fransisco. [*Preface*; *11*:2]

V. CHVÁTAL, P. ERDÖS (1972). A note on Hamiltonian circuits. *Discrete Math. 2*, 111-113. [*11*:3]

L. CLARK, R.C. ENTRINGER, D.E. JACKSON (1980). Minimum graphs with complete *k*-closure. *Discrete Math. 30*, 95-101. [*11*:3]

G. CLARKE, J.W. WRIGHT (1964). Scheduling of vehicles from a central depot to a number of delivery points. *Oper. Res. 12*, 568-581. [*12*:1,4]

A. COBHAM (1964). The intrinsic computational difficulty of functions. Y. BAR-HILLEL (ed.). *Proc. 1964 International Congress Logic, Methodology and Philosophy of Science*, North-Holland, Amsterdam, 24-30. [*3*:2]

E.G. COFFMAN, JR., M.R. GAREY, D.S. JOHNSON (1984). Approximation algorithms for bin-packing - an updated survey. G. AUSIELLO, M. LUCERTINI, P. SERAFINI (eds.). *Algorithm Design and Computer System Design*, CISM Courses and Lectures 284, Springer, Vienna, 49-106. [*5*:7]

W. CONOVER (1980). *Practical Nonparametric Statistics*, Wiley, New York. [*7*:2]

S. A. COOK (1971). On the complexity of theorem-proving procedures. *Proc. 3rd Annual ACM Symp. Theory of Computing*, 151-158. [*1*:6; *3*:3,4]

G. CORNUÉJOLS, D. NADDEF, W.R. PULLEYBLANK (1983). Halin graphs and the traveling salesman problem. *Math. Programming 26*, 287-294. [*8*:4]

G. CORNUÉJOLS, D. NADDEF, W.R. PULLEYBLANK (1985). The travelling salesman problem in graphs with 3-edge cutsets. *J. Assoc. Comput. Mach.*, to appear. [*4*:17]

G. CORNUÉJOLS, G.L. NEMHAUSER (1978). Tight bounds for Christofides' traveling salesman heuristic. *Math. Programming 14*, 116-121. [*5*:3]

G. CORNUÉJOLS, W.R. PULLEYBLANK (1982). The travelling salesman polytope and {0,2}-matchings. *Ann. Discrete Math. 16*, 27-55. [*8*:3]

G.A. CROES (1958). A method for solving traveling-salesman problems. *Oper. Res. 6*, 791-812. [*1*:5; *7*:3]

H. CROWDER, E.L. JOHNSON, M.W. PADBERG (1983). Solving large-scale zero-one linear programming problems. *Oper. Res. 31*, 803-834. [*9*:1,4]

H. CROWDER, M.W. PADBERG (1980). Solving large-scale symmetric travelling salesman problems to optimality. *Management Sci. 26*, 495-509. [*1*:8; *7*:3,4; *9*:1,2,4; *10*:5]

W. CUNNINGHAM (1984). Testing membership in matroid polyhedra. *J. Combin. Theory Ser. B 36*, 161-188. [*9*:1]

D.G. DANNENBRING (1977). Procedures for estimating optimal solutions for large combinatorial problems. *Management Sci. 23*, 1273-1283. [*7*:6]

G.B. DANTZIG (1960). On the significance of solving linear programming problems with some integer variables. *Econometrica 28*, 30-44. [*3*:3]

G.B. DANTZIG (1963). *Linear Programming and Extensions*, Princeton University Press, Princeton, NJ. [*3*:5; *8*:5]

G.B. DANTZIG, W.O. BLATTNER, M.R. RAO (1967). All shortest routes from a fixed origin in a graph. P. ROSENSTIEHL (ed.). *Theory of Graphs: International Symposium*, Gordon & Breach, New York, 85-90. [*3*:3]

G.B. DANTZIG, D.R. FULKERSON (1954). Minimizing the number of tankers to meet a fixed schedule. *Naval Res. Logist. Quart. 1*, 217-222. [*1*:4]

G.B. DANTZIG, D.R. FULKERSON, S.M. JOHNSON (1954). Solution of a large-scale traveling-salesman problem. *Oper. Res. 2*, 393-410. [*1*:4,5; *2*:4; *3*:5; *8*:2; *9*:1,2,3,4; *10*:1]

G.B. DANTZIG, D.R. FULKERSON, S.M. JOHNSON (1959). On a linear-programming, combinatorial approach to the traveling-salesman problem. *Oper. Res. 7*, 58-66. [*10*:1]

G.B. DANTZIG, J.H. RAMSER (1959). The truck dispatching problem. *Management Sci. 6*, 80-91. [*12*:1]

L. DE HAAN (1981). Estimation of the minimum of a function using order statistics. *J. Amer. Statist. Assoc. 76*, 467-469. [*7*:6]

V.M. DEMIDENKO (1979). The traveling salesman problem with asymmetric matrices (in Russian). *Vestsĭ Akad. Navuk BSSR Ser. Fĭz.-Mat. Navuk 1*, 29-35. [4:8]

U. DERIGS (1983). *On the Use of Confidence Limits for the Global Optimum in Combinatorial Optimization Problems*, Unpublished manuscript. [7:6]

C. DERMAN, M. KLEIN (1966). Surveillance of multi-component systems: a stochastic traveling salesman's problem. *Naval Res. Logist. Quart. 13*, 103-111. [2:5]

E.W. DIJKSTRA (1959). A note on two problems in connexion with graphs. *Numer. Math. 1*, 269-271. [10:3]

G.A. DIRAC (1952). Some theorems on abstract graphs. *Proc. London Math. Soc. 2*, 69-81. [11:3]

G.A. DIRAC (1960). In abstrakten Graphen vorhandene vollständige 4-Graphen und ihre Untereilungen. *Math. Nachr. 22*, 61-85. [11:2]

W.L. EASTMAN (1958). *Linear Programming with Pattern Constraints*, Ph.D. thesis, Harvard University, Cambridge, MA. [1:5; 10:1,2]

W.F. EDDY (1977). A new convex hull algorithm for planar sets. *ACM Trans. Math. Software 3*, 398-403. [7:4]

J. EDMONDS (1965a). Paths, trees, and flowers. *Canad. J. Math. 17*, 449-467. [1:5,6; 3:1,2; 11:2]

J. EDMONDS (1965b). Minimum partition of a matroid into independent subsets. *J. Res. Nat. Bur. Standards 69B*, 67-72. [3:3; 11:2]

J. EDMONDS (1965c). Maximum matching and a polyhedron with 0,1-vertices. *J. Res. Nat. Bur. Standards 69B*, 125-130. [3:5; 8:3; 10:5]

J. EDMONDS (1965d). The Chinese postman's problem (abstract). *Oper. Res. 13*, Suppl. 1, B73. [5:6]

J. EDMONDS (1967). Optimum branchings. *J. Res. Nat. Bur. Standards 71B*, 233-240. [9:2; 10:3]

J. EDMONDS (1970). Submodular functions, matroids, and certain polyhedra. R. GUY, H. HANANI, N. SAUER, J. SCHONHEIM (eds.). *Combinatorial Structures and Their Applications*, Gordon and Breach, New York, 69-87. [8:3; 9:2]

J. EDMONDS (1971). Matroids and the greedy algorithm. *Math. Programming 1*, 127-136. [8:3]

J. EDMONDS, E.L. JOHNSON (1973). Matching, Euler tours, and the Chinese postman. *Math. Programming 5*, 88-124. [5:6]

B. EFRON, C. STEIN (1981). The jackknife estimate of variance. *Ann. Statist. 9*, 586-596. [6:2]

S. EILON, C.D.T. WATSON-GANDY, N. CHRISTOFIDES (1971). *Distribution Management: Mathematical Modelling and Practical Analysis*, Griffin, London. [7:4]

P. ERDÖS, A. RÉNYI (1961). On the strength of connectedness of a random graph. *Acta Math. Acad. Sci. Hungar. 12*, 261-267. [11:4]

L. EULER (1759). Solution d'une question curieuse qui ne paroit soumise à aucune analyse. *Mem. Acad. Sci. Berlin 15*, 310-337. [1:2]

F. EWALD (1973). Hamiltonian circuits in simplicial complexes. *Geom. Dedicata 2*, 115-125. [11:5]

W. FELLER (1968). *An Introduction to Probability Theory ans Its Apllications, Volume 1*, Wiley, New York. [6:2; 11:4]

L. FEW (1955). The shortest path and the shortest road through *n* points. *Mathematika 2*, 141-144. [1:7; 6:2]

M.L. FISHER (1981). The Lagrangian method for solving integer programming problems. *Management Sci. 27*, 1-18. [10:3]

M.L. FISHER, R. JAIKUMAR (1978). *A Decomposition Algorithm for Large-Scale Vehicle Routing*, Report 78-11-05, Department of Decision Sciences, The Wharton School, University of Pennsylvania, Philadelphia. [12:2,3]

M.L. FISHER, R. JAIKUMAR (1981). A generalized assignment heuristic for vehicle routing. *Networks 11*, 109-124. [12:2,4]

M.L. FISHER, R. JAIKUMAR, L.N. VAN WASSENHOVE (1979). *A Multiplier Adjustment Method for the Generalized Assignment Problem,* Report 81-07-06, Department of Decision Sciences, The Wharton School, University of Pennsylvania, Philadeplphia. [*12*:4]

R.A. FISHER, L.H.C. TIPPETT (1928). Limiting forms of the frequency distribution of the largest or smallest member of a sample. *Proc. Cambridge Philos. Soc. 24,* 180-190. [*7*:6]

B. FLEISCHMANN (1981). *The Travelling Salesman Problem on a Road Network,* Working paper, Fachbereich Wirtschaftswissenschaften, Universität Hamburg. [*9*:4]

B. FLEISCHMANN (1982). *Linear Programming Approaches to Travelling Salesman and Vehicle Scheduling Problems,* Presented at the XIth International Symp. Mathematical Programming, Bonn, August 1982. [*9*:4]

H. FLEISCHNER (1974). The square of every two-connected graph is Hamiltonian. *J. Combin. Theory Ser. B 16,* 29-34. [*11*:6]

M.M. FLOOD (1956). The traveling-salesman problem. *Oper. Res. 4,* 61-75. [*1*:3,7; *7*:3]

L.R. FORD, D.R. FULKERSON (1956). Maximal flow through a network. *Canad. J. Math. 8,* 399-404. [*1*:4]

L.R. FORD, D.R. FULKERSON (1962). *Flows in Networks,* Princeton University Press, Princeton, NJ. [*3*:3; *9*:2]

J.J.H. FORREST, J.P.H. HIRST, J.A. TOMLIN (1974). Practical solution of large mixed integer programming problems with UMPIRE. *Management Sci. 20,* 736-773. [*10*:2]

B.L. FOX, J.K. LENSTRA, A.H.G. RINNOOY KAN, L.E. SCHRAGE (1978). Branching from the largest upper bound: folklore and facts. *European J. Oper. Res. 2,* 191-194. [*10*:2]

K.R. FOX, B. GAVISH, S.C. GRAVES (1980). An *n*-constraint formulation of the (time-dependent) traveling salesman problem. *Oper. Res. 28,* 1018-1021. [*2*:5]

G.N. FREDERICKSON (1979). Approximation algorithms for some postman problems. *J. Assoc. Comput. Mach. 26,* 538-554. [*5*:6]

G.N. FREDERICKSON, M.S. HECHT, C.E. KIM (1978). Approximation algorithms for some routing problems. *SIAM J. Comput. 7,* 178-193. [*5*:6]

A.M. FRIEZE, G. GALBIATI, F. MAFFIOLI (1982). On the worst-case performance of some algorithms for the asymmetric traveling salesman problem. *Networks 12,* 23-39. [*5*:6; *7*:5]

D.R. FULKERSON (1974). Packing rooted cuts in a weighted directed graph. *Math. Programming 6,* 1-13. [*10*:3]

S.H. FULLER (1972). An optimal drum scheduling algorithm. *IEEE Trans. Comput. C-21,* 1153-1165. [*4*:11]

E.YA. GABOVICH (1970). The small traveling salesman problem (in Russian). *Trudy Vychisl. Tsentra Tartu. Gos. Univ. 19,* 27-51. [*4*:3]

E.YA. GABOVICH (1976). Constant discrete programming problems on substitution sets (in Russian). *Kibernetika (Kiev) 5,* 128-134. Translation. *Cybernetics 12,* 786-793 (1977). [*4*:2]

H.N. GABOW, Z. GALIL, T.H. SPENCER (1984). Efficient implementation of graph algorithms using contraction. *Proc. 25th Annual IEEE Symp. Foundations of Computer Science,* 347-357. [*4*:10]

N.E. GAIKOV (1980). On the minimization of a linear form on cycles (in Russian). *Vestsĭ Akad. Navuk BSSR Ser. Fĭz.-Mat. Navuk 4,* 128. [*4*:14]

M.R. GAREY, R.L. GRAHAM, D.S. JOHNSON, A.C.-C. YAO (1976). Resource constrained scheduling as generalized bin packing. *J. Combin. Theory Ser. A 21,* 257-298. [*5*:7]

M.R. GAREY, D.S. JOHNSON (1979). *Computers and Intractability: A Guide to the Theory of NP-Completeness,* Freeman, San Francisco. [*1*:1,6; *3*:2,3,4,5; *5*:4,7; *9*:1; *11*:1]

M.R. GAREY, D.S. JOHNSON, R.E. TARJAN (1976). The planar Hamiltonian circuit problem is *NP*-complete. *SIAM J. Comput. 5,* 704-714. [*11*:5]

R.S. GARFINKEL (1973). On partitioning the feasible set in a branch-and-bound algorithm for the asymmetric traveling-salesman problem. *Oper. Res. 21,* 340-343.

[*10*:2]

R.S. GARFINKEL (1977). Minimizing wallpaper waste, part I: a class of traveling salesman problems. *Oper. Res. 25*, 741-751. [*2*:2; *4*:4,11]

R.S. GARFINKEL, K.C. GILBERT (1978). The bottleneck traveling salesman problem: algorithms and probabilistic analysis. *J. Assoc. Comput. Mach. 25*, 435-448. [*2*:5]

R.S. GARFINKEL, G.L. NEMHAUSER (1972). *Integer Programming*, Wiley, New York. [*9*:1; *10*:4]

T.J. GASKELL (1967). Bases for vehicle fleet scheduling. *Oper. Res. Quart. 18*, 281-295. [*12*:1,4]

B. GAVISH, K.N. SRIKANTH (1979). *Mathematical Formulations of the Dial-a-Ride Problem*, Working paper 7909, Graduate School of Management, University of Rochester, NY. [*12*:2]

B. GAVISH, K.N. SRIKANTH (1983). *Efficient Branch and Bound Code for Solving Large Scale Traveling Salesman Problems to Optimality*, Working paper QM8329, Graduate School of Management, University of Rochester. [*10*:3,6]

A.M. GEOFFRION (1974). Lagrangean relaxation for integer programming. *Math. Programming Stud. 2*, 82-114. [*10*:3]

R. GILES (1975). *Submodular Functions, Graphs, and Integer Polyhedra*, Ph.D. thesis, University of Waterloo. [*8*:3]

R. GILES, L.E. TROTTER, JR. (1981). On stable set polyhedra for $K_{1,3}$-free graphs. *J. Combin. Theory Ser. B 31*, 313-326. [*9*:1]

B.E. GILLETT, J.G. JOHNSON (1976). Multi-terminal vehicle-dispatch algorithm. *Omega 4*, 711-718. [*7*:4]

B.E. GILLETT, L.R. MILLER (1974). A heuristic algorithm for the vehicle dispatch problem. *Oper. Res. 22*, 340-349. [*12*:4]

P.C. GILMORE, R.E. GOMORY (1964). Sequencing a one state-variable machine: a solvable case of the traveling salesman problem. *Oper. Res. 12*, 655-679. [*1*:6; *2*:2; *4*:1,13]

B.L. GOLDEN (1976). *Recent Developments in Vehicle Routing*, Presented at the Bicentennial Conf. Mathematical Programming, Gaithersburg, MD, November 1976. [*12*:2]

B.L. GOLDEN (1977a). Evaluating a sequential vehicle routing algorithm. *AIIE Trans. 9*, 204-208. [*7*:5]

B.L. GOLDEN (1977b). A statistical approach to the TSP. *Networks 7*, 209-225. [*7*:6]

B.L. GOLDEN (1978). Point estimation of a global optimum for large combinatorial problems. *Comm. Statist. B - Simulation Comput. 7*, 361-367. [*7*:6]

B.L. GOLDEN, F.B. ALT (1979). Interval estimation of a global optimum for large combinatorial problems. *Naval Res. Logist. Quart. 26*, 69-77. [*7*:6]

B.L. GOLDEN, L.D. BODIN, T. DOYLE, W. STEWART, JR. (1980). Approximate traveling salesman algorithms. *Oper. Res. 28*, 694-711. [*7*:1,3,5]

B.L. GOLDEN, T.L. MAGNANTI, H.Q. NGUYEN (1977). Implementing vehicle routing algorithms. *Networks 7*, 113-148. [*12*:4]

B.L. GOLDEN, C. SKISCIM (1984). *Using Simulated Annealing to Solve Routing and Location Problems*, Unpublished manuscript. [*7*:3]

R.E. GOMORY (1958). Outline of an algorithm for integer solutions to linear programs. *Bull. Amer. Math. Soc. 64*, 275-278. [*1*:5]

R.E. GOMORY (1960). Solving linear programming problems in integers. *Proc. Sympos. Appl. Math. 10*, 211-215. [*1*:5]

R.E. GOMORY (1963). An algorithm for integer solutions to linear programs. R.L. GRAVES, P. WOLFE (eds.). *Recent Advances in Mathematical Programming*, McGraw-Hill, New York, 269-302. [*1*:5; *9*:1]

R.E. GOMORY (1966). The traveling salesman problem. *Proc. IBM Scientific Computing Symp. Combinatorial Problems*, IBM Data Processing Division, White Plains, NY, 93-121. [*1*:4,8; *8*:4,5]

R.E. GOMORY, T.C. HU (1961). Multi-terminal network flows. *SIAM J. Appl. Math. 9,* 551-556. [9:2,3]

D. GOYOU-BEAUCHAMPS (1982). The Hamiltonian circuit problem is polynomial for 4-connected planar graphs. *SIAM J. Comput. 11,* 529-539. [11:5]

R.L. GRAHAM (1966). Bounds for certain multiprocessing anomalies. *Bell System Tech. J. 45,* 1563-1581. [1:7; 5:7]

R.L. GRAHAM (1969). Bounds on multiprocessing timing anomalies. *SIAM J. Appl. Math. 17,* 416-429. [1:7; 5:7]

R.L. GRAHAM, E.L. LAWLER, J.K. LENSTRA, A.H.G. RINNOOY KAN (1979). Optimization and approximation in deterministic sequencing and scheduling: a survey. *Ann. Discrete Math. 5,* 287-326. [5:7]

E. YA. GRINBERG (1968). Plane homogeneous graphs of degree three without Hamiltonian circuits (in Russian). *Latv. Mat. Ezhegodnik 4,* 51-58. [11:5]

M. GRÖTSCHEL (1977a). *Polyedrische Charakterisierungen kombinatorischer Optimierungsplobleme,* Hain, Meisenheim am Glan. [8:3,4,5; 9:1,4]

M. GRÖTSCHEL (1977b). The monotone 2-matching polytope on a complete graph. *Oper. Res. Verfahren 24,* 72-84. [8:3,4]

M. GRÖTSCHEL (1980a). On the monotone symmetric travelling salesman problem: hypohamiltonian/hypotraceable graphs and facets. *Math. Oper. Res. 5,* 285-292. [3:5; 8:4]

M. GRÖTSCHEL (1980b). On the symmetric travelling salesman problem: solution of a 120-city problem. *Math. Programming Stud. 12,* 61-77. [9:1,4]

M. GRÖTSCHEL (1984). Developments in combinatorial optimization. W. JÄGER, J. MOSER, R. REMMERT (eds.). *Perspectives in Mathematics: Anniversary of Oberwolfach 1984,* Birkhäuser, Basel, 249-294. [8:2]

M. GRÖTSCHEL, M. JÜNGER, G. REINELT (1984). A cutting plane algorithm for the linear ordering problem. *Oper. Res. 32,* 1195-1220. [9:1,4]

M. GRÖTSCHEL, L. LOVÁSZ, A. SCHRIJVER (1981). The ellipsoid method and its consequences in combinatorial optimization. *Combinatorica 1,* 169-197. [9:1]

M. GRÖTSCHEL, M.W. PADBERG (1974). Zur Oberflächenstruktur des Travelling Salesman Polytopen. H.-J. ZIMMERMANN, A. SCHUB, H. SPÄTH, J. STOER (eds.). *Proc. Operations Research 4,* Physica, Würzburg, 207-211. [8:4,5]

M. GRÖTSCHEL, M.W. PADBERG (1975a). *On the Symmetric Travelling Salesman Problem,* Working Paper, Institut für Oekonometrie und Operations Research, Universität Bonn. [8:4]

M. GRÖTSCHEL, M.W. PADBERG (1975b). Partial linear characterizations of the asymmetric travelling salesman polytope. *Math. Programming 8,* 378-381. [8:5]

M. GRÖTSCHEL, M.W. PADBERG (1977). Lineare Charakterisierungen von Travelling Salesman Problemen. *Z. Oper. Res. 21,* 33-64. [8:5]

M. GRÖTSCHEL, M.W. PADBERG (1978). On the symmetric travelling salesman problem: theory and computation. R. HENN, B. KORTE, W. OETTLI (eds.). *Optimization and Operations Research,* Lecture Notes in Economics and Mathematical Systems 157, Springer, Berlin, 105-115. [8:4]

M. GRÖTSCHEL, M.W. PADBERG (1979a). On the symmetric travelling salesman problem I: inequalities. *Math. Programming 16,* 265-280. [1:5,8; 8:4; 9:1; 10:5]

M. GRÖTSCHEL, M.W. PADBERG (1979b). On the symmetric travelling salesman problem II: lifting theorems and facets. *Math. Programming 16,* 281-302. [1:5,8; 3:5; 8:4; 9:3; 10:5]

M. GRÖTSCHEL, W.R. PULLEYBLANK (1985). Clique tree inequalities and the symmetric travelling salesman problem. *Math. Oper. Res.,* to appear. [8:3,4]

M. GRÖTSCHEL, Y. WAKABAYASHI (1981a). On the structure of the monotone asymmetric travelling salesman polytope I: hypohamiltonian facets. *Discrete Math. 34,* 43-59. [8:5]

M. GRÖTSCHEL, Y. WAKABAYASHI (1981b). On the structure of the monotone asymmetric travelling salesman polytope II: hypotraceable facets. *Math. Programming Stud. 14,* 77-97. [8:5]

B. GRÜNBAUM (1967). *Convex Polytopes,* Wiley, London. [3:5; 8:1,5]

G. HADLEY (1964). *Nonlinear and Dynamic Programming,* Addison-Wesley, Reading, MA, 267-296. [2:5]

M. HALL (1967). *Combinatorial Theory,* Blaisdell, Waltham, MA. [10:2]

J.H. HALTON, R. TERADA (1982). A fast algorithm for the Euclidean traveling salesman problem, optimal with probability one. *SIAM J. Comput. 11,* 28-46. [6:1,2]

P.L. HAMMER, E.L. JOHNSON, U.N. PELED (1975). Facets of regular 0-1 polytopes. *Math. Programming 8,* 179-206. [8:2]

W.R. HAMILTON (1856). Memorandum respecting a new system of roots of unity (the Icosian calculus). *Philos. Mag. 12,* 446. [1:2]

W.R. HAMILTON (1858). On a new system of roots of unity. *Proc. Royal Irish Acad. 6,* 415-416. [1:2]

F. HARARY (1969). *Graph Theory,* Addison-Wesley, Reading, MA. [11:1]

F. HARARY, A.J. SCHWENK (1971). Trees with Hamiltonian squares. *Mathematika 18,* 138-140. [11:6]

W.W. HARDGRAVE, G.L. NEMHAUSER (1962). On the relation between the traveling salesman and the longest path problems. *Oper. Res. 10,* 647-657. [2:4]

D.B. HARTVIGSEN (1984). *Extensions of Matching Theory,* Ph. D. thesis, Department of Mathematics, Carnegie-Mellon University, Pittsburgh, PA. [8:3]

D. HAUSMANN (1980). *Adjacency on Polytopes in Combinatorial Optimization,* Hain, Meisenheim am Glan. [8:5]

R. HAYS (1967). *The Delivery Problem,* Report 106, Department of Management Science, Carnegie Institute of Technology, Pittsburgh, PA. [12:1]

M.S. HECHT, J.D. ULLMAN (1972). Flow graph reducibility. *SIAM J. Comput. 1,* 188-202. [4:16]

K. HELBIG HANSEN, J. KRARUP (1974). Improvements of the Held-Karp algorithm for the symmetric traveling-salesman problem. *Math. Programming 7,* 87-96. [10:3]

M. HELD, R.M. KARP (1962). A dynamic programming approach to sequencing problems. *SIAM J. Appl. Math. 10,* 196-210. [1:7; 3:2; 6:2]

M. HELD, R.M. KARP (1970). The traveling-salesman problem and minimum spanning trees. *Oper. Res. 18,* 1138-1162. [1:5; 8:3,4; 9:4; 10:3]

M. HELD, R.M. KARP (1971). The traveling-salesman problem and minimum spanning trees: part II. *Math. Programming 1,* 6-25. [1:5; 10:3]

M. HELD, P. WOLFE, H.P. CROWDER (1974). Validation of subgradient optimization. *Math. Programming 6,* 62-88. [10:3]

I. HELLER (1953). On the problem of shortest paths between points, I and II (abstract). *Bull. Amer. Math. Soc. 59,* 551-552. [8:5]

I. HELLER (1955). On the travelling salesman's problem. *Proc. Second Symp. Linear Programming, Vol. 2,* Washington, DC, January 1955, 643-665. [1:4; 8:5]

I. HELLER (1956). Neighbor relations on the convex of cyclic permutations. *Pacific J. Math. 6,* 467-477. [8:5]

I. HERSTEIN (1975). *Topics in Algebra,* Xerox College Pub., Lexington, MA. [4:1]

F.L. HITCHCOCK (1941). The distribution of a product from several sources to numerous localities. *J. Math. & Phys. 20,* 224-230. [1:4]

D.S. HOCHBAUM (1982). Approximation algorithms for the weighted set covering and node covering problems. *SIAM J. Comput. 11,* 555-556. [5:7]

S. HONG (1972). *A Linear Programming Approach for the Travelling Salesman Problem,* Ph.D. thesis, Johns Hopkins University, Baltimore, MD. [9:4]

S. HONG, M.W. PADBERG (1977). A note on the symmetric multiple traveling salesman problem with fixed charges. *Oper. Res. 25,* 871-874. [2:3]

J.E. HOPCROFT, R.M. KARP (1973). An $n^{5/2}$ algorithm for maximum matchings in bipartite graphs. *SIAM J. Comput. 2,* 225-231. [4:5]

J.E. HOPCROFT, R.E. TARJAN (1974). Efficient planarity testing. *J. Assoc. Comput. Mach. 21*, 549-558. [*3*:4]

J.E. HOPCROFT, J.D. ULLMAN (1979). *Introduction to Automata Theory, Languages and Computation*, Addison-Wesley, Reading MA. [*3*:2]

D.J. HOUCK, J.-C. PICARD, M. QUEYRANNE, R.R. VEMUGANTI (1980). The traveling salesman problem as a constrained shortest path problem: theory and computational experience. *Opsearch 17*, 93-109. [*10*:5]

T.C. HU (1969). *Integer Programming and Network Flows*, Addison-Wesley, Reading, MA. [*9*:2]

L.J. HUBERT, F.B. BAKER (1978). Applications of combinatorial programming to data analysis: the traveling salesman and related problems. *Psychometrika 43*, 81-91. [*2*:2]

O.H. IBARRA, C.E. KIM (1976). Fast approximation algorithms for the knapsack and sum of subset problems. *J. Assoc. Comput. Mach. 22*, 463-468. [*5*:4,7]

IBM CORPORATION (1970). *Vehicle Scheduling Program Application Description - VSPX*, Report GH 19-2000/0, White Plains, NY. [*12*:1]

A. ITAI, C.H. PAPADIMITRIOU, J. SZWARCFITER (1982). Hamiltonian paths in grid graphs. *SIAM J. Comput. 11*, 676-686. [*3*:4]

W. JAQUES (1859). *The Icosian Game*, published and sold wholesale by John Jaques and Son, London. [*1*:2]

D.S. JOHNSON (1974a). Approximation algorithms for combinatorial problems. *J. Comput. System Sci. 9*, 256-278. [*5*:7]

D.S. JOHNSON (1974b). Worst case behavior of graph coloring algorithms. *Proc. Fifth Conference Combinatorics, Graph Theory, and Computing*, Utilitas Mathematica, Winnipeg, 513-527. [*5*:7]

D.S. JOHNSON (1983). *Private Communication*. [*7*:3]

D.S. JOHNSON, A. DEMERS, J.D. ULLMAN, M.R. GAREY, R.L. GRAHAM (1974). Worst-case performance bounds for simple one-dimensional packing algorithms. *SIAM J. Comput. 3*, 299-325. [*5*:7]

S.M. JOHNSON (1954). Optimal two- and three-stage production schedules with setup times included. *Naval Res. Log. Quart. 1*, 61-68. [*1*:4]

P.-C. KANELLAKIS, C.H. PAPADIMITRIOU (1980). Local search for the asymmetric traveling salesman problem. *Oper. Res. 28*, 1086-1099. [*7*:5]

R.L. KARG, G.L. THOMPSON (1964). A heuristic approach to solving travelling salesman problems. *Management Sci. 10*, 225-248. [*9*:4]

N. KARMARKAR (1984). A new polynomial-time algorithm for linear programming. *Combinatorica 4*, 373-395. [*8*:1]

R.M. KARP (1972). Reducibility among combinatorial problems. R.E. MILLER, J.W. THATCHER (eds.). *Complexity of Computer Computations*, Plenum Press, New York, 85-103. [*1*:6; *3*:3]

R.M. KARP (1976). The probabilistic analysis of some combinatorial search algorithms. J.F. TRAUB (ed.). *Algorithms and Complexity: New Directions and Recent Results*, Academic Press, New York, 1-19. [*6*:1]

R.M. KARP (1977). Probabilistic analysis of partitioning algorithms for the traveling-salesman problem in the plane. *Math. Oper. Res. 2*, 209-224. [*1*:7; *5*:4,5; *6*:1,2]

R.M. KARP (1979). A patching algorithm for the nonsymmetric traveling-salesman problem. *SIAM J. Comput. 8*, 561-573. [*6*:3; *5*:7]

R.M. KARP (1983). *Private Communication*. [*11*:4]

R.M. KARP (1984). *An Upper Bound on the Expected Cost of an Optimal Assignment*, Computer Science Division, University of California, Berkeley. [*6*:3]

R.M. KARP, C.H. PAPADIMITRIOU (1982). On linear characterizations of combinatorial optimization problems. *SIAM J. Comput. 11*, 620-632. [*3*:5; *9*:1]

R.L. KEENEY, H. RAIFFA (1976). *Decisions with Multiple Objectives: Preferences and Value Tradeoffs*, Wiley, New York. [*7*:2]

L.G. KHACHIAN (1979). A polynomial algorithm in linear programming (in Russian).

Dokl. Akad. Nauk SSSR 244, 1093-1096. Translation. *Soviet Math. Dokl. 20*, 191-194 (1979). [*3*:2,5; *9*:1]

T.P. KIRKMAN (1856). On the representation of polyhedra. *Philos. Trans. Roy. Soc. London Ser. A 146*, 413-418. [*1*:2; *11*:1]

S. KIRKPATRICK (1984). Optimization by simulated annealing: quantitative studies. *J. Statist. Phys. 34*, 975-986. [*1*:8]

S. KIRKPATRICK, C.D. GELATT, JR., M.P. VECCHI (1982). *Optimization by Simulated Annealing*, IBM Computer Science/Engineering Technology report, IBM Thomas J. Watson Research Center, Yorktown Heights, NY. [*7*:3]

S. KIRKPATRICK, C.D. GELATT, JR., M.P. VECCHI (1983). Optimization by simulated annealing. *Science 220*, 671-680. [*7*:3]

V. KLEE, G.J. MINTY (1972). How good is the simplex algorithm? O. SHISHA (ed.). *Inequalities III*, Academic Press, New York, 159-175. [*3*:2]

S. KLEIN (1975). *Monte Carlo Estimation in Complex Optimization Problems*, Ph.D. thesis, The George Washington University, Washington, DC. [*7*:6]

P.S. KLYAUS (1976). Structure of the optimal solution of certain classes of traveling salesman problems (in Russian). *Vestsi Akad. Navuk BSSR Ser. Fiz.-Mat. Navuk 6*, 95-98. [*4*:8]

D.E. KNUTH (1976). The travelling salesman problem. W. SULLIVAN. Frontiers of science, from microcosm to macrocosm. *The New York Times*, February 24, 1976. [*9*:4]

J. KOMLÓS, E. SZEMERÉDI (1973). Hamiltonian cycles in random graphs. A. HAJNAL, R. RADO, V.T. SÓS (eds.). *Infinite and Finite Sets*, Colloq. Math. Soc. János Bolyai 10, 1003-1010. [*11*:4]

J. KOMLÓS, E. SZEMERÉDI (1983). Limit distribution for the existence of Hamiltonian cycles in a random graph. *Discrete Math. 43*, 55-63. [*11*:4]

T.C. KOOPMANS, M. BECKMANN (1957). Assignment problems and the location of economic activities. *Econometrica 25*, 53-76. [*2*:4]

A.D. KORŠUNOV (1976). Solution of a problem of Erdös and Rényi on Hamiltonian cycles in nonoriented graphs (in Russian). *Dokl. Akad. Nauk SSSR 228*, 529-532. Translation. *Soviet Math. Dokl. 17*, 760-764 (1976). [*11*:4]

P.D. KROLAK, W. FELTS, G. MARBLE (1971). A man-machine approach toward solving the traveling salesman problem. *Comm. ACM 14*, 327-334. [*7*:3,4; *9*:4]

P.D. KROLAK, W. FELTS, J.H. NELSON (1972). A man-machine approach toward solving the generalized truck dispatching problem. *Transportation Sci. 6*, 149-170. [*12*:1]

J.B. KRUSKAL, JR. (1956). On the shortest spanning subtree of a graph and the traveling salesman problem. *Proc. Amer. Math. Soc. 7*, 48-50. [*2*:4; *5*:3; *10*:3]

H.W. KUHN (1955a). On certain convex polyhedra (abstract). *Bull. Amer. Math. Soc. 61*, 557-558. [*1*:4; *8*:5]

H.W. KUHN (1955b). The Hungarian method for the assignment problem. *Naval Res. Logist. Quart. 2*, 83-97. [*10*:2]

A.H. LAND (1979). *The Solution of 100-City Symmetric Travelling Salesman Problems*, Research report, London School of Economics. [*9*:2,4]

A.H. LAND, A.G. DOIG (1960). An automatic method of solving discrete programming problems. *Econometrica 28*, 497-520. [*1*:5]

H.T. LAU (1980). *Finding a Hamiltonian Cycle in the Square of a Block*, Ph.D. thesis, School of Computer Science, McGill University, Montreal. [*11*:6]

H.T. LAU (1981). Finding EPS-graphs. *Monatsh. Math. 92*, 37-40. [*11*:6]

E.L. LAWLER (1963). The quadratic assignment problem. *Management Sci. 9*, 586-599. [*2*:4]

E.L. LAWLER (1971). A solvable case of the traveling salesman problem. *Math. Programming 1*, 267-269. [*4*:5]

E.L. LAWLER (1976). *Combinatorial Optimization: Networks and Matroids*, Holt, Rinehart and Winston, New York. [*Preface*; *2*:4; *5*:3,6; *9*:2; *10*:2]

E.L. LAWLER (1979). Fast approximation algorithms for knapsack problems. *Math. Oper. Res. 4*, 339-356. [5:4,7]

E.L. LAWLER, J.K. LENSTRA, A.H.G. RINNOOY KAN, D.B. SHMOYS (eds.) (1985). *The Traveling Salesman Problem: A Guided Tour of Combinatorial Optimization*, Wiley, Chichester.

A.J. LAZARUS (1979). *The Assignment Problem with Uniform* (0,1) *Cost Matrix*, B.A. thesis, Department of Mathematics, Princeton University, Princeton, NJ. [6:3]

J.K. LENSTRA (1974). Clustering a data array and the traveling-salesman problem. *Oper. Res. 22*, 413-414. [2:2]

J.K. LENSTRA, A.H.G. RINNOOY KAN (1975). Some simple applications of the travelling salesman problem. *Oper. Res. Quart. 26*, 717-733. [2:2]

J.K. LENSTRA, A.H.G. RINNOOY KAN (1978). On the expected performance of branch-and-bound algorithms. *Oper. Res. 26*, 347-349. [6:3; 10:6]

J.K. LENSTRA, A.H.G. RINNOOY KAN (1979). A characterization of linear admissible transformations for the *m*-travelling salesman problem: a result of Berenguer. *European J. Oper. Res. 3*, 250-252. [4:2]

J.K. LENSTRA, A.H.G. RINNOOY KAN (1981). Complexity of vehicle routing and scheduling problems. *Networks 11*, 221-227.

J.K. LENSTRA, A.H.G. RINNOOY KAN, P. BRUCKER (1977). Complexity of machine scheduling problems. *Ann. Discrete Math. 1*, 343-362. [3:4]

L. LESNIAK-FOSTER (1977). Some recent results in Hamiltonian graphs. *J. Graph Theory 1*, 27-36. [11:7]

L.A. LEVIN (1973). Universal sequential search problems (in Russian). *Problemy Peridachi Informatsii 9*, 115-116. Translation. *Problems Inform. Transmission 9*, 265-266 (1975). Better translation. *Ann. Hist. Comput. 6*, 399-400 (1984). [1:6]

H.R. LEWIS, C.H. PAPADIMITRIOU (1981). *Elements of the Theory of Computation*, Prentice-Hall, Englewood Cliffs, NJ. [1:5,6; 3:2,3]

S. LIN (1965). Computer solutions of the traveling salesman problem. *Bell System Tech. J. 44*, 2245-2269. [1:7; 7:3]

S. LIN, B.W. KERNIGHAN (1973). An effective heuristic algorithm for the traveling-salesman problem. *Oper. Res. 21*, 498-516. [1:7,8; 5:1,2,3; 7:3,4,5; 9:4; 10:3]

J.D.C. LITTLE, K.G. MURTY, D.W. SWEENEY, C. KAREL (1963). An algorithm for the traveling salesman problem. *Oper. Res. 11*, 972-989. [1:5; 10:1,2]

M. LOS, C. LARDINOIS (1982). Combinatorial programming, statistical optimization and the optimal transportation network problem. *Transportation Res. Part B 16*, 89-124. [7:6]

L. LOVÁSZ (1979). *Combinatorial Problems and Exercises*, Akadémiai Kiadó, Budapest. [4:11]

M. MARCUS, H. MINC (1964). *A Survey of Matrix Theory and Matrix Inequalities*, Allyn & Bacon, Boston. [9:1]

R.E. MARSTEN (1974). An algorithm for large set partitioning problems. *Management Sci. 20*, 774-787. [12:3]

J.F. MAURRAS (1975). Some results on the convex hull of Hamiltonian cycles of symmetric complete graphs. B. ROY (ed.). *Combinatorial Programming: Methods and Applications*, Reidel, Dordrecht, 179-190. [3:5; 8:4]

J.F. MAURRAS (1976). *Polytopes à sommets dans* {0,1}^{n}, Thèse de doctorat d'Etat, Université Paris VII. [8:4]

W.T. MCCORMICK, JR., P.J. SCHWEITZER, T.W. WHITE (1972). Problem decomposition and data reorganization by a clustering technique. *Oper. Res. 20*, 993-1009. [2:2]

K.L. MCROBERTS (1971). A search model for evaluating combinatorially explosive problems. *Oper. Res. 19*, 1331-1349. [7:6]

K. MENGER (1927). Zur allgemeinen Kurventheorie. *Fund. Math. 10*, 96-115. [11:2]

K. MENGER (1930). Das Botenproblem. [Menger 1932, 9. Kolloquium (5.II.1930), 12]. [1:2,7]

K. MENGER (ed.) (1932). *Ergebnisse eines Mathematischen Kolloquiums 2*, Teubner, Leipzig. [*Bibliography*]

P. MILIOTIS (1976). Integer programming approaches to the travelling salesman problem. *Math. Programming 10*, 367-378. [9:4]

P. MILIOTIS (1978). Using cutting planes to solve the symmetric travelling salesman problem. *Math. Programming 15*, 177-188. [9:4]

C.E. MILLER, A.W. TUCKER, R.A. ZEMLIN (1960). Integer programming formulations and traveling salesman problems. *J. Assoc. Comput. Mach. 7*, 326-329. [2:4]

T.R. MININA, V.T. PEREKREST (1975). On a method of approximating solutions of the traveling-salesman problem (in Russian). *Dokl. Akad. Nauk SSSR 220*, 31-34. Translation. *Soviet Math. Dokl. 16*, 26-30 (1975). [7:5]

G.J. MINTY (1980). On maximal independent sets of vertices in claw-free graphs. *J. Combin. Theory Ser. B 28*, 284-304. [9:1]

R.H. MOLE, S.R. JAMESON (1976). A sequential route-building algorithm employing a generalised savings-criterion. *Oper. Res. Quart. 27*, 503-511. [12:4]

B. MONIEN, I.H. SUDBOROUGH (1981). Bandwidth constrained NP-complete problems. *Proc. 13th Annual ACM Symp. Theory of Computing*, 207-217. [4:15]

S. MORAN (1982). *On the Length of Optimal TSP Circuits in Sets of Bounded Diameter*, Technical report 235, Computer Science Department, Technion, Haifa. [6:2]

F. MOSTELLER, R. ROURKE (1973). *Sturdy Statistics*, Addison-Wesley, Reading, MA. [7:2]

T. MOTZKIN, I.J. SCHOENBERG (1954). The relaxation method for linear inequalities. *Canad. J. Math. 6*, 393-404. [10:3]

H. MÜLLER-MERBACH (1983). Zweimal travelling Salesman. *DGOR-Bulletin 25*, 12-13. [1:3]

K.G. MURTY (1968). An algorithm for ranking all the assignments in order of increasing cost. *Oper. Res. 16*, 682-687. [10:2]

K.G. MURTY (1969). On the tours of a traveling salesman. *SIAM J. Control Optim. 7*, 122-131. [8:5]

C.ST.J.A. NASH-WILLIAMS (1970). *Valency Sequences Which Force Graphs to Have Hamiltonian Circuits: Interim Report*, Research report, Department of Combinatorics and Optimization, University of Waterloo. [11:3,7]

C.ST.J.A. NASH-WILLIAMS (1971). Edge-disjoint Hamiltonian circuits in graphs with vertices of large valency. L. MIRSKY (ed.). *Studies in Pure Mathematics*, Academic Press, London, 157-183. [11:3]

C.ST.J.A. NASH-WILLIAMS (1975). Hamiltonian circuits. D.R. FULKERSON (ed.). *Studies in Graph Theory*, Mathematical Association of America, Washington, D.C., 301-360. [11:7]

F. NEUMANN (1964). On a certain ordering of the vertices of a tree. *Casopis Pěst. Mat. 89*, 323-339. [11:6]

A. NIJENHUIS, H.S. WILF (1975). *Combinatorial Algorithms*, Academic Press, New York. [7:5,6]

T. NISHIZEKI (1980). A 1-tough nonhamiltonian maximal planar graph. *Discrete Math. 30*, 305-307. [11:5]

J.P. NORBACK, R.F. LOVE (1977). Geometric approaches to solving the traveling salesman problem. *Management Sci. 23*, 1208-1223. [7:3]

J.P. NORBACK, R.F. LOVE (1979). Heuristic for the Hamiltonian path problem in Euclidian two space. *J. Oper. Res. Soc. 30*, 363-368. [7:3]

R.Z. NORMAN (1955). On the convex polyhedra of the symmetric traveling salesman problem (abstract). *Bull. Amer. Math. Soc. 61*, 559. [8:4]

I. OR (1976). *Traveling Salesman-Type Combinatorial Problems and their Relation to the Logistics of Regional Blood Banking*, Ph.D. thesis, Northwestern University, Evanston, IL. [7:3]

O. ORE (1960). Note on Hamilton circuits. *Amer. Math. Monthly 67*, 55. [11:3]

O. ORE (1961). Arc covering of graphs. *Ann. Mat. Pura Appl. 55*, 315-321. [*11*:3]

C.S. ORLOFF (1974). A fundamental problem in vehicle routing. *Networks 4*, 35-64. [*5*:6]

M.W. PADBERG (1971). *Essays in Integer Programming*, Ph.D. thesis, Carnegie-Mellon University, Pittsburgh, PA. [*9*:1]

M.W. PADBERG (1973). On the facial structure of set packing polyhedra. *Math. Programming 5*, 199-215. [*9*:1,4]

M.W. PADBERG (1975). A note on zero-one programming. *Oper. Res. 23*, 833-837. [*8*:5]

M.W. PADBERG (1979). Covering, packing and knapsack problems. *Ann. Discrete Math. 4*, 265-287. [*8*:2]

M.W. PADBERG, S. HONG (1980). On the symmetric travelling salesman problem: a computational study. *Math. Programming Stud. 12*, 78-107. [*1*:8; *9*:1,2,3,4]

M.W. PADBERG, M.R. RAO (1974). The travelling salesman problem and a class of polyhedra of diameter two. *Math. Programming 7*, 32-45. [*8*:5]

M.W. PADBERG, M.R. RAO (1982). Odd minimum cut-sets and *b*-matchings. *Math. Oper. Res. 7*, 67-80. [*9*:1,3]

M.W. PADBERG, M.R. RAO (1985). The Russian method for linear inequalities III: bounded integer programming. *Math. Programming Stud.*, to appear. [*9*:1]

M.W. PADBERG, L.A. WOLSEY (1983). Trees and cuts. *Ann. Discrete Math. 17*, 511-517. [*9*:1,2]

C.H. PAPADIMITRIOU (1976). On the complexity of edge traversing. *J. Assoc. Comput. Mach. 23*, 544-554. [*3*:4; *5*:6]

C.H. PAPADIMITRIOU (1978). The adjacency relation on the traveling salesman polytope is NP-complete. *Math. Programming 14*, 312-324. [*3*:5; *8*:5]

C.H. PAPADIMITRIOU (1981). On the complexity of integer programming. *J. Assoc. Comput. Mach. 28*, 765-768. [*3*:3]

C.H. PAPADIMITRIOU (1984) On the complexity of unique solutions. *J. Assoc. Comput. Mach. 31*, 392-400. [*3*:5]

C.H. PAPADIMITRIOU, K. STEIGLITZ (1976). *Traps for the Traveling Salesman*, Presented at the ORSA Meeting, Florida, November 1976. [*9*:4]

C.H. PAPADIMITRIOU, K. STEIGLITZ (1977). On the complexity of local search for the traveling salesman problem. *SIAM J. Comput. 6*, 76-83. [*3*:5; *5*:2; *9*:4]

C.H. PAPADIMITRIOU, K. STEIGLITZ (1978). Some examples of difficult traveling salesman problems. *Oper. Res. 26*, 434-443. [*5*:2; *7*:6]

C.H. PAPADIMITRIOU, K. STEIGLITZ (1982). *Combinatorial Optimization: Algorithms and Complexity*, Prentice-Hall, Englewood Cliffs, NJ. [*Preface*; *3*:3,4,5; *5*:2,3,6,7]

C.H. PAPADIMITRIOU, U.V. VAZIRANI (1984). On two geometric problems related to the travelling salesman problem. *J. Algorithms 5*, 231-246. [*3*:5; *5*:3]

C.H. PAPADIMITRIOU, M. YANNAKAKIS (1982). The complexity of restricted spanning tree problems. *J. Assoc. Comput. Mach. 29*, 285-309. [*3*:5]

C.H. PAPADIMITRIOU, M. YANNAKAKIS (1984). The complexity of facets (and some facets of complexity). *J. Comput. System Sci. 28*, 244-259. [*3*:5; *8*:4]

R.G. PARKER, R.L. RARDIN (1984). Guaranteed performance heuristics for the bottleneck traveling salesman problem. *Oper. Res. Lett 2*, 269-272. [*11*:6]

N.R. PATEL, R.L. SMITH (1983). The asymptotic extreme value distribution of the sample minimum of a concave function under linear constraints. *Oper. Res. 31*, 789-794. [*7*:6]

K. PATON (1971). An algorithm for the blocks and cutnodes of a graph. *Comm. ACM 14*, 468-475. [*9*:3]

V.A. PEREPELIČA (1970). On two problems from the theory of graphs (in Russian). *Dokl. Akad. Nauk SSSR 194*, 1269-1272. Translation. *Soviet Math. Dokl. 11*, 1376-1379 (1970). [*11*:4]

R. PFAFFENBERGER, J. PATTERSON (1981). *Statistical Methods*, Irwin, Homewood, IL. [*7*:2]

J.C. PICARD, M. QUEYRANNE (1978). The time-dependent traveling salesman problem and its application to the tardiness problem in one-machine scheduling. *Oper. Res. 26*, 86-110. [2:5]

B.T. POLJAK (1967). A general method of solving extremum problems (in Russian). *Dokl. Akad. Nauk SSSR 174*, 33-36. Translation. *Soviet Math. Dokl. 8*, 593-597 (1967). [10:3]

L. PÓSA (1962). A theorem concerning Hamilton lines. *Magyar Tud. Akad. Mat. Kutató Int. Közl. 7*, 225-226. [11:3,4]

L. PÓSA (1976). Hamiltonian circuits in random graphs. *Discrete Math. 14*, 359-364. [11:4]

R.C. PRIM (1957). Shortest connection networks and some generalizations. *Bell System Tech. J. 36*, 1389-1401. [5:3; 10:3]

W.R. PULLEYBLANK (1973). *Faces of Matching Polyhedra*, Ph.D. thesis, University of Waterloo, Waterloo, Ontario. [9:1]

W.R. PULLEYBLANK (1983). Polyhedral combinatorics. A. BACHEM, M. GRÖTSCHEL, B. KORTE (eds.). *Mathematical Programming: the State of the Art - Bonn 1982*, Springer, Berlin, 312-345. [8:2]

M.R. RAO (1976). Adjacency of the traveling salesman tours and 0-1 vertices. *SIAM J. Appl. Math. 30*, 191-198. [8:5]

M.R. RAO (1980). A note on the multiple traveling salesmen problem. *Oper. Res. 28*, 628-632. [2:3]

H.D. RATLIFF, A.S. ROSENTHAL (1983). Order picking in a rectangular warehouse: a solvable case of the traveling salesman problem. *Oper. Res. 31*, 507-521. [4:15]

L. RÉDEI (1934). Ein kombinatorischer Satz. *Acta Sci. Math. (Szeged) 7*, 39-43. [6:2]

J. RIVERSDALE COLTHURST (1944). The Icosian calculus. *Proc. Royal Irish Acad. 50 Section A*, 112-121. [1:2]

H. RÖCK (1984). The three-machine no-wait flow shop is *NP*-complete. *J. Assoc. Comput. Mach. 31*, 336-345. [3:4; 4:13]

R.T. ROCKAFELLAR (1970). *Convex Analysis*, Princeton University Press, Princeton, NJ. [8:1]

D.J. ROSENKRANTZ, R.E. STEARNS, P.M. LEWIS II (1977). An analysis of several heuristics for the traveling salesman problem. *SIAM J. Comput. 6*, 563-581. [5:3; 7:3]

S. SAHNI, T. GONZALEZ (1976). *P*-complete approximation problems. *J. Assoc. Comput. Mach. 23*, 555-565. [1:7; 5:2]

C. SANDI (1979). Subgradient optimization. N. CHRISTOFIDES, A. MINGOZZI, P. TOTH, C. SANDI (eds.). *Combinatorial Optimization*, Wiley, Chichester, 73-91. [10:3]

V.I. SARVANOV (1980). On the complexity of minimizing a linear form on a set of cyclic permutations (in Russian). *Dokl. Akad. Nauk SSSR 253*, 533-534. Translation. *Soviet Math. Dokl. 22*, 118-120 (1980). [4:14]

R. SCHMIDT (1925). Ueber das Borelsche Summierungsverfahren. *Schriften d. Königsberger gel. Gesellschaft 1*, 205-256. [6:2]

R. SCHRADER (1982). Ellipsoid methods. B. KORTE (ed.). *Modern Applied Mathematics, Optimization and Operations Research*, North-Holland, Amsterdam, 265-311. [9:1]

A. SCHRIJVER (1983). Min-max results in combinatorial optimization. A. BACHEM, M. GRÖTSCHEL, B. KORTE (eds.). *Mathematical Programming: the State of the Art - Bonn 1982*, Springer, Berlin, 439-500. [8:2]

M. SEKANINA (1960). On an ordering of the set of vertices of a connected graph. *Publ. Fac. Sci. Univ. Brno 412*, 137-142. [11:6]

D.M. SHAPIRO (1966). *Algorithms for the Solution of the Optimal Cost and Bottleneck Traveling Salesman Problems*, Sc.D. thesis, Washington University, St. Louis, MO. [10:1]

J.F. SHAPIRO (1979). A survey of Langrangean techniques for discrete optimization. *Ann. Discrete Math. 5*, 113-138. [10:3]

T.H.C. SMITH (1975). *A LIFO Implicit Enumeration Algorithm for the Asymmetric*

Traveling Salesman Problem Using a One-Arborescence Relaxation, Chapter of Ph.D. thesis, Carnegie-Mellon University, Pittsburgh, PA. [*10*:3]

T.H.C. SMITH, V. SRINIVASAN, G.L. THOMPSON (1977). Computational performance of three subtour elimination algorithms for solving asymmetric traveling salesman problems. *Ann. Discrete Math. 1,* 495-506. [*10*:2,6]

T.H.C. SMITH, G.L. THOMPSON (1977). A LIFO implicit enumeration search algorithm for the symmetric traveling salesman problem using Held and Karp's 1-tree relaxation. *Ann. Discrete Math. 1,* 479-493. [*10*:3,6]

K. SPIELBERG (1979). Enumerative methods in integer programming. *Ann. Discrete Math. 5,* 139-183. [*10*:1]

J.M. STEELE (1981). Complete convergence of short paths and Karp's algorithm for the TSP. *Math. Oper. Res. 6,* 374-378. [*6*:1,2]

J.M. STEELE (1985). Probabilistic algorithm for the directed traveling salesman problem. *Math. Oper. Res.,* to appear. [*6*:2]

D. STEIN (1977). *Scheduling Dial-a-Ride Transportation Systems: An Assymptotic Approach,* Ph.D. thesis, Harvard University, Cambridge, MA. [*7*:6]

H.I. STERN, M. DROR (1979). Routing electric meter readers. *Comput. & Oper. Res. 6,* 209-223. [*12*:1]

W.R. STEWART, JR. (1977). A computationally efficient heuristic for the traveling salesman problem. *Proc. 13th Annual Meeting of S.E. TIMS,* 75-85. [*7*:3]

W.R. STEWART, JR. (1981). *New Algorithms for Deterministic and Stochastic Vehicle Routing Problems,* Ph.D. thesis, University of Maryland, College Park. [*7*:1,4]

J. STOER, C. WITZGALL (1970). *Convexity and Optimization in Finite Dimensions I,* Springer, Berlin. [*8*:1]

K.J. SUPOWIT (1981). *Topics in Computational Geometry,* Technical report UIUCDCS-R-81-1062, Department of Computer Science, University of Illinois, Urbana. [*5*:5]

K.J. SUPOWIT, E.M. REINGOLD, D.A. PLAISTED (1983). The traveling salesman problem and minimum matching in the unit square. *SIAM J. Comput. 12,* 144-156. [*5*:5]

M.M. SYSLO (1973). A new solvable case of the travelling salesman problem. *Math. Programming 4,* 347-348. [*4*:2]

R.E. TARJAN (1977). Finding optimum branchings. *Networks 7,* 25-35. [*10*:3]

C. THOMASSEN (1974). Hypohamiltonian and hypotraceable graphs. *Discrete Math. 9,* 91-96. [*8*:4]

C. THOMASSEN (1978). Hypohamiltonian graphs and digraphs. Y. ALAVI, D.R. LICK (eds.). *Theory and Applications of Graphs,* Lecture Notes in Mathematics 642, Springer, Berlin, 557-571. [*8*:4]

L.E. TTROTTER, JR. (1973). *Solution Characteristics and Algorithms for the Vertex Packing Problem,* Ph.D. thesis, Cornell University, Ithaca, NY. [*9*:1]

A.W. TUCKER (1983). *Letter to David Shmoys,* February 17, 1983. [*1*:3]

W.T. TUTTE (1946). On Hamiltonian circuits. *J. London Math. Soc. 21,* 98-101. [*11*:5]

W.T. TUTTE (1952). The factors of graphs. *Canad. J. Math. 4,* 314-328. [*11*:2]

W.T. TUTTE (1954). A short proof of the factor theorem for finite graphs. *Canad. J. Math. 6,* 347-352. [*11*:2]

W.T. TUTTE (1956). A theorem on planar graphs. *Trans. Amer. Math. Soc. 82,* 99-116. [*11*:5]

P. UNDERGROUND (1978). On graphs with Hamiltonian squares. *Discrete Math. 21,* 323. [*11*:6]

P. VAN DER CRUYSSEN, M.J. RIJCKAERT (1978). Heuristic for the asymmetric travelling salesman problem. *J. Oper. Res. Soc. 29,* 697-701. [*7*:5]

A.T. VANDERMONDE (1771). Remarques sur les problèmes de situation. *Histoire de l'Académie des Sciences (Paris),* 566-574. [*1*:2]

J. VAN LEEUWEN, A.A. SCHOONE (1985). Untangling a traveling salesman tour in the plane. *Theoret. Comput. Sci.,* to appear. [*5*:3]

S. VERBLUNSKY (1951). On the shortest path through a number of points. *Proc. Amer.*

Math. Soc. 2, 6. [*1*:8]

B. F. VOIGT (1831). *Der Handlungsreisende, wie er sein soll und was er zu thun hat, um Aufträge zu erhalten und eines glücklichen Erfolgs in seinen Geschäften gewiss zu sein,* Von einem alten Commis-Voyageur, Ilmenau. (Republished (1981) Verlag Bernd Schramm, Kiel.) [*1*:3]

T. VOLGENANT, R. JONKER (1982). A branch and bound algorithm for the symmetric traveling salesman problem based on the 1-tree relaxation. *European J. Oper. Res. 9*, 83-89. [*10*:3,6]

J. VON NEUMANN (1953). A certain zero-sum two-person game equivalent to the assignment problem. H.W. KUHN, A.W. TUCKER (eds.). *Contributions to the Theory of Games II,* Princeton University Press, Princeton, NJ, 5-12. [*3*:2]

D.W. WALKUP (1979). On the expected value of a random assignment problem. *SIAM J. Comput. 8*, 440-442. [*6*:3]

M.E. WATKINS, D.M. MESNER (1967). Cycles and connectivity in graphs. *Canad. J. Math. 19*, 1319-1328. [*11*:2]

M.H.J. WEBB (1971). Some methods of producing approximate solutions to travelling salesman problems with hundreds or thousands of cities. *Oper. Res. Quart. 22*, 49-66. [*7*:5]

B.W. WEIDE (1978). *Statistical Methods in Algorithm Design and Analysis,* Ph.D. thesis, Department of Computer Science, Carnegie-Mellon University, Pittsburgh, PA. [*6*:1]

H. WEYL (1935). Elementare Theorie der konvexen Polyeder. *Comment. Math. Helv. 7,* 290-306. Translation. H.W. KUHN, A.W. TUCKER (eds.). *Contributions to the Theory of Games I,* Princeton University Press, Princeton, NJ, 3-18 (1950). [*9*:1]

R.J. WILSON (1972). *Introduction to Graph Theory,* Oliver and Boyd, Edinburgh. [*Preface*; *11*:1]

J.J. WIORKOWSKI, K. MCELVAIN (1975). A rapid heuristic algorithm for the approximate solution of the traveling salesman problem. *Transportation Res. 9,* 181-185. [*7*:3]

D.R. WOODALL (1978). A sufficient condition for Hamiltonian circuits. *J. Combin. Theory Ser. B 25,* 184-186. [*11*:3]

E.M. WRIGHT (1973). For how many edges is a digraph almost certainly Hamiltonian? *Proc. Amer. Math. Soc. 41,* 384-388. [*11*:4]

P. YELLOW (1970). A computational modification to the savings method of vehicle scheduling. *Oper. Res. Quart. 21,* 281-283. [*12*:4]

S. ZANAKIS (1977). Computational experience with some nonlinear optimization algorithms in deriving maximum likelihood estimates for the three-parameter Weibull distribution. *TIMS Studies in the Management Sciences 7,* 63-77. [*7*:6]